A NEW LOOK

at a very

OLD BOOK

A Spirituality for the 21st Century

An Adult Analysis Of Sacred Scriptures
For Their Meaning

With emphasis on
The Hebrew and Christian Testaments

BY

Robert E. Mayer, PhD

Order this book online at www.trafford.com
or email orders@trafford.com

Most Trafford titles are also available at major online book retailers.

Print information available on the last page.

ISBN: 978-1-4251-1713-9 (sc)

Trafford rev. 05/14/2015

www.trafford.com

North America & international
toll-free: 1 888 232 4444 (USA & Canada)
fax: 812 355 4082

Ask *and it will be given to you; seek and you will find; knock and the door will be opened to you. For everyone who asks, receives; and the one who seeks, finds; and to the one who knocks, the door will be opened.* Matthew 7: 7-8

If one does not keep pace with one's companions,
Perhaps it is because one hears a different drummer.
Let one step to the music one hears, however measured
or far away.

Thoreau

And we speak about them not with words taught by human wisdom, but with words taught by the Spirit {of God}, describing spiritual realities in spiritual terms.

1 Corin 2:13

"Every time I read this great 'O BIBLOS' I see more mythology,
more meaning and deeper spirituality."

The Authors, 26 Feb 04

It does not concern me in the least that I be judged by you or any human tribunal; I do not even pass judgment on myself; I am not conscious of anything against me, but I do not thereby stand acquitted; the one who judges me is the Lord {God}.

I Corin 4: 3-4

It was so of old, and it is just so today. They criticize him who sits in silence; they criticize him who talks a lot. They even criticize him who speaks in moderation. There is not an author in the world who is not criticized.

Aphorism of Buddha #227 (~520 BC)

ACKNOWLEDGEMENT

So many forgotten names and faces of family, friends and teachers throughout my years of learning! They know who they are and when we meet again in eternity I shall thank them. Notable among them is Raymond E. Brown, SS who brought me unto the 20th century of modern scholarship and Albert C. Giaquinto, SS who taught me what true spirituality is. And then there was my special friend, Robert Moon, PhD, who argued each and every theological and biblical point in this book. His wisdom was greatly appreciated.

I've been so fortunate to have had the opportunity to study at so many different places of higher learning; fortunate indeed to have afforded them all. Ignorance is not bliss; it's expensive. But, believe me, education is also expensive, check any college tuition and the monthly cost of any high speed Internet. That Internet is truly a godsend. My friendly library, bookstore and the Internet were the sources of all this research. Assembling all the pieces took much mental sweat, energy and many a 2 AM curfew, with a bit of intuition and grace from above. I'm particularly grateful to my significant other, my wife, for her many hours of proofing and her critical reviews. And thanks to my son for his thought provoking honesty.

May you learn something about yourselves as I did and understand why you chose your beliefs and community.

TABLE of CONTENTS

APPENDICES

INTRODUCTION

SECTION ONE: Authors' Note

There is always a temptation to write what one believes to be absolute truth and accuse all others of blindness and untruth. I pray you don't get that impression because I am not in possession of anything absolute. Like you, the reader, I'm only a person who sees life through his own experiences and certainly does not have the last word on any topic. Well, maybe a couple! I recognize that there are some subjects with which I'm more than casually familiar; these include the Sciences of Nuclear Physics, Psychology, Theology and its associated Biblical Scholarship. Please don't be too impressed because it has taken me some 25 to 50 years of intensive and expensive study to get here by the sweat of my brow and what's behind and inside of it.

There is no deliberate intention to label anyone good or evil, ignorant or genius and/or conservative or liberal. We humans believe what we perceive. What you believe does not make you good or evil. Morality is determined by your behavior. We each have our own experiences and have chosen our own pathways through this quagmire we call life. This book speaks of my own footsteps as I have trodden here and there in search of what, to me, is the meaning and understanding of my life. We know very little of those who lived prior to the written word. However, many have preceded me and have made their own pathways known by their own writings or by the writings of their followers. My only claim is having read as many of these biographies as are available, few in the original language but most in translation.

This book's primary purpose is to share what I've observed and, of course, expose what I believe to be some of the pitfalls made within those biographical writings and what occurs in interpreting them. For the most part some humans have considered some of these to be Sacred Scriptures and, in most cases, have accepted each one at some revered level: from a hallowed respect for those writings that are "Traditional Guidelines to Meaning and Purpose" at one end of the spectrum up to worshiping those that are thought to be of "Divine Origin" at the opposite end. It has been my obsession to discover where one can place each of the World's Sacred Scriptures on such a spectrum. Believe me when I say that I'm not the only one who is driven by this obsession. Our names are legion!

My wish is that you read with the same questioning intensity that I have poured into this work. May you also find the joy of discovery, a serenity of spirit, a new relationship with your Higher Power and a compassionate respect for your neighbor ... all making your life full of meaning.

I ask you this question, "Why do you not judge for yourselves what is right? (Luke 12: 57)

SECTION TWO: Humans Meet Their God

As the dawn broke over the distant mountains tinting everything in a pink radiance, a two-legged, five-foot tall creature, partially visible under a large bearskin, hobbled out of a cave located on the southern portion of the mountainside about 100 feet above the valley floor. The creature steadied itself on the ledge with a tall smooth staff held tightly in its stubby right hand. One could see large dissimilar puffs of fur wrapped around each foot just up to the ankles, dark-skinned, hairy muscular shortish legs to the mid thigh, a large dark-skinned muscular right arm, a wild bush of hair protruded on each side of a bear's head hat which was apparently a part of the large skin that wrapped around its torso. Its face was almost hidden by a thick brown beard and a dark shadow covered its weathered face. The staff, bear's head and heavy build gave one the impression of the alpha male of a pre-historic clan in Eastern Europe some hundred thousand years ago.

He stared intently at the color of the Eastern sky and the foreboding clouds speeding towards his domain. The temperature was close to freezing for it was late winter and the sun just beginning to climb to its maximum azimuth. The Ice Age was still controlling the weather but today his clan's activities appeared to be threatened by the approaching clouds. A storm from the East would bring warming rain from the sea that was located a four-day forced march from where he stood. From his experience he judged that the storm would bring its furry with just enough time to collect wood for the morning meal and a little nestling around the warming embers till the storm ended. Others came out of the cave, listened to the grunting orders and scurried off to their assignments. Inside the cave one heard the bustling of adults and children. Then, a line of people came out dashing towards the nearby sanitary pits.

Moments later the women all marched back into the cave. After several minutes, the men returned with wood for the day and renewed the fires for cooking and heating the cave to remove the cold dampness.

After all had eaten, the weather became the center of interest since the day's hunting was going to be delayed by the severity and length of the storm. The Alpha Male rose and went outside to survey the sky. As he reached the edge of the rock precipice, lightning, thunder and a deluge of rain greeted him. He hardly had time to turn around and run for the protection of his cave when a modest bolt of lightning hit his staff. He was visibly shaken but only his staff bore the full current flow to ground. He was untouched but paralyzed with fear and amazement. The people in the cave grunted loudly at this phenomenon. The sound "Shaah-mah" was repeated several times by the shocked members of the clan and then, repeated again when the Alpha Male, soundly shaken by the incident, re-entered the cave. He opened his mouth and pronounced, "Shaah-mah", and all the members bowed to him ... silence followed.

Thus was created the first nature god, the god of lightning, and the first holy man who would now be THE messenger and interpreter of the divine for that clan. However, his was not an isolated event; for every clan would have its own unique epiphany. Each would identify with different mysterious, but natural, occurrences and have their own individual interpreter of the divine to lead and guide their activities. It would not be until humans learned to write that any spiritual experiences would be documented for posterity.

Only after the fifth millennium BC would there be picture writing in the pyramids by the Egyptians. By the fourth millennium BC triangular stick markings on clay tablets were used by the Sumerians. By about 1200 BC scrolls of commandments were carried about in an Ark by the Hebrews. Writings for the people of India and the people of China began to appear. People around the world were now documenting those ancient stories, told and re-told, within their cultural history. All of these legends and myths became the stuff from which later generations wrote of their own experiences of the mysteries of nature and life. In later years these writings grew to be regarded as their culture's own unique and profound scriptures.

Some period between 1400 and 1100 BC another epiphany took place. During his self-imposed exile after killing one of his countryman, a slave-master, an Egyptian prince named Moses would encounter what appeared to him to be a burning bush that wasn't being consumed. From within the fire a voice filled with compassion spoke to him. It chartered him to return to his homeland, confront his own father, the King, and seek the freedom of an enslaved suffering people. Thus empowered by the voice, he demanded that the Pharaoh give freedom to those foreigner slaves. This alpha male took his place as the leader of the band of *habiruh (*meaning*,* foreigners*)* taking them out of their slavery towards a new land filled with promise. While on that journey through the desert the prince stopped at a very large and tall mountain, climbed it and experienced an historic spiritual encounter within a dark storm of lightning and thunder; this atop the legendary Mt Sinai. This Prince, Moses, walked out of the storm down to the assembled mass of wanderers and delivered a covenant of commandments from the Unknowable, "I AM BECOMING" ... "yod-he-wav-he" of the future Hebrew Nation (the Israelites).

Once again a numinous encounter with the unknown created a messenger who shaped the divinity to be worshipped by his people.

A little more than a thousand years later a humble man emerged from an insignificant town, Nazareth by name, seeking a baptism in water and light. From that experience in the desert he returned to Galilee preaching a message of hope and behavior that had not been heard since the beginning of time nor has been superseded since. His birth split history into a "before" and an "after". The moment of his epiphany is still in question because his four biographers were inconsistent in their reports. His words and deeds amazed his followers but earned a death sentence on a cross from the ruling Romans because this man preached a "Kingdom" that threatened Rome. As though by Divine guidance his followers (identified as Christians) were empowered by this prophet's re-appearance from the dead. To his followers he made unusual claims, performed great deeds and explained the meaning of his life. His followers were motivated to share their experience of joy and hope to the rest of the world.

Close to the middle of that first century AD another epiphany was about to occur that would turn the Roman Empire upside down. A Pharisee with a group of jailors was traveling the road to Damascus in search of a disturbing sect (*heresis*, in Greek) of believers within the organized Jewish synagogue. His purpose was to remove these troublesome Hebrew heretics by civil or mortal means as he saw fit. It is told that he experienced a bolt of light from the sky that blinded him and knocked him off his horse while some of his party fell to the ground. Some saw the light and others did not. In the confusion he heard a voice that some of his fellow jailors heard and some others did not hear. This Pharisee, Saul, is reported to have claimed that the voice belonged to one named Yeshua, the teacher from Nazareth. The voice told him to stop persecuting those followers for they were his people. Saul now blinded (was that physical or psychological?) went directly to a holy man to get his sight returned (was it his spiritual sight?). The experience caused this Saul to undergo a personality change so dramatic that he joined the new sect, changed his name to Paul and became that sect's most important preacher and organizer. His preachings and writings changed the face of the Christian sect into an Institutional giant. The ensuing organization became the driving force for the next 1500 years, until another epiphany took place.

A well-to-do young German man was leaving a bookstore after having selected his textbooks for his entrance into law school. It was a stormy rainy day. As he walked away from the store he was hit by a bolt of lightning. We have very little details of his injuries and recovery but one note of information; he never went to law school. He changed his mind and entered a monastery instead. The monk, Martin Luther, later nailed a controversial document to a church door and shook the Institutional structure of Roman Catholicism to its very foundation. That protest became the trumpet call that has fractured Christianity into the hundreds of protesting denominations functioning today.

Thus in the course of human affairs several individuals experienced the light ... and things changed. New sects were born.

In this 21st century some of those very old stories and writings have taken on a more significant character and are referred to as "Sacred Scriptures" reflecting their importance in people's lives. In some cultures these Sacred Scriptures are known to be of human origin while in others they are held in such high regard that the people believe them to be of Divine origin. All Sacred Scriptures contain in many cases similar understandings of a Creator, creation, and rules for correct living, rewards and punishments. However, while the similarities are striking indeed, the dissimilarities are strangely contradictory, one Scripture to the other, and most unfortunately, within the body of each Scripture are some different inconsistencies and contradictions. Because of those differences, individuals have fought with one another, groups have performed atrocities against others, nations have declared war on other nations, and religious institutions have condemned other religious institutions. Fear, distrust, hatred, vengeance, murder and ethnic cleansing have prevailed. Humans have demonstrated a penchant for not tolerating differences: different skin colors, different languages, different dress, different religious practices, and different cultures and different differences. At the core of these prejudices lies the erroneous belief that if your name for God is not the same name that I know, then you must be wrong, religiously objectionable, evil and, therefore, must be annihilated.

Do not think that what you have just read is fictional and non-existent. It is alive, well and very active in every corner of our blue planet. It is a dysfunctional human virus present in homes, schools, churches and public places everywhere. It is the single most serious social pandemic affecting relationships, even those within religious communities.

The distrust, fear and hatred that permeates the soul's darker places owes its existence to the obsessive search for power, wealth and position that is freely lusted after by humans.

The only way to diffuse this sickness is to understand the nature and origin of those Sacred Scriptures that polarize cultures, nations, cities and neighbors. To know your own beliefs and know those of your neighbor may just be the right step in treating another's "Way" with respect and tolerance.

SECTION THREE: The Seeds of Research

The saddest experience that I've had to endure as a Christian Zenist is to be rejected and condemned by another Christian for being intellectual and not proclaiming that Christian's brand of Institutional Religion as absolute. Christian sectarianism and intolerance expressed so vociferously and prejudicially is not only a sin against civility but also a Christian embarrassment. What we have discovered is that several sects of Christianity claim themselves to be the one and only "Truth" and all other sects "False". Have you ever wondered in the past, while searching for the true God, "whatever happened to respect and love thy neighbor?" What shocked us most was those frequent incidents of criticism by adults (students) while in a Religious Studies Program at a Christian College. It has taken us a long time, since earning our degrees in that very program, to make sense out of the expressed anger voiced during those four years of summer school study. Today we're convinced that the behavior of sectarian institutional religious people is a function of what Karl Jung called, "the Collective Unconscious".

One of Jung's major psychiatric observations was that underneath the skull of all of us human beings is a subconscious memory of the experiences from the preceding generations that we received while growing up, being trained towards an old encultured mindset which directs our behavior. The relevant key to this phenomena is that every generation, since humans could first talk (guessed to be several million years ago), every child since that time, has been psychologically formatted into a unique family history, into a specific social group, in a particular isolated village or town, in a bordered country. In other words, we have not only been unconsciously encultured by our family's past history but also by our present distinct moment in history, our personal socializations and our religious indoctrination. From early on, humans feared differences, especially languages. People distrusted strangers. People looked to the mountains as fences that kept out their enemies, often the marauders and plunderers. These memories are firmly imprinted in our subconscious and unconsciously direct some of our behaviors.

In this 21st century the Collective Unconscious is mysteriously alive and active in every human who walks the planet. We inhabitants in the world still act as our ancestors did in order to survive; Catholics avoid Protestants, Blacks distrust Whites, Nations fight Nations (not for survival but for conquest), ethnic groups slaughter to cleanse the neighborhood. And humankind behaves worse than barbarians, worse than sociopaths, worse than demons. Who among us is without sin? When will someone turn the other cheek to stop the insanity?

xviii

There is one common factor that has precipitated this inhumanity. Its name is ignorance, ignorance of history, ignorance of the literature and ignorance of the roots of all religions: the Sacred Scriptures written within the period 3000 B.C. (B.C.E., if you prefer) to 700 AD (or CE). We truly believe that what the world needs now is not love, but study. Read your Sacred Scripture, get the facts, become aware that all are very similar in intent and realize that they are all filled with legends and myths. All state the existence of a single Creator; all defend the universal brother and sisterhood of the human race. Most importantly, all contain figurative literary constructs with pinches of salted history and none are tape-recorded words from the Divine. Therein lies the sum total of the most violently disputed postures in all of theology's history—Divine Inspiration. We kill today because those others have a book from their god with a name for their deity that differs from our own name in our Sacred Scripture. We disparage other religions because we perceive that only ours is truly from the One Creator. We are deeply prejudiced against anyone who questions the factuality of our Sacred Books.

Karl Jung uncovered that deeply rooted human dysfunction that began in very ancient pre-historic times, taught to every generation throughout every land throughout the ages and continues today to produce the mental illness infecting humanity, an illness in a population that is unaware of its origins and incapable of curing itself. Who is going to help us?

The original title for this book was going to be "Shocking Secrets of Sacred Scriptures" because we really thought that most readers would react exactly in that manner. However, we're not out to make it shocking as much as we wish to explain, clarify and present to the reader a new awareness of the nature and purpose of each culture's Revered Writings. We hope that you will discover and accept that conclusion. As human culture moved through the ages, there occurred a significant development and shift in the knowledge of science and religious thought. Those changes were introduced by well-intentioned charismatic dissidents who not only saw through the questionable traditional human practices but also suggested new and improved ones. Our problem is that we have little to no awareness of our history or how those alterations to the traditions have come down to us. They have, in fact, produced a plethora of conflicting, contradictory, sectarian groups within each major institutional religion.

There will be only one basic assumption made here: *there is ONE and only ONE Creator.* That fact has been intellectually voted upon in every single known Sacred Scripture! We will not dispute that popular observation. Each of us stands with Paul of Tarsus, "it is indeed obvious to the critical observer that this universe is many orders of complexity beyond our most sophisticated mathematical and physical sciences and still continues to be incomprehensible and mysterious. There is a Creator! " The Platos, Aristotles, Aquinases, Galileis, Copernicuses, Keplers, Einsteins, all scientists, philosophers, theologians, and many others who have but scratched the surface of knowing the Absolute. This book is my little scratch!

We are FIFES people: Free-willed - Imperfect - Frail - Existentialist - Seekers who admits to imperfection and to both physical and mental frailty, who choose to search everywhere, freely, in the yesterday and today, for a profound relationship with people in our world and with The Creator. Therefore, there are times when our choices or thinking will be correct and, equally probable, incorrect. Neither correct or incorrect is good or evil; correct or incorrect are just human fallible choices. However, incorrect can oftentimes be the result of intellectual dishonesty.

We do not push any specific name for the Creator. However, there is one teacher who appeals to our sense of the Divine. Yeshua was his name (the correct Aramaic name of the Carpenter from Nazareth). No other self acclaimed prophet fits the bill. Just so that you get our meaning, we believe that the word prophet means, "to speak for someone", NOT to predict the future. We clearly do not possess the only "truth" in the Universe. We respect each and every faith but not because they are "THE" truth. We humans are fallible and because of that condition no single person, religious Institution or self-appointed Church group actually possesses the absolute truth. "Absoluteness resides with and in THE DIVINE, alone." How arrogant and outrageous it is that any single institution whether Christian, Israelite, Muslim or Hindu proclaims itself as THE ONLY TRUTH and all others FALSE.

Our combined studies have convinced us that every Sacred Scripture has its own cultural uniqueness and each possesses deeply profound parts that nurture the individuals who were raised in that particular culture. That profoundness is visible to whomsoever takes the time to become familiar with those Scriptures with an inquiring intellect and a respectful compassion.

Our first purpose in this book, then, is to assist the reader in discovering the nature of ancient Sacred Scriptures that are available to us in Libraries across our nation in this 21st century. And, for your use and review, Appendix L contains information for downloading those Scriptures from the Internet.

The second purpose of this book is to demonstrate that your relationship with any or all people of a different faith is worthy of your compassionate respect, not because of their possession of Truth but because of their sincerity of faith in the same Divinity with whom you and us are in relationship.

Our basic axiom and observation is that people choose a religious community within their culture that offers acceptance, affection and a sense of belonging and meaning. It is in that context that Grace reaches out to meet them just as they are, in their now.

And thirdly, this book is our personal invitation to you to discover a religious posture and a purposeful spirituality that is free of hierarchy (gatekeepers), doctrine, dogma, ritual and legalisms. Doctrine and dogma don't encourage ecumenical acceptance very easily; ritual hypnotizes everyone into passivity; laws make hypocrites of legalistic people. This book is meant to expand your awareness of others, so don't walk away if at first you are confronted with an alleged contradiction to your belief structures. When you come against some difficulty in this text, understand, it's there to challenge your preconceived notions into which you have been programmed in your youth by those in authority: parents, teachers, public officials, religious leaders and your peers, etc. This is not the fault of the teaching; it comes about because children exhibit a cognitive limitation called "pre-critical naiveté"; they take everything they hear as absolute without any critical analysis of the information. Here's a little story about a community's confronting the modern world. I call it, "Johnny and the Owl".

XX

There once was a young lad who was very intelligent. In fact he usually got the highest grades in all his classes and he could stump most of the people in his community because of his general book knowledge and in particular in Biblical quotations from his Church training. Of course, there was only one Church in that small town and it was Southern Baptist. When the lad had finished the 8th Grade (his was the highest grade in that single classroom school), the town's people, actually the church members, decided that this lad was worthy of going on to college for a higher education. So they collected enough money to send him (at that time, only 100 dollars per year!).

Four years later the lad graduates college with very fine grades: honors. The Church people were so proud of their choice and his accomplishments that they asked him to speak at the Fourth of July celebration.

Now Johnny was a little anxious because this was the first time he had to tell the whole town what he had learned. He was going to choose his words carefully and practice his speech; he had learned many new things that he wanted to share with his community and friends.

He went to the back of the family barn and started to practice, out loud, "Friends and neighbors, I want to thank you all for your kind support in sending me to college. Today I would like to share with you all that it meant to me."

Suddenly, a great white snowy owl flew to a nearby tree and settled on a branch at the middle of the tree in clear view of Johnny. It surprised him but he continued. "In my first year I learned about Chemistry and Physics, especially, about Radioactivity. The instructors told me about how long these radioactivities have been decaying ... some for as long as 14 billion years."

At that moment the owl screeched "whoo ... whoo". Johnny was startled and looked up at the owl. The owl didn't move. Johnny continued, "In my second year I studied Zoology. Much to my surprise I found out that most of the animal kingdom is related and there are people-like bones that seem to have died well over three million years ago. Potassium-40 and Carbon-14 dating have substantiated it."

Once again the owl screeched out, "whoo ... whoo." Johnny turned and stared at the owl. Neither moved a twitch. And Johnny started to practice his talk again. "In my third year I took a course in Astronomy in which I learned about the size of the Universe ... over 14 billion years of galaxy travel that started with a unique moment of creation, called the Big Bang."

For the third time the owl interrupted Johnny's talk. This time it seemed to be an angry screech, "Whoo ... Whoo. Whoo ... Whoo." There was a long pause during which the owl shuffled its feet and moved as if disgusted and impatient. Johnny returned to his speech, "In my fourth year I studied the origins of our world and living beings. Putting all those facts together, I can only conclude very simply that ... God does not exist."

The owl fluttered its wings, jumped up and down on the branch and shouted out, "That's not true! That's not true!"

Johnny was stunned, "You can talk!"

"Of course I can." the owl replied.

"How come you only screech out "whoo ... whoo" all the time?" Johnny queried.

"Because, my purpose in life is to remind people that no matter what they learn and experience from life, they must never forget *WHO* made it all."

There are a couple of messages here: the first is that Johnny opened his mind to his new studies and secondly the owl helped him realize that there is a Creator no matter how much he learns from the places of higher education. You see, Science tells us HOW the universe was and is constructed and operating. Religion speaks about WHO did it. Science and Religion are two sides of the SAME coin. They complement each other! Ignorance and fear think otherwise!

SHE-HE "whoo" maintains the Universe is compassionate, full of mercy and forgiveness. Religious leaders who focus on condemnation of science or propose exclusive sectarianisms or threaten eternal punishment are not of God. All worthy prophets speak of: "changing your behavior", "sharing your wealth", "being just in your dealings", "being compassionate", "God's mercy", "God's forgiveness", "God's love", etc. Where is all this eternal torture theology coming from? We believe it comes from those who do not understand the nature of God and, more importantly, from those who refuse to forgive. In short, eternal torture is folk theology! When people are ignorant of their Sacred Scriptures, they can be easily led to the strangest of ideas by the charlatans of religion whose unquenchable greed for power will proffer any form of folk theology that gains them position and prestige. Personal knowledge of one's Sacred Scripture is one piece of mental armor needed to protect oneself. Compassion towards one's neighbor is the shield against hatred. And, finally, a relationship with one's Higher Power is the sword that slays one's deep-rooted prejudices and destroys the Demon, not the outside one, but the one residing inside the darker places of our free will! In total, the armor of knowledge, the shield of compassion and the sword of relationship are the components of a strong spirituality. Be informed, be compassionate and be in an active relationship with God, whoever SHE-HE is for you!

Join us in this Camelotian adventure to search for an awareness of all Sacred Scriptures. Remember, frequently, as you read these pages, this book is not about good or evil; it's about the psychological problem relating to a human's intellectual capacity to engage in mature critical thinking! That will be the true path to your authentic personal spirituality!

To end on a more humorous note, we offer this definition of the term "homo sapiens":

Homo stands for human,
S stands for social,
A stands for animal,
P stands for potentially,
I stands for intellectual,
E stands for emotional,
N stands for normally,
S stands for stupid.

Together now, it reads: a Human is a Social Animal, Potentially Intellectual and Emotional but Normally Stupid. ....Have a chuckle!

Aristotle about 2300 years ago wrote, "Perfection is a myth. We are frail, fallible and imperfect beings living in the human condition." If you perchance find any mistakes in punctuation, spelling or grammar, understand that even after ten reviews our humanity has reigned supreme. We ask your forgiveness. We may have unwittingly contributed to Aristotle's opinion and database.

CHAPTER ONE

JUST WHAT IS TRUTH?

A Philosophy and Psychology of Perception

It appears that there are three types of truth: subjective, objective and absolute. First, this subjective truth is really what we humans decide to adhere to in our minds because of what our senses perceive and interpret from our experiences. Ten people observe a situation and each recounts a different story. That's subjective truth! The second is objective truth that derives from a communal reproducible measurement of some observation of nature or behavior. In other words, a person observes a phenomenon; he or she interprets it to mean a specific thing. A second person observes that same phenomenon and comes to the same conclusion. More people repeat the experience and arrive at the very same conclusion. That's objective truth! In fact, scientists are those people who do that kind of work through experimentation in a controlled laboratory or environment. The third type of truth is what all recognize as absolute truth and it resides only in the Creator! Absolute truth is what the Creator knows has taken place (case one above) but the ten people didn't know. Therefore, NO HUMAN is privy to, nor in possession of absolute truth! We will now only discuss the first type of truth and demonstrate its fallibility and relativity.

We humans are peculiar beings: nothing comes into our minds except through our five physical senses and our intuitive sixth sense. This sixth sense is, we believe, a function of the mind's ability to integrate unrelated facts and produce new relationships, ideas or things. Psychology calls this an activity of the subconscious portion of the mind. Now, the bottom line is this: when we experience anything, it is registered in our mind and its meaning, as it applies to our life, is interpreted. That activity is what we mean by the word, perception. In the scheme of things, we humans believe what we perceive! Our perceptions determine all our courses of action and behavior. The question remains, do humans have absolute perception? Here's that word again! The answer is, humans do NOT have absolute perception. You see, human perception is a function of three factors: enculturation, cognitive development and psychological profile.

Before we get to the definitions of those three factors, let's review the characteristics of being human. A human exhibits five characteristics (certainly to a greater degree than an animal or other life forms): Emotions or Affect, Needs, Free Will or Choice, Intellect or Cognition and, lastly, Relationship.

1. The AFFECTING Characteristic (Human Emotions):

Each person is born with an active AFFECT. The baby emotes almost instantaneously in response to its physical or psychological needs. If parents don't answer the call, the baby turns up the volume and often its "temper-tantrum" button. Mother's radar system, which is being fine-tuned since conception, must learn and quickly translate what those messages require of her. Fathers take a few months to discover the significance of those noisy messages. As a matter of fact, most of us fathers need our wavelengths re-calibrated. But eventually we tune in accurately to the messages and translate the kiddy code.

It's at that early age that infants sense the proximity of Mothers (bonding) but that Fathers are somewhat distant. Could it be that Fathers never get properly trained to fathom AFFECT? In counseling most males are not in touch with their own feelings and, therefore, do not deal well with their own AFFECT nor with the AFFECT of others.

As the infant grows into childhood in its own nuclear family, it's absolutely necessary for it to experience the healthy use of adult AFFECT. Otherwise, the curse of dysfunctional behavior infects it to a lesser or greater degree depending upon the example of its parents and siblings. The difficulty in most households is that too few of its members understand the use of healthy adult affect. Let's make this point clear.

Emotions and feelings are to each person what light filters are to a camera. As a person tries to communicate, the emotional filters lock in place and distort what's being communicated. The more intense the feeling, the more the filter distorts. The only way that anyone can engage in distortion-free conversation is to be in touch with his/her emotions/feelings and articulate them out loud as the first step in speaking to another person. By doing so the mind comprehends that such a feeling is filtering the choice of words used to express whatever thought it's trying to convey. Identifying the pre-existing emotion relaxes the mind so that it has ready access to its own subconscious in which is stored one's own myriad of experiential knowledge and vocabulary. People who participate in "quiz" shows know only too well that they must be relaxed in order to have instant recall, i.e., instant access to one's subconscious. And, of course, the "quiz" show people do everything they can to increase the stress levels. Have you ever tried to remember some odd fact when you were under stress? Remember those high school exams that gave you the most trouble? Were they the SAT exams? What about your professional certification exams?

The key ideas we're trying to make are:

- **Emotions filter your listening and speech.**
- **Intense emotions can render you speechless.**
- **Be in touch with your feelings so you can identify them out loud which diffuses the filtering effect of your emotions.**

In other words, sense your gut reaction to situations, put a name to your feelings so that you can respond without stress. As a relaxed person you will be able to communicate very accurately, openly and honestly. In all of this so far I'm preparing you to accept the formal pattern for healthy communication.

A healthy person is
(a) aware of his/her feelings,
(b) can articulate those feelings,
(c) to the person with whom the feelings occurred,
(d) without blaming that other person.

Sounds simple! It actually is, but only to those persons who are in touch with their own feelings. Most people are simply not always cognizant of their affect. The result is the crippling behavior of "acting out". When we are hurt, we respond in anger, attack and destroy what or whomever it was that delivered the hurt. We do so without, in any way, sensing or being aware of our hurt. We humans experience that "acting out" behavior every day of our lives, if not first hand, then second hand from the media. Shootings, stabbings, fightings, all are initiated in misunderstandings and culminated in "acting out" our feelings. The final tally is always "lose/lose". The immediate solution appears to be win/lose, but the winner does seriously violate the human rights of the victim. What we're proposing here is a condition of being "in touch" so that no "acting out" occurs and the disagreement turns out to be a win/win conclusion. Both individuals win because each can voice their feelings to achieve accurate communication. There are no victims when open and honest dialogue takes place. Healthy communication starts with being "in touch" with our feelings.

The major experiences of our counseling have dealt with the inability of dysfunctional clients to communicate their AFFECT in a healthy way. Teaching people to become aware of their deeply personal, emotional content is always a lengthy and frequently tedious process.

Now, let's take a look at the many different kinds of AFFECT. Here are some names. Try to recall when you last experienced them (or, the last time you can recall having experienced them). The classical, four basic feelings are mad, glad, sad and scared. You probably know that each has several shades. One author, Robert Pluchik, in PSYCHOLOGY TODAY, February 1980, states that, as a starting point, there are eight basic (the Primary column) emotions with three levels (degrees) of intensity:

	MILD	**PRIMARY**	**INTENSE**
1	**Annoyance**	**Anger**	**Rage**
2	**Boredom**	**Disgust**	**Loathing**
3	**Pensiveness**	**Sadness**	**Grief**
4	**Distraction**	**Surprise**	**Amazement**
5	**Apprehension**	**Fear**	**Terror**
6	**Approval***	**Acceptance**	**Adoration**
7	**Delight***	**Joy**	**Ecstasy**
8	**Expectance***	**Anticipation**	**Vigilance**

Those three with the * were added by this Author. In addition to those 24 emotions, Robert Pluchik writes about complex emotions (dyads). Those are composed of the PRIMARY emotions, 1-2-3-4-5-6-7-8 listed individually above. The following are the complex emotions generated by combining two primaries.

1/2 - (Anger with Disgust)	Contempt
2/3 - (Disgust with Sadness)	Remorse (or Guilt)
3/4 - (Sadness with Surprise)	Disappointment
4/5 - (Surprise with Fear)	Awe
5/6 - (Fear with Acceptance)	Submission
6/7 - (Acceptance with Joy)	Love
7/8 - (Joy with Anticipation)	Optimism
8/1 - (Anticipation with Anger)	Aggressiveness

To help yourself get in touch with these 32 named emotions you can do the following exercises. First, write each of the 32 names on an individual card and place the 32 cards in a bag. Select one at a time and then tell a story involving that feeling to a person whose job it will be to identify the emotion with which you told the story. This is a fun game. It does help you to become familiar with words that portray a unique emotion. It also helps the other person put a name to the emotional content of the story.

2. The NEEDING Characteristic

According to Abraham Maslow, the renowned Psychologist, every human has five significant Needs: (1) one's physical-biological needs, (2) security needs relating to parents and home, (3) belonging needs for loving and being loved as well as knowing and being known, (4) needs related to self-esteem and, finally, (5) a need to self-actualize oneself.

3. The FREE WILL Characteristic

Choosing is only the first part of Free Will; the second part is choosing morally and ethically ; and the last is taking responsibility for one's choice.

4. The INTELLECT (COGNITION) Characteristic

There are several steps to being fully cognitive: (1) accurate sensing, (2) data storage into one's conscious or subconscious mind, (3) reasoning in a logical manner (deductively or inductively) or intuitively (creating new things or imagining new ideas/solutions), (4) understanding cognitively and empathically and (5) evaluating the moral and ethical situation or condition. These steps are all followed by one's actions

5. The RELATIONSHIP Characteristic

No human is an Island! Each must develop friends, best friends and sexual companions over the long term. Through those relationships one experiences personal psychological and spiritual growth by means of which one determines one's meaning.

The Behavioral Profiles

Lawrence Kohlberg and Eric Erickson have developed highly technical categories relating to the psychological behavioral profiles through which people pass in the course of their lives. We have interpolated them into seven categories, in keeping with their intent, using words that are easier to understand as well as to teach. Humans develop in seven stages through which they grow or into which they can get stuck. They are:

Stage 1. Egocentric: The child's demands are solely for its personal security and/or pleasure. Strangely, this also applies to dysfunctional adults who operate at that stage doing or taking anything solely for their personal security and/or pleasure without concern for others.

Stage 2. Reciprocity: We act in defense of our personal self-image and safety. If you do good to me, I'll do good to you. If you do me harm, I'll get even or punish you.

Stage 3: Personal Gain: I'll do anything to earn points towards, personal privileges, financial gain, favoritism and reward.

Stage 4: Legalistic: I act according to society's (and my religion's) laws and seek lawyers, the courts and ministers to solve my problems.

Stage 5: Autonomous: I seek all the information I can get and then choose actions that satisfy my needs without short-changing or hurting others.

Stage 6: Respect and Concern: I behave with concern for others and respect the social or religious choices that others make.

Stage 7: Self-Giving: My actions become focused on the needs of others, first in a limited way and then utter and complete self-giving.
Comrades in the battlefield have been known to sacrifice their own lives for those of another.

It is of interest to note that these seven stages also pertain to theological and spiritual profiles. In which profile one decides to behave most frequently depends to a great extent on whether he or she exhibits (a) pre-critical naiveté, (b) critical thinking or (c) post-critical thinking. If you take everything that authorities tell you, and accept them unconditionally, then be aware that you are a follower, the pre-critical naiveté stage/level. If, on the other hand, you think about the rationality of the demands on you and choose to accept what helps you and your community, and to reject what you know will not help, then you are a mature, critical-thinking person. When you stand up for your rights to behave in a manner that questions legalisms that infringe upon those rights, whether social or religious, then you are an adult behaving autonomously, that's what is called post-critical thinking and frequently labeled as wisdom.

Next we will examine the manner by which our perceptions become our personal truths.

It appears that the single most important problem is the difficulty for inexperienced people identifying and separating these three ways of experiencing TRUTH: (1) truth perceived by one's own human fallibility, our human nature; (2) truth taught by authority figures in what they require the person to learn and obey and (3) truth written into the legendary and mythic compositions of literature and, in particular, their Sacred Scriptures. The balance of this Chapter will develop, work out and offer some solutions to the first problem of truth: truth through one's personal perception and the second truth told to us via authority figures. Then, we will dissect perception into its components: enculturation, cognitive development and psychological profile. Chapter 2 will address truth in facts, fictions and myth (type 3).

Predisposing One's Attitude

At the start of such a complex project you must make a sincere attempt to clean your chalked slate, empty your mental hard drive, dump your deep prejudices and clear your stuffed mind, leaving yourself open for learning and growth. Don't discard all the logic you've learned, just make it fertile ground for new seeds. The Tao Te Ching has a two-liner that says,

6

"Clay is formed into a vessel.
It is because of its emptiness that the vessel is useful."

Make yourself full of use! And for beginners, here is a fitting Zen parable whose story line goes like this.

> One day a young woman entered the room of the Zen Master and asked if she could become a student of his and learn to be a Zen person. The Master was a bit surprised at first. Then he realized her seriousness and explained that she must first experience the introductory ceremony with him before she made a definite commitment. She agreed and followed him to the low table in the far corner. He placed a large pillow where he wanted her to sit. He asked her in a soft inviting voice, "Would you like a warming cup of tea?"
> "Yes" she replied, to which he went directly to the hibachis and placed a full pot of water on it. No words passed between them while he prepared for the ceremony. Moments later the water boiled, he took a spoonful of tealeaves, went to the table and sat opposite her with pot and tealeaves. He mixed the leaves into the pot with small, slow, stirring strokes for what seemed an eternity to the young lady. Then the Master reached across the table and poured the tea into her cup. When the cup was full he continued to pour more tea. The brew spilled over the cup into the saucer and, when it filled, the warm, wet tea spilled out of the saucer onto the table and then over the edge to her lap.
> "Stop!" she cried, "Can't you see the cup is full? You can't get any more tea into it!"
> "Yes, I see that." He said in a soft polite voice, and you will not learn anything about Zen if you enter here with a filled mind. You must first empty all your pre-conceptions that have filled your spirit and only then will you be ready to learn."

Can you not understand that to enter the quest for TRUTH, you, too, must be like an empty vessel, empty of all your pre-conditioning and pre-judg-ments? Well, please do remember your name, address and social security number (and where your keys are)! So, take a moment, hour or day to posture yourself serenely. The information you will examine may at first appear like a plethora of confusion. So, compose yourself to patiently assimilate it, bit-by-bit, thought-by-thought, without shaking your equilibrium nor falling into emotional distraction. If you are at peace, the jigsaw pieces of TRUTH will come together in a clear picture for you, just like solving one of those 1,000-piece puzzles, one piece at a time.

Well, what does all this mean to you? It may mean that the average person cannot distinguish which one among the entire world's alleged "Sacred Scriptures" is the TRUE WAY to the Creator. Therefore, consider this; maybe none is the absolute WAY. And further, each Sacred Scripture is the Creator's reaching out via a personal communication to a specific encultured person, in the only way possible, inspiring THAT individual from THAT culture to try his own human best to transcribe his/her experience and, of course, feelings of this sacred "moment of clarity". Is it not possible that there can never be Divine Dictation? Wouldn't that become absolute LAW thereby eliminating, and definitely violating, humankind's gift of free will that was bestowed at the creation of the human spirit?

7

What may have occurred is that our common Divinity has produced an epiphany, a "moment of clarity", unique to each culture and "let the chips fall where they may". Remember now, each mainstream religion reports that this Creator talked to an intimate friend (a member of that culture) and that friend wrote what he/she "remembered" of the conversation. How many people do you know who will recall exactly a several hundred-page story that was spoken the night before? Especially if the recipient was half asleep! If this Creator is dictating the absolute TRUTH, how come so many people got it differently in the writing? Was there far too much static on the telephone? Or, as we like to tell it, can you imagine the following happening on some dark night about 2 AM?

"Hello! Wake up, this is God! I want to tell you the meaning of life and all the rules I want you to follow ... Hey, wake up!"
"What do you want?"
"I'm God! You know, your Creator! Get up and get a pencil and paper! Quick now, move it!"
"Wait a minute. What's a pencil, what's paper?"
"OK, never mind those things, I don't have all night. Just listen carefully and remember! Tomorrow, tell it to a Scribe! I'm going to say this one time only, so pay attention! I started the whole world some 14 billion years ago and watched it..."
"Whoa, what's a billion mean?"
"Uh, it means a very long time!"
"OK. But there is no word in my language for this "billion". How about I use the word, *yowm*, Hebrew for day or long time or the hot part of the day?"
"OK, OK. But let's move on. Now, where was I ... *pause* ... Ah, I created everything over many, many *yowm*. On the first *yowm* I ... "
Say, I've got an idea, why not use seven? You know like 28 days for the moon to return and we have broken that down to seven days in a week and rest on the seventh day? And, every seven years we have a ..."
Ok, OK, I get the message. So be it. On the first yowm I made light."
"What's light?'
"You know, like the brightness of lightning but much brighter, like the intense light of the sun when you look directly at it but still very much more intense than your paltry sun!"
"So, where is that light now?"
"Hey, listen, I just told you it wasn't the sun but something much bigger. I made the sun on a different *yowm*. Please, remember the words and the story and don't try to understand the science."
"OH, what's science?"
"For Heaven's sake! I just want you to remember the story so human kind can know the meaning of life."
"Wait, what's this 'heaven" thing?"
Long pause and then God said. "I think you should go back to sleep and forget this strange dream. Goodnight."

Can it be that each of the recipients of Divine knowledge could have possibly misunderstood the message or forgotten parts of it? Can you just imagine that, on the next day, each related the remembered portions to a Scribe and the Scribe added a few personal touches to the story to make sense of it. Isn't it a fact that all of the recipients of God's Sacred Scriptures incorporated their own cultural slant to the story as they related it to the scribe who then transcribed it for posterity? For that matter, could it have been that the community heard the message (oral tradition) and some time later (maybe years, decades or centuries later) a scribe wrote what the communities remembered and passed down? The facts speak for themselves. When we examine the various Sacred Scriptures together, you, too, will discover (a) the similarities of God's message and, then, (b) the many encultured differences and lastly, (c) the different theological perceptions. Then, just maybe, you'll ponder the question, "What did God really inspire?"

Perception and its Role in Finding Truth

It's time now to formulate the final piece of human psychology that is the principal mechanism determining one's choices in one's life drama. The name of the process is perception. Our perception is the prime mover of our choices! Three factors influence perception: enculturation, cognitive development and psychological profile. Let's see why each person is so different.

Enculturation is a factor that includes the following life realities and experiences. First off is our DNA that gives us a body with all its peculiar physical characteristics and a few mannerisms, some charming others not quite so. We have no control over any of those DNA gifts. Secondly, we inherit a family of like DNA recipients. To a large degree they influence our psychological profile because our slate is clean at birth and it is filled with the examples around us. Humans emulate the social behavior and gender role models of the family members from their nuclear family. The real confusions arise from dysfunctional parents and the pandemic of divorces and remarriages that presents its cacophony of personal conflicts. It is no small wonder that the experiences of spousal love and sacrifice are absent in the children of divorce. Thirdly, humans are exposed to a legion of teachers from both the classroom and the streets, from both competent and incompetent state certified professionals and the informal lessons from our street buddies. Then there is the curriculum we select in high school (college, business or trades) followed by entry into college or the work force. Thus far, we haven't mentioned the influences of Institutional Religion if, in fact, there was any. Who indoctrinated you? Was the choice made by parents or, post 12th grade; or were you proselytized by a charismatic preacher? In either case, did you study the tenets of your religion? We have observed that the majority of Institutions do not provide significant adult education to their membership. If a program is in effect, it more often than not is conducted by a poorly informed director whose perception is very institutional. Throughout this list we haven't touched on the personal and social mores of the geographic area in which one has lived. Can you imagine the social influences if one has moved to many countries in the world during those formative first 18 years - the military life?

Basically we have said that in today's world, as it was in years past, each person who has ever lived on this planet is:

1. born with a parental DNA code that sets one's many physical features and eventual cognitive capabilities,
2. nurtured within a specific culture that socialized and, hopefully, civilized one into a specific set of cultural mores and beliefs.

Therein lies the difficulty identified as the first factor that influences one's perception; its name is enculturation. Enculturation, therefore, is an important factor influencing each human being and determining part of its adult behavior along with one's religious beliefs and the truths of life we cling to so tightly. In other words, what we as humans perceive is clouded, like having cataracts in our mind's eye, almost pre-judged by our enculturation. Do you really understand the immense influence one's enculturation exerts on our perception?

However, enculturation is only one factor in our choice making. **Cognitive development** is the second contributor. If our education and experiences have been limited, we will remain in the "pre-critical naïveté" state of cognition. Imagine those who cannot read or write! They are cursed to an existence of acquiescing to authority's directives. Can you remember from your history class in high school that just 500 years ago the world believed that the Earth was flat? The ignorant responded by assassinating those who preached a round spinning planet. That condition has its source in the pandemic of "pre-critical naïveté" that permeates the religious mind.

The second stage is the "critical" mind. There are those who can think for themselves in all situations and conditions of life. They consult knowledgeable professionals in serious matters and then make up their minds to act or not to act.

The third stage of cognitive development is "post-critical". Those people who have exhibited it are special indeed. Think of Buddha, Lao Tze, Confucius, Moses, Yeshua of Nazareth, Socrates, Plato, Aristotle, Pythagoras, Martin Luther, Galileo Galilei, Albert Einstein and so many more too numerous to include here. You know of them; they are legion.

These then are just two factors affecting one's perception: enculturation and cognitive development. We have yet to add psychological profile. Basically, personal perceptions are completely subjective and, as such, are relative, imperfect and not absolute. Ask any judicial officer! It is impossible for any human to know absolute truth. It is a contradiction to think that a finite being can have complete access to the infinite. Logic dictates that the infinite is not able to fit into a finite box. However, humans can know that abstracts exist but cannot fit the absoluteness of infinity into their minds. Yes, the Creator is infinite; this we know for certain. Who or what that Infinity is, is a truth that will always remain unknowable. Some author several centuries ago wrote a lengthy description of his understanding of the Divine Infinite. We know it as "The Cloud of Unknowing". He wrote about his relationship with this mysterious Higher Power we all seek. Read it! It's on the Internet. See if you get the drift

We have already stated the seven psychological behavioral profiles and you should easily see why they enter into the complexity of one's perception. They each are like a unique filter that distorts one's vision thereby influencing perception. Just imagine how an egocentric person interprets his or her perception! Just review the remaining profiles and evaluate what each profile will see:

What will a person of "reciprocity" see and do?

What will a person of "personal gain" see and do?

What will a person of "legalism" see and do?

What will a person of "respect and concern" see and do?

What will a person of "self giving" see and do?

Now add each of the three stages of cognitive development to the mix! Pre-critical naiveté, critical, post critical/ Can you envision the confusion?

Now add the effects of one's "enculturation". Is this becoming clear to you? We must understand that each believes exactly what he or she perceives and then acts accordingly for good or evil.

Intelligently or ignorantly?

Compassionately or indifferently?

Onward to Chapter Two!

11

12

On Legends

Father O'Connor said musingly, "Legends do have a grand way of receding into the past, and becoming tradition, and it is more authentic for a man to say, 'My old Dada heard it from his Dada,' than to say, I saw it myself, and I swear it by the saints.' No one believes a man, entirely, but the world has a curious way of believing legends, and the older the better, as if time gave them verity. It was harder for the Apostles to bear personal witness to the life of My Lord, they who had had the blessed grace to see Him alive among them—and they died for the witnessing—than it is today for a priest to bear the witness through the Church, the Holy Bible and tradition. For the priest teaches what he has been taught, but the Apostles taught what they had known and had seen for themselves and so the people, many of them, did not believe the Apostles, and killed them. Do men fear that all men are liars, then? I do not know. It is very puzzling that men will believe legends, which were first told by dead men, if those legends are old enough.

"It could be," said Father O'Flynn, "that men believe that a story which does not die must be true."

From "Grandmother and the Priests", Taylor Caldwell, Page 369

CHAPTER TWO

TRUTH
in
FACTS, FICTIONS AND MYTHS

When a book is published, do you know what criteria are used to determine whether that book is fact or fiction? This is not a trick question! The publisher's proofreader examines the book very carefully and checks the facts against reality. It's that simple. If the facts are not true, the story line not real or the history deliberately incorrect, the publisher calls the book fiction. On the other hand, if the author calls it fiction, the proofreader checks it to see whether the characters, setting and history are indeed fabricated and contain absolutely no reference to any living person or current situation which might prompt a legal problem. After all, the publisher doesn't want to be sued.

Now, struggle with this, the same rules apply to any Sacred Scripture. As a scientist, I had to search my own Sacred Scripture and question its veracity. Not because I had been taught that God had told the authors what to write but because I had to see for myself whether what was written contained facts, was historically fictitious or whether the characters and stories were mythical. It turned into a study of the history of religions to find out how those many books got to be so revered to the point of being worshiped by most of the Jewish, Christian and Islamic people I met. The result of my search is that all Sacred Scriptures are ... well, read on and make up your own mind.

This Chapter is going to deal with the world of facts and fictions, as they are understood in our daily lives. Let's discover in our descriptive language just how much truth is communicated in movies, literature and speech using fictions, fables and legends.

Let's start with Aesop's Fables, those wonderful stories about real life situations. Remember the fox and the "sour grapes". Now please tell me that you don't recognize the human truth in that fable (fictional story). How about "the boy who cried 'wolf'"? Most people haven't read the rest of Aesop's tales. But they too contain great observations of human behavior. So, how do I know for certain that these tales are not real? Do foxes talk? Do wolves eat humans? Do you know any little boys who play tricks on others? When, or if, you ever read the remaining tales, ask yourself whether it matters whether these tales are factual or not? Meaning doesn't require that the story be real! But understand, the meaning is what counts! The same obtains in all Sacred Scriptures. The deeper meaning does not depend on the veracity of the words and sentences. That's why that genre of literature is Sacred in the first place. It's the meaning that carries a profound, almost Divine, message.

Today, in this 21st century, more than ever, for the first time in history, our level of knowledge and information about the cultures and languages woven into all Sacred Scriptures from as far back as 4000 BC is greater than it was during the time of their writing. For example, within the past 200 years scholars have examined the mythologized structure of those Scriptures written prior to the Old Testament (O.T.)

written between 500 to 100 BC) and have compared some very important books of the O.T. to those very same stories discovered in the more ancient Scriptures from other cultures. That became possible because of the discovery of the "Rosetta Stone" in 1799 AD. What was found in the earliest Scriptures is the very same story reported in the O.T. but reformatted and woven with Hebrew theological traditions. In other words, the Hebrew authors demoted the nature gods of the Enuma Elish to the natural phenomena those names represent. The primary gods of the Enuma Elish (a very fictional myth) were replaced with the one-ness of the Hebrew God. The Noah and Job stories, written many centuries before, were transcribed into O.T. books and were, here again, Hebrew-icized. What were "collective unconscious" memories of the melting Ice Age (the flood) was described in the Epic of Gilgamesh and extracted and added to the book of Genesis. The Job story included what was the generally accepted cosmology of the times and transcribed into Chapter 38. Read it and experience that very primitive, but incorrect description of their world. Discover with us the difficulty in fathoming why the Divine Mind mis-understands its own creation. My only conclusion then is that much of the "alleged science" in Job and Genesis is not accurate, but just cultural ignorance and myth. If that is correct, it's easy to conclude that, for the most part, the Bible is composed from the culture's memories that were retold and massaged to include variations that only a culture can introduce to make its religious colloquial points more imbedded in the minds of the faithful.

The second reason for telling you all that history is to expose you to the problem of differentiating between fact and fiction that likewise bothered the early Christian Church. Thus, the confusions of Christianity's past history haven't helped us one bit. The very same confusions are alive and well in these modern times and continues to be a daily struggle among sectarian people for the reasons explained in the previous Chapter: that pesky, inaccurate, relative human perception influenced by enculturation (of the 1st century), cognitive development (at the level of pre-critical naiveté by both leaders and followers) and, finally, psychological profile (a God of reciprocity—the "eye for an eye" injustice).

Every day in our private lives we are called upon to decide what we read in the newspapers, hear on the radio or see on TV whether all of it, is fact or fiction. Have we not learned that facts are data that can be corroborated by testing their veracity? True facts can be checked! Fiction, on the other hand, is difficult to prove. Why? Because it isn't real in the first place and you'll have to go a long way to establish that this bit of data is actually false. For instance, gossip is one of the most vicious bits of misinformation for the sole reason that it is pure fiction woven with a few small factual threads. Sacred Scriptures, in a similar manner, contain lots of confusing threads of folk theology woven into historical memories within legends and myths of the author's culture.

So now, you should have a better grasp of the nature of facts and fictions. Well, since myth has now been introduced, let's prove to you that myth plays an integral role in the scheme of our own present lives. Myth is a made-up story, yes, and for the most part it is pure fiction! However, myth is like experiencing garlic; the full aroma is experienced only after its thick skin is taken off and the remaining layers peeled open. Myth reveals a profound truth about human behavior, or group dynamics, or simply a truth, only after the literal story is penetrated and the meaning of the figurative language is peeled away.

The Santa Clause myth is one of those fictions that parents keep alive in the retelling of the story during the Christmas holidays. Children learn about self-giving in that myth as do parents perpetuating it. The tooth fairy is another household myth. Let's see, do I have another example? Oh yes, the Easter bunny is one. But actually I don't know how it came about other than the occurrence of Spring and new life which the rabbit personifies in its bountiful creation of new bunnies. Somehow, the relationship of a chocolate Easter bunny candy to the Resurrection stories of the Carpenter from Nazareth is lost in antiquity or it just might be the secularization that has overtaken this country. Or, is it really an ancient Spring Ritual allegory! It's confusing isn't it?

Basically, this is my fundamental premise: myth is more powerful in its ability to convey profound truth than mere one-dimensional facts. In truth, myth is multi-dimensional because it can yield so many levels of meaning. Believe it, analyzing myth is just like peeling that clove of garlic; you've got to remove the superficial skin (the literal story) to reach the full aroma and flavor (the meaning).

There's another example for us to examine. It's reading the newspaper! What do you expect from reading the entire paper? Do you expect facts from the front page to the last page? Do you take some pages with a little pinch of salt? Oh yes, you do! (A pinch of salt is a metaphor and the expression means you don't actually believe everything you read.) How about the front-page news? Is that always absolutely true? And the comics? No, they're not facts, they're allegorical pictures! And your brain automatically looks for the deeper meaning the artist intended in the cartoon strip. How about the sports pages? Well, here's a laugh. The Tigers beat the Cubs! Do you accept that as fact? Were there real tigers or bear cubs in conflict? No, Tigers and Bears is sports talk! It's just figurative language talk! (Did you catch the subtle mistake? The Tigers team is baseball and the Bears team is football! They don't ever compete with each other.) Then how about the advertisements for goods, cars, furniture, etc.? Do you take them literally? No, you don't actually believe everything in the ads, right? Every day you adjust your mind to the facts, fictions and myths you find reading newspapers, listening to the radio, watching TV and in everything else you read, hear and see. And, that's a fact, isn't it? We humans are drowning in myth! The critical reader of Sacred Scriptures has the same problems; which parts are historically accurate and which are mythologized?

Tell me, what do you think about the movie, "The Wizard of Oz", the motion picture film? Later in life did you discover that it really is a great psychological story (mythologized) about a little girl lost in a confused world? Dorothy needed to go home (find herself and her place in life) but couldn't do it alone. She found the straw man who wanted a thinking brain (she sought intellectuality) so she invited him to go along. Later the tin man entered the story. He wanted a heart and she eagerly added him to her travels (she sought compassion, emotionality). Then, the lion showed up and he wanted courage (she sought the courage to choose). Together (in relationship) they all searched for someone who could help them achieve their goals. But the Wizard turns out to be just another human, a wise man who pointed out that one only has to believe in oneself (achieve self esteem and confidence) and all will be fine.

Think of it for a moment. That fable depicts a person who exhibited needs, developed relationships, sought intelligence, emotions and the will to choose. Those are exactly the five characteristics that define the nature of Homo Sapiens! Now, try to say that "the Wizard of OZ" is an empty story. Myth relates deeper meaning but must be worked over (peeled away) to reveal that deeper and, often, profound meaning.

16

If you need more facts about myth in these modern times, try analyzing the Star Trek movies and their deeper mythical meanings. Let's examine a bit of the "story line" along with the perceived deeper meaning of the first film. First though, think about the three principal characters: Spock, Kirk and McCoy. Kirk is the leader, planner and doer, Spock represents wisdom and McCoy is the healer. Does that give you any clue to what this trinity represents? Well, if you haven't seen any of these Star Trek movies, it's a good time to rent them and enjoy. Remember, look for the deeper meaning! Now, I'll just present my perception of that first movie. The rest are in Appendix AG and in the White Paper section on my Internet site: <whyseekmeaning.com>.

1, The first movie, titled, The Motion Picture, was about a Monster, destructive something or other, moving towards the Earth's space destroying everything in its path **...** behaving like a spoiled child. It took a while to uncover its purpose ... to communicate with someone ...all the while "*It*" was seeking its Creator. The Star Trek heroes Kirk, Spock, McCoy and company travel in the Enterprise to intercept the Monster, hoping to stop it. One of the crew is literally assimilated by the Monster and then she returns as a hologram to the Enterprise with a message for the heroes. "V-ger wants to connect with the Creator." The heroes actually fly through V-ger's vastness slowly approaching its core. They get to the center, leave the Enterprise and walk to an old space probe, Voyager (number one) whose purpose was to collect information and data about the Universe. There's a broken wire connection that prevents this space probe from downloading its data (knowledge) to the NASA creator. The heroes fix it and now Voyager can connect and download its collected Terabytes of data. A second crew member volunteers to be absorbed by Voyager Then, Voyager disappears happily into the Universe.
The End.

What's so great about this story? Its subtle meaning points to humans who operate on intelligence (IQ or facts) alone ending in much destruction. Spock hinted at this hidden meaning when he decided to leave Vulcan, the "Logic" planet, and be a member of the Enterprise's human staff. V-ger was the personification of data-knowledge gone awry. And, of course, the NASA group represents God. Returning to God to get full mature knowledge and meaning for our lives is a theme as old as human nature. The real fix is hinted at when the male crew member joins V-ger to be with the female to insure the balance between emotion and intelligence. Did you catch the "fix the disconnected wire"? Aren't we sort of disconnected from God in today's world? Cannot the Trinity fix us? You'll see this theme again in the remaining Star Trek Movies.

Now, wasn't that an interesting fable/Sci-Fi?

Many more of Hollywood's fictional productions are loaded with truths via mythical writing: Snow White, Pinocchio, Bambi, Star Wars Series, Oh God (George Burns and John Denver), Dances with Wolves, Dogma, Stigmata, Bruce Almighty, The Legend of Bagger Vance, Bedazzled, Lord of the Rings, Harry Potter series, The Chronicles of Narnia and so, so many more. Each is a fiction with undertones of Biblical, theological, modern psychological and behavioral themes. If we in modern times can create such popular mythical stories, why do we refuse to acknowledge their use in ancient times? The answer is that we humans find comfort in Divine Laws, or any laws for that matter. Laws tell us what to do and free us from making ourselves responsible for our choices. We humans relish passing the buck, just like Augustine (425 AD) did when he blamed the mythical Adam and Eve for his lustful youth. It was Augustine pf Hippo who created

"Original Sin"! And that has been nothing more than a supreme guilt-trip nurtured by folk-theology that separates us from God. We humans look into a mirror but only see a facial portrait while missing the soul's true visage much like the movie, The Picture of Dorian Grey, whose portrait displayed not just his face but also his true soul.

As you found out in the previous chapter, everybody sees things differently; people only see or hear what they want. That makes us humans limited by our own perception and its inherent subjectivity. It's our human condition. At least, that's what I tell people when they have a conflict of interest! Children are brought up by parents who see things differently. Therefore, children develop different criteria for determining what is truth. Now, translate that to the perceptions of the peoples of this world!

Before we proceed to the Job and Genesis stories, it's important that we examine one final misconception in the quest for truth in myth. When you hear the phrase, "Have a heart", what do you think you're being asked to do? All have used that phrase. Especially in the O.T.! I wonder if they knew what it meant. It's telling that person to have compassion! Now, examine the denotation of that phrase, its literal meaning. It's telling the person to have a heart, right? Isn't that kind of silly? We all have hearts! So why did they not understand that the phrase meant to chide the person to be compassionate? At one time the heart was thought to be the organ that produced the emotion of compassion. Today the educated know that the brain is the center of all emotions. However, that particular phrase has taken on a mythic quality. We all accept its deeper meaning because, not only has it been handed down through the centuries as one from the "collective unconscious" but that it also is believed to be true— "the heart is the center of emotions and intellect." See Appendix AE. Can you have a stone heart and live? They're metaphors, but the illiterate take it literally. Can you think of any other such phrase that carries a false meaning via a misunderstood metaphor?

How about "stiff necked"? What does "stone hearted" really mean? "You have a brain like concrete" (all mixed up and firmly set). Now, don't take that one personally, we're only quoting some of the more familiar metaphors. Here's one, "you're chicken"! OK, do you now give up and accept the reality that you do use figurative language in your everyday life?

We all know a lot about the types of myth we use in daily conversation. The problem is, we automatically, subconsciously, shift our interpretational mental mechanism depending upon the material we read, see or hear. However (and here is a very important observation), when it comes to Sacred Scriptures, our "pre-critical naiveté" training takes over and shifts our minds into a tape-recording mode in which the speaker is GOD. What we have to learn as adults is to shift into a critical or post critical mode when reading Sacred Scriptures exactly like we do reading our daily newspapers!

Why, you ask? Because we were all taught during childhood that our Sacred Scriptures came directly from God and our minds were never equipped to challenge that statement. Certainly, when you read Aesop's Fables, you read it as it should be understood; it's allegory and that's myth. "Sour Grapes" is a very meaningful phrase. It's so well known that we don't even have to translate it for you, you already know the meaning and the sting of hearing those two words spoken to you. No one can escape struggling with translational denotation and connotation. All good literature (even our newspaper) has built into itself the dictionary definitions as well as that which the words, and sentences, imply. When people read poetry and find allegories, similes, metaphors, parables, irony, all of which are mythic language, do they take it literally as opposed to the implied meaning? Of course not! That's the beauty in poetry and the beauty in myth: discovering the hidden meaning. One has to remove several layers of the garlic clove before getting to the powerful aroma. The Sacred Scriptures are powerful, not because they are factual or tape-recorded messages from Allah but because they contain "Power in their Myth" (Joseph Campbell's thesis). To be sure, there are many myths and each requires extensive peeling or excavation to reveal the intended and implied truth. But, in most cases, Bible Study, for example, has become an emotional dispute over sectarian doctrines, a most unbecoming, hateful sport. People, it seems, would rather guard their fort than examine and unravel the myths for their profound truths.

Here's a little story that is appropriate at this point. It's about a farmer's good or possibly bad fortune from his neighbor's point of view (perception). It's the story of Chin Li and it's called "What is Good? What is Evil?"

> There lived in a fertile valley somewhere in China a father and his son. They owned a farm and raised horses. One day the lead stallion ran off into the wilderness and didn't return. Chow Mein, the farmer's neighbor, came for a visit and after he heard the tale he remarked, "What an evil thing that has befallen you!" To which Chin Li said, "What is Evil? What is Good?"
>
> Within six months the stallion returned with seven mares, all healthy and strong. Chin Li and his son were pleased. When the neighbor heard of this, he immediately visited Chin Li and remarked, "What a wonderful good that has come your way." To which Chin Li responded, "What is Good? What is Evil?"
>
> Then when the son was breaking in the mares, he was thrown off the first one and broke his leg and arm in the fall. When the neighbor heard of this he came over to Chin Li and said sadly, " What a terrible evil that comes to your house." To which Chin Li remarked, " What is Evil? What is Good?"
>
> Now, it came to pass that the military was conscripting young men for its war. When they arrived at Chin Li's farm they expected to take his son away. However, upon seeing his infirmity, passed by without taking the boy. When Chow Mein heard that story he rushed over to Chin Li and told him, "What a shameful dishonor you must feel for your son that he was unable to fight for his country." To which Chin Li responded seriously, "What is dishonor? What is honor?
>
> Three months later news came that the army was decidedly beaten in their first battle and no one survived. As soon as the neighbor heard this news he ran over to Chin Li and congratulated him, saying, "What a happy occasion of Good fortune has blessed your house." To which Chin Li re-iterated softly, " What is Good? What is Evil?"

Now, ask yourself, what has life brought to you? When at a spiritual retreat many years ago, the Master asked us to make a time-line like a sine curve and date the good times (peaks) and the not-so-good times (valleys) that happened in our lives. That was a great little exercise! You might want to try it yourself sometimes and maybe do it with your spouse, if you are still fortunate enough to have one, or with a sibling. There's more to that little short story you've just read! When you did your own time-line, did you see the Good things and the not-so-Good things that happened to you or your family? Were they really Good or not-so-Good?

Here's the punch line! How about what is happening to you as you read this book? Have you been tempted to say that this material is not-so-Good for you? Or, have you found it interesting and challenging? If the former, please, don't give up. The better Good is yet to come. We are just in a re-building mode and must construct a strong new foundation so that when you rebuild your spiritual house it will rest on firm ground. Now, that's a good simile!

PART ONE: Myth in the Creation Stories of Sacred Scriptures

Most Sacred Scriptures have very little to say about creation. Check Appendix L for the Internet URL's for each of our listed Sacred Scriptures and find them on the Internet. Read a few of the beginning verses to discover what each writes about creation.

Section One: The Babylonian Myth

The Enuma Elish contains in its first several verses a strange tale of many gods starting with a male and a female god who populate the world with many sub-deities. There is no specific creation of all that exist. These two gods start from a barren planet. Apsu and Tiamat then create the remaining demi-gods some of whom turn evil and kill the god Apsu, the male progenitor, and leave Tiamat, the female goddess, untouched who now seeks revenge. Note that Good and Evil co-exist from the very beginning (that's the Babylonian Light and Darkness that later become the metaphor for good and evil in the Bible). The description in this Sacred Scripture of the Earth's original condition is a familiar format, almost story for story, appearing in the Hebrew Testament's Genesis story of creation. This leads many scholars to conclude that Genesis 1 & 2 were written after the Exile!

Section Two: The Hindu Myth

In reading the Upanishads, you will find these creation verses:

1. In KHANDOGYA-UPANISHAD Part 1, FIRST PRAPATHAKA. NINTH KHANDA: 1 *"'What is the origin of this world?' 'Ether',' he replied. For all these beings take their rise from the ether, and return into the ether. Ether is older than these, ether is their rest."*
2. In KHANDOGYA-UPANISHAD Part 2, THIRD PRAPATHAKA, NINETEENTH KHANDA: 1. *Aditya (the sun) is Brahman, this is the doctrine, and this is the fuller account of it: In the beginning this was non-existent. It became existent, it grew. It turned into an egg. The egg lay for the time of a year. The egg broke open. The two halves were one of silver, the other of gold. 2. The silver one became this earth, the golden one the sky, the thick membrane (of the white) the mountains, the thin membrane (of the yoke) the mist with the clouds, the small veins the rivers, the fluid the sea. 3. And what was born from it that was Aditya, the sun.*
3. In the FMYTH PRAPATHAKA, SEVENTEENTH KHANDA,: 1. *Pragapati brooded over the worlds, and from them thus brooded on he squeezed out the essences, Agni (fire) from the earth, Vayu (air) from the sky, Aditya (the sun) from heaven. 2. He brooded over these three deities, and from them thus*

brooded on he squeezed out the essences, the Rik verses from Agni, the Yagus verses from Vayu, the Saman verses from Aditya. Does this sound familiar?

4. And, finally, in the SIXTH PRAPATHAKA, SECOND KHAVDA: 1. *'In the beginning,' my dear, 'there was that only which is, one only, without a second. Others say, in the beginning there was that only which is not, one only, without a second; and from that which is not, that which is was born. 2. 'But how could it be thus, my dear?' the father continued. 'How could that which is, be born of that which is not? No, my dear, only that which is, was in the beginning, one only, without a second. 3. 'It thought, may I be many, may I grow forth. It sent forth fire. 'That fire thought, may I be many, may I grow forth. It sent forth water. 'And therefore whenever anybody anywhere is hot and perspires, water is produced on him from fire alone. 4. 'Water thought, may I be many, may I grow forth. It sent forth earth (food). 'Therefore whenever it rains anywhere, most food is then produced. From water alone is eatable food produced.*
   THIRD KHANDA: *1. 'Of all living things there are indeed three origins only, that which springs from an egg (oviparous), that which springs from a living being (viviparous), and that which springs from a germ. 2. 'That Being, (i. e. that which had produced fire, water, and earth) thought, let me now enter those three beings, (fire, water, earth) with this living Self (giva atma)', and let me then reveal (develop) names and forms. 3. 'Then that Being having said, Let me make each of these three tripartite (so that fire, water, and earth should each have itself for its principal ingredient, besides an admixture of the other two) entered into those three beings (devata) with this living self only, and revealed names and forms. 4. 'He made each of these tripartite; and how these three beings become each of them tripartite, that learn from me now, my friend!* FOURTH KHANDA: *1. 'The red colour of burning fire (agni) is the colour of fire, the white colour of fire is the colour of water, the black colour of fire the colour of earth. Thus vanishes what I call fire, as a mere variety, being a name, arising from speech. What is true (satya) are the three colours (or forms). 2. 'The red colour of the sun (aditya) is the colour of fire, the white of water, the black of earth. Thus vanishes what I call the sun, as a mere variety, being a name, arising from speech. What is true are the three colours. 3. 'The red colour of the moon is the colour of fire, the white of water, the black of earth. Thus vanishes what I call the moon, as a mere variety, being a name, arising from speech. What is true are the three colours. 4. 'The red colour of the lightning is the colour of fire, the white of water, the black of earth. Thus vanishes what I call the lightning, as a mere variety, being a name, arising from speech. What is true are the three colours. 5. 'Great householders and great theologians of olden times who knew this, have declared the same, saying, " No one can henceforth mention to us anything which I have not heard, perceived, or known'." Out of these (three colours or forms) they knew all. 6. 'Whatever they thought looked red, they knew was the colour of fire. Whatever they thought looked white, they knew was the colour of water. Whatever they thought looked black, they knew was the colour of earth. 7. 'Whatever they thought was altogether unknown, they knew was some combination of those three beings (devata). 'Now learn from me, my friend, how those three beings, when they reach man, become each of them tripartite. FIFTH KHANDA: 1. 'The earth (food) when eaten becomes threefold; its grossest portion becomes feces, its middle portion flesh, its subtilest portion mind. 2. 'Water when drunk becomes*

threefold; its grossest portion becomes water, its middle portion blood, its subtilest portion breath. 3. 'Fire (i.e. in oil, butter, &c.) when eaten becomes threefold; its grossest portion becomes bone, its middle portion marrow, its subtilest portion speech. 4. 'For truly, my child, mind comes of earth, breath of water, speech of fire.' 'Please, Sir, inform me still more,' said the son. Be it so, my child,' the father replied.

In these readings one can see that there are several problems for the reader: the Indian language is a barrier, the constant circumlocution and use of specific numbers (numerology was the thing back then!) and, finally, the science of a primitive culture. The authors struggled with the logic of an eternal, pre-existent single Being, a Being without any other. Thomas Troward in his "Edenborough Lectures on Mental Science" spends the entire first few chapters explaining why there can only be a single eternal, infinite Being.

Section Three: The Israelite Myth

Although Genesis 1 and 2 are the first stories of creation in the O.T. and later a similar story shows up in Job 38, let's examine Job 38 first. But right now, before we proceed further, please read Job Chapter 38. As you read it, make a mental note of what you think the punch lines are for each of the verses. You may even try constructing a picture of the world as described in Job 38.

OK, it's my turn now! let's analyze that worldview written in Job 38. First, clearly that Chapter can be readily proven to be a false cosmology. It says that the Earth (a plate) rests on pillars; the sky has gates that open for the rain to come down. The snow, hail and ice are each held in separate jars, darkness is placed in hiding when daylight appears and vice versa for light. Oh, please tell me where those pillars, gates, jars and hiding places are! They don't exist! The entire Chapter is one big incorrect cosmology. It's a mythic construct meant to challenge Job and those who think they know God's mind. The meaning of the entire Job story, and mythic a story it is, is simply to dispel the folk theology that being good receives rewards and doing wrong brings down God's wrath and punishment. It is a mythic tale of a person moving out of the second stage (Reciprocity) to a higher stage of the psychological profiles described in the preceding Chapter.

If God really dictated the Bible, Job 38 is a very BIG MISTAKE in communication. So ponder it! Why do so many still cling to such mis-information about the Universe? Or, is it the shock of finding out that some parts of the Bible are mythic stories? Let's get on with Genesis.

Sectiom Four: Evil and the Apple Eating Tale Myth

Even Jesus in the Synoptic Gospels believed that sickness was for bad behavior (sin) and could be cured by driving out the demons that caused the sickness. Read the completely fabricated theological story in John 9 for a terrific and slightly different approach to blindness. Please take notice of the statement that the blind man wasn't blind because of his parent's sin or his own sin. Doesn't that sound like a contradiction to the folk doctrine of original sin? It sure does! Augustine's original sin thesis is man's second attempt to blame someone else for his own choices. Do you know the first time in literature someone blamed the other for his sin? Yes, it was Adam who ate the apple, a terrific mythical and memorable drama along with Cain's murder of Able which most Jewish scholars believe to have been the first real sin. Oh, by the way, the apple allegory really means the developmental moment of human consciousness about personal and social wrongdoing. After many years as a psychotherapist I believe that somehow this consciousness has not occurred in a large fraction of humans. Be that as it may, I vote that real sin is in the Cain and Able story. A brief note of interest here about Genesis 2: Origen, a 2nd century Christian Church Father, wrote that the Garden of Eden and the Adam and Eve stories are not real, just great cosmic myths. Three cheers for Origen !

In Genesis 1 creation takes place stepwise over seven days. Most every scholar recognizes that it is simple poetry patterned after the seven days of the week and results in a Divine origin for the day of rest. Also, in Numerology, seven is considered to mean the "fullest" or "most bountiful " number, almost like a perfect number. Remember when Jesus (really Yeshua in Aramaic) was asked how many times should someone forgive, seven times? Jesus is reported to have answered, "No, seventy seven times" (Matt 18:22-NAB), a super abundant amount of perfect times (77)! It is not strange that the number seven is the key to forgiveness: 77 is certainly a full quantity of forgiveness. Note carefully: (1) Luke 17: 4 (NAB) writes "each of the 7 time he sins", (2) in the New Revised Standard it quotes both 77 and 490 times. Which is the correct number? Luke's "each time", Matthew's 77 or 490? If God inspired the writers, how come there are differences from author to author and Biblical translation to translation? Is it God's fault or the author's? Do you think that maybe there is no such communication from God to those authors? I'll present several reasons in Chapter Five

Ok, what about the individual days of creation.

Genesis 1: verse one says that when God started creating the earth and the heavens, there was in existence: the Earth as a formless wasteland, darkness over the abyss (beyond the oceans) and a mighty wind (or breath) that swept over the waters. The text is unclear whether these existed before the act of creation or did God make them first. I suspect, as do scholars, that the act of creation really starts when God creates "light". So, here we have our first dilemma! Enter Science! I believe that this first paragraph says that God's plan is to create the earth and the heavens and the first act was "light". So, just as Albert Einstein mathematically determined that Energy and matter co-exist, consider the possibility that poetic Earth, Abyss and Wind preexisted as fundamental nuclear particles with God in timelessness. God then brought all primary matter (to date, it's QUARKS) into Her bosom and, BEHOLD!, there was the Universe's first nuclear fusion explosion, a really big, BIG BANG. You may want to read Appendix X+Y for a different Creation Myth.

Well, it appears that God did not just create a star; it was instead an entire Universe-filling, noisy explosion of matter into the vacuum of infinite space. {For those of you who have a modicum of knowledge of physics, it was the energy (Mass Defect) that was released that heated all matter to molten missiles. This Mass Defect is the difference in mass between (a) the sum of the masses of the fundamental particles that constitute an element and (b) the resultant mass of the element formed.} That Big Bang did not create our solar system's sun because that came later. Now, a few billion years (remember the Hebrew word, *yowm,* also means a long time period!) passed before the whole fiery mass cooled and coalesced into huge stars and smaller planets of the Universe. {The technical name for that process is "accretion".} After that time the earth was definitely a formless wasteland, the abyss (salt water seas or the beyond) were in darkness and the winds were howling over the rivers and lakes formed by the condensing gaseous moisture surrounding the earth. What's being proposed is that the Genesis description (written about 500 BC) is pure poetry conveying not reality but the following truths: (1) God created everything, (2) everything is good, (3) the six days are structured to coincide with a six-day work week and a seventh day of rest in consort with the Hebrew nation's theology mythologized in the stories of the Exodus from the Oral Tradition. Since the Hebrew word for day is "yowm" whose secondary meaning is "a long time", it means that evolution turns out to be the mechanism by which the Universe, and particularly the Earth, developed, including precursors of chimpanzees developing into humans. You may wish to examine Appendix G and H for Geology's evidence of evolution,

Let's look at this personal experience that may help your perception of "evolution". Our family visited the USS Constitution in Boston, Mass. some years back and while walking below deck from compartment to compartment, I bumped my head at each doorway (the naval term is hatchway). It then dawned on me that the average sailor 200 years ago was shorter, by at least six inches, than the average sailor today. Well, if the average height of humans could get taller in a period of two hundred years, why couldn't humanity and the rest of creation change in billions of years? Evidently, people's problem with accepting evolution is not with its alleged contradiction with the Biblical age, it's because most people cannot comprehend the capacity of the Universe to change over a period of 14 - 16 billion years. Most aren't aware of the changes that have taken place in the last 200 years of American history, let alone imagine what the Universe was 7,000,000 years ago. Now, ask them to conceive of the changes over a billion years. It's much too large a number for the average mind to grasp! How would you spend 500 million dollars if you were to win some lottery? After a while you would own all the possible goods available and still there would be money left over. Could it be that given the enculturation most have received, we humans find it far easier to accept a literal description from the Divine than to struggle with a great meaningful mythical story.

I need to interrupt this for a line or two to make a point about why there is so much myth in the Bible. Let me remind you that I am a Scientist and a Christian with Nuclear, Theological and Psychological backgrounds. I firmly believe that the Bible is a great source of Godly information; but it's neither a Science or history text. Nor is it a tape recording of God's voice!

With the Big Bang explained and my observation that evolution IS God's plan for the Universe, let me make this clear: God's power keeps everything in existence and God's Spirit resides IN everything (that's called Pan-En-Theism). But don't confuse this with "God IS a thing" (Pantheism). God's Spirit could not find expression until there was a being in creation that was capable of voicing that expression. That being was Homo Sapiens who came into existence about some 7 million years ago on this planet. Homo Sapiens had to arrive here through the natural God-created order – Darwin recognized that order --- he called it evolution.

What is very impressive is the order of creation in the seven days (*yowm*) of Genesis One. According to one reference, *yowm* is the Hebrew word for day and a long time! That order starting with plant life is very close to, if not exactly, what biologists would predict from evolutionary science and, actually, what Geologists have observed in the Fossil Record. Therefore, can you perceive that the hidden message in the Genesis Myth is that Evolution is according to God's Natural Law? Again and again, one will find that myth in the Bible is bigger than just scientific facts, it's more than informative and it points to the mystery of our Divine origin. The real evidence is that the natural order of creation can be related closely to the divisions within the Geological times: Eons, Eras, Periods and Epochs (Look again at Appendix G and H):

1st Interval: (~7 Billion years): "Let there be Light!"—from a singularity (a white hole) to the Big Bang, a nuclear explosion that creates the molten elements for the entire Universe!! These would eventually coalesce into stars and planets, a process called "Accretion" observed during one of NASA's space flights. As a matter of astronomical fact, we have seen little bangs occurring in distant space. Of course that light-show may have taken all this time to traverse the distance between us. This hot radioactive universe took a very long time to expand and cool. The Force of the fusion pushed the expansion outwards and gravity kept the inertial force constant. As time and distance between galaxies increased, the Universe slowly moved away at a faster rate. Hubble discovered that acceleration in the last half of the 20th century.

2nd Interval (~3 Billion years): Of all that coalesced, one of the stars is our Solar System's sun and one of the planets in that System is Earth, along with the other planets in our system. [Note: except Venus, which has been suggested to have arrived from outside of the Milky Way.] This is the time written of in the Genesis Myth as Day One. Understand that the planet Earth had yet not totally cooled to the solid state; our core is still molten to this very day--volcanoes are proof of this molten center. Towards the end, last 0.5 billion, of this *yowm* the liquid surface slowly cools and apparently begins to form a solid surface and cause the moisture clouds surrounding the planet to condense. The surface hardens. The rains come. The resultant contractions will eventually produce mountains, visible cracks (like the Great Lakes) and other basins. The Oceans depress portions of the Earth and the land mass aligns at the equator and begins its extremely slow redistribution to form the continents. It did not slow down until about 50 million years prior to our present day. Within the past 50 years the US Naval Nuclear Submarine program has photographed the ocean floor with Sonar. That shifting is quite visible on maps printed by the National Geographic Magazine illustrating this phenomenon. At the end of the second day the Universe was then close to 10 billion years old and the barren Earth in existence for almost 1 billion years. This is identified in Appendix G as the Precambrian Eon.

3rd Interval (~2 Billion years): This interval begins with the surface sufficiently cooled with a gaseous atmosphere whose composition differed significantly from that of the modern world. For the past 1 billion plus years the surface has been contracting due to the surface cooling and thus compressing the molten liquid center forcing it to release its internal pressure outwards. Volcanic eruptions took place covering some of the surface with a thicker crust. Then plates that had solidified earlier cracked and caused all sorts of earthquakes and surface folding as well as the upwards thrust of the planet's mountains. The atmosphere cooled and it rained profusely carving out the rivers and most likely the Grand Canyon. There were turbulent and severe lightning storms. The ocean covered close to 75% of the Earth's surface and the land mass, originally one big continent about the equator, was now slowly reforming due to the shifting plates below the Earth's crust. The water, gases, the heat from excessive internal radiation contributed to the formation of single-cellular life. These were the beginning of evolution's many radiation induced mutations through the ages!

> [Note: This has been verified by a lab experiment in a container filled with Carbon Dioxide, Ammonia, Methane and Hydrogen (the suspected typical atmosphere at that time) exposed to high levels of Gamma radiation. Complex amino acids, the building blocks of DNA, were formed inside the vessel.]

Thus, the earliest and simplest life forms were initiated in the condensation when the planet cooled sufficiently. The ocean with all of its rich mineral content produced a myriad of single-celled microscopic forms that have been classified in the Fossil Record. These single-celled microscopic forms evolved into the plant and animal forms, identified as the Cambrian explosion (550 to 490 million years ago (re-examine Appendix H). Eventually the physical and atmospheric conditions caused the evolution of the ocean's and the landmass' plant and animal species to higher forms. In this period some of the water animals migrated to land. There were snakes, lizards, alligators, turtles and all sorts of evolved creatures except mammals. There is evidence that a mutation process, enhanced by the high levels of radiation, caused DNA changes that gave birth to new species. Here is a good theory. In Physics I learned that there are four forces in Nature: Gravity, Electro-Magnetic, Strong (Nuclear) and Weak (Chemical). Could it be that God created another force that we humans have not yet considered, a Life Force? The rules for it are simple: "Where and when there exists a possibility, no matter how small the probability, life will occur." Many hard line Literalists have tried to prove that it is statistically impossible for life to occur in just those few billions of years. Maybe this Life Force theory explains the Creator's intentions! This interval is called the Paleozoic Era. It ends with the Permian Period in which occurred the largest mass extinction of life on Earth recorded in the geological history. It affected many groups of organisms in many different environments, but it affected marine communities the most by far, causing the extinction of most of the marine invertebrates of the time. On land, a relatively smaller extinction cleared the way for other forms to dominate, and led to what has been called the "Age of the Dinosaurs". Also, the great forests of fern-like plants shifted to plants with their offspring enclosed within seeds. Modern conifers, the most familiar of today, first appear in the fossil record of the Permian. In all, the Permian was the end of time for some organisms and a pivotal point for others, and life on earth was never the same again. The Earth is approaching 4 billion years old and the Universe approximately 13.5 billion. It is interesting to note that as of this writing, scientists have calculated that the Universe may be as old as 16 billion years.

4th Interval (248 to 65 Million years: This interval, the Mesozoic Era, is the great age of the dinosaurs: Triassic, Jurassic and Cretaceous Periods. I needn't describe anything more because most have seen the "Jurassic Park" motion picture trilogy. So now after the dinosaurs have passed into history, the Universe is approaching 13.7 billion years old and Earth is closing in on 4.5 billion, and growing strong. The next *yowm* if you please!

5th Interval (65 to 1.8 Million years): The remaining interval to our present is the Cenozoic Era, divided into two Periods: the Tertiary and the Quaternary. So now, during this Tertiary Period the land and oceans experienced a renewed growth in the variety of plants and animals, and, most particularly, mammals. At first there was an evolutionary explosion of mammals, all of which were small and primitive. Then changes occurred in their development; the first elephants appeared along with horses and the many grasses that eventually produced vast grasslands and kelp in the oceans. During that time the polar caps began to grow significantly colder forming the great glaciers leading to the ice age. The age of the Universe was nearing its presently estimated value of 14-16 billion years and our blue planet about 4.5 billion. There is evidence that humankind began their development some 7 million years ago.

6th Interval (1.8 Million to 10,000 years): Then, between 7,000,000 to 500,000 years ago the precursors of Homo Sapiens appeared. The debate over the actual time is still ongoing. As new human bones are discovered and analyzed by radioactive dating, a better estimate of the beginning of human life may be discovered. Suffice it for the moment and consider that the cave drawings found throughout Europe and Asia confirm the presence of an intelligent species that existed between 300,000 to close to 50,000 years ago. The fossil record also confirms two types of intelligent beings in that landmass: the Neanderthals and the Cro-Magnons. Since these human races existed, their predecessors were also of human origin. It now becomes clear that humans were definitely on this planet far more than 500,000 years ago, which makes the previous estimates pretty much in the ballpark.

However, there is strong evidence that multi-genesis was the planet's process by which humans originated, not an Adam and not an Eve! Neanderthals possessed certain physical attributes that differed with their Cro-Magnon neighbors. And now, there is evidence that the Cro-Magnons race may have come from the southern tip of Africa and started to migrate throughout the entire surface of Earth sometime around 300,000 years ago. Mitochondrial DNA studies indicate that the people from all parts of the world have identical forms. That would imply that those Africans made a significant contribution to the "gene pool" of present-day Homo Sapiens. The other species were not annihilated but, I believe, simply integrated into the larger gene pool. {That hypothesis is available in VHS and DVD formats, look for "The Real Eve" from the Discovery Channel, accessible on the Internet.} Evidence for this is the existence of Neanderthal characteristics (eye-ridges and/or sloping foreheads) among some individuals today regardless of race, ethnic or geographical boundaries. The Universe is now just 10,000 years short of the 21st century.

7th Interval (10,000 years to Present) At this point it would seem plausible that the seventh day started shortly after the melting of the Ice Age, give or take a few thousand years. Humans were everywhere on the planet and were the ones who did all the creating. So, it does look like God rested. And, as one would expect, humans did a less than perfect job of it. Actually, humans did create written communication. Pictured walls and oral traditions were the primary means of transmitting knowledge during the past before the year 4000 BC. After 4000 BC writing became the vogue, human creativity myth-ed the real history. The only written information in our possession came from those cultures essentially located in the fertile regions of what is presently known as the Middle

East. Studies of their writings give evidence of a distinctly male dominated society that appears to have persisted to this day in that region and throughout Europe and Asia. The rest that happened is history, but not totally factual until way past the invention of the printing press. Well, folks, even some of the stuff I see printed today is still not totally factual! We have arrived at the 21st century. I hope you have had an interesting trip and digested all this material without any Tums!

PART TWO: An Analysis of Genesis 1 & 2

At this juncture, let's turn to the actual Genesis story in the Revised Standard Version (RSV). I will add comments after each day of the seven days.

RSV: BOOK OF GENESIS
Chapter One
1 In the beginning God created the heavens and the earth. 2 The earth was without form and void, and darkness was upon the face of the deep; and the Spirit {actually, a mighty wind or breath in Hebrew} of God was moving over the face of the waters. 3 And God said, "Let there be light"; and there was light. 4 And God saw that the light was good; and God separated the light from the darkness. 5 God called the light Day, and the darkness he called Night. And there was evening and there was morning, one day.

First comment: In verses 1 and 2 there are two interpretations possible: (a) God created earth, water and deep space; all of which are in chaos. God's "*ruah*" or "*ruwach*", breath, {spirit is a Latin word used by Jerome in 400 AD} was intimate with all three. That means verse zero would have said that God existed in only a spirit world, that is, nothing material. So creation out of nothing, "ex nihilo", transformed the chaos in verse 1 and 2 by means of "the light" in verse 3. [An interesting alternative theory can be found in Appendices X+Y.] The phrase, "Let there be light" initiated the nuclear fusion reaction bringing chemical order and physical law to all the molten elements. (b) There was no form, no light and only a void, a chaos of waters, meaning that all the fundamental nuclear particles were preexistent with God. Other translations have a "when" between beginning and God in the first verse. That conjunction implies that creation starts with verse 3, "Let there be light". Verse 4 identifies the nuclear light that pierced the infinite darkness as the first manifestation of material form and order. God was pleased. God put a human label on the difference between the black void of space and the brightness of this nuclear proliferation of matter. And, in addition, God was proclaiming that Good had just conquered Evil. Have you missed the simile, "light is Good" and "darkness is Evil"? My goodness, folks, that simile is in every book, every TV drama and every movie, especially, the westerns whose heroes wore white hats and the bad guys always wore black. Well, all except Paladin, the TV series of the 20th century. I'll talk about the mistake of the day and night thing later in Chapter Five.

6 And God said, "Let there be a firmament in the midst of the waters, and let it separate the waters from the waters." 7 And God made the firmament and separated the waters that were under the firmament from the waters that were above the firmament. And it was so. 8 And God called the firmament Heaven. And there was evening and there was morning, a second day.

Second Comment: Now, I begin to see that the remaining story is patterned after the flat earth cosmology found in Job 38 as well as the Enuma Elish that the exiled Israelites learned while in Babylon. Don't be confused by the repetitive use of the word, waters in verse 6. "Waters" refers not only to the ocean which bordered all the land mass and which leads to the abyss (the deep part of the ocean containing the horrible monsters) but also to the waters held above on the firmament that brings rain, hail and snow. [NOTE: firmament means an upside down bowl! You know, like the Earth as a plate, covered with an inverted bowl with gates on its interior to let the rain, hail and snow fall through to the earth.] This concept is a misunderstanding of the ancient atmosphere. Thus the reference to Heaven on the other side of the firmament has led us to use "up there" as the place of God's heavenly throne. The Space Program has debunked most of that description!

> *9 And God said, "Let the waters under the heavens be gathered together into one place, and let the dry land appear." And it was so. 10 God called the dry land earth, and the waters that were gathered together he called seas. And God saw that it was good. 11 And God said, "Let the earth put forth vegetation, plants yielding seed, and fruit trees bearing fruit in which is their seed, each according to its kind, upon the earth." And it was so. 12 The earth brought forth vegetation, plants yielding seed according to their own kinds, and trees bearing fruit in which is their seed, each according to its kind. And God saw that it was good. 13 And there was evening and there was morning, a third day.*

Third Comment: Here is the first real factual correlation with the Geology model above. The Earth is solidifying and the atmosphere is just super saturated with moisture. The surface cools and it is mostly covered with liquid. The land mass buckles somewhat to push a large section of itself upwards. All that in one verse! The story gets better. Once the place is wet, the ingredients are present, willing and able, to produce cellular life. (Remember the "Life Force"?) Cellular life mutates to multi-cellular life of the plant variety. However, the fossil record does not verify the immediate jump to seed bearing plant life. There is an excellent Internet reference to a Geology site where you can read about the fossil record and the classifications of the many different time periods from the beginning of the formation of Earth. See Appendix L, Internet References, and Appendix G for the geological designations.

> *14 And God said, "Let there be lights in the firmament of the heavens to separate the day from the night; and let them be for signs and for seasons and for days and years, 15 and let them be lights in the firmament of the heavens to give light upon the earth." And it was so. 16 And God made the two great lights, the greater light to rule the day, and the lesser light to rule the night; he made the stars also. 17 And God set them in the firmament of the heavens to give light upon the earth, 18 to rule over the day and over the night, and to separate the light from the darkness. And God saw that it was good. 19 And there was evening and there was morning, a fourth day.*

Fourth Comment: First off, please notice that the word "light" has different connotations (implications) thus far! If there was a literal "light" created early on, why have two more now? So, Literalists recalibrate that gray matter! Now, to Verse 14 that introduces an error in the evolutionary sequence; the stars were in their place and orientation by the end of the second *yowm*, not the fourth day. The same argument applies to the sun and the moon. There can be no day and night on Earth without the sun and moon.

Science/Geology 5 points, A Factual Genesis 0 points!

> *20 And God said, "Let the waters bring forth swarms of living creatures, and let birds fly above the earth across the firmament of the heavens." 21 So God created the great sea monsters and every living creature that moves, with which the waters swarm, according to their kinds, and every winged bird according to its kind. And God saw that it was good. 22 And God blessed them, saying, "Be fruitful and multiply and fill the waters in the seas, and let birds multiply on the earth." 23 And there was evening and there was morning, a fifth day.*

Fifth Comment: Now we're back to instant creation that doesn't jive with the fossil record. Geology proves a gradual evolutionary process. There is no mention here or in the next verses of the sixth day that God creates cannibalism: animals eating animals for nutrition. Ask yourself; was it a good thing that sea and land animals ate each other as part of the natural law? Was that a good thing?

> *24 And God said, "Let the earth bring forth living creatures according to their kinds: cattle and creeping things and beasts of the earth according to their kinds." And it was so. 25 And God made the beasts of the earth according to their kinds and the cattle according to their kinds, and everything that creeps upon the ground according to its kind. And God saw that it was good. 26 Then God said, "Let us make man in my image, after my likeness; and let them have dominion over the fish of the sea, and over the birds of the air, and over the cattle, and over all the earth, and over every creeping thing that creeps upon the earth." 27 So God created man in his own image, in the image of God he created him; male and female he created them. 28 And God blessed them, and God said to them, "Be fruitful and multiply, and fill the earth and subdue it; and have dominion over the fish of the sea and over the birds of the air and over every living thing that moves upon the earth." 29 And God said, "Behold, I have given you every plant yielding seed which is upon the face of all the earth, and every tree with seed in its fruit; you shall have them for food. 30 And to every beast of the earth, and to every bird of the air, and to everything that creeps on the earth, everything that has the breath of life, I have given every green plant for food." And it was so. 31 And God saw everything that he had made, and behold, it was very good. And there was evening and there was morning, a sixth day.*

Sixth Comment: The big day for humans has arrived. First, let's say something about the use of the pronoun "us" in verse 26. It simply means that the culture believed that there were other lesser spirits with God, angels, sons of God or Heaven, *angelos* in Greek means messenger. [Christian literalists believed that it implies Trinity. Trinitarianism is what caused the Jewish Christians to be excommunicated from the synagogue in 85 AD.] Later in Genesis these same sons of Heaven would descend to Earth and copulate with the human women (see Gen 6: 4). So at this point in v. 26 we come to "man" who is made in the "image" of God. Does that literally mean that God has a body like us? Does God have a heart like us? The answer is, NO! Metaphor and simile are the tools used to describe God. Wow, that surely is a simile deserving of a theological book or two. Can you actually write down what it means to you? Is it my body that's like God? If it is, then God is material! Oh, get this, God must then have both a male and a female body? If you take the Bible literally, God is a cross-gendered Being—one moment HE appears male and the next moment SHE appears female. And that's just the problem confronting the literalists who adhere to a factual, tape-recorded Bible or Sacred Scripture.

God is Spirit! God is not a "HE" nor is God a "SHE"! God has no hands, feet, throne, nor is God old. Therefore, the Bible is mistaken when it refers to God's hands, feet, throne or any other physical attribute. What we must get into our heads is that those references are similes, allegories, metaphors ... simply figurative language. That was the only literary style the "encultured" Bible writers could use to explain such mysteries of creation in a way that would be understandable to all people for all times.

Now, examine the rest of v. 26. Man, male and female, is given dominion over the rest of Earth and is told to subdue it in v. 28! In v. 29 we are to have all that is living as food. WOW! A smorgasbord! Let's consider the cattle and the creeping things. Folks, trilobites were in the fossil record billions of years before the mammals. The score is now 8 to 0! And personally, I don't consider cockroaches, spiders, and creepies a good thing for the Earth. For that matter, neither do I like Great White sharks. Then, what is the category for Beasts? Were these the dinosaurs? Obviously not; their remains are in the fossil record as having lived some 200 million years ago. To look at this Bible as a factual, tape-recording of God's spoken word is to exist in the world of make believe and cursed to worship a book. If the Bible is worshiped it then becomes a crutch alleviating the literalists of the responsibility for exercising their free will. In other words, as John Calvin concluded falsely, all people have been pre-destined without any consequences for their free-willed choices; do good or evil as you wish, you may already be appointed to eternal happiness. Not so! If it were so, then there would be no reason for the Prophets, especially, Yeshua and his cross.

So, how are we humans made in the imager of God? We have the breath of life, v. 30, free will, the power to create life and re-create the Earth. We have the intellectual capacity to know the difference between facts and myths, right from wrong! We are emotional and in relationships with each other and, I hope, with our God. Finally, God said, "It is all very good!"

Genesis Chapter Two (RSV)

1 Thus the heavens and the earth were finished, and all the host of them. 2 And on the seventh yowm God finished his work which he had done, and he rested on the seventh day from all his work which he had done. 3 So God blessed the seventh day and hallowed it, because on it God rested from all his work which he had done in creation.

Seventh Comment: Actually, the scribe who initiated chapter and verse made an error here! Chapter 2, v. : 4 should actually start Chapter 2. This concludes the first creation story in the Bible. Notice the two occurrences of the word "finished" and the three uses of the phrase "work which He had done". If everything is finished and all the work is done, why has such change taken place since the Big Bang? It's because the seven day structure was repeated from the Oral Tradition about the Exodus story (see Exodus 13: 6-7 which precedes the 10 Commandments) to impose a Divine authorship of a seven day week with a day of rest for humanity. To conclude these comments, I would remind you that, as a Christian, I see a very profound meaning to the Genesis Myth in the unraveling of its hidden layers. That is truly the essence of myth. Now, let's go to the second creation myth.

The Second Creation Myth (RSV)

4 These are the generations of the heavens and the earth when they were created. In the day that the LORD God made the earth and the heavens, 5 when no plant of the field was yet in the earth and no herb of the field had yet sprung up--for the LORD God had not caused it to rain upon the earth, and there was no man to till the ground; 6 but a mist went up from the earth and watered the whole face of the ground

First Comment: This story is obviously an abbreviated version of the first creation story. Why the author would add this to the first is more than likely because he heard of it in the oral tradition. Not knowing which story was the correct one caused him to add it to the book of Genesis ... well, Bruce Vawter proposed this in his book: a Commentary on Genesis. I agree that this is a plausible explanation. My logic is simple indeed. The two stories are in disagreement about the sequence of events; it goes from the creation of Heaven and earth directly to rain falling, mist rising and no man to till the earth. In the first story there was plant and animal life without man even in the picture.

7 Then the LORD God formed man of dust from the ground, and breathed into his nostrils the breath of life; and man became a living being. 8 And the LORD God planted a garden in Eden, in the east; and there he put the man whom he had formed.

Second Comment: This is a new twist that could be just explanatory. I do like the concept of a material body into which God breaths the Spirit of Life. Great mythic structure! Then, hocus-pocus, an Eden appears followed, kerplop, by an Adam in the garden. That, dear reader is in total contradiction to the sequence in Genesis One!

9 And out of the ground the LORD God made to grow every tree that is pleasant to the sight and good for food, the tree of life also in the midst of the garden, and the tree of the knowledge of good and evil. 10 A river flowed out of Eden to water the garden, and there it divided and became four rivers. 11 The name of the first is Pishon; it is the one which flows around the whole land of Havilah, where there is gold; 12 and the gold of that land is good; bdellium and onyx stone are there. 13 The name of the second river is Gihon; it is the one which flows around the whole land of Cush. 14 And the name of the third river is Tigris, which flows east of Assyria. And the fourth river is the Euphrates. 15 The LORD God took the man and put him in the Garden of Eden to till it and keep it. 16 And the LORD God commanded the man, saying, "You may freely eat of every tree of the garden; 17 but of the tree of the knowledge of good and evil you shall not eat, for in the day that you eat of it you shall die."

Third Comment: OH, there's some juicy stuff in this section. The Great Tree is the center of the plot. Eat and you shall die. Right? They eat but they don't die!! What's going on here? Does God lie? It appears SHE-HE does lie! Hang on to your roller coaster safety belts, here is the start of every scholar's curiosity and mine too. I would call it an initiation into the "critical cognitive" stage of development that was described in the previous Chapter. So, what God meant was that the soul would experience some kind of spiritual change from innocence to awareness; the body would continue to live while the mind (soul) matures.

And, that means these lines are allegorical to begin with. Thus, a perceptive theologian would interpret this apple-eating story as the moment that the individual person becomes aware of its conscience and recognizes the differences between good and evil, right from wrong. Is this not the moment that all humans lose their innocence? Truly, this is a mythical tale of profound proportions. And, now, the creation of woman and the perplexing blame pointing psychosis of humanity ... in myth. First, a comment about verses 10-14: these describe the geography of Iraq! Does this not give us another clue that Genesis was written after the Exile?

18 Then the LORD God said, "It is not good that the man should be alone; I will make him a helper fit for him." 19 So out of the ground the LORD God formed every beast of the field and every bird of the air, and brought them to the man to see what he would call them; and whatever the man called every living creature, that was its name. 20 The man gave names to all cattle, and to the birds of the air, and to every beast of the field; but for the man there was not found a helper fit for him.

Fourth Comment: So God makes all sorts of pets and man just can't swing it with pets alone. This too is out of sequence with Genesis Chapter One! The straw that foiled the show was that Adam was allergic to cats and dogs! So God thinks up another plot. Get ready for true chaos!

21 So the LORD God caused a deep sleep to fall upon the man, and while he slept took one of his ribs and closed up its place with flesh; 22 and the rib which the LORD God had taken from the man he made into a woman and brought her to the man. 23 Then the man said, "This at last is bone of my bones and flesh of my flesh; she shall be called Woman, because she was taken out of Man." 24 Therefore a man leaves his father and his mother and cleaves to his wife, and they become one flesh. 25 And the man and his wife were both naked, and were not ashamed.

Fifth Comment: Boy, are **we** going to have fun with this section! Ok, so the first woman came from a man. However, from that time forward every human comes from a woman. (See Reference to "The Real Eve" above!) And, the psychological blame game is put into motion in the next several verses. The snake is introduced! It tempts the woman; the woman tempts the man. God comes and recognizes that HER-HIS human creatures are now aware of good and evil. The man blames the woman. The woman blames the snake in the grass. The snake gets cursed and just wiggles off into the jungle with a poison bite that plagues humans for the rest of history. The bride and groom cover their shame (with leather from God!) and get kicked out of Eden. Humankind will forever yearn for the innocence of this imaginary Eden. OH shucks, they goofed and we suffer. Pity, pity on us all!

There is a terrific one liner in the Apocryphal Gospel of Mary Magdalene, line 25 and 26, that goes like this:

"Peter said to him, 'Since you have explained everything to us, tell us this also: What is the sin of the world'? 26 The Savior said, 'There is no sin, but it is you who make sin.'"

Yikes, what a shocking reply! Original sin from eating an apple is a folk myth devised by the author of Genesis to explain the presence of evil and how to pass the buck, but mostly to blame females! Please write this on your forehead for everyone to see: "Each individual is born pure and holy, whole before God and the world. The individual is the only person responsible for its own choices." I'll be writing about this much later in the book. In the meanwhile you may want to read John Chapter 9; it makes the very same point about the sin of the parents not passed down to children.

The Creation Myth in Genesis leaves us with awe when we interpret its mythical and poetic story:

1. Everything that was created is GOOD;
2. There is a sense of evolution in its stepwise order of creation;
3. The Universe was chaotic, void and in darkness all of which leads one to accept John duns Scotis' (13th century) premise of the existence of fundamental particles (the singularity or white hole of Stephen Hawking) co-existing with God before the Big Bang;
4. God acted out of "Unconditional Self-Giving" to share what is HER-HIS glory. We humans have the opportunity to jump on that bandwagon for an eternal joy-ride!

Here's a little real science to finish up this Chapter.

Is the Big Bang an objective or subjective truth? Depends on your personal education! The Nuclear Scientists and Geologists say it's objective—provable. The pigmy in New Guinea says it's irrational. And, most Literalists call it "the distraction of the Devil". The Big Bang existed; it is objective. Why it was started is anybody's guess, therefore, subjective. "Why" is the universal question which history has called speculative theology (or psychology).

The microwave distribution in the Universe is a scientific fact—objective! The cooling after a Big Bang follows natural law and that microwave measurement throughout space is in agreement with a Universe about 14-16 billion years old plus or minus a few years to account for any statistical errors in the measurement.

The direction and velocity of the Galaxies when extrapolated back from whence they came indicate a central point about 14-16 billion years ago. These measurements are made by means of the red shift exhibited by the movement away from our Earth. It's the same kind of shift you hear when a train whistle is high pitched as it approaches and a low pitch after it passes you. Only, for planets and galaxy movement, it's a shift of the emitted light into the red region of the spectrum when moving away from us.

As far as the age of the Universe goes, I've selected the average age of 14 billion (plus or minus a billion or two).

The Hubble telescope has taken pictures of the farthest galaxies and they figure to be about 14-16 billion years old One thing is certain; the Universe is definitely not just 10,000 years old! Nor is the Planet Earth that young!

The Nature of Myth in the Bible: An Overview

To summarize this Chapter, I pass this on to you. "The best way to tell a story that has a moral to it is ... write it in Myth." Myth is ... well, read Appendix M.

Mythology is all make-believe threaded with a few facts to make it appear to be real. However, it is never totally factual. Facts are one-dimensional. Myth is multi-dimensional: there's the surface story, many deeper stories, hidden meanings and timelessness. A great Prophet was asked why he spoke in parables? He said, "To test the hearer's comprehension". "Let him hear who has ears with which to hear". Let the person listening examine the other dimensions of the story! Now, wasn't that a metaphorical reply about one's mind being able to see and hear?

Sacred writings are NOT simply facts. They are stories to deepen ones understanding of the relationship between humans and God. And relationship with the Divine is commonly referred to as spirituality. Every culture (language) has a set of its own writings that have been enculturated with a unique message. The problem is that today's cultures are one-dimensional in assigning absolute factuality and truth to its Sacred Stories. When a culture doesn't comprehend the nature of Myth, it misses the deeper meaning. There is no "sacred" scripture! There are only literatures from the PERSPECTIVE of many observers. Remember what you read in Chapter One and understand that each observer had a unique and jaundiced vision of a profound and mysterious nature. Therefore, I believe there are "Profound Scriptures" in all cultures that tell us about Divine relationships available to man- and womankind. Be certain of this: "What your life means is whatever you want it to mean, and that is your own subjective truth!"

SUMMARY

The goal here was to identify the amount of myth that pervades our daily life and literature in order to increase our ability to distinguish how much myth exists in our alleged Sacred Scriptures. We in America have so much myth and folklore woven into our country's history that it seems ironic that we shut down our critical capacity when we read our Sacred Scripture. The quotation that introduces this topic is ever so appropriate. A lot has to do with one's psychological disposition, "pre-critical naïveté" and enculturation when we were taught religion from family and in Sunday school. Even Paul in 1 Corinthians 13: 11 wrote:

> *When I was a child, I used to talk as a child, think as a child, reason as a child; when I became a man, I put aside childish things.*

It is strange indeed that what we humans have learned in childhood sticks in our subconscious and is never challenged.

This Chapter demonstrated that Science and Religion are two sides of the SAME coin. Myth, as defined here, is more powerful in unwrapping meaning than any other literary form written to this date. It was necessary to employ a mythical style for meaning to be for all times. We actually practice that because of the stories of Santa, Tooth Fairy, Easter Bunny and others we retell to our children year after year. Myth is the vehicle by which we perpetuate meaning to the next generation. That is exactly the intent of the Biblical writers! And, of course, those writers of the other Sacred Scriptures!

The biggest deterrent to one's acceptance of a mythologized Bible or Sacred Scripture is not Science or Evolution. It is IGNORANCE of Science and IGNORANCE of the real history of Biblical times and the confusion between what is fact and what is faith.

I now invite you to the next Chapter; we're going to examine several Sacred Scriptures!

CHAPTER THREE

SACRED SCRIPTURES OF THE WORLD

Up to this point we've stated that there are special documents that people consider to be messages about their world, life and Deity. Some of these complicated works of literature are known to be of human origin, like a good mystery book, but unlike your favorites, these ancient writings are profoundly respected nonetheless. There are some others that cultures believe to be factual history that came as special dictation from their Deity to one or several messengers and written by a disciple, scribe or scribes. All these special literary works are what cultures have identified as Sacred Scriptures. The list is small and these are the principal written ones we will examine but not necessarily in this order:

TITLE	WRITTEN
1. The Enuma Elish	~1100 BC
2. The Upanishads	900 - 500 BC
3. The Hebrew (Old) Testament	800 - 100 BC
4. The Four Noble Truths	~525 BC
5. The Bhagavat Gita	500 - 200 BC
6. Dao de Jing (original name)	400 – 300 BC
7. The Christian (New) Testament	40 – 125 AD
8. The Qur'an	600 A D

As we analyze these Sacred Scriptures it should become obvious to you that none are factual, in the sense that they are "absolute" history, "accurate" science, and without errors. The real justifications for this posture lie in the following four observations that have lead people to challenge a factual, errorless scripture. First, there is a great deal of mysterious cosmology, like the "flat Earth" of Job 38. Second, there are historical stories or events that archeologists find difficult to substantiate, like Jericho vs Ai as in "the battle of ...". Third, there are some cultural descriptions that don't belong to that particular period, like straw vs. a clay roof (in Mark vs. Luke) . And, lastly, the scientific aspects are in most cases not quite what we know in this 21st century, for example the simplicity of seven 24-hour consecutive days in the Genesis creation story. No matter how hard we try to soften these observations, the science of ancient times is singularly and definitely primitive such that it leads us all to ask a profound question to those who insist that their Sacred Scripture is from the Divine lips.

"If the all-knowing Deity says that the Universe is flat in one part (Job 38) and suspended (string?) over nothing (Job 26: 7) in another part of its Sacred Scripture, how come this Deity is so ignorant of its own creation?" Or its corollary question, "Could it be that all Sacred Scriptures are totally of human encultured perceptions?"

Religion is a human invention whose purpose was and is to commune with the source of all those mysterious natural phenomena that beset the earliest human communities some 7 million years ago. Religion had its origin before writing was invented (sometime between 4000 and 3000 BC, the fourth millennium BC). Ebla, the 2500 BC Syrian city, contained a full library of clay tablets written with a well-developed cuneiform. Archeologists have no examples of writing before 4000 BC; they only have the cave pictures found throughout Europe and Asia from some 50,000 years ago. Pictures prove the existence of Homo Sapiens but pictures do not reveal their thoughts other than to tell us that they possessed intelligence and artistry. Knowing about the ancient peoples and their customs requires written documents. According to what is currently available in our textbooks, the Sacred Scriptures we know about and the approximate date of the manuscripts limit our knowledge about ancient cultures and their religious beliefs.

Now, having recovered from those two questions at the end (two paragraph ago) you should know that the answers to those questions are themselves profound. Assuredly, Sacred Scriptures are part fact, part science and part profoundly informative about the Nature of the Deity and its relationship with Humans. The other side of that coin is readily translatable to this: Sacred Scriptures are NOT totally factual, NOT totally scientific and NOT very much directly from any Deity's lips. It is expected that most, if not all, institutional officials will bolt at that sentence. Our problem here is to analyze those Scriptures to determine which parts are validly unknowable to human intelligence and which parts are observable and, therefore, known to human intelligence.

Read Deuteronomy 21:18 to 21 and decide whether you think that it is a divine law for all times. Before you can make up your mind, let's see what's written:

> *"18 "If a man has a stubborn and rebellious son, who will not obey the voice of his father or the voice of his mother, and, though they chastise him, will not give heed to them, 19 then his father and his mother shall take hold of him and bring him out to the elders of his city at the gate of the place where he lives, 20 and they shall say to the elders of his city, 'This our son is stubborn and rebellious, he will not obey our voice; he is a glutton and a drunkard.' 21 Then all the men of the city shall stone him to death with stones; so you shall purge the evil from your midst; and all Israel shall hear, and fear."*

Believe me! If that were truly a Divine Law for all times, there would be a very large pile of bones in most cities in the USA and the rest of civilization's crowded cities. Would you follow that law today? Do you believe that stoning is equivalent to psychiatric or psychotherapeutic intervention? Is there not sufficient evidence that the H.T. is replete with God's compassion and forgiveness? Is this paragraph in Deuteronomy from God or from the human clan's design to maintain public order and civility? After reading Jean M. Auel's historical novels (the first of which is "The Clan of the Cave Bear"), would you vote for the clan as the source of that horrible biblical law, as well as a great number of the other Deuteronomic laws and Levitical rituals? In addition, if you have been awake during the Afghanistan and Iraqi military actions, have you recognized the pre-historic culture of those countries that are just a few years advanced from the Neanderthal clan mentality of Jean Auel's novels?

Consider these: (a) if there is one statement that is erroneous, contradicts another statement or inconsistent with scientific fact, would you conclude that the one error dismisses Divine Dictation; (b) if there is a statement that opposes the Divine Nature, then, again Divine Dictation is dismissed. One cannot hold to a Divine Dictation under those criteria. What you will discover is that there are a plethora of errors, inconsistencies and scientific misunderstandings in every Sacred Scripture. We'll visit those errors in Chapter Five.

It's the same argument that goes like this: if the first floor of the Empire State building in New York city were constructed of balsa wood, then no matter how many beautiful floors are added on top of it, the entire building will collapse, and the taller it is, the quicker it will tumble. It remains to be shown that, not whether there are any errors and contradictions, but rather just how many there really are found in some so-called Divinely inspired Sacred Scriptures. The operative word here is really "inspiration"! It is a word with many degrees of human enlightenment and a word that has caused many disagreements among Institutional Religions at both ends of the spectrum. The actual problem of "inspiration" boils down to identifying these alleged errors and inconsistencies and deciding which ones of the Sacred Scriptures are actually of human origin.

This then will be our focus in this Chapter: to analyze each Sacred Scripture to see whether it is actually of a Divine origin. Or, are they simply legendary stories (tales woven with threads of facts) written by humans (with the community's approval) to explain their world-view, the Who and Why of their existence: "Is there a Creator?" "Who is that being?" "Why are we here?" "Why is there suffering?" "Why is there evil?" "Why is there death?" And, why and why!

Literary writers throughout history have demonstrated that the best way to propose and answer profound questions is to tell a story in allegory, metaphor, simile, irony or parable. In short, write a Fable or a Mythical Story, just like Aesop's Fables! Just like the parables of Yeshua, the carpenter from Nazareth! Myth is a strong, powerful, meaningful and timeless literary style. Myth explains and answers yesterday's questions that are translatable to today's needs and Myth will effectively speak to tomorrow's problems. The Greek myths are still validly meaningful for retelling in our present fictional literature and films. Myth is the only timeless style capable of achieving such largess throughout all of human history. Yesterday's facts were good for yesterday but not for today. Philosophies change according to the tides of life. Today's cultural complexity works only for today; it will be different tomorrow. No one can predict what will be tomorrow's life experiences. Ah, but myth is timeless and more profound than mere encultured history. Facts are one-dimensional; myth is multi-dimensional.

Sacred writings are NOT simply factual. They are the individual's and their community's stories describing relationships with the contemporary world and with that world's Creator. Sacred Scriptures addressed people's concerns for the meaning of their lives. And meaning is a question asked since humans could think. Sacred Scriptures talk of relationships between peoples and relationship with one's Deity. And the mythically constructed questions and conversations in Sacred Scriptures are the author's attempt to put his own faith-based profound solutions in the mouth of the Prophets and oftentimes on the lips of his Deity.

Every culture has a set of its own writings that contain a unique message that is both timely for that culture and timeless for its next generation. The problem in this 21st century is that we are accustomed to the facts of instant news, instant telephone conversation, instant food; we, humans, have become an instant "everything factual" culture. We are seekers of reality and legalistic in everything we touch, taste, hear, see and read. Our dysfunction is to take the Sacred Scriptures literally, factually, as a direct quote from a Deity's lips. That's why Deut 21: 18 to 21 along with the remaining regulations of the Torah are still accepted as God's Laws by the literalist individual and community.

We, all the people, need meaning and purpose in our lives and, unfortunately, we read only the literal words from the ancient writings. Our mind's eye misses the otherness of the mythic stories which leaves us puzzled and confused. The real problem is that Sacred Scriptures are not read with a critical mind. This book will challenge you, right this moment, to make a critical reading of those Sacred Scriptures with us.

PART ONE: Scriptures of Human Origin

Section 1: The Enuma Elish

The first Sacred Scripture to examine is the Enuma Elish (EE). We will call the present referenced copy EE II because we've discovered that there was a previous EE document that had little to no mention of the principal character, Marduk, found in this later edition, EE II. This EE II document was circulating in the Tigris and Euphrates basin (Mesopotamia) prior to the Babylonian Exile (587 BC to 539 BC). It cannot be emphasized enough that the Israelites who were exiled to Babylon were forced to participate in the local religious rituals and belief structure. Scholars suggest that the Genesis creation stories and the remaining pre-sixth century Oral Traditions were completed (See Nehemiah 8) after the Israelites were freed (539 BC). The inside joke is that the authors compiling Genesis weren't sure which of the two in circulation at that time, Gen 1 or 2, was the correct creation tale. Therefore, they inserted both to let the reader decide. The creation tale, found in Job 38, is not meant to be a creation story, but reveals the cosmological awareness prevalent during that period, likewise for Psalm 104 (found in NAB, RSV and KJV Bible translations). In that sense Job and Ps 104 do document the peoples knowledge of the mechanics of creation; we've chosen to regard them as a third and fourth creation story, albeit an incorrect cosmology. Strange, that Yahweh didn't know how the Universe was constructed! Ah, but that's another story to be addressed later in the Hebrew Testament section.

If you are wondering why the discussion of the Genesis story is in the Enuma Elish section, wonder no more. As we describe the Enuma Elish creation story you will see the peculiar similarity between the two Sacred Scriptures. Right in the first verse we find the existence of Apsu and Tiamat (the still earth water and the chaotic ocean water, respectively). Same as Genesis 1: 1! The other gods of EE II simply represent the unique powerful forces of Nature. At this juncture let's read this excerpt from EEII, Tablet One, verses 1 to 9.

> *"When on high the heaven had not been named,*
> *Firm ground below had not been called by name, (1) When primordial Apsu, their begetter, (2) And Mummu-Tiamat, she who bore them all, (3) Their waters mingled as a single body, (4) No reed hut had sprung forth, no marshland had appeared, None of the gods had been brought into being, (5) And none bore a name, and no destinies determined-- Then it was that the gods were formed in the midst of heaven." (6) And no field was formed, no marsh was to be seen; (7) When of the gods none had been called into being, (8) And none bore a name, and no destinies were ordained; (9) Then were created the gods in the midst of heaven,*

The story starts with a heaven and earth not yet in existence {not named!} (1) Alone with Apsu, the waters of heaven or earth (pure), and Tiamat, the waters of the ocean (chaotic). Apsu is the male image (2); Tiamat is the female counterpart (3). The imagery reflects the twofold nature of their existence; the mingling of the two waters produces offspring born by Tiamat (4). The barrenness of creation is confirmed as if to imply the order of creation and that nothing of the natural order had yet been created (5). The implication is that Nature's phenomena were deified and each given a separate name (6). Therefore, take out the names and you have just about the same format as Gen 1: 1 to 10, which reads:

> *"1 IN the beginning God created the heavens and the earth. 2 The earth was without form and void, and darkness was upon the face of the deep; and the Spirit of God was moving over the face of the waters. 3 And God said, "Let there be light"; and there was light. 4 And God saw that the light was good; and God separated the light from the darkness. 5 God called the light Day, and the darkness he called Night. And there was evening and there was morning, one day. 6 And God said, "Let there be a firmament in the midst of the waters, and let it separate the waters from the waters." 7 And God made the firmament and separated the waters which were under the firmament from the waters which were above the firmament. And it was so. 8 And God called the firmament Heaven. And there was evening and there was morning, a second day. And God said, "Let the waters under the heavens be gathered together into one place, and let the dry land appear." And it was so. 10 God called the dry land Earth, and the waters that were gathered together he called Seas. And God saw that it was good."*

Of course there is not a one-to-one, word for word, correlation because the Genesis story is fuller in description and actually slightly more hierarchically structured. And we admit that compared to the EEII creation story the Genesis story is the closest to what modern science has discovered, except that a "day" in Genesis is really many billions of years. Enough of Genesis, let's proceed to the EEII creation story. You can read the Enuma Elish commentary by Dennis Bratcher from the Internet, See Appendix O.

Here are some lines depicting the creation of the seven-day week and the twenty-eight-day month, Tablet V: 12 to 18:

> *12 "The Moon he caused to shine, entrusting the night to him. 13 He appointed him a creature of the night to signify the days, 14 And marked off every month, without cease, by means of his crown. 15 At the month's very start, rising over the land,16 You shall have luminous horns to signify six days,18 On the seventh day reaching a half-crown18 So shall the fifteen-day period be like one another-two halves for each month."*

Isn't this a remarkably coincidence to the seven days in Genesis with the seventh day being the Sabbath? Remember now, the moon has a 28 day cycle around the Earth; the Babylonians definitely had observed the night sky and the phases of the moon. To continue with the creation story, read this from Tablet V: 45 to 66:

> *(45) "After he had appointed the days to Shamash [the sun] And had established the precincts of night and day, Taking the spittle of Tiamat Marduk created . . .He formed the clouds and filled them with water. (50)The raising of winds, the bringing of rain and cold, Making the mist smoke, piling*

up . . .These he planned himself, took into his own hand. Putting her head into position he formed thereon the mountains, Opening the deep which was in flood, He caused to flow from her eyes the Euphrates and Tigris, Stopping her nostrils he left . . He formed from her breasts the lofty mountains, Therein he drilled springs for the wells to carry off the water. (60) Twisting her tail he bound it to Durmah,. . . Apsu at his foot, . . . her crotch, she was fastened to the heavens, Thus he covered the heavens and established the earth.. . . in the midst of Tiamat he made flow, . . . his net he completely let out, So he created heaven and earth . . . ,their bounds . . established."

And then Marduk created mankind in these two selections:

Tablet VII: 1 to 9:
"When Marduk heard the words of the gods,
His heart prompted him to fashion artful works.
Opening his mouth, he addressed Ea
To impart the plan he had conceived in his heart:
"I will take blood and fashion bone.
I will establish a savage, 'man' shall be his name.
truly, savage-man I will create.
He shall be charged with the service of the gods
That they might be at ease!"

Tablet VII: 23 to 36:
"Who was it that contrived the uprising,
And made Tiamat rebel, and joined battle?
Let him be handed over who contrived the uprising.
His guilt I will make him bear. You shall dwell in peace!"
The Igigi, the great gods, replied to him,
To Lugaldimmerankia, counselor of the gods, their lord:
"It was Kingu who contrived the uprising,
And made Tiamat rebel, and joined battle." (30)
They bound him, holding him before Ea.
They imposed on him his punishment and severed his blood vessels.
Out of his blood they fashioned mankind.
He imposed on him the service and let free the gods.
After Ea, the wise, had created mankind,
Had imposed upon them the service of the gods—"

Did you appreciate that the story makes Marduk the actual Creator and not Apsu nor Tiamat? Haven't Christians done the same with respect to God the Father and Jesus the Son, the mythical creator? EEII relates that bone was fashioned first. And, surprisingly, "savage man" is the creation! What was interesting in this rendering is the heavenly war to purge the Evil One, Kingu. Doesn't that ring a bell? Sounds like the revolt of Satan in the Hebrew Testament (H.T.). The last underlined text says that Ea, the wise, created mankind. Hasn't Jesus been identified with the "Wisdom" of Proverbs 8 and the creator of the world in later Christian texts? Finally, read this selection, Tablet I : 124 to 143

When Tiamat heard these words, she was pleased:
" . . . you have given. Let us make monsters,
. . . and the gods in the midst . . . .

. . . let us do battle and against the gods . . . !"
They banded themselves together and marched at the side of Tiamat.
Enraged, they plot without cease night and day,
They are set for combat, growling, raging, (130)
They form a council to prepare for the fight.
Mother Hubur, she who fashions all things,
Added matchless weapons, bore monster-serpents,
Sharp of tooth, unsparing of fang.
With venom for blood she has filled their bodies.
Roaring dragons she has clothed with terror,
Has crowned them with haloes, making them like gods,
Whoever beheld them, terror overcame him,
And that, with their bodies reared up, none might turn them back.
She set up the Viper, the Dragon, and the monster Lahamu, (140)
The Great-Lion, the Mad-Dog, and the Scorpion-Man,
Mighty lion-demons, the Dragon-Fly, the Centaur--
Bearing weapons that do not spare, fearless in battle.

That excerpt gives credence to the tempting serpent of Gen 2 originating out of the Enuma Elish.

Now it should be obvious to you that some portions of the Genesis story and other parts of the H.T. are not original. What the Genesis author did was to de-code the complex EEII and re-write it in the context of his nation's experience with the Divinity who spoke to Moses on the fiery mountain. Do you now understand that the process of "*inspiration*" could include plagiarizing from existing literature yet be limited by the culture's knowledge (or lack thereof) of cosmology, science and politics? The impetus to write may very well have originated in the Divine Mind but the actual words and story line put down to express that impetus appears to be of human origin.

If these selections interest you, Appendix L lists the Internet references at which you can read, or from which download, the entire text of most Sacred Scriptures.

Section 2: The Upanishads

One's first impression of the Upanishads is that it is a "Hierarchical Nature Dictionary", that is, it uses a single word to mean each and every separate observable physical phenomenon or action of humans and nature. The reasoning and relationships appear to be stepwise and circular. Let me quote an example or two.

(1) *KHANDOGYA-UPANISHAD Part 1: FIRST PRAPATHAKA: FIRST KHANDA*

1. *Let a man meditate on the syllable Om, called the udgitha; for the udgitha (a portion of the Sama-veda) is sung, beginning with Om. The full account, however, of Om is this: 2. The essence of all beings is the earth, the essence of the earth is water, the essence of water the plants, the essence of plants man, the essence of man speech, the essence of speech the Rig-veda, the essence of the Rig-veda the Sama-veda, the essence of the Sama-veda the udgitha (which is Om). 3. That udgitha (Om) is the best of all essences, the highest, deserving the highest place, the eighth.*

That was a stepwise example that ended in a circumlocution.

(2) The following one will illustrate the (often-confusing) circular relation.

KHANDOGYA-UPANISHAD Part 1: FIRST PRAPATHAKA: THIRD KHANDA

> *3. Then let a man meditate on the udgitha (Om) as vyana indeed. If we breathe up, that is prana, the up-breathing. If we breathe down, that is apana, the down-breathing. The combination of prana and apana is vyana, back-breathing or holding in of the breath. This vyana is speech. Therefore when we utter speech, we neither breathe up nor down. 4. Speech is Rik, and therefore when a man utters a Rik verse he neither breathes up nor down. Rik is Saman, and therefore when a man utters a Saman verse he neither breathes up nor down. Saman is udgitha, and therefore when a man sings (the udgitha, Om) he neither breathes up nor down.* {Therefore, OM is speech and we are right back where we started in verse 3!} *5. And other works also which require strength, such as the production of fire by rubbing, running a race, stringing a strong bow, are performed without breathing up or down. Therefore let a man meditate on the udgitha (Om) as vyana.*

It has been suggested that readings like that help us to look upon Hinduism more as a culture than a religion.

(3) Yet, there are passages that are distinctly religious. For example:

KHANDOGYA-UPANISHAD Part 2: 4th PRAPATHAKA: 11th KHANDA.

> *1. When from thence he has risen upwards, he neither rises nor sets. He is alone, standing in the centre. And on this there is this verse: 2. 'Yonder he neither rises nor sets at any time. If this is not true, ye gods, may I lose Brahman.' 3. And indeed to him who thus knows this Brahma-upanishad (the secret doctrine of the Veda) the sun does not rise and does not set. For him there is day, once and for all. 4. This doctrine (beginning with III, I, 1) Brahman (m. Hiranyagarbha) told to Pragapati (Virig), Pragipati to Manu, Manu to his offspring (Ikshvaku, &c.) And the father told that (doctrine of) Brahman (n.) to Uddalaka Aruni. 5. A father may therefore tell that doctrine of Brahman to his eldest son, or to a worthy pupil.*

In that selection there is the concept of doctrine or knowledge as handed down to sons or students. Notice in v. 3 the reward for someone who knows the knowledge of "the secret doctrine of the Veda". Take note of this "possessing of the knowledge"; it will show up in the early history of Christianity as "Gnosticism".

(4) In the following selection there is the appearance of a multiplicity of gods, the elements of fire, air and the sun.

KHANDOGYA-UPANISHAD Part 2: 4th PRAPATHAKA: *17th KHANDA*

> *1. Pragapati brooded over the worlds, and from them thus brooded on he squeezed out the essences, Agni (fire) from the earth, Vayu (air) from the sky, Aditya (the sun) from heaven. 2. He brooded over these three deities, and from them thus brooded on he squeezed out the essences, the Rik verses from Agni, the Yagus verses from Vayu, the Saman verses from Aditya.*

(5) However, this next excerpt identifies a single entity as the creator.

KHANDOGYA-UPANISHAD Part 3: 6th PRAPATHAKA: SECOND KHANDA

> *1. 'In the beginning,' my dear, 'there was that only which is, one only, without a second. Others say, in the beginning there was that only which is not, one only, without a second; and from that which is not, that which is was born. 2. 'But how could it be thus, my dear?' the father continued. 'How could that which is, be born of that which is not? No, my dear, only that which is, was in the beginning, one only, without a second.*

Finally, we have just read an interesting passage acknowledging the one-ness of the Creator. This was a necessary one to point out that another Sacred Scripture affirmed a single Creator-Being, just like the Genesis story. Did you catch the phrase, "without a second"? We will see this phrase again when we examine several passages from Isaiah (O.T.), the Gospels (N.T.) and the Qur'an. The Enuma Elish hints at it but is wrapped up in the mysteries and powers of nature. The Upanishads propose it as a statement of obvious logic yet gets entangled in the word "OM" and naming all things in relation to "OM". What surprised me was the identification of fire, air and the sun. It reminded me of the 19th century phlogiston theory.

(6) As a final selection, let's look at a little philosophy (24th K.) and psychology (26th K.) even though it is a bit off our primary target. Verse 2 is reminiscent of the Christian Testament, don't you think?

KHANDOGYA-UPANISHAD Part 4, 7th PRAPATHAKA.

24th KHANDA

> *'Where one sees nothing else, hears nothing else, understands nothing else, that is the Infinite. Where one sees something else, hears something else, understands something else, that is the finite. The Infinite is immortal, the finite is mortal.'*

26th KHANDA

> *The spirit (prana) springs from the Self, hope springs from the Self, memory springs from the Self; so do ether, fire, water, appearance and disappearance, food, power, understanding, reflection, consideration, will, mind, speech, names, sacred hymns, and sacrifices-aye, all this springs from the Self. 2. 'There is this*

verse, "He who sees this, does not see death, nor illness, nor pain; he who sees this, sees everything, and obtains everything everywhere.

That last verse also rings of Jeremiah 33:3, "3 *Call to me, and I will answer you; I will tell to you things great beyond reach of your knowledge."*

(7) Here's a quote that is related to Tao Te Ching! [That's the modern spelling.]

TALAVAKARA-UPANISHAD (or KENA-UPANISHAD,) 2nd Khanda.

V1 If thou thinkest I know it well, then thou knowest surely but little, V.2 'I do not think I know it well, nor do I know that I do not know it. He among us who knows this, he knows it, nor does he know that he does not know it.

(8) And this next one is reminiscent of Christianity

v 8 'The feet on which that Upanishad stands are penance, restraint, sacrifice; the Vedas are all its limbs, the True is its abode.

(9) Here is another example of circular logic. Note that '*prana*' is now breath rather than spirit as it was in the above passage, see *26th KHANDA*! Note we will see that the same definition and use exist in the Hebrew Testament with spirit and breath! It was the cultural understanding of that time period.

AITAREYA-ARANYAKA Part 2; 3rdADHYAYA. 1st Khanda

He who knows himself as the fivefold hymn (uktha), the emblem of Prana (breath), from whence all this springs, he is clever. These five are the earth, air, ether, water, and fire (gyotis). This is the self, the fivefold uktha.

(10) Here is the name of the second tier god who is but another manifestation of the Creator.

AITAREYA-ARANYAKA Part 2; 3rdADHYAYA 7th K,

V.1 Indra is the lord of all beings.

(11) This following lengthy selection indicates a hierarchical order in creation ending with man. Note the word, Ap, in verse 3 that means water and compare it with the word, Apsu, in EEII. Sounds related, doesn't it? Here there are two waters just like the Genesis story.

AITAREYA-ARANYAKA Part 3 ,4th ADHYAYA, 1st Khanda

Adoration to the Highest Self, Hari, Om

1. Verily, in the beginning all this was Self, one only; there was nothing else blinking whatsoever. 2. He thought: 'Shall I send forth worlds?' He sent forth these worlds, 3. Ambhas (water), Mariki (light), Mara (mortal), and Ap (water). 4. That Ambhas (water) is above the heaven, and it is heaven, the support. The Marikis (the lights) are the sky. The Mara (mortal) is the earth, and the waters under the earth are the Ap world. 5. He thought: 'There are these worlds; shall I send forth guardians of the worlds?' He then formed the Purusha (the person), taking him forth from the water. (Like humans are born out of women from a sack of water!) 6. He brooded on him , and when that person had thus been brooded on, a mouth burst forth like an egg. From the mouth proceeded speech, from speech Agni (fire), Nostrils burst forth. From the nostrils proceeded scent (prana), from scent Vayu (air). Eyes burst forth. From the eyes proceeded sight, from sight Aditya (sun). Ears burst forth. From the ears proceeded hearing, from hearing the Dis (quarters of the world). Skin burst forth. From the skin proceeded hairs (sense of touch), from the hairs shrubs and trees. The heart burst forth. From the heart proceeded mind, from mind Kandramas (moon). The navel burst forth. From the navel proceeded the apana (the down-breathing), from apana death. The generative organ burst forth. From the organ proceeded seed, from seed water.

That heart to mind phrase sounds like our modern metaphor.

SECOND KHANDA.

1. *Those deities (devata), Agni and the rest, after they had been sent forth, fell into this great ocean. Then he (the Self) besieged him, (the person) with hunger and thirst. 2. The deities then (tormented by hunger and thirst) spoke to him (the Self) : 'Allow us a place in which we may rest and eat food' He led a cow towards them (the deities). They said : 'This is not enough.' He led a horse towards them. They said: 'This is not enough.' He led man towards them. Then they said: 'Well done, indeed.' Therefore man is well done. 3. He said to them: 'Enter, each according to his place.'*

Did you not read between the lines and see how all that relates to a simplistic understanding of biology?

(12) In this next selection we read the Hindu definition of the SELF and all that SELF is and what the SELF has created. We read the Hindu understanding of God as described in the Bible. Also note the relationship between heart and mind. Note the trinity in v 4.

SIXTH ADHYAYA. FIRST KHANDA

2. Who is he whom we meditate on as the Self? Which is the Self? 3. That by which we see (form), that by which we hear (sound), that by which we perceive smells, that by which we utter speech, that by which we distinguish sweet and not sweet, and what comes from the heart and the mind, namely, perception, command, understanding, knowledge, wisdom, seeing, holding, thinking, considering, readiness (or suffering), remembering, conceiving, willing, breathing, loving, desiring? 4. No, all these are various names only of knowledge (the true Self). And that Self, consisting of (knowledge), is Brahman, it is Indra, it is Pragapati . All these Devas, these five great elements, earth, air, ether, water, fire, these and those which are, as it were, small and mixed, and seeds of this kind and that kind, born from eggs, born from the womb, born from heat, born from germs, horses, cows, men, elephants, and whatsoever breathes, whether walking or flying, and what is immoveable-all that is led (produced) by knowledge (the Self). 6. It rests on knowledge (the Self). The world is led (produced) by knowledge (the Self). Knowledge is its cause. 7. Knowledge is Brahman.

Is this some kind of secret "knowledge"? We'll read in our next Chapter about Gnosticism. Sounds like it was born in India.

(13) This next quote is a paraphrase of Proverbs 8. Or maybe, Proverbs is derived from it!

SIXTH KHANDA. Pg 143

Indra said to him: 'No one who chooses, chooses for another; choose thyself. Indra said to him: 'Know me only; that is what I deem most beneficial for man, that he should know me He who meditates on me as life and immortality, gains his full life in this world, and obtains in the Svarga world immortality and indestructibility. {Now here is a very modern theological concept.} *'This universe, before it was developed in the present form, was the existent one, Brahma, itself.'* {Universe in God's Mind!}

(14) A careful reading of Job 38 and, maybe, 26: 7-10 appears to ring true in this quote.

For it is said by the Bhagavat: "O Gautama, on what does the earth rest?" "The earth, O Brâhmana, rests on the sphere of water." "O Gautama, on what does the sphere of water rest?" "It rests on the air." "O Gautama, on what does the air rest?" "It rests on the ether (âkâsa)." "O Gautama, on what does the ether rest?" "Thou goest too far, great Brâhmana; thou goest too far, great Brahmana. The ether, O Brâhmana, does not rest. It has no support."

(15) Now these sentences are almost the very same words found in the Christian Testament.

a. 'The Self, smaller than small, greater than great, is hidden in the heart of that creature. A man who is free from desires and free from grief, sees the majesty of the Self by the grace of the Creator.' b. 'But he who has not first turned away from his wickedness, who is not tranquil, and subdued, or whose mind is not at rest, he can never obtain the Self (even) by knowledge. c. Wise men only, knowing the nature of what is immortal, do not look for anything stable here among things unstable

(16) Does this sound like God the Father and Yeshua the son?

BRAHMA was the first of the Devas, the maker of the universe, the preserver of the world. He told the knowledge of Brahman, the foundation of all knowledge, to his eldest son Atharva

(17) Is this next quote not the 4th Commandment?

> *Let thy mother be to thee like unto a god! Let thy father be to thee like unto a god!*

(18) Here is another slightly unique creation allegory.

> *'In the beginning this was non-existent (not yet defined by form and name). From it was born what exists. In the beginning this was Self alone, in the shape of a person (purusha). He looking round saw nothing but his Self. He first said, 'This is I;' Verily that Self consists of it; that Self consists of speech, mind, and breath. 4. These are the three worlds: earth is speech, sky mind, heaven breath. 5. These are the three Vedas: the Rig-veda is speech, the Yagur-veda mind, the Sama-veda breath. 6. These are the Devas, Fathers, and men: the Devas are speech, the Fathers mind, men breath. 7. These are father, mother, and child: the father is mind, the mother speech, the child breath*

(19) Well, these next three verses are right out of the 13th century AD, Summa Theologica of Thomas Aquinas who used a similar argument to prove the existence of God!

> *7. Let us know that highest great lord of lords, the highest deity of deities, the master of masters, the highest above, as god, the lord of the world, the adorable. 8. <u>There is no effect and no cause known of him</u>, no one is seen like unto him or better; his high power is revealed as manifold, as inherent, acting as force and knowledge. 9. There is no master of his in the world, no ruler of his, not even a sign of him. <u>He is the cause, the lord of the lords of the organs, and there is of him neither parent nor lord</u>.}*

(20) `Again, an example of the circular syllogisms in Hindu logic.

> *The syllable Om is the manifest greatness of Brahman, thus said one who well grounded (in Brahman) always meditates on it. Therefore by knowledge, by penance, and by meditation is Brahman gained There are two forms of Brahman, the material (effect) and the immaterial (cause). The material is false, the immaterial is true. That which is true is Brahman, that which is Brahman is light, and that which is light is the Sun. And this Sun became the Self of that Om.*

The theology within the Upanishads is quite similar to that which we find in the Western literature, the Bible. Where did these authors get that awareness, from God in a moment of inspiration or from their own common sense about what they observed? You decide! But consider this, if these ideas appear in both the Upanishads and in the Bible then these ideas are either from humankind's intelligent perception or they are both from the Divine lips --- inspiration! One cannot have an idea in one Sacred Scripture being from the Divine and the same idea in another Sacred Scripture being not from the Divine! That, dear literalist, is intellectual dishonesty.

So, if you wish to read more of the Upanishads, the Internet reference is in Appendix L. However, it is a very long read. We'll now turn our mind's eye to Siddhartha (he who has attained his goal) Gautama and Buddhism.

Section 3: Buddha and His Four Noble Truths

The life and legends of Buddha are available on the Internet, in libraries and in bookstores across this Nation. Appendix L lists suggested URL's and sites for your perusal. Right now, let's examine the tenets of Buddhism and thereby get a glimpse of the teacher and his followers. The Sacred Scripture of Buddhism is called "the Four Noble Truths and the Eightfold Paths".

THE FOUR NOBLE TRUTHS OF BUDDHA

The first truth: the knowledge of suffering.
Right off, Buddha's first observation is the misery of the people throughout his territory. If you have been to India you would almost come to the same conclusion. There were a great number of people who lived in abject poverty. It's almost impossible for us in the 21st century to imagine what it was like for so many in Buddha's time! Today in India pain and suffering associated with no jobs, little food and no shelter persists as it does elsewhere in the world. In some of the readings about Buddha and his times his view was that all in life is a type of suffering: birth, death and everything in between.

The second truth the origin of suffering.
Buddha identifies "desire and ignorance" as the principal causes of suffering. We think he would have a picnic in today's world judging by all the desires for power, money and consumer goods and services prevalent in the USA and the abject ignorance in many countries and communities around the globe.

The third truth: the destruction of suffering.
Buddha proclaims that suffering must be removed from one's life

The fourth truth: the way to this removal of suffering.
Peace and serenity can be achieved by following the Eightfold Path.
The Eightfold Paths:

1. Right knowledge or understanding.
   This is a familiar theme of the Gnostics who came centuries later:
   to know, intellectually, and comprehend the Four Noble Truths.

2 Right attitude or thought
   Here Buddha requires a behavioral and an intellectual serenity that is morally and ethically correct: internal peace and outward goodness to all along with an absence of all desires.

3. Right speech;
   What comes out of one's mouth must exhibit kindness, compassion and concern. One must guard against gossip, lying and treachery.

4. Right action
   Do good, not evil. Act forgivingly, seek not revenge. Be respectful of other's life, goods and family; hurt no one, steal nothing and engage in no illicit sex.

5. Right occupation
Choose a life's work that is ethical and does not lead to excess profit, luxury and greed at the expense of your neighbors.

6. Right effort
Strive to foster goodness, avoid evil, in what you do, say and think.

7. Right mindfulness or awareness
One must be aware of one's choices in order to prevent wrong desires and wrong actions in thought, emotion, word and deed.

8. Right composure
Meditation is the key to inner serenity; it will free one to accomplish one's goal: nirvana.

Now, this is an excerpt from Wulf Metz's article on the Internet site that truly hits the nail on the head as far as a crisp summary of Buddha's path to Nirvana.

> *"Essentially the Eightfold Path is concerned with three things: with morality (right speech, right action, right occupation); with spiritual discipline (right effort, right mindfulness, right composure), and with insight (right knowledge, right attitude). It is worth noting how far this is from any strictness or severity. It is a middle way, avoiding both the extreme of self-mortification or asceticism, and the extreme of sensuality, of giving oneself up to every impulse. This middle way cannot be called a compromise; it offers a demanding life-style that is both practical and balanced."*

Who do you think said it better, Buddha or Yeshua? You may wish to read the entire Internet article. There are many references to the New Testament (Christian Testament or C.T.) that might give you cause to consider that the Carpenter from Nazareth spent time in India prior to his ministry. Buddha's teachings (the Eightfold Paths) come close, very close, to those of the Carpenter. In the Bible's C.T. section we shall make a strong argument that the Prophet of Nazareth, like Buddha, never intended to create a new religion replete with hierarchical officials formulating any additional code of complex laws and dogmas. When you read the next section on the Tao Te Ching you will find some comments on what strict laws do to the people who must follow laws. Today, Zen Buddhism is an inclusive organizing non-religion for anyone interested. There are no restrictive laws and dogmas because there is no self-appointed, official managerial staff to re-formulate their personal interpretations and impose them on the membership. Christianity has failed miserably in that department.

However, no matter how clear and simple Buddha was, people love to re-organize and they did attempt to re-define his message. As one steeped in political science would predict, the entire following of monks began to debate over the exact interpretation intended by Buddha. The field narrowed down to two major groups: the conservatives (Theravada Buddhists) and the liberals (Mahayana Buddhists). Oh, shades of modern history and the divisiveness of us human folk! It seems that the conservatives were so strict that they tried to convinced everyone that Nirvana was unreachable but for a very select few. The wise liberals insisted that Buddhism was a way for everyone. Personally, the liberal position (could you tell?) is exactly what was preached 400 years later by our good friend Yeshua of Nazareth, the greatest liberal of all times. History does repeat itself, doesn't it? We now have a gamut of Christian denominations (See Appendix B for the list) from the strict ultra-conservative Calvinistic doctrines to the liberal, free, open arms policy of the non-denominational churches. Isn't it confusing why salvation became so burdened with legalisms and dogmatic restrictions within conservative Institutions when it is as plain as the nose on your face that the teachings of the Christian Testament extend salvation to whosoever chooses the Way of Right thinking, Right speaking and Right actions. Isn't that the definition of the "Kingdom of God" which Yeshua preached?

It is no small wonder why there are books recently published that compare Buddha with the Messiah, the Christ.

In a different vein, Buddha's interpretation of the world is close to the target. Look at this excerpt from Wulf Metz's commentary.

> *"According to Buddha, every part of the universe--not only human beings-- is subject to change and decay. Everything that is created must perish. Moreover, neither people nor the world are units complete in themselves and separated from other units. They are composed of many individual elements which are in a constant state of flux, always dissolving and combining with one another in new ways."*

Now that's so penetrating an observation that the Greeks, 200 years later, developed the exact same philosophy of a world in flux. Continuing with that excerpt:

> *"These components do not rearrange themselves at random. They are regulated by strict laws."*

Yes, Buddha recognized Natural Law: the existence of Physical and Mathematical regulations that order the Universe. Again, continuing this excerpt:

> *"In the case of human beings, the crucial factor is the law of karma, originally a Hindu idea. Karma, meaning roughly 'action' or 'works', is the quality that shows itself in the thoughts, words and deeds of an individual. It determines the nature of the individual's rebirth: good works automatically bring about a good rebirth, bad works a bad rebirth. So each rebirth is conditioned by the karma of the previous life. This is the moral order of the world, from which no one can escape."*

Although you won't ever see the word "Karma" in the Bible, this observation of Buddha is parallel to the teachings of the Nazarene in that we each are being judged by our actions in thoughts, words and deeds. Christianity's end is heaven or the other place; Buddhism camouflages its end with the rebirth process until such time as the individual reaches Nirvana. Sounds like the Catholic theory of Purgatory doesn't it?

Before we leave Buddhism there is another collection of Buddha's thoughts found in the Dhammapada. We've singled out several verses that caught our attention. Those of you familiar with the Christian Testament may find these aphorisms of Buddha quite similar to Yeshua's. The number at the end of each one identifies its position among all 423 of them.

53

The Dhammapada

A selection of the Aphorisms of Buddha

Occasions of hatred are certainly never settled by hatred. They are settled by freedom from hatred. This is the eternal law. 5

One's own misdirected thought can do one more harm than an enemy or an ill wisher. 42

It is not the shortcomings of others, nor what others have done or not done that one should think about, but what one has done or not done oneself. 50

Like a fine flower, beautiful to look at but without scent, fine words are fruitless in a man who does not act in accordance with them. 51

Like a fine flower, beautiful to look at and scented too, fine words bare fruit in a man who acts well in accordance with them. 52

Even if a fool lived with a wise man all his life, he would still not recognize the truth, like a wooden spoon cannot recognize the flavor of the soup. 64

Stupid fools go through life as their own enemies, doing evil deeds which have bitter consequences. 66

Like fresh milk a bad deed does not turn at once. It follows a fool scorching him like a smoldering fire. 71

Like one pointing out hidden treasure, if one finds a man of intelligence who can recognize one's faults and take one to task for them, one should cultivate the company of such a wise man. He who cultivates a man like that is the better for it, not worse. 76

He who drinks in the Truth will live happily with a peaceful mind. A wise man always delights in the Truth taught by the saints. 79

The wise find peace on hearing the truth, like a deep, clear, undisturbed lake. 82

Few are those among men who have crossed over to the other shore, while the rest of mankind runs along the bank. However those who follow the principles of the well-taught Truth will cross over to the other shore, out of the dominion of Death, hard though it is to escape. 85, 86

Freed by full realization and at peace, the mind of such a man is at peace, and his speech and action peaceful. 96

Do not think lightly of good that not the least consequence will come of it. A whole water pot will fill up from dripping drops of water. A wise man fills himself with good, just a little at a time. 122

Whoever does harm to an innocent man, a pure man and a faultless one, the evil comes back on that fool, like fine dust thrown into the wind. 125

Don't speak harshly to anyone. If you do people will speak to you in the same way. Harsh words are painful and their retaliation will hurt you. 133

Even when he is doing evil, the fool does not realize it. The idiot is punished by his own deeds, like one is scorched by fire. 136

An ignorant man ages like an ox. His flesh may increase, but not his understanding. 152

If one would only apply to oneself what one teaches others, when one was well disciplined oneself one could train others. It is oneself who is hard to train. 159

By oneself one does evil. By oneself one is defiled. By oneself one abstains from evil. By oneself one is purified. Purity and impurity are personal matters. No one can purify someone else. 165

Even if previously careless, when a man later stops being careless, he illuminates the world, like the moon breaking away from a cloud. 172

Blinded indeed is this world. Few are those who see the truth. Like a bird breaking out of the net, few are those who go to heaven. 174

A human birth is hard to achieve. Difficult is the life of mortals. To hear the true teaching is difficult, and the achievement of Buddhahood is difficult. 182

After enjoying the taste of solitude and the taste of peace, one is freed from distress and evil, as one enjoys the taste of spiritual joy. 205

It was so of old, Atula. It is not just so today. They criticize him who sits in silence; they criticize him who talks a lot. They even criticize him who speaks in moderation. There is not a man in the world who is not criticized. 227

But the supreme blight, ignorance, is the blight of blights. Destroying this blight, be free of blights. 243

Other people's faults are easily seen. One can winnow out other people's faults like chaff. One hides one's own faults though, like a dishonest gambler hides an unlucky throw. 252

He who seeks his own happiness by inflicting suffering on others, does not reach freedom from hatred, caught as he is in the toils of hatred. 291

Many of those dressed in the yellow robe are evil and unrestrained, and the evil end up in hell because of their evil deeds. 307

In the same way that a wrongly handled blade of grass will cut one's hand, so a badly fulfilled life in religion will drag one down to hell. 311

The gift of the Truth beats all other gifts. The flavor of the Truth beats all other tastes. The joy of the Truth beats all other joys, and the cessation of desire conquers all suffering. 354

Riches destroy a fool, but not those who are seeking the other shore. The fool destroys himself by his craving for riches, as he destroys others too. 355

One is one's own guard. What other guard could one have? One is one's own destiny. Therefore one should train oneself, like a merchant does a thoroughbred horse. 380

Does it not seem possible that the teachings of Buddha were the precursor to Yeshua's preaching? Many would agree that somehow the works of Buddha were influential in the development of Yeshua's theology and practical aphorisms. Clearly, both men ... were inspired of God!

Now, let's turn to the Chinese contributions

Section 4: The Tao Te Ching

This Sacred Scripture of China is more of a collection of good advice for the person of integrity, morality and ethical behavior than it is a prescription for a relationship with a Higher Power. One can find profound awareness of the world's affairs, guidance for success and inner serenity as well as humorous sayings all in the same paragraph. There is also recognition of a numinous being as you can read in its first paragraph:

I. The Tao that can be followed is not the eternal Tao.
The name that can be named is not the eternal name.
The nameless is the origin of heaven and earth
While naming is the origin of the myriad things.
Therefore, always desireless, you see the mystery
Ever desiring, you see the manifestations.
These two are the same--
When they appear they are named differently.
This sameness is the mystery,
Mystery within mystery;
The door to all marvels.

That introductory paragraph is the most theology that one will see in the Tao; there is a nameless mystery [creator] that is the door to all marvels. To those familiar with Paul's letters, the Tao Te Ching precedes by several hundred years his observation in Romans 1:19-20:

"19 For what can be known about God is evident to them, because God made it evident to them. 20 Ever since the creation of the world, his invisible attributes of eternal power and divinity have been able to be understood and perceived in what he has made".

In the Tao there is another paragraph here below that leads one to ponder its deeper meaning.

16. Effect emptiness to the extreme.
Keep stillness whole.
Myriad things act in concert.
I therefore watch their return.
All things flourish and each returns to its root.
Returning to the root is called quietude.
Quietude is called returning to life.
Return to life is called constant.
Knowing this constant is called illumination.
Acting arbitrarily without knowing the constant is harmful.
Knowing the constant is receptivity, which is impartial.
Impartiality is kingship.
Kingship is Heaven.
Heaven is Tao
Tao is eternal.
Though you lose the body, you do not die.

The Toa is full of paradoxes. Note the similarity to Buddhism's desires as seen in the following paragraph:

19. Get rid of "holiness" and abandon "wisdom" and the people will benefit a hundredfold.
Get rid of "altruism" and abandon "Justice" and the people will return to filial piety and compassion.
Get rid of cleverness and abandon profit, and thieves and gangsters will not exist.
Since the above three are merely words, they are not sufficient.
Therefore there must be something to include them all.
See the origin and keep the non-differentiated state.
Lessen selfishness and decrease desire.

Here is an observation of Nature that is translated into behavior:

23. *To speak little is natural.*
Therefore a gale does not blow a whole morning
Nor does a downpour last a whole day.
Who does these things? Heaven and Earth.
If even Heaven and Earth cannot force perfect continuity
How can people expect to?
Therefore there is such a thing as aligning one's actions with the Tao.
If you accord with the Tao you become one with it.
If you accord with virtue you become one with it.
If you accord with loss you become one with it.
The Tao accepts this accordance gladly.

Virtue accepts this accordance gladly.
Loss also accepts accordance gladly.
If you are untrustworthy, people will not trust you.

24. Standing on tiptoe, you are unsteady.
Straddle-legged, you cannot go.
If you show yourself, you will not be seen.
If you affirm yourself, you will not shine.
If you boast, you will have no merit.
If you promote yourself, you will have no success.
Those who abide in the Tao call these
Leftover food and wasted action
And all things dislike them.
Therefore the person of the Tao does not act like this.

It's interesting that the Tao recognizes the imperfection of nature and then states the foolishness of a requirement that humans be perfect! Did you catch the similarity between the line, "If you accord with the Tao you become one with it", and in John's Gospel, "being one with the Father"?

And this next paragraph borders on theology. Note the reference to a female Deity and the greatness of the human being (compare it to the quotation in Appendix P).

25. There is something that is perfect in its disorder
Which is born before Heaven and Earth.
So silent and desolate! It establishes itself without renewal.
Functions universally without lapse.
We can regard it as the Mother of Everything.
I don't know its name.

Hence, when forced to name it, I call it "Tao."
When forced to categorize it, I call it "great."
Greatness entails transcendence.
Transcendence entails going-far.
Going-far entails return.
Hence, Tao is great, Heaven is great, the Earth is great
And the human is also great
Within our realm there are four greatnesses and the human being is one of them.
Human beings follow the Earth.

Earth follows Heaven
Heaven follows the Tao
The Tao follows the way things are.

Then, in paragraph 26 there is an admonition to dictators.

How could the ruler of a large state
Be so concerned with himself as to ignore the people?

Here in paragraph 27 there is some good advice for people in the field of education. Notice: (a) that the sage is feminine, like wisdom in the Old Testament and (b) the Maslownian phrase *"the actualization of her luminosity"*.

It is in this manner that the sage is always skillful in elevating people.
Therefore she does not discard anybody.
She is always skillful in helping things
Therefore she does not discard anything.
This is called "the actualization of her luminosity."
Hence, the good are the teachers of the not-so-good.
And the not-so-good are the charges of the good.
Not valuing your teacher or not loving your students:
Even if you are smart, you are gravely in error.
This is called Essential Subtlety.

The Tao takes the middle road and cautions future leaders. Might this be a good message for elected officials in Washington?

29. If you want to grab the world and run it
I can see that you will not succeed.
The world is a spiritual vessel, which can't be controlled.
Manipulators mess things up.
Grabbers lose it. Therefore:
Sometimes you lead
Sometimes you follow
Sometimes you are stifled
Sometimes you breathe easy
Sometimes you are strong
Sometimes you are weak
Sometimes you destroy
And sometimes you are destroyed.
Hence, the sage shuns excess
Shuns grandiosity
Shuns arrogance.

Well, here is the best in ancient advice found in paragraph 30. Does this sound familiar? Imagine, it was written about 300 BC!

What goes around comes around.

But when you read it in context, there is a larger message, especially for our times of terrorism and retaliation. Note the warning in the last verse!

30. If you used the Tao as a principle for ruling
You would not dominate the people by military force.
What goes around comes around.
Where the general has camped
Thorns and brambles grow.
In the wake of a great army
Come years of famine.
If you know what you are doing

You will do what is necessary and stop there.
Accomplish but don't boast
Accomplish without show
Accomplish without arrogance
Accomplish without grabbing
Accomplish without forcing.
When things flourish they decline.
This is called non-Tao
The non-Tao is short-lived.

There is even a bit of good psychology here, too.

33. If you understand others you are smart.
If you understand yourself you are illuminated.
If you overcome others you are powerful.
If you overcome yourself you have strength.
If you know how to be satisfied you are rich.
If you can act with vigor, you have a will.
If you don't lose your objectives you can be long lasting.
If you die without loss, you are eternal.

34. The Tao is like a great flooding river
How can it be directed to the left or right?
The myriad things rely on it for their life but do not distinguish it.
It brings to completion but cannot be said to exist.
It clothes and feeds all things without lording over them.
It is always desireless, so we call it "the small."
The myriad things return to it and it doesn't exact lordship
Thus it can be called "great."
Till the end, it does not regard itself as Great.
Therefore it actualizes its greatness.

If you replace the word, TAO, with "Kingdom of God", this excerpt reads like what Yeshua is alleged to have spoken.

When the Tao appears from its opening
It is so subtle, it has no taste.
Look at it, you cannot see it.
Listen, you cannot hear it.
Use it
You cannot exhaust it. (Para. 35)

And for our National Security Officials this is their justification from of old.

The country's potent weapons
Should not be shown to its people.

These are the final selections from the Tao Te Ching. Their advice covers many subjects, some funny, some obvious, some practical and some profound. Yet all have been written within a culture that claims no divine inspiration. The Tao Te Ching demonstrates clearly the profound capacity of Homo Sapiens.

60

1. *The further you go, the less you know*

2. *No matter how much you manipulate*
   You can never possess the world.

3. *Though the Way is quite broad, People love shortcuts.*

4. *Therefore, take yourself and observe yourself.*

5. *Therefore, Tao gives birth.*
   Its virtue rears, develops raises, adjusts and disciplines,
   Nourishes, covers and protects, Produces but does not possess,
   Acts without expectation, Leads without forcing.
   This is called "Mysterious Virtue."

6. *One who knows does not speak.*
   One who speaks does not know.

7. *The more regulations there are,*
   The poorer people become.

8. *The more picky the laws are,*
   The more thieves and gangsters there are.

9. *When the government is nitpicking*
   The people have anxiety.

10. *Get involved without manipulating.*

11. *Handle things before they arise.*
    Manage affairs before they are in a mess.

12. *I have three treasures that hold and cherish.*
    The first is compassion,
    The second is frugality,
    The third is not daring to put myself ahead of everybody.

13. *There is no greater danger than under-estimating your opponent.*

14. When opponents clash
    The one who is sorry about it will be the winner.

15. There is nothing better than to know that you don't know.
    Not knowing, yet thinking you know--This is sickness.

16. The reason people starve is because their rulers tax them excessively.
    They are difficult to govern because their rulers have their own ends in mind.

17. The Heavenly Tao has no favorites:
    It raises up the Good.

18. True words are not fancy.

*19. My words are easy to understand and easy to practice.
Yet nobody understands them or practices them.*

For such a simplistic and short Sacred Scripture the Tao appears to be a way to a peaceful life. Since it was written close to 400 BC, is it possible that the Carpenter from Nazareth could have also spent some of his so-called missing years in China? Or, just maybe the teachings of the Tao came to Nazareth! There is a remarkable similarity between the teachings of the Tao and the tenets of the "Jesus Movement" which we will discuss later in Chapters Six and Seven.

PART TWO: Scriptures Alleged to be of Divine Origin

The key to understanding the Sacred Scriptures included in this Section is the definition of "inspired" which is a common response by the believers justifying the validity of their scripture. To some faithful, the word, "inspired" carries a kind of absoluteness to the scripture as though there were a Divine guarantee that each story, actually, the entire text, is historically accurate in every detail including the conversations therein. If in their Sacred Scripture one points out specific mistakes or contradictions, these believers rebuttal with the most astonishing convoluted justifications followed by epithets of severe condemnation. It appears that literalism requires a faith in the absolute veracity of the Sacred Scripture itself as well as its purpose and significance. Furthermore, it may be that if there are mistakes and contradictions, the literalist fears a loss of faith in the Sacred Scripture. We have a deep suspicion that literalists worship their Book and not the God about whom it speaks.

The modern scholar has a more balanced understanding of "inspired". The word denotes a level of creativity that ranges from simply (a) putting together two unrelated concepts to form a new concept to, (b) creating an absolute work of profound meaning and great social consequence up to (c) a Divine guarantee of absolute factual history, accurate science including the conversations. A literalist interprets the word "inspired" as in (c). Psychology recognizes the mental condition of people adhering to that third definition; it's called "cognitive dissonance". If one invests his or her total belief in the absoluteness of a chosen Sacred Scripture, then any attempt to discredit that Sacred Scripture is met with a logic barrier in the mind of that believer. That's what "cognitive dissonance" means.

We speak of artists being inspired to create a new technique. Henry Ford was inspired to engineer a new mode of transportation. Dante was inspired to write a shocking description of the hellish beyond. Beethoven was inspired to compose his beautiful music. Writers of spirituality texts are inspired to motivate people to re-consider the meaning of their lives. And finally, even the authors of the different Sacred Scriptures were inspired to write about the history and lives of important events and people that affect the meaning of their own and other lives. Yet none of the above was privy to the absolute knowledge of the Divine.

Therefore, we have chosen to use the word, "alleged" in the title of this section in reference to Sacred Scriptures. Can anyone prove that a Scripture is scientifically correct in its description of creation? Can anyone prove that a Scripture has not confused natural phenomenon with divinity? Can anyone prove that a Scripture is not contradictory and not full of mistakes? Alas! None can be proven! All Sacred Scriptures display their author's simplistic knowledge of their culture's awareness of the world about them. They all mistakenly interpret natural events as a divinity or as divinely caused. They all contain: human errors, mistakes in references, historical and cosmological inaccuracies and mostly re-written ancient legends.

In spite of these shortcomings, each Sacred Scripture contains lesser and greater profoundness worthy of the reader's consideration. It is in these portions of profoundness that reside true insights into the Divine mind; true human insights produced by the gift of intelligence from a self-giving Creator.

The prime reasons for challenging "The Divine Origin Belief" here, and every other claim to a Divine dictation, lies in some or all of the following:

1. There is far too much cultural scientific and cosmological ignorance;
2. The creation tales are in themselves contrary to the fossil record;
3. The presence of obvious contradictions in history and philosophy;
4. References from one statement to a previous statement or fact are wrong;
5. Cultural and geographical statements in the story line reflect the author's misconceptions.

Chapter Five will be devoted to listing as many of the above concerns that make modern scholars challenge the idea that God dictated the contents of a particular Sacred Scripture. For now, let's examine the profundities in the following Scriptures.

Section 5: The Bhagavad-Gita

Never have we seen so much profound theology that resembles the theology of the Bible. The depth and spirituality found in the Gita is awesome. Understand that the purpose of the Gita was to combine the principles of the Upanishads with Buddhism along with mainstream Hinduism. The attainment of Brahman knowledge and Buddha's righteous life without desire woven into the fabric of Hindi meditation through the practice of Yoga is truly a marvel of Indian spirituality. The Gita's doctrines are clear evidence that the One Creator of the Universe was actively communicating with humankind in that first millennium BC. That is, without dictating every word! When one examines the order of our eight written Scriptures, the evidence points to a systematic development in human understanding of this Supreme Being whose nature becomes more compassionate, merciful and forgiving as human cultures matured.

The total length of the Bhagavad Gita is relatively short compared to the Upanishads, the Qur'an and the Bible. Yet the spirituality, in most excerpts, is powerful to the analytical reader. There is a translation on the Internet, referenced in Appendix L. Your personal reading of the Gita will be very rewarding.

The story line in the Gita is interesting. The essence of God (Brahman) is the prime character, Lord Krishna (God's Human form), and the noble student is Arjuna the archer. The concern that gives birth to all the dialogue is that Arjuna is reluctant to begin a war that will result in the death of his relatives and countrymen. Lord Krishna explains the rules of existence that lead to one's choice of a life of happiness or of misery and death. The conversation during the eighteen chapters covers the ideas of the Upanishads, Buddhism and the spiritual culture of India. This is an intriguing presentation of their relationship with the Divine because it doesn't come across as a set of doctrines, dogma and rituals. Rather, one can see the minds of human genius culling and molding the three theologies into a single national spirituality. Too bad the Christian denominations couldn't get together and form a single-minded position about the meaning of their Holy Book.

The first chapter of the Gita will give you a clearer idea of the nature of this mythical text. Please, don't get too concerned about the names of the characters; after all, it takes place in India about 300 BC.

Chapter 1: Arjuna's Dilemma

Dhritaraashtra said: O Sanjaya, assembled in the holy field of Kurukshetra and eager to fight, what did my people and the Paandavas do? (1.01) Sanjaya said: Seeing the battle formation of the Paandava's army, King Duryodhana approached his guru, Drona, and spoke these words: (1.02) O master, behold this mighty army of the sons of Paandu, arranged in battle formation by your talented disciple, the son of Drupada. (1.03) There are many heroes and mighty archers equal to Bheema and Arjuna in war such as Yuyudhaana and Viraata; and the great warrior, Drupada; (1.04) Dhrishtaketu, Chekitaana, and the heroic King of Kaashi; Purujit, Kuntibhoja, and the great man Saibya; (1.05) The valiant Yudhaamanyu, the formidable Uttamauja, the son of Subhadraa, and the sons of Draupadi; all of them are great warriors. (1.06) Also know, O best among the twice born, the distinguished ones on our side. I name the commanders of my army for your information. (1.07) Yourself, Bheeshma, Karna, and the victorious Kripa; Ashvatthaamaa, Vikarna, and the son of Somadatta. (1.08) And many other heroes who have risked their lives for me. They are armed with various weapons, and all are skilled in warfare. (1.09) Our army, commanded by Bheeshma, is invincible; while their army, protected by Bheema, is easy to conquer. (1.10) Therefore all of you, occupying your respective positions on all fronts, protect Bheeshma only. (1.11) The mighty Bheeshma, the eldest man of the Kuru dynasty, roared as a lion and blew his conch loudly bringing joy to Duryodhana. (1.12) After that, conches, kettledrums, cymbals, drums, and trumpets were sounded together. The commotion was tremendous. (1.13)

Then Lord Krishna and Arjuna, seated in a grand chariot yoked with white horses, blew their celestial conches. (1.14) Krishna blew His conch, Paanchajanya; Arjuna blew his conch, Devadatta; and Bheema, the doer of formidable deeds, blew (his) big conch, Paundra. (1.15) The son of Kunti, King Yudhishthira, blew (his conch) Anantavijaya, while Nakula and Sahadeva blew Sughosha and Manipushpaka conches, respectively. (1.16) The King of Kaashi, the mighty archer; Shikhandi, the great warrior; Dhristadyumna, Viraata, and the invincible Saatyaki; (1.17) King Drupada, and the sons of Draupadi; the mighty son of Subhadraa; all of them blew their respective conches, O lord of the earth. (1.18)The tumultuous uproar, resounding through earth and sky, tore the hearts of the Kauravas. (1.19) Seeing the sons of Dhritaraashtra standing; and the war about to begin; Arjuna, whose banner bore the emblem of Hanumana, took up his bow; and (1.20) Spoke these words to Lord Krishna: O Lord, (please) stop my chariot between the two armies until I behold those who stand here eager for battle and with whom I must engage in this act of war. (1.21-22)

I wish to see those who are willing to serve the evil-minded son of Dhritaraashtra by assembling here to fight the battle. (1.23) Sanjaya said: O King, Lord Krishna, as requested by Arjuna, placed the best of all the chariots in the midst of the two armies; (1.24) Facing Bheeshma, Drona, and all other Kings; and said to Arjuna: Behold these assembled Kurus! (1.25)

There Arjuna saw his uncles, grandfathers, teachers, maternal uncles, brothers, sons, grandsons, and comrades. (1.26) Seeing fathers-in-law, all those kinsmen, and other dear ones standing in the ranks of the two armies, (1.27) Arjuna was overcome with great compassion and sorrowfully said: O Krishna, seeing my kinsmen standing with a desire to fight, (1.28) My limbs fail and my mouth becomes dry. My body quivers and my hairs stand on end. (1.29) The bow, Gaandeeva, slips from my hand and my skin intensely burns. My head turns, I am unable to stand steady and, O Krishna, I see bad omens. I see no use of killing my kinsmen in battle. (1.30-31) I desire neither victory nor pleasure nor kingdom, O Krishna. What is the use of the kingdom, or enjoyment, or even life, O Krishna? (1.32) Because all those, for whom we desire kingdom, enjoyments, and pleasures, are standing here for the battle, giving up their lives and wealth. (1.33) Teachers, uncles, sons, grandfathers, maternal uncles, fathers-in-law, grandsons, brothers-in-law, and other relatives. (1.34) I do not wish to kill them, who are also about to kill, even for the sovereignty of the three worlds, let alone for this earthly kingdom, O Krishna. (1.35) O Lord Krishna, what pleasure shall we find in killing the sons of Dhritaraashtra? Upon killing these felons we shall incur sin only. (1.36) Therefore, we should not kill our brothers, the sons of Dhritaraashtra. How can we be happy after killing our kinsmen, O Krishna? (1.37) Though they, blinded by greed, do not see evil in the destruction of the family, or sin in being treacherous to friends. (1.38) Why shouldn't we, who clearly see evil in the destruction of the family, think about turning away from this sin, O Krishna? (1.39) With the destruction of the family, the eternal family traditions are destroyed, and immorality prevails due to the destruction of family traditions. (1.40) And when immorality prevails, O Krishna, the women of the family become corrupted; when women are corrupted, social problems arise. (1.41) This brings the family and the slayers of the family to hell, because the spirits of their ancestors are degraded when deprived of ceremonial offerings of rice-ball and water. (1.42) The everlasting qualities of Varna and family traditions of those who destroy their family are ruined by the sinful act of illegitimacy. (1.43) (Note: Varna means color, or the make up and the hue of mind; a social division or order of society such as caste in India.) We have been told, O Krishna, that people whose family traditions are destroyed necessarily dwell in hell for a long time. (1.44) Alas! We are ready to commit a great sin by striving to slay our kinsmen because of greed for the pleasures of the kingdom. (1.45) It would be far better for me if the sons of Dhritaraashtra should kill me with their weapons in battle while I am unarmed and unresisting. (1.46) Sanjaya said: Having said this in the battle field and casting aside his bow and arrow, Arjuna sat down on the seat of the chariot with his mind overwhelmed with sorrow. (1.47)

****

From here on to the end, the quoted passages illustrate noteworthy theological similarities to other Sacred Scriptures. The capitalized titles indicate their significance (as best we perceive them to be significant!).

THIS VERSE SPEAKS OF THE SOUL OR SPIRIT: This Atma cannot be cut, burned, wetted, or dried up. It is eternal, all pervading, unchanging, immovable, and primeval. (2.24) [*This is the standard abbreviation for Chapter Two, Verse twenty-four]*.

WHAT IS WRONG BEHAVIOR: The resolute determination (of Self-realization) is not formed in the minds of those who are attached to pleasure and power; and whose discernment is obscured by such (ritualistic) activities. (2.44)

THIS SOUNDS LIKE A MASLONIAN ACTUALIZATION: A Karma-yogi gets freedom from both vice and virtue in this life itself. Therefore, strive for Karma-yoga. Working to the best of one's abilities without getting attached to the fruits of work is called Karma-yoga. (2.50)

REMINDS ONE OF THE LITERALIST'S CREDO: One falls down (from the right path) when reasoning is destroyed. (2.63)

A PRINCIPAL OF BUDDHISM: A disciplined person, enjoying sense objects with senses that are under control and free from likes and dislikes, attains tranquility. (2.64)

THE POTENTIAL IN HUMAN NATURE (LIKE IN GENESIS): Brahman, the creator, in the beginning created human beings together with [selfless service and unselfish work], and said: By [these] you shall prosper and ... shall fulfill all your desires. (3.10)

BUDDHISM'S SIMILARITY TO CHRISTIANITY: The righteous who eat the remnants of the [selfless service and unselfish work] are freed from all sins, but the impious who cook food only for themselves (without sharing with others in charity) verily eat sin. (3.13)

MASLONIAN SPIRITUALITY: A Self-realized person does not depend on anybody (except God) for anything. (3.18)

CHRISTIAN SPIRITUALITY: Dedicating all works to [Brahman] in a spiritual frame of mind, free from desire, attachment, and mental grief, do your duty. (3.30) Those who always practice this teaching of [Brahman], with faith and free from cavil, are freed from the bondage of [fate]. (3.31) But, those who carp at [Brahman] teachings and do not practice it, consider them as ignorant of all knowledge, senseless, and lost. (3.32)

THIS IS PURE CHRISTIAN AND MASLONIAN PSYCHOLOGY: Attachments and aversions for the sense objects remain in the senses. One should not come under the control of these two, because they are two stumbling blocks, indeed, on one's path of Self-realization. (3.34)

CAUSE OF SIN, BUT NOTE THAT THIS DEFINITION IS NOT WHAT PEOPLE UNDERSTAND TODAY: Arjuna said: O Krishna, what impels one to commit sin as if unwillingly and forced against one's will? (3.36) The supreme Lord said: It is Karma [*free will choices affecting one's future*] and anger born of Rajo Guna [*passionate desire for all sensual and material pleasures*]. Karma is insatiable and is a great devil. Know this as the enemy. (3.37)

MOSES' RELATIONSHIP WITH YAHWEH (Exo 33: 12): Today I (Lord Krishna) have described the same ancient science (science of right action) to you, because you are my sincere devotee and friend. (4.03)

THE THEOLOGY OF THE HEBREW TESTAMENT I {Lord Krishna (Brahman)} am eternal, imperishable, and the Lord of all beings (4.06)

BIBLICAL QUOTE: Freed from attachment, fear, and anger; fully absorbed in [Brahman], taking refuge in Me, and purified by the fire of Self-knowledge, many have attained Me. (4.10) [See Pro 8: 34-36, Eph 3: 17-19]

THE TEACHING OF GNOSTICISM: The knowledge sacrifice is superior to any material sacrifice, O Arjuna because, all actions in their entirety culminate in knowledge. (4.33) Even if one is the most sinful of all sinners, yet one shall cross over the ocean of sin by the raft of <u>knowledge alone</u>. (4.36) {"Into all literature some error must creep!" our comment.}

FAITH AND REASON: The one who has faith, and is sincere, and has mastery over the senses, gains this knowledge. Having gained this, one at once attains the supreme peace. (4.39) But the ignorant, who has no faith and is full of doubt (about the Self) perishes. There is neither this world nor the world beyond nor happiness for the one who doubts. (4.40)

THIS APPROXIMATES A YESHUA SAYING: One who does all work as an offering to the Lord, abandoning attachment to the results, is as untouched by sin as a lotus leaf is untouched by water. (5.10)

SPIRITUALITY: One who neither rejoices on obtaining what is pleasant nor grieves on obtaining the unpleasant, who is undeluded, who has a steady mind, and who is a knower of Brahman; such a person abides in Brahman. (5.20) The wise, O Arjuna, do not rejoice in sensual pleasures. (5.22) One who is able to withstand the impulse of lust and anger before death is a yogi, and a happy person. (5.23) One who finds happiness with the Self, who rejoices the Self within, and who is illuminated by the Self-knowledge; such a yogi becomes one with Brahman and attains supreme nirvana. (5.24)

THE SEAT OF FREE WILL: One must elevate, not degrade, oneself by one's own "mind". The mind alone is one's friend as well as one's enemy. (6.05) The mind is the "friend" of those who have control over it, and the mind acts like an enemy for those who do not control it. (6.06) One who has control over the mind is tranquil in heat and cold, in pleasure and pain, and in honor and dishonor; and is ever steadfast with the Supreme Self. (6.07)

MEDITATION: Let the yogi -- seated in solitude and alone -- having mind and senses under control and free from desires and attachments for possessions, try constantly to contemplate on the Supreme Self. (6.10) Sitting (in a comfortable position) and concentrating the mind on a single object, controlling the thoughts and the activities of the senses, let the yogi practice meditation for self-purification. (6.12) 3. Thus, by always keeping the mind fixed on the Self, the yogi whose mind is subdued attains peace of the Supreme nirvana by uniting with Me. (6.15)

PARAPHRASE OF Verse 77 FROM THE GOSPEL OF THOMAS: Those who see Me in everything and see everything in Me [Lord Krishna], are not separated from Me and I am not separated from them. (6.30)

THIS IS CLOSE TO A YESHUA SAYING: One is considered the best yogi who regards every being like oneself, and who can feel the pain and pleasures of others as one's own, O Arjuna. (6.32)

A BIT OF HUMOR RIGHT OUT OF PROVERBS: Because the mind, indeed, is very unsteady, turbulent, powerful, and obstinate, O Krishna. I think restraining the mind is as difficult as restraining the wind. (6.34)

ABOUT THE MYSTERY OF GOD: Scarcely one out of thousands of persons strives for perfection of Self-realization. Scarcely any one of the striving, or even the perfected persons, truly understands Me [Lord Krishna]. (7.03)

JUST LIKE IN GENESIS: Brahman is the origin as well as the dissolution of the entire universe. (7.06)

OUR PERSONAL THEOLOGY OF "GOD MEETS US WHERE WE ARE": Whosoever desires to worship whatever deity (using whatever name, form, and method) with faith, I make their faith steady in that very deity. (7.21) Endowed with steady faith they worship that deity, and fulfill their wishes through that deity. Those wishes are, indeed, granted only by Me. (7.22)

AGE OF EARTH: Those who know that the day of Brahma lasts one thousand Yugas (or 4.32 billion years) and that his night also lasts one thousand Yugas, they are the knowers of day and night. (8.17)

LIFE OR DEATH OF DEUTERONOMY: The path of light (of spiritual practice and Self-knowledge) and the path of darkness (of materialism and ignorance) are thought to be the world's two eternal paths. The former leads to nirvana and the latter leads to ... [guess where?]. (8.26) (Deut 30: 19)

BIBLICAL STATEMENT: The Supreme Lord said: I shall reveal to you, who do not disbelieve, the most profound secret of Self-knowledge and Self-realization. Having known this you will be freed from the miseries of worldly existence. (9.01) [Jer 33:3]

FOURTH GOSPEL STATEMENT: The ignorant ones, not knowing My supreme natures as the great Lord of all beings, disregard Me when I assume human form. (9.11)

THE DESCRIPTION OF THE BIBLICAL CREATOR: But great souls, O Arjuna, who possess divine qualities know Me as the (material and efficient) cause of creation and imperishable, and worship Me single-mindedly. (9.13) I am the supporter of the universe, the father, the mother, and the grandfather. I am the object of knowledge, the purifier, the sacred syllable OM, and ... (9.17) I am the goal, the supporter, the Lord, the witness, the abode, therefore, the friend, the origin, the dissolution, the foundation, the substratum, and the imperishable seed. (9.18)

A CONTRADICTION WITH (7. 21 & 22) ABOVE: O Arjuna, even those devotees who worship demigods with faith, they too worship Me, but in an improper way. (9.23)

A CHRISTIAN SAYING: O Arjuna, whatever you do, whatever you eat, whatever you offer as oblation to the sacred fire, whatever charity you give, whatever austerity you perform, do all that as an offering unto Me. (9.27)

AN AXIOM OF PAN-EN-THEISM: The Self is present equally in all beings.

A STATEMENT OF CONTRADICTION: There is no one hateful or dear to Me.

A FOURTH GOSPEL SAYING But, those who worship Me with devotion, they are with Me and I am also with them. (9.29)

THE FORGIVING GOD OF YESHUA AND THE SAUL-PAUL OF ACTS: Even if the most sinful person resolves to worship Me with single-minded loving devotion, such a person must be regarded as a saint because of making the right resolution. (9.30) Such a person soon becomes righteous and attains everlasting peace. Be aware, O Arjuna, that My devotee never falls down. (9.31)

THE INCLUSIVE NEW BUDDHISM: Anybody, including women, merchants, laborers, and the evil-minded can attain the supreme goal by just surrendering unto My will (with loving devotion), O Arjuna. (9.32)

BIBLICAL STATEMENT: One who knows Me as the unborn, the beginningless, and the Supreme Lord of the universe, is considered wise among the mortals, and gets liberation from the bondage of: (10.03) Discrimination, knowledge, non-delusion, forgiveness, truthfulness, control over the mind and senses, pleasure, pain, birth, death, fear, fearlessness; (10.04). Nonviolence, equanimity, contentment, austerity, charity, fame, and ill fame; all these diverse qualities in human beings arise from Me alone. (10.05)

BIBLICAL STATEMENT (Jer 33:3): I give the knowledge, to those who are ever united with Me and lovingly adore Me, by which they come to Me. (10.10)

THE GREAT "I AM" OF MOSES: The Supreme Lord said: O Arjuna, now I shall explain to you My prominent divine manifestations, because My manifestations are endless. (10.19) O Arjuna, I am the Atma abiding in the heart of all beings. I am also the beginning, the middle, and the end of all beings. (10.20) I am the beginning, the middle, and the end of the creation, O Arjuna. Among the knowledge I am knowledge of the supreme Self. I am logic of the logician. (10.32) I am the letter "A" among the alphabets, among the compound words I am the dual compound, I am the endless time, I am the sustainer of all, and have faces on all sides (or I am omniscient). (10.33) I am the all-devouring death, and also the origin of future beings. Among the feminine nouns I am fame, prosperity, speech, memory, intellect, resolve, and forgiveness. (10.34) I am the origin or seed of all beings, O Arjuna. There is nothing, animate or inanimate, that can exist without Me. (10.39)

MOSES WISHES TO SEE GOD'S GLORY (EX 33: 17-23): O Lord, You are as You have said, yet I wish to see Your divine cosmic form, O Supreme Being. (11.03) O Lord, if You think it is possible for me to see this, then O Lord of the yogis, show me Your imperishable Self. (11.04) The Supreme Lord said: O Arjuna, behold My hundreds and thousands of multifarious divine forms of different colors and shapes.(11.05) But, you are not able to see Me with your physical eye; therefore, I give you the divine eye [PAUL'S VISION OF NATURE IN POMANS] to see My majestic power and glory. (11.08)

THE TRANSFUGURATION OF YESHUA: If the splendor of thousands of suns were to blaze forth all at once in the sky, even that would not resemble the splendor of that exalted being. (11.12)

REMEMBER THE STORY LINE of this B-G? HERE IS ITS JUSTIFICATION FOR WAR THAT IS SIMILAR TO THE "JEHAD" OF THE QUR'AN: The Supreme Lord said: I am death, the mighty destroyer of the world, out to destroy. Even without your participation all the warriors standing arrayed in the opposing armies shall cease to exist. (11.32) Therefore, you get up and attain glory. Conquer your enemies and enjoy a prosperous kingdom. All these (warriors) have already been destroyed by Me. You are only an instrument, O Arjuna. (11.33)

GOD'S COVENANT TO THE ISRAELITES: But, to those who worship Me as the personal God, renouncing all actions to Me; setting Me as their supreme goal, and meditating on Me with single minded devotion; (12.06) I swiftly become their savior, from the world that is the ocean of death and transmigration, whose thoughts are set on Me, O Arjuna. (12.07) Therefore, focus your mind on Me alone and let your intellect dwell upon Me through meditation and contemplation. Thereafter you shall certainly come to Me. (12.08)

THOSE DEAR TO GOD: One who does not hate any creature, who is friendly and compassionate, free from (the notion of) "I" and "my", even-minded in pain and pleasure, forgiving; and (12.13) The yogi who is ever content, who has subdued the mind, whose resolve is firm, whose mind and intellect are engaged in dwelling upon Me; such a devotee is dear to Me. (12.14) The one by whom others are not agitated, and who is not agitated by others; who is free from joy, envy, fear, and anxiety; is also dear to Me. (12.15) One who is free from desires; who is pure, wise, impartial, and free from anxiety; who has renounced (the doership in) all undertakings; and who is devoted to Me, is dear to Me. (12.16) One who neither rejoices nor grieves, neither likes nor dislikes, who has renounced both the good and the evil, and who is full of devotion, such a person is dear to Me. (12.17) The one who remains the same towards friend or foe, in honor or disgrace, in heat or cold, in pleasure or pain; who is free from attachment; and (12.18) The one who is indifferent or silent in censure or praise, content with anything, unattached to a place (country, or house), equanimous, and full of devotion; that person is dear to Me. (12.19) But those devotees who have faith and sincerely try to develop the above mentioned immortal virtues, and set Me as their supreme goal; are very dear to Me. (12.20)

PAN-EN-THEISM (GOD IN ALL THINGS): the creator exists in the creation by pervading everything. (13.13) He is inside as well as outside all beings, animate and inanimate. He is incomprehensible because of His subtlety. He is very near as well as far away. (13.15) The light of all lights, He is said to be beyond darkness. He is the knowledge, the object of knowledge, and seated in the hearts of all beings, He is to be realized by the knowledge. (13.17) The Supreme Spirit in the body is also called the witness, the guide, the supporter, the enjoyer, and the great Lord or Paramaatma. (13.22) Some perceive God in the heart by the intellect through meditation; others by the yoga of knowledge; and others by the yoga of work (or Karma-yoga). (13.24) The one who sees the imperishable Supreme Lord dwelling equally within all perishable beings truly sees. (13.27) When one perceives diverse variety of beings resting in One and spreading out from That alone, then one attains Brahman. (13.30)

BUDDHISM AND CHRISTIANITY: The Supreme Lord said: Fearlessness, purity of heart, perseverance in the yoga of knowledge, charity, sense restraint, sacrifice, study of the scriptures, austerity, honesty; (16.01) Nonviolence, truthfulness, absence of anger, renunciation, equanimity, abstaining from malicious talk, compassion for all creatures, freedom from greed, gentleness, modesty, absence of fickleness; (16.02) Splendor, forgiveness, fortitude, cleanliness, absence of malice, and absence of pride; these are the qualities of those endowed with divine virtues, O Arjuna. (16.03)

THE CAPITAL EVILS: There are two types of human beings in this world: the divine, and the demonic. The divine has been described at length; now hear from Me about the demonic, O Arjuna. (16.06) Hypocrisy, arrogance, pride, anger, harshness, and ignorance [*who are these guys?*]; these are the marks of those who are born with demonic qualities, O Arjuna. (16.04) Persons of demonic nature do not know what to do and what not to do. They neither have purity nor good conduct nor truthfulness. (16.07) They say that the world is unreal, without a substratum, without a God, and without an order. The world is caused by lust (or Karma) alone and nothing else. (16.08} *Authors Note: No one is born with demonic qualities; we are all born with free will that oftentimes leads to demonic behavior!*

THE LOST SOULS: Obsessed with great anxiety until death, considering sense gratification as their highest aim, convinced that this (sense pleasure) is everything, (16.11) Bound by hundreds of ties of desire and enslaved by lust and anger; they strive to obtain wealth by unlawful means for the fulfillment of desires. They think: (16.12) This has been gained by me today, I shall fulfill this desire, this is mine and this wealth also shall be mine in the future; (16.13) That enemy has been slain by me, and I shall slay others also. I am the Lord. I am the enjoyer. I am successful, powerful, and happy; (16.14) I am rich and born in a noble family. I am the greatest. I shall perform sacrifice, I shall give charity, and I shall rejoice. Thus deluded by ignorance; (16.15) Bewildered by many fancies; entangled in the net of delusion; addicted to the enjoyment of sensual pleasures; they fall into a foul hell. (16.16)

THE RITUALISTS: Self-conceited, stubborn, filled with pride and intoxication of wealth; they perform Yajna only in name, for show, and not according to scriptural injunction. (16.17) *Yajna means sacrifice, selfless service, unselfish work, Seva, meritorious deeds, giving away something to others, and a religious rite in which oblation is offered to gods.*

LITERALISM, EVEN IN THE GITA!: One who acts under the influence of their desires, disobeying scriptural injunctions, neither attains perfection nor happiness nor the supreme goal. (16.23) Therefore, let the scripture be your authority in determining what should be done and what should not be done. You should perform your duty following the scriptural injunction. (16.24)

FREE WILL: O Arjuna, the faith of each is in accordance with one's own nature or Sanskaara. A person is known by the faith. One can become whatever one wants to be (if one constantly contemplates on the object of desire with faith). (17.03)

A YESHUA STATEMENT: Acts of sacrifice, charity, and austerity should not be abandoned, but should be performed, because sacrifice, charity, and austerity are the purifiers of the wise. (18.05)

BUDDHISM AND CHRISTIANITY: The person whose mind is always free from attachment, who has subdued the mind and senses, and who is free from desires, attains the supreme perfection of freedom from (bondage) through renunciation. (18.49)

FOURTH GOSPEL AND 2 CORINTHIANS 12: 9: One attains the eternal imperishable abode by My grace, even while doing all duties, just by taking refuge in Me. (18.56)

BIBLICAL STATEMENT: When your mind becomes fixed on Me, you shall overcome all difficulties by My grace (II Cor 12: 9) . But, if you do not listen to Me due to ego, you shall perish. (MOSES TO ISRAELITES) (18.58)

THE TRUE TEACHER: The one who shall propagate this supreme secret philosophy (or the transcendental knowledge of the Gita) amongst My devotees, shall be performing the highest devotional service to Me and shall certainly attain (or come to) Me. (18.68) No other person shall do a more pleasing service to Me, and no one on the earth shall be more dear to Me. (18.69)

Now that you've read all these passages, can you not see God's communication at work? These previous Sacred Scriptures are just as inspired, to a lesser or greater degree proportional to the author's ability to receive the signals, as any other Sacred Scripture is, including the Bible. There may be some inconsistencies but the value of the Gita lies in its profound meaning, all of which is wrapped in its Mythic structure.

And now, let's look at the power within the stories of the Bible.

Section 6: The Bible's Hebrew Testament

Sub-Section One: Overview

It is our personal opinion that the whole Bible is singularly the most insightful of all Sacred Scriptures. This Ο ΒΙΒΛΟΣ (its Greek name meaning "The Book") is an extraordinarily profound human saga of good and evil, sin and faithfulness, faith and disbelief, hate and love, joy and sorrow, failure and success, integrity and egotism, despair and hope, strength and weakness, the mundane and the divine, comedy and tragedy and every other imaginable pair of opposites. The Bible is a saga of humankind's evolution towards spirituality composed of poetry and legends with threads of history mythologized from the imperfect Oral Traditions of Israel. There are many (people and nations) who look to it for discernment, comfort and meaning in their lives. There are those who perceive the Way to eternal life and those who trivialize and mock the experiences written in its lines and between those lines. Among those who fathom meaning in their life from the Bible, there are two opposing groups: those followers of the Letter of the Bible and those who follow the Spirit of the Bible.

These dichotomous tensions exist because, while a large number of readers are deeply entrenched in worshiping the words, per se, as divinely dictated factoids, formulas and commands, others understand the timeless meaning of the legendary and mythologized stories some of which originated before the human experiences of the Israelite communities. Note clearly, both groups claim to understand the implications of those godly principles that are proffered and by which humanity must live and will be judged. The latter's attitude is the result of recent (past 200 years) discoveries of ancient, pre-biblical and early Christian writings that have shed new light on a realistic, mature interpretation of biblical history and events. The uncritical acceptance of so-called accurate oral and written traditions by the literalists are being challenged by today's awareness of inherent errors (misconceptions, inconsistencies and contradictions) in the canonical Judeo-Christian Bible. The posture that "God doesn't lie" (Titus 1: 2) is a Literalist's argument for a Bible that is absolutely accurate in every scientific, historical and theological detail because they are allegedly Divinely guaranteed. The modern analysts have discovered the legendary mythic nature of very many portions of the Biblical books and have reassessed their meaning, which is valid, whether or not the stories are factual. It's almost as though the Literalists would loose their faith if they found out that the Bible was legendary and mythical in nature and not absolutely factual. Here is a story composed several years ago that put to test the true faith of a friend. It went like this:

> "On a certain day in the near future you died and went to the pearly gates and were met by a man whom you didn't recognize. He said he was Yeshua the Nazarene and he welcomed you to Heaven and said that he understood that you were a good man of integrity and in your lifetime you helped many people find meaning. A place waiting for you in Heaven is behind the door on the right . He then added, 'But I want you to understand that even though you were a good Baptist, the true and normative Institution was Roman Catholicism. '
>
> "My Calvinistic Baptist friend, with a face turned red, blurted out angrily, "What? I'm going to the other door!'"

That response was a surprise almost to the point of incredulity. After recovering, my curiosity got the better of me and I asked "what is 'the other door'?" He said, "it must be Heaven because that person was lying; the Catholic Church is NOT the true Church!" However, the one he chose was not heaven!

Well, was this pride at its stubborn best or simple hatred for the Catholic Church (at any cost!)?

A few days later in our Interfaith Group Greek class, I told the very same story to our attending Catholic Prelate, a personal friend. However, for him I reversed the story; the Baptist Church was the true normative church this time. I anxiously awaited his response.

He turned to me and said calmly, "I would tell this Yeshua that I had done the best I could and proceed into the door leading to where he pointed."

I've used that story many times since and it received close to a comparable response from Literalists every time. They seem to choose the other place. However, most modern Christians and those who, although representing various other religions, are more concerned with meaning than with the controversy of "divine inspiration" vs "human interpretation", seem to accept their fallibility and walk into heaven knowing that the God of Mercy and Absolute Knowledge accepted their best efforts.

The "God doesn't lie" justification not only speaks of the uncritical mindset but also, in a deeper sense, relinquishes one's personal responsibility for one's thinking and free choices. Could it be "intellectual dishonesty"? Among the Biblical communities there has grown three distinct groups: the hard line traditionalists (Literalists), the middle of the road followers and the critical modernists. Please, don't think that this is any new revelation! The arenas of religion and politics have always behaved in exactly a parallel manner: once the original is set in place the re-interpreters disagree on the meaning and then comes (a) the conservatives clinging to a strict verbatim factual translation; (2) the liberals seeing the world in a constant state of flux in culture and knowledge and recognizing that growth and change are the order of the day; and, finally, (c) those who walk the middle way not because they have any definite doctrine but because they can't fathom either extreme. Thus, there are always three groups: two polarized groups (each to opposite ends), and one paralyzed, independent middle group.

If you haven't guessed it yet, we're definitely in the modernist camp. For us, the Bible is a great book that speaks of God through the life experiences of a nation that feels it is a chosen people. The Bible is a product of those authors who saw a special, personal relationship with God during previous generations such that they each wrote God into the equation as the active agent in every success and failure, reward and punishment of earlier times. The major portion of this great (H.T.) book was not written shortly following the incidents. Rather, the many books were penned decades and even many centuries later. Modern scholarship estimates that the H.T. was assembled around 500 BC by Ezra while the Temple was being rebuilt. The stories are, therefore, simple constructs of literature whose authors believed that God was very intimate in directing the course of their nation's history, i.e., personally involved in daily situations, eager to be in holy relationship with the Israelites. Since the psychological mindset of those times was that of Profile # 2, Reciprocity, the God of the Chosen People was a "follow My Laws in the Torah or suffer the punishments for the evil doers and dis-believers". The stories in the Torah substantiate that primitive premise quite clearly. The God of the Torah was viewed by the people as One who displayed anger, temper tantrums and a quick "shot-from-the-hips" punishment at the slightest hint of unfaithfulness or disloyalty. If Yeshua is any indicator of what God is really like, then the whole Judeo-Christian-Islamic world needs to re-assess their belief in a punishing God. The bottom line is: humans of the 21st Century need to grow out of a faith based on Profile # 2 and mature to one of Profile # 6 and #7! (Do you remember the seven behavioral profiles from Ch 1?)

On the other hand, if you read the following Hebrew Testament passages you will discover the God of LOVE extending Her-His arms out of the biblical pages. Ladies and Gentlemen, God doesn't punish, we punish ourselves! Our Free Will causes evil! We chose whom we will become in every single free choice we make at every moment of our daily lives. Those choices lead us to our successes and failures; God desires only that we let Her-Him into our lives. As Paul writes in II Corin 12: 9: *"My Grace is sufficient for you, My power is made perfect (will be perfect to help) in (your) weakness".* Is that the angry God of the Torah? How about Isaiah 49: 14-16:

> *14 But Zion said, "The LORD has forsaken me; my Lord has forgotten me." 15" Can a mother forget her infant, be without tenderness for the child of her womb? Even should she forget, I will never forget you. 16 See, upon the palms of my hands I have written your name; your walls are ever before me."*

And look in Joel 2: 13:

> *13 Rend your hearts, not your garments, and return to the LORD, your God. For gracious and merciful is he, slow to anger, rich in kindness, and relenting in punishment.*

The God of the Torah is rather harsh because the writers made God that way due to their personal, immature, Profile #2 perceptions. They wrote into their stories only what their community could understand. Authors wrote conversations into the mouths of the principal actors, what they thought those characters would say, based solely on their own mis-directed belief in a punishing God.

Later in the Christian Testament analysis (Chapter Four) there will be many other indicators of God's compassion, forgiveness and mercy. And, a few surprises in Chapters Six and Seven!

Sub-Section Two: Legends and Myths in the Hebrew Testament

So, the real problem is to determine which of the three groups (Literalists, Modernists or the middle-of-the-Roaders) wrote the H.T. in the first place. It is our personal suspicion that none of them wrote the whole H.T. But one can determine the simple prejudices of each author woven into the individual books as long as the reader maintains a mental microscope focused on the author's subliminal, personal intentions. Now, there is a great tale that illustrates an author's disguised intent. That author happens to be a Christian Prelate but we'll show why it is relevant to the Bible as a whole.

Augustine of Hippo led a lecherous youth, so he wrote in his book, "Confessions". In it he writes of his regrets and makes a great discovery of the true cause of all sin by all people; he blames Adam and Eve (with the principal blame on Eve). Therefore, he concludes, "It was the first sin by our original parents that infects us all." And, thus, Original Stain was created; a sin that we all are marked with upon conception (like it's a molecule on our genetic code—DNA). Augustine blamed someone else for his free choices to lead a life of promiscuity. From that time onward the world fell victim to his new definition. Would you believe that the Bible says there is no such thing as Original Sin, nor that it is passed down to the next generation? It's true! Just read John 9:1-3 in which the author puts the answer on Jesus' lips.

> *(1) As he passed by, he saw a man blind from his birth. (2) And his disciples asked him, "Rabbi, who sinned, this man or his parents, that he was born blind?" (3) Jesus answered, "It was not that this man sinned, or his parents, but that the works of God might be made manifest in him.*

There is no such thing as the transfer of parental sin to the offspring, so says Yeshua. So please decide, whom do you believe, Augustine or John's Jesus? Any psychologist knows that children imitate their parent's beliefs and behavior! However, each child is born pure and holy.

That was an illustration of how one person can manipulate you if you are not a vigilant reader. Therefore, let's be vigilant readers as we peruse the H.T. for some deeper meanings woven within its alleged historically accurate stories.

To comment on each book of the H.T. is a task far greater than we wish to attempt here. Our purpose is overview and to note the profound qualities of its mythical stories. It is to point out the similarities and differences in primary beliefs in Sacred Scriptures from different cultures that have been mis-interpreted leading to the polarization of peoples of different cultures. To do that we have to examine the historical and scientific accuracy and the author's intended meaning. We will do just that but in different sections of this book. In this Chapter we will focus on the deeper meaning contained in selected H.T. books. In Chapter Four, we'll look for meaning as well as the development of Christian theology and doctrine. In Chapter Five, we'll examine the errors that challenge the nature and belief in a Divinely inspired Bible. It now remains to discover the hidden nature of the God of Israel.

Sub-Section Three: Chronology of Hebrew History

At first glance it would seem logical to accept that the Books of the H.T., as they have been assembled and ordered into the Bible, as the actual historical order of those events and the order in which they were written. That observation is far from accurate. The order of events is as follows:

1. The Singular most defining moment for Israel was the Exodus;
2. The Conquest of the lands forming the 12 nations of Israel;
3. The Period of the Judges;
4. The Period of the Kingdoms;
5. The Construction of the Temple;
6. The Decay of the Kingdom following the reign of Solomon;
7. The Pre-Exilic Prophets
8. The Destruction of the Temple and the Exile;
9. The Return to Israel and the re-construction of the Temple;
10. The Formal collection and writing of the Life and Times of Israel into the books of the TANAK as remembered in the Oral Tradition. We are not certain exactly which books came first but the clues will be discussed momentarily.

The caution here is simply to be aware that the chronological order of penning the books of the Hebrew Testament does not reflect the sequence as it exists in our present day H.T. In other words, Genesis was not the first book written nor was Exodus the second book written, followed by the remaining books as they appear in our present Hebrew Testament canon. Rather, they were mostly written bit by bit between 800 BC and 100 BC as short vignettes documenting the Oral Tradition. But most likely each book was assembled by Ezra after the Exile when Israelites returned to their Promised Land. When the Hebrew Testament was finally canonized in the second century BC, the order of books in our present day H.T. was conveniently arranged to represent the alleged historical development of Israel. In 270 BC the existing H.T. was translated into Greek at Alexandria: it's called the Septuagint. Shortly thereafter, the book of Daniel was added to both the Hebrew and Greek texts, also some other books too. When Christianity moved out of Israel to the Gentile world, they only used the Greek Septuagint as their Bible. At that time the Hebrew text contained different books than the Septuagint. In the seventh century the Massoretes added a vowel pointing system to the Hebrew text in order to preserve the pronunciations of the Hebrew words. In the seventeenth century the English translators of the entire Bible elected to use the Hebrew version and they dismissed the Septuagint as an unauthorized version. The Catholic Church chose to include the Septuagint books. That controversy is still alive today. The New Revised Standard Version is the only other English translation that includes the books from both the Massoretic and Septuagint texts.

With that said, let's turn to the meaning of this Sacred Scripture.

Sub-Section Four: Comments on the Books of the Hebrew Testament

It would appear that each Sacred Scripture documented the religious or theological history of that culture and thus established a code of behavior for its future believers. The H.T. Torah does it up like a lawyer and gives the term "code of behavior" new meaning. The tablets of Ten Commandments constitute the primary code that, even to this day, is the basic (but minimal) religious rules of life for the Jewish, Christian and Islamic peoples. Then after the Tablets and rules in Exodus, additional particulars were expounded in Deuteronomy, Leviticus and Numbers. In these four, one finds the basis of temple worship, strict food cautions, rituals of animal offerings, social mores and snippets of folk history. The Torah, that collection of the first five books of the H.T., is the fundamental Sacred Scripture of Israel.

The Torah:

(1) **Genesis**: In order to understand the nature of the book of Genesis, one must come to grips with the development of language, specifically the pre-existence of language prior to the presence of Humans. After all, language, i.e., communication by means of sound and signals, presently exists in the animal kingdom and must have existed in the animal kingdom since the earliest times when animal forms first lived on this planet. However, in the case of Humans, that very same type of "sound-noise-grunting-signing" communication developed further over time into what we have in this present age. Then, somewhere in the pre-historic period humans changed grunting-screeching into specific tonal words and primitive sign language. From there picture-words were created as found in the caves throughout Western and Eastern Europe and Asia. In Egypt picture-words were refined into a great language. And last of all, there were alphabets and written words. But, do you know that Chinese and Japanese writing is in picture words? That means we have to make a SWAG, Scientific Wildly Analytical Guess, to classify the time periods of pre-history. When we look to our records, we bump into a wall at 4000 BC. However, we do have the Fossil Record. Therefore, Earth history can now be divided into four periods, (a) the physical history from Earth's formation at about 4.5 to 3.5 billion years ago; (b) our Fossil Record —3.5 billion to about 7,000,000 years ago, (c) the artifacts and pictured history from about 7,000,000 years to 4000 BC and, finally, (d) the written history 4000 BC to today. In case you forgot what has already been written, review Appendix N for the same story-like tale of Creation from our 21st century's knowledge.

Unrecorded history has been classified and dated by Archeologists, Nuclear Chemists, Paleoanthropologists and other professionals of that ilk. All have constructed our Fossil Record so aptly assembled from the remains of many living and non-living creatures unearthed out of the mineral deposits that have accumulated over time. Please examine Appendices G and H. Pictured history was recognized when children initially discovered drawings in a cave not only in Western Europe and throughout Eastern Europe and Asia but also recently discovered outside of that continent. Written history began with the Egyptian hieroglyphics, Asian character-words and Sumerian cuneiform followed by the Hebrew alphabet and other alphabetized languages. It is from those Oral Traditions and the written myths about the remembered tales and legends of the third period (c) that we find the sources for the book of Genesis.

Thus, the book of Genesis (authored between 800 BC and 100 BC, but suspected to be closer to 500 BC, in Ezra's time) contains mythologized stories whose purpose was to explain the human conditions of the world: a creator, creation, the tale of the source of the knowledge of Good and Evil along with the perpetrators of disobedience and suffering in this world and the great murder of Abel that many consider the first sin. That covered the earliest history of the world. Then, the authors of Genesis needed to build a bridge between the curse of Cain and the great Hebrew migration (Exodus) that terminated in the establishment of a national country, Israel. Hence, the tale of the flood from the Epic of Gilgamesh, the genealogy of Noah's sons, the tower of Babel (the cause of different languages) a mythic explanation of the Egyptian pyramids covered the Pictured History period. Then from the Oral Traditions Genesis extracted the elaborate stories of Abram (changed to Abraham), Isaac and Jacob (changed to Israel) and the eventual sale of Joseph to get him and his people, the foreigners from Hebron, into Egypt. After Joseph dies, the Hebrews were forced into slavery by the following Pharaohs.

Thus the stage was set for the great Hebrew revolt under Moses' leadership followed by the great migration (Exodus) to a distant promised land.

Genesis is indeed the finest mythical construct of all times in its attempt to explain God, creation, disobedience, suffering, and the sin of murder, the Sumerian flood tales remembered from the tales at end of the Ice Age. Then comes the reconciliation (covenant) between God and the father of the Israelite nation (Abraham) and the genetic and anthropological connection to the Egyptian slaves. And finally, Act Two with the curtain opening to an enslaved class poised to fulfill the will of their God to inherit the Promised Land. As an added bonus, the myth gave credence and authenticity to a divinely established weekly day of rest. Hold it! The actual Book of Genesis was penned hundreds of years after the Exodus event! The seven-day week was a Babylonian standard practice long before the Exile during which the Israelites were first exposed to it and wrote it into their Exodus and Genesis stories. The Creation myth in Genesis was written by the Priestly authorities and the Author of the seven-day week was none other than God, as far as the Israelites were concerned. The same logic applies to Exodus. It is recognized in scholarly quarters that Moses did not author any book of the Torah.

The authors of Genesis would unravel the story of a God, the playwright and prime puppeteer, who was the controlling force of each and every action and event of Israelite history. God was the rewarder and punisher in the script that was acted out by the Israelite people; God's will be done. In other words, the players understood that God was the Author and Power behind their lives and their destiny. The actual writers of Genesis, employing the Backward-Looking literary style, saw God in intimate control and relationship with the people of the Covenant formed with Abraham.

These authors constructed those fifty mythic chapters to place the progeny of Abraham in Egypt to be able to set the stage for the Exodus. There is a very thin thread of remembered history woven into the fabric of Genesis as well as a large dose of the legendary tales remembered from the Oral Tradition explaining the causes of suffering and meaning in Human existence.

In spite of the preponderance of that mythic quality in Genesis, the authors included several meaningful sub-tales that are loaded with implied theology and spirituality. Let's examine a few of them!

It is noteworthy to point out that the Hebrew words (*ruwach elohiym*) translated into the KJV English bible as "the spirit of God" in Gen 1: 2 really means "the breath of God". This will be discussed in Chapter Five because it turns out to be the earliest synonym for God but misunderstood by the Christian communities as the Holy Spirit. We will also point out its use in the Book of Isaiah 63: 10-11.

Now, let's turn to the commentary.

THE PUNISHMENT OF WOMEN: Gen 3: 16 *To the woman he {God} said: I will intensify the pangs of your childbearing; in pain shall you bring forth children. Yet your urge shall be for your husband, and he shall be your master."*

THE COMPASSION OF GOD: Gen 3: 21 *For the man and his wife the LORD God made leather garments, with which he clothed them.*

THE FIRST DENIAL OF HUMAN RESPONSIBILITY: Gen 4: 9 *Then the LORD asked Cain, "Where is your brother Abel?" He answered, "I do not know. Am I my brother's keeper?"*

THE FIRST CONTRADICTION [WHERE DID THE OTHER PEOPLE COME FROM?]: Gen 4: 13 *Cain said to the LORD: "My punishment is too great to bear. 14 Since you have now banished me from the soil, and I must avoid your presence and become a restless wanderer on the earth, anyone may kill me at sight." 15 *"Not so!" the LORD said to him. "If anyone kills Cain, Cain shall be avenged sevenfold." So the LORD put a mark on Cain, lest anyone should kill him at sight.*

INTIMACY WITH GOD: Gen 6: 8 *But Noah found favor with the LORD. 9 These are the descendants of Noah. Noah, a good man and blameless in that age, 10 for he walked with God,*

THE FIRST CATHOLIC MASS AND THE LAW FOR TITHING: Gen 14: 18 *Melchizedek, king of Salem, brought out bread and wine, and being a priest of God Most High, he blessed Abram with these words: 19 *"Blessed be Abram by God Most High, the creator of heaven and earth; 20 And blessed be God Most High, who delivered your foes into your hand." Then Abram gave him a tenth of everything.*

THE FIRST NAME CHANGE SYNDROME: Gen 17: 5 *No longer shall you be called Abram; your name shall be Abraham, for I am making you the father of a host of nations.*
That is a significant event for monastics. Men and women who wish to enter the Establishment are required to change their names to connote a new relationship with God!!

THE MORMON JUSTIFICATION FOR POLYGOMY, THE FIRST FAMILY FEUD, THE FIRST DIVORCE AND THE GREAT DIVISION OF ARAB AND ISRAELITE CULTURES: Gen 21: 9 *Sarah noticed the son whom Hagar the Egyptian had borne to Abraham playing with her son Isaac; 10 so she demanded of Abraham: "Drive out that slave and her son! No son of that slave is going to share the inheritance with my son Isaac!" 11 Abraham was greatly distressed, especially on account of his son Ishmael. 12 But God said to Abraham: "Do not be distressed about the boy or about your slave woman. Heed the demands of Sarah, no matter what she is asking of you; for it is through Isaac that descendants shall bear your name. 13 As for the son of the slave woman, I will make a great nation of him also, since he too is your offspring."*

THE SACRIFICE OF ISAAC: Gen 22 That is a story to explain why the Israelites no longer engaged in infant sacrifice!

THE OCCURRENCE OF SACRED NUMBERS [7 AND 40]: Gen 29: 20 & 27 *Jacob worked for two sets of seven years;* in Gen 31: 23 pursued for 7 days; the flood story involved 40 days and nights; creation took place over seven days! How mythic can you get?

ANOTHER NAME CHANGE: Gen 32:29 A name change for Jacob to Israel after he fought God and Human beings, and prevailed.

SACRED NUMBERS: Gen 33: 3 *He himself went on ahead of them, bowing to the ground seven times, until he reached his brother.*

NAMES FOR GOD: Gen 33: 8 *Then Esau asked, "What did you intend with all those droves that I encountered?" Jacob answered, "It was to gain my lord's favor."* The title "Lord" [the Hebrew word is "*adonai*"] is used here because Yahweh is revealed only in Exodus. Gen 33: 20 *He set up a memorial stone there and invoked "El, the God of Israel."*

FROM HERE TO THE END OF GENESIS THE STORY OF JOSEPH PREVAILS: Gen 37: 19 *They said to one another: "Here comes that master dreamer!*

THE INTRODUCTION OF SHEOL—place of the Dead!: Gen 37: 35 *Though his sons and daughters tried to console him, he refused all consolation, saying, "No, I will go down mourning to my son in the nether world." Thus did his father lament him.*

EVERYTHING IS GOD'S DOING: Gen 45*: 5 But now do not be distressed, and do not reproach yourselves for having sold me here. It was really for the sake of saving lives that God sent me here ahead of you.*
*Gen 45: 7 God, therefore, sent me on ahead of you to ensure for you a remnant on earth and to save your lives in an extraordinary deliverance. 8 *So it was not really you but God who had me come here; and he has made of me a father to Pharaoh, lord of all his household, and ruler over the whole land of Egypt. 9 *"Hurry back, then, to my father and tell him: 'Thus says your son Joseph: God has made me lord of all Egypt; come to me without delay. .*
Gen 50: 20 *Even though you meant harm to me, God meant it for good, to achieve his present end, the survival of many people.*
Gen 40: 24 Joseph said to his brothers: "I am about to die. God will surely take care of you and lead you out of this land to the land that he promised on oath to Abraham, Isaac and Jacob." 25 Then, putting the sons of Israel under oath, he continued, "When God thus takes care of you, you must bring my bones up with you from this place." 26 Joseph died at the age of a hundred and ten. He was embalmed and laid to rest in a coffin in Egypt.
NOTE: These all sound like "Backward-Looking" by the authors who put the Genesis story together after the Exile in Ezra's time.

SACRED NUMBERS AGAIN: Gen 50: 3 *they spent forty days at it, for that is the full period of embalming; and the Egyptians mourned him for seventy days.*
Gen 50:1 0 *When they arrived at Goren-ha-atad, which is beyond the Jordan, they held there a very great and solemn memorial service; and Joseph observed seven days of mourning for his father.*

Thus, Genesis establishes the source of this world and frames pre-Israelite history with the constructed ancestry of the peoples of Abraham, Isaac and Jacob, along with a host of pre-written fables like the flood (to restart human creation) and the Tower of Babel (that tale of the origin of languages!). Did the pyramids look that tall to the Israelite slaves?

The real value of Genesis lies in its spirituality of a loving God who shares existence by creating the Universe and humans in HER image—intelligent, emotional, free willed, needy and in relationships!

(2) **Exodus** introduces Moses, prince of Egypt, as the great Hebrew hero who leads the Israelites to the Promised Land and their first encounter with God at the legendary Mt. Sinai and the Tablets of the 10 Commandments of the Covenant.

After finishing reading this book, it should become obvious to you that there is a great deal of misaligned history. Parts of the revelation of the Covenant, at the mountain of the 10 Commandments, are included in various sections of Exodus as though they are already a part of the knowledge and experience of the Israelites even prior to their departure from Egypt. Now, that's strange! Yet, when we realize that the author(s) is (are) writing from the Oral Traditions passed down from the twelfth century to the sixth century BC, it becomes patently obvious that they (authors) know exactly what is going to happen and they deviate from the historical sequences of the real events. This phenomenon occurs very frequently throughout the book of Exodus. In addition, there is about 20 per cent of the story that is repeated in a disorderly manner. Our theory about this is that the author(s) didn't recognize which of the source materials was the true story; so he (they) included them all. The exact same thing happened in the book of Genesis in the two creation stories. A note of interest here! If the book of Exodus was written prior to the book of Genesis, then the statement in Ex 20: 11 about the creation taking place over six days was the impetus for the Gen 1 creation myth whose choreography authenticated the sacred day of rest! That alone should alert the average reader to the possibility that the Bible was never intended to be a work of science or history. The Bible's purpose is "Salvation through a relationship with God" and a respect for one's neighbor. We will expand on that topic later on in our sixth and seventh chapters. Don't quit just yet!

There are two significant incidents of a profound nature: Moses' epiphany at the burning bush and when Moses asks God to see God's glory (face). Both of these are what one would identify as a "Moment of Clarity" (It's discussed in Chapter Seven). Maybe you've read about peak experiences, Brahman, Nirvana, Satori, Oceanic View and Beautific Vision. These terms are, respectively, from psychology, Hinduism, Buddhism, Zen, general literature and the experience of Saints of the Roman Tradition, notably, Thomas Aquinas in the 13th century AD. Their meaning is the same—a deep emotional soul-moving experience of God that leaves a person in an altered state of joy or silence without the words to explain what happened (some might even call it a moment of confusion!). Moses could only ask himself, "Why wasn't the bush consumed?" The story in Ex 3 ends in Moses' silence. Check it out! Have you never asked why? The answer may be simpler than you realize! We suggest that the burning bush represents God's consuming love for HER creation but it will never burn us. It is a metaphor! The meaning of Ex 33: 17-23 is that one never understands the moment that God interacts in one's life; one sees meaning only after the fact, from the behind of the event. Often, even with the passage of a lengthy period, the event remains a silent persistent memory. When the mind is ready, the event takes on its true meaning and one's life grows fuller with the understanding. After many hours and days on top of the mountain Moses would come down with a radiant visage that struck fear in the hearts of the Israelites so much so that they suggested he wear a veil over his face. (Ex 34: 30 to 35) Moses obliged his onlookers because he knew what that meant! In like manner one will become aware of the change in one's spirit, as Moses did. Much more will be discussed in Chapter Seven. The rest of Exodus is a shadowy history reworked and re-defined through the Oral Tradition. But it was written many centuries later as an extraordinary mythic tale woven with threads of significant moments in the life of a chosen people. Here are some of those many moments:

1. EX 3:2-22 the encounter with the burning bush and the sacredness of the Earth upon which Moses walks; God's name; the plan and the spoils.
GOD'S NAME HERE (3: 14) IS NOT THE SAME AS FOUND IN GENESIS AND IN EX 3: 15 IT IS THE TETRAGRAMMATON. ("The Hebrew word for God, consisting of the four letters *yod, he, wav,* and *he,* transliterated consonantally usually as *YHVH,* now pronounced as *"Adonai"* in substitution for the original pronunciation forbidden since the 3rd or 2nd century BC. Cf. Yahweh." Quoted from Webster's Dictionary.)

2. EX 4: 1-17 the several miracles to convince the Pharaoh and the Israelites.
HUMANS NEED A LOT OF MIRACLES TO ACCEPT GOD INTO THEIR LIVES BUT THOSE WERE NOT MIRACLES. THEY WERE NATURAL EVENTS OCCURRING EACH YEAR ON THE NILE RIVER AND INCORPORATED INTO THE STORY TO GIVE AUTHENTICITY TO GOD'S POWER.

3. EX 7: 1-2; *The LORD answered him, "See! I have made you as God to Pharaoh, and Aaron your brother shall act as your prophet. 2 You shall tell him all that I command you. In turn, your brother Aaron shall tell Pharaoh to let the Israelites leave his land.*
GOD SETS A NEW GAME PLAN.

4. EX 7: 3-5; *Yet I will make Pharaoh so obstinate that, despite the many signs and wonders that I will work in the land of Egypt, he will not listen to you. Therefore I will lay my hand on Egypt and by great acts of judgment I will bring the hosts of my people, the Israelites, out of the land of Egypt, so that the Egyptians may learn that I am the LORD, as I stretch out my hand against Egypt and lead the Israelites out of their midst."*
GOD DOESN'T MAKE PEOPLE "OBSTINATE"! PEOPLE CHOOSE TO BE THAT WAY. SINCE THE AUTHORS ALREADY KNOW THE OUTCOME OF THEIR TALE, THE TECHNIQUE OF BACKWARD-LOOKING WRITING PRODUCES A DISTORTED HISTORY—LIKE THEY CAN'T HELP BUT REVEAL THEIR SECRET KNOWLEDGE.

5. EX 7: 25 *Seven days passed after the LORD had struck the river.*
ANOTHER USE OF THE SACRED NUMBERS.

6. EX 9: 12 *But the LORD made Pharaoh obstinate, and he would not listen to them, just as the LORD had foretold to Moses.*

WHY IS GOD STOPPING PHARAOH FROM LETTING THE ISRAELITES GO?? BECAUSE PHARAOH REALLY CHOSE TO DO IT! BUT THE AUTHOR ASCRIBES EVERY ACTION TO GOD IN THE BACKWARD-LOOKING * LITERARY STYLE!
* This is a term borrowed from Scott Atran's book, "In Gods We Trust".

7. EX 10: 22 *So Moses stretched out his hand toward the sky, and there was dense darkness throughout the land of Egypt for three days.*
MORE SACRED NUMBERS

8. EX 12: 6 *You shall keep it until the fourteenth day of this Month, and then, with the whole assembly of Israel present, it shall be slaughtered during the evening twilight.*
TWO TIMES SEVEN!!

9. EX 12: 15- 16 *For seven days you must eat unleavened bread. From the very first day you shall have your houses clear of all leaven. Whoever eats leavened bread from the first day to the seventh shall be cut off from Israel. On the first day you shall hold a sacred assembly, and likewise on the seventh. On these days you shall not do any sort of work, except to prepare the food that everyone needs.*
SACRED NUMBERS RELATING TO THE MOON'S CYCLE ! NOTE: THIS OCCURS BEFORE RECEIVING THE TEN COMMANDMENTS!

10. EX 12: 18 *From the evening of the fourteenth day of the first month until the evening of the twenty-first day of this month you shall eat unleavened bread. For seven days no leaven may be found in your houses.*
MORE SACRED NUMBERS ! 21 IS 3 X 7

11. EX 12: 21-24 *Moses called all the elders of Israel and said to them, "Go and procure lambs for your families, and slaughter them as Passover victims. *Then take a bunch of hyssop, and dipping it in the blood that is in the basin, sprinkle the lintel and the two doorposts with this blood. But none of you shall go outdoors until morning. For the LORD will go by, striking down the Egyptians. Seeing the blood on the lintel and the two doorposts, the LORD will pass over that door and not let the destroyer come into your houses to strike you down. "You shall observe this as a perpetual ordinance for yourselves and your descendants.*
TAKE NOTE OF ANOTHER REPITITION OF CERTAIN MATERIAL. IT SHOULD TWEEK YOUR SENSES THAT THE AUTHOR HAD A SECOND SOURCE FOR THE STORY AND INCLUDED, ONCE AGAIN, THE SECOND SOURCE MATERIAL BECAUSE HE DIDN'T KNOW WHICH WAS THE CORRECT TALE. JUST LIKE THE TWO GENESIS CREATION TALES!

12. EX 13: 4 *This day of your departure is in the month of Abib.*
THAT IS THE DETERMINING DATE FOR ALL INSTITUTIONS TO SELECT THE EASTER DATE (PASSOVER).

13. EX13: 6-7 *For seven days you shall eat unleavened bread, and the seventh day shall also be a festival to the LORD. Only unleavened bread may be eaten during the seven days; no leaven and nothing leavened may be found in all your territory.*
SACRED NUMBER. AGAIN, BEFORE THE TABLETS OF COMMANDMENTS

14. EX 13: 21-22 *The LORD preceded them, in the daytime by means of a column of cloud to show them the way, and at night by means of a column of fire to give them light. Thus they could travel both day and night. Neither the column of cloud by day nor the column of fire by night ever left its place in front of the people.*
DUST DEVILS PREVAIL IN THE DESERT AND FIRE MAY BE THE METHANE BURNING OFF FROM THE OIL DEPOSITS!

15. EX 14: 4 *Thus will I make Pharaoh so obstinate that he will pursue them. Then I will receive glory through Pharaoh and all his army, and the Egyptians will know that I am the LORD." This the Israelites did.*
WHAT KIND OF A GOD IS THIS THAT MAKES THE EGYPTIANS DESTROY THEMSELVES? THIS IS AN EXAMPLE OF BACKWARD-LOOKING WRITING THAT ASCRIBES EACH AND EVERY DETAILED ACTION TO THE HAND OF GOD.

16. EX 15: 4 *Pharaoh's chariots and army he hurled into the sea; the elite of his officers were submerged in the Red Sea.*
ACTUALLY THE HEBREW WORD IS "CWPH", which means REED . THE TRANSLATORS IN 1611 AD MADE A MISTAKE!

17. EX 15: *26 "If you really listen to the voice of the LORD, your God," he told them, "and do what is right in his eyes: if you heed his commandments and keep all his precepts, I will not afflict you with any of the diseases with which I afflicted the Egyptians; for I, the LORD, am your healer."*
THAT IS THE SOURCE OF "A GOD OF RECIPROCITY"

18. EX 15: 27 *Then they came to Elim, where there were twelve springs of water and seventy palm trees, and they camped there near the water.*
THE QUR'AN MAKES REFERENCE TO THIS, BUT CONFUSES IT WITH THE SPRING AT HOREB (# 20 BELOW)!

19. EX 16: 23 *he told them, "That is what the LORD prescribed. Tomorrow is a day of complete rest, the sabbath, sacred to the LORD. You may either bake or boil the manna, as you please; but whatever is left put away and keep for the morrow."*
FINALLY THE SACRED DAY OF REST. BUT THIS PRECEEDS THE ACTUAL GIVING OF THE TEN COMMANDMENTS IN WHICH THE SABBATH IS DEFINED. IT IS AN EXAMPLE OF BACKWARD-LOOKING WRITING.

20. EX 17: 6 *I will be standing there in front of you on the rock in Horeb. Strike the rock, and the water will flow from it for the people to drink." This Moses did, in the presence of the elders of Israel.*
IN CONTRAST TO THE TWELVE SPRINGS IN EX 15:27 ABOVE. MISQUOTED IN THE QUR'AN

21. EX 18: 16 *Whenever they have a disagreement, they come to me to have me settle the matter between them and make known to them God's decisions and regulations."*
THE REAL ORIGEN OF MOSAIC LAW!!

22. EX 18: 17 to 26; *17 "You are not acting wisely," his father-in-law {Reuel in Ex 2: 18 but Jethro in the rest of Exodus?} replied. 18 "You will surely wear*

yourself out, and not only yourself but also these people with you. The task is too heavy for you; you cannot do it alone. 19 Now, listen to me, and I will give you some advice, that God may be with you. Act as the people's representative before God, bringing to him whatever they have to say. 20 Enlighten them in regard to the decisions and regulations, showing them how they are to live and what they are to do. 21 But you should also look among all the people for able and God-fearing men, trustworthy men who hate dishonest gain, and set them as officers over groups of thousands, of hundreds, of fifties, and of tens. 22 Let these men render decisions for the people in all ordinary cases. More important cases they should refer to you, but all the lesser cases they can settle themselves. Thus, your burden will be lightened, since they will bear it with you. 23 If you do this, when God gives you orders you will be able to stand the strain, and all these people will go home satisfied." 24 Moses followed the advice of his father-in-law and did all that he had suggested. 25 He picked out able men from all Israel and put them in charge of the people as officers over groups of thousands, of hundreds, of fifties, and of tens. 26 They rendered decisions for the people in all ordinary cases. The more difficult cases they referred to Moses, but all the lesser cases they settled themselves.
THE ORIGIN OF INSTITUTIONAL RELIGION'S LEGALISMS.

23. EX 19: 4, *tell the Israelites: You have seen for yourselves how I treated the Egyptians and how I bore you up on eagle wings and brought you here to myself. 5 Therefore, if you hearken to my voice and keep my covenant, you shall be my special possession, dearer to me than all other people, though all the earth is mine. 6 *You shall be to me a kingdom of priests, a holy nation. That is what you must tell the Israelites."*
THE ORIGIN OF THE OBSESSION WITH PRIESTHOOD AND HOLINESS IN ISRAEL. BUT NOTE THAT ONLY A FEW WERE PRIESTS !? LATER IN THE C.T. PETER WILL QUOTE THIS VERSE TO JUSTIFY THAT CHRISTIANS ALL BELONG TO THE ROYAL PRIESTHOOD! SEE 1 PETER 2: 9

24. EX 19: 9-23 *The LORD also told him, "I am coming to you in a dense cloud, so that when the people hear me speaking with you, they may always have faith in you also." When Moses, then, had reported to the LORD the response of the people, 10 the LORD added, "Go to the people and have them sanctify themselves today and tomorrow. Make them wash their garments <u>11 and be ready for the third day; for on the third day the LORD will come down on Mount Sinai before the eyes of all the people.</u> 12 Set limits for the people all around the mountain, and tell them: Take care not to go up the mountain, or even to touch its base. If anyone touches the mountain, he must be put to death<u>. 13 No hand shall touch him; he must be stoned to death or killed with arrows. Such a one, man or beast, must not be allowed to live. Only when the ram's horn resounds may they go up to the mountain."</u> 14 Then Moses came down from the mountain to the people and had them sanctify themselves and wash their garments. 15 He warned them, "Be ready for the third day. Have no intercourse with any woman."16 On the morning of the third day there were peals of thunder and lightning, and a heavy cloud over the mountain, and a very loud trumpet blast, so that all the people in the camp trembled. 17 But Moses led the people out of the camp to meet God, and they stationed themselves at the foot of the mountain. 18 Mount Sinai was all wrapped in smoke, for the LORD came down upon it in fire. The smoke rose from it as though from a furnace and the whole mountain trembled violently. 19 The trumpet blast grew louder and louder, while Moses*

was speaking and God answering him with thunder. 20 When the LORD came down to the top of Mount Sinai, he summoned Moses to the top of the mountain, and Moses went up to him. 21 Then the LORD told Moses, "Go down and warn the people not to break through toward the LORD in order to see him; otherwise many of them will be struck down. 22 The priests, too, who approach the LORD must sanctify themselves; else he will vent his anger upon them." 23 Moses said to the LORD, "The people cannot go up to Mount Sinai, for you yourself warned us to set limits around the mountain to make it sacred."
THIS MUST HAVE BEEN A SMALL VOLCANO TO HAVE AFFECTED THE PEOPLE THAT MUCH. BUT NOTE VERSE 11; COULD THIS BE THE REFERENCE FOR YESHUA'S 3 DAYS IN THE TOMB? AND, WHY THE DISCIPLES WERE TO MEET HIM ON A MOUNTAIN? AND, DON'T MISS THE HORRIBLE COMMAND IN V. 13 ; THAT'S NOT THE GOD OF YESHUA.

25. EX 20 11 *In six days the LORD made the heavens and the earth, the sea and all that is in them; but on the seventh day he rested. That is why the LORD has blessed the sabbath day and made it holy.*
THIS CONFIRMS THAT THE AUTHORS WROTE EXODUS AND GENISIS TOGETHER AFTER THE EXILE!

26. *EX 20: 18 When the people witnessed the thunder and lightning, the trumpet blast and the mountain smoking, they all feared and trembled. So they took up a position much farther away 19 and said to Moses, "You speak to us, and we will listen; but let not God speak to us, or we shall die." 20 Moses answered the people, "Do not be afraid, for God has come to you only to test you and put his fear upon you, lest you should sin." 21 Still the people remained at a distance, while Moses approached the cloud where God was.*
THE PRIMITIVE MISUNDERSTANDING OF SMOKE, THUNDER AND LIGHTNING, EACH AS SIGNS AND VOICE OF THE DIVINE!

27. EX 21: THE WHOLE SECTION DEALS WITH CIVIL LAW AND ITS APPROPRIATE PENALTIES.

28. EX 22: MORE CIVIL LAW

29. EX 23: 1 to 19 THE END OF CIVIL LAW.

30. EX 23: *20 "See, I am sending an angel before you, to guard you on the way and bring you to the place I have prepared. 21 *Be attentive to him and heed his voice. Do not rebel against him, for he will not forgive your sin. My authority resides in him. 22 If you heed his voice and carry out all I tell you, I will be an enemy to your enemies and a foe to your foes. 23 "My angel will go before you and bring you to the Amorites, Hittites, Perizzites, Canaanites, Hivites and Jebusites; and I will wipe them out.*
BACK TO THE TALE AND NOW AN ANGEL WILL LEAD THE ISRAELITES TO THE PROMISED LAND.

31. EX 23: *31 I will set your boundaries from the Red Sea to the sea of the Philistines, and from the desert to the River; all who dwell in this land I will hand over to you to be driven out of your way. 32 You shall not make a covenant with them or their gods.*
THE BOUNDARIES OF THE OLD AND NEW ISRAEL!!

32. EX 24: 4 & 7; 4. *Moses then wrote down all the words of the LORD and, rising early the next day, he erected at the foot of the mountain an altar and twelve pillars for the twelve tribes of Israel; 7 Taking the book of the covenant, he read it aloud to the people, who answered, "All that the LORD has said, we will heed and do."*
THE WRITING OF THE COVENANT AND THE PEOPLE'S CONFIRMATION! BUT WAY BEFORE MOSES HAD THE 10 COMMANDMENTS. AND THE TABLETS

33. EX 24: 15 *After Moses had gone up, a cloud covered the mountain. 16 The glory of the LORD settled upon Mount Sinai. The cloud covered it for six days, and on the seventh day he called to Moses from the midst of the cloud. 17 To the Israelites the glory of the LORD was seen as a consuming fire on the mountaintop. 18 But Moses passed into the midst of the cloud as he went up on the mountain; and there he stayed for forty days and forty nights.*
THE SACRED NUMBERS AGAIN! NOTICE HOW AND IN WHAT FORM THE ISRAELITES EXPERIENCE GOD

34. EX 25: THE CONSTRUCTION OF THE ARK AND ALTER TABLE.

35. EX 26 THE FABRICATION OF THE VEILS

36. EX 27 THE CONSTRUCTION OF THE ALTER

37. EX 28 THE FABRICATION OF THE RITUAL ROBES AND DRESS

38. EX 29 THE ANOINTING RITUAL OF THE PRIESTS OF AARON'S FAMILY

39. EX 30: 18 *"For ablutions you shall make a bronze laver with a bronze base. Place it between the meeting tent and the altar, and put water in it. 19 Aaron and his sons shall use it in washing their hands and feet. 20 When they are about to enter the meeting tent, they must wash with water, lest they die. Likewise when they approach the altar in their ministry, to offer an oblation to the LORD,*
THE SOURCE OF THE ROMAN CHURCH'S HOLY WATER FONT AND THE WATER WASHING OF THE PRIEST'S HANDS BEFORE THE CONSECRATION IN THE MASS.

40. EX 30: 22 *The LORD said to Moses, 23 "Take the finest spices: five hundred shekels of free-flowing myrrh; half that amount, that is, two hundred and fifty shekels, of fragrant cinnamon; two hundred and fifty shekels of fragrant cane; 24 five hundred shekels of cassia-all according to the standard of the sanctuary shekel; together with a him of olive oil; 25 and blend them into sacred anointing oil, perfumed ointment expertly prepared.*
THE COMPOSITION OF THE ANOINTING OIL REMEMBER, "TO ANOINT" IN HEBREW IS "*MASHACH*". HENCE, MESSIAH IS THE WORD FOR "ANOINTED ONE"

41. EX 30: 34 *The LORD told Moses, "Take these aromatic substances: storax and onycha and galbanum, these and pure frankincense in equal parts; 35 and blend them into incense.*
THE SACRED INCENSE. IS THIS WHAT CHURCHES USE?

42. EX 31: 12 *The LORD said to Moses, 13 "You must also tell the Israelites: Take care to keep my sabbaths, for that is to be the token between you and me throughout the generations, to show that it is I, the LORD, who make you holy.*
NOTE, NOT THE THINGS YOU DO BUT GOD WHO MAKES PEOPLE HOLY!!

43. EX 31: 17 ... *for in six days the LORD made the heavens and the earth, but on the seventh day he rested at his ease." 18 When the LORD had finished speaking to Moses on Mount Sinai, he gave him the two tablets of the commandments, the stone tablets inscribed by God's own finger.*
A LOT OF REPITITION AND NOTE THE FINGER OF GOD WRITING THE TABLETS? DIDN'T MOSES JUST DO THAT IN # 32 ABOVE? NOW, CHECK # 48 BELOW!

44. EX 32: 20 *Taking the {golden} calf they had made, he fused it in the fire and then ground it down to powder, which he scattered on the water and made the Israelites drink.*
IF GOLD WERE FUSED IN A FIRE IT WOULD COME OUT AS A BIG HARD LUMP. I DON'T THINK THEY HAD THE ABILITY TO GRIND IT TO A POWDER AND THEN DISPERSE IN WATER. THE DRINKING OF THAT WATER WOULD DO NOTHING, GOLD IS INERT! YOU CAN QUESS WHERE IT WOULD THEN RE-APPEAR! HOWEVER, WE DO USE SILVER COINS SUSPENDED IN OUR SWIMMING POOLS TO PURIFY THE WATER !?

45. EX 32: 27 *and he (Moses) told them, "Thus says the LORD, the God of Israel: Put your sword on your hip, every one of you! Now go up and down the camp, from gate to gate, and slay your own kinsmen, your friends and neighbors!" 28 The Levites carried out the command of Moses, and that day there fell about three thousand of the people.*
THIS IS TOO HARD TO BELIEVE!! IS THIS THE GOD OF YESHUA? NO, IT'S THE GOD OF THE AUTHOR!

46. EX 33: 17 *The LORD said to Moses, "This request, too, which you have just made, I will carry out, because you have found favor with me and you are my intimate friend." 18 Then Moses said, "Do let me see your glory!" 19 He answered, "I will make all my beauty pass before you, and in your presence I will pronounce my name, 'LORD'; I who show favors to whom I will, I who grant mercy to whom I will. 20 But my face you cannot see, for no man sees me and still lives. 21 Here," continued the LORD, "is a place near me where you shall station yourself on the rock. 22 When my glory passes I will set you in the hollow of the rock and will cover you with my hand until I have passed by. 23 Then I will remove my hand, so that you may see my back; but my face is not to be seen."*
THUS, GOD AFFIRMS GOD'S PRIVACY THAT NO MAN SHALL SEE GOD'S GLORY NOR FACE!!! HOWEVER, THERE IS A POWERFUL MESSAGE HERE. WE DON'T UNDERSTAND GOD'S ACTION IN OUR LIVES UNTIL MUCH AFTERWARDS.

47. EX 34: 14 *You shall not worship any other god, for the LORD is 'the Jealous One'; a jealous God is he. VERY CONFUSING!*

48. *EX 34: 28 So Moses stayed there with the LORD for forty days and forty nights, without eating any food or drinking any water, and he wrote on the tablets the words of the covenant, the ten commandments.*
THIS TIME MOSES WROTE THE TABLETS!!!

49. EX 34: 14 *You shall not worship any other god, for the LORD is 'the Jealous One'; a jealous God is he.* Repeat of 47 above! Which one is correct? WAS GOD JEALOUS WHEN THE THREE THOUSAND WERE KILLED BY GOD'S DICTATE? (# 45 ABOVE)

50. EX 35 TO EX 40 ARE CHAPTERS OF REPITITICIOUS RITUALISTIC MATERIAL!

We may not have picked up all the problems in Exodus but we will identify them in Chapter Five.

(3) **Leviticus** is a priestly book of ritual ordination and sacrifice, of social and legal order and of health/purity considerations (the concepts of cleanness and uncleanness) all allegedly from God's lips to Moses for the Israelites to follow in obedience to the Divine Covenant.

(4) **Numbers** starts and ends with a census of the Israelites over a period of about 38 years during which they engaged in a hate/love relationship that (a) incurred God's punishing wrath that kept Moses and the first generation of the Israelites from entering the promised land, (b) the 38 year wanderings in the desert and (c) the eventual forgiveness and entry into the promised lands.

(5) **Deuteronomy:** In it we find a series of contradictions: (a) in Deut 5:4, the author says that the Lord spoke to the people face to face; in Deut 5: 24, the people acknowledged that they saw God's face and glory and still lived! Are we missing something? Didn't God already tell Moses that he couldn't see God's glory and live? We suggest that Deut and Ex were written by two separate authors who didn't know what the other wrote! Then, there is the Great Schema of the H.T., Deut 6:4—*God is alone*! This is echoed in the Qur'an with great repetitive emphasis along with the phrase, "God has no partners". Deut 6: 4 will turn out to be the theological reason for the expulsion of Christian Jews from the Synagogue in 85 AD.

Deut 7: 10, there is a neat reason for Purgatory, the Catholic doctrine that makes God to be a score-keeper and One who requires retribution from sinners. May we ask what happened to forgiveness and mercy? In Deut 8: 3, we have the great quote that the C.T. authors put on the lips of Jesus, 40 days in the desert, that he used to ward off Satan: "not by bread alone but by every word that comes from the mouth of the Lord". In Deut 9: 4, God is destroying the inhabitants of the Promised Land and sending in the Israelites to fill the vacancy. That certainly doesn't sound like a loving God! And, nor does it jive with our present day archeological discoveries of a mingling of peoples when the Israelites moved into the land! Well, how many quotes must we make to show you that Deuteronomy is a centuries old piece of literature that confuses the Exodus story because the community has reworked and embellished the dickens out of the oral traditions and doesn't have the first edition to check? If you believe that God dictated this book, better rethink your belief structure.

Early History Books:

(6) Joshua, Judges, Ruth, 1 & 2 Samuel, 1 & 2 Kings, 1 & 2 Chronicles, Ezra, Nehemiah, Tobit, Judith, Esther and the two Apocryphal Books (1 & 2 Maccabees).

In the first nine books the largest fraction of Israelites move across the Jordan River into their Promised Land. From that point onwards, the petulant Israelites begin their bickering and eventually establish a Kingdom. The next several decades turn out to be the glory years for the country under the leadership of Saul, David and Solomon. Then corruption sets its sharp claws into the culture and the ruling class corrodes like a nail in stagnant water and the Promised Land crumbles like a dried piece of toast. Israel is conquered and the Temple is destroyed. The people of the Exile then create a dream tale that yearns for an Ultimate King who will bring Israel to a new glory for the rest of existence. The Anointed One of God, the Ultimate King, will come! You know that the word Anointed in Hebrew is *mashiyach,* do you not? That's from whence the word Messiah comes. This coming of the Messiah began with the dream of future glory and has continued to this day in the prayers of every Jewish person at the Seder Meal celebrated prior to the Passover. If you have never attended a Seder with a Jewish family, then we highly recommend it; it is an impressive and moving evening of remembrance of the persecutions and sufferings of God's people over the last 3000 years.

Then come the "begot" lists from which the literalists calculate the date of the creation to be about 10 to 8 thousand years ago? Nice try guys and gals, the Universe is about 14-16 Billion years old and the Solar system and Earth are approximately 4.5 Billion years old in which 3.5 Billion Earth years are in the Geological Fossil Record. Read the remaining books yourself. They have inspired many a good movie. Read, especially, the Books of Ezra and Nehemiah because they speaks of Ezra's attempt to re-establish the H.T. Mosaic Law and document the Torah that was lost in the destruction of the Temple in 587 BC. The books of Ezra and Nehemiah took place after the Exile. We're not sure when the remaining books were written, but the NAB Introductions would make good reading.

The Wisdom Books

Job, Psalms, Proverbs, Ecclesiastes, Songs and two Apocryphal books (Wisdom & Sirach).

There are some very profound literary passages in these books.

(7) The Job story is a psychological drama of people stuck in the Reciprocity mode (Profile #2 from Chapter One). Note that the primary theme is the question of suffering. The answer to the why of suffering has been dissected so many times in the past and present that we thought it would be refreshing to take a slightly different approach to it. First, we see suffering totally related to these two qualities of life: human free will and the statistical vagaries of existence—Hollywood would call it "the revenge of Mother Nature". Life on this Planet is the result of the randomness of Natural Laws that govern the variety of occurrences around us. If Nature had to make everything perfectly as the H.T. authors depicted, this world would be scripted without wonderment and change; people would be nothing more than puppets. Think about it!

Good without evil is boring!
Life without choice is boring!
Reward without accomplishment is boring!
And, Evil without consequences is absurd!

Now, back to our thesis; To misunderstand suffering caused by a God of Profile #2, Reciprocity, is a function of primitive cultures or a person whose cognitive development never grew out of a pre-critical naiveté. Reciprocity is a consuming belief in "Reward and Punishment". That pervasive mindset, which still persists in the 21st Century, is simply this: "If I follow God's Laws, I will be rewarded with earthly riches; if I sin against God's Laws, I will be punished with sickness and loss of riches. With that said, let's get to the dilemma of Job.

The opening scene shows Job as a well-to-do landowner. This is followed by a heavenly discussion between God and the Great Archangel Satan (a son of God or Heaven as in Genesis 6) who suggests that Job is loyal because he is rich. Satan challenges God to take away all Job's possessions to see if Job would remain loyal. God thinks that Job would remain loyal. Now the plot thickens! Job's life experiences an ill wind, hot and fiery, caused by God! His friends reprimand Job, because they believe in God's Reciprocity punishing (Profile #2) Job for his alleged sins. The reader misinterprets it too and lays it on the angel, Satan--satanic comes to mind. Job counters with his conviction that God isn't in the Reciprocity business because Job's condition is simply a roll of the Natural Law dice. Job remains faithful to God his Savior and eventually wins back his personal glory, as well as achieving a psychological transition to Profile #3 and # 4. There is another twist to this story; the Good Archangel Satan becomes such a convincing advocate against Job that the whole of the Human race begins to associate him with evilness; Satan become the Archetype of Evil—Lucifer--the Supreme Ruler of the Underworld—Hell. Actually, the Babylonians believed that there was a supreme Good and a supreme Evil. Henceforth, the Devil (the dragon-snake from the Enuma Elish) becomes the tempter in the story of the Fall from Grace. Understand this, the Job story is an ancient one pre-dating the biblical times of Israel. It's another re-write with a Hebrew theological twist and a drama of psychological development in the style of Piaget/Kohlberg, referenced in Ch 1.

(8) The Psalms are good spiritual prayers but one of them is historically important. It's Psalm 2, the words for the royal ceremony used in the coronation to kingship, which we might add, is not thoroughly understood by John and Jane Doe. Let's read it in Appendix S.

Verses 6 and 7b are words spoken by God. [Actually, they are the author's words put into God's mouth to give them authenticity, a favorite ploy of biblical writers.] The meaning of the two verses are: (a) in verse 6, God makes the Kingship for the Israelites in response to the people's cry (See 1 Samuel 8); and (b) in verse 7b, the King reveals his relationship with God, "God is my Father and I am His son". The King is God's son, and henceforth the Israelites will refer to their King as "a son of God". Since the King is anointed with a 55-gallon drum of special oil (Ex 30: 22), the anointed King is also referred to as the Messiah, the anointed One. And for those of us in the English speaking community, the Biblical Hebrew word in Strong's Concordance, anointed, # 4899 (the word in Psalm 2, verse 2) is *machiyach* defined as "usually in reference to a king". #4899 is a past tense variation of the noun form, #4886, *mashach,* "to rub with oil, to anoint". Where is this leading to, you might be thinking. Here it is: The existing King, and every King thereafter, is promoted to the rank of a son of God along with the other sons of God (Angels?) in the presence of God (See Job 1: 6 and Job 38: 7) and then the King's name became known as the Messiah, the anointed one.

When, after years of war, oppression and exile, the Israelites begin to wonder when God would give them a final Messiah King who would come to return the Israelites to their former glory under David and Solomon. This hope has been resident on the lips of the Jewish people since even before the Diaspora (587 BC to 539 BC) and it resounds in their hearts at every Seder Meal celebrating the Passover from Egypt to the Promised Land. This anticipation of the Final Coming of the Messiah has taken on a new life of its own that we will address in the Book of Daniel and in our Chapter Four when we will comment on the Christian Testament in which the titles for the King become synonyms, i.e., Messiah, the Anointed One and son of God. A final note, Psalm 2: verse 9 and 11 are another indication that the author is pushing a God of Reciprocity.

(9) In Proverbs, there is a multitude of humorous social material and there is one powerful passage, Chapter 8. Here it is:

Chapter 8

1 Does not Wisdom call, and Understanding raise her voice?
2 On the top of the heights along the road, at the crossroads she takes her stand;
3 By the gates at the approaches of the city, in the entryways she cries aloud:
4 "To you, O men, I call; my appeal is to the children of men.
5 You simple ones, gain resource, you fools, gain sense.
6"Give heed! for noble things I speak; honesty opens my lips.
7 Yes, the truth my mouth recounts, but the wickedness my lips abhor.
8 Sincere are all the words of my mouth, not one of them is wily or crooked;
9 All of them are plain to the man of intelligence, and right to those who attain knowledge.
10 Receive my instruction in preference to silver, and knowledge rather than choice gold.
11 (For Wisdom is better than corals, and no choice possessions can compare with her.)
12 "I, Wisdom, dwell with experience, and judicious knowledge I attain.
13 (The fear of the LORD is to hate evil;) Pride, arrogance, the evil way, and the perverse mouth I hate.
14 Mine are counsel and advice; Mine is strength; I am understanding.
15 By me kings reign, and lawgivers establish justice;
16 By me princes govern, and nobles; all the rulers of earth.
17 "Those who love me I also love, and those who seek me find me.
18 With me are riches and honor, enduring wealth and prosperity.
19 My fruit is better than gold, yes, than pure gold, and my revenue than choice silver.
20 On the way of duty I walk, along the paths of justice,
21 Granting wealth to those who love me, and filling their treasuries.

22 "The LORD begot me, the first-born of his ways, the forerunner of his prodigies of long ago;
23 From of old I was poured forth, at the first, before the earth.
24 When there were no depths I was brought forth, when there were no fountains or springs of water;
25 Before the mountains were settled into place, before the hills, I was brought forth;
26 While as yet the earth and the fields were not made, nor the first clods of the world.
27 "When he established the heavens I was there, when he marked out the vault over the face of the deep;
28 When he made firm the skies above, when he fixed fast the foundations of the earth;
29 When he set for the sea its limit, so that the waters should not transgress his command;
30 Then was I beside him as his craftsman, and I was his delight day by day, Playing before him all the while,
31 playing on the surface of his earth; and I found delight in the sons of men.
32 "So now, O children, listen to me;
33 instruction and wisdom do not reject! Happy the man who obeys me, and happy those who keep my ways,
34 Happy the man watching daily at my gates, waiting at my doorposts;
35 For he who finds me finds life, and wins favor from the LORD;
36 But he who misses me harms himself; all who hate me love death."

Here are two opinions to the nature and meaning of this passage: the first is that it is a prophetic (you know, a futuristic thing) reference to Yeshua as the Wisdom figure and the other interpretation is an allegory about the Wisdom of God. Our focus and belief is on the second issue. It's fascinating to read the verses relating to knowledge (vs. 9 & 10), the feverish human search/pursuit of Wisdom (God) in v 17 and 32 to 35 and, finally, the warning in v. 36. Later in this book (Chapter Seven) we will discuss the "Moment of Clarity" and the "Metanoia Instant", both of which are offshoots of Proverbs 8. Of special note is the warning in verse 36. It is a free will statement of one's personal responsibility to avoid harming oneself because that results in one's choice of {eternal} death! This appears to be another statement like Deut 30: 19: *I place before you Life and Death, choose Life!*

Now, for some teeth in our analysis; examine this quote from the Upanishads:

> *"Indra said to him: 'No one who chooses, chooses for another; choose thyself.'*
> *Indra said to him. 'Know me only; that is what I deem most beneficial for man, that he should know me.*
> *He who meditates on me as life and immortality, gains his full life in this world, and obtains in the Svarga world immortality and indestructibility"*

Makes one wonder whether God was inspiring any other people, doesn't it?

Chapter 31: 10-31 of Proverbs is an interesting male perspective about wives. We wonder if there are any complementary verses from women's perspective about husbands? Well, actually, there are very few. So much for that male society! The rest of Proverbs appears to be "conventional wisdom" some of which are quite humorous. Enjoy!

(10) Ecclesiastes is a philosophical soliloquy dealing with life's puzzling questions about meaning. Occasionally the author gets a little pessimistic about his experiences. Read it, you might dig out more than we wish to discuss here.

(11) Wisdom is a book that reiterates the principal themes of the Covenant: seek God in an intimate relationship by following a righteous path. In Chapter 1: 12 &13, the author cautions:

> *12 Court not death by your erring way of life, nor draw to yourselves destruction by the works of your hands.*
>
> *13 Because God did not make death, nor does he rejoice in the destruction of the living.*

The significant phrases are: verse 12 "draw to yourselves destruction by the works of your hands" and verse 13 "God did not make death". The first one identifies "free will" (just like Proverbs 8: 36) and the second one puts death in the hands of human choice and it implies God's compassion for life (a refutation of God's choice to kill people or nations). Destroying people is an opinion of the authors of the H.T., not a choice of God to punish. Choosing sin and death is a human choice! Before leaving this topic, let's add this thought. Allah, in the Qur'an, recites a similitude that says, "do you not see that going to sleep at night and waking up in the morning is a similitude for death and resurrection?" So, we ask you, do you see that forms of myth can have a deeper significance?

One passage is appropriate for our times, Wis 13: 1, which reads:

> *"For all men were by nature foolish who were in ignorance of God, and who from the good things seen did not succeed in knowing Him who is, and from studying the works did not discern the artisan;"*

The whole problem we are having in the USA is that our basic principles of Church-State Separation are getting fuzzy and overlapping when the efforts of Atheists are focused on the removal of any mention of God from anything governmental and the Religious Right are trying to impose their own brand of morality in all public matters. It appears that Atheists are unaware of our country's primary law: majority rules. And the Religious Right do not know the history of the Pilgrims who, persecuted, left England. These people forget that the entire reason for the existence of America was to have the freedom to worship the God of one's choice. Existence is a gift of the Creator not a perk of the State.

(12) **Song of Solomon**, on the other hand, is a beautiful poem expressing the love that a man has for a woman. Some say it is God wooing Israel! Read this erotic little book!

(13) **Sirach** is another apocryphal book taken from the Septuagint (only available in the Catholic New American, NAB, and Jerusalem, JB, Bibles and the Protestant

New Revised Standard Version, NRSV, translations). It was used extensively in the early Christian community for teaching. There is just one paragraph from the Forward by the author/translator that is very significant to the readers of any English document translated from ancient writings, especially the Bible. It reads:

> *"You are now invited to read it (Sirach) in a spirit of good will, with indulgence for any apparent failure on our part, despite earnest efforts, in the interpretations of particular passages. For words spoken originally in Hebrew are not as effective when they are translated into another language. That is true not only of this book but of the law, the prophets and the rest of the books, which differ no little when they are read in the original."*

Those who have labored in love and sincerity to translate the many Sacred Scriptures of the World are well aware of that caution. However, the uneducated believers have, throughout the ages, misunderstood this problem and have significantly distorted the meanings of their Sacred Scriptures. That is very evident when one examines the denominational chasms that separate and polarize every religious community. Well, for that matter, every Institutional religion seems to be infected by that perverse mental virus, "If you don't believe my way, you are evil!"

The Major Prophets

Before we delve into the category of Prophetic Literature, there needs to be some definitions established. The word "prophet" applies to a seer who recognizes some serious infractions of moral and ethical behaviors within the community and/or the rulers of that community (and in some cases especially the King/Ruler). The prophet is apparently moved by the Spirit of God to speak out against those infractors and warn them of their duty to God, to rethink their behavior and change it for the benefit of the people they serve. Note clearly, a prophet speaks for God to the existing conditions of his time. In other words, the prophet is NOT predicting the future. So many people in this day and age are so focused on prophesy, its future-ness, in these books that they visualize all sorts of nonsense, up to and including the end of the world, to the detriment of sensible everyday believers. Words, phrases and paragraphs are interpreted in such ways as to be just this side of psychotic and poisonous to a community's spiritual health and in some cases, physical health. There have been three such instances in recent times: the Jim Jones incident, David Koresh and the Comet worshipers. The worse part is that such interpretations only fuel the formation of more denominationalism and disdain for knowledgeable believers.

The only solution for people of that ilk is to provide an adequate educational program about the true mythical nature of the biblical writings, all of which were penned several decades and mostly centuries after the actual events took place (a literary style that we've called, "Backward-Looking" history – a term used in "In Gods We Trust" by Scott Atran). The community's memories were, without a doubt, altered in proportion to the interval over which the stories were retold to the following generations. Facts became myths with a dash of salted history. We have already proven that with the three Creation tales and one Garden of Eden myth. Myth is multi-dimensional but if accepted as literal, can be fertile ground for crystal gazers who lust to be the first to see the future, to enlighten others about their visions and to be the center of attention. So be it! Now let's peek into the Prophetic literature.

(14) Isaiah is a masterful story containing several clarifying passages about worship and the people who are loyal to God. Chapter 1 tells of God's disgust with the empty rituals of Israel. God requires works of empathy, compassion and concern for three classes of people. Read it here:

> *ISA 1: 10-20 Hear the word of the LORD, princes of Sodom! Listen to the instruction of our God, people of Gomorrah! 11 What care I for the number of your sacrifices? says the LORD. I have had enough of whole-burnt rams and fat of fatlings; In the blood of calves, lambs and goats I find no pleasure. 12 When you come in to visit me, who asks these things of you? 13 Trample my courts no more! Bring no more worthless offerings; your incense is loathsome to me. New moon and Sabbath, calling of assemblies, octaves with wickedness: these I cannot bear. 14 Your new moons and festivals I detest; they weigh me down, I tire of the load. 15 When you spread out your hands, I close my eyes to you; Though you pray the more, I will not listen. Your hands are full of blood! 16 Wash yourselves clean! Put away your misdeeds from before my eyes; cease doing evil; 17 learn to do good. Make justice your aim: redress the wronged, hear the orphan's plea, defend the widow. 18 Come now, let us set things right, says the LORD: Though your sins be like scarlet, they may become white as snow; Though they be crimson red, they may become white as wool. 19 If you are willing, and obey, you shall eat the good things of the land; 20 But if you refuse and resist, the sword shall consume you: for the mouth of the LORD has spoken!*

That is one powerful passage. The Prophet, speaking for God, says that ritual is disgusting and he names all of those that are useless. Then the prophet, again speaking for God, says what are the important works that are acceptable to God in verse 17: (a) learn to do good; (b) make justice your aim; (c) redress the wronged; (d) hear the orphan's plea; and (e) defend the widow. The sum and substance is: RITUAL ROTS, THEREFORE, DO GOOD WORKS. Seems a few Institutions will be upset by that statement! Oh my, it turns out that "do good works" appears to contradict Paul's "Faith Alone" followers and, we think, this passage puts James (Chapter 2) back in the forefront for his "not just by faith but also by good works" Epistle. For your edification and perusal, here is the actual passage in the Epistle of James:

> *14 What good is it, my brothers, if someone says he has faith but does not have works? Can that faith save him? 15 If a brother or sister has nothing to wear and has no food for the day, 16 and one of you says to them, "Go in peace, keep warm, and eat well," but you do not give them the necessities of the body, what good is it? 17 So also faith of itself, if it does not have works, is dead. 18 Indeed someone might say, "You have faith and I have works." Demonstrate your faith to me without works, and I will demonstrate my faith to you from my works. 19 You believe that God is one. You do well. Even the demons believe that and tremble. 20 Do you want proof, you ignoramus, that faith without works is useless? 21 Was not Abraham our father justified by works when he offered his*

> *son Isaac upon the altar? 22 You see that faith was active along with his works, and faith was completed by the works. 23 Thus the scripture was fulfilled that says, "Abraham believed God, and it was credited to him as righteousness," and he was called "the friend of God." 24 See how a person is justified by works and not by faith alone. 25 And in the same way, was not Rahab the harlot also justified by works when she welcomed the messengers and sent them out by a different route? 26 For just as a body without a spirit is dead, so also faith without works is dead.*

Doesn't that passage have a terrific concluding message? The person of faith must walk the talk in good works. Can it be any plainer? Those of you who think "that attending the weekly ritual will save" must make a serious re-evaluation!

Now back to Isaiah for a special section that has been so mistranslated as to cause the word "prophet" to mean a "predictor of the future". The word in 7: 14 is the Hebrew "*almah*", a young woman, a maiden. It is the feminine form of the Hebrew "*elem*", lass. Therefore, *almah* does not specifically mean "virgin". All the other books in the H.T. use the word, *bethuwlah*, when referring to a virgin, except Gen 24:43 and Songs 1:3 and 6:8 which translate with the word, "maiden"! Well, the entire Christian community interpreted *almah* to mean the Virgin Mary, mother of Jesus. Certain denominations still refuse to alter their opinion. Thus, another case of "folk theology" has arisen and forever more the word, *almah*, will, in the minds of literalists, be mis-translated as well as misinterpreted.

The book of Isaiah is considered to be a three-part book written by three different authors from three different periods in Israelite history. Chapters 1 to 39 were written by a disciple of the original Isaiah; 40 to 55, by a disciple who lived some time after Isaiah; and 56 to 66, by a post-Diaspora disciple, probably by Ezra. The more famous passages from Isaiah are in the Messianic chapters from 40 to 55 written by a disciple identified as Deutero-Isaiah. They are about the life and times of the Israelites who are depicted as the "Suffering Servant". Here again, unfortunately, the literalist community interprets those chapters as referring precisely to Yeshua of Nazareth. Deutero-Isaiah's material written after Isaiah's life and the later chapters written over one hundred and fifty years after the death of Isaiah are not very likely to be an accurate portrayal of Isaiah's mindset and those Chapters are quite mythologized.

It is most interesting that in Isa 63: 10-11 there are two references to God: both called God the Holy Spirit! The Hebrew words used are, *ruwach godesh* meaning "sacred breath". In the next Chapter we will elaborate on Paul's and Luke's use of the Greek translation of "sacred breath".

It is in the myth that a reader sees personal experiences and allusions to future events. Personally, we see a lot of our friend's life, and even our own, in the Bible in general and in Isaiah in particular. Therein are examples of the beauty and the mystery of the Bible's mythical structure.

(15) **Jeremiah** holds a very special meaning. First, this little story of the prophet's struggles.

> "One day Jeremiah had just proclaimed the Word of God to this little village and, to his dismay, the villagers weren't in the mood to hear what he had to say. They not only kicked him out of town but threw him into the village cistern (the one that held the town's waste). Jeremiah got out, walked briskly away gazing to the sky and muttering to himself, 'W-w-why d-d-did y-y-you sel-l-lect m-m-me?' A period of silence followed as he stumbled down the path kicking a few stones out of his way. 'I w-w-as o-o-only d-d-doing Y-Y-our w-w-work! ... W-why m-m-me? E-E-everyw-w-where I ... I go, th-th-they t-t-treat m-m-me b-b-badl-l-ly! W-why m-m-me?' Suddenly, a cloudy sky opened a small hole and a beam of light shown directly on Jeremiah. From within the beam a gentle voice spoke, ' I-I-I ch-ch-chose y-y-you b-b-bec-c-cause y-y-you t-t-talk l-l-like M-M-Me!'"

I told this story to a friend whose son had a bad case of frequent stuttering. The boy listened to his father telling the story and from that day on his stuttering diminished. If it was OK for God, then it was OK for him. Now, that's how I feel too, not because I stutter, but because of my frailty, flawed and imperfect nature, the nature of humanity. This "Be Ye Perfect" guilt-trip is not from God. (Note: the word "perfect" is a mistranslation of the Greek word used for athletes.) What is from God is, "Strive to do the best you can under your individual circumstances!" And, that's exactly what Jeremiah did!

The next message from Jeremiah is 31: 31 to 34—probably the singularly most important passage in the entire H.T.! It reads:

> *31 The days are coming, says the LORD, when I will make a new covenant with the house of Israel and the house of Judah. 32 It will not be like the covenant I made with their fathers the day I took them by the hand to lead them forth from the land of Egypt; for they broke my covenant and I had to show myself their master, says the LORD. 33 But this is the covenant which I will make with the house of Israel after those days, says the LORD. <u>I will place my law within them, and write it upon their hearts</u>; I will be their God, and they shall be my people. <u>34 No longer will they have need to teach their friends and kinsmen how to know the LORD</u>. All, from least to greatest, shall know me, says the LORD<u>, for I will forgive their evildoing and remember their sin no more.</u>*

The three monumental underlined passages say that: (a) God's relationship will be compassionately inscribed onto human's soul, (b) humans will have a direct experience of God, and (c) that the relationship will be so intimate that God will forget their errors. Now, that's exactly what the Carpenter taught. Try putting this together with an eternal punishing God! How can God punish people if SHE has forgotten their sins?

For those who think that God and mystery are unknowable, please look at 33: 3: *"Call to me, and I will answer you; I will tell to you things great beyond reach of your knowledge."* We have experienced this ever since we took it upon ourselves the task to discover what this great book has to offer. We're convinced that you too can experience that spiritual adrenaline. One caution, "knowledge" used in the Bible oftentimes means "experience", it usually doesn't mean head/book knowledge, per se! But it does suggest one uses one's intellect!

(16) Ezekiel is called to be God's spokesman at the very beginning of the Diaspora (about 597 BC) in Babylon. The Temple is finally destroyed in 587 BC, a date that has been referred to as the time when the final wave of Israelites were removed from Israel. Ezekiel is given strict guidelines for what he is to proclaim. Here in Chapter 2 Ezekiel's duties are described. In verse 2 the use of the word "spirit" (Hebrew is "*ruwach*" meaning breath or wind!) seems to refer to God's spirit. We will have much to say about Paul's use of that word in Romans 8: 9-16 in our Chapter Four as well as in Chapter Five in relation to the mis-use of the title, Holy Spirit, in the C.T.! Notice in verse 8 that Ezekiel is told to eat what is given to him; that is a much-used phrase in literature meaning to absorb the material in a deeply intellectual, compassionate and spiritual manner, and walk your talk!

> *"1 Son of man, stand up! I wish to speak with you.*
> *2 As he spoke to me, spirit entered into me and set me on my feet, and I heard the one who was speaking*
> *3 say to me:*
> NOTE the bad verse numbering!
> *Son of man, I am sending you to the Israelites, rebels who have rebelled against me; they and their fathers have revolted against me to this very day.*
> *4 Hard of face and obstinate of heart are they to whom I am sending you. But you shall say to them: Thus says the Lord GOD!*
> *5 And whether they heed or resist--for they are a rebellious house--they shall know that a prophet has been among them.*
> *6 * But as for you, son of man, fear neither them nor their words when they contradict you and reject you, and when you sit on scorpions. Neither fear their words nor be dismayed at their looks, for they are a rebellious house.*
> *7 (But speak my words to them, whether they heed or resist, for they are rebellious.)*
> *8 As for you, son of man, obey me when I speak to you: be not rebellious like this house of rebellion, but open your mouth and eat what I shall give you.*
> *9 It was then I saw a hand stretched out to me, in which was a written scroll*
> *10 which he unrolled before me. It was covered with writing front and back, and written on it was: Lamentation and wailing and woe!"*

And again in Chapter 3, verse 20:

> *"20 If a virtuous man turns away from virtue and does wrong when I place a stumbling block before him, he shall die. He shall die for his sin, and his virtuous deeds shall not be remembered; but I will hold you responsible for his death if you did not warn him."*

In Chapter 4: 5-6 Ezekiel is told that the sinfulness of Israel has taken place over the last 390 years and the Diaspora will last for 40 years. This 40 years value is definitely a recurring number and may very well be a folk myth number. From 587 to 539 BC is 48 years! God can't count!

In this book the author uses the title of "Son of Man" for Ezekiel. That title shows up in the Book of Daniel and is then interpreted to be the future final judge who will come riding in on a cloud. Since the C.T. authors have applied that same title (in English) to Yeshua, some Christians have re-interpreted the Book of Revelations as predicting a second coming, a Parusia, at which time Yeshua will take up all the believers into heaven and then destroy all the non-believers. We'll talk more on this subject when we examine Daniel.

Chapter 7 announces that the Exile is about to happen and Chapter 11 speaks of God's forgiveness:

> *"19 I will give them a new heart and put a new spirit within them; I will remove the stony heart from their bodies, and replace it with a natural heart,*
> *20 so that they will live according to my statutes, and observe and carry out my ordinances; thus they shall be my people and I will be their God."*

Chapter 14 contains an interesting statement about when this book was most likely put to print. Since Daniel was written during the Jewish "apocalyptic" period (167-164 BC), this reference may well mean that after the Exile some more material may have been added to the book of Ezekiel. Both books employ the "Backward-Looking" literary form. "Backward-Looking" makes the Daniel story appear that it is describing an actual event at the beginning of the Exile. It is no wonder that the people of today's world think that Daniel was a real prophet predicting the future with such accuracy. The author contrived it that way because he already knew the outcome. It has been suggested that the Daniel of Ez 14: 20 is not the Daniel written into the Book of Daniel!

> *Eze 14: 20 "even if Noah, Daniel, and Job were in it, as I live, says the Lord GOD, I swear that they could save neither son nor daughter; they would save only themselves by their virtue."*

There are several very insightful passages in Ezekiel that deal with (a) Original Sin (Eze 18: 19), (b) Free Will (Eze 18:13 ff) and (c) the sinful shepherds, princes and priests of Israel. (Eze 34). Does this condemnation of priests sound familiar to our current situation with pedophilia in the ministry?

> (a) Eze 18: 19 *You ask: "Why is not the son charged with the guilt of his father?" Because the son has done what is right and just, and has been careful to observe all my statutes, he shall surely live.* No Original sin!

> (b) Eze 18: 13, 14, 17, 19-20 and 27
> 13 *lends at interest and exacts usury--this son certainly shall not live. Because he practiced all these abominations, he shall surely die; his death shall be his own fault.*
> *14 On the other hand, if a man begets a son who, seeing all the sins his father commits, yet fears and does not imitate him;*
> *17 who holds off from evildoing, accepts no interest or usury, but keeps my ordinances and lives by my statutes--this one shall not die for the sins of his father, but shall surely live.*

19 You ask: "Why is not the son charged with the guilt of his father?" Because the son has done what is right and just, and has been careful to observe all my statutes, he shall surely live.
20 Only the one who sins shall die.
27 But if a wicked man, turning from the wickedness he has committed, does what is right and just, he shall preserve his life;"

(c) Eze 34:1-24
1 "*Thus the word of the LORD came to me*
2 Son of man, prophesy against the shepherds of Israel, in these words prophesy to them (to the shepherds): Thus says the Lord GOD: Woe to the shepherds of Israel who have been pasturing themselves! Should not shepherds, rather, pasture sheep?
3 You have fed off their milk, worn their wool, and slaughtered the fatlings, but the sheep you have not pastured.
4 You did not strengthen the weak nor heal the sick nor bind up the injured. You did not bring back the strayed nor seek the lost, but you lorded it over them harshly and brutally."
5 So they were scattered for lack of a shepherd, and became food for all the wild beasts. My sheep were scattered
6 and wandered over all the mountains and high hills; my sheep were scattered over the whole earth, with no one to look after them or to search for them.
7 Therefore, shepherds, hear the word of the LORD:
8 As I live, says the Lord GOD, because my sheep have been given over to pillage, and because my sheep have become food for every wild beast, for lack of a shepherd; because my shepherds did not look after my sheep, but pastured themselves and did not pasture my sheep;
9 because of this, shepherds, hear the word of the LORD:
10 Thus says the Lord GOD: I swear I am coming against these shepherds. I will claim my sheep from them and put a stop to their shepherding my sheep so that they may no longer pasture themselves. I will save my sheep, that they may no longer be food for their mouths.
11 For thus says the Lord GOD: I myself will look after and tend my sheep.
12 As a shepherd tends his flock when he finds himself among his scattered sheep, so will I tend my sheep. I will rescue them from every place where they were scattered when it was cloudy and dark.
13 I will lead them out from among the peoples and gather them from the foreign lands; I will bring them back to their own country and pasture them upon the mountains of Israel (in the land's ravines and all its inhabited places).
14 In good pastures will I pasture them, and on the mountain heights of Israel shall be their grazing ground. There they shall lie down on good grazing ground, and in rich pastures shall they be pastured on the mountains of Israel.
15 I myself will pasture my sheep; I myself will give them rest, says the Lord GOD.
16 The lost I will seek out, the strayed I will bring back, the injured I will bind up, the sick I will heal (but the sleek and the strong I will destroy), shepherding them rightly.

17 As for you, my sheep, says the Lord GOD, I will judge between one sheep and another, between rams and goats.
18 Was it not enough for you to graze on the best pasture, that you had to trample the rest of your pastures with your feet? Was it not enough for you to drink the clearest water, that you had to foul the remainder with your feet?
19 Thus my sheep had to graze on what your feet had trampled and drink what your feet had fouled.
20 Therefore thus says the Lord GOD: Now will I judge between the fat and the lean sheep.
21 Because you push with side and shoulder, and butt all the weak sheep with your horns until you have driven them out,
22 I will save my sheep so that they may no longer be despoiled, and I will judge between one sheep and another.
23 I will appoint one shepherd over them to pasture them, my servant David; he shall pasture them and be their shepherd.
24 I, the LORD, will be their God, and my servant David shall be prince among them. I, the LORD, have spoken."

It's of interest that in verses 9 to 11 above, God says that SHE will be the shepherd. Verses 23 and 24 reflect the hope of Israel for a future Messiah in the appointment of David as shepherd. Confusing, isn't it? Remember now, David will return; David was the anointed king; anointed is *messiah*; the coming shepherd is the Messiah figure. In the following excerpt we read again that David will be their shepherd. But David is dead! One should learn that in the Hebrew mindset, a person lives on into the future by means of his DNA carried in the succeeding generations. Therefore, these verses are the author's expressed hope for a future Davidic Messiah, that's why the gospel writers wrote that Yeshua was of the house of David:

Eze 37 24 *"My servant David shall be prince over them, and there shall be one shepherd for them all; they shall live by My statutes and carefully observe My decrees.*
25 They shall live on the land which I gave to My servant Jacob, the land where their fathers lived; they shall live on it forever, they, and their children, and their children's children, with My servant David their prince forever."

Now, this following passage speaks to Ezekiel and his responsibility:

Eze 33: 5 *"He heard the trumpet blast yet refused to take warning; he is responsible for his own death, for had he taken warning he would have escaped with his life.*
6 But if the watchman sees the sword coming and fails to blow the warning trumpet, so that the sword comes and takes anyone, I will hold the watchman responsible for that person's death, even though that person is taken because of his own sin.
7 You, son of man, I have appointed watchman for the house of Israel; when you hear me say anything, you shall warn them for me."

Here again, we have a statement of God's compassion for converting a wicked person:

Eze 33: 11 "*Answer them: As I live, says the Lord GOD, I swear I take no pleasure in the death of the wicked man, but rather in the wicked man's conversion, that he may live. Turn, turn from your evil ways! Why should you die, O house of Israel?"*

In Eze 33: 14 below there is a hint of the policy in the 12 steps of Alcoholics Anonymous and verse 16 confirms God's forgiveness and mercy:

33: 14 "*And though I say to the wicked man that he shall surely die, if he turns away from his sin and does what is right and just,*
15 giving back pledges, restoring stolen goods, living by the statutes that bring life, and doing no wrong, he shall surely live, he shall not die. 16 None of the sins he committed shall be held against him; he has done what is right and just, he shall surely live."

The Minor Prophets
Lamentations to Malachi

Of all the Minor Prophets there are only two that will be discussed here: Daniel and Zechariah. Daniel has special meaning to the future looking believers and Zechariah to Matthew's reference of the 30 pieces of silver that Judas threw back into the temple.

(17) Zechariah will be a short discussion. We'll make this point quickly. In Matt 27: 9 he refers to Jeremiah when quoting the H.T. as the source of the prophecy of Judas Iscariot's remorse and throwing his recently acquired 30 pieces of silver back into the Temple (Matt 27: 2-9). When one reads the entire book of Jeremiah one is hard pressed to find any reference to 30 pieces of silver. Poor Matthew, he made a mistake! The reference he should have stated was Zechariah 11: 11-13 which reads:

Zec 11: 11 "that day it was broken off. The sheep merchants who were watching me understood that this was the word of the LORD. 12 I said to them, "If it seems good to you, give me my wages; but if not, let it go." And they counted out my wages, thirty pieces of silver. 13 But the LORD said to me, "Throw it in the treasury, the handsome price at which they valued me." So I took the thirty pieces of silver and threw them into the treasury in the house of the LORD."

You may wish to read the verses which precede that passage. It's surely an eye opener. Then, go back to Mathew 27; that's good reading too. But who made the mistake? God? Matthew? Then, explain "inspiration"!

(18) Daniel has some very peculiar implications of great concern to those waiting for the end-days and, as we will see in the next Chapter on the Christian Testament, the second coming of Yeshua. Upon examining the book of Daniel under a critical microscope, we found a few perplexing passages:

1. In Daniel 7: 13, the use of the Aramaic phrase "*bar enach*" (Strong's # 606) translates to "a son of man" and the single word "*enach*" meaning man or a Human person. The word "man" in the rest of Daniel means

the very same thing, except that each Aramaic or Hebrew word differs in what kind of man it implies. The problem is that Yeshua spoke Aramaic and is reported to have used the Aramaic phrase, *bar enach*, in response to questions about his identity. However, Mark wrote it in Greek as a title, *huios* tou *anthropos* (son of man), which looses the idiomatic understanding of the Aramaic. In Mark 8: 27-31, the author writes that Jesus refers to himself as the son of man. Does that mean that Jesus understands himself as the man on Daniel's cloud or as a simple human person acting as teacher/prophet like many other prophets in Israelite history? Or is it Mark who translates the Aramaic phrase, *bar enach*, into Greek and misses its correct idiomatic meaning and thereby makes it appear that Yeshua means the Greek title? There is serious doubt that Yeshua understood himself as that Daniel type. Yeshua's real response may very well have been that he was simply a human person, a response that coincides with 2nd John 1: 7.

2. There are some clues indicating that this is not an authentic story:
   - History does not record such a 60 cubit tall golden statue as described in 3: 1;
   - In 4: 7-8 the dream tree is seen at the ends of the Earth. That's a flat Earth cosmology;
   - The story takes place during the early years of the Exile. A Daniel shows up in the writings about Ezekiel (Eze 28: 3) yet there is no evidence that this Daniel, who is associated with Noah et al, is the person of the book of Daniel;
   - Scholars report that this book gives clues that show it was written in and about 167 BC, a perfect example of the "Backward-Looking" literary style.

The book of Daniel is the author's way of writing about a fictitious person who lives about 400 years previously and meets certain challenging situations and solves his problems with the help of Divine interventions (visions). Within the story line this Daniel interprets the King's dreams that give rise to the hope of all Israel that there will be justice at the end of days by a fictitious human-like cloud-rider, David or the Davidic Messiah and thereby impresses the non-believers that the Living God of Israel is the TRUE God of justice. Now, since the author knows what has already happened in the Joseph story in Genesis, he patterns the particulars of the Daniel story. The audience reads the book of Daniel and is amazed at Daniel's great power to portend such wonders, especially the "son of man" coming on a cloud IN POWER at the end times. The readers are filled with hope at such a confirmation of their beliefs that God will finally justify Israel.

Daniel's fabled book was written for his downtrodden community to infuse a bit of hope. The time during which Daniel was written is called the "apocalyptic" period. And Daniel was not the only piece of literature written then. Some scholars suspect that much of the material found in the Book of Revelations was also a product of those "apocalyptic" years but it was re-Christianized for the new sect.

There are two considerations here with which the average believer may not be familiar. The first relates to the translation of the Aramaic expression "*bar enach*", a human person, into a Greek title, "son of man". (This is analyzed in

Appendix AA.) The second relates to identifying this Daniel as one who lived before the beginning of the Exile.

Further commentary on Daniel can be found in the Internet Article, "Old Testament Life and Literature, Chapter 29, by Gerald A. Larue (See Appendix L for the URL).

A Transition

Up to this point the Bible in general and the Hebrew Testament in particular has been suggested to be our standard by which other Sacred Scriptures are evaluated. The result of the analysis is that all Sacred Scriptures have a similarly basic theology of a single Creator who communicated various degrees of knowledge about its creation and the nature of the Universe in proportion to the culture's capacity to grasp its significance. The communication to the primitive culture of the Exodus people resulted in the establishment of a ritualistic, doctrinal and legal Institutional Religion that ruled the Israelites—just like similar cultures did to all their people during the 1st millennium BC. In other words, God inspires only that material which the culture could observe and absorb, for example, a flat Earth cosmology. From the earliest of recorded history humans have always exhibited a ritualistic and sacrificial type of religion: Abraham was about to sacrifice his son. The Incas and Mayans conducted human sacrifices; the Hawaiians engaged in young female offerings to the volcano deity. The ancestral story of God's stopping Abraham from sacrificing his own son was, for the Israelites, a command to cease human sacrifice and to begin their religious history with animal sacrifice. They interpreted the storm and lightning at the mythical Mt. Sinai as divine revelation that they wrote into ritualistic, sacrificial rules and regulations that became the Mosaic Law. The Law grew into regulatory subsets of social, dietary, health and bodily cleanliness and later expanded to include spiritual cleanliness of the soul, all defined in the Torah that was put to pen centuries after the events. Following those Deuteronomic and Levitical rules and regulations became the pathway to holiness and, as Paul wrote in Romans, following those rules became know as "performing the works of the Law".

In opposition to that interpreted tradition, the Christian Testament will reveal a more sophisticated theology and a radically new social behavioral teaching of non-aggression and negate the need for a ritualistic and doctrinal Institutional religion. The context of the "Good News" was that it was possible to have a personal relationship with the Divine outside of the Mosaic Law and without any intermediary. In Chapter Four our examination will determine whether the Christian Movement did, in fact, accomplish that objective.

For now we will address ourselves to the study of the second to the last Sacred Scripture, the Qur'an.

Section 7: The Qur'an

The Qur'an appears to be a written set of local preachings for different audiences throughout Muhammad's ministry. The reason for this opinion is the recurring themes in each of the individual chapters or sermons. The major theological ideas presented in each chapter appear simply to be repetitions of the Hebrew Testament stories. For example, these quotes appear from the earlier chapters of the Qur'an:

> 5: 48 *And unto thee have We revealed the Scripture with the truth, confirming whatever Scripture was before it, and a watcher over it. So judge between them by that which Allah hath revealed, and follow not their desires away from the truth which hath come unto thee. For each We have appointed a divine law and a traced-out way. Had Allah willed He could have made you one community. But that He may try you by that which He hath given you (He hath made you as ye are). So vie one with another in good works. Unto Allah ye will all return, and He will then inform you of that wherein ye differ.*
>
> 2:164 *Lo! In the creation of the heavens and the earth, and the difference of night and day, and the ships which run upon the sea with that which is of use to men, and the water which Allah sendeth down from the sky, thereby reviving the earth after its death, and dispersing all kinds of beasts therein, and (in) the ordinance of the winds, and the clouds obedient between heaven and earth: are signs (of Allah's Sovereignty) for people who have sense.*
>
> 5:68 *Say O People of the Scripture! Ye have naught (of guidance) till ye observe the Torah and the Gospel and that which was revealed unto you from your Lord.*
>
> 12:111 *In their history verily there is a lesson for men of under-standing. It is no invented story but a confirmation of the existing (Scripture) and a detailed explanation of everything, and a guidance and a mercy for folk who believe.*
>
> 14: 4 *And We never sent a messenger save with the language of his folk, that he might make (the message) clear for them.*
>
> 32: 4 *Allah it is Who created the heavens and the earth, and that which is between them, in six Days. Then He mounted the Throne. Ye have not, beside Him, a protecting friend or mediator. Will ye not then remember?*
> 32: 5 *He directeth the ordinance from the heaven unto the earth; then it ascendeth unto Him in a Day, whereof the measure is a thousand years of that ye reckon.*
>
> 2:35 *And We said: O Adam! Dwell thou and thy wife in the Garden, and eat ye freely (of the fruits) thereof where ye will; but come not nigh this tree lest ye become wrong-doers.*
> *2:36 But Satan caused them to deflect therefrom and expelled them from the (happy) state in which they were; and We said: Fall down, one of you a foe unto the other! There shall be for you on earth a habitation and provision for a time.*
> *2:37 Then Adam received from his Lord words (of revelation), and He relented toward him. Lo! He is the relenting, the Merciful.*
>
> 5:27 *But recite unto them with truth the tale of the two sons of Adam, how they offered each a sacrifice, and it was accepted from the one of them and it was not accepted from the other. (The one) said: I will surely kill thee. (The other) answered: Allah accepteth only from those who ward off (evil).*
>
> 2:50 *And when We brought you through the sea and rescued you, and drowned the folk of Pharaoh in your sight.*

2:51 And when We did appoint for Moses forty nights (of solitude), and then ye chose the calf, when he had gone from you, and were wrong-doers.
2:52 Then, even after that, We pardoned you in order that ye might give thanks.
2;53 And when We gave unto Moses the Scripture and the criterion (of right and wrong), that ye might be led aright.
2:54 And when Moses said unto his people: O my people! Ye have wronged yourselves by your choosing of the calf (for worship) so turn in penitence to your Creator, and kill (the guilty) yourselves. That will be best for you with your Creator and He will relent toward you. Lo! He is the Relenting, the Merciful.

2:60 *And when Moses asked for water for his people, We said: Smite with thy staff the rock. And there gushed out therefrom twelve springs (so that) each tribe knew their drinking-place. Eat and drink of that which Allah hath provided, and do not act corruptly, making mischief in the earth.*
[Note, Exodus does indicate that there were twelve springs, only not at the rock]

2:133 *Or were ye present when death came to Jacob, when he said unto his sons: What will ye worship after me ? They said: We shall worship thy God, the God of thy fathers, Abraham and Ishmael and Isaac, One God, and unto Him we have surrendered.*
[The Qur'an changes the middle name to Ishmael, the father of the Arab Nations]

6:84 *And We bestowed upon him Isaac and Jacob; each of them We guided; and Noah did We guide aforetime; and of his seed (We guided) David and Solomon and Job and Joseph and Moses and Aaron. Thus do We reward the good.*
6:85 And Zachariah and John and Jesus and Elias. Each one (of them) was of the righteous.
6:86 And Ishmael and Elisha and Jonah and Lot. Each one (of them) did We prefer above (Our) creatures,

3:3 *He hath revealed unto thee (Muhammad) the Scripture with truth, confirming that which was (revealed) before it, even as He revealed the Torah and the Gospel.*

57: 27 *Then We caused Our messengers to follow in their footsteps; and We caused Jesus, son of Mary, to follow, and gave him the Gospel, and placed compassion and mercy in the hearts of those who followed him. But monasticism they invented - We ordained it not for them - only seeking Allah's pleasure, and they observed it not with right observance. So We give those of them who believe their reward, but many of them are evil-livers.*

Muhammad accepts the whole Bible as actual historical facts reported accurately by its authors. Yet, he adds a unique twist here and there! He says repeatedly that they are inspired by Allah and in this sense, the word inspired means that the words of Allah are true because they have been whispered into Muhammad's ear and he wrote it down immediately (it's what I've called the "tape-recording syndrome" that guarantees the historical and scientific accuracy that literalists require in order to believe in their Sacred Scriptures).

Muhammad insists that every major character in his entire list of biblical messengers was sent by Allah. What is surprising is that the list of messengers includes those people in the Christian Testament as well. Muhammad repeats the Hebrew "schema", *"Hear Oh Israel, the Lord thy God is one (alone)"*, in practically every sermon, only in the Qur'an it reads, "2:163 *Your God is One God; there is no God save Him, the Beneficent, the Merciful."* However, the Qur'an frequently adds,

"*And Allah needs no partner*!" Muhammad's theology is clearly a condemnation of those who hold to many gods and, specifically, the Christian error of elevating Jesus to an equal partnership with God.

> 6:*19 Say (O Muhammad): What thing is of most weight in testimony ? Say: Allah is Witness between me and you. And this Qur'an hath been inspired in me, that I may warn therewith you and whomsoever it may reach. Do ye in sooth bear witness that there are gods beside Allah? Say: I bear no such witness. Say: He is only One God. Lo! I am innocent of that which ye associate (with Him).*
>
> 6:21 *Who doth greater wrong than he who inventeth a lie against Allah or denieth His revelations ? Lo! the wrongdoers will not be successful.*
> *6:22 And on the day We gather them together We shall say unto those who ascribed partners (unto Allah): Where are (now) those partners of your make-believe ?*
>
> 5:72 *They surely disbelieve who say: Lo! Allah is the Messiah, son of Mary. The Messiah (himself) said: O Children of Israel, worship Allah, my Lord and your Lord. Lo! whoso ascribeth partners unto Allah, for him Allah hath forbidden paradise. His abode is the Fire. For evildoers there will be no helpers.*
> *5:73 They surely disbelieve who say: Lo! Allah is the third of three; when there is no God save the One God. If they desist not from so saying a painful doom will fall on those of them who disbelieve.*
>
> 5:75 *The Messiah, son of Mary, was no other than a messenger, messengers (the like of whom) had passed away before him. And his mother was a saintly woman. And they both used to eat (earthly) food. See how We make the revelations clear for them, and see how they are turned away!*
>
> 12:106 *And most of them believe not in Allah except that they attribute partners (unto Him).*
>
> 16:51 *Allah hath said: Choose not two gods. There is only One God. So of Me, Me only, be in awe.*
>
> 16: 98 *And when thou recitest the Qur'an, seek refuge in Allah from Satan the outcast.*
> *16: 99 Lo! he hath no power over those who believe and put trust in their Lord.*
> *16: 100 His power is only over those who make a friend of him, and those who ascribe partners unto Him (Allah).*
>
> 17: 111 *And say: Praise be to Allah, Who hath not taken unto Himself a son, and Who hath no partner in the Sovereignty, nor hath He any protecting friend through dependence.*
>
> 18: 38 *But He is Allah, my Lord, and I ascribe unto my Lord no partner.*

112. AL-IKHLAS: THE UNITY

1 Say: He is Allah, the One!
2 Allah, the eternally Besought of all!
3 He begetteth not nor was begotten.
4 And there is none comparable unto Him.

The thrust of Muhammad's scripture is that the majority of Israelites and Christians have rejected those previous messengers. Nevertheless, Allah accepts those who believe in Him:

> 2:62 Lo! *Those who believe (in that which is revealed unto thee, Muhammad), and those who are Jews, and Christians, and Sabaeans - whoever believeth in Allah and the Last Day and doeth right - surely their reward is with their Lord, and there shall no fear come upon them neither shall they grieve.*

Then, in this next verse Allah states that He became very disappointed with those of the Israelites who rejected His H.T. covenant and the C.T. message of Jesus:

> 2:86 *Such are those who buy the life of the world at the price of the Hereafter. Their punishment will not be lightened, neither will they have support.*
> 2:87 *And verily We gave unto Moses the Scripture and We caused a train of messengers to follow after him, and We supported and We gave unto Jesus, son of Mary, clear proofs (of Allah's sovereignty), him with the Holy spirit. Is it ever so, that, when there cometh unto you a messenger (from Allah) with that which ye yourselves desire not, ye grow arrogant, and some ye disbelieve and some ye slay ?*
> Note; Holy spirit as used here means Allah is present in Jesus the prophet as God is present in every prophet!

> 2:101 *And when there cometh unto them a messenger from Allah, confirming that which they possess, a party of those who have received the Scripture fling the Scripture of Allah behind their backs as if they knew not.*

Now, Allah has conscripted Muhammad who will re-state the message and straighten out humanity one last time through the Arab nation as the other branch of the chosen people (note the inclusion of Ishmael in the list of ancient fathers, Abraham, Ishmael, Isaac and Jacob):

> 3:84 *Say (O Muhammad): We believe in Allah and that which is revealed unto us and that which was revealed unto Abraham and Ishmael and Isaac and Jacob and the tribes, and that which was vouchsafed unto Moses and Jesus and the prophets from their Lord. We make no distinction between any of them, and unto Him [Allah] we have surrendered.*

> 5:19 *O People of the Scripture! Now hath Our messenger come unto you to make things plain unto you after an interval (of cessation) of the messengers, lest ye should say: There came not unto us a messenger of cheer nor any warner. Now hath a messenger (Muhammad) of cheer and a warner come unto you. Allah is Able to do all things.*

> 2:105 *Neither those who disbelieve among the people of the Scripture nor the idolaters love that there should be sent down unto you any good thing from your*

Lord. But Allah chooseth for His mercy whom He will, and Allah is of Infinite Bounty.

2:106 Nothing of our revelation (even a single verse) do we abrogate or cause be forgotten, but we bring (in place) one better or the like thereof [Muhammad is the new prophet]. Knowest thou not that Allah is able to do all things ?
2:107 Knowest thou not that it is Allah unto Whom belongeth the Sovereignty of the heavens and the earth; and ye have not, beside Allah, any guardian or helper?
Allah is ALONE!

2:111 *And they say: None entereth paradise unless he be a Jew or a Christian. These are their own desires. Say: Bring your proof (of what ye state) if ye are truthful.*
2:112 Nay, but whosoever surrendereth his purpose to Allah while doing good, his reward is with his Lord; and there shall no fear come upon them neither shall they grieve.
2:113 And the Jews say the Christians follow nothing (true), and the Christians say the Jews follow nothing (true); yet both are readers of the Scripture. Even thus speak those who know not. Allah will judge between them on the Day of Resurrection concerning that wherein they differ.

2:119 *Lo! We have sent thee (O Muhammad) with the truth, a bringer of glad tidings and a warner. And thou wilt not be asked about the owners of hell-fire.*
2:120 And the Jews will not be pleased with thee, nor will the Christians, till thou follow their creed. Say: Lo! the guidance of Allah (Himself) is Guidance. And if thou shouldst follow their desires after the knowledge which hath come unto thee, then wouldst thou have from Allah no protecting guardian nor helper.

2:136 *Say (O Muslims): We believe in Allah and that which is revealed unto us and that which was revealed unto Abraham, and Ishmael, and Isaac, and Jacob, and the tribes, and that which Moses and Jesus received, and that which the prophets received from their Lord. We make no distinction between any of them, and unto Him [Allah] we have surrendered.*

2:144 *We have seen the turning of thy face to heaven (for guidance, O Muhammad). And now verily We shall make thee turn (in prayer) toward a qiblah which is dear to thee. So turn thy face toward the Inviolable Place of Worship, and ye (O Muslims), wheresoever ye may be, turn your faces (when ye pray) toward it. Lo! Those who have received the Scripture know that (this revelation) is the Truth from their Lord. And Allah is not unaware of what they do.*

In the Qur'an you will experience the duality of Allah, God of Muhammad, as both a compassionate, merciful, forgiving God and, on the other hand, a very angry and punishing Divinity. I call that kind of Divinity, a God of "do what I say, or else ...". Allah is a God of "reciprocity"! He is a Profile # 2 defined as "I do good to my believers and I punish those who disbelieve in Me".

First, let's look at Allah from the believer's point of view :

5:54 *Such is the grace of Allah which He giveth unto whom He will.*
(Like II Corin 12: 9)

2:148 *And each one hath a goal toward which he turneth; so vie with one another in good works. Wheresoever ye may be, Allah will bring you all together. Lo! Allah is Able to do all things.*
2:149 And whencesoever thou comest forth (for prayer, O Muhammad) turn thy face toward the Inviolable Place of Worship. Lo! it is the Truth from thy Lord. Allah is not unaware of what ye do.
2:150 Whencesoever thou comest forth turn thy face toward the Inviolable Place of Worship; and wheresoever ye may be (O Muslims) turn your faces toward it (when ye pray) so that men may have no argument against you, save such of them as do injustice - Fear them not, but fear Me! - and so that I may complete My grace upon you, and that ye may be guided.
2:151 Even as We have sent unto you a messenger from among you, who reciteth unto you Our revelations and causeth you to grow, and teacheth you the Scripture and wisdom, and teacheth you that which ye knew not.
2:152 Therefore remember Me, I will remember you. Give thanks to Me, and reject not Me.
2:153 O ye who believe! Seek help in steadfastness and prayer. Lo! Allah is with the steadfast.

2:160 *Except those who repent and amend and make manifest (the truth). These it is toward whom I relent. I am the Relenting, the Merciful.*

2:195 Spend your wealth for the cause of Allah, and be not cast by your own hands to ruin; and do good. Lo! Allah loveth the beneficent.

2:199 *Then hasten onward from the place whence the multitude hasteneth onward, and ask forgiveness of Allah. Lo! Allah is Forgiving, Merciful.*

2:218 *Lo! those who believe, and those who emigrate (to escape the persecution) and strive in the way of Allah, these have hope of Allah's mercy. Allah is Forgiving, Merciful.*

2:225 *Allah will not take you to task for that which is unintentional in your oaths. But He will take you to task for that which your hearts have garnered. Allah is Forgiving, Clement.*

2:243 *Bethink thee (O Muhammad) of those of old, who went forth from their habitations in their thousands, fearing death, and Allah said unto them: Die; and then He brought them back to life. Lo! Allah is a Lord of Kindness to mankind, but most of mankind give not thanks.*

3:31 *Say, (O Muhammad, to mankind): If ye love Allah, follow me; Allah will love you and forgive you your sins Allah is Forgiving, Merciful.*

4:57 *And as for those who believe and do good works, We shall make them enter Gardens underneath which rivers flow - to dwell therein for ever; there for them are pure companions - and We shall make them enter plenteous shade.*

So now, let's take a look at the punishing Allah:

4:84 ... *Allah is stronger in might and stronger in inflicting punishment.*

6:157 *We award unto those who turn away from Our revelations an evil doom because of their aversion.*

5:86 *But those who disbelieve and deny Our revelations, they are owners of hell-fire.*

7:50 *And the dwellers of the Fire cry out unto the dwellers of the Garden: Pour on us some water or some wherewith Allah hath provided you. They say: Lo! Allah hath forbidden both to disbelievers (in His guidance),*

2:178 O ye who believe! Retaliation is prescribed for you in the matter of the murdered; the freeman for the freeman,
and the slave for the slave, and the female for the female. And for him who is forgiven somewhat by his (injured) brother, prosecution according to usage and payment unto him in kindness. This is an alleviation and a mercy from your Lord. He who transgresseth after this will have a painful doom.

3: 11 *Like Pharaoh's folk and those who were before them, they disbelieved Our revelations and so Allah seized them for their sins. And Allah is severe in punishment.*
3: 12 Say (O Muhammad) unto those who disbelieve: Ye shall be overcome and gathered unto Hell, an evil resting-place.

3:21 *Lo! those who disbelieve the revelations of Allah, and slay the prophets wrongfully, and slay those of mankind who enjoin equity: promise them a painful doom.*

3:77 *Lo! those who purchase a small gain at the cost of Allah's covenant and their oaths, they have no portion in the Hereafter. Allah will neither speak to them nor look upon them on the Day of Resurrection, nor will He make them grow. Theirs will be a painful doom.*

3:84 *Say (O Muhammad): We believe in Allah and that which is revealed unto us and that which was revealed unto Abraham and Ishmael and Isaac and Jacob and the tribes, and that which was vouchsafed unto Moses and Jesus and the prophets from their Lord. We make no distinction between any of them, and unto Him [Allah] we have surrendered.*
3:85 And whoso seeketh as religion other than the Surrender (to Allah) it will not be accepted from him, and he will be a loser in the Hereafter.

3:131 *And ward off (from yourselves) the Fire prepared for disbelievers.*

3:177 *Those who purchase disbelief at the price of faith harm Allah not at all, but theirs will be a painful doom.*

4:10 *Lo! Those who devour the wealth of orphans wrongfully, they do but swallow fire into their bellies, and they will be exposed to burning flame.*

4:55 And of them were (some) who believed therein and of them were (some) who turned away from it. Hell is sufficient for (their) burning.
4:56 Lo! Those who disbelieve Our revelations, We shall expose them to the Fire. As often as their skins are consumed We shall exchange them for fresh skins that they may taste the torment. Lo! Allah is ever Mighty, Wise.

6:70 *Those are they who perish by their own deserts. For them is drink of boiling water and a painful doom, because they disbelieved.*

8:50 *If thou couldst see how the angels receive those who disbelieve, smiting faces and their backs and (saying): Taste the punishment of burning!*

13: 32 *And verily messengers (of Allah) were mocked before thee, but long I bore with those who disbelieved. At length I seized them, and how (awful) was My punishment!*

13: 35 *A similitude of the Garden which is promised unto those who keep their duty (to Allah): Underneath it rivers flow; its food is everlasting, and its shade; this is the reward of those who keep their duty, while the reward of disbelievers is the Fire.*

14: 49 *Thou wilt see the guilty on that day linked together in chains,*
50 Their raiment of pitch, and the Fire covering their faces,
51 That Allah may repay each soul what it hath earned. Lo! Allah is swift at reckoning.

17: 97 *And he whom Allah guideth, he is led aright; while, as for him whom He sendeth astray, for them thou wilt find no protecting friends beside Him, and We shall assemble them on the Day of Resurrection on their faces, blind, dumb and deaf; their habitation will be hell; whenever it abateth, We increase the flame for them.*

22: 19 *These twain (the believers and the disbelievers) are two opponents who contend concerning their Lord. But as for those who disbelieve, garments of fire will be cut out for them; boiling fluid will be poured down on their heads,*
20 Whereby that which is in their bellies, and their skins too, will be melted;
21 And for them are hooked rods of iron.
22 Whenever, in their anguish, they would go forth from thence they are driven back therein and (it is said unto them): Taste the doom of burning.

23: 76 *Already have We grasped them with punishment, but they humble not themselves unto their Lord, nor do they pray,*
23: 77 Until, when We open for them the gate of extreme punishment, behold! they are aghast thereat.

24: 4 *And those who accuse honourable women but bring not four witnesses, scourge them (with) eighty stripes and never (afterward) accept their testimony - They indeed are evil-doers –*

47: 15 *A similitude of the Garden which those who keep their duty (to Allah) are promised: Therein are rivers of water unpolluted, and rivers of milk whereof the flavour changeth not, and rivers of wine delicious to the drinkers, and rivers of clear- run honey; therein for them is every kind of fruit, with pardon from their Lord. (Are those who enjoy all this) like those who are immortal in the Fire and are given boiling water to drink so that it teareth their bowels?*

73: *11 Leave Me to deal with the deniers, lords of ease and comfort (in this life); and do thou respite them awhile.*
12 Lo! with Us are heavy fetters and a raging fire,
13 And food which choketh (the partaker), and a painful doom
14 *On the day when the earth and the hills rock, and the hills become a heap of running sand.*

In this next set of quotes Muhammad states Allah's code as: (1) do good works, (2) believe in Allah's Messengers, (3) establish worship of Allah alone, making no other a partner of Allah, and (4) pay the "poor-due". Here are some of the verses that substantiate that:

5:12 *Allah made a covenant of old with the Children of Israel and We raised among them twelve chieftains, and Allah said: Lo! I am with you. If ye establish worship and pay the poor-due, and believe in My messengers and support them, and lend unto Allah a kindly loan, surely I shall remit your sins, and surely I shall bring you into Gardens underneath which rivers flow.*

11: 114 *Establish worship at the two ends of the day and in some watches of the night.*

23: 78 *So establish worship, pay the poor-due, and hold fast to Allah. He is your Protecting friend. A blessed Patron and a blessed Helper!*

23: *1 Successful indeed are the believers*
2 Who are humble in their prayers,
3 And who shun vain conversation,
4 And who are payers of the poor-due;
5 And who guard their modesty -
6 Save from their wives or the (slaves) that their right hands possess, for then they are not blameworthy,
7 But whoso craveth beyond that, such are transgressors -
8 And who are shepherds of their pledge and their covenant,
9 And who pay heed to their prayers.
10 These are the heirs
11 Who will inherit paradise. There they will abide.

24: 30 *Tell the believing men to lower their gaze and be modest. That is purer for them. Lo! Allah is aware of what they do.*
24: 31 And tell the believing women to lower their gaze and be modest, and to display of their adornment only that which is apparent, and to draw their veils over their bosoms, and not to reveal their adornment save to their own husbands or fathers or husbands' fathers, or their sons or their husbands' sons, or their brothers or their brothers' sons or sisters' sons, or their women, or their slaves, or male attendants who lack vigour, or children who know naught of women's nakedness. And let them not stamp their feet so as to reveal what they hide of their adornment. And turn unto Allah together, O believers, in order that ye may succeed.

24: 32 And marry such of you as are solitary and the pious of your slaves and maid- servants. If they be poor, Allah will enrich them of His bounty. Allah is of ample means, Aware.
24: 33 And let those who cannot find a match keep chaste till Allah give them independence by His grace. And such of your slaves as seek a writing (of emancipation), write it for them if ye are aware of aught of good in them, and bestow upon them of the wealth of Allah which He hath bestowed upon you.

Now we will see a compassionate Allah. This next passage repeats the first Chapter of Isaiah.

93: 9 Therefore the orphan oppress not, 10 Therefor the beggar drive not away, *11 Therefore of the bounty of thy Lord be thy discourse.*

98: 5 And they are ordered naught else than to serve Allah, keeping religion pure for Him, as men by nature upright, and to establish worship and to pay the poor-due. That is true religion.

107. AL-MA`UN: THE DAILY NECESSARIES

1 Hast thou observed him who belieth religion?
2 That is he who repelleth the orphan,
3 And urgeth not the feeding of the needy.
4 Ah, woe unto worshippers
5 Who are heedless of their prayer;
6 Who would be seen (at worship)
7 Yet refuse small kindnesses!

There are some dietary laws and health codes to follow that appear to be copied right out of the Torah. As you read above, the believers are promised "Gardens under which rivers flow" as their eternal reward and the disbelievers are to be punished most severely with eternal tortures of fire, molten metals poured on them and only boiling water to drink, to name a few. Doesn't that sound like a God who understands a people of the desert? But what about the rest of the world's people?

Judgment Day is called by many names. One can see the comparison of Blessed vs. Cursed at the end time by the very designations used in those names. The Doom; The Appointed Day; the Hour; the Day of Resurrection; Day of Reckoning; Day of Decision; the doom of a tremendous Day; the day of coming forth; the doom of thy Lord; The threatened Hour; the day of the Summoner; the Last Day; the Day of Assembling; the True Day; the Shout; an Awful Day; the Promised Day; the Night of Predestination; The Terrible Calamity; Day of Discrimination; the Day of Meeting; the Day of the Approaching (doom); the Day of Immortality; ! the Doom of thy Lord.

31: 34 *Lo! Allah! With Him is knowledge of the Hour. He sendeth down the rain, and knoweth that which is in the wombs. No soul knoweth what it will earn tomorrow, and no soul knoweth in what land it will die. Lo! Allah is Knower, Aware.*

It is interesting that Muhammad preaches a ONE-God theology. The very backbone of Christianity is the theology of the "WORD is God", a partner!

> 4: 171 *O People of the Scripture! Do not exaggerate in your religion nor utter aught concerning Allah save the truth. The Messiah, Jesus son of Mary, was only a messenger of Allah, and His word which He conveyed unto Mary, and a spirit from Him. So believe in Allah and His messengers, and say not "Three" - Cease! (It is) better for you! - Allah is only One God. Far is it removed from His Transcendent Majesty that He should have a son. His is all that is in the heavens and all that is in the earth. And Allah is sufficient as Defender.*

> 23: 52 *And lo! this your religion is one religion and I am your Lord, so keep your duty unto Me.*
> *23: 53 But they (mankind) have broken their religion among them into sects, each group rejoicing in its tenets.*
> *23: 54 So leave them in their error till a time.*

Understanding the Stories of God in the Qur'an is essentially to understand the use of figurative language in the form of simile.

> 24: 35 *Allah is the Light of the heavens and the earth. The similitude of His light is as a niche wherein is a lamp. The lamp is in a glass. The glass is as it were a shining star. (This lamp is) kindled from a blessed tree, an olive neither of the East nor of the West, whose oil would almost glow forth (of itself) though no fire touched it. Light upon light. Allah guideth unto His light whom He will. And Allah speaketh to mankind in allegories, for Allah is Knower of all things.*

> 25: 47 *And He it is Who maketh night a covering for you, and sleep repose, and maketh day a resurrection.*

> 29: 43 *As for these similitudes, We coin them for mankind, but none will grasp their meaning, save the wise.* (Right out of the C.T.)

> 30: 58 *Verily We have coined for mankind in this Qur'an all kinds of similitudes.*

So it is that the Qur'an speaks to a chosen nation again in the hope of bringing its inhabitants to an intimate relationship with Allah, the Creator. The author of the Qur'an reflects on the previous Sacred Scripture of the Israelites and that of the Christians as the basis or foundation of this new revelation to the Arab Nation. Allah's proclamations, voiced through Muhammad, are that the earlier messengers were rejected and that Allah is now making a compassionate plea anew to another chosen people.

The commandments of the Qur'an are simple, indeed, in contrast to the Torah and the severe interpretations (or is it the misinterpretations?) of the formal Jewish and Christian Institutions. If you wish to see what happened to Islam after the death of Muhammad, read Appendix I.

SUMMARY of SACRED SCRIPTURES

When you first read these Sacred Scriptures it should become obvious that they share several similarities, among them are:

1. The "One Creator with Many Names" (as many as the alphabet! See Appendix W) and with many "Prophets" are the common denominators of all Cultures except Christianity which has only one teacher/prophet.
2. Sacred Scriptures range from simplistic mythic stories (Enuma Elish) to complex historical legends and myths (Bible): unintelligible fantasy to profoundly meaningful myths.
3. The literary style in the writings of Alleged Divinely Inspired Sacred Scriptures is a "Faith Interpreted Backward-Looking" literature.
4. Eastern Thought of Right Living counters Western Doctrinalized Religions
5. Bible's Hebrew (Old) Testament books are legends and myths with threads of Human interpretations laced with remembered mythologized history
6. Islamic roots are from the mythologized Bible of Judaism without complex Doctrinalizations
7. Literalism vs. modern Science and Technology--a Problem of Education and Pre-critical Naiveté. The Big Bang and Fossil Record do not negate a creation by a Deity; they only contradict the Creationism of Literalists.

B. Specific Comments:

Each sacred scripture contains at least one verse concerning the existence of a Creator. The Upanishads restates a well-known Thomas Aquinas proof for the existence of God, "an Uncaused Being, who is the only explanation for the existence of the Universe". The Upanishads actually reads:

> *"He (the golden person, called ut) is lord of the worlds beyond that (sun), and of all the wishes of the Devas (inhabiting those worlds)."* And in another passage, *"He is indeed the udgitha (Om = Brahman), greater than great (parovariyas), he is without end."*
> Yet another, "Verily, in the beginning all this was Self, one only; there was nothing else blinking whatsoever." An identical reading occurs in the Bhagavad-Gita: 'For it is said by the Bhagavat:

"O Gautama, on what does the earth rest? The earth, O Brâhmana, rests on the sphere of water. O Gautama, on what does the sphere of water rest? It rests on the air. O Gautama, on what does the air rest? It rests on the ether (âkâsa)? O Gautama, on what does the ether rest? Thou goest too far, great Brâhmana; thou goest too far, great Brahmana. The ether, O Brâhmana, does not rest. It has no support."

One can understand that in all Sacred Scriptures there is one Creator and many fables from the pre-historic oral traditions. Each Scripture reflects the science of their own day; each clearly mirrors their own psychological profile in their description of their divinity and its relationship to human beings. It appears that the divinity of all the Sacred Scriptures is a Being steeped in reciprocity—an eye for an eye morality and ethic. We recognize that the author is describing exactly the behavior of his culture. Therefore, the divinity or creator is seen in terms of the culture's perceptions of itself and its own worldview.

From a scientific perspective each Sacred Scripture suffers from plain old lack of knowledge about the nature of the planet Earth and the Universe. The problem that ensues is simply that the world before 1700 AD interpreted their Sacred Scripture from their ignorance of the physical, psychological and theological sciences. It is unfortunate that each particular culture had developed a mindset of divine authorship that to this very 21st century denies the actual dependence on the human authorship of their Sacred Scripture. At this point you may understand that if these Scriptures were absolutely historical and theologically correct, there would be no mistakes, errors or inconsistencies. It remains for us in Chapter Five to add just a few more points to the list of inconsistencies, errors and mistakes!

Nevertheless, each Sacred Scripture does contain many human as well as godly recommendations about the manner in which humans can lead a happy social and private life. Those have been pointed out in this review and, as you have undoubtedly recognized, they have been compared to the basic tenets contained in the Western Sacred Scripture, the Bible, to illustrate their similarity. You've also noticed that the Christian (New) Testament was not included in this Chapter. It is our opinion that this New Testament is refreshingly counter-cultural to the general interpretation and practice of every preceding and other Sacred Scripture. In spite of that, many in this present hedonistic, radical terrorist and fundamentalist world deny the veracity of the superiority of the Christian Testament. We will now turn to that Christian Testament and examine the challenging social guidance, theology and spirituality found in its "not-exactly-factual" content.

One last thought! One should be puzzled by the fact that the ideas in one Sacred Scripture are labeled as Divinely inspired and the very same ideas in another Sacred Scripture are labeled NOT Divinely inspired. Could it be that all Sacred Scriptures are in some small or large manner actually human epiphanies? Understand that "inspire" doesn't mean "inerrant content by virtue if its divine source". Rather, inspire means simply to pen new experiences of one's God in terms to which the author and his community can relate!

INTERMISSION TIME

At this juncture it would be appropriate to take a brief moment to reflect on and meditate over our observations and conclusions thus far. In this 21st century a great deal of technological progress has been made. Included in this new awareness is the psychology of us humans and what our minds are capable of accomplishing. We are privy to a large portion of our own nature and its tendency to frailty, imperfection and fallibility. One of our human tendencies manifests itself when we hear a long story, followed by a short time delay; we fail to repeat it exactly in every detail. When we tell that story to another and have that person pass it on, then we humans tend to embellish the story by reinforcing that which we believe to be the highlights of the important meanings of that story. Well, as the story is passed through several people over a few weeks, mythologizing takes place. Can you imagine if that story is passed down through the years, decades or even centuries, what will be left of the original? That's exactly what has taken place with the Bible stories.

Today, we humans no longer believe in either fortune telling prophets or the ability of oral traditions to preserve the past without mythologizing it. We believe in facts! We understand the mathematical basis of the Universe in which God's engineering included evolution, especially and particularly of Homo Sapiens.

With all that in mind, we have just examined a selected list of Sacred Scriptures and found each and every one to be lacking in veracity (both historical and scientific) and, confusing the situation further, to contain myths and legends evolved via the defective, human oral tradition. The Sacred Scriptures thusfar presented point to a Creator with borderline characteristics of a God of Reciprocity, merciful yet punishing. Some Sacred Scriptures contain a subtle indication of a God who is in love with Her creation. The Hebrew Testament is schizophrenic in that it can not decide which best depicts Yahweh. We are left with our own dilemma!

On critical examination of the Christian Testament, we will discover from our suggested chronological format that there were changes taking place because of this prophet and teacher from Nazareth, Yeshua. It has been our purpose to dig deeply into those very teachings and unwrap a counter-cultural non-religion {non-institutional, non-ritualistic and non-doctrinal) spirituality. The Jesus Movement is that unique spirituality! Our biggest problem will be to decode what the Apostles handed down that developed differently in each individual community bringing the end of the 1st century into a complete confusion concerning the nature of Yeshua. At first Yeshua was totally human and in the end there was great confrontations about who he really was: (1) Human; (2) a physical body with God inside; (3) a Divine Being, like an Angel; or (4) an equal Partner of the Hebrew God, Yahweh. Four distinct Christologies are clearly found in the chronological reading of the Christian Testament. In addition, a third Divine Partner arose out of the flowery language of the famous Paul of Tarsus. A simple name of the Hebrew God was shortened and repeated so inaccurately that the abstract Holy Spirit and the spirit of holiness (See Appendix AD) were personified into this third equal Being of the Godhead. Then came the dissenters and Christendom erupted in intellectual, emotional and physical conflict.

The humanity of the historical Yeshua was lost in the transmissions of the oral tradition. The actual words and deeds of Yeshua fell to the embellishments of storytellers. The center of the Christian Movement focused on the glorified risen Messiah.

In addition, what is now identified as the "Jesus Movement" (that which the historical Yeshua taught) was replaced with an organized Institution of doctrine by none other than the learned Paul, the one time Pharisee. Of course, the plethora of apocryphal writings had a lot to do with the resultant local doctrinal confusions. There was no official collection of canonical writings until 400 AD. Therefore, each Christian community developed its own variant doctrine concerning the nature of the Good News and of Yeshua himself. So, from the 2nd century to the beginning of the 5th century Christendom was in theological chaos. Then, in 312 AD Constantine made a fatal error by making the Catholic Church leaders take over the responsibilities of judicial officer within the Empire. From that day forward we have experienced the intertwining of religion and politics, a Church- State, right up to the battle to remove "under God" from the American pledge.

Some people have a little difficulty with God having a second partner. Some others have a problem with that third partner, the Holy Spirit. We will review that issue a little more carefully. The Hebrew Testament very often refers to God as "the Holy One of Israel", "the spirit of holiness" and the "Holy Spirit (of God)", isn't that so? As you will find out, throughout the Christian Testament, there are a variety of phrases using the word, Spirit. We will pay very special attention to the verses in Paul's letter to the Romans, written as early as 57 AD, in Romans 8: 9-16.

As a companion problem, we've often wondered that if Yeshua were totally God and knew the future outcome, wouldn't his sacrifice be like a short walk on the beach? If we have to be Divine in order to live a life as Yeshua did, then, there is really no hope at all for humanity's salvation. However, if Yeshua was just a man like all of us humans (according to Genesis, all humans are in the form/image of God), then His sacrifice has infinite meaning to John and Jane Doe. The statements in Romans 1: 3-4, Philippians 2: 8-9 and the three special verses in Acts would be "right on"! Oh my! What a concept! Someone, human like us, made it and his example means, so can we!

It is our opinion, alone, that Institutionalism and the imperfections in human nature have distorted the central message, Deified the messenger out of his humanity and now makes worshiping the Book or the Institutional Dogma, Doctrines and Rituals the primary route to guaranteed salvation. Oh, do you think this passage from the Fourth Gospel placed on the lips of Yeshua by the authors has any significance here?

> *"John 5: 39 You search the scriptures, because you think you have eternal life through them; even they testify on my behalf."*

Once again a select few have gained a large margin of control over the interpretation of the message with the distortion "we teach what the Apostles have handed down". Can anyone really say that we definitely know exactly what the Apostles handed down? We think not, especially when we read the Gospels first! Christianity today is composed of two camps: the Book worshipers and the Bread worshipers ... mind you, both in violation of the first Commandment! A very low percentage of Christians really understand and practice what we now call the "Jesus Movement". Many are still caught in empty ritualistic ruts. When challenged with intelligent questions, we've frequently heard the classic response, "Pay, Pray and Obey!" It is therefore necessary to point out to both sides that the Book and the Bread are falsely worshipped. And to make our interpretations more complex, God doesn't want nor need worship! Just read Isaiah 1: 10 20 again.

Our efforts must be focused on re-forming a correct basis for interpreting the message, on understanding the messenger and on developing a sound personal spirituality in consort with what Yeshua taught. Martin Luther started to do this in the Western World but became cocooned in the affairs of state. Mahatma Gandhi made his attempt in the Eastern World and was assassinated by one of his own people. We in the USA experienced the life and times of Martin Luther King, Jr. and witnessed his destruction. Yes, every person who speaks an authentic version of God's words is murdered just like the prophets of both Hebrew and Christian Testaments.

> _"Alas, poor Hebrew Prophets, I knew all of you because you were human just like me. Then the last one was mythologized, placed on a large marble monument and Deified, such that, who he really was, I can hardly see!"

Come with me to the next portion and join in the search for the REAL Yeshua and what he REALLY taught. Then, come and experience the errors, mistakes, reworked legends and myth making, woven into the Bible. Maybe we can re-assemble a WAY out of people's confusions and dissentions.

Before you turn the page, there is just one thing that has to be cleared up. We humans are born with the need to belong. When we look for meaning and companionship we will always choose a person or a community that shows us acceptance and affection no matter what their or our fundamental belief structure is. It is at that time, place of community and companionship when God meets us as we are. Don't you ever forget God's love for us, all of us!

OK, Helmets on, sword in hand and shields poised?

Onward to Chapter Four !!!

CHAPTER FOUR

THE CHRISTIAN TESTAMENT IN ITS CHRONOLOGICAL ORDER OF AUTHORSHIP

Part One: A Little Necessary Overview

For millennia upon millennia humankind has suffered in relative ignorance of any clear meaning to life. Then a little more than three thousand years ago an army of slaves bravely left their captivity under the leadership of an Egyptian Prince. This army of foreigners (called ha-bi-ruw) journeyed over the sands of troubling times and eventually established a country of their own with a set of religious rules and rituals that have remained almost intact to this very day. From out of that nation two thousand years ago, there arose a great Prophet who offered a new WAY to live life. After his crucifixion several of his followers regrouped and began explaining the meaning to life's mysteries. Have you ever paused for a moment to ponder the fact that the existence of Christianity is the result of one single event in history? That's true, you know! That event was the Resurrection. Had it never occurred, those men and women wouldn't have regrouped, re-motivated and re-empowered such that they chose not to return to their mundane existence and chose to bring their experience to the rest of the world.

The miracle of the Resurrection spoke clearly of a new dawn of hope for human understanding and existence. We have a record, albeit, a slightly figuratively written one, of the impact of that singular event. That record is the Christian Testament (C.T.). With a literary style prevalent in that 1st century's culture. This Christian Testament described the remembered teachings of one Yeshua the Carpenter from Nazareth. He, and he alone, proposed a counter-cultural lifestyle that turned the normal way of doing business upside down. He spoke in such simple terms, parables, allegories, metaphors and similes, that no one listening with a clear mind could misinterpret his recommendations. Most simply chose not to believe him. Who he was and what he did and said were authenticated by means of that Resurrection.

The Good News (Gospel) itself had the misfortune of having been written by men who were not eyewitnesses. Historians cannot judge the historicity of those stories because each story cannot be completely substantiated. Especially, when we read that some facts in them are contradicted in another Gospel or Letter. Even though that seems like the bad news, you can work through it by taking it upon yourself to analyze the collection of those acceptable (canonized) 27 books to determine their significance in your own personal life. The task is not an easy one; your mind's eye must weed out the myth to find the man and then discern the meaning. That leads you to face that cross and despair .. until you behold the real truth of that Resurrection, just like those disciples and their followers.

Read the amazing tale in this Christian Testament! It will change your life. However, read it again in its newly arranged chronological order, as it was historically written. Your observations and conclusions will be affected by the nuances and striking differences from what you have been taught or heard. Our objective in this Chapter is to point out these significant differences. You have definitely missed the fuller meaning if you read this Testament in its present canonical order! The reason will become apparent as we examine each book in our recommended sequence found in Appendix U. Please understand that our purpose is to fathom the stages of Christianity's historical development among the various communities of the people who received the message from the Apostles.

Understand further that the writings in the Christian Testament reflect the cultural beliefs within the literary style of their authors. The one that comes to mind is Paul's writing that God established the order of authority in the local communities (first letter to the Corinthians Chapter 12, verse 28—written 1 Corin 12: 28 for short). It's fairly obvious that Paul set it up yet he assigned the responsibility to God (a commonly used ploy to give it authenticity). You've already seen the seven-day cycle in Genesis 1 that gave authenticity and authority to the day of rest -- the Sabbath! {Of course, you now know that the Exodus was the time and place in which a day of rest was first established and that Genesis, written centuries after the Exodus just emulated the seven-day sequence in its first creation myth!} The point is that one needs to be critical of these C.T. readings because the authors were writing faith stories, not necessarily accurate history. History has already shown that other cultures older than Israel recognized the four periods of the Moon and its 28-day cycle!

OK, that was the good news! Now here's the not-so-good news. Unfortunately, it comes in two parts:

A: The first observation is related to the mindset of the Christian authors. Let's state this in another way. The writer's mindset consisted of the following perceptions (enculturation, cognitive development and psychological profiles, from Chapter One):

- That every word written in the Hebrew (Old) Testament (H.T.) was a tape-recording of God's direct dictation to those writers. Incidentally, that biblical book (H.T.) in use by the Christian communities in the 1st century throughout the Roman Empire was the Septuagint, a Greek translation performed in Alexandria about 270 BC;

- That the Hebrew Testament was a collection of books that were, by definition, absolutely factual in identifying the people in the stories (they were believed to have been real people) and its portrayal of history and scientifically accurate, including all of the conversations;

- That the Christian Testament writers knew the end result of the "Jesus the Christ" story (called a Backward-Looking literary style);

- That these Christian writers correlated their stories with the Hebrew Testament to show that God was fulfilling those alleged predictions relating to a David-like, Messianic fulfillment which was, of course, Jesus the Carpenter from Nazareth;

- That the writers not only had not experienced the historical Jesus but also got their information from second, third and even fourth generation Christians in written and/or oral form. The exceptions are the books of James, 1st Peter, Jude and John's letters.

As it turns out, what we've just written above is a perfect description of a Literalist! Now, that produces a significant slant on all the writings in the Christian Testament, doesn't it? Well, we'll need to reconsider this and re-interpret these first century writings to show the effect on that which was passed on to this 21st century.

B: The second observation is that today we have access to hundreds of writings from the first century's early Christian biblical and theological world. These writings have prompted the scholarly community to wonder whether Christian doctrines and dogmas of the first few centuries were a correct reflection of who Jesus was (later we will explain why his real Aramaic name was Yeshua) and what he, Yeshua, said and did. Therefore, after re-examining certain parts of the Christian Testament, we will point to some peculiar contradictions and inconsistencies demanding further critical analysis.

Do you think that these two discoveries, A and B above, produce a significant slant in all of the author's writings? We believe their interpretations were affected and, sadly, distorted the real Yeshua's life and meaning! That opinion leads to the thesis of this Chapter, there is an entirely different doctrinal perspective when one critically reads the Chronological C.T. incorporating our 21st century information. For instance, we are led to the following concerns:

1. Were the Apostles fully knowledgeable about Yeshua's divinity? Unequivocally, NO!

2. What is the authentic Aramaic name of this carpenter from Nazareth. It is Yeshua! Modern English scholars discovered that the letter "J" was introduced to the world more than a thousand years after the Resurrection. Hebrew has no "J"; Greek also had no "J". And neither did Latin. So, what was his real name? It was "yod-shin-wav-he" in Hebrew/Aramaic. Those letters are "y-sh-w-ah" without vowels. In the sixth century the Massoretes added vowels to the Hebrew alphabet by means of a sophisticated pointing system to preserve the commonly accepted vowel soundings. With these newly assigned vowels the name becomes Yeshua (with or without the letter "h" at the end, but since it is parallel with Joshua, we prefer to leave out the "h".). Now, the corollary to this is that all the words beginning in "J" in the King James Version (1611 AD) must now begin with "Y" in order to be authentic. Words like, Joshua must now be Yoshua; Jericho must now be Yericho; Jerusalem must be Yerusalem. We're sorry to give you this information but that's the way it was! We prefer the use of Yeshua in our prose but will continue to use Jesus when quoting the Bible.

3. When pushed for a response by his disciples, Yeshua replied that he was only, *bar enash,* a son of a man – an Aramaic phrase meaning a "human being".

For you "do it yourself" scholars, see the 1976 Concordance by Strong: the Hebrew Section #606 and #1247. Three problems come to mind:

- The first is that this phrase means a simple human being, "a son of a human";
- The second is that this expression is used in Daniel in the phrase, "like a human being on a cloud". That second interpretation is loaded with all sorts of "end time" theology (eschatology)!
- The third arose when translated into Greek; the literal idiomatic "*bar enach*" (son of a human) became a three-word Greek title, *huios ho anthropos*, the son of man (a human). The Greek became a title!

Thus, as it has been written: "The translator becomes a traitor!" This Greek translation contributed to the confusion by not preserving the intent or connotation of the Aramaic phrase. Today, there are biblical scholars who are attempting to retrofit the nature of the man of history, Yeshua, and clarify whether he refers to himself as that man riding the cloud or as a simple human being. Then again, did Yeshua actually say those words or did the authors put them on his lips? The Nicene Creed (~350 AD) voted for the cloud rider but the Chalcedon doctrine (451 AD) defining Yeshua's humanity voted for the human being. Score tied! Nobody's dogma can solve our confusion. You can already guess what the tension is between what a literalist believes or a modernist can rationalize. The real question is; what did Yeshua believe? And, that, dear Reader, will never be answered. We can examine the Gospels but they are tainted because they are "Backward-Looking" FAITH stories in which the authors already had a fixed mindset about who Yeshua was, and is, for them! The argument will live its own life until we meet the One who really knows ... absolutely. And, that won't happen for quite some time, that's for sure!

While planning the remainder of this Chapter, a light came on! Most readers will have read or heard the major portions of the Christian Testament and will, by now, be well versed. [Nice pun!] With that in mind we would just like to present a few items that may have eluded the average believer. This for the sake of pointing out some traps and pitfalls, namely, the literalist's position within the Christian Movement:

1. No one can miss the fact that Paul, also a literalist, was a terrific organizer. He wrote that God (the Puppeteer!) assigned to the local communities the following pecking order (found in 1st Corinthians Chapter 12: verse 28, whose short form is 1 Corin 12: 28)

   > *"And God has appointed in the church first apostles, second prophets, third teachers, then workers of miracles, then healers, helpers, governor {administrators}, speakers in various kinds of tongues."*

   The Greek word, *kubernesis*, is translated as (a) "administrators" in the Revised Standard Version, (RSV), (b) "forms of leadership" in the New Revised Standard Version (NRSV) and (c) governor in the New American Bible (NAB). This administrator is the second from the bottom in the list of responsible authorities in the passage above. {Note, the speaker in tongues is last, but there are a few present day denominations in which the tongue speakers run the show!} In the local Christian communities around the late 60's AD, the administrator's Greek name was changed to *episkopos,* overseer or bishop. By the time Constantine conscripted the Christian leaders to run the judicial system in his empire, the *episkopos* had climbed to the top of Paul's ladder and were called Patriarchs! You see, Constantine conscripted those Church leaders to be the Supreme Court officials of his Empire:

Constantine planted the seeds for a future Church-State. {Does the book, The Peter Principle, ring a bell?} In our present century that Episcopal person is the local "district manager" in charge of everything from the teachings to the tokens and the tariff (administrative collector) within that Christian denomination. Some denominations have a Senior Bishop or Archbishop leading the flock and some have a hierarchy like an ancient kingdom model straight out of the medieval ages and clothed in the finest, expensive medieval costumes one can procure. The point is that this hierarchical model derives from Paul's list in his Epistle. Paul organized those assignments to achieve some sort of order and civility in the local community's operations. Unfortunately, God did not dictate that kind of order nor did Yeshua desire that type of community. Even the Buddha defined religion's six stages: Authority, ritual, explanations (doctrines), tradition, grace and mystery. (See Houston Smith's book, World's Religions.) Well, like many thoughts in this book, it's only our research and personal perceptions. And you know how much coffee that will buy! Besides, Institutionalism means rules and regulations that usually stifle spirituality. An in-depth examination of the Gospels (Chapter Seven) hints that Yeshua had no specific directions to the Apostles and disciples to start any formal institution. Rather, only Matthew was tuned in to an authoritative dictatorship (Matt 16: 17-20). As a matter of fact, one can say that the majority of these afore-mentioned communities were definitely influenced by Paul and were definitely Pauline in doctrine and government.

2. The 27 books of the Christian Testament were chosen from the plethora of material to reflect what the official leaders believed to be an acceptable account of the life and times of the Carpenter from Nazareth. Those 27 books were compiled and approved (canonized—made acceptable) by normative Christian Officials that were known then as the Catholic Church. It is essentially the only C.T. Canon in circulation today which when added to the Septuagint (the Greek translation of the Hebrew Text) forms today's Catholic Bibles, the New American Bible (NAB) and the New Jerusalem Bible (NJB). However, there are many more writings, Gospels and Epistles, which were not approved by the early Church authorities (~ 400 AD). Therefore, one must understand that all the writings about Yeshua and his disciples were circulating throughout the Mediterranean Basin for the previous 300 years. Note carefully, not every community had all the documents; most had but a few, some of the future canonical and many of the rejected writings. Because of that situation, each Christian community had developed its own idea about the nature of this Prophet from Nazareth based solely on the literature available to them and the stories brought to them by traveling missionaries—the Oral Tradition.

3. Who the historical Yeshua was has been discussed, debated and re-analyzed ever since Yeshua entered the prophetic scene with his first preaching. And, mind you, that discussion is alive and very actively pursued today in the forum of the group known as the "Jesus Seminar" (a membership of more than 100 scholars from most every denomination of Christianity and then some). Needless to say, much confusion existed back then in the 4th century (the 300's) because all of the

Christians and their leaders were "literalists". That alone caused sufficient confusions, which have continued, up to and including this 21st century. A chasm now exists between Literalists and Modernists concerning the physical and spiritual nature of this Teacher from Galilee whose core preachings are presently identified as that "Jesus Movement" (as opposed to the "Christian Movement" initiated by the Apostles, but particularly by Paul). The fourth century was indeed a very trying period for Christianity's official leaders whom Constantine early on (312 AD) had conscripted to be the judicial officers of his empire. In a good way, Constantine required Christianity to clean up its act. In another not-so-good way, Church and State became intimately entwined and inseparable for the next 1400 years until nipped in the bud first by Martin Luther followed by the French and the American Revolutions.

Well, wasn't that a brief revealing history lesson? Small wonder why these United States of America wanted nothing to do with a Church-State government in charge of and legislating policies for the people. Yet, there is much Christianity in our Declaration of Independence, Bill of Rights and Constitution!

Part Two: Two Recommended Solutions

We are proposing two very significant solutions to those troublesome problems.

1. The first one is that the Gospels were actually composed by five separate and theologically distinct communities that can be confirmed in the writings of those five major authors.

2. The second solution involves re-reading and re-analyzing the 27 books in their CHRONOLOGICAL ORDER, the order in which they were written and distributed.

The basis for these derives in part from the Jerome Biblical Commentary. It analyzed the letters of the New Testament in its correct order but placed the four Gospels first. That in itself was a grievous mistake because Paul's Epistles were written some 30 years prior to the writing of Mark, the first Gospel. Paul's letters contain a photocopy of the basic teachings of the Apostles and, as such, they establish the approximate contents of "what the Apostles handed down" to the Christian communities during the first 37 years after the Resurrection. What Paul wrote is authenticated in three separate passages in the book of Acts that we will discuss a little later.

Section One: The Five Distinct Christologies of Yeshua

First, let's delineate who those authors were; here's that list:

(1) **Paul** (40-67 AD) who is the first one to write about the Christian movement, who proselytized the Mediterranean Countries under Roman control;
(2) **Mark** (65-70 AD) the alleged author of the first canonical Gospel put to pen; he is believed to be a disciple of Paul;
(3) **Matthew** (68-80 AD) the alleged author of that Gospel was a Christian of Jewish nationality;
(4) **Luke** (70-80 AD) a person of Greek nationality and a physician who was a disciple of Paul; and finally,
(5) **John** (90-100 AD) who is suspected to be the beloved disciple (not actually proven); who may have written (also not proven) the skeletal version of the

Fourth Gospel along with four other contributing authors who made significant additions. We'll present a very different commentary of that Fourth Gospel in Ch 6.

These authors lived in different communities and were directly and indirectly responsible for the five major Christological Moments in the first century. A Christological Moment is the time that each author pointed to when Yeshua was promoted to Messiahship (son of God, King and Anointed One). We have identified these Moments as follows:

a. Messiah/Divinity at the Resurrection: During the Apostolic Period—from ~33 AD to ~67AD, the Resurrection up to Paul's death. See Rom 1: 1-4, Acts 2: 36, Acts 5: 30-32 and Acts 13: 30-33.
b. Messiah/Divinity at the Baptism: in Mark's Gospel —from 67 AD to about 80 AD (but prior to the appearance of Matthew's and Luke's Gospels). See Mk 1: 9-11.
c. Messiah/Divinity at the Conception: Matthew (IIIA) and Luke (IIIB)—about 80 AD to about 95 AD (but particularly before the Fourth Gospel was written). See Mt 1 and Lk 2, their respective Infancy Narratives.
d. Messiah/Divinity from Eternity: The Post Biblical Period—starts with the appearance of the Fourth Gospel. See Jn 1: 1-18.

Each of these Periods represents the Gospels author's opinion about the time at which Yeshua received the title of Messiah. This title, Messiah, implies the following directly from the H.T.: Anointed One (*mashiyach* in Hebrew, Strong's 4899), King, Son of God, Savior, etc. They are all titles of the Israelite Kings. However, not until the writing of the Fourth Gospel was the title, Son of God, considered to mean equality with God (for some Christians is still doesn't!). Note carefully, Messiah does not actually mean "the Son" of God. But, when the canon was established with the Gospels up front and read first, it became the common understanding that Messiah was equivalent to "the Son" of God and not "a son" of God as in Gen 6. The Nicene Creed (312 to 350 AD) dogmatized the equality to God.

In the Apostolic Period (I) Yeshua was preached to have been "raised from the dead by God and then given the title of Messiah by means of the Resurrection" (Romans 1: 3-4). In other words, God raised Yeshua and, in the raising, God certified that Yeshua was God's real messenger. It was God's way of authenticating Yeshua's ministry as the true WAY of living a whole and holy life. Remember, the concept of a future King (Davidic Messiah) to return Israel to its former glory was a deep Israelite cultural expectation that grew out of the suffering during the Babylonian Exile (587 to 539 BC). We will rest our case on (a) Romans 1: 3-4 (the earliest teaching) and on (b) three passages in Luke's Acts that are recollections of the early teachings handed down by the Apostles: Acts 2: 36, Acts 5: 30-32 and Acts 13: 30-33.

In the Baptism Period (II) Yeshua was preached to have received the title of Messiah at John's Baptism (when the words from the voice spoke the coronation formula of Psalm 2). This occurred because Mark's theme was about a Messiah who had a secret. If Yeshua didn't know who he was, then he couldn't have a secret! And Mark's proposed secret was that Yeshua learned that he was the Messiah at his baptism, but wasn't going to tell anyone until later in that Gospel. In our commentary one can examine all this with a critical eye and easily discover Mark's theme.

Some real questions immediately come to mind!

(a) Did Yeshua get his title at the Resurrection or at his Baptism?
(b) Did Mark's community nearly 40 years after the Resurrection forget what Paul wrote in Romans? Actually Mark could not have known what Luke wrote in Acts.
(c) Or did Mark formulate his own Christological Moment (the moment when Yeshua knew who he was—the Messiah of God)?
(d) Did Mark's community believed it to be at the Baptism and Mark simply constructed a beautiful story about that belief?

Our personal choice and interpretation is (c) and (d).

In the Conception Period (III) two different communities believed that Yeshua was made Messiah (and all the Kingly Titles thereby implied) at conception, sometimes referred to as the Annunciation. So we have III A and III B because of the difference in the Infancy Narratives with their conflicting genealogies, trip to Egypt and hometowns of Mary and Joseph (they are all tricky deductions that we will analyze in Chapter Five). Additionally, Matthew's allegorical thread is that Yeshua was a new Moses while Luke's thread was that Yeshua was a new and the final prophet in the style of the Old Testament prophets.

To make matters worse, the Fourth Gospel initiates the Eternal Period (IV) in which Yeshua is proclaimed to have been the Son of God, equal to God even before the Big Bang, existing and equal to God from eternity. OK, how frustrating can this puzzle be? The Fourth Gospel contradicts the previous writings. Is this a mess or what?

So, tell me now, which of the four Christological Moments is correct? Was it the Resurrection, Baptism, Conception or from Eternity? It's not logical that this Bible contradicts itself ... after all, do not people believe that it's the Word of God, inerrant in all matters? Is that what's at stake here? Is there an answer? Yes! Can we straighten this out? Yes! We'll present our perceptions here in this Chapter and any additional correctives in Chapter Five.

This, now, is exactly the nature of our thesis: there were five separate communities that evolved four different Christological Moments. It happened because there was little to no communication between communities and each community possessed only a few, if in fact they had any, canonical writings but they had many apocryphal (rejected in 400 AD) Gospels and Epistles. By the year 70 AD Bishops were guarding their flocks from false missionaries (see 1 Tim 6: 3-5). They were isolating themselves and justified that posture by claiming to be hanging onto "what the Apostles had handed down" to their community. After close to 40 to 60 years following the Resurrection, who really remembered exactly, word for word, what the Apostles handed down? We will see that Paul's writings were not only confusing but also were the major fuel igniting these problems from the very first Epistle to the last, but, especially the Letter to the Romans.

I. The Apostolic Period: The Man Yeshua, Messiah at the Resurrection

It is known that Paul did write the majority of his Epistles; however, his disciples wrote several of the latter ones. Those that were written in this period are listed in Appendix U. These will, in parts, parrot the teachings of the Apostles. The problem for

Paul is his flowery and often-poetic language that, at times, embellishes what he has heard from the leaders and Christians in the period between his own epiphany and the beginning of his ministry. And, do not underestimate the fact that Paul was a Pharisee, highly educated for his time and knowledgeable about the Hebrew Testament. Our commentary will try to highlight the verses that corroborate his agreement with those Apostolic teachings. In additions, we will point out any other significant teaching that originates from Paul.

It should be obvious that the Pauline Churches believed what Paul taught. Before we proceed too far down the road, there is one word that appears to have been mistranslated in the 1611 AD King James Version (KJV) of the Bible. The Greek word is "didache" which means a teaching; the KJV used the word "doctrine" that implies a harder meaning. We must be a bit more careful from now on when we read the word "doctrine" when it points to that which Yeshua preached. In Paul's letter to the Romans you will find his fundamental teaching that is in complete agreement with that handed down by the Apostles, as documented in Luke's Acts. This is without a doubt a very important teaching concerning Yeshua whom Paul preaches. In Romans 1: 1-4, we can read (from the following five Bible translations) what Paul wrote to testify to his concurrence with the Apostolic teachings regarding Yeshua's appointment to Messiahship, known as the Christological Moment:

King James Version (KJV):

> Paul, a servant of Jesus Christ, called to be an apostle, separated unto the gospel of God, (Which he had promised afore by his prophets in the holy scriptures,) Concerning his Son Jesus Christ our Lord, which was made of the seed of David according to the flesh. And declared to be the Son of God with power, according to the spirit of holiness, by the resurrection from the dead.

New King James Version (NKJV):

> Paul, a servant of Jesus Christ, called to be an apostle, separated unto the gospel of God, (Which he had promised afore by his prophets in the holy scriptures,) Concerning his Son Jesus Christ our Lord, which was made of the seed of David according to the flesh; And declared to be the Son of God with power, according to the spirit of holiness, by the resurrection from the dead:

Revised Standard Version (RSV):

> "Paul, a servant of Jesus Christ, called to be an apostle, set apart for the gospel of God. which he promised beforehand through his prophets in the holy scriptures, the gospel concerning his Son, who was descended from David according to the flesh and designated Son of God in power according to the Spirit of holiness by his resurrection from the dead, Jesus Christ our Lord."

New Revised Standard Version (NRSV):

> Paul, a servant {Gk [slave]} of Jesus Christ, called to be an apostle, set apart for the gospel of God, which he promised beforehand through his prophets in the holy scriptures, the gospel concerning his Son, who was descended from David according to the flesh and was declared to be Son of God with power according to the spirit {Or [Spirit]} of holiness by resurrection from the dead, Jesus Christ our Lord,

New American Bible (NAB):

> Paul, a slave of Christ Jesus, called to be an apostle and set apart for the gospel of God, which he promised previously through his prophets in the holy scriptures, the gospel about his Son, descended from David according to the flesh, but established as Son of God in power according to the spirit of holiness through resurrection from the dead, Jesus Christ our Lord.

There are several points to be examined because (1) each Bible translation contains what appears to be an accurate translation of the same Greek text, but (2) when it comes to a Greek word for an English word, there are significant different theological connotations. An obvious one is the mis-translation of the Greek word, *euaggélion*", which literally means "good message" or "good news". The word Gospel is a 1611 AD translation! In the first phrase in the KJV and NKJV Bibles use the word "separated" while the others write, "set apart". The meaning in the KJV translation is not only awkward but we consider it actually misleading. The KJV and NKJV use "the seed" which implies that David is the biological father of Yeshua while the RSV, NRSV and NAB use "descended according to the flesh" which means from the Davidic genetic line. Does one have to be a scholar to recognize that the KJV and its modern descendents are not quite up to a translational par with the other Bibles? Finally, the use of "the" resurrection in the KJV as opposed to the "his" resurrection in the RSV, yet neither "the" nor "his" is in the NRSV and NAB. Now, PLEASE tell me that you see that there's something suspicious in the KJV and NKJV translations. Well, those are minor points but there are some others that will be coming up that are truly mis-translations of theological significance! Therefore, the NAB and the NRSV are our recommended Bible translations because they have both historical and theological introductions to each book; they use modern English and their translation are recent. However, in the NAB there are a few incorrect English words present only because of doctrinal and dogmatic requirements by that authorizing Institution. My other choice, the NRSV, has a modern English word for each Hebrew or Greek word. Both of those are the better of the bunch. Of course, you have another choice, if you read Biblical Hebrew and Koine Greek, then, by all means, purchase (or download) copies of the originals and understand that you'll have to sort out which of the several original texts will suit your interests best. It "ain't" an easy, simple world out there, is it? So, back to our theme, five different Christologies of which the bottom line is that Paul is in agreement with Apostolic teachings. But what are those teachings?

Before we leave this part, can you decide just who the "spirit of holiness" is? Remember, it is the same phrase that appears in Isaiah 63: 10-11 and in Daniel (NAB). It's the ONE GOD! Therefore, the earliest, up to 70 AD, Apostolic teaching was that God raised Yeshua and appointed certain titles to Yeshua, titles Yeshua did not have previously..

Continuing, let's revisit the following Hebrew Testament facts. Now, understand this, there are no capitol letters in biblical Hebrew. The King of the Israelites is confirmed (with an oil bath) by the words of Psalm 2 and called the Anointed One (which is *mashiyach* in Hebrew and *Christos* in Greek); he is viewed as God's representative—a son of God. Then, in the Hebrew Testament angels are referred to as "sons of God" or "sons of Heaven" (pointed out in the previous Chapter). Well, for that matter, humans are also spoken of by the term "sons and daughters of God". Those titles and facts will be very important when we examine the titles that the Christian Testament applied to Yeshua in later writings.

Now, let's look at that passage by Paul in Romans. He states right up front in 1: 1-4 by writing that he preaches exactly what the Apostles preach, so the Roman community can trust him. And later we will see in Phil 2: 8-9 that Paul stated the same truth (God gives Yeshua the NAME above every name). It is important too that you understand that Paul says that Yeshua is now the Anointed One, the Messiah, and can also be called "son of God **in** power", like the Israelite Kings are so titled. Most importantly, Paul states that this title was bestowed by God at the Resurrection. Now here is the proof! The very same statements of God's bestowing onto Yeshua those identical titles (and a few similar ones) are confirmed by an examination of three more passages found in the Acts of the Apostles (written by Luke). They are recollections of what the Apostles handed down!

In the Acts of the Apostles (80-85 AD) Luke states the very same doctrine written by Paul in Romans and Philippians; these in Acts are presented in the following selections:

> **Acts 2: 36** *"Therefore let the whole house of Israel know for certain that God has made him both Lord and Messiah, this Jesus whom you crucified."* [Note: from the Greek text, "Messiah" should be translated as "the Christ"]
>
> **Acts 5: 30-32** *"The God of our ancestors raised Jesus, though you had him killed by hanging him on a tree. God exalted him at his right hand as leader and savior to grant Israel repentance and forgiveness of sins.."*
>
> **Acts 13: 30-33, 37** *"But God raised him from the dead, and for many days he appeared to those who had come up with him from Galilee to Jerusalem. These are (now) his witnesses before the people. We ourselves are proclaiming this good news to you that what God promised our ancestors he has brought to fulfillment for us, (their) children, by raising up Jesus, as it is written in the second psalm, 'You are my son; this day I have begotten you.'"* **...**
> *37 "But the one whom God raised up did not see corruption".*

So, the Apostolic Christian communities believed that God raised Yeshua from the dead and God then anointed Yeshua with the titles, Messiah, Son of God, Lord, King, gave Yeshua Power, and made Yeshua both leader and savior. All those are titles of an Israelite King, a human person, but were given or bestowed on Yeshua by means of and at the time of the Resurrection. The only conclusion one can logically make about this is that before 67 AD the major Pauline Christian communities believed that Jesus was totally human and then was promoted to the position of a divine being (like an Angel) at the Resurrection but was NOT considered to be eternally equal to God!

We do hope that this assertion doesn't shock you too severely. Stop and take a deep breath and gather your intellectual composure and slowly re-read all of the above material from your Bible. Confirm what was written here because it is actually quite simple and an uncompromisingly correct interpretation of those four quotations!

In a few pages we will examine the writings of Paul, James and Peter: In their writings we will experience a gradual incorporation of those titles in the individual letters as Christianity aged. First, however, we will take a brief peek at what the other authors said about their community's belief. Now, once a community formally accepts a particular position or belief, that belief becomes "doctrine".

II. The Baptism Period: The Man, Yeshua, Messiah at the Baptism

Mark's community may have been leaning more towards a human Yeshua whose family thought him a bit out of his mind (Mk 3: 20-21 which will be found in the commentary on Mark's Gospel). In spite of that, Mark's Gospel puts the moment of Messiahship at the baptism of Yeshua. We know this because of Mark's use of the coronation formula from Psalm 2 during the baptism of Yeshua, administered by John the Baptist. In Mark you can read:

> **1: 9-11** *"It happened in those days that Jesus came from Nazareth of Galilee and was baptized in the Jordan by John. On coming up out of the water he saw the heavens being torn open and the Spirit, like a dove, descending upon him. And a voice came from the heavens, "You are my beloved Son; with you I am well pleased."*

Once again the use of a paraphrased Psalm 2 is evidently the moment of appointment to Kingship, Messiahship and the other title, son of God, just like they are used for the anointing of the Kings in Hebrew Testament times. Of course, Mark throws in a few elaborations (metaphors) to make his point: "the heavens opening" and "the Spirit, descended". The phrase "the heavens opening" is quite similar to a lightning strike or a bright light that you may have read about previously in Paul's epiphany. The phrase "the Spirit, descended" could be a metaphor for God's gift of awareness (knowledge) and the Spirit definitely refers to God's Spirit as we shall see in our commentary on Romans 8: 9-16 later on in this Chapter. Since Mark wrote in the 70's the single term "Spirit" was frequently used to represent either the "Spirit of God" or the "Spirit of Yeshua" depending upon the textual construct. Scholars suspect that Mark's theme of the "Messiah with a secret" led him first to making Yeshua aware of his being the Messiah and therefore gradually letting it out to the Disciples over the 16 Chapters of his Gospel. These instances will be identified as we comment on his Gospel.

III. The Conception Period: The Man, Yeshua, Messiah at Conception

Keep in mind that the term Messiah carries with it the other titles of the King of Israel, son of God, Anointed One, Savior, etc. At this point in history, Messiah still doesn't mean Divinity in the sense of equality with God.

In opposition to Mark, both Matthew and Luke (80-90 AD) give the titles of son of God and Messiah at the Annunciation to Mary (within their birth narratives). That is a totally different doctrine ascribed to by the communities of Matthew and Luke. Now, we have three different interpretations about the time of Yeshua's anointing! When we examine the details of each of these two Gospels we will take notice that, in Matthew, Yeshua is looked upon as the new Moses and Luke considers Yeshua the new and final prophet. Even though they assign son of God at the same instant, Matthew and Luke differ in several areas that make us identify Matthew as the IIIA community and Luke as the IIIB community. These differences will be discussed in Chapter Five when we try to synchronize their Infancy Narratives. Well, the Messianic Moment issue may (or may not!) have been resolved here. We have reported three different moments and thereby discovered a significant inconsistency, that is, if one considers the Word of God to be historically correct and true in every aspect of the two Testaments, in other words, the True "Words of God" -the Literalists position.

IV. The Eternal Period: Yeshua Eternally Divine

The plot thickens further when we read in the Fourth Gospel (1: 1-2) that Yeshua is the Son of God even before the "Let there be light!" in Genesis 1---the Big Bang.

John 1: 1-2 *In the beginning was the Word, and the Word was with God, and the Word was God. He was in the beginning with God.*

The problem with the Fourth Gospel is that there may have been four other contributors who made significant additions to the original. The first 18 verses in Chapter 1 were apparently a later addition written by another author, maybe not a disciple of John. (That posture is discussed in Raymond E. Brown's Commentary on the Gospel of John, a Two Volume work in the Anchor Bible Series.) This puts a very high Christology on the historical Yeshua especially since this Gospel was written some 60 plus years after the Resurrection. This novel definition written by a person who never experienced the human Yeshua makes for a very suspicious theology, to say the least.

Chapter One of this Gospel starts with a play on the Greek term "Logos", "word" in English. God's spoken words in Genesis possessed the miraculous power that created the Universe. Yeshua's "Words and Deeds" in the Gospels were the miraculous revelation of the Nature of God. One author called Yeshua, "The Human Face of God"! Sounds similar to Sri Krishna as the physical manifestation of Brahman in the Bhagavad-Gita!

The first Chapter of the Fourth Gospel contains a theology of "the Christ" that heretofore was not found in any other written source. That author is presently believed NOT to have been John the Apostle nor is there any confirmation that this John was the Beloved Disciple! The style and vocabulary of the first 18 verses is not that of a fisherman; it is that of a refined scholar of the Greek language. That Christology (the study of Yeshua's Nature and Messiahship) emanated from a fifth and different Christian community. It was an addition by that community's spokesperson. If you find this extraordinary, then, you'll have to read Raymond E. Brown's two-volume commentary on the Fourth Gospel for yourself. {Note: Father Brown was the Chairman of the Pontifical Biblical Commission for the Roman Catholic Church.}

The remainder of the Fourth Gospel portrays Yeshua as a Divine Being in possession of absolute knowledge, in total control of his life and death. This knowledgeable person is the quintessential Gnostic hero. That comparison almost kept this Gospel out of the Canon! But since the Bishops were Literalists, it made it into the Canon in the 5th century. There will be more, much more, about this Gospel in Chapter Six.

Another Little Thought

Thus, the five distinctly different postures concerning the nature of the personhood and alleged divinity of Yeshua indicate NOT a slow development by the entire Christian community's common awareness of the nature of Yeshua. Our thesis is that there are five dissimilar Christologies written by five different communities. Recognize, please, these different communities still identified themselves as Christian, whose beliefs developed independently of each other over the 30 to 70 year interval after the Resurrection. They were Christians who accepted the meaning of Yeshua's teachings and were not violently polarized over their Christologies. That violence erupted much later in the second and third centuries. We are convinced that the meaning of Yeshua's teachings should be what unites Christians. Doctrines, dogmas, Institutional regulations and rituals are barriers, not only to one's personal journey but also to the spirituality of each and every denominational community. Those very same doctrines, dogmas, Institutional regulations and rituals inhibit one's respect for the beliefs of all other Christian communities and affect how Christians relate to other religious communities of differing faiths as well.

Section Two: What's Important about a Chronological Reading?

In order to help you understand the actual growth and development of the Christian Movement in those different communities, it will be necessary to analyze the writings in the Christian Testament in the order of their approximate date of publication as a more historical way of reading and understanding these 27 books. The dating used here can be found in part in the Jerome Biblical Commentary and in most of the Introductions to each book found in the New American and New Revised Standard Bibles. Again, please refer to Appendix U. It will aid you in seeing the order and the theological relationships, all on one page!

At the start, please recognize that the Christian Testament contains three types of literature:

(1) the historical Letters (Epistles) written by the various principal leaders;

(2) the Gospels as Faith Statements woven with reconstructed and often fabricated history derived from each author's own community and unique sources. We'll discuss each profile as we comment on each book. Lastly,

(3) the apocalyptical, mythical (as in Appendix M) Revelation, a composite of past and present challenges to, cautions for and sufferings of the Jewish and Christian peoples.

Item 1: The Epistles are considered to be historical with mostly admonitions to the various communities. They contain valuable information about the social mores, religious beliefs and living conditions during Christianity's early years. These Letters speak of conflicts with the traditional hard-line Jewish communities and persecutions by the Roman authorities. We find internal disagreements among the Christians concerning the nature of the organization, interpretations of Yeshua's teaching/doctrines and interpersonal behavior. Well, when you read these Epistles, you too will see the same conflicts in those early years as you currently experience in your own present day personal, social and religious life. Remember too, the authors are LITERALISTS in their interpretations of the Hebrew Testament!

Item 2: The Gospels, on the other hand, are short on history and long on both faith and alleged prophecy in the sense that the New is simply a fulfillment of the Old Testament's mythologized stories (see Appendix M, "The Styles of Mythology"). The events from one Gospel do not always line up with the events of another Gospel and, moreover, the words of Yeshua are the words of the author re-interpreted from the community's remembered meaning of Yeshua's teachings---that's the Oral Tradition. This is especially true in the Fourth Gospel. The Jesus Seminar members, as well as a number of the world's scholars, have concluded, based upon their analysis of the Gospels and the doctrinal history of Christianity, that Yeshua could not have spoken many of the sentences assigned by the Fourth Gospel's writers. The evidence for this opinion will be discussed in Chapter Five when we examine all the recognized conflicts discovered in the Christian Testament in particular and the Bible in general. In addition, we will share our personal re-interpretation of this allegorical Fourth Gospel in terms of its meaning, not its suspicious historicity.

Item 3: The apocalyptic book, Revelation, is altogether another problem. The soothsayers of the 21st century are having a feast on that material. We swear it's like the behavior of a pack of wolves having just discovered a ton of raw meat in the middle of the Artic tundra in mid-winter. There is the wildest profusion of interpretations that are just plain scary. But, any student of history already knows that this fever pitch has occurred several times before and each one was for naught. Personally, that mythical book for the most part speaks to the time period within which it was written and has very little to do with the future. It has the same intent as the Israelite prayerful yearning at the Passover celebrations for a military Messiah, but, in the case of John's Revelation, is referred to as the destruction of the Evil Prince and a future court of Divine Justice.

A few words about the Canonical Text are in order here. A most unfortunate occurrence took place in the fifth century. At that time the Catholic Church was a highly organized Hierarchical Institution. It justified its authority from Matthew 16: 15-19 presented here:

> *15 He said to them, "But who do you say that I am?" 16 Simon Peter said in reply, "You are the Messiah, the Son of the living God." 17 Jesus said to him in reply, "Blessed are you, Simon son of Jonah. For flesh and blood has not revealed this to you, but my heavenly Father. 18 And so I say to you, you are Peter, and upon this rock I will build my church, and the gates of the netherworld shall not prevail against it. 19 I will give you the keys to the kingdom of heaven. Whatever you bind on earth shall be bound in heaven; and whatever you loose on earth shall be loosed in heaven."*

If you wanted the world to comprehend your position of authority, what would you put up front in your literature? You got it! Quote the above-alleged authoritative words of Yeshua and have everyone read them first. The result, Matthew's Gospel comes first in the Canon! Then, put the other biographies of Yeshua next. Follow that with Luke's Acts of the Apostles and then all the letters. Of course, end it with the Super description of the "End Times" predictions of John's Revelation. It's perfectly natural to assemble all your advertising in the way that best portrays your belief structure. And that translates into maintaining power and control over both the Church and the Government of one's Empire. Constantine inaugurated that situation in 312 AD and it prevailed until the collapse of The Roman Petrine Tradition at the time of Martin Luther. Oh, did I mention that absolute power brought the Inquisition, multiple popes in conflict, the Crusades and a spiritual vacuum?

Part Three: Quoting the Christian Testament

Prior to starting the commentary, some mention must be made about taking single verses and contriving an entire theology. Much has been made of Paul's "justification by faith" referenced in Romans 5: 1-2, Heb 11 and Gal 3: 8-10 (See the

Commentary for these passages) while one of the strongest and important postures is in Gal 2: 16 which reads:

> *"16 ... a person is not justified by works of the law but through faith in Jesus Christ, even we have believed in Christ Jesus that we may be justified by faith in Christ and not by works of the law, because by works of the law no one will be justified. "*

The thrust of the Protestant Reformation rested on that and similar passages in Paul's Letters. However, they have been misused to be that one is saved "by faith alone" (as in Hebrews 11) implying that good works are not required. Paul's real statement about works is, "... a person is not justified by works of the law ..." The "works of the law" puts an entirely different spin on the whole matter. Works of the Law are the Ten Commandments, the Deuteronomic rules and the Levitical ritualistic regulations! Everyone already knew that the Israelites did not follow the 10 Commandments! And, for that matter, neither has the rest of the World followed them completely. Notice that in Romans 2:5-7 Paul writes:

> "5. *By your stubbornness and impenitent heart, you are storing up wrath for yourself for the day of wrath and revelation of the just judgment of God, who will repay everyone, according to his works, eternal life to those who seek glory, honor, and immortality through perseverance in good works."*

Therefore, one must understand that "Good Works" is not the same as "works of the Law". When reading the Bible, one must factor in the whole picture! Now, read James' comment about Paul's thesis; James 2: 14-26 gives a different slant to interpreting Paul. We'll present the whole passage when we comment on James' Letter. For now, here is the final verse:

> James 2: 26 *for just as a body without a spirit is dead, so also faith without works is dead."*

Please consider our interpretation about what these two Epistles are trying to say about Faith and good works. Think about this, isn't it that first comes God's knock on our door that can only be opened from the inside of our hearts? Second, do we not choose to accept God's Grace of perfect Love and welcome God into our spirit, our life? If we do accept, then an infusion of Faith follows. And in that spirit of Faith in God and Yeshua, there emerges a natural self-giving in the form of good works towards one's neighbor. This, of course, is just a humble opinion derived from a pursuit of the deeper Biblical meaning. Literalist Christians, or for that matter all religious Literalists, have a theological myopia in their DNA for single verse Biblical quotes. It is a myopia that creates arrogance, distrust and eventually looks upon others as false and evil, only because they differ in their subjective perception of Biblical meanings. Did we all miss Yeshua's words about loving and respecting one's neighbor? Have you ever read that there is any doctrinal, ethnic, color or creedal restrictions to that love and respect spoken by Yeshua? Did you?

There are two major dynamics in the Christian Testament: "Kingdom of God" and "Metanoia". Yeshua preached that one must be a member of the Kingdom of God to be in commune with God. He told his audience that the Kingdom of God was all around and entry was by "metanoia". Metanoia is a Greek word meaning "to change one's mind". That word implied that one had to re-evaluate one's life style and change it to the Way of

God—that enigmatic "righteousness". That word, metanoia, has been mistranslated as repent or repentance, to be sorry. Unfortunately, the word repent is a French word meaning to re-think. So many believers do the "being sorry" thing but never re-think or change their life style.

Peter and Paul in their letters wrote that, "Reading the scriptures (a) is a good thing because they are (b) inspired by God". Well, that's OK as long as you know that it's the Greek Septuagint to which each is referring. You see, it was the Greek text that was distributed throughout the Mediterranean area because Greek was the written and spoken language of that day and every Synagogue had a Greek Septuagint, alone with a Hebrew Torah. In fact that's exactly why the Christian Testament was written in Greek! Therefore, the Septuagint (270 BC) with its apochcryphal books was the authoritative translation of the Hebrew (Old) Testament for the newly formed Greek Christian communities until ~400 AD. When the Old and the New Testaments were translated into Latin (400 AD), Jerome opted to utilize the Hebrew Testament but included the four apochcryphal books from the Septuagint. This Latin translation (Vulgate, meaning common) stood the test of time up to the seventeenth century when the good King James of England decided to authorize a new translation and, strangely, included the apocryphal books that were protected from removal by an edict of death to anyone who did. Today there are more than 25 different translations. Personally, the New American Bible (NAB) and the New Revised Standard Version (NRSV) are much better because of the excellent introductory explanations preceding each book of the Bible. Two scholars (both editors of the Jerome Biblical Commentary) recommended the NAB H.T. translation as the most recently upgraded. The King James Bibles (KJV and NKJV) are the least acceptable because they have many translational errors. But when pushed for a contrasting Biblical viewpoint, we quote the KJV and many of its daughter translations as corroborating material.

Before we leave that paragraph, that (b) in the second line needs some further explanation. Inspired has many implications! It could mean "was energized to write", "what was written contains significant meaning" or "God told the author to write exactly what she was telling the author". It is our scholarly opinion that "inspired" really means the first two implications. However, there are legions of devout believers who only accept the third one. We will defend our position in Chapter Five.

Before we go to each book of the C.T., let's explain a very simple situation that causes a great deal of theological argumentation. There are really two parts to the life and times of Yeshua: the first is labeled the "historical Jesus" and the second is called the "Post-Resurrectional Jesus". According to the Council at Chalcedon in 451 AD, Yeshua was a fully human person. That meant that the authoritative leaders of the Christian movement (the Roman Catholic Church of that period) recognized that Yeshua was exactly as we humans are today, in the flesh, with all our propensities for frailty and, most importantly, ignorance. Some of the writings of the C.T. have not considered Yeshua's humanity in their works because they were trying to convert outsiders to Christianity and wrote what they heard and believed after the Resurrection rather than what they believed about the historical Yeshua. After all folks, the Resurrection was the major thrust producing the FAITH in the Good News. The Gospels and all those letters do contain "Faith" statements and are "Backward-Looking" literature. That means that the authors knew the outcome of Yeshua's life and teachings and were interested only in presenting the meaning of the Resurrection, i.e., their faith story of salvation into eternal life. Therefore, in the decades that followed, when human memory started to fade, a few activities of the Post-Resurrectional Yeshua were inserted into the life of the historical

Yeshua. Talk about confusion! The Divine Yeshua walked on water, underwent the Transfiguration and raised the dead; he probably did a few other things of a very miraculous nature without it being identified as "post-Resurrectional". When the authors mistakenly inserted them into the life of the historical Jesus, what do you think an average reader in the 21st century is going to believe? Then, add the Fourth Gospel's eternally Divine Yeshua to the mix and what results is a human Yeshua having the quality and appearance of an all-knowing God. It does appear that the Gospel authors put the Christological Moment whenever the author thought it necessary to complement his tale: at the Resurrection, Baptism, Conception, or from eternity! And, that makes each Gospel a mythologized work because all four could not have been simultaneously correct; only one is factual, maybe only one and, possibly, none are correct. That's right; maybe no single Gospel is correct! To have been eternally Divine is unquestionably an inherent contradiction to the ignorance and suffering that the human Yeshua experienced!

The Christian Testament is a collection of books about the Resurrected Yeshua (the Christ) and the Good News about salvation in his name as the one human who has been certified by God and raised to divinity according to Ephesians 3: 17-19. Read that passage here!

> *... and that Christ may dwell in your hearts through faith; that you, rooted and grounded in love, may have strength to comprehend with all the holy ones what is the breadth and length and height and depth, and to know the love of Christ that surpasses knowledge, so that you may be filled with all the fullness of God.*

The single most difficult task for Christians of all ages is to digest the last clause of that passage! Think now, what will it be like to "be filled with the fullness of God?" Will it not depend on your perception of WHO God IS, don't you think? Is this what happened to Yeshua after the Resurrection? Yes! In the eyes of his followers, Yeshua was experienced as a Being who possessed the fullness of God! And that was the essence of the Good News! There is a physical eternal life after one's physical existence on Earth ends! Don't you want to be one of those fortunate people? Don't you?

Before we examine the specific books of the C.T. we need to put to rest one more notion of designating one specific person to be the spokesperson for God on Earth and all that he thereby transmits to us pilgrims is an infallible Divine directive. That person is a product of only the Matthean Community and no other! If Peter were granted such authority during the ministry of Yeshua, how come there is no record of any election to replace him after his death, about 67 AD? Opps! Guess what? Nobody was chosen because everyone understood that he wasn't appointed in the first place. Just one more example of selective reading! One might be tempted to make a little pun about that situation by pointing out that Matthew's mis-interpretation is the supreme example of the Peter Principle. But alas, somebody punned it already!

A long time ago during a Christian Testament class, attended with my wife, a priest asked the instructor (a noted scholar) whether Peter was the first Pope. The Instructor stopped his talk, turned toward him and walked across the room right up to within 4 feet of the priest and said, "You are asking the wrong question. You should have asked 'whether there was recorded an election of another person to take Peter's place?'"

Before any other question surfaced, the instructor turned, walked back to his lectern and continued his presentation where he left off without missing a beat. My wife and I suspect that he was not willing to commit to a fuller explanation because, you see, he was a priest teaching in a Catholic College. Two years later, the priest who asked the question resigned his position, left the priesthood, got married and disappeared into a distant community. In retrospect he must have discovered that the Institutional Dogma of Matthew was a perception of a single sect of Christianity. Was that priest's response to that perception a courageous act of liberation, do you think?

Part Four: The Nature of the "Good News"

When the Apostles and disciples first made their announcement of Yeshua's Resurrection, they used the words, "Good News", (actually Paul, in his Letter, 1 Thessalonians 1: 5, uses the Greek word, *euaggelion*, meaning a good message). That phrase implies something very significant! The first of "the Good News" is that Yeshua had risen from the dead. That confirmed the deepest need of all humans --- life has a meaning, here in the NOW and for ETERNITY. All will experience a resurrection. Oh Gosh, maybe not all! The second significant point, there is a compassionate God who has just sent the biggest message to humanity; THERE WILL BE JUSTICE. {A brief note here: be assured, it will be God's Justice NOT Human justice!} The third point is that the teachings of Yeshua are the REAL THING! The Way of God is a personal, self-giving and non-violent response to human evil. The phrase, "the Kingdom of God", was Yeshua's allegory for those who aggressively sought a relationship with God and practiced godly behaviors in their daily lives. In this 21st century we would most likely call that "kingdom", "the Community of God". Therefore, within that community, its members would be aptly described by the Matthean and Lukan Beatitudes. The welcoming doors to God's community were now opened to all of society even, and especially, those falsely labeled by society to be unworthy of membership. This "Good News" heralded a freedom from the traditional religious conduct: ritual sacrifice of animals, circumcision, dietary laws, and cultural-religious definitions of what constitutes clean and unclean living. And, finally, it clarified who were the children of God. The "Good News" turned the "conventional way of doing business" upside down. From that moment on, it was to be "God's Way" or The Hellsway, Guys and Gals! That "Good News" is delineated in Chapter Six and is identified as the "Jesus Movement".

However, we shall see that the "Good News" didn't last very long. Human nature being what it is, a new religion developed in which ritual, doctrine, dogma and legalisms once more took center stage. If one examines the history of Christianity, one soon recognizes the seeds of dissention being planted within 20 years following the Resurrection and one reads all about it in Paul's letters.

It's now time to turn to reading and commenting on the Christian Testament's VERY NEW CHRONOLOGICAL ORDER OF AUTHORSHIP.

Part Five: An Analysis and Reading of the VERY NEW Chronological Christian Testament (The C.C.T.) in its order of Authorship

Section One: Preface

The historical sequence of the appearance of the books of the Christian Testament is in Appendix U. Our first encounter with the idea of a chronological reading and critical examination of the Christian Testament came from our study of the Jerome Biblical Commentary (Editors: Raymond E. Brown, S.S., Joseph A. Fytzmyer, S.J. and Roland E.

Murphy. O. CARM.). Having studied under Fathers Brown and Murphy while in Grad school, we found it necessary to read their work. In addition, John Dominic Crossan's short Internet article, "An Inventory of the Jesus Tradition by Chronological Stratification", convinced us that our approach had merit. [See Appendix R for the URL to Crossan's Article.]

However, it is not our intent to spend a lot of print on each book. If your desire is to have a complete commentary relating to the interpretations contained here, then read the "New Jerome Biblical Commentary" as your first choice or the Anchor Bible Series as your second. And, mind you, that would commit you to about a five-year reading assignment. Better seek out a perfectly secluded cave in which to hide and read! Did we just explain what the biblical game, "hide and seek," means?

For something less consuming there is a list (in Appendix R) of excellent reading materials and inexpensive paperbacks, probably found in your local public library, well worth investing your time picking them up and reading them. There are two special books you may want to consider "must reading": Marcus Borg's, "Meeting Jesus Again for the First Time" and "The God We Never Knew". They would start you off in a good direction.

Well, let's go! Keep in mind that my purpose as a Christian author will be to:

(1) focus on the development of doctrine that will support the interpretation of five separate and independent theological and Christological communities;
(2) point out the significant thoughts contributed by the biblical authors relating to that subject, and,
(3) Present and discuss the many inconsistencies, mistakes and theological misinterpretations (Ch 5) in order to re-build a consistent Biblical message.

In case it has slipped your mind, I am a Christian who believes that the Bible is woven with threads of history remembered yet essentially mythologized. In spite of that, I completely understand that the Bible is primarily a book of meaning, more demanding than its actual alleged history appears to be. Once you see the nature of these five different Christian belief-structures in the early 1st century, you will understand why the denominational varieties in this 21st century exist and, hopefully, you will see them in a different light. The fact is that all Christian communities struggle with their own set of perceived doctrines, no one better than the other, exactly like the 1st century Christian communities. Read on and discover the "way it was" so that today you can understand and respect the "way it is"!

One last note, you should have your Bible (preferably a New American Bible or a New Revised Standard Version) next to you. The King James Versions are certainly not our first choice because they still have several 17th century mis-translations never upgraded to today's English, except, of course, the NRSV. But, that's only our perception. Maybe, just maybe, you'll get to appreciate that viewpoint as you read through these commentaries!

Section Two: The Books of the Apostolic Period (up to 67 AD): One God and the Appointment of the Messiah

1. First Thessalonians (51 AD):

In general, this five–chapter letter is an admonition to the Thessalonians to return to wholeness and an exhortation to stay the spiritual course brought to them by Paul. Can you recognize the primitive doctrines in this letter written about 15 years after the Resurrection? As we proceed through the other books, be alert to the gradual doctrinal shifts in these same topics. Get out your Bible and put it close to you so that you can certify that we are correctly quoting that particular verse, or passages, and the associated verses so that our explanations will make sense. If you are using any other Bible, take care to focus on the meaning of the verse.

Within these verses there are a few important statements by Paul:

1:2 *we give thanks to God always for all of you, remembering you in our prayers, unceasingly*
God is the principal to be thanked and prayed to.

1: 10 and *to await his Son from heaven, whom he raised from (the) dead, Jesus, who delivers us from the coming wrath.*
Jesus has the rank of Lord and doesn't appear to be equal to God in the phrase "*Jesus was raised by God*" as was pointed out above in the passages from Romans and Acts. Also, this same verse echoes Daniel's cloud prediction and the "*coming wrath*" (sooner or later). Take notice of the use of the "wrath" presumably of God, a recognition that God is perceived as a being of reciprocity.

2: 8-9 *With such affection for you, we were determined to share with you not only the gospel of God, but our very selves as well, so dearly beloved had you become to us. You recall, brothers, our toil and drudgery. Working night and day in order not to burden any of you, we proclaimed to you the gospel of God.*
Paul points to the Gospel of God that hints at the primacy of God and the secondary role of Yeshua as God's messenger. So Paul considers that God's Good News represents God's mercy, forgiveness and grace. That's important.

2: 13 *And for this reason we too give thanks to God unceasingly, that, in receiving the word of God from hearing us, you received not a human word but, as it truly is, the word of God, which is now at work in you who believe.*
Paul's use of "*the word of God*" is the belief of a Literalist who believes that God was the voice behind the H.T. and Yeshua's lips. At this point we must refresh your memory of the previous study of the Sacred Scriptures that preceded Yeshua since they proclaimed exactly the same teachings. Is it not reasonable to assume that God was the voice behind the authors of those earlier Sacred Scriptures that proffered the same teachings? You may want to revisit the aphorisms of Buddha in the Dhammapada (in Ch 3).

2: 14 *for you, brothers, have become imitators of the churches of God that are in Judea in Christ Jesus. For you suffer the same things from your compatriots as they did from the Jews,*
The "churches of God" appears again and the anti-Semitic phrase "the Jews" takes on a new meaning because of the disagreements between Orthodox Jews

and Christian Jews in the Synagogues where Paul first preached to the Gentile world. It is interesting that the Greek word for churches is *ekklesia* which means "a calling out" of people to the community. The word, churches, is a seventeenth century translation! The translation of *ekklesia* to churches really misses the "calling out" of people to belong to and interact with the membership of the community of God.

4: 14 *for if we believe that Jesus died and rose, so too will God, through Jesus, bring with him those who have fallen asleep.*
Paul points to God as the driving force in the Resurrection once again.

4: 15 *Indeed, we tell you this, on the word of the Lord, that we who are alive, who are left until the coming of the Lord, will surely not precede those who have fallen asleep.*
Paul expects the second coming to occur in his lifetime, a theme that Yeshua predicts in one Gospel but claims ignorance of its schedule in another Gospel.

4: 17 *Then we who are alive, who are left, will be caught up together with them in the clouds to meet the Lord in the air. Thus we shall always be with the Lord.*
This is a continuation of the thought in v. 15 and thereby originates the folk theology of the "Christians being caught up into the cloud with Yeshua", the Parousia.

5:1 *concerning times and seasons, brothers, you have no need for anything to be written to you.*
Paul's use of "brothers" implies the second-class nature of women. Paul's use of "sisters" occurs much later.

5: 3 *when people are saying, "Peace and security," then sudden disaster comes upon them, like labor pains upon a pregnant woman, and they will not escape.*
There is a prediction relating to the "peace and security" as the principal chant of the people near the end times.

And, finally, 5: 21 "*Test everything, retain what is good*".
And, that is exactly what we are doing right this minute, testing everything, with your reading of this book!

2. Second Thessalonians (52 AD):

1: 4 *accordingly, we ourselves boast of you in the churches of God regarding your endurance and faith in all your persecutions and the afflictions you endure.*
We see the phrase, "*the churches of God*" which for Paul is simply the Greek translation of "*Beth El*", Hebrew for House of God, this being a familiar name for one's local synagogue. But Paul is not referring to a synagogue, he means "the people who are called out to God's new community of believers in Yeshua". Again, *ekklesia* is the Greek word used by Paul. Also, it is easy to understand why many early Christians referred to their organization as "the Church of God" because of the Hebrew "Beth El".

2: 1-2 *We ask you, brothers, with regard to the coming of our Lord Jesus Christ and our assembling with him, not to be shaken out of your minds suddenly, or to*

be alarmed either by a "spirit," or by an oral statement, or by a letter allegedly from us to the effect that the day of the Lord is at hand.
Words of Paul hinting at the proximity of the end times. Note the hint of false epistles implied in the word *allegedly*!

2:3-4 *Let no one deceive you in any way. For unless the apostasy comes first and the lawless one is revealed, the one doomed to perdition, who opposes and exalts himself above every so-called god and object of worship, so as to seat himself in the temple of God, claiming that he is a god*
This is an indirect pointing to the Caesars of Rome.

2: 11-12 *Therefore, God is sending them a deceiving power so that they may believe the lie, that all who have not believed the truth but have approved wrongdoing may be condemned.*
God doesn't do such things! It's a person's free will that chooses evil or confusion. That passage is just one more indication (See 1 Kings 22: 23) of an immature "folk theology" that points to God's perceived controlling role in our life. It is a function of the "Backward-Looking" literary style of that day.

3: 10-11 *In fact, when we were with you, we instructed you that if anyone was unwilling to work, neither should that one eat. We hear that some are conducting themselves among you in a disorderly way, by not keeping busy but minding the business of others.*
Well, it appears that things were the same then as now; times haven't changed much, have they?

3. Galatians (54-55 AD):

This letter is a hot one because it substantiates James as the BROTHER of Yeshua (1: 19), especially since Paul knows the word for cousin (see Col 4: 10). That will, of necessity, give credence to Mark's reference to Yeshua's brothers and sisters. Another important note is that James is the Leader in Jerusalem, not Peter! {That certainly contradicts Matthew (Mt 16: 13-20), doesn't it? More in Ch 5.}

1: 6-9 *I am amazed that you are so quickly forsaking the one who called you by (the) grace (of Christ) for a different gospel (not that there is another). But there are some who are disturbing you and wish to pervert the gospel of Christ. But even if we or an angel from heaven should preach (to you) a gospel other than the one that we preached to you, let that one be accursed! As we have said before, and now I say again, if anyone preaches to you a gospel other than the one that you received, let that one be accursed!*
Denominationalism existed in the early Church community. Sounds just like today's troubles. The real difficulty is, "What exactly did the Apostles hand down?" We'll see the "handed down" stuff in Romans and Acts in a few pages from here. OH, the word for accursed is *anathama* in Greek! That word appears frequently in the Inquisition times.

2: 11-13 *And when Kephas came to Antioch, I opposed him to his face because he clearly was wrong. For, until some people came from James, he used to eat with the Gentiles; but when they came, he began to draw back and separated himself, because he was afraid of the circumcised. And the rest of the Jews*

(also) acted hypocritically along with him, with the result that even Barnabas was carried away by their hypocrisy.
This certainly puts credence to the fact that James was the titular head of Christianity and not Peter

3: 1-29 Paul argues for a faith based Christianity as opposed to "works of the Law" doctrine. We don't always fathom his logic, but do recognize his zeal for "justification by faith". Have you ever wondered what these "works of the Law" allude to in today's world? It may be worthwhile for you to read this Chapter in Galatians.

3: 27-29 *For all of you who were baptized into Christ have clothed yourselves with Christ. There is neither Jew nor Greek, there is neither slave nor free person, there is not male and female; for you are all one in Christ Jesus. And if you belong to Christ, then you are Abraham's descendant, heirs according to the promise.*
Here is poetry in motion. This is the center of Paul's egalitarian understanding of the Jesus Movement: women are equal to men in all things, including apostleship, discipleship, prophecy, teaching, service and administration and speaking in tongues. Unfortunately, the clan mentality of the Middle East resides too deeply in the masculine psyche to accept females as equals. History shows that by the end of the fifth century the ecclesial works of women leaders were erased from the records and that women were not eligible to hold office in the Christian Churches except one of silence and servitude as a deaconess. And that, dear reader, is why the Roman Petrine Curia is so adamantly intolerant of women's right to priesthood! Yes, in spite of there being regulations for deaconesses described in canon law records! Go figure!

4:6 *As proof that you are children, God sent the spirit of his Son into our hearts, crying out, "Abba, Father!"*
There are two very powerful statements, *"God sent the spirit of his son" and "Abba".* I thought that the spirit was the third Christian God! It appears that it was just Yeshua after all. Abba doesn't mean Father; it is Aramaic for "daddy" (the cry of a very young child) which now gives it a decidedly different implication. I prefers "Mommy".

4:9 *but now that you have come to know God, or rather to be known by God, how can you turn back again to the weak and destitute elemental powers? Do you want to be slaves to them all over again?*
Paul is confused. Doesn't God know those people before then? Can you see that Paul is saying that God just now knows those who have accepted His Grace? An interesting confirmation that God changes when a newborn enters the World. God must get to know that new person. Think about it! It's sure to put a chink in someone's perception!

4:13-14 *you know that it was because of a physical illness that I originally preached the gospel to you, and you did not show disdain or contempt because of the trial caused you by my physical condition, but rather you received me as an angel of God, as Christ Jesus.*
This raises a question: is Paul saying that an angel of god is who Jesus was? That's a WOW, for sure. Strong's concordance offers many meanings of "as" but there are two for "like". My goodness, Paul, you may have made a pretty

important statement: Yeshua is like an angel of God which is equivalent to "son of God", but not God, according to H.T. theology!

4: 21-31 Paul is using allegory to explain something of importance. I guess there is myth in the Bible! You may want to re-read this passage and Appendix M again!

5: 13 *For you were called for freedom, brothers. But do not use this freedom as an opportunity for the flesh; rather, serve one another through love*.
"Called for Freedom" is a "free will" statement. The underlined is what James will write about; Faith and Good Works that proceed from the grace of Love. A significant note is required here. In 1904 a writer named Thomas Troward wrote, Liberty without Love is Destruction and Love without Liberty is Despair. Sounds like he caught Paul's point.

5: 19-21 *Now the works of the flesh are obvious: immorality, impurity, licentiousness, idolatry, sorcery, hatreds, rivalry, jealousy, outbursts of fury, acts of selfishness, dissensions, factions, occasions of envy, drinking bouts, orgies, and the like. I warn you, as I warned you before, that those who do such things will not inherit the kingdom of God.*
This is a great description of the 21st century, isn't it?

5: 22-23 *In contrast, the fruit of the Spirit is love, joy, peace, patience, kindness, generosity, faithfulness, gentleness, self-control. Against such there is no law.*
That reads like the Boy Scout law. Take note of "the Spirit". Who is that Spirit? God? Jesus? Welcome to Paul's use of the single word, Spirit, without any clear definition. At this writing he means, the Spirit of God!

6: 5 and 6:7 "5. *for each will bear his own load.*" and "7. *Make no mistake, God is not mocked, for a person will reap only what he sows*".
Paul acknowledges free will again. How John Calvin reached his theology of "pre-destination" is a mystery to us.

6: 16 "*Peace and mercy be to all who follow this rule and to the Israel of God.*"
I think we need this prayer today.

4. Philippians (56-57):

There are three important issues that appear in this Letter: the first is the use of the title, overseer, *episkopos*, in 1: 1. That is the name of our friendly Bishop who has ruled the individual Christian community since the middle of the first century (See Comments on Timothy and Titus for confirmation). The second is the use of the word for deacons and deaconesses, *diakonos and diakonissai*, those male and female servants of the early Christian communities. And lastly, but certainly one of the most controversial bits of confusing theology that Paul has ever penned in 2: 6-11, the hymn to Yeshua the Christ as God's agent in the salvation of humankind. The confusion lies in the interpretation of that hymn after reading the four Gospels. However, reading it before the Gospels reveals nothing more than what Paul will write in Romans 1:3-4 and what appears in Genesis 1 and 2. When we get to Ephesians 3: 17-19, the very same sentence, as in 2:9, below will be expanded further. Mind you, Philippians was written way before the Gospels. So it is evident that the Gospels may have copied what Paul believed and expanded it to something more! That hymn will be deciphered below. Be certain you spend a little extra time with it so that Paul's theology becomes clear. And, please, be sure that you don't muddle it with any argument or justification from the Gospels.

The remainder of this Epistle is typical of Paul and here are several important passages. Because these passages are so theologically loaded, they are quoted with significant words and phrases underlined:

1: 1 *Paul and Timothy, slaves of Christ Jesus, to all the holy ones in Christ Jesus who are in Philippi, with the overseers and ministers:*
These are the bishops and deacons, *episkopos* and *diakonos*. A note below will include female deaconesses!

1: 6 *I am confident of this, that the one who began a good work in you will continue to complete it until the day of Christ Jesus.*
Paul's use of "good works" and his identification of the "last days".

1: 9-10 *And this is my prayer: that your love may increase ever more and more in knowledge and every kind of perception, to discern what is of value, so that you may be pure and blameless for the day of Christ,*
There are four key words here:

Knowledge— information for your intellect, learned through study or experience
Perception— what enculturation, cognition and psyche compel and limit your mind's eye
Discern— what you are able to understanding (a cognitive ability)
Value— what is important and meaningful to you

Do you remember what you read in Chapter One about those very words? There are days when conversing with literalists that we cringe when told that knowledge is Gnostic and therefore evil. Knowledge is NOT evil and anyone who says that flunked out of education in the second grade! Discern and pick what is of value. You do that every day when you go out to purchase anything. Why not do your homework about understanding what the Bible is really about? Always test the person from whom you are learning about the Bible. Literalism is a fog producing intellectual dishonesty.

1: 19 *for I know that this will result in deliverance for me through your prayers and support from the Spirit of Jesus Christ.*
It is important that we recognize that there is a person and that we can talk or write about the spirit of that person and not mean a different being. Again, there is the appearance of the phenomenon of "personification" of an ideal, like, Beauty becoming a person and Love used to define God. Later in Chapter Five we'll discuss the Spirit of God and its synonym from Isa 63:10, the Spirit of Holiness

2: 6-11 This is the famous controversial hymn that begs a longer explanation!
" *Who, though he was (a) in the form of God, did (b) not regard equality with God something to be grasped. Rather, he emptied himself ,(c) taking the form of a slave, coming in human likeness; and found human in appearance, he humbled himself, becoming obedient to death, even death on a cross. Because of this, (d) God greatly exalted him and (e) bestowed on him the name that is above every*

<u>name</u>, that at the name of Jesus every knee should bend, of those in heaven and on earth (f) and under the earth, and every tongue confess that Jesus Christ is (g) Lord, to the glory of God the Father."

(a) This is Paul's way of saying what is in Gen 1: 26 *"Then God said: 'Let us make man in our image, after our likeness'".* Of course most translate the "us" as the Trinity. Sorry folks, it only refers to God and the Angels. Most of Genesis 1 & 2 was written after the Exile!
(b). That means he didn't make himself equal to God like Adam & Eve tried to do in the Garden of Eden when they ate the forbidden fruit (Gen 3:1-13); especially verse 5 *"No, God knows well that the moment you eat of it your eyes will be opened and you will be like gods who know what is good and what is bad."* The word *"grasped"* refers to picking a fruit to cause one's transformation, you know, grabbing and eating a fruit and getting the reward of divinity. And don't jump on the pronouns "us" and "our", those refer to the sons of God or sons of heaven and in some cases they are the familiar editorial forms of writing used by a single person referring to him or herself (like the pronouns, we, us and our, we're using in this book!). It doesn't speak to trinity! It is God speaking to the Angels who are identified as sons of God throughout the H.T.
(c) It means that Yeshua did not want to be worshiped; he chose to serve! Yeshua was human in likeness and appearance just like Adam! Other Sacred Scriptures also referred to humans as slaves of the gods.
(d). This is a repetition of Ro 1:3-4 and
(e). This is exactly what is written in Eph 3: 17-19

> *17 and that Christ may dwell in your hearts through faith; that you, rooted and grounded in love, 18 may have strength to comprehend with all the holy ones what is the breadth and length and height and depth, 19 and to know the love of Christ that surpasses knowledge, so that you may be filled with all the fullness of God.*
> In other words, God gave Yeshua the "fullness of Divinity" but NOT eternal equality.

(f). This is Paul's cultural cosmology along with his comprehension of the location of *Sheol* (the Hebrew word for the place of the dead).

(g) In this case the word "Lord" does not mean God! If it did, then it would contradict (b) above. You may want to review Strong's Concordance for the appearance of the word "Lord", *"adonai"*. It is used interchangeably for master and king. In Hebrew the word *"adonai"* is used whenever YHWH occurs; the Israelite would offend God were he to pronounce the Tetragrammaton.

This entire passage, Phi 2: 6-11, has been so mis-translated because all readings of this Epistle to the Philippians have taken place after reading the Gospels, Acts and the other letters which precede it in the Canonical order. What we are doing now is definitely a simple solution to this complexity. Therefore, it behooves us to continue READING THE CHRISTIAN TESTAMENT IN ITS CHRONOLOGICAL ORDER OF AUTHORSHIP!

Surprisingly, we all may find that many of Christianity's so-called doctrinal and dogmatic postures will disappear! The bottom-line thus far in our reading is that Yeshua is believed to be nothing other than a human person acknowledged as someone very special, Lord, in that he taught Godly truths. There is much evidence that he was murdered because of his preaching of the Kingdom of God and his attack on the moneychangers in the Temple. Paul writes that Yeshua was raised to divinity as a true son of God (that's equal to the angels) and given the name above all names at the Resurrection (Phil 2:8-9 below). Up to this point in our chronological reading, those are the very words and meaning written by Paul! And most importantly, they are the beliefs of the Apostles who approved Paul's ministry. To believe otherwise is somewhat illogical and intellectually dishonest. However, you should know that this whole approach is only our humble opinion, isn't it? If it upsets you, take ownership of your emotions and search your compassionate intellect for a solution you can live with. If your intellectual ulcer persists, consult a qualified Psychologist, but not a minister until you finish this book! Let's continue with Philippians.

> 2: 8-9 *he humbled himself, becoming obedient to death, even death on a cross. Because of this, God greatly exalted him and bestowed on him the name that is above every name,*
> If Yeshua were God eternally, why does God promote him now? This is surely a promotion to divinity with God in much the same way as Eph 3: 17-19 (we will address this quote again later in the letter to the Ephesians). Note carefully, the very same offer is extended to each and every person who imitates the behavior of Yeshua the Christ!
>
> 3:3 *For we are the circumcision, we who worship through the Spirit of God, who boast in Christ Jesus and do not put our confidence in flesh,*
> Here again we see the "Spirit" as that belonging to God, not a third persona.
>
> 3: *9 and be found in him, not having any righteousness of my own based on the law but that which comes through faith in Christ, the righteousness from God, depending on faith*
> There is the tendency here to interpret this as a "Faith alone" theology!

5. 1st Corinthians (Spring 57):

"For the person studying this letter, it seems to raise as many more questions than it answers, but without it our knowledge of church life in the middle of the first century would be much poorer." (From the Introduction in the NAB) You should definitely read this Introduction. Remember, you can read the NAB from the Internet, see Appendix L.

The theological stance of Paul in this letter remains consistent with his previous letters. However, because of the many local problems Paul makes several departures from what he understood about what the Apostles reported Yeshua to have said. There are a few bizarre practices going on in Corinth by those early Christians.

There is no doubt that male dominance is a thriving attitude based on the concerns expressed in this letter in spite of Paul's preaching and teachings at their conversion to Christianity. Seems, they are just like what situations are making the news in this 21st century. The Introduction (in the NAB) conveniently lists these problems that do appear to be similar to our own times (the Chapters listed are from 1 Corin):

"Divisions in the Church, Chapter 3
Moral Disorders, Chapter 5
Marriage and Virginity, Chapter 7
The Lord's Supper, Chapter 10
The Problem of Speaking in Tongues, Chapter ***14***
The Teachings about the Resurrection of the Christ and the Dead as well as the Manners for Christians, Chapter 15"

Pay special attention to your readings in this Epistle!

1:10-12 *I urge you, brothers, in the name of our Lord Jesus Christ, that all of you agree in what you say, and that there be no divisions among you, but that you be united in the same mind and in the same purpose. 11 For it has been reported to me about you, my brothers, by Chloe's people, that there are rivalries among you. I mean that each of you is saying, "I belong to Paul," or "I belong to Apollos," or "I belong to Kephas," or "I belong to Christ."*
Paul writes of the divisive perceptions of people in the early church (seems familiar, doesn't it?). Notice the call to sameness! Could it be that each person listed is preaching his very personal perception of what constitutes Christianity?

1:18-31 For such long passages please read them from your Bible or the Internet.
Paul explains how God, through Yeshua, turned the World upside down by means of the cross, a foolish act to the intelligentsia and arrogant, but sanctifying to the common person; unreal to the rich but rich in grace to the humble. This passage implies that God acted through Yeshua as though God were a Puppeteer pulling all the strings. We would suggest that Yeshua acted out of his own experiences of God in his personal life and from his own observations of life around him. The prophets of old spoke in like manner from within their own experiences of Yahweh. One might just consider that Yeshua knew of the teachings of Buddha because of their similarities to God's messiah through Yeshua. After all, God shows no partiality! See the following:

Jonah 4: 11 *And should I not be concerned over Nineveh;*
Col 3: 23-25 *Whatever your task, work heartily, as serving the Lord and not men, knowing that from the Lord you will receive the inheritance as your reward; you are serving the Lord Christ. For the wrongdoer will be paid back for the wrong he has done, and there is no partiality;*
Eph 6: 9 *Masters, act in the same way toward them, and stop bullying, knowing that both they and you have a Master in heaven and that with him there is no partiality;*
Gal 2: 6 *But from those who were reputed to be important (what they once were makes no difference to me; God shows no partiality)--those of repute made me add nothing;*
Rom 2: 10-13 *But there will be glory, honor, and peace for everyone who does good, Jew first and then Greek. There is no partiality with God. All who sin outside the law will also perish without reference to it, and all who sin under the law will be judged in accordance with it. For it is not those who hear the law who are just in the sight of God; rather, those who observe the law will be justified;*

> ***Luke 20: 21*** *They posed this question to him, "Teacher, we know that what you say and teach is correct, and you show no partiality, but teach the way of God in accordance with the truth;*
> ***Acts 10: 34-35*** *Then Peter proceeded to speak and said, "In truth, I see that God shows no partiality. Rather, in every nation whoever fears him and acts uprightly is acceptable to him.)*
> So, why can't God reveal Her truths to whomever He chooses to offer salvation?

2: 11-14 *Among human beings, who knows what pertains to a person except the spirit of the person that is within? Similarly, no one knows what pertains to God except the Spirit of God. 12 We have not received the spirit of the world but the spirit that is from God, so that we may understand the things freely given us by God. 13 And we speak about them not with words taught by human wisdom, but with words taught by the Spirit, describing spiritual realities in spiritual terms. 14 Now the natural person does not accept what pertains to the Spirit of God, for to him it is foolishness, and he cannot understand it, because it is judged spiritually.*
Here is an important passage because it clearly identifies the Spirit as the Spirit of God, not a partner! Nevertheless, it is confusing in verses 12 and 13 but cleared up in verse 14. At this point in time, there is no conclusive proof that the word "Spirit" means anything other than the "Spirit of God"! Re-read Isaiah 63: 10-11.

3: 16 *Do you not know that you are the temple of God, and that the Spirit of God dwells in you?*
Again, the Spirit of God. But take note of the intimacy of God in us!

5: 9 *I wrote you in my letter not to associate with immoral people, 10 not at all referring to the immoral of this world or the greedy and robbers or idolaters; for you would then have to leave the world. 11 But I now write to you not to associate with anyone named a brother, if he is immoral, greedy, an idolater, a slanderer, a drunkard, or a robber, not even to eat with such a person. 12 For why should I be judging outsiders? Is it not your business to judge those within? 13 God will judge those outside. "Purge the evil person from your midst."*
This illustrates the Hebrew Testament's influence on Paul and the early Christians to isolate the evildoers and purge them from the community. Didn't Yeshua associate with those very people? Yes and no! Yeshua encouraged "metanoia" for those who desired reform but those whom society called sinners were, in fact, mis-labeled. Paul gets persnickety to protect the flock from backsliding into serious evil.

6: 9 *Do you not know that the unjust will not inherit the kingdom of God? Do not be deceived; neither fornicators nor idolaters nor adulterers nor boy prostitutes nor practicing homosexuals 10 nor thieves nor the greedy nor drunkards nor slanderers nor robbers will inherit the kingdom of God.*
This is the justification used by Literalist Christians in our times to condemn certain people.

6: 19 *Do you not know that your body is a temple of the holy Spirit within you, whom you have from God, and that you are not your own?*
This is not a Trinitarian statement! It repeats what is in 2: 12 and 3: 16 above. The Spirit within you is the Spirit of God; you are its temple!

7: 1 ff There are some very peculiar understandings of marriage in this Chapter some of which are Paul's own prejudices that demean females. But read it for yourself and then decide. Note: the "ff", it is a common symbol meaning "and the following verses".

7: 29 *I tell you, brothers, the time is running out. From now on, let those having wives act as not having them,*
This is especially offensive to the sacredness of marriage! It may be excusable only because Paul considers the end time to be approaching. Otherwise, this is male chauvinism!

7: 38 *So then, the one who marries his virgin does well; the one who does not marry her will do better.*
This, too, speaks of male chauvinism!

11: 8 *For man did not come from woman, but woman from man; 9 nor was man created for woman, but woman for man;*
An excellent example of the literal nature of the early Christians. Paul, you certainly goofed here! One more example that not everything in the Bible is God's Words, just a male thing and just cultural ignorance and chauvinism!

12: 1 ff There is a great metaphor in this Chapter comparing the human body to the spiritual body of the Christ in which Christians occupy many parts. Please take time to absorb this Chapter.

12: 3 *Therefore, I tell you that nobody speaking by the spirit of God says, "Jesus be accursed." And no one can say, "Jesus is Lord," except by the holy Spirit.*
These passages of Paul's do leave a lot of theology in question. To be sure, the holy Spirit (the spirit of holiness) here is none other than the Spirit of God. (Isaiah 63: 10-11 and Rom 1: 1-4)

13: 1 ff This is the magnificent soliloquy on Love and its true practical meaning! It's worthwhile reading, do look it over. And then, look it over again!

6. 2nd Corinthians (Autumn 57 AD):

Right in the first verse Paul writes about the church (called out people) of God, not of Yeshua; he writes, "trust in God who raises the dead", this is in keeping with his understanding that God raised Yeshua and then promoted Yeshua to the fullness of God.

1: 9 *Indeed, we had accepted within ourselves the sentence of death, that we might trust not in ourselves but in God who raises the dead.*
This is another precursor to Romans 1: 3-4.

1: 20-22 *For however many are the promises of God, their Yes is in him; therefore, the Amen from us also goes through him to God for glory. 21 But the one who gives us security with you in Christ and who anointed us is God; 22 he has also put his seal upon us and given the Spirit in our hearts as a first installment.*
Paul again writes simply that God anointed him and his two disciples and God's spirit was placed in his soul. There is no implication that God's spirit is another

person! (That is, unless you read the Gospels first and get theologically mis-directed.)

2:12 *When I went to Troas for the gospel of Christ, although a door was opened for me in the Lord,*
Paul's Greek really says, Good News. Gospel is a modern word (1611 AD modern) . Believe it, the more Paul rethinks his epiphany the more elaborate and complex his description becomes (see Paul's epiphany in Acts 9, 22, and 26—oops, or is it Luke who gets it twisted?).

3: 17-18 *Now the Lord is the Spirit, and where the Spirit of the Lord is, there is freedom. 18 All of us, gazing with unveiled face on the glory of the Lord, are being transformed into the same image from glory to glory, as from the Lord who is the Spirit.*
First of all, the Greek word, *kunos*, is the generic word for master, Lord, God. Paul makes two astounding theological statements, "*the Lord IS the Spirit*" and "*the Spirit IS the Lord*". The previous verses seem to imply that God, LORD, is the Spirit. However, it just might mean Yeshua is that SPIRIT. The word Spirit is not a third person nor is the Spirit of God or of Yeshua a third person. This Pauline theology is that of the "Shema" in Deut 6:4: God is ONE! And, as the Qur'an so aptly states it, "nor does God have any partners." This topic will be treated more fully in Chapter Five.

4: 4-6 *in whose case the god of this age has blinded the minds of the unbelievers, so that they may not see the light of the gospel* {good news} *of the glory of Christ, who is the image of God. For we do not preach ourselves but Jesus Christ as Lord, and ourselves as your slaves for the sake of Jesus. For God who said, "Let light shine out of darkness," has shone in our hearts to bring to light the knowledge of the glory of God on the face of (Jesus) Christ.*
Paul refers to the Christ as the image of God, another stepwise development of Paul's theology. But we already know that all humans are the image of God, don't we? He continues with a second phrase in the build up of a more complex theology. Yeshua is "The Human Face of God"—a book by J.A.T. Robinson, and it is a good one! Note: this glory on the face of Jesus is a copycat of the glory on the face of Moses. Not too original!

4: 14 *knowing that the one who raised the Lord Jesus will raise us also with Jesus and place us with you in his presence.*
Here we see some of the words of Romans 1: 3-4 being articulated,

5: 16 *Consequently, from now on we regard no one according to the flesh; even* *<u>If we once knew Christ according to the flesh, yet now we know him so no longer</u>.*
This is a true description of us in this 21st century. We have forgotten that Yeshua was as we are, a complete mortal in the flesh, including ignorance. Now, he, Yeshua, has been promoted to the fullness of God by means of the Resurrection and that's how the disciples will remember Yeshua.

6: 4 *on the contrary, in everything we commend ourselves as ministers of God, through much endurance, in afflictions, hardships, constraints,*
Paul refers to himself "*as a minister of God*" not as a minister of Yeshua.

6: 18 *and I will be a father to you, and you shall be sons and daughters to me, says the Lord Almighty.*
Well, finally, Paul acknowledges women. But note that God is LORD Almighty! This phrasing comes directly from the Hebrew, *El Shadday*.

11:3 "*But I am afraid that, as the serpent deceived Eve by his cunning, your thoughts may be corrupted from a sincere [and pure] commitment to Christ.*" Paul shares the belief of the 1st century culture, the H.T. is factual. But we know it's just history MYTHOLOGIZED, don't we? More in that vein in Chapter Five.

11: 7 *Did I make a mistake when I humbled myself so that you might be exalted, because I preached the gospel of God to you without charge?*
Here is another "*gospel of God*" in the NAB. The NRSV uses "good news". We in this 21st century read "gospel" and immediately think that Paul has read the four Gospels! Very wrong! They haven't been written yet?

12: 9 "*Three times I begged the Lord about this, that it might leave me, but he said to me, "My grace is sufficient for you, for power is made perfect in weakness."*
This is our favorite verse; God's grace is powerful enough to overcome our weaknesses, including our sins!

13: 14 *The grace of the Lord Jesus Christ and the love of God and the fellowship of the holy Spirit be with all of you.*
It appears that by 57 AD there is the hint of the grace of Yeshua and of God and Spirit. The breath (*ruwach*) of God in Gen 1 is now being personified. Nevertheless, there is no certainty that this is Trinitarian. Paul's literary style leaves a lot to be desired as far as his defining the use of the single word, Spirit or the phrases, "holy Spirit" and "Spirit of Holiness", for God but it doesn't imply a partner. The real confusions come about AFTER one first reads the four Gospels and Acts!

7. Romans (Winter 57-58 AD):

We are now approaching the 20th year of Paul's ministry when he is about to travel to Rome. In order to clear up any misunderstandings with the Roman community, he states his beliefs. After all, a while back he was a principal persecutor. In the first verse Paul writes clearly that "he has been called to be an apostle and set apart for {the purpose of} the good news from God". Then he continues with his Christology that demonstrates that he teaches exactly what the Apostles teach (1: 3-4). We presented this previously along with passages from Acts 2, 5 and 13 that detailed the same Christology: "God raised Yeshua, and gave Yeshua the titles and powers by means of (through or at) the Resurrection." As we proceed through Romans, be alert to the Christological statements. In addition, the term "gospel" is not meant to be understood as any of the four Gospel writings but rather should be understood as "Good News". Can you articulate what this "Good News" is for you? You could start with 1: 16, "*For I am not ashamed of the good news. It is the power of God for the salvation of everyone who believes: for Jew first, and then Greek.*" The good news is that there is eternal life available to anyone who has an intimate relationship with their Higher Power and loves his/her neighbor and performs "good works" as implied in the "good Samaritan" parable!

Verse 1:20 is especially pertinent for Atheists and Agnostics, *"Ever since the creation of the world, his invisible attributes of eternal power and divinity have been able to be understood and perceived in what he has made. As a result, they have no excuse".*

Then in 1: 21-32 there is a very timely description of our present day problem of perversity in this country. Notice that it is a continuation of 1: 20. This one reads:

> 1: 21-32 *for although they knew God they did not accord him glory as God or give him thanks. Instead, they became vain in their reasoning, and their senseless minds were darkened. While claiming to be wise, they became fools and exchanged the glory of the immortal God for the likeness of an image of mortal man or of birds or of four-legged animals or of snakes. Therefore, <u>God handed them over to impurity through the lusts of their hearts for the mutual degradation of their bodies.</u> They exchanged the truth of God for a lie and revered and worshiped the creature rather than the creator, who is blessed forever. Amen. Therefore, <u>God handed them over to degrading passions</u>. Their females exchanged natural relations for unnatural, and the males likewise gave up natural relations with females and burned with lust for one another. Males did shameful things with males and thus received in their own persons the due penalty for their perversity. And since they did not see fit to acknowledge God, <u>God handed them over to their undiscerning mind</u> to do what is improper. They are filled with every form of wickedness, evil, greed, and malice; full of envy, murder, rivalry, treachery, and spite. They are gossips and scandalmongers and they hate God. They are insolent, haughty, boastful, ingenious in their wickedness, and rebellious toward their parents. They are senseless, faithless, heartless, ruthless. Although they know the just decree of God that all who practice such things deserve death, they not only do them but give approval to those who practice them.*
>
> Note the underlined! God, the Puppeteer, interfered with Human free will. That isn't God; it's the mis-conceptions of the culture. It was difficult for the people of that time to understand "free will" because they all believed that God was in control of every choice and action. Even Paul didn't recognize "free will" as the driving force in human behavior.

Did you actually read all of Paul's Letters first? It would be a great exercise because you would read some excellent metaphors and allegories as well as experience much of Paul's theology, sometimes beautiful and at other times confusing. We've tried to point them all out in this commentary. Then, pay particular attention to his allegories about the relationship between the Christ and the Christian membership as (1) a vine (11: 16-24) with Yeshua as the root and Christians as the branches and (2) as the body of believers (12: 4-8) with Yeshua as the head and Christians the body parts. Aren't these two allegorical (myth) comparisons full of meaning? Read them below.

Now, let's start the commentary from the beginning:

> 1: 4 *but established as Son of God in power according to <u>the spirit of holiness</u> through resurrection from the dead, Jesus Christ our Lord.*
>
> This is a reference to the Spirit of God. Further discussion will be found in Chapter Five.

> 1: 17 *For in it is revealed the righteousness of God from faith to faith; as it is written, "The one who is righteous by faith will live."*

That quotation is one of the seeds for Martin Luther's protest.

1: 24 *Therefore, God handed them over to impurity through the lusts of their hearts for the mutual degradation of their bodies*
We are going to see a lot of this God doing something to stop us humans from understanding or using our free will. That is NOT the nature of God! It is the simplistic mindset of the Hebrew Testament's folk theology that God is the Puppeteer with humans on Her strings.

2: 4 *Or do you hold his priceless kindness, forbearance, and patience in low esteem, unaware that the kindness of God would lead you to repentance?*
The Greek word for "repentance" is "*metanoia*" which means, "change of mind or behavior". Yes, there is sorrow but that misses the real meaning, because sorrow doesn't always lead to change.

2: 5-7 *By your stubbornness and impenitent heart, you are storing up wrath for yourself for the day of wrath and revelation of the just judgment of God, who will repay everyone according to his works: eternal life to those who seek glory, honor, and immortality through perseverance in good works*
The first underlined is the fodder for the same phrase that is overworked in the Qur'an—a punishing God The second underlined implies exactly what James in his letter wrote about good works. We suspect that Martin Luther overlooked these lines!

2: 9 *Yes, affliction and distress will come upon every human being who does evil, Jew first and then Greek.*
This is cute; the Greek text has "*psuche anthropos*" meaning "the soul of man" that is translated by "human being"! I guess Freud wasn't first after all! The Greek Psychologists were first and Paul and then Freud copied them.

2: 14-16 *For when the Gentiles who do not have the law by nature observe the prescriptions of the law, they are a law for themselves even though they do not have the law. They show that the demands of the law are written in their hearts, while their conscience also bears witness and their conflicting thoughts accuse or even defend them on the day when, according to my gospel, God will judge people's hidden works through Christ Jesus.*
And those outside of any Institution will be judged by the works of their own choosing. Sounds like one doesn't have to be Christian to be saved, true? Yes, it's very true!

3: 27-28 *What occasion is there then for boasting? It is ruled out. On what principle, that of works? No, rather on the principle of faith. For we consider that a person is justified by faith apart from works of the law".*
THIS is also a biggie that has been misinterpreted as we mentioned earlier! Recall, "works of the Law" does not mean "good works"! Romans 4 is one long explanation of his thesis—Faith vs. works of the Law. Wow, a heavy chapter, even when read several times, that may still give one an Excedrin headache.

5: 1 *Therefore, since we have been justified by faith, we have peace with God through our Lord Jesus Christ,*

The thesis of Paul again. And when quoted leads to a misunderstanding.

5: 5 *and hope does not disappoint, because the love of God has been poured out into our hearts through the holy Spirit that has been given to us.*
The Holy Spirit is mentioned for the second time but, again, it refers to God the Father who dispenses all grace. What makes this so confusing is that the Greek reads either "spirit of holiness" or" holy spirit". However, in the H.T. and in 1: 3-4 it is "spirit of holiness"; they are synonyms!

5:12-14 *Therefore, just as through one person sin entered the world, and through sin, death, and thus death came to all, inasmuch as all sinned for up to the time of the law, sin was in the world, though sin is not accounted when there is no law. But death reigned from Adam to Moses, even over those who did not sin after the pattern of the trespass of Adam, who is the type of the one who was to come.*
Paul blames Adam for the first sin. Too bad that the Adam story is pure fiction and one of the many mythic tales in the Hebrew Testament. It is obvious that the first Apostles and Disciples had a touch of Literalism in their belief that the H.T. was factual history and science. For that matter, it took the world about 2000 years to clear up the science issue and it will probably take another several hundred years for Christians to be convinced that the Bible has deeply significant meanings without it being a tape-recording of a Divine lecture. The second underlined is a reference to the humanity of Yeshua!

5: 15 *But the gift is not like the transgression. For if by that one person's transgression the many died, how much more did the grace of God and the gracious gift of the one person Jesus Christ overflow for the many.*
For the Star Trekies among you, this is the source for Spock's aphorism at the end of the second movie, "The needs of the many are greater than the needs of the one."

6: 15-25 *What I do, I do not understand. For I do not do what I want, but I do what I hate. Now if I do what I do not want, I concur that the law is good. So now it is no longer I who do it, but sin that dwells in me. For I know that good does not dwell in me, that is, in my flesh. The willing is ready at hand, but doing the good is not. For I do not do the good I want, but I do the evil I do not want. Now if (I) do what I do not want, it is no longer I who do it, but sin that dwells in me. So, then, I discover the principle that when I want to do right, evil is at hand. For I take delight in the law of God, in my inner self, but I see in my members another principle at war with the law of my mind, taking me captive to the law of sin that dwells in my members. Miserable one that I am! Who will deliver me from this mortal body? Thanks be to God through Jesus Christ our Lord. Therefore, I myself, with my mind, serve the law of God but, with my flesh, the law of sin.*
Psychologically speaking, this passage sounds like a big buck passing soliloquy by a person who is not aware of his own free will. He feels that someone or thing is in control of his body. It may very well be the idea that there are demons who force him to perform evil deeds. We'll see the same belief in the Gospels that write about evil spirits causing illness and demon possession.

8:2-3 *For the law of <u>the spirit of life</u> in Christ Jesus has freed you from the law of sin and death. For what the law, weakened by the flesh, was powerless to do, this God has done: by <u>sending his own Son in the likeness of sinful flesh</u> and for the sake of sin, he condemned sin in the flesh,*
Again a "spirit of" is used. Could Paul be confused about giving a "spirit" to everything and not understand that "a spirit of something or someone" is still that thing or that person? The distinction is not clear! We'll see in the following comment for 8: 9-16 that the confusion persists even to the point of suggesting a new personage in the already crowded Godhead! The second underlined is the powerful sentence that positively states that Yeshua was a complete human including ignorance!

BE ALERT FOR WHAT FOLLOWS; IT'S THE MOST CHALLENGING SECTION IN ALL THE C.T.!
8: 6-16 *The concern of the flesh is death, but the concern of <u>the spirit</u> is life and peace. 7 For the concern of the flesh is hostility toward God; it does not submit to the law of God, nor can it; 8 and those who are in the flesh cannot please God. 9 But you are not in the flesh; on the contrary, you are <u>in the spirit</u>, if only the <u>Spirit of God</u> dwells in you. Whoever does not have <u>the Spirit of Christ</u> does not belong to him. 10 But if Christ is in you, although the body is dead because of sin, <u>the spirit</u> is alive because of righteousness. 11 <u>If the Spirit</u> of the one who raised Jesus from the dead dwells in you, the one who raised Christ from the dead will give life to your mortal bodies also, through <u>his Spirit</u> that dwells in you. 12 Consequently, brothers, we are not debtors to the flesh, to live according to the flesh. 13 For if you live according to the flesh, you will die, but if <u>by the spirit</u> you put to death the deeds of the body, you will live. 14 For those who are led by <u>the Spirit of God</u> are children of God. 15 For you did not receive <u>a spirit of slavery</u> to fall back into fear, but you received <u>a spirit of adoption</u>, through which we cry, "Abba, Father!" 16 <u>The Spirit</u> itself bears witness with <u>our spirit</u> that we are children of God,*
There are two parts to this selection.
(I) The verses 6 to 8 are totally confusing in that they condemn the flesh rather than acknowledge the role of free will. Paul is way out of his literal mind in verses 7-8 because of his (a) ignorance of human psychology and biology, (b) his Pharisaic prejudices and (c) his constant poetic literary style that, in itself, leads to confusion. It is no small wonder why so many have been misled by Paul's pontifications! The only thing that we can think is that those verses are completely metaphorical in which the flesh means sin. But even then they leave a bad taste in our minds, especially in light of the way a literalists would understand them.
(II) There are several "spirits" and "Spirits of" that Paul refers to in the remaining verses that introduce a serious confusion about whom he is speaking. He starts with "the spirit" followed later by "in the spirit, ..." both God's , then "the Spirit of God dwells...", followed by "the Spirit of Christ ...", and "the Spirit of One (God's) who raised...", then "his Spirit ..." (God's), now it's "the spirit..." (lower case, but whose "spirit" is this?), again, "the Spirit of God...", now there is "a spirit of slavery" along with "a spirit of adoption" (both of which are lower case and rhetorical of abstractions), then "Abba, Father" (Abba means Daddy which places an entirely different weight on the word, Abba), and, finally, "the Spirit itself..."(God's) and "our spirit".
There are four problems here: (1) has Paul used the metaphor for holy Spirit, "sacred breath" from Isaiah 63: 10-11? (2) did Paul write in uncials (all caps) or

lower case Greek?; (3) are capital or lower case Spirits or spirits due to the interpretation by the translator?; (4) if one reads the Gospels before reading Romans, the confusion is magnified because we already know about Father, Son and Holy Spirit (the Trinity) in Matthew, 80 AD. Now, if one reads the Christian Testament in its chronological order, then there is no Trinity and Paul is just waxing poetically! It would appear that this kind of poetry (*ruwach qodesh*, the Hebrew or the Greek, pneuma hagios, both for "sacred breath") is the principal cause of much of the turmoil that arose among Christian communities with respect to the doctrine of Trinity (325 AD at Nicaea) and later to the physical disturbances that gave rise to Constantine's demand for a Council of Bishops at Nicaea. This passage is clearly evidence of such a conflicted doctrine. Therefore, it is our strong belief that at the year 57 AD the concept of Trinity was not yet in existence.

8: 26-27 *In the same way, the Spirit too comes to the aid of our weakness; for we do not know how to pray as we ought, but the Spirit itself intercedes with inexpressible groanings. And the one who searches hearts knows what is the intention of the Spirit, because it intercedes for the holy ones according to God's will.*
In these verses it would seem that the "Spirit" has a life of its own. However, Paul has already laid the groundwork that this Spirit is God's. Check out the similarities to 2 Corin 12: 9 ! Also recall that in Rom 1:3-4 above Paul calls God "the spirit of holiness", the very same two Greek words, *pneuma hagiosune*, that are translated Holy Spirit, in Greek, *pneuma hagios*, later on in the Gospels and Acts.

8:28-30 *"We know that all things work for good <u>for those who love God</u>, who are called according to his purpose. <u>For those he foreknew he also predestined to be conformed to the image of his Son</u>, so that he might be the firstborn among many brothers. <u>And those he predestined he also called</u>; and those he called he also justified; and those he justified he also glorified."*
Here we see the basis for John Calvin's five-point "Predestination" theology. However, we can understand that Johnnie C. made a mis-calculation by not taking into account the pre-condition of, *"for those who love God"*. God did not, nor ever will, throw any dice to come up with those who would love God and those who would not! Those who first choose to love God make the cut; those who choose not to love God miss the boat. Once more biblical myopia is blind to God's gift of free will to Homo Sapiens: the gift that made us in God's image, to love or not to love, to choose or not to choose, to be or not to be! Oh, bless the perception of Shakespeare; Hamlet said it so clearly!

9: 1 *I speak the truth in Christ, I do not lie; my conscience joins with the holy Spirit in bearing me witness*
The title of Holy Spirit is very reminiscent of the Hebrew Testament's name for God, the Holy One of Israel or a different way to write the Spirit of holiness that Paul used in Rom 1: 1-4. PS: Paul should have written, "I believe what I perceive; my truth is in the Christ."

9: 4 *They are Israelites; theirs the adoption, the glory, the covenants, the giving of the law, the worship, and the promises; theirs the patriarchs, and <u>from them, according to the flesh, is the Messiah</u>. God who is over all be blessed forever. Amen.*

That is Paul's acknowledgement of Yeshua's humanity.

9: 15-16 *For he says to Moses: "I will show mercy to whom I will, I will take pity on whom I will ." So it depends not upon a person's will or exertion, but upon God, who shows mercy.*
The first sounds more like the Jonas Tale and the second one seems to mean that God can fathom the will or a person's intent so that God can give mercy when mercy is justified by the person's choice and action.

9: 18 Consequently, *he has mercy upon whom he wills, and he hardens whom he wills.* [7]
NO, NO! That is NOT God's WAY. Mercy, YES, harden NO!

9: 21 *Or does not the potter have a right over the clay, to make out of the same lump one vessel for a noble purpose and another for an ignoble one?*
Actually, the potter does! However, the allegory is flawed. Clay is not human! God gives us free will and God not only does not, but cannot, violate our free will! "Love without free will is despair!" Thomas Troward circa 1910 AD.

10:13 Here is a very special verse. *"For everyone who calls on the name of the Lord will be saved."* Yet, in the Gospel of Matthew 25: 34-40 there is a parable of a person who is saved because he clothed the naked and fed the hungry without knowing the name of Yeshua! There is a statement (Matt 7: 21) that says *"not everyone who cries, "Lord, Lord" will be saved".* Can you not see that Matt 7: 21 contradicts Rom 10: 13? Yet, Paul wrote 10:13 several years before the Gospels appeared! Tell me which is the word of God? Or is She a fickled God who changes Her mind at a snap of an author's finger? "Ain't" life just full of surprises and unanswerable questions?

10: 21 *But regarding Israel he says, "All day long I stretched out my hands to a disobedient and contentious people."*
Now, this is the God of Yeshua! Always seeking those who are spiritually blind and deaf.

11: 8 *as it is written: "God gave them a spirit of deep sleep, eyes that should not see and ears that should not hear, down to this very day."*
Paul is much too poetic at times for his own good. There is no such thing as a *spirit of deep sleep* . As far as God blinding men and making them deaf, it's not God's WAY.

11: 16- 27 *If the first fruits are holy, so is the whole batch of dough; and if the root is holy, so are the branches. But if some of the branches were broken off, and you, a wild olive shoot, were grafted in their place and have come to share in the rich root of the olive tree, do not boast against the branches. If you do boast, consider that you do not support the root; the root supports you. Indeed you will say, "Branches were broken off so that I might be grafted in." That is so. They were broken off because of unbelief, but you are there because of faith. So do not become haughty, but stand in awe. For if God did not spare the natural branches, (perhaps) he will not spare you either. See, then, the kindness and severity of God: severity toward those who fell, but God's kindness to you, provided you remain in his kindness; otherwise you too will be cut off. And they also, if they do not remain in unbelief, will be grafted in, for God is able to graft them in again.*

For if you were cut from what is by nature a wild olive tree, and grafted, contrary to nature, into a cultivated one, how much more will they who belong to it by nature be grafted back into their own olive tree. I do not want you to be unaware of this mystery, brothers, so that you will not become wise (in) your own estimation: a hardening has come upon Israel in part, until the full number of the Gentiles comes in, and thus all Israel will be saved, as it is written: "The deliverer will come out of Zion, he will turn away godlessness from Jacob; and this is my covenant with them when I take away their sins."
That is a powerful allegory that conveys God's Love for us humans. Note clearly, this is not a God who deliberately stops humans from accepting grace. Only we humans can reject that love because, as far as God is concerned, God's Love is an act of unconditional self-giving. Grace is never withheld; it can only be refused!

12: 1-21 *This* Chapter is probably the closest summation of the meaning of Yeshua's teachings in the C.T. Go, read the whole Chapter! And. if that doesn't impress you, then re-read 1 Corin 13: 1-13. Of special note is the use of the phrase, "the renewal of your mind", in v. 2; that's *metanoia*. Psychologically speaking, all emotional and intellectual activities take place in the brain (mind) not in the heart! Mechanical heart transplants don't change one's basic personality. These and others like it are great metaphors for compassion or the lack of it.

15: 5 *May the God of endurance and encouragement grant you to think in harmony with one another, in keeping with Christ Jesus, that with one accord you may with one voice glorify* <u>*the God and Father of our Lord Jesus Christ*</u>.
We think this should put to rest the idea that Paul considers Yeshua to be equal to the Father in any other manner than by gift according to Eph 3: 17-19.

15: *19 by the power of signs and wonders, by the power of the Spirit of God so that from Jerusalem all the way around to Illyricum I have finished preaching the gospel* {good news} *of Christ*. (from the NAB)
This is very interesting! There are three Greek texts which differ in the Greek of this phrase: (1) one says Spirit, (2) the other says Holy Spirit and (3) the last says Spirit of God. That should convince anyone that (a) Paul is far too poetic with his confusing use of "Spirit" and (b) the translators can't agree on which meaning Paul intended. For Paul and his communities, there is ONE God (Deut 6: 4) and one gifted (Eph 3: 17-19) with the fullness of God, Yeshua. We could be next, n'est pas?

8. Philemon (61-63)

There are two subjects worthy of comment in this Letter: the first is the topic of slavery which is acceptable to Paul (and to the rest of the world until Lincoln freed them). Yet slavery still exists in many other parts of the world! The second is the mention of a Mark and a Luke who are co-workers of Paul.

The "Introduction" to this Letter in the NAB suggests that Paul had no other choice but to be neutral to slavery. What would have happened to the Christians if they were to speak out publicly against this profitable political evil? Yep, another persecution! So, silence was the order of the day! Well, Paul did handle it very diplomatically, didn't he?

The second problem relates to the names of the two co-workers! Was Mark the author of the first Gospel? Then, why did his Christology take such a turn contrary to Paul's and the Apostolic teachings? If it is a different Mark from another community, it would explain the Christological shift and answer the question of authorship. Luke's name raises a similar question. He is apparently the author of the Gospel and the "Acts of the Apostles" (but in which order?). What is more puzzling is his quoting the Romans 1: 3-4 formula in Acts (recall the three Chapters-2, 5 and 13) but, in his Gospel, changing the Christological moment to the Annunciation (in his Infancy Narrative). That seems, again, contrary to Paul's and the Apostles' teachings. Well, for the moment, maybe one does have to accept a few unanswered questions. But, just for this moment!

One possibility is that Luke has access to Mark's Gospel and decides to write an improved Christology to counter Mark's Baptism Christology. That would seem appropriate since by 80 AD the nature of Yeshua was causing theological issues with the Israelites in the synagogues. After all, Christians were beginning to worship Yeshua (using the word, Lord, in reference to him, just like the Israelites use "Lord" for God). Recall your history, the Christian sect was excommunicated from Judaism in 85 AD.

A second possibility is that by that time, 35 years after the Resurrection, the stories of Yeshua and the apocryphal Gospels and Letters have succeeded in putting Yeshua so high up on the marble pedestal that Luke fell victim to them and included an Infancy Narrative to make the claim stick as well as justify Yeshua's wisdom and authority.

A third and real possibility was the positioning of Yeshua as an equal to the Roman emperor by making an identical birth myth about God's *ruwach,* breath or spirit, (Gen 1: 1), impregnating an earthly female thus making the child a true Son of God just like all the Greek and Roman myths of his day! (Actually the Infancy Narratives of Matt and Luke are completely mythic, just like Hercules in Greek Myth!) And then, how about the Nephilim in Gen 6:1-4?

We've got our money on the third one! Why discuss this here? Should I have not waited until we get to Luke's Gospel? The answer is simple. Paul mentions Luke and Mark as his followers and the followers learn about Yeshua from what Paul tells them. Is Paul beginning to shift his own Christology and may have shared it with these two followers. Additionally, it may be that (a) neither of these are the Authors of the Mark and Luke Gospels and (b) the different Christologies in the next Gospels will reveal the answer to our puzzlement. We can now be prepared to examine those differences more carefully.

9. Colossians (61-63 AD):

Colossians is the first Epistle to direct its teachings at a community in conflict and dissent because of false teachings. Mind you, those new preachings are focused on different ways to regard the personage of Yeshua. Paul considers these teachers opposed to his and the Apostles' teachings concerning Yeshua. In other words, those teachings presented a threat to the community's conformity. It appears that during that period many false documents and false teachings were beginning to circulate around the Empire. Paul almost gets theologically tongue-tied in this dissertation to save the souls at Colossae. By now you should be convinced that Christians have been literalists from day one (actually starting Monday morning the day after the Resurrection). As you read the commentary, keep these observations in mind as well as the date of this letter; Paul is approaching the end of his life.

1: 5-6 For Paul to write "*the word of truth, the gospel*" is a clear indication of his enculturation that he perceives his own and the Apostles "good news" to be absolute truth about Yeshua. That truth, according to Paul, comes directly as a tape-recording of God's voice. However, he does recognize that "*to know the grace of God in truth*" is part of being Christian. Could that truth be Paul's faith?

1: 10 Now, this quote is right on target: "*to live in a manner worthy of the Lord, so as to be fully pleasing, in every good work bearing fruit and growing in the knowledge of God*".
What we are doing here is to encourage you to use all your faculties to gain that "*knowledge of God*".

1: 15-20 "*He is the image of the invisible God, the firstborn of all creation. 16 For in him were created all things in heaven and on earth, the visible and the invisible, whether thrones or dominions or principalities or powers; all things were created through him and for him. 17 He is before all things, and in him all things hold together. 18 He is the head of the body, the church. He is the beginning, the firstborn from the dead, that in all things he himself might be preeminent. . 19 For in him all the fullness was pleased to dwell. 20 and through him to reconcile all things for him, making peace by the blood of his cross [through him], whether those on earth or those in heaven.*"
This is believed to be a hymn about Yeshua. But the claims in the poem simply confuse the human Yeshua with the Resurrected Yeshua. Let's examine this further! To begin, it should be pointed out that portions of this passage are paraphrased from Proverbs 8 that speaks of the God's wisdom that Christians interpreted to be Yeshua. You might want to re-read that before proceeding.

Welcome back. This is fun, isn't it? Have you considered taking anything for your aching mind and blurry eyes?

The first point is that this whole hymn is out of context with the theology that preceded this letter. Yeshua is the "image of the invisible God" like Adam and Eve and the rest of us who are in the image of God. {Please note, Paul believes in the Adam and Eve Cosmic Myth, but it is just a myth.} Verses 16 and 17 are a confusing bit of Paul's, or the Christian community's, interpretation of Proverbs 8. The second underlined says that Yeshua is the firstborn. Does that mean that God created Yeshua first? If Yeshua is the firstborn of all the dead, then he must not be equal to God. In other words, Yeshua was the first to be resurrected! Now, all else will revolve around Yeshua. It means that Yeshua entered into eternal life before everyone else; yes, after the Resurrection. In v. 19 Yeshua is the human, now divine (Eph 3: 17-19), as the leader of the Christian movement. Verse 20, according to Paul, ties the whole passage together by affirming God's plan to assign to Yeshua the responsibility to re-form God's creation into a whole unified (heaven and earth) and holy existence. The implication is that God wants a former human to judge the remainder of humanity! Note that the "ekklesia" is the called out community, not a church (a word from 1611 AD when people came to a building on Sunday). Christianity is a community not a building! Christianity is a behavior not a ritual.

2: 8-9 "*See to it that no one captivate you with an empty, seductive philosophy according to human tradition, according to the elemental powers of the world and not according to Christ. For in him dwells the whole fullness of the deity bodily*"
The fallacy in verse 8 is that human Christian traditions have really considered that all the writings in the Bible are tape-recorded voice mail from God and that's the fallacy which is perpetuated by Christian interpreters who have failed to understand that the history, science and just about all conversations were mythologized to begin with. Take note, Paul is really talking about the philosophies of his day! Verse 9 sets the tone for Eph 3: 17-19 and repeats verse 1: 19 above for emphasis. The last underlined refers to the Resurrected Yeshua.

3: 12-14 "*Put on then, as God's chosen ones, holy and beloved, heartfelt compassion, kindness, humility, gentleness, and patience, bearing with one another and forgiving one another, if one has a grievance against another; as the Lord has forgiven you, so must you also do. And over all these put on love, that is, the bond of perfection.*"
This passage is definitely from God and Yeshua. Notice that Paul doesn't write about doctrine, dogma, or Institution as Christian characteristics!

3: 18-23 "*Wives, be subordinate to your husbands, as is proper in the Lord. Husbands, love your wives, and avoid any bitterness toward them Children, obey your parents in everything, for this is pleasing to the Lord. Fathers, do not provoke your children, so they may not become discouraged. Slaves, obey your human masters in everything, not only when being watched, as currying favor, but in simplicity of heart, fearing the Lord. Whatever you do, do from the heart, as for the Lord and not for others,*"
AH, at last, a glimpse of first century AD culture. Does it pain anyone to realize that it was a male dominated society? So, ladies, what's so strange about this? Male domination still persists, even in some Christian Institutions, doesn't it? Note the two heart metaphors that refer to compassion.

4: 10 Mark's name comes up. Could he be the author of the first Gospel?

4: 14 Well, finally, the correct identification of who Luke is: the beloved physician, the author of the Gospel and the Acts of the Apostles.

10. Ephesians (61-63)

"Since the early nineteenth century, however, much of critical scholarship has considered that: (a) this letter's literary style and vocabulary (especially when compared with Colossians), (b) its concept of the church, and (c) other points of doctrine put forward by the writer are grounds for serious doubt about Paul's authorship. Yet the comments assume that the author is Paul or at the very least one of Paul's followers." (From the Introduction in the NAB) In case you haven't used the NAB, the Intro to Ephesians in it is quoted here because it's important to the commentary.

Regardless of authorship, Ephesians contains some mighty powerful theological passages worthy of your keenest attention. Let's begin.

1: 13 *In him you also, who have heard* the word of truth, the gospel {good news} *of your salvation, and have believed in him, were sealed with the promised holy Spirit,*
Holy Spirit!? Who? God or Yeshua? Yes, still God's Spirit! Why? Because the Gospels haven't been published yet! And, this may not be Paul's writings! We will discuss this "Holy Spirit" problem further in Chapter Five.

2: 2 *in which you once lived following the age of this world, following the ruler of the power of the air, the spirit that is now at work in the disobedient.*
You might think of Satan at first but don't be fooled. Paul is talking about evil choices by evil people who have evil spirits. You've got to look up the comic strip, "Pogo", in a Library. One of the daily strips showed Pogo staring into his mirror and saying to himself, " I have discovered the enemy! And the enemy is us."

2:5 *even when we were dead in our transgressions brought us to life with Christ (by grace you have been saved).*
Yes, It's true and when grace is offered, humans can and often refuse it!

2: 8 *For by grace you have been saved through faith, and this is not from you; it is the gift of God;*
Also true and it is because we choose to have faith in God. There are some who know (i.e., intellectual certainty) that there is a creator.

2: 17-18. *He came and preached peace to you who were far off and peace to those who were near, for through him we both have access in one Spirit to the Father.*
A classic "Paulism" which lends itself to much confusion. The one spirit is our oneness with Yeshua, or does Paul mean a third God ? You see, we really don't know which!

3: 9 *and to bring to light (for all) what is the plan of the mystery hidden from ages past in God who created all things,*
Now, folks, who created all things? God did and only God did; God needs no help. Nice contradiction to the Yeshua's present day assignment as creator, n'est pas? Now, if this is correct, then Yeshua was created and is not equal to God! Chew on that!

3: 17-21 *and that Christ may dwell in your hearts through faith; that you, rooted and grounded in love, 18 may have strength to comprehend with all the holy ones what is the breadth and length and height and depth, 19 and to know the love of Christ that surpasses knowledge,* ***so that you may be filled with all the fullness of God****. 20. Now to him who is able to accomplish far more than all we ask or imagine, by the power at work within us, 21. to him be glory in the church and in Christ Jesus to all generations, forever and ever. Amen.*
This passage has been worked over before, yet there is one more thought: God can accomplish more than we will ever be able to imagine! Recall, 2 Corin 12: 9. Please notice that the pronoun "him" (underlined) refers to God! Don't forget to define for yourself what that highlighted passage means. Also what does it mean by "the fullness of God"?

4:4-6 *one body and one Spirit, as you were also called to the one hope of your call; 5 one Lord, one faith, one baptism; 6 one God and Father of all, who is over all and through all and in all.*
Can any of Paul's thoughts be clearer than this? He and the Apostles believed in ONE God and Yeshua was just "Lord"! Language! Always a problem with language!

4: 26 *Be angry but do not sin; do not let the sun set on your anger,*
This is a great admonition. So, for all you para-psychologists, anger is not a sin!

4: 30 *And do not grieve the holy Spirit of God, with which you were sealed for the day of redemption.*
Has it not yet sunk in that in these Apostolic times Paul's use of "Holy Spirit" is just another name for God?

4: 32 *(And) be kind to one another, compassionate, forgiving one another as God has forgiven you in Christ.*
Another good bit of advice.

5: 23-28 *For the husband is head of his wife just as Christ is head of the church, he himself the savior of the body. <u>As the church is subordinate to Christ, so wives should be subordinate to their husbands in everything</u>. Husbands, love your wives, even as Christ loved the church and handed himself over for her to sanctify her, cleansing her by the bath of water with the word, that he might present to himself the church in splendor, without spot or wrinkle or any such thing, that she might be holy and without blemish. So (also) husbands should love their wives as their own bodies. He who loves his wife loves himself.*
The passage is very lofty and covers much. But, please forgive all of us who believe that Paul is totally encultured in verse 24 and in error for today's world! So many sermons have just missed the point that the world has changed and this advice of Paul, or whomever wrote this, is outdated because it is NOT from God; it is just male chauvinism of the first century AD! In the last part of this quote, Paul begins to see the light.

5: 33 *In any case, each one of you should love his wife as himself, and the wife should respect her husband.*
Now, Paul has regained his common sense.

5: 17 *And take the helmet of salvation and the sword of the Spirit, which is the word of God.*
OH, glory be! The Bible is a Spirit ... but absolutely the "words of men" writing about their relationship with God. And those human words are flowing with myth and not least of all—deep meaning!

11. James (62 AD)

The Introduction to James in the NAB identifies this author as the "brother of the Lord" (Gal 1: 19) who was stoned to death about 62 AD, that is, according to Josephus, a Jewish historian. It would be advantageous for you to read this whole NAB Introduction to get a fuller flavor of what is in contest within today's scholarly community. Now, let's turn to the commentary.

1: 13-15 *No one experiencing temptation should say, "I am being tempted by God"; for God is not subject to temptation to evil, and he himself tempts no one. Rather, each person is tempted when he is lured and enticed by his own desire. Then desire conceives and brings forth sin, and when sin reaches maturity it gives birth to death.*
How great this passage is! Folks, there is free will after all. Once again the myopia of the literalists reads only one verse and proceeds to formulate the mind in confusion. Poor, J. Calvin, he needed a better Bible as well as better reading glasses.

1: 19-20 *Know this, my dear brothers: everyone should be quick to hear, slow to speak, slow to wrath, for the wrath of a man does not accomplish the righteousness of God.*
Somehow, we've got to get this message to the Middle East and especially the Islamic terrorists.

1: 25 *But the one who peers into the perfect law of freedom and perseveres, and is not a hearer who forgets but a doer who acts, such a one shall be blessed in what he does.*
Another statement about "good works" speaking more loudly than a quotation of dogma and doctrine.

1: 27 *Religion that is pure and undefiled before God and* <u>*the*</u> *Father is this: to care for orphans and widows in their affliction and to keep oneself unstained by the world.*
That's exactly what Yeshua preached, Isaiah wrote in Ch 1: 10-20, and what James states here in this Letter. Note: The article is not in the Greek text. It should read "before God and Father" which means a single person!

2: 14-19 *What good is it, my brothers, if someone says he has faith but does not have works? Can that faith save him? If a brother or sister has nothing to wear and has no food for the day, and one of you says to them, "Go in peace, keep warm, and eat well," but you do not give them the necessities of the body, what good is it? So also faith of itself, if it does not have works, is dead. Indeed someone might say, "You have faith and I have works." Demonstrate your faith to me without works, and I will demonstrate my faith to you from my works.* <u>*You believe that God is one. You do well.*</u> *Even the demons believe that and tremble.*
This is James' explanation of a balanced life "of faith which produces good works". There is also a re-statement of Deut 6: 4!

2: 24 & 26 *See how a person is justified by works and not by faith alone.* 26 *For just as a body without a spirit is dead, so also faith without works is dead.*
The whole of James 2 is a magnificent definition and explanation of the problem with "faith alone" with which some theologians struggle. It seems that Paul did have a reputation for lofty confusing words. So, faith produces good works! Yet it all starts with faith in the meaning of Yeshua's life and Resurrection.

3: 7-8 *For every kind of beast and bird, of reptile and sea creature, can be tamed and has been tamed by the human species, but no human being can tame the tongue. It is a restless evil, full of deadly poison.*

Wow, can James get to the heart of a matter? You bet. And it's all simile and metaphor!

3: 10-11 *From the same mouth come blessing and cursing. This need not be so, my brothers. Does a spring gush forth from the same opening both pure and brackish water?*
Oh, confession time! This little quote has very personal meaning. It was the one that my friend said to me way back in 1974 that jolted my soul and started me off reading the Bible. For the next three years I was a Literalist and read the KJV voraciously. It was the answer that my soul sought for so long. Today, I are a Christian. {That's an old Engineering joke about the English training they don't get!} Well, by today's standards my theology is quite modern because of 25 years of personal study. Some of my companions put it less politely— Lib Rebel ! However, I'm really just an inquiring Christian. In Zen that's a Seeker.

5: 14 *Is anyone among you sick? He should summon the presbyters of the church, and they should pray over him and anoint (him) with oil in the name of the Lord,*
This is the justification for the Roman Catholic sacrament of "Anointing the Sick".

12. 1st Peter (64 AD)

There is quite a confusion concerning the authorship of this Letter. Some suspect a disciple of Peter who wrote it just after Peter died, a scribe, Silvanus (5: 12), who fills in and improves Peter's vocabulary and literary style. Some allusions to conditions not easily documented in history seem to cloud the dating of this Epistle. The NAB Introduction is a good read, so take a peek at it; it may give you more insight into the real problems that scholars have in acknowledging the authorship and dating of the Christian Testament literature.

1: 1-3 *Peter, an apostle of Jesus Christ, to the chosen sojourners of the dispersion in Pontus, Galatia, Cappadocia, Asia, and Bithynia, in the foreknowledge of God the Father, through sanctification by the Spirit, for obedience and sprinkling with the blood of Jesus Christ: may grace and peace be yours in abundance. Blessed be <u>the God and Father</u> of our Lord Jesus.*
Three points to be explained: one, foreknowledge is a primitive quality assigned to God but, as for us, we suspect that God doesn't know the future. Granted that God knows the past and is totally aware of the present. However, we believe that a respect for human free will prevents God's knowing our future. Knowing the future is tantamount to a Calvinistic predestination! Each new child born causes God to adapt to a new relationship—God changes—a new relationship forced by human choice to create children implies a freely chosen and a statistical future. In Genesis 1 God turns the future over to humankind. And you already know that we humans will do what we choose. Two: the Spirit referred to here is the Spirit of God, not a third persona. Three: this sentence says in clear Greek that the Lord Jesus has a God and Father. I ask you, do we not have God as our Father? Are we God? Neither is Yeshua!

1: 11 *investigating the time and circumstances that the Spirit of Christ within them indicated when it testified in advance to the sufferings destined for Christ and the glories to follow them.*

Again, this is an example of a person having a spirit but it isn't a separate person. The spirit of someone is an expression that speaks of a person's character and power source.

1: 21 *who through him believe in God who raised him from the dead and gave him glory, so that your faith and hope are in God.*
This is a repeat of Rom 1: 3-4 and the three passages from Acts 2, 5 and 13 that expressed Yeshua's humanity and God's promoting him to glory (Eph 3: 17-19), like what Moses wanted to see! Now, realize that this is about the year 62 AD and this letter confirms the Apostolic preaching that Yeshua was graced with Messiahship at the Resurrection!

2: 9 *But you are "a chosen race, a royal priesthood, a holy nation, a people of his own, so that you may announce the praises" of him who called you out of darkness into his wonderful light.*
Yes, you've read that correctly, we—all Christians-- are a Royal Priesthood. So, what need we of any hierarchically anointed males? Didn't Paul write that a community should elect their own leaders? We'll see in a few years from this publication that in Paul's letters to Timothy and Titus he spells out the social and personal characteristics of a person to be elected. How come those directions are so perverted in this 21st century?

2: 15-16 *For it is the will of God that by doing good you may silence the ignorance of foolish people. Be free, yet without using freedom as a pretext for evil, but as slaves of God.*
Shall we hang this in our courtrooms? It appears to be a genuine need. Can you see that the Bible is a book that contains some profound wisdom? And, don't miss the "Be free!" because we are free willed".

3: 1-5 *Likewise, you wives should be subordinate to your husbands so that, even if some disobey the word, they may be won over without a word by their wives' conduct when they observe your reverent and chaste behavior. Your adornment should not be an external one: braiding the hair, wearing gold jewelry, or dressing in fine clothes, but rather the hidden character of the heart, expressed in the imperishable beauty of a gentle and calm disposition, which is precious in the sight of God. For this is also how the holy women who hoped in God once used to adorn themselves and were subordinate to their husbands;*
It surely appears that males were in power and defined what a wife should be and should do. It must go back to the prehistory of the European and Asian Neanderthal clan cultures. But then again, it still persists today in the world but practiced to extreme in the Middle Eastern countries.

: 7-9 *Likewise, you husbands should live with your wives in understanding, showing honor to the weaker female sex, since we are joint heirs of the gift of life, so that your prayers may not be hindered. Finally, all of you be of one mind, sympathetic, loving toward one another, compassionate, humble. Do not return evil for evil, or insult for insult; but on the contrary, a blessing, because to this you were called, that you might inherit a blessing.*
Well, the first is fighting words for women but for the second, at least the author tried to balance the scales.

3: 15-16 *but sanctify Christ as Lord in your hearts. Always be ready to give an explanation to anyone who asks you for a reason for your hope, 16 but do it with gentleness and reverence, keeping your conscience clear, so that, when you are maligned, those who defame your good conduct in Christ may themselves be put to shame.*
And thus, we urge you to use your reason, brain, intellect and discernment to be able to explain why you are a Christian. But mostly, does your behavior match your Christianity? You know, the walk your talk thing!

3: 18 *For Christ also suffered for sins once, the righteous for the sake of the unrighteous, that he might lead you to God. Put to death in the flesh, he was brought to life in the spirit.*
Is the author trying to say that Yeshua was resurrected as a spirit or that the Resurrection brought Yeshua into the spirit of God? Sometimes these biblical sayings are too vague to tell what the author really means. Yeshua was a fully Resurrected human, in the flesh. Otherwise, there wouldn't have been any disciples so motivated to unpack, remain in Jerusalem and proclaim Yeshua risen!

4: 6-8 *For this is why the gospel (good news) was preached even to the dead that, though condemned in the flesh in human estimation, they might live in the spirit in the estimation of God. The end of all things is at hand. Therefore, be serious and sober for prayers. Above all, let your love for one another be intense, because love covers a multitude of sins.*
There was a belief that the end of the world was at hand mostly because Yeshua was reported to have said that the final judgment would come while some of his disciples were still alive. Sounds like Yeshua didn't really know about that subject after all. The world is still here. The second underlined is a powerful aphorism.

5: 1 *So I exhort the presbyters among you, as a fellow presbyter and witness to the sufferings of Christ and one who has a share in the glory to be revealed.*
This may very well indicate that Peter is not the author because he was an Apostle and never referred to as a presbyter.

5: 10 *The God of all grace who called you to his eternal glory through Christ (Jesus) will himself restore, confirm, strengthen, and establish you after you have suffered a little.*
Early Christians assigned the giving of all grace to God. Has Christianity truly lost touch with the meaning of the Christian Testament because of its politicizing of hierarchy, ritualistic priesthood and its dogma and doctrinal structures? Are we not all called to God's glory?

5: 13 *The chosen one at Babylon sends you greeting, as does Mark, my son.*
What, pray tell, does this author mean by "the chosen one?"
On closer examination it appears that he is in Rome, commonly referred to as Babylon and in the first verse of this letter, Peter is addressing the "chosen sojourners". Seems like this is a play on that address; Peter is one of the chosen of the chosen sojourners. And here is another "Mark". Could this have been the author of that Gospel?

13. 1st Timothy (66)

Well, here again is a dispute concerning the authorship of this Letter. It does contain a lot of Paul's theology, so the first choice is Paul as its author. Please read the NAB Introduction.

1: 11 *according to the glorious gospel of the blessed God, with which I have been entrusted.*
Gospels are what have been written by men, the Greek word must be translated "Good Message" or "Good News" both of which connote a deeper meaning,

1: 17 *To the king of ages, incorruptible, invisible, the only God, honor and glory forever and ever. Amen.*
This is addressed to God and here again is Paul's signature, the ONLY God!

2: 3-4 *This is good and pleasing to God our savior, who wills everyone to be saved and to come to knowledge of the truth.*
In this one Epistle written just before his death there is confirmation of Paul's theology. God is the Savior and God wills everyone to be saved. John Calvin, eat your heart out! That last phrase is really neat: knowledge will lead to the truth, ignorance will never cut it!

2: 5 *For there is one God. There is also one mediator between God and the human race, Christ Jesus, himself human,*
Can you ask for anything more definitive than this? There is one God and one mediator—Yeshua the Christ who was HUMAN ! It would appear that the men at Nicaea hadn't read this letter!

2: 11-15 *A woman must receive instruction silently and under complete control. I do not permit a woman to teach or to have authority over a man. She must be quiet. For Adam was formed first, then Eve. Further, Adam was not deceived, but the woman was deceived and transgressed. But she will be saved through motherhood, provided women persevere in faith and love and holiness, with self-control.*
OH Brother Paul, you are perpetrating the worst kind of male chauvinism in that first verse! You then make theology from the creation MYTHS; get real! In the story, Adam was just as culpable as Eve, shame on you! Well Bro, you should visit us in this century. You won't find any similarity between your Christianity and ours! Yes, and you won't find very many real Christians either! OH, keeping silent is a prerequisite even today! Very few priests allow questions; it's still pray, pay, and obey!

3: 2-4 *Therefore, a bishop must be irreproachable, married only once, temperate, self-controlled, decent, hospitable, able to teach, not a drunkard, not aggressive, but gentle, not contentious, not a lover of money. He must manage his own household well, keeping his children under control with perfect dignity;*
Have any of you found a modern-day Bishop with that profile? For one thing, there are a lot of Bishops of certain Institutions who are closing Churches because the community is poor and can't afford its weekly tithe to the Chancellery, not to mention the game of dispersing the parishioners (does that sound like a modern Diaspora to you?).

3: 15 *But if I should be delayed, you should know how to behave in the household of God, which is the church of the living God, the pillar and foundation of truth.*
There ain't none of those in this 21st century! (There goes our grammar, again!)

4: 4 *For everything created by God is good, and nothing is to be rejected when received with thanksgiving, for it is made holy by the invocation of God in prayer.*
How about that? Augustine of Hippo better change his pet theory about Original Sin. It no longer holds black water.

4: 7 *Avoid profane and silly myths.*
This is IRONIC! Every writer of the Bible believes that the writings of this book, O Biblos (the Greek title) are absolute history and science and every conversation is as true as though it were tape-recorded. Furthermore, Paul has the unmitigated gall to tell Christians to avoid silly myths. What a joke! OH Pahleeaze, sell Paul the Brooklyn Bridge!

4: 14 *Do not neglect the gift you have, which was conferred on you through the prophetic word with the imposition of hands of the presbyterate.*
That's the ordination of priests, ministers, deacons and hierarchs.

5: 17 *Presbyters who preside well deserve double honor, especially those who toil in preaching and teaching.*
Oh yes, they do get it ... from the till.

5: 23 *Stop drinking only water, but have a little wine for the sake of your stomach and your frequent illnesses.*
By George, that's the best advice written in many a verse!

6:10 *For the love of money is the root of all evils, and some people in their desire for it have strayed from the faith and have pierced themselves with many pains.*
Does that sound familiar? Look, it's not money that's evil; it's the love of it. The Lord knows, we all need that gold stuff to live in these times!

14. Titus (66):

Wow! Paul is surely in a tizzy in this Epistle over the troubles in Crete! He got one big burr in his saddle and even his donkey is jumping mad!

There are plenty of good recommendations written down for Titus to work on but there're also a few little goofs too. Let's go directly to the comments and discover what's going on.

1: 1 *Paul, a slave of God and apostle of Jesus Christ for the sake of the faith of God's chosen ones and the recognition of religious truth,*
Part A is Paul-talk which he chose to refer to Yeshua in Philippians 2: 6-11; well, Part B is a tough one to swallow—since truth is perception and perception is psychologically and, in this case, theologically relative!

1: 2 *in the hope of eternal life that God, who does not lie, promised before time began,*

That's certainly true ... but God didn't write the Bible! May we suggest you read 1 Kings 22: 23 before you leave this topic. Now tell me that God doesn't lie! Or is it that God just deceives? PS: it's the author again who puts these thoughts in the letter.

1: 3 *who indeed at the proper time* *revealed his word in the proclamation with which I was entrusted* *by the command of* *God our savior,*
First underlined appears to say that Paul received the "word of God" to preach. If so, why did he spend so much time in Damascus getting his act together? The second suggests that God the Father is the Savior!

1: 4 *to Titus, my true child in our common faith: grace and peace from God the Father and Christ Jesus our savior.*
A definite overlay which surely added to the confusion at Niceae. So, who is the savior? Compare v. 1: 3 with v.1: 4!

1: 5 *For this reason I left you in Crete so that you might set right what remains to be done* *and appoint presbyters* *in every town, as I directed you,*
What happened to letting the communities select their leaders?

1: 7 *For a bishop as God's steward must be blameless, not arrogant, not irritable, not a drunkard, not aggressive, not greedy for sordid gain,*
I guess Paul just forgot to list homosexuality and Pedophilia.

1: 9 *holding fast to the true message as taught so that he will be able both to exhort with sound doctrine and to refute opponents.*
It would appear that "holding to what the Apostles taught" was too difficult to nail down then as it is to discover today, isn't it!

1: 11 *It is imperative to silence them, as they are upsetting whole families by teaching for sordid gain what they should not.*
No you won't, not in this age of reason, Science and free speech.

1: 12 *One of them, a prophet of their own, once said, "Cretans have always been liars, vicious beasts, and lazy gluttons."*
Sounds like prejudice to me! Even, stereotyping!

1: 13-14 *Therefore, admonish them sharply, so that they may be sound in the faith, instead of paying attention to Jewish myths and regulations of people who have repudiated the truth.*
Hey, Paul, those are the very Jewish myths in Genesis and the rest of the Hebrew Testament that you believe in! Now, please realize that Paul and the rest are just Literalists!

1: 15-16 *To the clean all things are clean, but to those who are defiled and unbelieving nothing is clean; in fact, both their minds and their consciences are tainted. They claim to know God, but by their deeds they deny him. They are vile and disobedient and unqualified for any good deed.*
What does Paul mean by "defiled"? And, what deeds are they doing that so perturbs Paul? That is some strong condemnation, isn't it? Nobody is unqualified; God's grace can overcome anything! You may have to read all 16 verses to catch the gist of these few quotes.

2: 1-5 *As for yourself, you must say what is consistent with sound* _doctrine_, *namely, that older men should be temperate, dignified, self-controlled, sound in faith, love, and endurance. Similarly, older women should be reverent in their behavior, not slanderers, not addicted to drink, teaching what is good, so that they may train younger women to love their husbands and children, to be self-controlled, chaste, good homemakers,* _under the control of their husbands_, *so that the word of God may not be discredited.*
Now the word translated as doctrine is actually a variant of "*didache*" which is better translated as "teaching". Of the 20 Bibles we've checked, nine of them translate it as teaching(s). Later in Chapter Seven we'll see that Yeshua taught no doctrines. This last underline does really sound like male chauvinism, doesn't it? It rings of Proverbs 31: 10-31: rules for women but none for men!

2: 10 *or stealing from them, but exhibiting complete good faith, so as to adorn the doctrine of God our savior in every way.*
Here's that doctrine word again. For this verse six of fifteen Bibles use teaching; the rest, doctrine! Doctrine is really a 17th century word. For the second time in this letter we see "God our Savior". . It's getting harder to know who the actual Savior was or is?

2: 13 *as we await the blessed hope, the appearance of the glory of the great God and of our savior Jesus Christ,*
Here's that confusion again!

3: 4 *But when the kindness and generous love of God our savior appeared,*
Now, we are really getting mixed up!

3: 6 *whom he richly poured out on us through Jesus Christ our savior,*
OK, score tied on this title.

3: 8 *This saying is trustworthy. I want you to insist on these points, that those who have believed in God be careful to devote themselves to good works; these are excellent and beneficial to others.*
Paul is finally getting it straight. And, thanks to James!

3: 10 *After a first and second warning, break off contact with a heretic,*
Little do you know, Paul, that by 325 AD your Christology will be heretical too!

3: 14 But let our people, too, learn to devote themselves to good works to supply urgent needs, so that they may not be unproductive .
Good for you, Paul, you're finally getting straight the place of "good works"!

13. 2nd Timothy (67)

This Epistle marks the end of the Apostolic Period in which there were the preachings, teachings and proselytizing all over the Mediterranean Countries by the first generation disciples of Yeshua, the Carpenter from Nazareth. Paul was a second generation Apostle but intimately accepted by those who knew Yeshua. This letter to Timothy is Paul's last writing and Paul counsels Timothy to "preserve and spread the Christian message" which Paul had delivered to him. Paul reiterates his familiar

Christology that one can easily recognize: the One God, the One Lord and the One Truth. Paul refers to the Spirit of God, the Spirit of Yeshua and the spirit of a person in such a manner that the phrase, holy Spirit, often means that of God or that of Yeshua in various verses of Paul's extensive writings. In later years "Holy Spirit" becomes a seed in the minds of the Christian community who then "personify" it into a third Deity. We will see that it grows steadily for the next 20 years and blossoms out within certain communities along with the eternal Divinity of Yeshua to become the most agonizing distraction that Christianity will experience for many a decade and even centuries. As we examine this Epistle, please take mental note of the basic Pauline Christology and the use of the word, spirit, throughout the four Chapters.

1: 1 *Paul, an apostle of Christ Jesus by the will of God for the promise of life in Christ Jesus,*
Two points: Paul states his Apostleship and the Good News, the promise of LIFE, eternal LIFE!

1: 3 *I am grateful to God, whom I worship with a clear conscience as my ancestors did,*
This may very well be that Paul still holds to a theology of Deut 6:4 (One God!), Hold on now, we shall see a little later in this letter what that means.

1: 6 *For this reason, I remind you to stir into flame the gift of God that you have through the imposition of my hands.*
Ordination by Authority!

1: 7 *For God did not give us a spirit of cowardice but rather of power and love and self-control.*
Now Paul introduces four new spirits. It would seem that anything can have a spirit. The clue is, they are all metaphors!

1: 9 *He {God} saved us and called us to a holy life, not according to our works but according to his own design and the grace bestowed on us in Christ Jesus before time began,*
This first is a bit strange in that it seems to imply that God the Puppeteer calls us by HER own design. This all may be part of Calvin's confusion but we see "God's design" only as a call to relationship made to every human in all cultures of all times. Humans have Free Will and God cannot violate that which SHE imbued! Remember Thomas Troward's "Love without Liberty is Despair!" The second implies God's eternal offer of grace as a component of salvation. Now, this "before time began" presents a real inconsistency. It implies that God wrote the whole play including who will make it and who will not. And that is a falsehood. It is incorrect because it dismisses our little old friend, Free Willie! To imply in any fashion that God has this Universe held on a set of puppeteer's strings that She orchestrates or manipulates every planetary action that did, is or will takes place is simply outrageously ignorant! But, remember, Paul and those early Christians were literalists in knowledge and behavior. And, in deference to the grace of God, they "did the best they could for who they were" during those times. If only all of us did our compassionate best ... in this 21st century.

1: 10 *but now made manifest through the appearance of our savior Christ Jesus, who destroyed death and brought life and immortality to light through the gospel* {good News}

Paul is predictably changing his mind about whom he calls "savior".

1: 14 *Guard this rich trust with the help of the holy Spirit that dwells within us.*
OK, is it God's Spirit, Yeshua's Spirit or simply a reference to our own spiritual character infused at birth by God's graceful gifts of existence?

2: 7 *Reflect on what I am saying, for the Lord will give you understanding in everything.*
I surely hope so; seems that a lot of us could use more understanding, compassion and respect towards others.

2: 14 *Remind people of these things and charge them before God to stop disputing about words. This serves no useful purpose since it harms those who listen.*
Looks like the distortions of "perception" were alive and proactive. Imagine that! They had just as much dissension among the troops as we have denominations today! We sometimes wonder how Paul could be so concerned about what words others use and not apply the same concerns about his own confusing selection of words.

2: 23 *Avoid foolish and ignorant debates, for you know that they breed quarrels.*
Looks like nobody read this letter. The quarrels continued and continued and are still kicking around today! Why? Paul's language and word selection were the cause!

3: 1-9 *But understand this: there will be terrifying times in the last days. People will be self-centered and lovers of money, proud, haughty, abusive, disobedient to their parents, ungrateful, irreligious, callous, implacable, slanderous, licentious, brutal, hating what is good, traitors, reckless, conceited, lovers of pleasure rather than lovers of God, as they make a pretense of religion but deny its power. Reject them. For some of these slip into homes and make captives of women weighed down by sins, led by various desires, always trying to learn but never able to reach a knowledge of the truth. Just as Jannes and Jambres opposed Moses, so they also oppose the truth--people of depraved mind, unqualified in the faith. But they will not make further progress, for their foolishness will be plain to all, as it was with those two.*
OH MY GOODNESS, PAUL PREDICTS THE 21ST CENTURY! In the last verse Paul didn't acknowledge CULTS.

3: 14-15 *But you, remain faithful to what you have learned and believed, because you know from whom you learned it, and that from infancy you have known (the) sacred scriptures, which are capable of giving you wisdom for salvation through faith in Christ Jesus.*
Does that mean we must be "literalists"?

3: 16 All *scripture is inspired by God and is useful for teaching, for refutation, for correction, and for training in righteousness,*
This is definitely the fundamentalist manifesto! However, in their defense, there are many, many profound truths to be discovered in Scripture as long as one understands that myth is an appropriate literary style with which to convey God's message. After all, Yeshua used parable and allegory constantly throughout his preaching! One other thing, the Scripture that Paul refers to is the Septuagint, a

Greek translation (around 270 BC) of the Hebrew Testament and used throughout Christianity for the first three centuries! Paul does not refer to the Christian Testament because it wasn't in existence then.

4: 3-4 *For the time will come when people will not tolerate sound doctrine but, following their own desires and insatiable curiosity, will accumulate teachers and will stop listening to the truth and will be diverted to myths.*
This is one big problem with a Christian population of the first century AD under the leadership of literalists: (a) understand that "sound doctrine" (really, Paul's sound teachings) has nothing to do with spirituality or Yeshua's teachings; (b) listening to the truth is impossible with a leadership whose perceptions are uneducated, encultured, and at the primitive "pre-critical naiveté" cognitive stage; (c) the people of that day had strong beliefs that their Sacred Scripture was absolute history, science and a tape-recording of the Divine voice! All that mindset because God had personal control of every event in history, past, present and future! The Bible is not a tape recording of God's voice! It isn't the "Word of God"; it is the work of men who are definitely imperfect and fallible.

4: 22 *The Lord be with your spirit. Grace be with all of you.*
Here in this last verse, the use of the word "spirit" means that a person possesses a soul that both defines and empowers a person. My spirit is not another me! One's spirit is not a separate being. The Spirit of God and the Spirit of Yeshua are not two more separate entities of God or of Yeshua. The title "holy Spirit" was never intended to be a third entity; it was only meant to be another title for God's character and nature. (See Isaiah 63: 10-11) However, after Paul's death the fabric of Apostolic teaching begins to fray. As we shall see next, when Mark's Gospel hits the streets, a rift in Christian theology gives birth to confusion and dissention among the many ethnic communities. You will appreciate this observation when you become familiar with the Apochcryphal writings listed in Appendix E. We hope you realize that many of the troubled communities had several of these unacceptable Gospels and Epistles in their libraries!

Summary of the First Period:

In closing this Apostolic Period, a restatement of the prevalent teachings of the Christian leaders is in order. In this Chronological Christian Testament, we have thus far seen the writings of Paul, James and Peter as well as investigated the Christology of Apostolic preachings in Paul's Rom 1:3-4 and 4: 24, Phil 2: 6-11, Luke's Acts 2, 5 and 13. In all of these, the principal teaching concerning Yeshua was that he was raised by God who then at the Resurrection gave Yeshua the titles of Son of God, the Anointed One (the Christ in Greek or the Messiah in Hebrew), Savior, the name above all names, etc. The Resurrection demarcated the Christological Moment. Therefore, at the end of Paul's life, 67 AD, there was but ONE God and ONE Lord, Yeshua, who is not equal to God.

Next is the problem of the use and mis-use of the word, SPIRIT, especially by Paul in the Letter to the Romans 8: 9: 16. In that passage there are several different applications of the word "spirit": to God, Yeshua and individuals along with two abstractions, slavery and adoption. It's reviewed above. The confusion that results contributed to the decision of the Council at Nicaea to consider a third person equal to God, naming it the Holy Spirit. But that is a term used throughout the Hebrew Testament referring to God as the Holy One of Israel and thus, a Holy Spirit. Paul's flowery language muddied the concept. As far as literalists are concerned, it was carved on marble for the next 2000 years. It's time to discard that tablet!

Those, dear reader, are the contradictions found in the previous writings that we have just struggled through. It may be painful and shocking, but they are real contradictions. Take a deep breath and begin to deal with it!

Section Two: One God, One Lord, Messiah at Baptism, and the Personification of God's Spirit

14. Gospel of Mark (70 + AD):

First, a brief look at the word Gospel. Our software reports that it first shows up around 1500's AD and is composed of two Old English words, God and Spell. God you understand but spell (the second definition) means, "supposed to have magic power"; "charm; incantation"; "a state or period of enchantment"; "any dominating or irresistible influence". One can visualize the spell that Yeshua had over the people, like a great speaker, and the word "God's Spell" would imply the power, enchantment or irresistible influence that God or Yeshua held over people. When time gets its hands on tricky words and phrases, the tricky words and phrases have a tendency to change. Well, such is the case here. Instead of God's Spell over the people, the term became "Go-spel" by dropping the "d's" from "God's" and an "L" from "spell". Voila! Mon ami ... Gospel! The secondary problem with Paul's use of the word "gospel" is that he didn't use it! The Greek word he wrote is "*euaggelion*" which means "Good News". The first translators into English (see Appendix L for the URL to a "History of the English Bible") mis-translated that Greek word and have consistently mis-translated it ever since! As far as we are concerned, the word "Gospel" should be replaced with "Good News"!

Mark's Gospel is not signed; there is no autograph! Authors of the second century wrote that is was a Mark who was the author. It's just an Oral Tradition reflecting a turning point in Christology because the Baptism of Yeshua was made to be the instant of Messiah-ship. This change in the Christological Moment is assigned to the Baptism because the author believed that Yeshua's wisdom could only have come from an earlier approval of Yeshua as the Messiah. It was that shift in doctrine that identified Mark's community as one whose belief structure was indeed different from Paul, Peter and James. That difference puts Mark in a new light; this Mark was not a disciple of Paul, nor the son of Peter, nor had he any direct, long term contact with the early Apostles and disciples. Mark's sources were of second or third generation Christians who carried the stories to Mark's community. If Mark had been associated with the eyewitnesses, his Christology would have reflected the identical Apostolic Resurrectional origin contained in Romans 1: 3-4! Thus, the significance of the royal ritual of Psalm 2 in the Baptism of Yeshua in Mark implies a new dimension and direction for Christian teachings. It will be shown that the remaining three Gospels actually introduce further differences and dimensions within the Christian doctrinal world.

It is a mistake to read this Gospel, or any of the other three, as though the author is telling an unbiased historical story. In the first place, the author wrote a faith centered text to preserve the Yeshua story and to teach those who are to become Christians. Mark knows exactly what outcome is necessary in order to convince the reader of Yeshua's authoritative and authentic teaching about the Divine. The author was not an eyewitness but relied mostly on oral traditions and maybe some written sources including some apocryphal writings. As in all Biblical writings, the Backward-Looking literary style of this Gospel has been influenced by the author's faith and his perceptions of the Hebrew Testament's alleged prophetic accuracies. If an author already believes that the Hebrew Testament is absolutely true in all things, then what he writes is his perception of truth and the story he tells becomes a total construct of his belief structure and not an objective report about the life and times within his story. Mind you, we're not saying that his faith is faulty, only that the factuality of the history and conversations of the reported events are not accurate.

Each reader of the Christian Testament must be aware that a human person is fabricating a tale so that the reader can experience an identical belief and faith in this Carpenter, Yeshua of Nazareth. The apostles lived, ate and slept with Yeshua throughout his entire ministry but were so disappointed and discouraged when Yeshua died on the cross that they were heading home, defeated! Were they all asleep during Yeshua's preachings? Well, maybe yes and maybe no! The point made here is that the author makes it appear that Yeshua is in command and totally aware of the outcome when, in actuality, it's Mark, or whoever this author is, who knows the outcome and puts all that awareness on Yeshua's lips and in the tale itself. Scholars recognized this and labeled it Mark's little secret.

Mark's Gospel contains clues about Yeshua. the real man, equal to us in every respect including ignorance (as later confirmed and defined in the Council of Chalcedon, circa 451 AD). Mark's Gospel presents Yeshua as a very human person who is misunderstood by his own family, experiences human emotions, curses a fig tree, tries to heal but doesn't heal on the first attempt, is tempted, makes mistakes (see the commentaries below: Mk 2: 26, Mk 9: 1 and Mk 13: 30) yet exhibits a rare wisdom about the personage of God and what our relationship to God ought to be and can be. Therefore, Mark's Gospel contains many profound truths about relationship and respect, that is, if we can sift through all the faith-myths (especially those made up conversations) and historical inaccuracies written in by the author.

Let's now proceed to our commentary on specific verses of interest and hopefully you will experience Mark's style and his profound Faith in the risen Anointed One, the Christos, as well as, the good news about the Kingdom of God.

You may wish to read the entire Gospel first and then return to the comments. That will hopefully step up your awareness of the subtlety of Mark's "between the lines" intentions. Of course, you may cheat a little and read the comments as you read the Gospel. If you are fortunate enough to have a New American Bible or access to the Internet where you can read the NAB, then definitely read the Introduction; it's very informative and rewarding.

1: 1 The beginning of the gospel of Jesus Christ (the Son of GOD).
Gospel is supposed to mean good message or good news. Mark used the Greek word "euaggelion" that means "Good News". After reading the Gospels the translator into English used the word "gospel" (mind you, a 14th to 17th AD English word along with a literalist's mindset!).

1: 2 *As it is written in Isaiah the prophet:*
There will be a lot of introductions like this because the author of the Gospel believes that the prophets of old predicted the future. We'll discuss "predicting the future" in Chapter Five.

1: 4 *John (the) Baptist appeared in the desert proclaiming a baptism of repentance for the forgiveness of sins.*
The Greek word, "metanoia", means to change one's mind or behavior. It doesn't mean to be sorry (repent) although sorrow does come with one's awareness of the wrongs that one has done! For you linguists, repent is a French word (*re-pense*) meaning to "think it over again".

1: 7 *And this is what he proclaimed: "One mightier than I is coming after me. I am not worthy to stoop and loosen the thongs of his sandals.*
It has been suggested that this verse was included to dismiss John as the Messiah, a position held by many. If John says he is not the Messiah then the confusion is resolved.

1: 8 *I have baptized you with water; he will baptize you with the holy Spirit."*
Actually this is a reference to the spirit of holiness; the same Greek words that are used in Rom 1: 4. However, from now through to the end of this book there is no certainty that the author had personified the Spirit of God into a third person.

1: 10-11 *On coming up out of the water he saw the heavens being torn open and the Spirit, like a dove, descending upon him. And a voice came from the heavens, "You are my beloved son; with you I am well pleased."*
The first underlined is from Isaiah 11: 2. It is fairly clear that "the Spirit" is God, not a third person. The second underlined is principally from Psalm 2 and Isaiah 42: 1 with overtones from Isa 61:1 and 63: 7 ff. This thought about the Spirit will be treated further in Chapter Five.

1: 12 *At once the Spirit drove him out into the desert,*
The early Christians still believed that God was the driving force in every action. Yet, the comment in 1: 8 still remains.

1: 18 *Then they abandoned their nets and followed him.*
This description is quite simple here. But there must have been more conversation to motivate two men to abandon their livelihood and families!

1: 22 *The people were astonished at his teaching, for he taught them as one having authority and not as the scribes.*
Mark presents Yeshua as a very confident man. Thus begins Mark's secret.

1: 26 *The unclean spirit convulsed him and with a loud cry came out of him.*
The people of this time period believed that illness was caused by invading evil spirits! This is a reconstructed tale to illustrate Yeshua's powers. The 1st century medical awareness was indeed faulty; they firmly believed in demons. We know better! And, if God dictated the contents (you know, inspired), then God doesn't know anything. But God does know everything past, therefore, the word "inspired" is NOT a guarantee of any type of accuracy, neither of history nor of science!

1: 34 *He cured many who were sick with various diseases, and he drove out many demons, not permitting them to speak because they knew him.*
This is a slight exaggeration to further Mark's secret. Evil spirits know things that people don't (a falsehood), so Mark was dropping hints about Yeshua's secret.

1: 44 *Then he said to him, "See that you tell no one anything, but go, show yourself to the priest and offer for your cleansing what Moses prescribed; that will be proof for them."*
Yeshua is a good Israelite; he respects the Mosaic Law. We don't believe that Yeshua would do this to provide proof of his Messiahship. Mark more than likely made this up so that it would appear to the reader that Yeshua was the Messiah.

2: 4 *Unable to get near Jesus because of the crowd, they opened up the roof above him. After they had broken through, they let down the mat on which the paralytic was lying.*
The Greek word for "roof" is *stege* [Strong's Greek Number, 4721: a "thatch" or "deck" of a building, a roof]. This may seem odd to you but in Luke's Gospel he refers to the roof as a clay tile roof. Store this in the back of your mind because we will compare the same story in Luke's Gospel again in Chapter Five.

2: 5 *When Jesus saw their faith, he said to the paralytic, "Child, your sins are forgiven."*
This starts the conflict with the Israelite authorities. Some scholars suspect that Mark was reflecting the result of the Resurrection and the theme of Yeshua's sacrifice to remit the sins of humankind.

2: 15 *While he was at table in his house, many tax collectors and sinners sat with Jesus and his disciples; for there were many who followed him.*
Sinner is a name applied to people who were not actually committing sin but only labeled unclean by the Mosaic Law. And just like us in the 21st century, people dislike tax collectors.

2: 26 *How he went into the house of God when Abiathar was high priest and ate the bread of offering that only the priests could lawfully eat, and shared it with his companions?"*
Opps! Yeshua doesn't know his Hebrew Testament history. Read 1 Sam 21: 1-5 and discover that the High Priest was Ahimelech!! Now, folks, we ask you, who made the mistake? Was it Yeshua, Mark or God's inspiration? Tune in to Chapter Five for the answer!

2: 27-28 *Then he said to them, "The sabbath was made for man, not man for the sabbath. That is why the Son of Man is lord even of the sabbath."*
The first sentence is apparently from Yeshua! But this last one is more likely a Markan addition. Mark is the first one to use "son of man" in reference to Yeshua. Scholars are still not certain that Yeshua referred to himself as Daniel's "son of man". Appendix AA presents an analysis of this problem.

3: 5-6 *Looking around at them <u>with anger and grieved</u> at their hardness of heart, he said to the man, "Stretch out your hand." He stretched it out and his hand was restored. The Pharisees went out and immediately took counsel with the Herodians against him <u>to put him to death</u>.*

That first one speaks of an emotional Yeshua, first anger, then sadness. The second one is the beginning of the BIG plot!

3: 11 *And whenever unclean spirits saw him they would fall down before him and shout, "You are the Son of God."*
This is certainly a Markan construct to further the secret. We suspect that no spirit actually became visible and bowed down! But who really knows what lurks in the mind of a 1st century literalist.

3: 16-19 *(he appointed the twelve:) Simon, whom he named Peter; James, son of Zebedee, and John the brother of James, whom he named Boanerges, that is, sons of thunder; Andrew, Philip, Bartholomew, Matthew, Thomas, James the son of Alphaeus; Thaddeus, Simon the Cananean, and Judas Iscariot who betrayed him.*
We will check out the accuracy of this list in the other Gospels and in Acts. The result will again be in Chapter Five. We will comment on Judas Iscariot and his recently publicized Gospel in Chapter Five.

3: 21 *When his relatives heard of this they set out to seize him, for they said, "He is out of his mind."*
This is great! The family doesn't know who Yeshua is! The Greek word is "*exhistemi*" which comes from "*ex*" meaning "out" and "*istemi*" which is related to "*stao*" meaning to stand. Yeshua's mind is standing out of his self, a synonym for crazy. Matthew and Luke, who both copied much of Mark's writings, left this incident out. One might theorize that each felt this to be embarrassing to the memory of Yeshua and his family. This material will be reviewed in Chapter Five.

3: 29 *But whoever blasphemes against the Holy Spirit will never have forgiveness, but is guilty of an everlasting sin."*
Theologians have been trying to figure out this statement for centuries. Is there a sin that God cannot forgive? Yes! There is! It's a person's free choice to reject every aspect of God's JUSTICE: forgiveness and mercy, but especially God's forgiveness of those whom we want punished. Keep this in mind when we read the parable of the daily workers and the one talent given to each worker no matter how long each labored!

3: 31 *His mother and his brothers arrived. Standing outside they sent word to him and called him*
Why? Because they don't know what Yeshua was doing in there! Of course, the whole family is concerned. This incident implies that Yeshua didn't tell any family member what he was planning. Could Mark be just making this up to enhance Yeshua's secret? This makes us question whether Yeshua had such a secret or did Mark make it all up?

4: 11-12 *He answered them, "The mystery of the kingdom of God has been granted to you. But to those outside everything comes in parables, so that 'they may look and see but not perceive, and hear and listen but not understand, in order that they may not be converted and be forgiven.'"*
This is Mark's quote of a common H.T. expression. this verse is an enigma. Supposedly, the disciples got the message but we'll see later that they didn't. Remember, a literalist believes that God makes everything happen. For Mark, that's why the crowd didn't understand Yeshua's parables; God inhibited it.

Actually, Yeshua spoke in mythical terms as the best way to teach his profound intimacy with Yahweh. And the reality is that God doesn't hinder anyone's understanding, people choose to ignore it! Then again, Mark may just be telling us that there are a lot of people in the world who are morally deaf, dumb and blind!

4: 23 *Anyone who has ears to hear ought to hear."*
A colloquial saying to prompt a person to examine the deeper meaning of the story.

4: 34 *Without parables he did not speak to them, but to his own disciples he explained everything in private.*
The Bible does speak in mythic styles. Some will understand. But the early Christians believed that God (and Yeshua) deliberately made certain people hard of hearing to stop them from understanding. And, that is called "folk-theology" which is always a distortion of reality! It's one's mind's eye that blinds one's heart. (Good metaphors!) If you think a bit more about this, you will recognize the "tree of knowledge of good and evil" as the source of why people believed that God hindered a person/s understanding. Remember, God didn't want humans to know good and evil in the Garden, maybe as a way of preserving their innocence. Of course, this is pure conjecture on the part of the author of Genesis and, as a result, Genesis is just about totally mythologized and constructed history ... it is the stuff of legends.

4: 36-41 *Leaving the crowd, they took him with them in the boat just as he was. And other boats were with him. A violent squall came up and waves were breaking over the boat, so that it was already filling up. Jesus was in the stern, asleep on a cushion. They woke him and said to him, "Teacher, do you not care that we are perishing?" He woke up, rebuked the wind, and said to the sea, "Quiet! Be still!" The wind ceased and there was great calm. Then he asked them, "Why are you terrified? Do you not yet have faith?" They were filled with great awe and said to one another, "Who then is this whom even wind and sea obey?"*
A Post-Resurrectional story misplaced. But the part about the disciples confusion is historical.

5: 26 *She had suffered greatly at the hands of many doctors and had spent all that she had. Yet she was not helped but only grew worse.*
Sounds like a a modern day, retired person living on just Social Security getting less than good medical help.

6: 3 *Is he not the carpenter, the son of Mary, and the brother of James and Joses and Judas and Simon? And are not his sisters here with us?" And they took offense at him.*
Gadsooks folks, Mary had other children.! Somebody has been giving its membership a line of ... bu ..... mis-information about Mary's perpetual virginity!

6: *4 Jesus said to them, "A prophet is not without honor except in his native place and among his own kin and in his own house."*
Ain't that the truth! To think, we didn't need Yeshua to tell us that! Notice, Yeshua implies that he is a prophet. He does not use "son of man" or "son of God".

6: 8-9 *He instructed them to take nothing for the journey but a walking stick--no food, no sack, no money in their belts. They were, however, to wear sandals but not a second tunic.*
A far cry from today's Ministers!

6: 34 *When he disembarked and saw the vast crowd, his heart was moved with pity for them, for they were like sheep without a shepherd; and he began to teach them many things.*
Many of today's church members.

6: 49 *But when they saw him walking on the sea, they thought it was a ghost and cried out.*
That's a Post-Resurrectional incident again, misplaced via the Oral Tradition.

7: 6-8 *He responded, "Well did Isaiah prophesy about you hypocrites, as it is written: 'This people honors me with their lips, but their hearts are far from me; In vain do they worship me, teaching as doctrines human precepts.' You disregard God's commandment but cling to human tradition."*
The problem that exists today is that many people do not understand that the Hebrew Testament is mostly myth constructed by human authors. Yet, notably, its deeper meaning is still there. Both words are "didache" in Greek but the second Greek word is best translated as "doctrines".

7: 18-23 *He said to them, "Are even you likewise without understanding? Do you not realize that everything that goes into a person from outside cannot defile, since it enters not the heart but the stomach and passes out into the latrine?" (Thus he declared all foods clean.) "But what comes out of a person, that is what defiles. From within people, from their hearts, come evil thoughts, unchastity, theft, murder, adultery, greed, malice, deceit, licentious-ness, envy, blasphemy, arrogance, folly. All these evils come from within and they defile."*
Yeshua has just implied that there is no Satan or devils making us do things! Humans choose freely! Demons don't affect our choices neither does God; we do the choosing ... and we do it freely! Notice that he believes that the Heart is the center of thought, a misconception of the times.

8: 27-30 *Now Jesus and his disciples set out for the villages of Caesarea Philippi. Along the way he asked his disciples, "Who do people say that I am?" They said in reply, "John the Baptist, others Elijah, still others one of the prophets." And he asked them, "But who do you say that I am?" Peter said to him in reply, "You are the Messiah." Then he warned them not to tell anyone about him.*
We will examine this further in Matthew and Luke's Gospels to determine what those two authors wrote about this conversation. Then we will know who said what to whom. This passage is really a little glimpse of Mark's story line---Yeshua's secret.

9: 4 *then Elijah appeared to them along with Moses, and they were conversing with Jesus.*
Definitely a Post-Resurrectional event misplaced by Mark because his sources misplaced it. Or, just maybe, another folk tale!

9: 9 *As they were coming down from the mountain, he charged them not to relate what they had seen to anyone, except when the Son of Man had risen from the dead.* "
Remember Chalcedon and the "humanity of Yeshua", including ignorance? Well, Yeshua could not have said this! Mark's Backward Looking put those words on Yeshua's lips to authenticate his own belief. Really now, this is the author's way of revealing the "secret". Now, the "Son of Man" as a title is problematic and the solution is presented in Appendix AA.

9: 10 *So they kept the matter to themselves, questioning what rising from the dead meant.*
Again, Mark's construct.

9: 23 *Jesus said to him, " 'If you can!' Everything is possible to one who has faith."*
Well, almost everything! But, it likely is from Yeshua.

9: 24 *Then the boy's father cried out, "I do believe, help my unbelief!"*
Us too.

9: 27-29 *But Jesus took him by the hand, raised him, and he stood up. When he entered the house, his disciples asked him in private, "Why could we not drive it {The demon} out?" He said to them, "This kind can only come out through prayer."*
This verse is the justification for the Catholic Institution's Rite of Exorcism.

9: 35 *Then he sat down, called the Twelve, and said to them, "If anyone wishes to be first, he shall be the last of all and the servant of all."*
Oh, please someone tell this to the Hierarchy of the Roman Petrine Tradition.

9: 50 *Salt is good, but if salt becomes insipid, with what will you restore its flavor? Keep salt in yourselves and you will have peace with one another."*
A good Chemistry simile! When salt (that which gives flavor) of that locale absorbed moisture, the NaCl dissolved out and left Calcium Sulfate that has no taste. Some Christians and Ministers appear to have lost their Sodium Chloride!

10: 21-22 *Jesus, looking at him, loved him and said to him, "You are lacking in one thing. Go, sell what you have, and give to (the) poor and you will have treasure in heaven; then come, follow me." At that statement his face fell, and he went away sad, <u>for he had many possessions</u>.*
Like many of us today!

10: 26-27 *They were exceedingly astonished and said among themselves, "Then who can be saved?" Jesus looked at them and said, "For human beings it is impossible, but not for God. <u>All things are possible for God</u>."*
And, for that, we sinners are grateful.

10: 45 *For the Son of Man did not come to be served but to serve and to give his life as a ransom for many."*
This sentence is totally Mark's Backward-Looking words placed on Yeshua's lips! But the title, son of man, occurs because of the mis-translation from Aramaic, *bar enach*, to Greek, *huios ho anthropos*. See Appendix AA for my analysis.

11: 13-14 *Seeing from a distance a fig tree in leaf, he went over to see if he could find anything on it. When he reached it he found nothing but leaves; it was not the time for figs. And he said to it in reply, "May no one ever eat of your fruit again!" And his disciples heard it.*
Why curse the fig tree? It wasn't its time? Was this some kind of temper tantrum? No! Just a folk tale!

11: 20 *Early in the morning, as they were walking along, they saw the fig tree withered to its roots.*
It died the next day! Another one for Chapter Five! Why? Because in the next Gospel we'll read that it died instantaneously. Which is correct? Inspiration? No! Human error? Yes!

11: 25 *When you stand to pray, forgive anyone against whom you have a grievance, so that your heavenly Father may in turn forgive you your transgressions."*
Ouch! Ouch! Forgiven ONLY when we forgive!!

12: 10 *Have you not read this scripture passage: 'The stone that the builders rejected has become the cornerstone;*
Mark's Backward-Looking knowledge placed on Yeshua's lips.

12: *27 He is not God of the dead but of the living. You are greatly misled."*
Not only is this a companion thought to Deut 30: 19 but also a clue to what happens after the final judgment! Think about it! God is alive with the living. Where are the dead? Wouldn't one have to be alive to experience the fire and brimstone? Oh, Oh, could it be that there's no fire and brimstone, no eternal torture! We'll discuss this later in Chapter Five.

12: 28-34 *One of the scribes, when he came forward and heard them disputing and saw how well he had answered them, asked him, "Which is the first of all the commandments?" Jesus replied, "The first is this: 'Hear, O Israel! The Lord our God is Lord alone!* {DEUT 6:4, GOD IS ONE!} *You shall love the Lord your God with all your heart, with all your soul, with all your mind, and with all your strength.' The second is this: 'You shall love your neighbor as yourself.' There is no other commandment greater than these."*
YOU GOT IT! RELATIONSHIP AND RESPECT!
The scribe said to him, "Well said, teacher. You are right in saying, 'He is One and there is no other than he.' And 'to love him with all your heart, with all your understanding, with all your strength, and to love your neighbor as yourself' is worth more than all burnt offerings and sacrifices." And when Jesus saw that (he) answered with understanding, he said to him, "You are not far from the kingdom of God." And no one dared to ask him any more questions.
This is a powerful passage because Yeshua (really Mark) acknowledges that there is One God and no other. Then, our problem is, "What does the Nicene Creed mean?" More on this subject in Chapter Five.

12: 38-40 *In the course of his teaching he said, "Beware of the scribes, who like to go around in long robes and accept greetings in the marketplaces, seats of honor in synagogues, and places of honor at banquets. They devour the houses of*

widows and, as a pretext, recite lengthy prayers. They will receive a very severe condemnation."
Watch out, Hierarchs! Abandoning poor parishes because they don't pay your tribute is scribal behavior, n'est pas?

13: 2 *Jesus said to him, "Do you see these great buildings? There will not be one stone left upon another that will not be thrown down."*
A Backward-Looking comment by Mark about his personal knowledge of the destruction of the Temple about 70 AD. This is what actually dates the Gospel!

13: 9 *"Watch out for yourselves. They will hand you over to the courts. You will be beaten in synagogues. You will be arraigned before governors and kings because of me, as a witness before them.*
Mark writes about his own times but puts the words in the lips of Yeshua as aggrandizement for Yeshua.

13: 30 *Amen, I say to you, this generation will not pass away until all these things have taken place.*
Opps! It did pass and the end times never came. Sounds like somebody has no foreknowledge after all! Was it Yeshua or faulty inspiration from God? Hint, hint, it's all Yeshua's human knowledge---he doesn't know the future!! However, if you can't tolerate Yeshua's ignorance, then blame it on God!

14: 14 *Wherever he enters, say to the master of the house, 'The Teacher says, "Where is my guest room where I may eat the Passover with my disciples?"'*
If Yeshua wanted a new Institution, why is he doing the Jewish Seder thing?

14: 22-25 *While they were eating, he took bread, said the blessing, broke it, and gave it to them, and said, "Take it; this is my body." Then he took a cup, gave thanks, and gave it to them, and they all drank from it. He said to them, "This is my blood of the covenant, which will be shed for many. Amen, I say to you, I shall not drink again the fruit of the vine until the day when I drink it new in the kingdom of God."*
This is a ritualistic re-interpretation of a Seder meal by non-Jewish Christians. We'll examine this later. Yep, in Ch 5!

14: 27-28 *Then Jesus said to them, "All of you will have your faith shaken, for it is written: 'I will strike the shepherd, and the sheep will be dispersed.' But after I have been raised up, I shall go before you to Galilee."*
Mark's Backward-Looking knowledge placed in Yeshua's mouth. Just a small comment; the quote doesn't apply to Yeshua. It comes from Zec 13: 7 and applies to the coming Exile! Remember these people in the 1st century are LITERALISTS; they all believe that the H.T. is future-looking. It ain't!

14: 36 *he said, "Abba, Father, all things are possible to you. Take this cup away from me, but not what I will but what you will."*
"Abba" means Daddy. The formal word, Father, appears to be Mark's mis-understanding of Aramaic. There is one problem here. How can Mark know what Yeshua said when the Gospel specifically states that no one was with him in the Garden? Check out verses 35 and 37.

14: 49 *Day after day I was with you teaching in the temple area, yet you did not arrest me; but that the scriptures may be fulfilled."*
A pre-critical naiveté understanding that the prophets predicted the future. It's "folk-theology" for sure from the Literalist camp.

14: 62 *Then Jesus answered, "I am; and 'you will see the Son of Man seated at the right hand of the Power and coming with the clouds of heaven.'"*
A Chalcedon man could not have said that! It's Mark's Backward-Looking construct from the book of Daniel..

16: 5 *On entering the tomb they saw a young man sitting on the right side, clothed in a white robe, and they were utterly amazed.*
We will compare the Tomb stories in each of the Gospels in Chapter Five.
Take note! Where are the Apostles? Could it be that these three women (in 16: 1) were the Apostles!

16: 16 *Whoever believes and is baptized will be saved; whoever does not believe will be condemned.*
This is not what Paul wrote in Romans. It's much too harsh for Yeshua also.
Note: this is from the longer version of the three different endings of Mark's Gospel. No one seems to be able to state for certain which one is authentic!

Summary of the Second Period:

Let me remind you that no one really knows who wrote Mark's Gospel! However, we've used the commonly accepted name. The theme of this biography is that this author believes Yeshua to be the Messiah whom the people believed that God promised (allegedly, that is!). Since Yeshua preached such an amazing revelation about who God is and what is necessary for salvation, Mark had to place the Christological Moment at the beginning of Yeshua's ministry so that Yeshua could carry with him an awareness of his mission and the role he played in God's plan. That awareness was sprinkled throughout this Good News tale as "The Secret". As plots go, it turns out that the "Secret" was revealed on several occasions throughout the story.

Another topic enters Christendom: the role of John the Baptist which heretofore was of no concern in Paul's writings. Suddenly a group of disciples popped up with the belief that John was the Messiah. From this time onwards that posture had to be addressed in each Gospel. John was the precursor, nothing more.

It's also important to realize that this "Good News" may not have circulated to every Christian community over the following ten years. One thing for sure, Matthew and Luke both had a copy. You will next see that they too had a different story to tell and they changed the Christological Moment as well.

Section Three: The Conception Period: One God, One Lord, Son of God at the Annunciation and this Holy Spirit

15. Gospel of Matthew (68-80):

A: The Confusions in the Gospel of Matthew

The first difficulty is that Matthew's Christology introduces a new concept not found in the previous canonical readings. Yeshua is Messiah at the conception! I wonder what Paul would think of this? Alas! We'll never know the answer until the end of time. This third doctrinal position takes place along the pathway of a very complex Christological development within some, or even a few, of the early Christian communities.

The second problem comes when we begin our reading of the Canonical Christian Testament. We find this Gospel right up front, in first place followed by the other Gospels. It actually was written close to fifty years after Yeshua's ministry ended. It appears that Matthew may not have had any contact with the Apostles and, most likely, not with any eye witnesses either; he probably only had an oral tradition from third and forth generation Christians. Further, Matthew utilizes Mark's Gospel as a skeleton onto which he adds material from two written sources, the Q (same as Luke's Q source) and the M (his own unique Matthean source). {Some parts of the Q Source are found in Appendices K & Q.} To make matters more complicated, Matthew rejects certain of Mark's descriptions that give Yeshua a negative image. He then ties all of this together with his own literary style and a great deal of Hebrew Testament verses (actually 26 references) that he believes speak directly about the future Messiah (by way of God's inspirational conversations with the Prophets). In Matthew's mind's eye, it is impossible to refute what he writes since God has already told the prophets exactly who, where and when this Messiah would appear and then live a life exactly according to God's absolute foreknowledge and plan. To load the deck further, Yeshua is not just human but God's Son in a shell of a human body. This interpretation, of course, will be refuted at Chalcedon in 451 AD. As a matter of history, we have thus far shown that trouble was brooding in Christendom in the Pauline communities and those troubles became more infectious as the years passed. Have you managed to look over the list of apocryphal writings in the early years (listed in Appendix E)? They are clearly indicative of a great deal of mis-information about Yeshua, what he said and did. Then in 312 AD Constantine politicized Christianity and he demanded (in 325 AD) that the Church-State Judicial officials resolve their doctrinal infighting for the sake of peace and civility within the Empire. Thus, the Nicene Creed came into being. It reconfigured Matthew's theology, along with Mark's, Luke's, Paul's, Peter's and especially the Fourth Gospel into the most earth-shattering dogma—Yeshua was always God, and the infancy narrative in Matthew and Luke erred in placing the Christological moment at the birth, as well as Mark's baptism, including Paul's and Acts Resurrectional assignments. Well, they all appear to have been incorrect! Except, there was one winner—the Fourth Gospel's authors! The real problem was, and still is, the existence of some Christian communities that don't accept the Nicene dogma. What do we do now? Our personal question is, what happened to "inspiration" and God's true Words?

The third problem occurs within the Gospel of Matthew with the inaccuracy of the genealogy when compared with the one in Luke. And worse still, Matthew used a numerological metaphor of three lists of fourteen names each. When one puts numbers to the three Hebrew letters of King David's name, Daleth (the 4th letter) + Wav (the 6th letter) + Daleth (the 4th), the sum becomes 14. This secret code stuff is common in most writings of that time period, like the number of the Beast in Revelations, 666. Therefore from David to Yeshua there are 28 generations. In Luke there are 72 generations from God to Yeshua but 40 from David to Yeshua. This is a good time for you to count them yourself. In Appendix J you'll find the list and in Chapter Five we'll examine the names, the reason for and the consequence of this inconsistency.

The fourth problem exists in our own time when one starts reading the Christian Testament with Matthew's Gospel placed up front by the primitive, literalistic Christian membership whose primary tenet is that (a) the Hebrew Testament is a true history and accurate scientific description of ages past, (b) God is the single driving force (Puppeteer Model) in every past, present and future event and (c) the Hebrew Testament is a platform from which God's holy prophets predicted the future events relating to the Messiah. After the typical reader absorbs the first four Gospels, Acts and the letter to the Romans, the remaining books are seen and interpreted solely as continuations of the Gospel events, the players, the conversations and, not the least of all, the alleged predictions of the Hebrew Testament's prophets. That makes the average readers wince with far too much theological baggage that both clouds and confuses their assimilation of the postures of the remaining authors. Be particularly attentive to the different theological and Christological moments in the other 21 books. Most have missed and mis-interpreted them because they have read Matthew first and innocently accepted Matthew's theological biography. The Matthean Gospel represents the view of a single Christian community in the Mediterranean basin in 80 AD. i

Those are the problems that helped determine the reading and commentary schedule found in Appendix U. It is the posture of this book that the development of a Christian theology and its companion Christology can be properly understood only if one reads the Christian Testament in its chronological order of authorship!

B: Prophets of the Hebrew Testament and Future Predictions

It was mentioned a few lines ago that Matthew's Gospel contains 26 references from the H.T. that predicted Yeshua's biography. Let's review those in the context of a fuller reading of the Hebrew Testament. At this juncture you should already be familiar with this Backward-Looking literary style employed by the H.T. authors. Let's restate it to refresh your memory! (1) The authors already know the result of events that they will write about. (2) The writing of each book takes place decades and oftentimes centuries after the event and much of the detailed material has been circulating in the Oral Tradition for those previous years. (3) The nature of the Oral Tradition is such that the stories become more elaborate and only the significant details are recalled—this is what is called "mythologizing" history. (4) Mythologized stories contain the deeper meaning of those events but not the literal facts or literal words. (5) The words in those remembered H.T. stories are themselves very general and apply only to the historical event in question. (6) However, to a primitive people who believe that their God is the Master Puppeteer and cause of every major and minor event in their own lives and the life of their nation, those mythologized stories become the Divine dictates that predict the future.

In our present world with its Archeological research and fossil records, along with our recent discoveries of ancient writings, DNA knowledge and the radioactivity dating measurements, we are able to detect and identify the age and veracity of the physical document containing the mythologized tales. All the data collected points to an incongruity within the Biblical stories themselves. It is tempting to wager that any one of us could write his/her own story using Hebrew Testament predictions with a few connecting constructs of his/her own dated experiences!

Now, it's appropriate to turn to the details.

C: Comments on the Gospel of Matthew

The author of Matthew's Gospel, whoever he was, constructed this 28 chapter book using the basic structure of Mark's Gospel woven with selected portions from two written sources (Q and M) whose alleged facts were then justified by the Hebrew Testament's generic mythologized stories.

1: 1-17 The genealogy of Yeshua, as written by Matthew, is in itself a contradiction to Luke's genealogy! Matt states that there are 28 generations from David to Yeshua while Luke indicates that there are 40 generations. It should be noted that 12 generations is NOT a small difference. Apparently each has a different idea about the life span of a single generation: Matt (36 years) and Luke (24 years). There is one more problem: Joseph's father (Jacob) here is different from Luke's (Heli)! These will be expanded further in Chapter Five.

1: 18 - 2: 23 This entire Infancy Narrative is in serious conflict with Luke's and will be dealt with in Chapter Five.

3: 1-17 This Chapter is a copy of Mark's baptism of Yeshua. Obviously, Ol' Matthew didn't recognize the significance of the light, dove and quote from Psalm 2!

4: 1-11 The desert experience from Mark with a Matthean elaboration. You will read about a similar elaboration in the commentary of Luke's Gospel.

4*: 17 From that time on, Jesus began to preach and say, "Repent, for the kingdom of heaven is at hand."*
The Greek word is "*metanoia*" which means change your mindset. Being "sorry" misses the point. The English word repent comes from a French word, *repenser*, to think again; "Changing your behavior" is the correct translation! It's noteworthy that the English language had a large influx of French when the Normans conquered them in 1066 AD. Yo'al remember that date from your history courses! Yes, sure you do!

5: 1 *When he saw the crowds, he went up the mountain, and after he had sat down, his disciples came to him.*
This is the second hint that Matt considers Yeshua to be the new Moses who went up Mt Sinai. The first was in the Infancy Narrative in which Matt threads his tale with the life story of Moses. Note, we will see in Luke, however, that Yeshua teaches on the plains.

5: 2-11 These are Matthew's 8 beatitudes (Blessed's). Luke uses 4 "Blessed's" and 4 "Woe to's"!

5: 16 *Just so, your light must shine before others, that they may see your good deeds and glorify your heavenly Father.*
Notice the words, good deeds. Even as late as 80 AD we see that faith and good deeds (works) belong together.

5: 17-18 *Do not think that I have come to abolish the law or the prophets. I have come not to abolish but to fulfill. Amen, I say to you, until heaven and earth pass away, not the smallest letter or the smallest part of a letter will pass from the law, until all things have taken place.*
These words of Yeshua seem to imply that the purpose of the "Jesus Movement" was only to fulfill and complete God's work. In Ch 7 we'll see that the Jesus Movement only pointed to a new behavior <u>within Judaism</u>.

5: 23-24 *Therefore, if you bring your gift to the altar, and there recall that your brother has anything against you, leave your gift there at the altar, go first and be reconciled with your brother, and then come and offer your gift.*
This is indeed a powerful recommendation by Yeshua! "Don't ask for forgiveness unless you have first forgiven your brother and sister."

5: 28-32 *But I say to you, everyone who looks at a woman with lust has already committed adultery with her in his heart. If your right eye causes you to sin, tear it out and throw it away. It is better for you to lose one of your members than to have your whole body thrown into Gehenna. And if your right hand causes you to sin, cut it off and throw it away. It is better for you to lose one of your members than to have your whole body go into Gehenna. "It was also said, 'Whoever divorces his wife must give her a bill of divorce.' But I say to you, whoever divorces his wife (unless the marriage is unlawful) causes her to commit adultery, and whoever marries a divorced woman commits adultery.*
My gosh, Yeshua believes in a punishing God like the rest of the people. Yet later on Yeshua speaks of a merciful and forgiving God! What do you believe? Note that Yeshua makes some mighty harsh and hard statements. These are especially difficult for Americans, particularly, the lust and divorce thing!

5: 37 *Let your 'Yes' mean 'Yes,' and your 'No' mean 'No.' Anything more is from the evil one.*
Don't lie, "say what you mean and mean what you say"! Sounds like good Psychology to us! Notice the "evil one"! Yeshua believes in demonology.

5: 43-48 "You have heard that it was said, 'You shall love your neighbor and hate your enemy.' But I say to you, love your enemies, and pray for those who persecute you, that you may be children of your heavenly Father, for he makes his sun rise on the bad and the good, and causes rain to fall on the just and the unjust. For if you love those who love you, what recompense will you have? Do not the tax collectors do the same? And if you greet your brothers only, what is unusual about that? Do not the pagans do the same? <u>So be perfect, just as your heavenly Father is perfect.</u>
These are the toughest of Yeshua's sayings. But the aphorism in v. 48 is a mis-translation! The word "perfect" should read, "do the best you can as an athlete tries". Then, it's within reach of us imperfect humans. The Greek word is *teleo,* a

term meaning work at making yourself better. The implication seems to be that God is working to make things better. Does this mean that God is "becoming", like growing and changing? Something to ponder! We'll be addressing that topic in Chapter Seven.

6: 1-34 This whole Chapter is worthy of a careful reading; these words are the closest we can come to actually listening to Yeshua! Check the prayer formula in v. 9-15 and pay special attention to the warning in v.14 and 15. When we get to Luke we will examine the prayer. But it's different! Did Yeshua give us two "Our Father's"? If you are curious, go to Luke 11: 1-4 and be surprised!

7: 1-29 Notice among all these teachings that the following stand out: v. 7-8; v. 12; v. 14; v. 21; v. 29.

> v. 7-8 Ask *and it will be given to you; seek and you will find; knock and the door will be opened to you. For everyone who asks, receives; and the one who seeks, finds; and to the one who knocks, the door will be opened.*
>
> v. 12 *Do to others whatever you would have them do to you. This is the law and the prophets.*
>
> v. 14 *How narrow the gate and constricted the road that leads to life. And those who find it are few.*
>
> v. 21 *Not everyone who says to me, 'Lord, Lord,' will enter the kingdom of heaven, but only the one who does the will of my Father in heaven.*
>
> V 29 *for he taught them as one having authority, and not as their scribes.*

8: 1 *When Jesus came down from the mountain, great crowds followed him.*
Like Moses, Yeshua comes down from the mountain!

8: 11-12 *I say to you, many will come from the east and the west, and will recline with Abraham, Isaac, and Jacob at the banquet in the kingdom of heaven, but the children of the kingdom will be driven out into the outer darkness, where there will be wailing and grinding of teeth.*
Now, this one puzzles me. What do you think the "children of the kingdom" means? Our first guess is that these are the chosen people of Israel who didn't choose the Kingdom of God that Yeshua preached! What say you?

8: 23-27 *He got into a boat and his disciples followed him. Suddenly a violent storm came up on the sea, so that the boat was being swamped by waves; but he was asleep. They came and woke him, saying, "Lord, save us! We are perishing!" He said to them, "Why are you terrified, O you of little faith?" Then he got up, rebuked the winds and the sea, and there was great calm. The men were amazed and said, "What sort of man is this, whom even the winds and the sea obey?"*
This has all the earmarks of a post-Resurrectional event. And, copied from Mark!

8: 28-34 *When he came to the other side, to the territory of the Gadarenes, two demoniacs who were coming from the tombs met him. They were so savage that no one could travel by that road. They cried out, "What have you to do with us, Son of God? Have you come here to torment us before the appointed time?" Some distance away a herd of many swine was feeding. The demons pleaded with him, "If you drive us out, send us into the herd of swine." And he said to them, "Go then!" They came out and entered the swine, and the whole herd rushed down the steep bank into the sea where they drowned. The swineherds ran away, and when they came to the town they reported everything, including what had happened to the demoniacs. Thereupon the whole town came out to meet Jesus, and when they saw him they begged him to leave their district.*
Here we have a great folk-tale. It's a 1st century belief that demons cause illness, both physical and mental. For a country that doesn't eat pork chops, there sure are a lot of piggies around town. Notice that the people were more frightened of Yeshua than the demons. Just goes to show you: we humans are more likely to stay with the pain we know or experience rather than change to something unfamiliar!

9: 9-10 *As Jesus passed on from there, he saw a man named Matthew sitting at the customs post. He said to him, "Follow me." And he got up and followed him. While he was at table in his house, many tax collectors and sinners came and sat with Jesus and his disciples.*
Could this be the Author telling his own story here?

9: 13 *Go and learn the meaning of the words, 'I desire mercy, not sacrifice.' I did not come to call the righteous but sinners."*
This is a direct reference to Isaiah 1: 17 in which the author speaks for God's compassion towards others rather than a ritualistic religion.

9: 22 *Jesus turned around and saw her, and said, "Courage, daughter! Your faith has saved you." And from that hour the woman was cured.*
Here's a Pauline reference about the saving nature of Faith.

9: 36 *At the sight of the crowds, his heart was moved with pity for them because they were troubled and abandoned, like sheep without a shepherd.*
There are two important components to this verse: Yeshua's pity, compassion or empathy for people and the fact that these were without a shepherd, a theme found in Ezekiel 34. Incidentally, is Ezekiel 34 an allegory or is Ezekiel talking about real shepherds?

10: 2-4 Here is a neat list of the Twelve chosen Apostles. Write these down somewhere because when we get to Chapter Five, we're going to compare them with the list of the 12 Apostles in the writings by the other C.T. authors.

10: 5-16 *Jesus sent out these twelve after instructing them thus, "Do not go into pagan territory or enter a Samaritan town, Go rather to the lost sheep of the house of Israel. As you go, make this proclamation: 'The kingdom of heaven is at hand.' Cure the sick, raise the dead, cleanse lepers, drive out demons. Without cost you have received; without cost you are to give. Do not take gold or silver or copper for your belts; no sack for the journey, or a second tunic, or sandals, or walking stick. The laborer deserves his keep.*

Whatever town or village you enter, look for a worthy person in it, and stay there until you leave. As you enter a house, wish it peace. If the house is worthy, let your peace come upon it; if not, let your peace return to you. Whoever will not receive you or listen to your words--go outside that house or town and shake the dust from your feet. Amen, I say to you, it will be more tolerable for the land of Sodom and Gomorrah on the Day of Judgment than for that town. "Behold, I am sending you like sheep in the midst of wolves; so be shrewd as serpents and simple as doves.
Now, that's a great message worthy of a few comments! First, Yeshua sends the 12 out to spread the Good News, the Kingdom of God is here and now, for the asking. Don't go outside of Israel! I guess Matthew didn't know about Paul's mission to the rest of the world nor of Yeshua's visit to the woman at the well in Samaria. Read the whole selection and ask yourself, "Do our ministers practice these directives?" Then, check out the last verse. We suggest that in the past 50 years some ministers took the serpent directive too literally but forgot the dove thing.

10: 20 *For it will not be you who speak but the Spirit of your Father speaking through you.*
Ah Ha! It's God's Spirit! It is hard to comprehend that a simple people would confuse this with the existence of a third person.

10: 23 *When they persecute you in one town, flee to another. Amen, I say to you, you will not finish the towns of Israel before the Son of Man comes.*
Is this a mistaken understanding of God who inspired Matthew, or Matthew's mistake or was it Yeshua who expected the end times to occur soon? Obviously, the end didn't arrive. You must re-read 1 Thess 4: 15 to 5: 10 for Paul's understanding of the end times. This hints of the Parousia.

10: 38 *and whoever does not take up his cross and follow after me is not worthy of me.*
Definitely a Post-Resurrectional observation written by Matthew and placed on the lips of the historical Yeshua. Definitely Backward-Looking

11:1 *When Jesus finished giving these commands to his twelve disciples, he went away from that place to teach and to preach in their towns.*
Note, Yeshua sent all 12 out to preach in 10: 5, now it appears that he goes alone or with minor disciples to their (Apostles) towns to preach and encounters John the Baptist's disciples. This whole Chapter addresses the problem of who John is, THE Messiah or the final messenger? This Chapter is just a polemic or disclaimer to discredit John the Baptist as the Messiah.

11: 14 *And if you are willing to accept it, he is Elijah, the one who is to come.*
Yeshua says that John may be Elijah! So, maybe Matthew believed in reincarnation! We suspect that Matthew put those words on the lips of Yeshua to discredit John as the Messiah.

11: 27-30 *All things have been handed over to me by my Father. No one knows the Son except the Father, and no one knows the Father except the Son and anyone to whom the Son wishes to reveal him. "Come to me, all you who labor and are burdened, and I will give you rest. Take my yoke upon you and learn*

from me, for I am meek and humble of heart; and you will find rest for your selves. For my yoke is easy, and my burden light."
These verses are faith statements from Matthew's community not the real words of Yeshua. The problem here is the Chalcedon doctrine of Yeshua's humanity. As a human, Yeshua cannot be in possession of such knowledge. Please re-read that Chalcedon doctrine of 451 AD and understand that being human includes ignorance! Oh, by the way, how come there is no mention that the Spirit isn't privy to the Father's or Son's knowledge? Does this mean that by Matthew's time there was no Trinity? Later you will read the formula of baptism in which there is the Trinity; it's not Matthew's. Or, it may be a later addition by some Trinitarian!

12: 3-4 *He said to them, "Have you not read what David did when he and his companions were hungry, how he went into the house of God and ate the bread of offering, which neither he nor his companions but only the priests could lawfully eat?*
Here Matthew decided to copy Mark's story but left out the name of the High Priest. Why? Because Mark got it wrong and Matthew doesn't want to make the same mistake. See 1 Sam 21: 1-5 & Mark 2: 26!!!

12: 8 *For the Son of Man is Lord of the Sabbath.*
First, throughout the C.T. Yeshua's use of the Son of Man title is doubtful. This sentence is a poor quote of Mark and misses the Markan point. This is more likely another of Matthew's constructs. It appears that the Commercial Industry has made a mockery of the "day of rest"! Actually, we in the USA have now destroyed the true meaning of the "Day of Rest" more so than Yeshua's disciples picking grain. Where is the outcry of the Institutional ministers? All are silent! You may reply, "But the Bible also says, 'the sabbath was made for man'"! All well and good, but have you considered that there is no day of rest anymore. We use that day to work our youth and poor for commercial gain! Did humankind forget another gift from God. Or was it Moses who made it a day of rest? Think about it!

12: 17-21 *This was to fulfill what had been spoken through Isaiah the prophet: "Behold, my servant whom I have chosen, my beloved in whom I delight; I shall place my spirit upon him, and he will proclaim justice to the Gentiles. He will not contend or cry out, nor will anyone hear his voice in the streets. A bruised reed he will not break, a smoldering wick he will not quench, until he brings justice to victory. And in his name the Gentiles will hope."*
This is a classic quote from Isaiah that is a standard reference to the king of Israel but was re-interpreted to point to Yeshua. See Isaiah 42: 1-4. Note the spirit; it is God! The problem with "his name" is that Jesus is not his name; it's Yeshua!

12: 28 *But if it is by the Spirit of God that I drive out demons, then the kingdom of God has come upon you.*
Another reference to God's Spirit but not a third persona.

12: 39-40 *He said to them in reply, "An evil and unfaithful generation seeks a sign, but no sign will be given it except the sign of Jonah the prophet. Just as Jonah was in the belly of the whale three days and three nights, so will the Son of Man be in the heart of the earth three days and three nights.*

This is definitely a "Backward- Looking" statement! Just think Chalcedon and you'll agree. This is simply Matthew's reflection. Yeshua was in the tomb for almost two nights Friday about 3 PM to Sunday morning 6 AM (that's about 40 hours. There's that number again)!

12: 47-50 *(Someone told him, "Your mother and your brothers are standing outside, asking to speak with you.") But he said in reply to the one who told him, "Who is my mother? Who are my brothers?" And stretching out his hand toward his disciples, he said, "Here are my Mother and my brothers. For whoever does the will of my heavenly Father is my brother, and sister, and mother."*
Another instance of Matthew's deliberate selective copying. There is much more to this story in Mark but Matthew will not copy a verse that points to Yeshua's family thinking him a bit out of his mind!

13: 11 *He said to them in reply, "Because knowledge of the mysteries of the kingdom of heaven has been granted to you, but to them it has not been granted.*
This is again a total misunderstanding of who God is! God does not deliberately clog a person's mind, only the "Shadow" does that! We humans choose what we wish to believe. Granted that not everyone understands Albert's Theory of Relativity; that has to do with education, but can we understand that it is not God's will to give us hardness of mind and heart.

13: 14-16 *Isaiah's prophecy is fulfilled in them, which says: 'You shall indeed hear but not understand you shall indeed look but never see. Gross is the heart of this people, they will hardly hear with their ears, they have closed their eyes, lest they see with their eyes and hear with their ears and understand with their heart and be converted, and I heal them.' "But blessed are your eyes, because they see, and your ears, because they hear.*
Another misinterpretation by Matthew; free will precludes such a statement by Yeshua and for that matter even by Isaiah! The underlined is again one of the many metaphors about a thinking and emoting heart. Hearts don't think nor do they emote! They just pump! The metaphor is about compassion, understanding with compassion!

13: 17 *Amen, I say to you, many prophets and righteous people longed to see what you see but did not see it, and to hear what you hear but did not hear it.*
Matthew is expressing his own opinion here. Yeshua could not have said this about himself; it is a contradiction to the Doctrine of Chalcedon and, as you will see later stated in 1 John!

13: 55 *Is he not the carpenter's son? Is not his mother named Mary and his brothers James, Joseph, Simon, and Judas?*
A Markan quote repeated by Matthew that confirms Mary's children. There is no "J" in Greek. The Greek is "Ioses". 3 of 15 Bibles use Joses, Joseph the rest.

13: 58 *And he did not work many mighty deeds there because of their lack of faith.*
Notice that Yeshua cannot perform any healing without a person's faith!

14: 23 *After doing so, he went up on the mountain by himself to pray. When it was evening he was there alone.*
Another comparison to Moses!

14: 24-32 *Meanwhile the boat, already a few miles offshore, was being tossed about by the waves, for the wind was against it. During the fourth watch of the night, he came toward them, walking on the sea. When the disciples saw him walking on the sea they were terrified. "It is a ghost," they said, and they cried out in fear. At once (Jesus) spoke to them, "Take courage, it is I; do not be afraid." Peter said to him in reply, "Lord, if it is you, command me to come to you on the water." He said, "Come." Peter got out of the boat and began to walk on the water toward Jesus. But when he saw how (strong) the wind was he became frightened; and, beginning to sink, he cried out, "Lord, save me!" Immediately Jesus stretched out his hand and caught him, and said to him, "O you of little faith, why did you doubt?" After they got into the boat, the wind died down.*
This story is surely a Post-Resurrectional one and copied from Mark.

14: 33 *Those who were in the boat did him homage, saying, "Truly, you are the Son of God."*
This is a faith pronouncement by Matthew. Son of God refers to Kings, the Messiah and to angels in the Hebrew Testament. Yeshua was appointed a Divine Being but definitely not equal to God.

15:15-20 *Then Peter said to him in reply, "Explain (this) parable to us." He said to them, "Are even you still without understanding? Do you not realize that everything that enters the mouth passes into the stomach and is expelled into the latrine? But the things that come out of the mouth come from the heart, and they defile. For from the heart come evil thoughts, murder, adultery, unchastity, theft, false witness, blasphemy. These are what defile a person, but to eat with unwashed hands does not defile."*
The first underlined make it clear how the disciple were simple people unable to plumb the meaning of parables. Note the heart metaphors. Also, human foolishness to think that bodily cleanliness is related to Godliness; it's spiritual cleanliness that's important!

16: 4 *An evil and unfaithful generation seeks a sign, but no sign will be given it except the sign of Jonah." Then he left them and went away.*
Matthew just wrote this above in 12: 39-40. Yeshua was in the tomb only about 40 hours.

16: 12 *Then they understood that he was not telling them to beware of the leaven of bread, but of the teaching of the Pharisees and Sadducees.*
Three Cheers for the gallery; they finally understood Yeshua's metaphors.

16: 13-19 When Jesus went into the region of Caesarea Philippi he asked his disciples, "Who do people say that the Son of Man is?" They replied, "Some say John the Baptist, others Elijah, still others Jeremiah or one of the prophets." He said to them, "But who do you say that I am?" Simon Peter said in reply, "You are the Messiah, the Son of the living God." Jesus said to him in reply, "Blessed are you, Simon son of Jonah. For flesh and blood has not revealed this to you, but my heavenly Father. And so I say to you, you are Peter, and upon this rock I will build my church, and the gates of the netherworld shall not prevail against it. I will give you the keys to the kingdom of heaven. Whatever you bind on earth shall be bound in heaven; and whatever you loose on earth shall be loosed in heaven."

This is a story that only appears in Matthew's Gospel. It has become patently obvious that only the Matthean community accepted Peter as the singular leader of the Christian movement. The Roman Petrine Tradition has repeated this story to its followers every year for the past 1700 years primarily to convince, instill and indoctrinate the world (especially Catholics) about Pope-ism and infallibility. The biblical facts are that Peter was never the *episkopos* of Rome nor was there an election to replace him. James was the head of the church ,called out people.

16: 21-28 *From that time on, Jesus began to show his disciples that he must go to Jerusalem and suffer greatly from the elders, the chief priests, and the scribes, and be killed and on the third day be raised. Then Peter took him aside and began to rebuke him, "God forbid, Lord! No such thing shall ever happen to you." He turned and said to Peter, "Get behind me, Satan! You are an obstacle to me. You are thinking not as God does, but as human beings do." Then Jesus said to his disciples, "Whoever wishes to come after me must deny himself, take up his cross, and follow me. For whoever wishes to save his life will lose it, but whoever loses his life for my sake will find it. What profit would there be for one to gain the whole world and forfeit his life? Or what can one give in exchange for his life? For the Son of Man will come with his angels in his Father's glory, and then he will repay everyone according to his conduct. Amen, I say to you, there are some standing here who will not taste death until they see the Son of Man coming in his kingdom."*
This entire passage is a Matthean Backward-Looking construct. Now, it sounds like Matthew is quoting Daniel referencing the cloud rider. But that prediction simply reflects the yearnings of the Israelites for a Messiah. Daniel is, as we have seen, pure myth.

17: 1-9 After *six days Jesus took Peter, James, and John his brother, and led them up a high mountain by themselves. And he was transfigured before them; his face shone like the sun and his clothes became white* ***as light.*** *And behold, Moses and Elijah appeared to them, conversing with him. Then Peter said to Jesus in reply, "Lord, it is good that we are here. If you wish, I will make three tents here, one for you, one for Moses, and one for Elijah." While he was still speaking, behold, a bright cloud cast a shadow over them, then from the cloud came a voice that said, "This is my beloved Son, with whom I am well pleased; listen to him." When the disciples heard this, they fell prostrate and were very much afraid. But Jesus came and touched them, saying, "Rise, and do not be afraid." And when the disciples raised their eyes, they saw no one else but Jesus alone. As they were coming down from the mountain, Jesus charged them, "Do not tell the vision to anyone until the Son of Man has been raised from the dead."*
This is a direct re-write of Moses going up Mt Sinai. Second, the story is more than likely a Post-Resurrectional one, if, in fact, it is a true event rather than a faith statement by Matthew. Third, recall that Mark used the same expression during the Baptism in the Jordan (the first half of the quote). The second half is from Deut 18: 15. Fourth, the last verse is another contradiction to Chalcedon but essentially one of the "Backward-Looking" faith constructs by Matthew.

17: 27 *But that we may not offend them, go to the sea, drop in a hook, and take the first fish that comes up. Open its mouth and you will find a coin worth twice the temple tax. Give that to them for me and for you."*
This is a pure folk-tale story! Yeshua did no magic tricks!

18: 1-4 *At that time the disciples approached Jesus and said, "Who is the greatest in the kingdom of heaven?" He called a child over, placed it in their midst, and said, "Amen, I say to you, unless you turn and become like children, you will not enter the kingdom of heaven. Whoever humbles himself like this child is the greatest in the kingdom of heaven.*
This is really packed with meaning. First, it says that we must be full of faith and innocence like that of a child. Secondly, we must not be childish, i.e., pre-critical naiveté, as Paul wrote in 1 Corin 13: 11!

18: 17-18 *If he refuses to listen to them, tell the church. If he refuses to listen even to* <u>*the church*</u>*, then treat him as you would a Gentile or a tax collector.*
18 Amen, I say to you, whatever you bind on earth shall be bound in heaven, and whatever you loose on earth shall be loosed in heaven.
The NAB states that, in this verse, Matthew is the first to use "church". Unfortunately that's the awareness of a literalist's mindset. Matthew wrote in this Gospel in 80 AD! Paul had used the Greek word, "*ekklesia*", much earlier. And, to make matters worse, the real meaning of "*ekklesia*" is "called out" (people, understood) which today is a congregation. The Latin Vulgate used *ecclesiae* in its translation of the Greek. Church is an English word from the 14th to the 17th century AD that loses the true meaning of a "called our people". In verse 18 Peter's privilege (See 16: 19) appears to be somewhat out of place except that here it is given to the disciples!. Check out the first few verses in this chapter.

18: 20 *For where two or three are gathered together in my name, there am I in the midst of them."*
This verse is bothersome! Does it imply that any group that gathers to decide on doctrine will be guided by Yeshua? Is it possible then that each Christian denomination is doctrinally OK? Or, maybe it doesn't refer to doctrinal meetings! Yeshua's presence does not guarantee doctrinal infallibility to the group!

18: 21 *Then Peter approaching asked him, "Lord, if my brother sins against me, how often must I forgive him? As many as seven times?"*
Ah, Peter shows up. This must mean that the Apostles have returned. Or, did Matthew miss something in his narrative?

18: 22 *Jesus answered, "I say to you, not seven times but seventy-seven times.*
In Luke 17: 4 Yeshua answers every time. That's a bit different. The NRSV says either 77 or 70 times 7 (490). Chalk up one more inconsistency! But really, it does mean that one must never stops forgiving.

18: 34-35 *Then in anger his master handed him over to the torturers until he should pay back the whole debt. So will my heavenly Father do to you, unless each of you forgives his brother from his heart."*
WOW! Here comes that punishing God again. Tell me, where does this idea come from? Is it Matthew's? Is it Yeshua who believes that God is a punisher? Or, is God's inspiration correct? Is God a punisher who will beat us for eternity with all sorts of physical torture like it is written in the Qur'an? We really think not! Whoever believes in such a dysfunctional being also believes in the Big Bad Wolf! Personally, we like the Good Fairy. Besides, people who want this kind of justice are frequently those who choose not to forgive!

19: 24 *Again I say to you, it is easier for a camel to pass through the eye of a needle than for one who is rich to enter the kingdom of God."*
This is a great simile! The eye of the needle is an actual hole in a wall. But the hole is so small that one can only go through with great difficulty.. OH my, this must really bother some people!

20: 1-16 *"The kingdom of heaven is like a landowner who went out at dawn to hire laborers for his vineyard. After agreeing with them for the usual daily wage, he sent them into his vineyard. Going out about nine o'clock, he saw others standing idle in the marketplace, and he said to them, 'You too go into my vineyard, and I will give you what is just.' So they went off. (And) he went out again around noon, and around three o'clock, and did likewise. Going out about five o'clock, he found others standing around, and said to them, 'Why do you stand here idle all day?' They answered, 'Because no one has hired us.' He said to them, 'You too go into my vineyard.' When it was evening the owner of the vineyard said to his foreman, 'Summon the laborers and give them their pay, beginning with the last and ending with the first.' When those who had started about five o'clock came, each received the usual daily wage. So when the first came, they thought that they would receive more, but each of them also got the usual wage. And on receiving it they grumbled against the landowner, saying, 'These last ones worked only one hour, and you have made them equal to us, who bore the day's burden and the heat.' He said to one of them in reply, 'My friend, I am not cheating you. Did you not agree with me for the usual daily wage? Take what is yours and go. What if I wish to give this last one the same as you? (Or) am I not free to do as I wish with my own money? Are you envious because I am generous?' Thus, the last will be first, and the first will be last."*
Now, here in this parable the real God of Yeshua shows up! It is a God of kindness and generosity. God gives the eternal reward to even those who only worked a short time. But notice the jealousy of those who want justice! Ponder this: those who want justice are those who refuse to forgive or may not be generous enough to forgive or not very generous at all. This parable is the cornerstone of Christianity and truly makes one question whether God is a torturing God! And, if not, then what of Hell? See you in Chapter Five for my answer.

21: 19 *Seeing a fig tree by the road, he went over to it, but found nothing on it except leaves. And he said to it, "May no fruit ever come from you again." And immediately the fig tree withered.*
Whoa neighbor, didn't that Figgie die the next day. Yes, and this will be discussed in Chapter Five. In the meanwhile you might want to refresh your memory by re-reading Mk 11: 20-22.

22: 36-40 *"Teacher, which commandment in the law is the greatest?" He said to him, "You shall love the Lord, your God, with all your heart, with all your soul, and with all your mind. This is the greatest and the first commandment. The second is like it: You shall love your neighbor as yourself. The whole law and the prophets depend on these two commandments."*
Two real Laws: Relationship with God and Respect for neighbor.

22: 44-46 *'The Lord said to my lord, "Sit at my right hand until I place your enemies under your feet"'? If David calls him 'lord,' how can he be his son?"*

No one was able to answer him a word, nor from that day on did anyone dare to ask him any more questions.
This has a built-in difficulty. If you read Psalm 110 you will find that the meaning of "Lord" refers to God and "my lord" refers to the king. Most literalists assign the "my lord" to Yeshua because they assume that David is the psalmist. Remember that the H.T. uses "Lord" in place of the Tetragrammaton and "lord" for the king or a master!

23: 23-36 *"Woe to you, scribes and Pharisees, you hypocrites. You pay tithes of mint and dill and cummin, and have neglected the weightier things of the law: judgment and mercy and fidelity. (But) these you should have done, without neglecting the others. Blind guides, who strain out the gnat and swallow the camel! "Woe to you, scribes and Pharisees, you hypocrites. You cleanse the outside of cup and dish, but inside they are full of plunder and self-indulgence. Blind Pharisee, cleanse first the inside of the cup, so that the outside also may be clean. "Woe to you, scribes and Pharisees, you hypocrites. You are like whitewashed tombs, which appear beautiful on the outside, but inside are full of dead men's bones and every kind of filth. Even so, on the outside you appear righteous, but inside you are filled with prophets and adorn the memorials of the righteous, and you say, 'If we had lived in the days of our ancestors, we would not have joined them in shedding the prophets' blood.' Thus you bear witness against yourselves that you are the children of those who murdered the prophets; now fill up what your ancestors measured out! You serpents, you brood of vipers, how can you flee from the judgment of Gehenna? Therefore, behold, I send to you prophets and wise men and scribes; some of them you will kill and crucify, some of them you will scourge in your synagogues and pursue from town to town, so that there may come upon you all the righteous blood shed upon earth, from the righteous blood of Abel to the blood of Zechariah, the son of Barachiah, whom you murdered between the sanctuary and the altar. Amen, I say to you, all these things will come upon this generation.*
OUCH. Have the ministers of Christianity really read this? Seems a few in the 19th to 21st century have missed it! Just replace the words, Pharisees and scribes with ministers and you'll get our drift!

24: 1-34 This whole chapter is great fodder for Hollywood up to verse 34. Then the bubble bursts. Many self-appointed prophets have made predictions but, alas, none have come true yet. And, most unfortunately, neither did Yeshua's. Ah, but was it Yeshua who spoke those words? We suspect that Matthew's community made them up.

24: 36 *"But of that day and hour no one knows, neither the angels of heaven, nor the Son, but the Father alone.*
That seems to us that Yeshua is admitting to his human ignorance, doesn't it?

25: 13 *Therefore, stay awake, for you know neither the day nor the hour.*
This verse is more like it. Nobody knows the appointed hour! If Nuclear Science has anything to say, our sun will run out of fuel in about 5 billion years from now.

25: 31-46 *"When the Son of Man comes in his glory, and all the angels with him, he will sit upon his glorious throne, and all the nations will be assembled before him. And he will separate them one from another, as a shepherd separates the sheep from the goats. He will place the sheep on his right and the goats on*

his left. Then the king will say to those on his right, 'Come, you who are blessed by my Father. Inherit the kingdom prepared for you from the foundation of the world. For I was hungry and you gave me food, I was thirsty and you gave me drink, a stranger and you welcomed me, naked and you clothed me, ill and you cared for me, in prison and you visited me.' Then the righteous will answer him and say, 'Lord, when did we see you hungry and feed you, or thirsty and give you drink? When did we see you a stranger and welcome you, or naked and clothe you? When did we see you ill or in prison, and visit you?' 40 And the king will say to them in reply, 'Amen, I say to you, whatever you did for one of these least brothers of mine, you did for me.' Then he will say to those on his left, 'Depart from me, you accursed, into the eternal fire prepared for the devil and his angels. For I was hungry and you gave me no food, I was thirsty and you gave me no drink, a stranger and you gave me no welcome, naked and you gave me no clothing, ill and in prison, and you did not care for me.' Then they will answer and say, 'Lord, when did we see you hungry or thirsty or a stranger or naked or ill or in prison, and not minister to your needs?' He will answer them, 'Amen, I say to you, what you did not do for one of these least ones, you did not do for me. And these will go off to eternal punishment, but the righteous to eternal life."
These verses present Matthew's understanding of who gets to heaven! It is important to grasp that some don't know exactly who Yeshua is. But in their acts of concern and kindness they do "good works" which are the "get home free" cards for acceptance into heaven! Note this carefully: All the dogma and doctrines of all the various Institutional Religions are but sticky dung piles strewn across the pathway of the searchers of true spirituality.

26: 2 *"You know that in two days' time it will be Passover, and the Son of Man will be handed over to be crucified."*
This is a perfect example of Matthew's Backward-Looking style

26: 12-13 *In pouring this perfumed oil upon my body, she did it to prepare me for burial. Amen, I say to you, wherever this gospel is proclaimed in the whole world, what she has done will be spoken of, in memory of her."*
Same comment as the one for 26: 2 above.

26: 14 *Then one of the Twelve, who was called Judas Iscariot, went to the chief priests*
This verse begins the complex weaving of the story in Zechariah 11: 13 into Matthew's passion story.

26: 31 *Then Jesus said to them, "This night all of you will have your faith in me shaken, for it is written: 'I will strike the shepherd, and the sheep of the flock will be dispersed';*
Here is another reference to Zechariah 13: 7.

26: 52 *Then Jesus said to him, "Put your sword back into its sheath, for all who take the sword will perish by the sword.*
Terrorists need to re-examine this verse.

26: 64 *Jesus said to him in reply, "You have said so. But I tell you: From now on you will see 'the Son of Man seated at the right hand of the Power' and 'coming on the clouds of heaven.'"*

There is some doubt that Yeshua saw himself as that 'Son of Man'. It is more likely and very reasonable that Matthew's community saw it that way. Or it could very well be that the "*bar enach*" was mistranslated into the "son of man" title!

26: 69-70 Now *Peter was sitting outside in the courtyard. One of the maids came over to him and said, "You too were with Jesus the Galilean." But he denied it in front of everyone, saying, "I do not know what you are talking about!"*
This is a great story and speaks about the public behavior of all of us Christians at some time or other in our lives.

27: 3-10 *Then Judas, his betrayer, seeing that Jesus had been condemned, deeply regretted what he had done. He returned the thirty pieces of silver to the chief priests and elders, saying, "I have sinned in betraying innocent blood." They said, "What is that to us? Look to it yourself." Flinging the money into the temple, he departed and went off and hanged himself. The chief priests gathered up the money, but said, "It is not lawful to deposit this in the temple treasury, for it is the price of blood." After consultation, they used it to buy the potter's field as a burial place for foreigners. That is why that field even today is called the Field of Blood. Then was fulfilled what had been said through Jeremiah the prophet, "And they took the thirty pieces of silver, the value of a man with a price on his head, a price set by some of the Israelites, and they paid it out for the potter's field just as the Lord had commanded me."*
Here is an example of confusion in Matthew's story. He takes four obscure passages from the Hebrew Testament, ties them into one prophecy and says in verse 9 that Jeremiah is the source (Jer 18: 2-10; Jer 19: 1-13; Jer 32: 6-15) of this prediction. Actually, Jeremiah's references have little to do with the story, except for a single word or two taken out of context. The real thrust is in Zechariah 11: 13! Once again the confusion lies within the author's mind. We'll explore the significance of this in Chapter Five.

27: 19 *While he was still seated on the bench, his wife sent him a message, "Have nothing to do with that righteous man. I suffered much in a dream today because of him."*
This is purely a Matthean construct to heighten the drama and reflect the first century's interpretation of dreams.

27: 52 *tombs were opened, and the bodies of many saints who had fallen asleep were raised.*
Here's the use of "saints". Did you know that the Greek word is *hagios* and it really means a special object set aside for worship. Christians understood it to mean a person set aside for God; in other words a holy person. It's a short jump to go to the Latin word "sacred" and to the English "saints"!

27: 56 *Among them were Mary Magdalene and Mary the mother of James and Joseph, and the mother of the sons of Zebedee.*
Those two are the names of Yeshua's brothers but Mary is not identified as Yeshua's mother. The Fourth Gospel writes that she was there. Chapter Five material again!

28: 1-20 Most everyone is familiar with the Resurrection story. However, most are unaware of the inconsistencies and contradictions existing among the four Gospels. Chapter Five will address them individually for your edification.

28: 16 *The eleven disciples went to Galilee, to the mountain to which Jesus had ordered them*
Another Moses reference, "to the mountain"! Did you catch the demotion of the Apostles to disciples? Could it be that the term "Apostles" is actually a term of respect introduced by Paul in 1 Thes2: 7 (~51 AD)?

28: 18-*19* *Then Jesus approached and said to them, "All power in heaven and on earth has been given to me. Go, therefore, and make disciples of all nations, baptizing them in the name of the Father, and of the Son, and of the holy Spirit,*
This is definitely a Matthean construct. But maybe, just maybe, it's a later addition to authenticate Trinitarianism! This lends veracity to our suspicions that Trinitarianism is ill founded.

18. Gospel of Luke (70-80):

Luke's Gospel has much in common with Matthew's Gospel. Yet, some of the material is quite different and actually contradictory. Christians for far too many years have mentally shuffled the four Gospels into one continuous story. It's mostly due to their reading the gospels first and not even blinking an eye at the tiny details. Then, again, the preachers have contributed to that confusion. Take note of the Infancy Narrative, the Our Father and the setting for the Beatitudes in Luke's Good News story. They're not the same as those found in Matthew.

It is very interesting to read what's in the Introduction to Luke's Gospel and Acts in the NAB. A portion reads as follows:

(1) "The stated purpose of the two volumes is to provide Theophilus and others like him with certainty--assurance--about earlier instructions they have received."
(2) "To accomplish his purpose, Luke shows that the preaching and teaching of the representatives of the early communities are grounded in the preaching and teaching of Jesus, who during his historical ministry prepared his specially chosen followers and commissioned them to be witnesses to his Resurrection and to all else that he did."
(3) " This continuity between the historical ministry of Jesus and the ministry of the apostles is Luke's way of guaranteeing the fidelity of the Apostolic preachings to the teachings of Jesus."

In the first item: Luke wants to provide justification for all that he is going to write an affirmation of what the Apostles have passed on. The problem is that he misrepresents much of what he writes in Acts and what Paul wrote in Romans! His facts are mostly mythologized material and the stuff of legends. In the second item: Yeshua did not establish any new Institution; Paul did and did it on his own authority. In other words, he made it appear as though God/Yeshua did it. In the third item: by the time of Luke's writing the Christian communities were already steeped in legend as witnessed by the existence of a plethora of apocryphal Gospels and Epistles from second or even third generation Christians (remember, they never knew the historical Yeshua!).

Luke's three Introductory items are intellectually dishonest postures but innocent of sin. They were understandably just human perceptions for Luke and people of that century. However, they are not acceptable for modern Christianity. Please read on and examine the comments carefully.

1: 3 *I too have decided, after investigating everything accurately anew, to write it down in an orderly sequence for you, most excellent Theophilus,*
After all these commentaries written thus far, it is our opinion that the criteria employed in the first century to determine TRUTH is contrary to our 21st century criteria. Demonology is not the cause of illness; our cosmology is based on scientific affirmation; gods don't impregnate women to produce demi-gods; our modern concept of history is based upon observed facts not legends and myths; our literary styles are similar but well defined; most knowledgeable people no longer curse the gods for what befalls them; and, lastly, we believe in personal free will and a God of mercy who is not a Puppet Master.

1: 5 *In the days of Herod, King of Judea, there was a priest named Zechariah of the priestly division of Abijah; his wife was from the daughters of Aaron, and her name was Elizabeth.*
Female order of descendency! Very Greek! But it's not the Hebrew way.

1: 10 *Then, when the whole assembly of the people was praying outside at the hour of the incense offering,*
Catholic Church rituals copied from the Temple times in Israel.

1: 11-15 *the angel of the Lord appeared to him, standing at the right of the altar of incense. Zechariah was troubled by what he saw, and fear came upon him. But the angel said to him, "Do not be afraid, Zechariah, because your prayer has been heard. Your wife Elizabeth will bear you a son, and you shall name him John. And you will have joy and gladness, and many will rejoice at his birth, for he will be great in the sight of (the) Lord. He will drink neither wine nor strong drink. He will be filled with the holy Spirit even from his mother's womb,*
How does Luke know this private stuff about the conversation between the angel and Zechariah? He makes it up! This Holy Spirit is a Paulism referring to God the Father. Remember, the Holy One of Israel, the Spirit of Holiness in Romans and Isaiah 63: 10-11!

1: 31 Behold, you will conceive in your womb and bear a son, and you shall name him Jesus.
What happened to Immanuel (see Isaiah 7: 14)?? The next problem is that in Aramaic his name is Yeshua! "Jesus" is an English KJV translation (1611 AD). There is no "J " in Hebrew, Greek or Latin!

1: 32 *He will be great and will be called Son of the Most High, and the Lord God will give him the throne of David his father,*
First, this is Luke's faith statement; note the future tense According to the Fourth Gospel, he already has it? Another in the list of contradictions!

1: 35 *And the angel said to her in reply, "The holy Spirit will come upon you, and the power of the Most High will overshadow you. Therefore the child to be born will be called holy, the Son of God.*
Again, Backward-Looking stuff! What happened to the Rom 1: 3-4 and the three quotes of Acts? Note carefully, the holy Spirit is equated with the Most High! And the child will be Son of God; that's not very Trinitarian! Should not Yeshua then

be the son of the Spirit? Seems like poetry. Easy answer, that's just God, the Spirit of Holiness!

1: 43 *And how does this happen to me, that the mother of my Lord should come to me?*
If this be true, how come Mark 3:21??? Wouldn't Mary then know who Yeshua is going to become?

1: 48 *For he has looked upon his handmaid's lowliness; behold, from now on will all ages call me blessed.*
I don't think she said that! Luke is putting these words on the lips of a 13 year old girl. Again, if this be true, how come Mark 3:21???

1: 64-66 *Immediately his mouth was opened, his tongue freed, and he spoke blessing God. Then fear came upon all their neighbors, and all these matters were discussed throughout the hill country of Judea. All who heard these things took them to heart, saying, "What, then, will this child be?" For surely the hand of the Lord was with him.*
Is this for real? Once again a contradiction with Mark 3: 21! If everyone is discussing this, then how come people were not aware of its significance when Yeshua began preaching (see Mark 3: 21)?

1: 67-80 is nothing more than Backward-Looking Faith stories!

2: 1-3 *In those days a decree went out from Caesar Augustus that the whole world should be enrolled This was the first enrollment, when Quirinius was governor of Syria. So all went to be enrolled, each to his own town.*
None of this is accurate! The date when that enrollment took place in the history books is 10 BC! Yeshua was born 6-4 BC.

2: 11 *For today in the city of David a savior has been born for you who is Messiah and Lord.*
Not yet, according to Rom 1: 3-4 and definitely contrary to the Fourth Gospel!

2: 17 *When they saw this, they made known the message that had been told them about this child.*
And then Mary forgot it!

2: 19 *And Mary kept all these things, reflecting on them in her heart.*
And then, Mary forgot them also!

2: 35 *(and you yourself a sword will pierce) so that the thoughts of many hearts may be revealed."*
Yes, and she forgot this too!

2: 36-37 *There was also a prophetess, Anna, the daughter of Phanuel, of the tribe of Asher. She was advanced in years, having lived seven years with her husband after her marriage, and then as a widow until she was eighty-four. She never left the temple, but worshiped night and day with fasting and prayer.*
Too hard to believe she stayed up every night and hardly ate!

2: 39 *When they had fulfilled all the prescriptions of the law of the Lord, they returned to Galilee, to their own town of Nazareth.*
What happened to the Egyptian trip? Notice, Luke's understanding is that Mary and Joseph returned to THEIR OWN town! But in Matthew they returned from Egypt to their own town, Bethlehem! Let me be among those who suggest that Yeshua was not born in Bethlehem!

2: 49-50 *And he said to them, "Why were you looking for me? Did you not know that I must be in my Father's house?" But they did not understand what he said to them.*
Above, it said that all this was explained !? (1: 64-66) Somehow, they missed it!

3: 7 *He said to the crowds who came out to be baptized by him, "You brood of vipers! Who warned you to flee from the coming wrath?*
Opps, God of Wrath now!

3: 9 *Even now the ax lies at the root of the trees. Therefore every tree that does not produce good fruit will be cut down and thrown into the fire."*
Such an allegory of a vengeful God!

3: 16 *John answered them all, saying, "I am baptizing you with water, but one mightier than I is coming. I am not worthy to loosen the thongs of his sandals. He will baptize you with the holy Spirit and fire.*
Argument against those who believed that John was the anticipated Messiah and were following John!

3: 17 *His winnowing fan is in his hand to clear his threshing floor and to gather the wheat into his barn, but the chaff he will burn with unquenchable fire."*
The punishing God still haunts Luke!

3: 23 *When Jesus began his ministry he was about thirty years of age. He was the son, as was thought, of Joseph, the son of Heli,*
That's hint at an illegitimate father. But Matthew wrote that Jacob was Joseph's father (Matt 1: 16). Who is correct? God? Matthew? Luke? Guess what! Nobody knew the name of Joseph's father!

3: 23-38 Luke reports 72 generations (40 from David to Yeshua). But Matt says 28 from David!? What gives here with this discrepancy? Must be old math?

4: 1 *Filled with the holy Spirit, Jesus returned from the Jordan and was led by the Spirit into the desert*
Is this Spirit a third persona? No way, it's still God the One and Only!

4: 2 *for forty days, to be tempted by the devil. He ate nothing during those days, and when they were over he was hungry.*
Magic number from Exodus! If you have read anything about Siddhartha, you would remember the story of his period of testing in the forest by Mara, the Evil One—three classic trials!

4: 1-13 *Filled with the holy Spirit, Jesus returned from the Jordan and was led by the Spirit into the desert for forty days, to be tempted by the devil. He ate nothing during those days, and when they were over he was hungry. The devil*

said to him, "If you are the Son of God, command this stone to become bread." 4 Jesus answered him, "It is written, 'One does not live by bread alone.'" Then he took him up and showed him all the kingdoms of the world in a single instant. The devil said to him, "I shall give to you all this power and their glory; for it has been handed over to me, and I may give it to whomever I wish. All this will be yours, if you worship me." Jesus said to him in reply, "It is written: 'You shall worship the Lord, your God, and him alone shall you serve.'" Then he led him to Jerusalem, made him stand on the parapet of the temple, and said to him, "If you are the Son of God, throw yourself down from here, for it is written: 'He will command his angels concerning you, to guard you,' and: 'With their hands they will support you, lest you dash your foot against a stone.'" Jesus said to him in reply, "It also says, 'You shall not put the Lord, your God, to the test.'" When the devil had finished every temptation, he departed from him for a time.
Isn't this a good allegory to represent Yeshua's humanity and his temptations as a human. It stems from the Messiah from conception story and the folk tales of Yeshua's amazing wisdom. However, it does make a strong point about Yeshua's humanity. If Jesus went into the dessert alone, how come these authors know the details of his conversations? Hint: they made it up! Just like the Buddha story.

4: 14 *Jesus returned to Galilee in the power of the Spirit, and news of him spread <u>throughout the whole</u> region.*
What exactly does this mean? The power of God the Father! The Greek phrase for *throughout the whole* is "kath 'oles " (phonetically, olace) the source of the word "catholic"! See also Acts 9: 31 below.

4: 23 *He said to them, "Surely you will quote me this proverb, 'Physician, cure yourself,' and say, 'Do here in your native place the things that we heard were done in Capernaum.'"*
There may have been some physical scars from a previous illness that caused the crowd to challenge Yeshua to first cure himself!

4: 28-30 *When the people in the synagogue heard this, they were all filled with fury. They rose up, drove him out of the town, and led him to the brow of the hill on which their town had been built, to hurl him down headlong. But he passed through the midst of them and went away.*
Yeshua surely got them all stirred up! Has your ministers stirred you up lately?

4: 34-35 *"Ha! What have you to do with us, Jesus of Nazareth? Have you come to destroy us? I know who you are--the Holy One of God!" Jesus rebuked him and said, "Be quiet! Come out of him!" Then the demon threw the man down in front of them and came out of him without doing him any harm.*
Part of the myths of the 1st century!

4: 39 *He stood over her, rebuked the fever, and it left her. She got up immediately and waited on them.*
Magic again!

4: 41 *And demons also came out from many, shouting, "You are the Son of God." But he rebuked them and did not allow them to speak because they knew that he was the Messiah.*
Who's kidding whom? This is Luke's faith speaking out.

4: 43 *But he said to them, "To the other towns also I must proclaim the good news of the kingdom of God, because for this purpose I have been sent."*
Is this the big picture from Luke? Or, Yeshua's real words? It's just a Lukan faith statement!

5: 1 *While the crowd was pressing in on Jesus and listening to the word of God, he was standing by the Lake of Gennesaret.*
Backward-Looking comment by the author! What Yeshua spoke is elevated to the importance of "the word of God". However, it is noteworthy that Luke considers Yeshua to be the final prophet and as such would use the familiar words that the prophets of old used (See Ezekiel 2;1: "THUS SAYS THE LORD GOD").

5: 19 *But not finding a way to bring him in because of the crowd, they went up on the roof and lowered him on the stretcher through the tiles into the middle in front of Jesus.*
Oops! Mark 2: 4 said a thatch roof (the Greek word is just "thatch"!) Oh, these mistakes are beginning to add up. How many will it take to convince you of the mythologized stories in the Bible?

5: 22 *Jesus knew their thoughts and said to them in reply, "What are you thinking in your hearts?*
Like NOT in any one's lifetime! No human reads minds! Nor does God violate one's thoughts!

5: 36-39 *And he also told them a parable. "No one tears a piece from a new cloak to patch an old one. Otherwise, he will tear the new and the piece from it will not match the old cloak. Likewise, no one pours new wine into old wineskins. Otherwise, the new wine will burst the skins, and it will be spilled, and the skins will be ruined. Rather, new wine must be poured into fresh wineskins (And) no one who has been drinking old wine desires new, for he says, 'The old is good.'"*
What exactly does this mean? People are more comfortable with the pain they know rather than change to what is new!! So, many people rejected Yeshua! Could this be the source of the new wine allegory in the marriage story at Cana in the Fourth Gospel? Or, is this a parable of new teachings by Yeshua vs. old Mosaic Law? We'll write more in Chapter Six about the Cana marriage in the Fourth Gospel commentary.

6: 3-5 *Jesus said to them in reply, "Have you not read what David did when he and those (who were) with him were hungry? (How) he went into the house of God, took the bread of offering, which only the priests could lawfully eat, ate of it, and shared it with his companions." Then he said to them, "The Son of Man is lord of the sabbath."*
At this telling, Luke doesn't quote the name of the high priest because he knows Mark made a mistake! Remember now, Luke copied much of the Markan material for his own Gospel. Here is one of the arguments for the phrase, "Son of Man", being a mis-translation. In Aramaic the idiomatic phrase is "*bar enach*" that means a son of a human (a man in general). When translated into Greek it becomes a non-idiom, "*huios ho anthropos*", a son of a man. The Literalist's authors of the 1st century interpreted the "*bar enach*" into a title as used in Daniel. See Appendix AA for that analysis.

6: 17-26 *And he came down with them and stood on a stretch of level ground. ... 20 And raising his eyes toward his disciples he said: "Blessed are ...* followed by the 4 Blessed's and the four Woe's.
Here Luke places the event on a plain while Matthew says it took place on the mountainside. Luke also changes four of Matthew's "blessed's" to "woes". Well, so much for the accuracy of Luke! In all fairness, this is not a major doctrinal situation. Its importance lies only in the erroneous belief that the Bible is an accurate, errorless book because it is "God's Word" and "God doesn't lie". We do agree that God doesn't lie (except men in the H.T. wrote that God did lie through His prophets, see 1 Kings 22: 20-23) but we fully understand that the Bible was really written by men who very often distorted and elaborated the oral traditional material, you know, like our fish stories.

7: 28 *I tell you, among those born of women, no one is greater than John; yet the least in the kingdom of God is greater than he."*
Very enigmatic! Is Yeshua saying that John is greater than he is?

8: 2 *and some women who had been cured of evil spirits and infirmities, Mary, called Magdalene, from whom seven demons had gone out,*
This is the famous quote that Christians have used to say that Mary of Magdala was a prostitute. Wrong Mary! Luke's mistake!

8: 8 *And some seed fell on good soil, and when it grew, it produced fruit a hundredfold." After saying this, he called out, "Whoever has ears to hear ought to hear."*
Challenge to the listener to interpret the allegory.

8: 9-10 *Then his disciples asked him what the meaning of this parable might be. He answered, "Knowledge of the mysteries of the kingdom of God has been granted to you; but to the rest, they are made known through parables so that 'they may look but not see, and hear but not understand.'*
It is not God's way to inhibit a person's understanding. It's people's own ignorance or hardness of heart (that's a good metaphor!).

8: 11-15 *"This is the meaning of the parable. The seed is the word of God. Those on the path are the ones who have heard, but the devil comes and takes away the word from their hearts that they may not believe and be saved. Those on rocky ground are the ones who, when they hear, receive the word with joy, but they have no root; they believe only for a time and fall away in time of trial. As for the seed that fell among thorns, they are the ones who have heard, but as they go along, they are choked by the anxieties and riches and pleasures of life, and they fail to produce mature fruit. But as for the seed that fell on rich soil, they are the ones who, when they have heard the word, embrace it with a generous and good heart, and bear fruit through perseverance.*
A story of free will and choice that may very well be authentically Yeshua's.

8: 19 –21 *Then his mother and his brothers came to him but were unable to join him because of the crowd. He was told, "Your mother and your brothers are standing outside and they wish to see you." He said to them in reply, "My mother and my brothers are those who hear the word of God and act on it."*
What happened to Mark's portrayal of Yeshua as one who was beside (actually crazy) himself?? Luke was too embarrassed to include it!

8: 28 *When he saw Jesus, he cried out and fell down before him; in a loud voice he shouted, "What have you to do with me, Jesus, son of the Most High God? I beg you, do not torment me!"*
Who heard this story? No one! Author's addition to stress Yeshua's power but mostly the author's faith!

8: 30 *Then Jesus asked him, "What is your name?" He replied, "Legion," because many demons had entered him.*
Part of the 1st century myths concerning demonology!

8: 31 *And they pleaded with him not to order them to depart to the abyss.*
1st century demonology and cosmology! The abyss was at the edge of the Earth!

8: 32-39 *For if you love those who love you, what credit is that to you? Even sinners love those who love them. And if you do good to those who do good to you, what credit is that to you? Even sinners do the same. If you lend money to those from whom you expect repayment, what credit (is) that to you? Even sinners lend to sinners, and get back the same amount. But rather, love your enemies and do good to them, and lend expecting nothing back; then your reward will be great and you will be children of the Most High, for he himself is kind to the ungrateful and the wicked. Be merciful, just as (also) your Father is merciful. "Stop judging and you will not be judged. Stop condemning and you will not be condemned. Forgive and you will be forgiven. Give and gifts will be given to you; a good measure, packed together, shaken down, and overflowing, will be poured into your lap. For the measure with which you measure will in return be measured out to you." And he told them a parable, "Can a blind person guide a blind person? Will not both fall into a pit?*
Part of Yeshua's preachings in the form of aphorisms—pithy teachings.

8: 46 *But Jesus said, "Someone has touched me; for I know that power has gone out from me."*
Definitely a Lukan embellishment!

9: 1 *He summoned the Twelve and gave them power and authority over all demons and to cure diseases,*
Even Yeshua believed in demons! However, this may very well be Luke's own spin on some oral tradition.

9: 3-5 *He said to them, "Take nothing for the journey, neither walking stick, nor sack, nor food, nor money, and let no one take a second tunic. Whatever house you enter, stay there and leave from there. And as for those who do not welcome you, when you leave that town, shake the dust from your feet in testimony against them."*
What happened to this regulation? Where are these ministers hiding?

9: 16 *Then taking the five loaves and the two fish, and looking up to heaven, he said the blessing over them, broke them, and gave them to the disciples to set before the crowd.*
The model of the Eucharist! Recall that Paul wrote about the Eucharistic celebrations way before this Gospel was written!

9: 17 *They all ate and were satisfied. And when the leftover fragments were picked up, they filled twelve wicker baskets.*
Another magic number! 12 tribes, 12 Apostles, etc. We today have a lot of 12's: how many in a dozen, inches in a foot, the 12 Steps in AA, etc.

9: 20-21 *Then he said to them, "But who do you say that I am?" Peter said in reply, "The Messiah of God." He rebuked them and directed them not to tell this to anyone.*
Where is Matthew's "keys to the kingdom" and the Papacy appointment? Not here, nor anywhere else, cause it only existed in Matthew's mind!

9: 43 *And all were astonished by the majesty of God. While they were all amazed at his every deed, he said to his disciples, ...*
God's work or Yeshua's power?

9: 45 *But they did not understand this saying; its meaning was hidden from them so that they should not understand it, and they were afraid to ask him about this saying.*
Part of Mark's "secret" depicted here.

9: 50 *Jesus said to him, "Do not prevent him, for whoever is not against you is for you."*
The honest sectarian is acceptable to Yeshua. Same as saying "Don't get hung up on anyone's doctrine or dogma!"

9: 51 *When the days for his being taken up were fulfilled, he resolutely determined to journey to Jerusalem,*
Backward-Looking.

9: 54-55 *When the disciples James and John saw this they asked, "Lord, do you want us to call down fire from heaven to consume them? "Jesus turned and rebuked them,*
Yeshua was a compassionate person!

10: 3-9 *Go on your way; behold, I am sending you like lambs among wolves. Carry no moneybag, no sack, no sandals; and greet no one along the way. Into whatever house you enter, first say, 'Peace to this household.' If a peaceful person lives there, your peace will rest on him; but if not, it will return to you. Stay in the same house and eat and drink what is offered to you, for the laborer deserves his payment. Do not move about from one house to another. Whatever town you enter and they welcome you, eat what is set before you, cure the sick in it and say to them, 'The kingdom of God is at hand for you.'*
A far cry from today's ministers!

10: 15 *And as for you, Capernaum, 'Will you be exalted to heaven? You will go down to the netherworld.'"*
The Hebrew name for our Hell, Sheol in Hebrew..

10: 16 *Whoever listens to you listens to me. Whoever rejects you rejects me. And whoever rejects me rejects the one who sent me."*
A hint of the justification of infallibility for the Petrine Tradition.

10: 17-18 *The seventy (-two) returned rejoicing, and said, "Lord, even the demons are subject to us because of your name." Jesus said, "I have observed Satan fall like lightning from the sky.*
Now, that's only a metaphor; some do take it literally!

10: 22 *All things have been handed over to me by my Father. No one knows who the Son is except the Father, and who the Father is except the Son and anyone to whom the Son wishes to reveal him."*
A faith statement! And, where is the third person of the Trinity? Left out?

10: 25 to 37 *There was a scholar of the law who stood up to test him and said, "Teacher, what must I do to inherit eternal life?" Jesus said to him, "What is written in the law? How do you read it?" He said in reply, "You shall love the Lord, your God, with all your heart, with all your being, with all your strength, and with all your mind, and your neighbor as yourself." He replied to him, "You have answered correctly; do this and you will live." But because he wished to justify himself, he said to Jesus, "And who is my neighbor?" Jesus replied, "A man fell victim to robbers as he went down from Jerusalem to Jericho. They stripped and beat him and went off leaving him half-dead. A priest happened to be going down that road, but when he saw him, he passed by on the opposite side. Likewise a Levite came to the place, and when he saw him, he passed by on the opposite side. But a Samaritan traveler who came upon him was moved with compassion at the sight. He approached the victim, poured oil and wine over his wounds and bandaged them. Then he lifted him up on his own animal, took him to an inn and cared for him. The next day he took out two silver coins and gave them to the innkeeper with the instruction, 'Take care of him. If you spend more than what I have given you, I shall repay you on my way back.' Which of these three, in your opinion, was neighbor to the robbers' victim?" He answered, "The one who treated him with mercy."*
Jesus said to him, "Go and do likewise."
The crux of Yeshua's teachings! Salvation by two laws: an intimate relationship with God and love of one's neighbor. Now, that's a serious simplification of the old ways of ritual and cleanliness, isn't it? Note the reply, "D*o this and you will live."* Does this remind you of Deut 30: 19?

11: 1-4 *He was praying in a certain place, and when he had finished, one of his disciples said to him, "Lord, teach us to pray just as John taught his disciples." He said to them, "When you pray, say: Father, hallowed be your name, your kingdom come. Give us each day our daily bread and <u>forgive us our sins for we ourselves forgive everyone in debt to us</u>, and do not subject us to the final test."*
That's the Lukan "Our Father" prayer. Note its different simplistic and personal tone compared to Matthew's formal language in his "Our Father" (Matt 6: 9-12). And please re-read the underlined again and ponder its significance in your daily life! And it just doesn't mean money!

11: 9-10 *"And I tell you, ask and you will receive; seek and you will find; knock and the door will be opened to you. For everyone who asks, receives; and the one who seeks, finds; and to the one who knocks, the door will be opened.*
A most important axiom of the "Jesus Movement". Didn't Jeremiah, 33: 3 suggest something similar?

11: 29-30 *While still more people gathered in the crowd, he said to them, "This generation is an evil generation; it seeks a sign, but no sign will be given it, except the sign of Jonah. Just as Jonah became a sign to the Ninevites, so will the Son of Man be to this generation.*
The sign is 3 days and 3 nights. Yeshua was in the tomb for about 40 hours! Oh well, they need a Math 101 class! On the other hand, this could not be a numbers game but a sign of salvation; Jonah saves Nineveh, Yeshua saves the Gentiles. Think about it! Wait, don't get us wrong, Jonah is still a myth tale! And, Luke has made this up too. But the difference is that it's Luke's faith speaking here in this Lukan construct.

11: 31-32 *At the judgment the queen of the south will rise with the men of this generation and she will condemn them, <u>because she came from the ends of the earth to hear the wisdom of Solomon</u>, and there is something greater than Solomon here. At the judgment the men of Nineveh will arise with this generation and condemn it, because at the preaching of Jonah they repented, and there is something greater than Jonah here.*
This is another faith statement by Luke! Note the cosmology underlined.

11: 39 *The Lord said to him, "Oh you Pharisees! Although you cleanse the outside of the cup and the dish, inside you are filled with plunder and evil.*
Does this ring a pedophile bell?

11: 42 to 54 *Woe to you Pharisees! You pay tithes of mint and of rue and of every garden herb, but you pay no attention to judgment and to love for God. These you should have done, without overlooking the others. Woe to you Pharisees! You love the seat of honor in synagogues and greetings in marketplaces. Woe to you! You are like unseen graves over which people unknowingly walk." Then one of the scholars of the law said to him in reply, "Teacher, by saying this you are insulting us too." And he said, "Woe also to you scholars of the law! You impose on people burdens hard to carry, but you yourselves do not lift one finger to touch them. Woe to you! You build the memorials of the prophets whom your ancestors killed. Consequently, you bear witness and give consent to the deeds of your ancestors, for they killed them and you do the building. Therefore, the wisdom of God said, 'I will send to them prophets and apostles; some of them they will kill and persecute' in order that this generation might be charged with the blood of all the prophets shed since the foundation of the world, from the blood of Abel to the blood of Zechariah who died between the altar and the temple building. Yes, I tell you, this generation will be charged with their blood! Woe to you, scholars of the law! You have taken away the key of knowledge. You yourselves did not enter and you stopped those trying to enter." When he left, the scribes and Pharisees began to act with hostility toward him and to interrogate him about many things, for they were plotting to catch him at something he might say.*
Reminds us of the priest who said that Yeshua never upset the people! Looks like that priest didn't read the Bible for its deeper meaning! And, is this the reason that Literalists dislike and ignore modern scholars? Modern scholars are not "scholars of the Law"? They are people seeking historical accuracy as well as personal spirituality! Do give them a break and listen or read them carefully!

12: 1 Meanwhile, so many people were crowding together that they were trampling one another underfoot. He began to speak, first to his disciples, "Beware of the leaven--that is, the hypocrisy--of the Pharisees.
Could this be applied to today's ministers and priests? Does the word "pedophile" strike a familiar note?

12: 8-10 I *tell you, everyone who acknowledges me before others the Son of Man will acknowledge before the angels of God. But whoever denies me before others will be denied before the angels of God. "Everyone who speaks a word against the Son of Man will be forgiven, but the one who blasphemes against the holy Spirit will not be forgiven.*
This is very interesting! Many have offered an explanation but no one knows what it means absolutely. May we suggest that it refers to a person who rejects God's forgiveness for him-herself, but especially rejects God's forgiveness for others whom that person wishes to be punished!

12: 24 *Notice the ravens: they do not sow or reap; they have neither storehouse nor barn, yet God feeds them. How much more important are you than birds!*
What is disturbing is the starvation of so many in Africa! Where is God now? Wait, isn't it part of the Genesis myth that God turned over the responsibility to humans? Shouldn't we ask, "What are we doing to solve the problem?"

12: 51 *Do you think that I have come to establish peace on the earth? No, I tell you, but rather division.*
How true that is! And, divisions and divisiveness we humans do have! Luke recognizes that condition existing in his time. We suspect that this passage is Luke's observation, not Yeshua's words.

12: 57 *"Why do you not judge for yourselves what is right?*
And, that, dear Reader, is exactly what this book is all about! Read and judge for yourself!

13: 11-13 *And a woman was there who for eighteen years had been crippled by a spirit; she was bent over, completely incapable of standing erect. When Jesus saw her, he called to her and said, "Woman, you are set free of your infirmity." He laid his hands on her, and she at once stood up straight and glorified God.*
That wasn't a spirit. It was a bad case of scoliosis!

13: 16 *This daughter of Abraham, whom Satan has bound for eighteen years now, ought she not to have been set free on the sabbath day from this bondage?"*
Even Yeshua believed in demonology! Didn't God inspire the truth? Just one more instance of the human-ness of the Bible!

13: 33 *Yet I must continue on my way today, tomorrow, and the following day, for it is impossible that a prophet should die outside of Jerusalem.'*
Lukan Backward-Looking again.

13: 34 *"Jerusalem, Jerusalem, you who kill the prophets and stone those sent to you, how many times I yearned to gather your children together as a hen gathers her brood under her wings, but you were unwilling!*
Female imagery of God!

14: 12-14 *Then he said to the host who invited him, "When you hold a lunch or a dinner, do not invite your friends or your brothers or your relatives or your wealthy neighbors, in case they may invite you back and you have repayment. Rather, when you hold a banquet, invite the poor, the crippled, the lame, the blind; blessed indeed will you be because of their inability to repay you. For you will be repaid at the resurrection of the righteous."*
When was the last time you did this? The Salvation Army has been doing it all along! How about that!

14: 26-27 *"If any one comes to me without hating his father and mother, wife and children, brothers and sisters, and even his own life, he cannot be my disciple. Whoever does not carry his own cross and come after me cannot be my disciple.*
Ouch! This is a real tough one, isn't it? But the cross sentence is from Luke's Backward-Looking, not from Yeshua's lips!

14: 33 *In the same way, everyone of you who does not renounce all his possessions cannot be my disciple.*
Boy, these are getting tougher by the verse!

14: 34 *"Salt is good, but if salt itself loses its taste, with what can its flavor be restored? 35 It is fit neither for the soil nor for the manure pile; it is thrown out. Whoever has ears to hear ought to hear."*
This is an intriguing parable and simile! Did you know that the salt used in that country came from the Dead Sea? It was a mixture of Sodium Chloride and Calcium Sulfate. Now, in the wet season the NaCl absorbed moisture and it dissolved out of the salt container leaving the Ca_2SO_4 which has no taste. When that happens the contents are useless and are thrown out. This is surely one fine simile about living one's Christianity, isn't it?

15: 1-32 There are three great parables in this Chapter: the Lost Sheep, the Lost Coin and the Lost Son. And God yearns for each to be found! When was the last time you hugged a lost sheep?

16: 14-15 *The Pharisees, who loved money, heard all these things and sneered at him. And he said to them, "You justify yourselves in the sight of others, but God knows your hearts; for what is of human esteem is an abomination in the sight of God.*
Another tough one to consider!

16: 19-31 *"There was a rich man who dressed in purple garments and fine linen and dined sumptuously each day. And lying at his door was a poor man named Lazarus, covered with sores, who would gladly have eaten his fill of the scraps that fell from the rich man's table. Dogs even used to come and lick his sores. When the poor man died, he was carried away by angels to the bosom of Abraham. The rich man also died and was buried, and from the netherworld, where he was in torment, he raised his eyes and saw Abraham far off and Lazarus at his side. And he cried out, 'Father Abraham, have pity on me. Send Lazarus to dip the tip of his finger in water and cool my tongue, for I am suffering torment in these flames.' Abraham replied, 'My child, remember that you received what was good during your lifetime while Lazarus likewise received what was bad; but now he is comforted here, whereas you are tormented.*

Moreover, between us and you a great chasm is established to prevent anyone from crossing who might wish to go from our side to yours or from your side to ours.' He said, 'Then I beg you, father, send him to my father's house, for I have five brothers, so that he may warn them, lest they too come to this place of torment.' But Abraham replied, 'They have Moses and the prophets. Let them listen to them.' He said, 'Oh no, father Abraham, but if someone from the dead goes to them, they will repent.' Then Abraham said, 'If they will not listen to Moses and the prophets, neither will they be persuaded if someone should rise from the dead.'"
This is a chilling parable, isn't it? Another story that's very meaningful! Read it twice to help it sink in!

17: 20-21 *Asked by the Pharisees when the kingdom of God would come, he said in reply, "The coming of the kingdom of God cannot be observed, and no one will announce, 'Look, here it is,' or, 'There it is.' For behold, the kingdom of God is among you."*
Do you know that today it's still here, just for the joining!

18: 17 *Amen, I say to you, whoever does not accept the kingdom of God like a child will not enter it."*
This is one of those sayings of Yeshua that is often mis-understood. A child accepts the security provided by its parents. Those who desire the Kingdom of God must do likewise. This simile doesn't mean that one should be childish and unthinking; Yeshua is speaking of the child's sincerity and innocence! Take a moment and mull this one over.

18: 20-22 *You know the commandments, 'You shall not commit adultery; you shall not kill; you shall not steal; you shall not bear false witness; honor your father and your mother.'" And he replied, "All of these I have observed from my youth." When Jesus heard this he said to him, "There is still one thing left for you: sell all that you have and distribute it to the poor, and you will have a treasure in heaven. Then come, follow me."*
Wow! Luke sure knows how to challenge us, doesn't he?

18: 26-27 *Those who heard this said, "Then who can be saved?" And he said, "What is impossible for human beings is possible for God."*
Here's that sincerity and acceptance again! Try re-reading 2 Corin 12:9 again.

18: 31-33 *Then he took the Twelve aside and said to them, "Behold, we are going up to Jerusalem and everything written by the prophets about the Son of Man will be fulfilled. He will be handed over to the Gentiles and he will be mocked and insulted and spat upon; and after they have scourged him they will kill him, but on the third day he will rise."*
This is a perfect example of Luke's Backward-Looking literary style. A human person has no knowledge of the future. Chalcedon determined that Yeshua was a total human!

19: 11 to 27 The Parable of the Ten Gold coins, go read it. It's an onion waiting to be peeled! It's an intriguing parable! It's about making money but its deeper meaning has nothing to do with making money! Isn't that ironic? Read it again and see what you can make of it! Here's a hint. Use your talents to do the best you can with what you have been given and do it with integrity and honesty to all with whom you come in contact. And, fear not!

19: 37-38 *and now as he was approaching the slope of the Mount of Olives, the whole multitude of his disciples began to praise God aloud with joy for all the mighty deeds they had seen. They proclaimed: "Blessed is the king who comes in the name of the Lord. Peace in heaven and glory in the highest."*
Believe it or not, but being called "King" by the crowd is what got Yeshua crucified by the Romans! Have you ever contemplated why the crowd chanted "King"? Well, to apply the title of Messiah brought with it the other titles of an Israelite King—Anointed One; Son of God and King. Just go back to the H.T. and re-read the books of Samuel and Kings.

21: 20-22 *"When you see Jerusalem surrounded by armies, know that its desolation is at hand. Then those in Judea must flee to the mountains. Let those within the city escape from it, and let those in the countryside not enter the city, for these days are the time of punishment when all the scriptures are fulfilled.*
This is Luke's retelling of the destruction of Jerusalem in 70 AD as though it were predicted by Yeshua!

21: 23-28 *Woe to pregnant women and nursing mothers in those days, for a terrible calamity will come upon the earth and a wrathful judgment upon this people. They will fall by the edge of the sword and be taken as captives to all the Gentiles; and Jerusalem will be trampled underfoot by the Gentiles until the times of the Gentiles are fulfilled. "There will be signs in the sun, the moon, and the stars, and on earth nations will be in dismay, perplexed by the roaring of the sea and the waves. People will die of fright in anticipation of what is coming upon the world, for the powers of the heavens will be shaken. And then they will see the Son of Man coming in a cloud with power and great glory. But when these signs begin to happen, stand erect and raise your heads because your redemption is at hand."*
These verses are a continuation of the previous passage that leads directly into the end time prediction (v. 27). As a matter of history, it hasn't arrived yet! Who got it wrong? (a) Was it God in her inspiration? (b) Was it Yeshua in his prediction? (c) Or, was it Luke in his attempt at Backward-Looking? Yep, C.

22: 3 *Then Satan entered into Judas, the one surnamed Iscariot, who was counted among the Twelve,*
A Myth! It was Judas' personal free will that chose to do what Yeshua asked of him! We'll revisit this in the Gospel of Judas in Ch 5 for a startleling discovery.

22: 17-20 *Then he took a cup, gave thanks, and said, "Take this and share it among yourselves; for I tell you (that) from this time on I shall not drink of the fruit of the vine until the kingdom of God comes." Then he took the bread, said the blessing, broke it, and gave it to them, saying, "This is my body, which will be given for you; do this in memory of me." And likewise the cup after they had eaten, saying, "This cup is the new covenant in my blood, which will be shed or you.*
These are the formulaic words that the community evolved 50 years after the Resurrection. They do not reflect the words of a Seder Meal. See your local Rabbi for the script. The "fruit of the vine" is wine not grape juice! Every Jewish person and all historians know that. Please stop saying that Yeshua lips

never touched alcohol. Nobody could drink the water in those days! You all know what happens then. Joachim Jeremais wrote a fine book about those very words called, "The Eucharistic Words of Jesus". It's out of print but a decent Christian bookstore may have a clue to its whereabouts. We found it on Amazon.com (about $35).

22: 24-27 Then *an argument broke out among them about which of them should be regarded as the greatest. He said to them, "The kings of the Gentiles lord it over them and those in authority over them are addressed as 'Benefactors'; but among you it shall not be so. Rather, let the greatest among you be as the youngest, and the leader as the servant. For who is greater: the one seated at table or the one who serves? Is it not the one seated at table? I am among you as the one who serves.*
Seems, our ministers and priests have it mixed up?

23: 18 *But all together they shouted out, "Away with this man! Release Barabbas to us."*
The people demand the release of a person whose name, Barabbas, is the title of Yeshua, Son of God ("bar abba" in Aramaic means a son of daddy!). Luke is definitely engaging in a bit of irony here!

23: 39-43 Now *one of the criminals hanging there reviled Jesus, saying, "Are you not the Messiah? Save yourself and us." The other, however, rebuking him, said in reply, "Have you no fear of God, for you are subject to the same condemnation? And indeed, we have been condemned justly, for the sentence we received corresponds to our crimes, but this man has done nothing criminal." Then he said, "Jesus, remember me when you come into your kingdom." He replied to him, "Amen, I say to you, today you will be with me in Paradise."*
This is Luke's version of the two thieves. It differs significantly from Matthew's story (Matt 27: 44). Go and read it and understand that "God's inspiration is no guarantee that the author will not make historical mistakes." (A paraphrase from the Jerome Biblical Commentary.) In Chapter 5 we will be pointing to many, many such mistakes.

24: 6-7 *He is not here, but <u>he has been raised</u>. Remember what he said to you while he was still in Galilee, that the Son of Man must be handed over to sinners and be crucified, and rise on the third day."*
That phrase is partly what Paul (Rom 1: 3-4) and Acts restate about God raising Yeshua. This is different than what was written about Yeshua previously. Yeshua is reported to have used the words "the sign of Jonah" which is a 72-hour period. This saying is only about a 40 hour period.

24: 10 *The women were Mary Magdalene, Joanna, and Mary the mother of James; the others who accompanied them also told this to the apostles,*
In this Gospel it's the women who experience the two men standing by the tomb! Read in Chapter Five what the other Gospel writers wrote!

24: 13 *Now that very day two of them were going to a village seven miles from Jerusalem called Emmaus,*
To this day a village called Emmaus has never been located! Isn't that strange?

24: 19 *And he replied to them, "What sort of things?" They said to him, "The things that happened to Jesus the Nazarene, who was a prophet mighty in deed and word before God and all the people,*
Well, once again we have an evaluation of Yeshua as a prophet. Does this reflect Rom 1: 3-4?

24: 25-27 *And he said to them, "Oh, how foolish you are! How slow of heart to believe all that the prophets spoke! Was it not necessary that the Messiah should suffer these things and enter into his glory?" Then beginning with Moses and all the prophets, he interpreted to them what referred to him in all the scriptures.*
Another Lukan faith statement and interpretation! Definitely not Yeshua's words! They are Luke's justification for the content of Apostolic preachings and teachings, but especially the prophetic references from the H.T.

24: 30 *And it happened that, while he was with them at table, he took bread, said the blessing, broke it, and gave it to them.*
Another example of Christian ritual and a Catholic justification.

24: 50-51 *Then he led them (out) as far as Bethany, raised his hands, and blessed them. As he blessed them he parted from them and was taken up to heaven.*
A good metaphor, but only first century cosmology.

Continued in Acts!

19. Acts of the Apostles (80-85 AD):

Yeshua defined the Kingdom of God with its (1) *metanoia*, (2) awareness of God's mercy and forgiveness, (3) a direct relationship with God, (4) love of neighbor, (5) concern for the well-being of all others with (6) a powerful reinforcement of Isaiah's (a) dismissal of ritual, (b) concern for widows, (c) orphans, and (d) those jailed unjustly (read Isaiah 1: 10 to 20 if you have any doubts). Modern scholarship calls these several items a synopsis of the "Jesus Movement" described within the mythologized four Gospels. The story of the "Christian Movement" is described in Acts.

[NOTE: We are using the title "Christian Movement" advisedly to separate the teachings of Yeshua as opposed to the formulaic church that develops out of Paul's ministry on the northern shore of the Mediterranean Sea and his eventual organizational directives. There are other areas of Christian development not mentioned in the Christian Testament: Alexandria, Syria and points East.]

Luke, a companion of Paul, follows the early preachings of the Apostles and then focuses on the life and times of Paul. Luke pays homage to the power of God's Spirit as the active impetus for the entire development. He refers to that power in terms of these four titles: the Spirit, the Holy Spirit, the Spirit of Yeshua; and the Spirit of God. It is uncertain whether he is using his literary license to use three synonyms for God and one for Yeshua or actually creating a third persona of the Godhead. As a disciple of Paul he repeats exactly those titles for God and Yeshua that Paul uses in his letters. This evidently is a problem until one reads that other people in the story are referred to as "the spirit of Stephen" in Acts 6: 10; the Spirit of Jesus in 16: 7. This may be the one clue that puts to rest the idea that Christology had a slow development throughout the Empire. Our thesis is that it was a sporadic and haphazard process in separate communities! To reinforce this perplexity we find the Spirit (breath) of God employed throughout the Hebrew Testament and certainly no Israelite would speak of a second or third person in the Godhead. In the Christian Testament the word "Spirit" was applied with a more diffused definition. This phenomenon is common in Greek philosophy, poetry and the Gospels, i.e., to raise an abstract idea to personhood, for examples, as in Beauty, Goodness and Love. Each of those three eventually became special gods in Greek mythology. As you have read in the Gospels, the authors referred to God as the Good and God is Love. Hey, case made! This tendency is part and parcel of the encultured Greek background of the majority of the newly baptized Gentile Christian membership. Much to our dismay in this 21st century, the title, Holy Spirit, had already evolved over the past 20 centuries and, like our modern concrete, is thoroughly mixed up and firmly set into our legends as an unchangeable biblical absolute. We will discuss that very subject in Chapter Five.

Concurrently, the teachings, handed down by the Apostles and Paul, spoke of Yeshua as a total human person anointed to Messianic status at and by means of the Resurrection. This and the above clearly make the Trinitarian Dogma very suspect. The circuitous and suspect development of Trinitarianism becomes crystal clear only when the New Testament is re-read in its chronological order of authorship. The contributing factors to the posture of the Nicene Creed were the plethora of apocryphal literature and the general confusion within the ranks of the presbyters and bishops of a widely uninformed membership of the Christian community. The fundamental difficulty lies in the cognitive development of that population of primitive leaders and members who, through no fault or sin of their own, were stuck at the pre-critical naiveté stage. Note this statement in Acts

> 4: 13 *Observing the boldness of Peter and John and perceiving them to be uneducated, ordinary men, they were amazed, and they recognized them as the companions of Jesus.*

This was very evident particularly at the 325 AD Council at Nicaea. And, then, when the Christian Testament was canonized around 400 AD, the translator, St. Jerome, placed the books into their commonly accepted present order, especially the Matthean Gospel that contained the banner justification of the Institutional Roman Catholic Church. WOW! Such a far-reaching historical mistake! By the time those two events took place, the traditions had developed into concretized legends of unbelievable mythical proportions.

Here are some specific comments to titillate your gray matter:

1. The term "Holy Spirit" occurs three or four times in the Hebrew Testament and 41 times in Acts; "Spirit" occurs 5 times; the "Spirit of the Lord" appears twice ; the "Spirit of Jesus" appears once; and then there were 2 evil spirits. Needless to say, Acts is a book powered by the "Spirit" but whose Spirit is it? Our vote is, its God's Spirit but misunderstood by a simplistic community of Christians who later personified it into a third person!

2. The three statements in Acts that repeat the theology of Paul expressed in Romans 1: 3-4 are in Acts 2: 36; 5: 31 and 13: 30-33 which we have

pointed out earlier in our discussions. But, please read them over again to capture their flavor and imprint them into your consciousness.

3. Check out the three stories of Paul's conversion and tell me that they are spoken by the one and only Paul and are without contradictions. What makes it humorous is that Luke actually wrote each one! The important points are: Who saw the light? Who fell down? And who heard the voice? When you add up your answers, you'll find the contradictions and be just as puzzled as we are. The real problem is, "Who is to blame for these inconsistencies? Is it God's failure to inspire correctly? Is it Luke's failing hearing aid, or sloppy editing? It looks very suspiciously like human error! Wasn't it so nice of God to inspire Luke and the rest of the authors to make such glaring mistakes. Then us regular Jane and Joe Does wouldn't worship this Book.

   Acts 9: 3-9 First Story of Paul's Epiphany
   On his journey, as he was nearing Damascus, a light from the sky suddenly flashed around him. He fell to the ground and heard a voice saying to him, "Saul, Saul, why are you persecuting me?" He said, "Who are you, sir?" The reply came, "I am Jesus, whom you are persecuting. Now get up and go into the city and you will be told what you must do." The men who were traveling with him stood speechless, for they heard the voice but could see no one. Saul got up from the ground, but when he opened his eyes he could see nothing; so they led him by the hand and brought him to Damascus. For three days he was unable to see, and he neither ate nor drank.

   Acts. 22: 6-9 Second Story
   "On that journey as I drew near to Damascus, about noon a great light from the sky suddenly shone around me. I fell to the ground and heard a voice saying to me, 'Saul, Saul, why are you persecuting me?' I replied, 'Who are you, sir?' And he said to me, 'I am Jesus the Nazorean whom you are persecuting.' My companions saw the light but did not hear the voice of the one who spoke to me.

   Acts 26: 13-18 Third Story
   At midday, along the way, O king, I saw a light from the sky, brighter than the sun, shining around me and my traveling companions. We all fell to the ground and I heard a voice saying to me in Hebrew, 'Saul, Saul, why are you persecuting me? It is hard for you to kick against the goad.' And I said, 'Who are you, sir?' And the Lord replied, 'I am Jesus whom you are persecuting. Get up now, and stand on your feet. I have appeared to you for this purpose, to appoint you as a servant and witness of what you have seen (of me) and what you will be shown. I shall deliver you from this people and from the Gentiles to whom I send you, to open their eyes that they may turn from darkness to light and from the power of Satan to God, so that they may obtain forgiveness of sins and been consecrated by faith in me.'

OK, let's plot those out :

Story	***Saw Light***	***Heard Voice***	***Fell Down***
First:			
Paul	***Yes***	***Yes***	***Yes***
Companions	***No***	***Yes***	***No***
Second:			
Paul	***Yes***	***Yes***	***Yes***
Companions	***Yes***	***No***	***No***
Third:			
Paul	***Yes***	***Yes***	***Yes***
Companions	***Yes***	***No***	***Yes***

Well, at least Luke was consistent about Paul, but, not the story about the companions. This repeated story of Paul's epiphany should be sufficient to alert one's intellect to the fact that God did not dictate or inspire Acts. Luke wrote what he remembered and what the oral tradition brought to him. Yes, a C.T. that is Man-Made in Israel!

Now, let's turn to the commentary:

1: 7 *He answered them, "It is not for you to know the times or seasons that the Father has established by his own authority.*
No one knows the final Judgment Day, not even Yeshua! Does this contradict what the Gospels say? You bet it does!

2: 16-17 *No, this is what was spoken through the prophet Joel: 17 'It will come to pass in the last days,' God says, 'that I will pour out a portion of my spirit upon all flesh. Your sons and your daughters shall prophesy, your young men shall see visions, your old men shall dream dreams.*
In this passage (Joel 3: 1 –NAB), that Spirit which is poured out is the Spirit of God! Luke is not too clear here. The "last days" alludes to the period from the resurrection to the end time!

2: 22 *You who are Israelites, hear these words. Jesus the Nazorean was a man commended to you by God with mighty deeds, wonders, and signs, which God worked through him in your midst, as you yourselves know.*
This is a re-statement of Yeshua's humanity and that God worked through Yeshua. One little problem, the word Nazorean means a holy dedicated man, not the town Nazareth! Seems to be a metaphor!

2: 27 *because you will not abandon my soul to the netherworld, nor will you suffer your holy one to see corruption.*
An H.T. reference to God and now Luke applies it to Yeshua, and it applies to Christians in general.

2: 36 *Therefore let the whole house of Israel know for certain that God has made him both Lord and Messiah, this Jesus whom you crucified."*

Here, as plain as day, is the Lukan statement of the earliest preachings of an Apostle that God appointed certain titles on Yeshua. Obviously, Yeshua didn't have those titles previously—a definite contradiction to the Fourth Gospel!

2: 42 *They devoted themselves to the teaching of the apostles and to the communal life, to the breaking of the bread and to the prayers.*
The Apostolic teaching gets distorted with time; the Eucharist takes on greater significance with time. So, the problem is what exactly are the Apostolic teachings for this 21st century now that we realize that it changed with the telling over the ages? We'll look at one possibility in Chapter Six.

2: 46 *Every day they devoted themselves to meeting together in the temple area and to breaking bread in their homes. They ate their meals with exultation and sincerity of heart,*
The Eucharist in the home of the members? So why is it only the province of ministers today in the Church building?

3: 14-15 *You denied the Holy and Righteous One {a} and asked that a murderer be released to you. The author of life {b} you put to death, but God raised him from the dead {c}; of this we are witnesses.*
These are three confusing designations: (a) is a confusing title; is it a designation for the God of the H.T. or a poetic reference to Yeshua; (b) is again confusing, is it the God of Genesis or a new title for Yeshua; and (c) if you think that the first two are pointing to Yeshua, then why does the Father have to raise Yeshua from the dead? Cannot the "author of life" raise himself up? Remember, Yeshua explained everything to the disciples! So, why the confusion? Or was that explanation a construct of the C.T. authors?

4: 13 *Observing the boldness of Peter and John and perceiving them to be uneducated, ordinary men, they were amazed, and they recognized them as the companions of Jesus.*
Simple men but nevertheless at the same cognitive stage of pre-critical naiveté as Luke is.

5: 30-32 *The God of our ancestors raised Jesus, though you had him killed by hanging him on a tree. God exalted him at his right hand as leader and savior to grant Israel* repentance *and forgiveness of sins. We are witnesses of these things, as is the holy Spirit that God has given to those who obey him."*
Thus is the second statement that Luke recalls from the earliest preachings of the Apostles. God raised Yeshua and gave him titles; titles Yeshua never had before! Repentance here in Greek is *metanoia*!

7: 33 *But the Lord said to him, 'Remove the sandals from your feet, for the place where you stand is holy ground.*
That was a great perception by the author of Exodus {the Universe is sacred}. Remember, it was spoken to Moses at the burning bush. Or was that also a myth?

7: 35 *This Moses, whom they had rejected with the words, 'Who appointed you ruler and judge?' God sent as (both) ruler and deliverer, through the angel who appeared to him in the bush.*

Now it's an angel!? Wasn't it God? It is strange indeed that first it's a messenger (angel) at the burning bush but as soon as it speaks, it's Yahweh!

7: 48-49 *Yet the Most High does not dwell in houses made by human hands. As the prophet says: "The heavens are my throne, the earth is my footstool. What kind of house can you build for me?" says the Lord, or what is to be my resting place?*
The Catholic practice of God in the Tabernacle is contradicted here.

8: 25-40 This is a long story, please read it.
There is a slight of hand in this tale. First an angel talks to Philip (v. 26). Later it turns out to be "a Spirit" (v. 29). The same thing occurred in Exodus at the burning bush. "Me thinks" this is a literary construct! Then in verse 39 we have a bit of magic when "the Spirit of the Lord" snatches Philip away. Whose Spirit is this? God's or Yeshua's? With each verse we examine, the distinctions get cloudier and cloudier!

9: 31 *The church <u>throughout all</u> Judea, Galilee, and Samaria was at peace. It was being built up and walked in the fear of the Lord, and with the consolation of the holy Spirit it grew in numbers.*
This "throughout all" is a special Greek phrase, "*kath holace*". It became the designating word for the Christian Institution in later years. It shortens to "Catholic"!

A special note about Acts 10 is in order. First, it is to make the transition from Jewish Christianity to the efforts to accept Gentiles into the membership. Secondly, The thrust to convert Gentiles is authenticated by the angelic vision to Peter. Thirdly, a holy person, no matter where he or she lives and no matter his or her religious preference is acceptable to God (next quoted verse), Fourthly, there is an affirmation of the belief that God raised Yeshua and the physical resurrection is verified (the "10: 40-41" referenced below).

10: 34-35 *Then Peter proceeded to speak and said, "In truth, I see that God shows no partiality. Rather, in every nation whoever fears him and acts uprightly is acceptable to him.*
Evidence of God's justice to all who have a good heart, even, and particularly, when they have not yet encountered Yeshua! We think the Evangelicals need take notice!

10: 40-41 *<u>This man</u> God raised (on) the third day and granted that he be visible, not to all the people, but to us, the witnesses chosen by God in advance, who ate and drank with him after he rose from the dead.*
The man Yeshua! A confirmation of Chalcedon! They ate and drank with him as proof of his humanity and bodily resurrection! Now, this idea that God chose these witnesses in advanced is the culture's concept of a Puppeteer Divinity who wrote the play in Genesis 1 and has pre-destined all of creation down to the jot and tittle of every word and deed since creation. That belief, dear Reader, negates Free Will. Pre-destination is the stuff of childishness (see I Corin 13: 11)!

13: 32 *We ourselves are proclaiming this good news to you that what God promised our ancestors he has brought to fulfillment for us, (their) children, by*

raising up Jesus, as it is written in the second psalm, 'You are my son; this day I have begotten you.' And that he raised him from the dead never to return to corruption he declared in this way, 'I shall give you the benefits assured to David.' That is why he also says in another psalm, 'You will not suffer your holy one to see corruption.' Now David, after he had served the will of God in his lifetime, fell asleep, was gathered to his ancestors, and did see corruption. But the one whom God raised up did not see corruption. You must know, my brothers, that through him forgiveness of sins is being proclaimed to you, (and) in regard to everything from which you could not be justified under the law of Moses, in him every believer is justified.
This is the third Lukan recollection of the earliest preachings of the Apostles. Once again, it confirms Paul's statement in Romans 1: 1-4. How much clearer can it be that Yeshua was preached to be a fully human person and NOT equal to God but given the fullness of God by way of gift (Eph 3: 17-19).

14: 22 *They strengthened* <u>*the spirits of the disciples*</u> *and exhorted them to persevere in the faith, saying, "It is necessary for us to undergo many hardships to enter the kingdom of God."*
Can you not now comprehend the confusion in the 1st century Christian communities with understanding the word "spirit"?

16: 6-7 *They traveled through the Phrygian and Galatian territory because they had been prevented by the holy Spirit from preaching the message in the province of Asia. When they came to Mysia, they tried to go on into Bithynia, but the Spirit of Jesus did not allow them,*
This is not like the Yeshua of the Gospels nor like the God of Love in the Fourth Gospel! It derives its theology from the "Puppeteer God" of the folklore mindset of these authors.

17: 30-31 *God has overlooked the times of ignorance, but now he demands that all people everywhere repent because he has established a day on which he will 'judge the world with justice'* <u>*through a man*</u> *he has appointed, and he has provided* <u>*confirmation for all by raising him from the dead*</u>*."*
The doctrine of Chalcedon (451 AD) is given substance here. God is the agent who has appointed Yeshua, the man, whom God has raised from the dead. How many statements do you need to grasp that Yeshua was, and is, NOT equal to God? The "repent" is again "*metanoia*".

18: 25-26 *He had been instructed in the Way of the Lord and, with ardent spirit, spoke and* <u>*taught accurately*</u> *about Jesus, although he knew only the baptism of John. He began to speak boldly in the synagogue; but when Priscilla and Aquila heard him, they took him aside and explained to him the Way (of God) more accurately.*
God has been called Lord throughout the H.T.. Yeshua is also called Lord. Even though the first appears to reference Yeshua, the second points to God the Father. Therein lie the seeds of Trinitarian confusion! Did you catch the "taught accurately"? That's an oxymoron if we ever read one!

20: 7 *On the first day of the week when we gathered to break bread, Paul spoke to them because he was going to leave on the next day, and he kept on speaking until midnight.*
This is the beginning of the shift to Sunday as the day of rest and of Worship.

26: 25 *But Paul replied, "I am not mad, most excellent Festus; I am speaking words of truth and reason.*
Yes, Reason and intelligence are part of adult faith! But, grasp the fact that it is also just Paul's perceived truth, his alone.

28: 25-26 Without *reaching any agreement among themselves they began to leave; then Paul made one final statement. "Well did the holy Spirit speak to your ancestors through the prophet Isaiah, saying: 26 'Go to this people and say: You shall indeed hear but not understand. You shall indeed look but never see.*
This is very interesting! No small wonder why the Synagogue Jews rejected Paul and Christianity; they know too well the statement of Deut 6: 4 !! What they didn't know was that Paul was referring to the Spirit of the ONE GOD. If you read Psalm 51: 13 (NAB or Psalm 51: 11 in either the NRSV or any other KJV daughter translations), you will discover the use of the phrase, "holy spirit". Of special interest is the translation "the spirit of holiness" in the New Jerusalem Bible!! That definitely refers to God the Father who is simply God, the One and Only—without any partners!

20. Revelation (81-96):

This book is one of the most mystifying in the entire Bible. It contains such a complex content of the entire range of mythic styles that it defies interpretation. Therefore, we recommend that you read the Introduction in the NAB and ponder your personal interpretation. For us, the book is a secret message of hope for the primitive Christian who is being persecuted by Rome and those Israelites angered at the new Christian theology. You definitely must read between the lines to make any sense out of the author's writing. But in spite of the brouhaha that literalists today make of this alleged future pointing book, it was actually intended to be a coded message for the people of that time, coded in myth to avoid the wrath of the Roman persecutors.

21. Jude (90)

Although a very short letter; Jude does contain several passages that are worthy of comment. They are informative in the sense that they point out the basic nature of the Christian mindset with respect to interpreting the writings of their times.

1: 1 *Jude, a slave of Jesus Christ and brother of James, to those who are called, beloved in God the Father and kept safe for Jesus Christ:*
He is the Brother of James and, logically, the brother of Yeshua.

1: 3 *Beloved, although I was making every effort to write to you about our common salvation, I now feel a need to write to encourage you to contend for the faith that was once for all handed down to the holy ones.*
This speaks of "a faith that was handed down" that means an oral tradition which was uncritically received. Could this community not have read the four gospels yet? This theme, "tradition that is handed down", is repeated in many writings of the early Church Fathers. That tends to be a sort of religious fundamentalism due primarily to a "pre-critical naiveté" stage of cognitive development prevalent throughout early Christendom. AND, up to the 21st century!

1: 9 *Yet the archangel Michael, when he argued with the devil in a dispute over the body of Moses, did not venture to pronounce a reviling judgment upon him but said, "May the Lord rebuke you!"*
Here in this underlined passage we see a reference to an apocryphal writing, the Assumption of Moses that was considered to be an acceptable source by many Christian communities. No wonder the Catholic Church authorities had a difficult time deciding what was correct doctrine (teachings) and what was faulty.

1: 14 *Enoch, of the seventh generation from Adam, prophesied also about them when he said, "Behold, the Lord has come with his countless holy ones ..."*
Again there is a reference to an apocryphal writing, the Book of Enoch. This gives us a hint as to the confusion among the Christian communities that came to a crescendo of conflict around 300 AD that led to the Council at Nicaea in 325 AD.

1: 25 *to the only God, our savior, through Jesus Christ our Lord be glory, majesty, power, and authority from ages past,*
Here is a unique statement about the ONLY God, our Savior. It almost appears to be a corrective of the "equal to God" beliefs that circulate among Christian communities. Then comes the Lord Jesus Christ as though the two are separate beings who are not equals! Makes one re-think the doctrine of Trinity!

Summary of the Third Period:

We find it strange that Luke posits a Messiah at Birth and yet includes a Messiah at the Resurrection in his early Chapters in Acts !? Then the Letter of Jude uses the phrase, "the Only God". To say the least, those were confusing times. We are firmly convinced that there is sufficient evidence to re-think the Trinitarian Dogma. The literature doesn't support a triune Godhead. What is clear is that there are communities whose theology is fractured because of the many apocryphal writings in circulation. Wouldn't it be great if Yeshua wrote a 50 page document telling us exactly what we should believe and how we should act? Do you know what would happen then? Just like the Zen koan in which the master points to the life-giving energy of the sun and the disciples get in a quandary debating the nature of that sun which is too blinding to see and end up worshiping the master's finger which they can see! If you replace a few key words you'll get the picture: the Prophet, Yeshua, points to the God of Israel, the Holy One, as the true source of all power. The listeners begin to argue about the nature of the Father whom they cannot see and end up worshipping the prophet whom they can see.

Section Four: The Eternal Period: A Father God, a Son God from Eternity and the Holy Spirit God

22. Hebrews (70-90):

Thus far, the previous Epistles and Gospels have led us through three stages of Christian Messianic Theology (Appendix U). Here in this Epistle the author gives every indication of the fourth and last stage of Christian beliefs about who they perceived Yeshua to have been. However, the Epistle to the Hebrews presents several problems due to the following: (1) there is no signature identifying the author; (2) the literary style precludes Paul as that author; (3) the Christology is closer to that of the Fourth Gospel because the phrase in Heb 1: 1-4, *through whom he created the universe*, (with the "*whom*" referring to Yeshua and the "*he*" referring to God) implies that Yeshua is the co-existent member of the Trinity or possibly a high ranking angel, eh?

The key to resolving the first two problems is best stated in the Introduction to Hebrews in the New American Bible.

> "As early as the end of the second century, the church of Alexandria in Egypt accepted Hebrews as a letter from Paul, and that became the view commonly held in the East. Pauline authorship was contested in the West into the fourth century, but then accepted. In the sixteenth century, doubts about that position were again raised, and the modern consensus is that the letter was not written by Paul. There is, however, no widespread agreement on any of the other suggested authors, e.g., Barnabas, Apollos, or Prisc(ill)a and Aquila. The document itself has no statement about its author."
>
> "Among the reasons why Pauline authorship has been abandoned are the great differences in vocabulary and style between Hebrews and Paul's confirmed letters, the alternation of doctrinal teaching with moral exhortation, the different manner of citing the Old Testament, and the resemblance between the thought of Hebrews and that of Alexandrian Judaism. The Greek of this letter is in many ways the best in the New Testament."

Understanding the final factor is somewhat more complicated in that it lies in the belief structure of the Epistle's author. To him the Hebrew Testament is a future-pointing composition of prophecies, especially, Proverbs 8 in which Wisdom is poured forth from the beginning. Every Christian in the world who clings to the literal intent sees the wisdom metaphor in Proverbs 8 referring to Yeshua. Since this Christian author is not of that ilk, the 8th Chapter of Proverbs is simply nothing more than a metaphorical dissertation on the Wisdom of God ... alone. Chapter Five should help you re-consider the real evidence for Trintarianism.

The reason for associating Wisdom with Yeshua lies in two factors: the depth of meaning in the preachings of Yeshua as allegedly reported in all the previously written books of the Christian Testament and the experience of the risen Yeshua. The Resurrection was the singular most befuddling experience for the primitive apostolic mind. The discouraged disciples witnessing the post-Resurrectional glorified being of Yeshua became empowered and the rest is history, but history mythologized. However, in the context of their Jewish enculturation (literalists) Paul and the other Christian writers found explanations in the Hebrew Testament's stories and in the Messianic anticipations. To them and their belief that God was the pro-active architect in all things, they believed that the Hebrew Testament was factual in every detail including future pointing. How would you, possessing such an encultured belief structure, speak, preach or write about Yeshua had you encountered him that Easter?

Consider this! What would be the response of a present day, illiterate fisherman from the backwaters of Lake Victoria in Africa if his great grandfather came back from the dead? Actually, what would you feel if your spiritual leader returned from the dead? Better still, how about Muhammad or Martin Luther King, Jr.? Run that through your mind and try to imagine your emotional response! What could you learn from such a visitor and think what you would then tell someone else about that experience? Then again, you might just pass it off as too many hot green Mexican peppers at your last meal!

Can you now imagine what the experience of the risen Yeshua did for those disciples who actually saw, touched, ate and spoke with Yeshua? Then, there are those who received the "good news" second and third hand! How would they write about the risen Yeshua if they too believed that the Gospels were factual, tape-recordings of a Divine dictation? Voila! You would become a literalist! Well, unfortunately you live in the 21st century, a time of science and reason (hopefully).

Bishop John Shelby Sponge (Episcopalian) wrote a book, "Christianity must Change or Die". He asked similar questions! Marcus Borg another modern theologian and biblical scholar has voiced a deep concern for Biblical meaning without taking the Bible literally. In Appendix R you can find a list of their writings and other serious books on modern Biblical interpretation.

Hebrews itself is for the most part a literal interpretation and uses the Hebrew Testament to provide the community with the doctrinal meaning to the life of Yeshua, the carpenter from Nazareth. Hebrews is an exhortation to Jewish Christians written between 70 and 95 AD. From a few phrases of a preexistent Wisdom in the H.T. the author has extrapolated to a pre-existent Yeshua. It is the Christology of a different community than that of Paul, James and Peter! It is a more complicated Christology than Mark, Matthew or Luke-Acts. Hebrews is very close to that of the authors of Fourth Gospel. In the remaining chronological readings of the Christian Testament we will find the last bit of evidence for the thesis of this book: five separate Christian communities existing, side by side, with both minor and major dissentious interpretations of the nature of this Yeshua. These communities will multiply and show up in force over the early 200 years. See Appendix A for the list of the principal beliefs (alleged heresies, courtesy of Nicaea). When Constantine conquers the civilized world in 312 AD, he makes the supreme blunder of installing Christianity's leaders to the Empire's Judicial offices throughout his new conquest. Then concurrently with the Constantine unification of the Mediterranean Basin, the disputing communities raised their ugly Christological conflicts. To stop those disputes Constantine ordered the Catholic leadership to define Christianity's doctrines to quell the disruptive infighting. The result was the Nicene Creed! The conflict has never been totally resolved! Nor has the flame of prejudicial doctrines been extinguished!

Let's proceed to the commentary of Hebrews.

1: 1 *In times past, God spoke in partial and various ways to our ancestors through the prophets;*
The use of the words *partial* and *various* has significances that are missed by the average reader. Partial means that only part of the full message was sent and various means that God spoke in different styles including mythology (as previously defined in Appendix M). What the author is saying is that the prophets only received a portion of the truth and the message could have been clothed in diverse literary styles, much like our daily newspapers!

1: 2 *in these last days, he {God} spoke to us through a son, whom he made heir of all things and through whom he created the universe,*
These *last days* are the days after the Resurrection; *a son* is what all Israel Kings are called, but they are not considered to be equal to God; *he {God} made heir* means that God appointed (as in Romans 1: 3-4) Yeshua to be heir (Psalm 2: 8) in the sense that a human will judge the rest of humanity; and the last phrase is the author's mis-interpretation of Proverbs 8 in which the metaphorical meaning of God's Wisdom was reinterpreted to be Yeshua. It is common for metaphors to be interpreted in several ways but metaphors must have a primary meaning based on the context of the whole, in this case, the whole of Proverbs. The authors of Proverbs are focused on the One God of Deut 6:4. Therefore, the metaphor must be another way to talk about the One God. The secondary reason for the misplacement is the belief that the Hebrew Testament is totally factual which, of course, has been proven to be a primitive incorrect belief. Chapter Five will attempt to formalize that proof, once and for all. The third reason for the mis-placement is the belief that all prophets speak to the future rather than to their present. The authors of the C.T. constantly look back (the Backward-Looking style) in order to understand their present, thereby, reading more into the past than what was originally intended. Remember, prophets speak for someone --- God; they do not predict the distant future! The phrase, "according to the scriptures" will always indicate the primitive and "pre-critical Naiveté" mindset of these Christian writers.

1: 3 *who {Yeshua} is the refulgence of his {God} glory, the very imprint of his {God} being, and who {God} sustains all things by his mighty word. When he {Yeshua} had accomplished purification from sins, he {Yeshua} took his seat at the right hand of the Majesty on high {God}.*
Clearly, the 1st, 5th and 6th { } are right out of Eph 3: 17-19 ; the purification of sins is confirmed by means of the Resurrection; and, seating at the right hand is from Acts 5: 31.

1: 4 *as <u>far superior to the angels</u> as <u>the name he has inherited is more excellent than theirs.</u>*
These two underlined are complementary titles because God raised Yeshua and gave him those titles (Rom 1:3-4, Acts 2: 32-33, Acts 5: 31 and Acts 13: 33). Therefore Yeshua inherited the name above all names, even superior to the Angels (as Eph 3: 17-19 says for all people who imitate Yeshua). This agrees with Pail's Christology.

1: 5-14 *For to which of the angels did God ever say: "You are my son; this day I have begotten you"? Or again: "I will be a father to him, and he shall be a son to me"? And again, when he leads the first-born into the world, he says: "Let all the angels of God worship him." Of the angels he says: "He makes his angels winds and his ministers a fiery flame"; but of the Son: "Your throne, O God, stands forever and ever; and a righteous scepter is the scepter of your kingdom. (v.9) You loved justice and hated wickedness<u>; therefore God, your God, anointed you</u> with the oil of gladness above your companions"; and: "At the beginning, O Lord, you established the earth, and the heavens are the works of your hands. They will perish, but you remain; and they will all grow old like a garment. You will roll them up like a cloak, and like a garment they will be changed. But you are the same, and your years will have no end." But to which of the angels has he ever said: "Sit at my right hand until I make your enemies your footstool"?*

Are they not all ministering spirits sent to serve, for the sake of those who are to inherit salvation?
The author makes a series of quotes from a variety of Psalms and Acts. These formulas are specifically for the anointing of a new King of Israel. In the NAB they are from Ps 2, Ps 89:19 (the Holy One of Israel, our king!), Psalm 45 (an example of a confusion with the references to the King of Israel who is considered to be a god and son of God and, allegedly, Yeshua's being God's Son), Ps 102 and Acts 2 and 5 which are Messianic titles applied to Yeshua at the Resurrection. The one catch is that underlined phrase: "therefore God anointed you, He who is your God, ..." (here paraphrased for clarity). We checked several KJV daughters and the Catholic Bibles and each one writes *"God, your God, anointed you ..."!* So the translations into English MUST read*: "God, who is your God, anointed you ...".* Now this puts Yeshua in a poor position to be equal to God the Father, does it not? The real difficulty lies in the use of the commas. If the two words between the commas are removed it reads, "therefore God has anointed you". That is exactly what Romans 1: 1-4 means and what the three quotes from Acts mean. Pretty strong evidence that here in Hebrews is a remembrance of the original teachings of the Apostles! Now, one must show the other way to read this underlined phrase. If you take out the commas, it can read "therefore God (pause) your God anointed you". Opps, it now reads like the author is addressing Yeshua as God. OH Boy, a big problem! The Greek has no punctuation, What this phrase really means is up for grabs. We'll never absolutely know the truth. Whatever the outcome, Yeshua is NOT equal to God is the correct psychological interpretation due to the cognitive level of the people in that time period.

2: 17 *therefore, he had to become like his brothers in every way, that he might be a merciful and faithful high priest before God to expiate the sins of the people.* This verse states that Yeshua became like his brothers in every way. Well, looks like Old Hebrews hit the nail on the head! That's Chalcedon 451 AD; Yeshua is human in every way including ignorance!

3: 7-12 *Therefore, as the holy Spirit says: "Oh, that today you would hear his voice, 'Harden not your hearts as at the rebellion in the day of testing in the desert, where your ancestors tested and tried me and saw my works for forty years. Because of this I was provoked with that generation and I said, "They have always been of erring heart, and they do not know my ways." As I swore in my wrath, "They shall not enter into my rest."''*
In this passage (from Ps 95: 7-11) there is no Holy Spirit. God is the one speaking! The author of Hebrews puts that Psalm on the lips of his own understanding of the Holy Spirit! The confusion persisted up to and possibly further in time than this Letter to the Hebrews. Catch the "wrath" again! It's just angry Christians wanting punishment for their persecutors. You may wish to review Appendices AB and AC for the biblical uses of the word Spirit and Vine's Dictionary definition of *"ruwach"* and *"pneuma"*, the Hebrew and Greek words for breath.

6: 18 *so that by two immutable things, in which it was impossible for God to lie, we who have taken refuge might be strongly encouraged to hold fast to the hope that lies before us.*
A quote from Gen 22: 16 in which God takes an oath on himself and makes promises. Then the author of Hebrews adds that "God can't lie"! The literalist translates that to mean that the Bible is absolutely and truthfully God's Word and,

thus, extrapolates to a conviction that the Bible doesn't lie either! However, as other Biblical Scholars have written, one mistake in the Bible is one too many. Look to Chapter Five for a partial listing of the many mistakes contained in the Bible in order to challenge the literalists to acknowledge a mythologized Bible!

12: 5-8 You *have also forgotten the exhortation addressed to you as sons: "My son, do not disdain the discipline of the Lord or lose heart when reproved by him; for whom the Lord loves, he disciplines; he scourges every son he acknowledges." Endure your trials as "discipline"; God treats you as sons. For what "son" is there whom his father does not discipline? If you are without discipline, in which all have shared, you are not sons but bastards.*
These are harsh statements about a God who disciplines those whom He loves. That's not the God of Yeshua! It is the God of folk-theology and Old Legends.

12: *17 For you know that later, when he wanted to inherit his father's blessing, he was rejected because he found no opportunity to change his mind, even though he sought the blessing with tears*
Finally the phrase "change of mind" is translated correctly from the Greek, *metanoia*. Repentance is not meant! "Change the way you behave" is what is meant.

It is important to reflect on this Epistle because it is the product of a Christian who is basically a literalist. The entire letter is packed full of folk theology extracted from the Hebrew Testament which this author of Hebrews considers to be a factual history, a scientific document and an accurate dictation from God's lips. Unfortunately, none of these is correct. But, don't despair! The Bible has immense meaning written between the lines. Just be patient; Chapters Six and Seven will re-fresh you with the REAL "Good News".

23. 2 Peter (90+):

First off, there are a lot of confusing statements made in this Epistle! It is becoming more certain that the Christian writers and interpreters are all from the literalist camp. That condition was prevalent in those times. As a matter of fact, the history of the Christian movement up to and including the Galileo, Copernicus and Kepler age reeked of literalism. Now, that doesn't mean those people were evil and sinful; it just means they were simple people like any "pre-critical naiveté" child of today. The humor in this is that most of today's children at age 12 are much more educated than any person who lived prior to Martin Luther, he of the 16th century. And even with the level of education in the world in this 21st century, many, many are trained by well-intentioned religious leaders who themselves are literalists. Look out for the word "knowledge"! There are many uses of that word, i.e., gaining information and experience (See Appendix Z). However, (in Greek it's *gnosis* or *epignosis* for knowledge and full knowledge) in this letter it may carry the meaning of "secret knowledge". Some simple people believe that this *"gnosis"* always means Gnosticism. Knowledge in any of the Christian Testament books doesn't always mean the same as what we in the 21st century understand it to mean--- gaining information and experience. Remember the dissertation on cognitive development in Chapter One and how it affects one's interpretive abilities! So much for Educational Psychology 210!

The next important revelation is the age of this letter. Here is a quote from the New American Bible's Introduction to 2 Peter:

> "many [Scholars] think it is the latest work in the New Testament and assign it to the first or even the second quarter of the second century. The principal reasons for this view are the following. The author refers to the apostles and "our ancestors" as belonging to a previous generation, now dead (2 Pet 3: 2-4). A collection of Paul's letters exists and appears to be well known, but disputes have arisen about their interpretation (2 Pet 3: 14-16). The passage about false teachers (2 Pet 2: 1-18) contains a number of literary contacts with Jude 1: 4-16, and it is generally agreed that 2 Peter depends upon Jude, not vice versa. Finally, the principal problem exciting the author is the false teaching of "scoffers" who have concluded from the delay of the Parousia that the Lord is not going to return. This could scarcely have been an issue during the lifetime of Simon Peter."

With that said, let's turn to the commentary of 2 Peter.

1: 1-2 *Symeon Peter, a slave and apostle of Jesus Christ, to those who have received a faith of equal value to ours through the righteousness of our God and savior Jesus Christ: may grace and peace be yours in abundance through knowledge of God and of Jesus our Lord.*
The translation of verse 1 leads to a problem for the reader to decide whether the author intended to mean that Yeshua is "God and Savior". However, in the second verse the exact opposite is conveyed by the two prepositional phrases (of God and of Jesus, our Lord) that indicate that they are two separate persons.

To illustrate the difficulty in interpreting this passage, let's examine the NRSV Bible translation:

> NRSV: 2 Peter 1:1-2 *Simeon {Other ancient authorities read [Simon]} Peter, a servant {Gk [slave]} and apostle of Jesus Christ, To those who have received a faith as precious as ours through the righteousness of our God and Savior Jesus Christ: {Or [of our God and the Savior Jesus Christ]} May grace and peace be yours in abundance in the knowledge of God and of Jesus our Lord.*

It is clear that there is a hermeneutical difficulty in distinguishing the absolute meaning and intent of the author!

1: 2, 3, 5, 6 and 8 In these five verses the word knowledge and full knowledge appear! Keep it straight in your mind that the meaning here does not mean Gnosticism!

1: 12 *Therefore, I will always remind you of these things, even though you already know them and are established in the truth you have.*
Another truth statement; but, is it absolute or a relative perception? What is "truth" for you? Is it the same "truth" as your neighbor's? I think NOT!

1: 16-18 We did not follow cleverly devised myths when we made known to you the power and coming of our Lord Jesus Christ, but we had been eyewitnesses of

his majesty. For he received honor and glory from God the Father when that unique declaration came to him from the majestic glory, "This is my Son, my beloved, with whom I am well pleased." We ourselves heard this voice come from heaven while we were with him on the holy mountain.
Actually, every literalist does follow those myths in the Hebrew Testament and is especially susceptible to the mythologizing found in the Christian Testament. And the eyewitness statements in 17 and 18 are without doubt the author's exaggeration because he wasn't Peter. But, we know that in those years authors frequently sign their letters as though their mentor were the originator.

1: 20-21 *Know this first of all, that there is no prophecy of scripture that is a matter of personal interpretation, for no prophecy ever came through human will; but rather human beings moved by the holy Spirit spoke under the influence of God.*
Well, to say that God put all those prophetic words on the lips of the Prophets of old is to deny the errors found throughout the Hebrew Testament because those Christians also believed that the Bible was a Divine dictate without errors. Be patient, Chapter Five is just a leap and a jump around a paragraph or two from here!

2: 1-18 *Therefore, we must attend all the more to what we have heard, so that we may not be carried away. 2 For if the word announced through angels proved firm, and every transgression and disobedience received its just recompense, 3 how shall we escape if we ignore so great a salvation? Announced originally through the Lord, it was confirmed for us by those who had heard. 4 God added his testimony by signs, wonders, various acts of power, and distribution of the gifts of the holy Spirit according to his will. 5 For it was not to angels that he subjected the world to come, of which we are speaking. 6 Instead, someone has testified somewhere: "What is man that you are mindful of him, or the son of man that you care for him? 7 You made him for a little while lower than the angels; you crowned him with glory and honor, 8 subjecting all things under his feet." In "subjecting" all things (to him), he left nothing not "subject to him." Yet at present we do not see "all things subject to him," 9 but we do see Jesus "crowned with glory and honor" because he suffered death, he who" for a little while" was made "lower than the angels," that by the grace of God he might taste death for everyone. 10 For it was fitting that he, for whom and through whom all things exist, in bringing many children to glory, it should make the leader to their salvation perfect through suffering. 11 He who consecrates and those who are being consecrated all have one origin. Therefore, he is not ashamed to call them "brothers," 12 saying: "I will proclaim your name to my brothers, in the midst of the assembly I will praise you"; 13 and again: "I will put my trust in him"; and again: "Behold, I and the children God has given me." 14 Now since the children share in blood and flesh, he likewise shared in them, that through death he might destroy the one who has the power of death, that is, the devil, 15 and free those who through fear of death had been subject to slavery all their life. 16 Surely he did not help angels but rather the descendants of Abraham; 17 therefore, he had to become like his brothers in every way, that he might be a merciful and faithful high priest before God to expiate the sins of the people. 18 Because he himself was tested through what he suffered, he is able to help those who are being tested*
This is without a doubt the most complicated chapter to read and understand. The Author quotes many passages from the H.T., mis-interprets most of them

moving back and forth between the literal and figurative meanings. Let me show you. Verse 7 says that Yeshua was lower than angels; does that mean human? Then in verse 17 Yeshua is like his brothers in every way; that means totally human including ignorance. Well if so, how come the Fourth Gospel makes Yeshua all knowledgeable including future predicting? Problem two, in verses 1 and 3 the Author implies that we should "hold on to what we have heard". What exactly did he hear? There is nothing about what Paul wrote in Rom 1: 1-4; nothing about the Christology of Mark, Matthew and Luke. His focus is on the alleged prophesies in the H.T. Does all this mean that he read none of the canonical books, heard none of the previous Apostolic preachings? .It would appear that this Author is a Jewish convert in the late first century who is convinced that the H.T. is the center of God's revelation. He assigns Yeshua to the role of creator in verse 10 in the first part and then says that Yeshua had to be perfected through suffering. What's this about? First Yeshua is creator and then he must suffer to be perfect! Doesn't this seem like the Author is contradicting himself? It does to me. Well, I believe that all this confusion owes its origin in two factors: first, there are many who come with different, false stories about what Yeshua said and did, no one had the inside tract about the life and times of Yeshua, and seconf, the people were literalists who believed that their Scriptures were absolutely true, a pre-critical naiveté. Anyone need Excedrin?

3: 4 *and saying, "Where is the promise of his coming? From the time when our ancestors fell asleep, everything has remained as it was from the beginning of creation."*
Is it believable that "*everything has remained as it was from the beginning of creation.?"* OH, definitely NOT! Does the word "evolution" ring a bell?

3: 5 *They deliberately ignore the fact that the heavens existed of old and earth was formed out of water and through water by the word of God;*
Another misuse of the word, "fact". Looks like the Genesis myth again!

3: 7 *The present heavens and earth have been reserved by the same word for fire, kept for the day of judgment and of destruction of the godless.*
How about this! It's the source of the belief that the Universe will end in fire! Well, what do you know, he may be correct in that a few mis-fired Hydrogen bombs may be the instruments of the Lord (through some terrorist!).

3: 8 *But do not ignore this one fact, beloved, that with the Lord one day is like a thousand years and a thousand years like one day.*
Finally, a truism! But no respectable literalist applies this to Genesis 1 & 2! OH well, life is surely full of inconsistent perceptions, isn't it?

3: 15-16 *And consider the patience of our Lord as salvation, as our beloved brother Paul, according to the wisdom given to him, also wrote to you, speaking of these things as he does in all his letters. In them there are some things hard to understand that the ignorant and unstable distort to their own destruction, just as they do the other scriptures.*
Ah, brother Paul and his writings now come under attack as far too complicated for the average Christian to comprehend. Our author warns the recipient community to beware of false interpreters. What a joke! The Christian community for the next 1500 years has trouble understanding Paul (as many

today still do!). Actually, there have been troubles understanding the entire Bible (as many today still do!). Ain't that right, Eh?

3: 18 *But grow in grace and in the knowledge of our Lord and savior Jesus Christ. To him be glory now and to the day of eternity. (Amen.)*
How can one grow in knowledge when one considers the Christian Testament to be literal, true and absolutely a Divine dictate! Seems very contradictory.

24. 1 John (90-100):

The Introduction (in the NAB) states that the Gospel and letters of John are the product of the same school of Johannine Christianity. However, read the comments on the other two letters before you concur. Actually, reading the "Introductions" to all the letters and especially the Gospel is very necessary to unearth the plethora of sectarianisms present in this Christian Testament.

The main theme in this first letter appears to be as described in this quote from the NAB:

> "The author affirms that authentic Christian love, ethics, and faith take place only within the historical revelation and sacrifice of Jesus Christ. The fullness of Christian life as fellowship with the Father must be based on true belief and result in charitable living; knowledge of God and love for one another are inseparable, and error in one area inevitably affects the other."

Here are two worthy ideals: (a) "the historical revelation", not the Post-Resurrectional one, and (b) Christian fellowship "must be based on true belief" which leaves us with someone's personal perception! Oh my, will the confusion ever end? Let's explain further.

The Resurrection of Yeshua (which we believe to be a true bodily occurrence) was an event in which God confirmed, certified and authenticated the teachings of Yeshua. Christianity operates based upon the Teachings of Yeshua. However, the Christian communities could not make up their minds exactly what those teachings were. The result turned out individual pockets of believers debating the nature of Yeshua rather than following the teachings. "Ain't" that ironic? Another finger to worship instead of what the Master was pointing to!

Ok, here are the comments:

1: 1 *What was from the beginning, what we have heard, what we have seen with our eyes, what we looked upon and touched with our hands concerns the Word of life*
The confirmations of the humanity of Yeshua.

1: 8 *Whoever sins belongs to the devil, because the devil has sinned from the beginning. Indeed, the Son of God was revealed to destroy the works of the devil.*
Literalism's belief in the veracity of the Hebrew Testament's myths. Well, somebody is full of it! And, did you catch the joke in the last line? Yeshua may have destroyed the evil works of the Devil but the evil works of humans is still

alive and flourishing!!! That's because Yeshua didn't know that the Devil is a myth!!!!!

1: 5-7 *Now this is the message that we have heard from him and proclaim to you: God is light, and in him there is no darkness at all. If we say, "We have fellowship with him," while we continue to walk in darkness, we lie and do not act in truth. But if we walk in the light as he is in the light, then we have fellowship with one another, and the blood of his Son Jesus cleanses us from all sin.*
Examples of the many uses of METAPHOR! Note the light vs. the darkness; it's a primitive Babylonian myth that associates good with the light of day and evil with the darkness of night.

2: 9-11 Whoever *says he is in the light, yet hates his brother, is still in the darkness. Whoever loves his brother remains in the light, and there is nothing in him to cause a fall. Whoever hates his brother is in darkness; he walks in darkness and does not know where he is going because the darkness has blinded his eyes.*
Additional uses of METAPHORS. But take heed of the condemnation of "hatred".

2: 18 *Children, it is the last hour; and just as you heard that the antichrist was coming, so now many antichrists have appeared. Thus we know this is the last hour.*
OOPS! The last hour has NOT come; 2: 18 is not a correct observation! It's only poor perception ... or is it poor reception? Chuckle!

2: 20 *But you have the anointing that comes from the holy one, and you all have knowledge.*
Who is the holy one? God the Father! Check the implied Gnosticism in the last phrase.

3: 12 *unlike Cain who belonged to the evil one and slaughtered his brother. Why did he slaughter him? Because his own works were evil, and those of his brother righteous.*
Quoting the Cosmic Myth of creation and the literalism's belief in that Myth.

3: 17-18 *If someone who has worldly means sees a brother in need and refuses him compassion, how can the love of God remain in him? Children, let us love not in word or speech but in deed and truth.*
This is the heart of the Jesus Movement, good works!

4: 2 *This is how you can know the Spirit of God: every spirit that acknowledges Jesus Christ come in the flesh belongs to God,*
This definitely demands the belief in Yeshua's humanity.

4: 3 *and every spirit that does not acknowledge Jesus does not belong to God. This is the spirit of the antichrist that, as you heard, is to come, but in fact is already in the world.*
There is no special Antichrist. The evil that humans choose is the Antichrist! And evil occurs in one's every-day bad choices, ever since Humans started to walk this Earth—almost 7 million years ago .

4: 7 Beloved, *let us love one another, because love is of God; everyone who loves is begotten by God and knows God.*
The true message of Yeshua, the Christos!

4: 20 *If anyone says, "I love God," but hates his brother, he is a liar; for whoever does not love a brother whom he has seen cannot love God whom he has not seen.*
Again, the true message of the Jesus Movement.

5: 14 *And we have this confidence in him, that if we ask anything according to his will, he hears us.*
This is a very difficult thing to comprehend. If we humans have free will, then, God is unable to stop our choices. What is mis-understood here is that God wishes (Her Will) that everyone gain eternal life. It is not God's will to force or require anyone to go against his or her own willful choice. God is NOT a puppet master controlling the life of every human!

5: 20 *We also know that the Son of God has come and has given us discernment to know <u>the one who is true</u>. And we are in <u>the one who is true</u>, in his Son Jesus Christ. <u>He is the true God</u> and eternal life.*
This is somewhat perplexing. Is this saying that Yeshua is God the Father? A statement like this causes much confusion about the nature of Yeshua. As you read this verse, consider that each underlined refers to God the Father!

25. Gospel of John (90-100)

The Fourth Gospel is such a complex writing that we are at a loss, at this time, to add more than the Introduction found in the New American Bible (NAB). It is imperative that you read that Introduction. (See Appendix L for the Internet source.) We will explain this Fourth Gospel in Chapter Six and demonstrate its relevance even though it is predominantly a mythologized and an allegorical version of the Life and Times of Yeshua!

Our major conclusion that the words of Yeshua are NOT reliably remembered is a shocking statement to those who worship every printed word in the Bible as true, accurate history and Divinely dictated. The bottom line here is that this mythologized (allegorical and metaphorical) Gospel is the most spiritually centered book, more so than any of the other 26 books in the Christian Testament.

Don't fret! We are postponing the analysis of this Gospel until the Sixth Chapter when we will set out our plan for re-discovering the nature of the "Jesus Movement" and re-forming the Way (ancient and modern) to a more authentic human Spirituality.

26. 2 John (90-100):

This and the third letter are very short. Their authors were John's disciples; read the Introduction in the NAB. Two important verses appear in this letter.

1: 7 *Many deceivers have gone out into the world, those who do not acknowledge Jesus Christ as coming in the flesh; such is the deceitful one and the antichrist.*

This and other verses are the source material of Chalcedon 451 AD, the humanity of Yeshua, including his human ignorance. This is also clearly the writing of the Johannine School that confirms the position that the 1st 18 verses of the Fourth Gospel are a later addition and NOT from the Johannine School.

1: 9 *Anyone who is so "progressive" as not to remain in the teaching of the Christ does not have God; whoever remains in the teaching has the Father and the Son.* Ok, so what are the real teachings when all the early Christians were literalists? Note the lack of the Holy Spirit! Do John's disciples not hold to a Trinitarian theology?

27. 3 John (90-100):

According to the "Introduction" in the NAB: "The problems of the Presbyter in this short letter provide us with valuable evidence of the flexible and personal nature of authority in the early church." This translates to the autonomy resident in the local Bishop! Then, another quote from the NAB says, "...he {*the Bishop*} perhaps exemplifies the cautious and sectarian nature of early Christianity; for its own protection the local community mistrusted missionaries as false teachers." This is exactly what caused the development of the wide variety of theological postures throughout the Christian communities. Probably the underlying contributor was the lack of good mail service thrown in with a generous portion of intellectual pre-critical naiveté, also known as, Literalism or Fundamentalism. And that brings us to the actual conditions in this 21st century; we experience a gradual (then again, it may not be so gradual!) change in technology, medicine, special effects in the movie industry, better this and better that, including our planetary news coverage. Dear Reader, none of that existed in the World until the last 100 years. And in the 1st century there was mass ignorance, with very little communication. The World then knew only that the Earth was flat and that the gods were puppeteers controlling each and every social, natural and economic occurrence. And demons were attacking them at every corner causing pain, sickness and poverty as punishment for their transgressions. Small wonder why myth was so prevalent in all their writings.

1: 3-4 *I rejoiced greatly when some of the brothers came and testified to how truly you walk in the truth. Nothing gives me greater joy than to hear that my children are walking in the truth.*
Notice how vague these statements are. Whose "truth" is this author talking about and what is that "truth"?

1: 11 *Beloved, do not imitate evil but imitate good. Whoever does what is good is of God; whoever does what is evil has never seen God.*
The problem with this is the implication that "to have seen Yeshua" is to have seen God. However, in this and the first letter the author implies that good-doers have seen God when there are several statements that no one can see God the Father! So, who is correct? Or is all this metaphor again?

The Summary of Chapter Four

WOW! Was Chapter Four a shot in the arm or what! Do you realize what you've experienced? Our thesis is that a chronological reading of the Christian Testament in the order of Authorship will draw a new portrait of Christianity. Look at the topics that were covered:

(a) A more realistic historical development of Christianity,
(b) The real teachings of the Apostles in the Early Church,
(c) A new and distinctly different position concerning the Christological Moments,
(d) The influence of the plethora of apocryphal writings that brought confusion to Christian communities,
(e) The effect of Paul's confusing use of the word, spirit,
(f) The theological conflicts throughout Christendom,
(g) The mythologizing that crept into the Gospel "Good News" tales,
(h) The presence of a profound literalism in the perceptions of the authors of the Christian Testament (not to mention the Legends and Myth in the Hebrew Testament) and, finally,
(i) The struggles that Christianity had with Yeshua's humanity and his Divinity along with the on-again-off-again Holy Spirit as a separate being and a third member of the Godhead. Chapter Five and Appendix AD will put an entirely new slant on the use of "Spirit of Holiness".

Well, that's a lot of material to digest. Yet the best we can tell you is that we're casting just one more vote for the legends, myth and confusion in the 1st century! Our next step is to attempt to demonstrate that the Bible, as a whole, is neither the literal nor errorless Word of God but just a collection of Godly messages that you need take seriously (Re: Marcus Borg). The catch is that you must make a personal choice (Deut 30: 19) to commit or not commit to a relationship with this intimate friendly and merciful God and do it outside of Institutional doctrine, dogma, ritual and legalisms. This is not to say that you cannot belong to an accepting and affectionate community. If you are seeking God, you will find Her-Him ... or is it that God has always been there for you, just waiting for you to crack open the door that isolates you so that God can come in to your heart (an acceptable metaphor, but spirit would be a better choice).

The real proof of your faith is the acceptance and affection you extend to your neighbor and enemies in the good works you do because you have discovered that it is truly "God's WAY".

. Now for the real heart-stopper! Oxygen ... anyone? Let's proceed to Chapter Five and the Millions of Errors in the Bible. Millions? Some may call that an overstatement! Yes it is, but it does capture your attention.

Now, let's start counting ...

THE RECONSTRUCTION

(OK, so the framework has aged! But now, just how decayed is it?)

In the film, OH God, staring George Burns and John Denver, the question, "Why is there Evil?" is thrust at God. God replies, "You wouldn't know what good is unless there was evil!" Thus, we place this before you; you will only understand what is true when someone identifies what is false. It is our intent to be objective in this chapter by pointing to what is blatantly false. That, dear Reader, is not a negative activity.

"How many times do you have to experience something counter to your beliefs or expectations before you are willing to alter your position"

R.D. Moon, PhD, 2003

"Something happens when a person takes an immutable position on a question. Then, there is little room for adjustment when new data come to the fore. The very classic example is the 16th century discovery of the shape of the planet Earth and the size of the Universe. That problem is exactly what Literalists face in this 21st century when biblical scholars discovered the many errors, mistakes and inconsistencies in the Hebrew Testament's legends and myths and in the Christian Testament's written accounts of the life and times of Yeshua."

R.D. Moon, PhD, 2003

CHAPTER FIVE

GOOD HEAVENS!

THERE'RE SOME SERIOUS CONFUSIONS IN THE BIBLE!

Part One: A Zen Parable

Once upon a time in a border village somewhere in the Far East along this country's western edge there was a community of merchants plying their skills and deceits to obtain the riches of those who traveled through this important intersection leading to the principal East-West and North-South trade routes. Needless to mention, the streets were bustling with people. The cacophony of noise hung heavy in the air. The many resident shopkeepers were bartering with the travelers to determine who would profit the most. Frequently, several heated sessions would burst out from one of the ancient narrow side streets while one person or the other was seeking financial redress. It was not uncommon that the noise would be cut to whispers at a gunshot echoing out of a recessed shop. There was no official constabulary to investigate the origin of the shooting or who, if any, were the victims. Yes, this was the state of affairs in this village -- without rule, without conscience, without trust.

One day a group of ten Buddhist monks journeying westward stopped to rest in the center of the village. They were astonished at the noise, the angered bartering and the lack of civility there. It occurred to the Master that this bustling community might benefit from their presence and decided to stay here as his personal calling.

It took several years for the residents to accept and re-learn the way of the Buddha. All passing through were shocked at the transformation that had taken place because of the efforts of the monks. Even the residents themselves were pleased with the changes. People experienced trust; shopkeepers developed a social conscience; peace ruled the whole village.

The principals of the village decided to formally accept the monks and planned to erect a Temple for them in which all residents and travelers could find quiet meditation. There was no room in the center so the principals chose an acre two miles out of the village to construct their Temple. When the edifice was completed there was much celebration for what they had built and for the changes that had taken place in the affairs of the village.

Some years passed and the Master noticed that with time, the attendance of villagers and travelers diminished to the level of a handful of loyal members. One morning just as dawn was cutting the darkness of night, the Master left the Temple and visited the village center. He found what he suspected. The village residents had returned to their previous habits and the residents were behaving exactly as the monks found them so many years ago.

The Master returned to the Temple late that evening. Moments later at the smell of smoke the nine other monks came running out of their residence. There they saw the Master holding a burning torch in his hand watching the Temple in such flames that no one could save it from destruction.

One brave monk approached the Master and queried, "Master, why have you burnt down the Temple?"

The Master turned and in a soft voice replied, "When we first came to this village we found the people without a Buddha heart. We taught them the peace and they accepted Buddha's heart into their lives. Then, out of gratitude they constructed this Temple. They removed their Buddha hearts and placed them in the Temple. Tonight I destroyed this Temple in the hope that we can put Buddha's heart back into the lives of the people."

Part Two: The Plan

God is not in the hearts of people in this generation. God has been surgically removed by years of Institutionalism's control over doctrines, dogmas and rituals. Do you think that we could discover the origin of Institutionalism and, perhaps, adjust our paradigms and practices?

We believe that the first step is to take an intellectually and emotionally honest re-examination of those Sacred Scriptures and, maybe, just maybe, we'll be able to re-construct a mature interpretation appropriate for the message to be more meaningful and applicable to our times. We don't mean to wipe out the traditional core of spirituality but to rebuild a model that fits in with the basic teachings of those whom we claim to follow. It all starts with recognizing that all Scriptures were actually written by men, fallible and imperfect. We'll show you the evidence for that observation. It's a list of errors and mistakes that only we humans could make; God is far too intelligent to have made those mistakes, and, was mistaken to that extent! We think that the primitive Scriptural authors totally missed (or should we say, mythed?) the factual story in order to convey their personal faith stories. Isn't that what "perception" is all about?

Mind you, in the case of each cultural Sacred Scripture the authors did their job out of innocence and sincerity (no maliciousness, no foul!). Our concern here is with those Sacred Scriptures that claim to be divinely inspired, i.e., accurate and without errors in history, science and even the conversations. In a previous Chapter we listed those Scriptures: the Bhagavad-Gita, the Hebrew Testament, the Christian Testament and the Qur'an. Of those four the principal one is the Christian Testament. Our rationale is simple; it is the only one that depicts an authentic portrait of the REAL Divinity. Its actual truth lies in the preachings of the "Jesus Movement" which will be delineated in Chapters Six and re-analyzed, filled out in Chapter Seven. Since similar ideas and teachings in the Bhagavad-Gita precede simplistically those in the Bible and the Qur'an takes its cue from the prophets of the Hebrew Testament, it is most natural to make the rest of this Chapter an in-depth examination of the accuracy and precision of the Bible's claim that God doesn't lie. To the Literalist, the Bible is God's infallible Word. The meaning of the Gita and the Qur'an will then become apparent.

God did a mighty work in and through his devoted prophets: Moses, the major and minor H.T. prophets and, especially, Yeshua. However, God only certified one of them! Only Yeshua was authenticated by means of a bodily Resurrection. The Resurrection was the only thing that could motivate a completely dejected group of disciples to return to Jerusalem to preach the "Jesus Movement" to their deaths! Their experience of the Risen Yeshua was such an awesome thing that it not only altered their lives but also changed human history as well. Apostles and disciples simply responded to the teachings of the historical Yeshua, the human person. It appears that the first decade following the empty tomb was indeed a growing, living and vibrant "Jesus Movement" (the core or central teachings of Yeshua). Then came the Apostolic Period, 40 AD to about 65 AD that turned the Christian Movement afoul. Paul's drive to organize, institutionalize and legalize those teachings through his organizational expertise became the turning point that eternally defined the role of Christian authority in the community and what those communities must hold as doctrinally authentic. Today we recognize that history has proven that Institutionalism has failed and has failed miserably!

OK, so God loves us anyway! Our focal objective now is to examine the Bible to determine exactly what leads us to the conclusion that the Bible fails the "Divine Inspiration" test. It is a simple test! If there are significant inaccuracies or contradictions in theology, history and science, then, with a bit of common sense, the specific Sacred Scripture will have to be labeled, "Made by Humans" (or, "Made in Israel" in the case of the Bible) whether it originates from Mecca, China, India or wherever! All Sacred Scriptures are composed by human authors with natural stories assembled from legends and myths! However, we shall not make the classic mistake of discharging the baby along with the bath water. Let's hope that our saving grace is going to be the re-discovery of the authentic "Jesus Movement" from our Bible and the significant meaning in other Sacred Scriptures. And this we promise to do!

Now, let's turn our attention to the Mythed List.

Part Three: The Major Myths

Scholars and others (that's me, folks) have identified several major myths in the Bible, so let's look there first:

A The Genesis Creation CH 1 & 2 [re-edited from the Enuma Elish],
B The Tutty Fruit story [Israel's explanation for the occurrence of evil and the ever popular "put-down of women],
C. The Flood Story [the Hebrew interpretation of the Epic of Gilgamesh]
D. The Birth of Moses, a real Arab Prince,
E. The Infancy Narratives of Matthew and Luke [written to compete with the alleged divinity of the Caesars],
F. The Sunday Resurrection Stories [the imperfect oral tradition at work],
G. The Trinitarian Conspiracy [a clear case of Guilty as charged!],
H. The Metaphors of that muscle we call the Blood-Pump and, lastly,
I. The Puppeteer God of Good for good and Evil for evil.

A. The Genesis Creation Story - CH 1 & 2

We have written profusely about the Creation Myths vs. Geology's Fossil Record; there are no additional words that can be added to force you to accept the scientific data which points to a Universe that's about 14-16 billion years old and a Solar System about

4.5 billion years old i.e., give or take 20%.. Well, you could go back to University and major in Geology or Nuclear Physics! A mind that holds to a 9000 years old Universe is indeed obdurate and paralyzed by its own pre-critical naiveté along with a pinch of Cognitive Dissonance. If God really dictated the biblical contents, how do you explain Job 38? Psalm 104 (Appendix T)? If God really dictated the biblical cosmology, how come the Earth is not flat as described in those Bible references, specifically, Job 38? If God really dictated the biblical order of Creation, how come the order is different in the first two chapters of Genesis?

The answer to all those questions is that those stories contain simple poetic messages, the only kind that a primitive culture could construct and understand. When a "pre-critical naiveté" mind is taught that this Bible is absolutely true, one misses the significant and meaningful message from the author(s):

1. God created it all;
2. Creation was an orderly evolutionary process over an extremely long period of time;
3. God said that it was all Good;
4. God turned over the responsibility to us humans about 7 million years ago to create new life and take care of this planet.

Aren't those simple enough truths? And, please, get off the creationism bandwagon and accept that God is the Supreme Scientist who ordered evolution. We ask you, like God asks Job in chapter 38, were you there? Science is not the culprit, ignorance is! But let's not end this thought right here. Ignorance is not an evil thing, unless, of course, it nourishes the seeds of hatred. Then, hatred is the evil! On the other side of that coin, education is the bleach that removes the stains of ignorance. And, we humans can obtain as much of that commodity (education) as we choose. Choosing to educate ourselves is our saving grace, so to speak, isn't it?

B. The Tutty Fruit Tale

There are two parts to this great Adam and Eve story. The first relates to our very recent discoveries concerning the transition from animal to human some seven million years ago. The human-like bones found in Africa give credence to several mutations pointing to creatures with significant differences to suggest multiple geneses. This may explain the Neanderthal presence in Europe as a migration of one species out of Africa and then, thousands of years later, the migration of a second species and the appearance of Cro-Magnons. These latter seem to have overwhelmed the Neanderthals who then disappeared off the planet. However, we suspect that the Neanderthal DNA survived by having been absorbed into the gene pool! Absorbed? Now that's a kind and polite way of saying it!

The second part of the Adam and Eve Genesis story may very well be a cosmic myth imagined by a primitive culture as its simplistic understanding of the creation of humankind. Two facts point to this observation: the two different stories and the unusual sequence of creation that differentiates Gen Ch 1 from Ch 2 and the outlandish and unbelievable descriptions in Job 38. Because of these we firmly believe the Genesis tale to be totally mythical. However, because of its mythologizing it is full of meaning. Let's re-examine them in search for some meaning!

Adam and Eve didn't have to sneak a bite of tutty fruity to possess the knowledge of good and evil. God had imbued free will into each and every Human; free choice in and by itself leads one to understand building friendships (the Good) vs. destroying relationships (the Evil). The great 2nd century Christian Author, Origen of Alexandria (185 to 254 AD) considered one of the greatest of all Christian theologians, wrote that the tutty fruity tale was a cosmic myth designed to explain the transition from innocence to social awareness and personal responsibility which really are the transitional stages from "pre-critical naiveté" to critical adulthood. The myth is a psychological allegory of the stages of cognitive development. Those authors of Genesis were not PhD Psychologists; they were simple observant men and women who experienced the meaning of life. Have you forgotten your own youthful experiences in discovering forbidden adult secrets like smoking, the taste of alcohol and the power of money in your pockets? Do you have any recollections of other adult experiences you might be too embarrassed to acknowledge to your own children or speak openly about? If you haven't figured it out yet, all children go through those very same experimental growth experiences. We each in the middle of our youth take a wee bite of the tutty fruity juice and become aware of good and evil! The beauty of this particular myth is that it triggers the memories we have of our own private life experiences, doesn't it? So, believe the meaning but acknowledge the myth.

C. The Flood Frolic

There is scientific evidence that there was a flood story floating around (nice pun!) in the oral tradition. Our first indication was the discovery of the Epic of Gilgamesh slightly before 1872 AD. Its estimated time of writing is somewhere between 2750 and 2000 BC. Very recently a theory was presented that the flood could have affected the area of the Black Sea and it occurred around the end of the Ice Age some 12,000 years ago. Now, we certainly haven't found any conclusive evidence of Noah's boat nor do we think that the whole world was under water. A simple calculation of the amount of water that would have to be available quickly disproves the submergence of the entire planet up to its highest peak (Ugh, 35,000 feet!). Therein lies the mythology. Yes, the event happened but not to the details written in the Hebrew Testament. That myth was to explain God's role in cleaning out the population of evil people and leaving just Noah and his family to inhabit the Earth. (Are we all Jewish?) It appears to be just a second creation tale allowing the authors to focus on the Israelites as God's chosen people. It is not a sin to aggrandize one's national heroes to further the importance and centrality of Israel. In a way, we suspect, that the authors of the Genesis stories felt necessary to write an adequate, believable transition starting from the beginning of time to illustrate God's plan for creation. It was a way to get to the start of Israel's history as slaves in Egypt on the doorstep of the Exodus. The Chosen People believed they were an integral part of God's plan to transmit the message of salvation to the Human race, a salvation necessary because of Adam and Eve's disobedience and loss of the idyllic life of happiness and innocence in the Garden of Eden. The fly in the ointment was that Israel thought more of being the Chosen People rather than sharing the message: exclusiveness rather than inclusiveness!

D. The Birth of Sargon and Moses

The birth story of Moses was considered for many centuries to be accurately transmitted via the Oral Tradition. However, in the following quote from the Internet article by Gerald A. Larue (See Appendix L, Item 9) you will learn otherwise:

"The birth story of Moses (Exo2:1-10), probably recorded well past the tenth century B.C., reflects the pattern found in the birth account of King Sargon of Agade who lived near the end of the third millennium B.C. The Sargon account reads:

'Sargon, the mighty king of Agade, am I. My mother was a changeling, my father I knew not. The brothers of my father loved the hills. My city is Azupiranu which is situated on the banks of the Euphrates.. My changeling mother conceived me in secret she bore me She set me in a basket of rushes, with bitumen She sealed my lid. She cast me into the river which rose not over me. The river bore me up and carried me to Akki, the drawer of water. Akki, the drawer of water, lifted me out as he dipped his ewer. Akki, the drawer of water, took me as his son and reared me. Akki, the drawer of water, appointed me as his gardener. While I was a gardener, Ishtar granted me her love, And for four and . . . years I exercised kingship.'

"The similarity of the Moses and Sargon accounts is obvious. Actually both stories reflect literary patterns often associated with heroes. The life of the hero is threatened when he is still a child; he escapes; he is unrecognized until he achieves his full status as a messiah or savior of the people. Very often his life pattern reflects the way in which a people consider their early history, for they look back upon their humble and troublous beginnings and marvel at what they have become. The life of the hero embodies the struggle of a nation or a group to achieve greatness. Having detected the hero motif in the Moses literature, one must consider the question of how much of the Moses cycle may be labeled "legend," and how much "history."

The Larue Reference: "The Moses story reflects accurate details concerning adoption procedures as known from Mesopotamian documents, cf. B. S. Childs, "The Birth of Moses," *Journal of Biblical Literature,* LXXIV (1965), 109-122."

It is our personal suspicion that the Israelite author, as well as transmitters of the Oral Tradition, did not want an Egyptian Arab to be their Messenger and Leader of the Chosen People! Therefore, he copied Sargon's infancy legend to soften history. It is most probable that Israel's greatest hero was an Egyptian Arab Prince after all! One more note: Moses' father-in-law is named Reuel in Ex 2: 18-21 and Jethro in Ex 3: 1 and Ex 18: 1-6. Mighty peculiar, ain't it? Imagine, two father-in-laws and one spouse!!

E. The Infancy Narratives of Matthew and Luke

If you are interested and brave enough, you can get a library copy of "The Birth of the Messiah," by Raymond E. Brown, SS. Read its 570 pages and really discover a wealth of information about the mythic contents of the Matthean and Lukan Infancy Narratives. Now, the book is not an easy read but don't you just feel like rising to the challenge? OK, so you want a little preview! Here's his resume followed by a few examples of inconsistencies, contradictions and outright errors in the two Infancy Narratives as reported in Father Brown's book.

Raymond E. Brown, SS, whose soul now rests peacefully, was the Chairman of the Pontifical Biblical Commission. He was the world's premier scholar of the Fourth Gospel and the three letters of John. He authored over a dozen books trying to bring the Catholic people and Hierarchs into the 20th century. Having been a student and disciple of this great and humble man, I can vouch for his character and knowledge. Don't think that this does justice to this holy man; there's much more too voluminous to repeat here! So, that's a peek at the man, now let's check out his book!

The inconsistencies between the Matthean and Lukan Gospels portraits, and the errors that each made, are many more than what we'll illustrate in this short list. Examine the following very carefully:

1. The genealogies differ in that Matthew has 28 generations from David to Yeshua while Luke has 40 generations. That is an IMPOSSIBLE gap! We are genuinely convinced that God could not have made that mistake! In Matt 1: 16 the father of Joseph is Jacob; in Luke 3: 23 it's Heli. Since every Israelite has only one name, and an identifier of his profession or town, it doesn't take an Einstein to recognize that contradiction! See Appendix J for the Genealogic list.

2. The next biggie is the actual list of names. So, look at the second page of Appendix J and compare the actual names. It's an incomprehensible mess! If you take the time to analyze the two columns and then try to align the names ... you get a mess of inconsistencies. Of course most Christians never do that. When a person believes it's all literally accurate, then why would that person challenge it? Both evangelists got their names from different sources (mostly from 1 Chron) and they each wrote what they thought was correct. Their innocence does not make the list accurate! But most importantly, how come God got it so messed up?

3. Matthew has Mary and Joseph living in Bethlehem; Luke has them in Nazareth. Check Matt 2: 22 and examine the word "there" and decide where "there" really is. Ah Ha, Matthew implies that it's Bethlehem where they lived before the birth! Herod was the ruler of Bethlehem but not the ruler of Nazareth! However, Dr. Luke clearly places them in Nazareth before the birth. OK, tell me that God dictated that!

4. According to the recorded history of that decade, the census edict to enroll the locals in their hometown was made in 10 BC. There was no Yeshua at that time! Yeshua was born between 6 and 4 BC. Come on folks, 5 years to get to your hometown? They both goofed; there was no census that brought the parents to Bethlehem. Yeshua was most likely born and raised in Nazareth! The authors were trying to force the birth of Yeshua to Bethlehem because the Messiah was prophesized to be of Davidic genealogy. David was born in Bethlehem.

5. The myth of Divine impregnation is really a counter to the Augustus Caesar's divine conception and also a take off of Gen 6: 1-4 which reads:

> *1 When men began to multiply on earth and daughters were born to them, 2 the sons of heaven saw how beautiful the daughters of man were, and so they took for their wives as many of them as*

> *they chose. 3 Then the LORD said: "My spirit shall not remain in man forever, since he is but flesh. His days shall comprise one hundred and twenty years." 4 At that time the Nephilim appeared on earth (as well as later), after the sons of heaven had intercourse with the daughters of man, who bore them sons. They were the heroes of old, the men of renown.*

The other reason for a Divine impregnation is to assign to Yeshua the same sort of Divinity as was written about Caesar Augustus that gave authenticity to his divinity as Emperor of Rome.

6. The Angelic messenger speaks to Joseph in Matthew (male centered society) but speaks to Mary in Luke (female equality society). Did husbands and wives talk to each other in those days? If that happened to this married couple, there would be a lot of discussions! In addition, it's nice that Luke writes that Mary got the picture, shared it with Elizabeth and kept it in her heart, while Mark (3: 21 ff) writes that Mary and Yeshua's brothers and sisters had no idea what Yeshua was doing when he began his preaching ministry. Did Mrs. Mary Christ forget such an angelic visit? All her words with Lizzie? And, the Magnificat, too? The Infancy Narratives are great drama, but quite unsubstantiated history, especially since the two authors disagree on the details! Where is inspiration for this mythic tale?

7. In Matt (1: 23) there are two problems: Isaiah 7: 14 is quoted but the word "virgin" is an incorrect translation; it should be "young woman" as is found in the NRSV. This may seem a bit picayune but the only reason we see "virgin" is because a certain Institution wants Mary to be a perpetual virgin! See Isa 62: 5 because the Hebrew word is *Bethulah*, which is commonly translated as virgin. Go figure! Not in the lifetime of any married couple! The second is that if the child is to be named "Emmanuel", how come he's called Yeshua? NOTEBENE: the Hebrew words, *almah* in Isa 7: 14 vs. *bethulah* in Isa 62: 5 are different!

8. In Matthew the family escapes to Egypt to avoid the massacre ordered by Herod. The real stumbling block is that Josephus, the Jewish historian, who is most assuredly not one of Herod's friendly biographers, makes no mention of any massacre. How's that for a "condition contrary to fact"? OH, wait one minute; Luke also makes no mention of the Egyptian side trip nor any massacre! Didn't Dr. Luke write something about the true facts of Yeshua's birth? How come God didn't "inspire" these guys with the correct story?

9. Poor Matt (2: 23) he calls Yeshua a Nazorean because he lived in Nazareth. Sorry, old chum, Nazorean doesn't mean you came from Nazareth; it means you have dedicated yourself to become holy unto God, a personal vow. On the other hand, maybe Matthew was implying the "Vow" part of Yeshua's holiness! Which is it? OH, please hang on; it gets better!

10. Matthew actually copies the Moses story and edits it to be a Jesus story because he believes that Yeshua is the new Moses. As opposed to that thesis, Luke re-tells a Greek Myth of gods impregnating a human female so that the son can be called a god. Try to understand, Luke is just employing a commonly accepted literary style. Not all of us in this century buy it. But those in the early

centuries ate it up as though it were God's very dictation; and, sadly, today many still do believe it is true.

11. Again, Matthew re-writes the Egyptian Exodus story of Moses and places Yeshua in Egypt to return to Judea just like in the Exodus story. The similarity is very dramatic but significantly legendary.

12. Then there is the problem of Luke's story of John the Baptist as a relative of Yeshua in Luke 1: 36 *And behold, Elizabeth, your relative, has also conceived a son in her old age, and this is the sixth month for her who was called barren.* Well, it's different in John 1: 30-34 *He is the one of whom I said, 'A man is coming after me who ranks ahead of me because he existed before me.' 31 I did not know him, but the reason why I came baptizing with water was that he might be made known to Israel." 32 John testified further, saying, "I saw the Spirit come down like a dove from the sky and remain upon him. 33 I did not know him, but the one who sent me to baptize with water told me, 'On whomever you see the Spirit come down and remain, he is the one who will baptize with the holy Spirit.' 34 Now I have seen and testified that he is the Son of God." !*
    The authors write in the Fourth Gospel that John didn't know Yeshua. Weren't they cousins in Luke, living in the same town? One more inconsistency!

13. Luke's Magnificat of Mary in 1: 46-55 is nothing more than a re-write of Hannah's Canticle in 1 Samuel 2:1-10 in much the same way the flood legend is a re-write of the "Epic of Gilgamesh, Chapter 11". Look it up yourself on the Internet.

F. The Sunday Resurrection Stories

The Resurrection stories by comparison have fewer inconsistencies but they're equally significant:

1. Those crucified along side of Yeshua:
    a. Mark & Matt: they both abused Yeshua
    b. Luke: The Good Thief asked forgiveness.

2. The people arriving at the empty tomb:
    a. Mark's Gospel:
       Mary Magdalene, Mary mother of James the Apostle and Salome
    b. Matthew's Gospel:
       Mary Magdalene and the other Mary
    c. Luke's Gospel:
       Mary Magdalene, Joanna, and Mary the mother of James
    d. Fourth Gospel:
       Only Mary of Magdala followed by Apostles (after she tells them).

3. The messengers at the tomb:
    a. Mark's Gospel: A young man in white
    b. Matthew's Gospel: The women saw an angel of the Lord descended
    c. Luke's Gospel: two men in dazzling garments

d. Fourth Gospel: two angels in white sitting there with the unrecognizable Yeshua.

OK Folks, multiple guess! Who is correct? Answer, none are!

4. What Yeshua said to the Apostles:

   a. Mark's Gospel reads:
   16: 15-18 *He said to them, "Go into the whole world and proclaim the gospel to every creature. Whoever believes and is baptized will be saved; whoever does not believe will be condemned. These signs will accompany those who believe: in my name they will drive out demons, they will speak new languages. They will pick up serpents (with their hands), and if they drink any deadly thing, it will not harm them. They will lay hands on the sick, and they will recover."*
   Did you catch the "in my name they will drive out demons"? Even the risen Yeshua still believes in demons! Is that or isn't it a clue to who wrote the story?

   b. Matthew's Gospel reads:
   28: 18-20 *Then Jesus approached and said to them, "All power in heaven and on earth has been given to me. Go, therefore, and make disciples of all nations, baptizing them in the name of the Father, and of the Son, and of the holy Spirit, teaching them to observe all that I have commanded you. And behold, I am with you always, until the end of the age."*

   c. Luke's Gospel reads:
   24: 25-27 *And he said to them, "Oh, how foolish you are! How slow of heart to believe all that the prophets spoke! Was it not necessary that the Messiah should suffer these things and enter into his glory?" Then beginning with Moses and all the prophets, he interpreted to them what referred to him in all the scriptures.*

   28: 18-20 *Then Jesus approached and said to them, "All power in heaven and on earth has been given to me. Go, therefore, and make disciples of all nations, baptizing them in the name of the Father, and of the Son, and of the holy Spirit, teaching them to observe all that I have commanded you. And behold, I am with you always, until the end of the age."*

   d. Fourth Gospel reads:
   20: 15-17 *Jesus said to her, "Woman, why are you weeping? Whom are you looking for?" She thought it was the gardener and said to him, "Sir, if you carried him away, tell me where you laid him, and I will take him." Jesus said to her, Mary!" She turned and said to him in Hebrew Rabbouni," which means Teacher. Jesus said to her, "Stop holding on to me, for I have not yet ascended to the Father. But go to my brothers and tell them, 'I am going to my Father and your Father, to my God and your God.'"*
   That sounds very much like monotheism to us!

20-: 21-23 *(Jesus) said to them again, "Peace be with you. As the Father has sent me, so I send you." And when he had said this, he breathed on them and said to them, "Receive the holy Spirit. Whose sins you forgive are forgiven them, and whose sins you retain are retained."* That sounds like Matt 16!

20: 27-29 *Then he said to Thomas, "Put your finger here and see my hands, and bring your hand and put it into my side, and do not be unbelieving, but believe." Thomas answered and said to him, "My Lord and my God!" Jesus said to him, "Have you come to believe because you have seen me Blessed are those who have not seen and have believed."*

As you have just read, there appear to be several inconsistencies. The questions that we would like to put to you are:

1. Why two stories about the two bad guys crucified along side of Yeshua?

2. How many women did go to the tomb on Sunday? Why so many different ones? And, who is this mysterious Mary of Magdala?

3. Notice that there were either one or two men and one or two angels!

4. Why so many directions from Yeshua to the Apostles?

The answer to all those apparent inconsistencies is very simple. Each author actually didn't have Yeshua's conversation on tape and, therefore, wrote what he had heard in a version of the oral tradition that managed to get to his ears. It simply cannot be ascribed to a Divine dictation. If it were, then even God didn't remember very well what took place. As one noted Catholic scholar wrote in The Jerome Biblical Commentary, "Inspiration is no guarantee that the writer will produce accurate history!" When the recollections about the nature of Yeshua and what he said and did are mythologized as much as the Christian Testament was, then "poetic license" governed the author's intentions to explain the meaning of his own and his community's faith experiences. There is little literal accuracy to this great Bible; its universal worth lies within the depth of its mythic structure. The Bible is itself a large parable, often larger than large, of relationship with and fidelity to the God of Love. From a purely literary point of view, the Bible is one large saga of a nation (or the human race) as it struggles seeking spirituality—a deep intimate relationship with the Loving Creator.

G. The Trinitarian Conspiracy

G-1: The Problem of Perception

Before we start a lengthy discussion on this very sensitive subject, we would like to address, once more, the mindset of the people of the 9th century BC to the 5th century AD. In the first chapter of this book we wrote of the human problem of perception that we suggested was directly related to three factors; (1) enculturation, (2) cognitive development and (3) psychological profile. We are firmly convinced that these three played the primary role in understanding and interpreting the biblical languages, both in definition and implication of specific Hebrew and Greek terms used by a primitive culture.

And to make matters worse, the problem continued up to about the time of the discovery of the Rosetta Stone, 1799 AD.

The perceptions of these ancient people were ones that had little understanding of nature, of science, of technology and of the universe. Their language was likewise a primitive one compared to our 21st century. The root problems of perception lie in the following:

1. Enculturation is a function of one's DNA, influences from family and friends, education, peer pressure, religious awareness, local mores and so many other conditionings too numerous to list (revisit Chapter One).

2. Cognitive development occurs in three stages: (a) pre-critical naiveté (when one believes everything that authority dictates as though it were all absolute); (b) critical (when one starts to recognize that some authoritative requirements and stories are fables); (c) post-critical (when one takes control and responsibility for one's choices and actions after much study of the problems of life and relationships with society). The entire population, save but for a few prophets and philosophers, were stuck at the pre-critical naiveté stage!

3. The last factor, psychological profile deals with how one behaves in personal and social circumstances. Most were in Profile 2, eye for an eye, Reciprocity. And, yes, their gods were gods of Reciprocity as well! You may want to take a quick peek back at Chapter One and review the seven profiles again.

It may be difficult to empathize with those ancients who were unable to cope with reality, as we know it in our modern world. The mass of humanity was struggling with the hardships of staying alive, the cruelties of their conquers, sickness and taxation by the wealthy and so much more. Legends and myths ruled the oral tradition that was their only source of information about the happenings outside their local community or in the world. Remember one little tidbit, there was no Department of Education in any part of that world! The majority of people could not read or write; there was no written communications to the masses except a Regal letter now and then that was read or posted at the public watering hole. Under all these conditions, try to imagine what your perceptions of life would be.

Perception is the primary source of language and its vocabulary. In a primitive culture definitions are vague and, more often than not, incorrect, difficult to translate into a sophisticated language. The case in point is Hebrew into Greek. Biblical Hebrew is a conditioned language of consonants; the Massoretes introduced vowel-pointing starting in the 6th century AD.

You may wish to read a more definitive work [Old Testament Life and Literature, Gerald A. Larue, Ch 32] on the Internet at the following URL:
http://www.infidels.org/library/modern/gerald_larue/otll/index.shtml

The bottom line is that when translating from an older language, scholars have had to try to consider the perceptions of the authors, their enculturation, cognitive development and psychological profile as well as their theological convictions.

G- 2: The Literary Style and Vocabulary of the Bible

First, there are two camps here: the Literal Believers and the Modern Believers. The first group claims that God inspired (actually dictated) the entire Bible to the different authors and God is the guarantor of their complete historical and scientific accuracy even down to every reported conversation. The second group professes to mostly human authorship as they documented their personal experiences and faith. They wrote in the literary style of their day--legends and myths re-interpreted, allegories, parables, similes, irony—basically, mythologically as defined in Appendix M. You don't have to guess which group is our choice. The remainder of this Chapter will, hopefully, convince you of the modern position.

In our attempt to understand the vocabulary of these two Testaments, we conducted a word search for the occurrence of "spirit", "Holy Spirit" and "heart" in the New International Version (NIV). We chose those three because of their theological significance in the Catholic Church's dogmatic postures over the past two thousand years. There were well over 500 appearances in this English translation of the word "spirit" from the Hebrew *ruwach* and the Greek *pneuma*. See Appendices AB and AC. To begin with, those two have a primary meaning recorded in Strong's Concordance, 1976 Ed.—wind or breath. However, when combined with *elohiym,* Hebrew for God, "the breath of God" became "the spirit of God". That was not the only interpretation of the Hebrew, *ruwach*! When *ruwach* was used alone, the English word became "spirit", with and without a capital "S", a synonym of "Spirit of God", the "spirit of a person", "soul", "mind", "heart", "a fortune teller", "a medium", a "familiar spirit", a "necromancer", "behavior", "courage", "strength", "hostility", a "temper", an "enchanter" and something of God that God could pour into humans. Our biggest surprise was the discovery of the Hebrew *ruwach qodesh (sacred breath)*, translated as Holy Spirit, also, translated as Spirit of Holiness in Isaiah 63: 10-11 which is a derivative of the phrase, "the Holy One of Israel" and from Psalm 105: 3, "the holy name". You can verify these in any Bible Version you choose! [Note: there are 17 occurrences of "the Holy One of Israel" in the book of Isaiah-RSV]

G-3: The mysterious third person of the alleged Trinity begins to be unveiled.

After having read the Christian Testament in our logical chronological order of authorship in Chapter Four, did you not experience the Apostolic confusions that start with Paul's complex poetic use of the Hebrew Testament's references to God, especially in Romans 8: 9-16. Reading the Christian Testament in the order prescribed by Jerome in the 5th century, ratified by the, then, Catholic Church and accepted by all future Christian denominations, does nothing but render the developing doctrines and theology inconsistent. Hopefully, reading it in the new order re-arranged your pre-critical naiveté acceptance of the concept of Trinity and re-pointed you to Deut 6: 4. By analyzing the appearance of the many titles for God in terms of Spirit, Spirit of Holiness and Holy Spirit we have uncovered the threads of the Trinitarian Conspiracy.

The Greek word for breath is "*pneuma*"; for the Holy Spirit it is "*pneuma hagios".* Similar to the H.T., the C.T. contains several interpretations of "*pneuma*": breath, wind, God's Spirit, soul and body ("*psuche*" and "*soma*" in Greek), spirit of humans or a certain person, mind (a figurative use of spirit but usually "*nous*" is mind), spirit of the Lord (Yeshua or, maybe, God), soul, way or manner in 2 Corin 12: 18, behavior, attitude, truth, ghost, demon and fervor. See Appendix AC. There is in 1 Corin 12: 9, 12-13 a references to "the one Spirit", that of God the Father.

To finish this Section, consider the history of the Hebrew Testament and its translation into Greek (the Septuagint, LXX) in 270 BC at Alexandria. That LXX was THE Bible for all the Gentiles. It's clearly the source of all the Greek C.T. uses and interpretations. The Septuagint really set the tone for the people to understand the many synonyms for God, none of which imply a third Person in the Godhead. The confusion arose from the general illiteracy among the Christians themselves. It is, in simpler terms, the problem of taking a primitive language and trying to conserve the meaning into a sophisticated and philosophical language and the conviction, or perception, that the new language accurately captures both the definitions and implications of the older language. Greek has greater precision than Hebrew! The lack of our 21st century science and technology is not the problem; the problem is ignorance of the old languages. Remember this; we only discovered how to read hieroglyphics and cuneiform at the end of the 18th century (the Rosetta Stone discovered in 1799 AD), a mere two centuries ago. There is no evil or sin in ignorance; evil and sin result when ignorance turns to violence and hatred. And we all know how much of that existed and exists in the affairs of humans throughout history!

G-4: A Little History and our Conclusions

The first disciples were simple Jewish fishermen and housewives living in and around Nazareth and the corridor to Jerusalem where Yeshua preached. The major believers, then, were people living in the towns and villages in Israel. They all were familiar with the Hebrew Bible that is divided into three collections: the Law, the Prophets, and the Writings. The Hebrew names of these collections are Torah, Nevi'im, and Ketuvim, often referred to as the TANAK. When Yeshua, a faithful Israelite, preached, his basic themes were directly from the known Hebrew Testament. After his death and Resurrection, these simple disciples proclaimed Yeshua's Messiahship and the Good News to the people of Israel. What they professed to the crowds was the fulfillment of the alleged future predictions of a coming Messiah that were written in that Hebrew Testament. The words they used to express their faith in the Risen "*Christos*", and the meaning of those words, were those contained in the Hebrew (and Greek Septuagint) TANAK and understood in the context of a unique history of a Chosen People in relationship with the God of Israel. On this basis the words spoken and later written in the Christian Testament were solely copied from the words and phrases found in the Greek translation of the Hebrew Testament. Added to this situation was the cognitive development stage of the world of that century. A simple people with a mindset at the "Pre-critical Naiveté" stage; what they believed was that the Hebrew Testament was accurate history and science and what was spoken by the prophets was infused into the authors' mind by the very breath of God—the process of inspiration.

Our point is that some of those designations for God were then repeated exactly as previously written or by using synonyms that introduced theological confusions in the minds of the new Christians. The problems that arose were a direct result of the (1) inaccuracies of the Oral Traditions, (2) personal perceptions and interpretations of the visiting missionaries, (3) the lack of communications between communities, (4) the presence of apocryphal writings, (5) the literary style of certain canonical writings, specifically, (6) the disagreement among the four gospels about the nature of the Messiah and, finally, (7) the confusing vocabulary found in Paul's letters, and, most importantly, (8) the use of the Septuagint throughout the Gentile world. All of these issues, and there are others, contributed to a Christianity that formulated as many different and contradictory beliefs as there were Christian members. This we know as factual due in part from the very letters of Paul to his converted communities. Years later we find the many sectarian issues (heresies labeled by the Catholic leadership) in violent and deadly conflict within the politicized Church-State of Constantine's Empire.

A. The Problem with Hebrew and Greek Vocabularies:

In the Hebrew Testament there are several passages in which God is referred to as the "spirit", "Holy Spirit" or "the Spirit of Holiness". Be mindful that this is in the OLD Testament in which the prevailing theology is Deut 6: 4 {*God ... is ONE (ALONE)*}. To speak or write about one's spirit is a synonym for that person. Your personhood and your spirit represent one and the same unique individual, YOU alone, not two people. Those readings are:

Psalm 51: 12-14
12 A clean heart create for me, God; renew in me a steadfast spirit. 13 Do not drive me from your presence, nor take from me your spirit. 14 Restore my joy in your salvation; sustain in me a willing spirit. In the NAB it reads "holy spirit". That makes us loose faith in the NAB

Isa 44: 24
Thus says the LORD, your redeemer, who formed you from the womb: I am the LORD, who made all things, who alone stretched out the heavens; when I spread out the earth, who was with me? No one!

Isaiah 63: 10-11
10 But they rebelled, and grieved his holy spirit; So he turned on them like an enemy, and fought against them. 11 Then they remembered the days of old and Moses, his servant; Where is he who brought up out of the sea the shepherd of his flock? Where is he who put his holy spirit in their midst;

NOTEBENE Mark 1: 10-11 *On coming up out of the water he saw the heavens being torn open and the Spirit, like a dove, descending upon him. And a voice came from the heavens, "You are my beloved son; with you I am well pleased."* The first underlined is from Isaiah 11: 2. It is fairly clear that it is the Spirit of God, not a third person. The second underlined is principally from Isaiah 42: 1 with overtones from Isa 61:1 and 63: 7 ff. It is indisputable that these two titles are in reference to God!

Daniel 13: 45 (NAB & RSV)
45 As she was being led to execution, God stirred up the holy spirit of a young boy named Daniel,
In this case it is evident that the holy spirit of Daniel is, in fact, Daniel himself. This demonstrates that the spirit of God and the Holy Spirit, both, refer to God, not a third person.

Wisdom 9: 13-17
13 For what man knows God's counsel, or who can conceive what our LORD intends? 14 For the deliberations of mortals are timid, and unsure are our plans. 15 For the corruptible body burdens the soul and the

earthen shelter weighs down the mind that has many concerns. 16 And scarce do we guess the things on earth, and what is within our grasp we find with difficulty; but when things are in heaven, who can search them out? 17 Or who ever knew your counsel, except you had given Wisdom and sent your holy spirit from on high?
Again, God is the Holy Spirit. Wisdom is not a person but only an intellectual gift.

B. The Problem with Christian Vocabulary:

- Paul is singularly responsible for the principal confusions of the use of synonyms for God, i.e., the Spirit, the Spirit of Holiness and the Holy Spirit, as well as Yeshua and the Spirit of Yeshua in the following:

  Romans 8: 9-16
  9 But you are not in the flesh; on the contrary, you are in the spirit, if only the Spirit of God dwells in you. Whoever does not have the Spirit of Christ does not belong to him. 10 But if Christ is in you, although the body is dead because of sin, the spirit is alive because of righteousness. 11 If the Spirit of the one who raised Jesus from the dead dwells in you, the one who raised Christ from the dead will give life to your mortal bodies also, through his Spirit that dwells in you. 12 Consequently, brothers, we are not debtors to the flesh, to live according to the flesh. 13 For if you live according to the flesh, you will die, but if by the spirit you put to death the deeds of the body, you will live. 14 For those who are led by the Spirit of God are children of God. 15 For you did not receive a spirit of slavery to fall back into fear, but you received a spirit of adoption, through which we cry, "Abba, Father!" 16 The Spirit itself bears witness with our spirit that we are children of God,

  The first thing we must impress upon you is that the original Greek texts are written in "uncials" that means all capital letters! The words that are capitalized in this passage were selected by the translators. Therefore, don't get confused if one "Spirit" is capitalized and another "spirit" is in lower case! The difficulty in this passage is to distinguish which person is being referenced in each of the phrases when "spirit" is written. If you return to Chapter Four, in Paul's letter to the Romans, you can re-read the comments concerning this passage.

- The words "Holy Spirit" are used approximately 90 times in the Christian Testament as opposed to 4 times in the Hebrew Testament. Paul in his letters uses it 21 times; Luke uses it 13 times in his Gospel and 41 times in Acts while the three other Gospels together use it 12 times. Doesn't it seem odd that Paul initiates the confusion and his disciple, Luke, uses it profusely? Between Paul and Luke we have 74 out of 90 uses of the term "Holy Spirit". Paul and Luke use that expression 82 % of the total. Does the pupil follow the teacher? The remainder of the C.T. uses it 18 % of the total. Of all the times "Holy Spirit" is written, only Matthew's interpretation indicates a third person! It's Matt 28: 19, *Go, therefore, and make disciples of all nations, baptizing them in the name of the Father, and of the Son, and of the holy Spirit.* The other passage is not as clear, it's John 14:

> 26 *The Advocate, the holy Spirit that the Father will send in my name--he will teach you everything and remind you of all that (I) told you.*

Our observation is that only Matthew is a Trinitarian; everyone else in the Christian Testament is a Monotheist. The two Dogmas of the Nicene Creed are without a doubt suspect. They were voted upon by a "pre-critical naiveté" leadership, all Literalists who had no awareness of the mythologized nature of the biblical writings. Matthew's theology was simply an error in human "perception"! How this FAITH MINDSET can be reversed is anyone's guess. It may well be one of those "flat Earth" beliefs that require several millennia to understand and resolve.

H. The Metaphors of the Heart, the Muscle We Call the Blood-Pump

> EZE 11 19 *And I will give them <u>one heart</u> {leb}, and I will put <u>a new spirit</u> within you; and I will take the <u>stony heart</u> {lebab eben} out of their flesh, and will give them <u>an heart of flesh</u> {lebab basar}:* [The {} are the Hebrew words for different meanings of Heart.]

It is truly amazing what a good search engine can do to obtain information. A dear friend gave me a special "search" software program and I have found myself in research paradise. This research would not have been completed if it were not for that little gift.

First off, did you know that there were 545 uses of "heart" in the Bible (See Appendix AE) and just about each one ascribes some distinct emotional quality to the heart? The verse from Ezekiel is typical! Of course, that rests on the belief that the heart is, in fact, the center of all human emotion as well as moral and ethical behavior. It also appears that there is a large portion of people in this 21st century who agree with that posture! Our FIRST difficulty is the Hebrew language itself. Why? There are two words in Hebrew that are used for our English word, heart. The generic word "*leb*" in Hebrew is a "general reference to the heart", like, "God is going to give us a new heart" in the verse from Ezekiel above. The specific word "*lebab*" along with *a* modifier means a "deeper heart", like, a heart full of emotions or in the case of the Ezekiel verse above, it refers to a "stony heart" or a "heart of flesh". One would not know this unless one could read Biblical Hebrew. In addition, the word "lebab" is frequently used to mean mind, soul or the center of all emotions. "The translator is a traitor", is a favorite among those who understand the complexity of converting an ancient language into a modern tongue! A second difficulty is that since heart transplants have become common in our times, 20th and 21st centuries, each person who has had one of those operations has NOT had a personality change. Judging by the biblical exactness (guaranteed by the alleged "Divine Inspiration" perception), a person receiving another person's heart should exhibit a different personality. And if someone received a pig's heart, then that recipient would really have a new look on life. Then, what about receiving a mechanical pump, a non-corrosive super-alloy, absolutely compatible with the human body? Would that person have zero personality after the zipper was closed? The answer is; no change takes place! One should be able to comprehend the simple fact that all the Biblical uses of the word "heart" are, for the most part, metaphors!

The HEART is not the center of emotions, not of morality and certainly not of ethical behavior. It is just a pump! Please read some or all of the biblical uses of the word heart in Appendix AE. If you don't read any of those verses, you're missing some great metaphors. Which brings up a point of interest!

The Bible contains many powerful allegories, similes, parables and metaphors. These are what mythologize the Bible. We remember in Graduate classes someone telling us about Albert Schweitzer (or was it Dietrich Bonhoffer) who said, "The Bible can only be understood if we de-mythologize its history, science and conversations." Today's single biggest problem is understanding the Bible. The persistence of the Literalists' position is that the Bible is absolute history, science and conversation. Their source is a little known verse (Titus 1: 1-3) that says that God doesn't lie! And if you compare this with Paul's letter to Tim 3: 16 that reading the Scriptures is beneficial, one does conclude that the Bible is absolutely God's Word. Of course, the Literalists do not remember 1 Kings 22: 21-23 in which God sends a lying spirit to confuse the prophets! Nor do they recognize that the very same quote occurs in 2 Chron 18: 20-22 that confirms that God ordered a lying spirit to confound them. I don't know what you perceive in all this, but the Bible confirms that God does deceitful things and causes people to lie. Now, that's a Literalist nightmare! If you believe that the Bible is absolute, you had better be absolutely sure that your perception is also absolute! "God doesn't lie" is absolutely true; it's the Bible (that is written by men) that is sometimes a lie!

The conclusion is that all references to the emotional character of one's heart are myth statements---metaphors. We now refer you to the beginning of this Chapter and the quotation:

> "How many times do you have to experience something counter to your beliefs expectations before you are willing to alter your position?"
>
> This following quote from James' letter should put an end to the "God MADE HIM NOT UNDERSTAND" camp.
> James 1: 13-15 *No one experiencing temptation should say, "I am being tempted by God"; for God is not subject to temptation to evil, and he himself tempts no one. Rather, each person is tempted when he is lured and enticed by his own desire. Then desire conceives and brings forth sin, and when sin reaches maturity it gives birth to death.*

I. The Puppeteer God of Good for good and Evil for evil.

In the earliest days of the Oral Traditions humanity considered that both good and evil emanated from the many gods concocted in their imaginations. This belief continued up to and into the Israelite enculturation and has pervaded human thought ever since. As a matter of interest, these quotes challenge the "God doesn't lie" position; so SHE doesn't lie but does a little evil on the side! See these six remembrances within the following verses in the first book of Samuel (1SA):

> 1SA 16: 14-16 *But the SPIRIT of the LORD departed from Saul, and an evil SPIRIT from the LORD troubled him. 15 And Saul's servants said unto him, Behold now, <u>an evil SPIRIT from God</u> troubleth thee. 16 Let our lord now command thy servants, [which are] before thee, to seek out a man, [who is] a cunning player on an harp: and it shall come to pass, when <u>the evil SPIRIT from God</u> is upon thee, that he shall play with his hand, and thou shalt be well.*

1SA 16: 23 *And it came to pass, when the [evil] SPIRIT from God was upon Saul, that David took an harp, and played with his hand: so Saul was refreshed, and was well, and the evil SPIRIT departed from him.*

1SA 18: 10 *And it came to pass on the morrow, that the evil SPIRIT from God came upon Saul, and he prophesied in the midst of the house: and David played with his hand, as at other times: and [there was] a javelin in Saul's hand.*

1SA 19: 9 *And the evil SPIRIT from the LORD was upon Saul, as he sat in his house with his javelin in his hand: and David played with [his] hand.*

Not only did that attitude exist in the Hebrew writings but it crept into the mindset of early Christian theology as well. Even in this most modern of times we frequently hear, "Why is there so much suffering?", "Why does God allow this condition?", "What have I done to deserve this cancer?" We blame God for the evil that befalls us! Did you miss Yeshua's meaning when he said that God closed the eyes and ears of some listeners so they wouldn't understand the parables' meaning? Now, isn't that a great example of Carl Jung's concept of the Collective Unconscious? We got it from the previous generation and the generations before them.

Part Four: The Miscellaneous Mythed List of Millions of Errors

Section 1. The True Words of Yeshua

We will now focus on the problem known as "ipsissima verba" (Latin for the very truest words) as it relates to Yeshua's alleged spoken words.

As much as we prefer the meaning within the Fourth Gospel rather than its factuality, we must acknowledge that it is the most mythologized of all the books in the Christian Testament, excluding Revelation, of course. It does constitute the first 990,000 simple and complex distortions of the life and times of Yeshua, the Theologian Extraordinaire from Nazareth. Yes, the list of errors is very long but we'll only highlight a few.

First of all, the Fourth Gospel was written by five authors the list of whom may not have included John the Apostle. It is not a problem to find out that John's disciples may well have written the Gospel since Christians accepted the Gospel as John's thoughts and beliefs. You'll have to do a great deal of personal research to confirm that conclusion offered by Raymond E. Brown, SS and several scholars of the "Jesus Seminar". To that end, we intend to present a few simple arguments and hope our logic will convince you. If you haven't read the Introduction to the Fourth Gospel in the NAB, then, now would be a very opportune time to do so. Remember, it's available on the Internet listed in Appendix L.

In our Greek classes we found the writing style of the first part of the Chapter 1: 1-18 to be more elegant than what a simple fisherman could write. Most scholars agree. In the body of the Gospel there were large portions injected that appear not to belong to the mainstream story. Check out the last verse of John 14: 31 and recognize that it connects to the first verse in John 18: 1. The Intro suggests that John 15 to 17 were additions made by another editor. Raymond Brown and the Jesus Seminar members suggest the same thing. The last chapter (21), pretty much stands out like orange polka dots on a purple wall, a true addition to the actual ending in Chapter 20.

The principal errors occur in all the words spoken by Yeshua. Yes, some of the individual words may very well be from Yeshua's mouth. That's not the problem. It's the sentences that are unreal; the content could not have been from Yeshua because the sentences all issue from a person who is in full knowledge of his personal Divinity along with some future knowledge. That is not what a fully human could know (See 1 John 4: 2). Yeshua is far too Divine in this Fourth Gospel, so much so, that his humanity is virtually non-existent. The Synoptic Gospels, on the other hand, would then be totally false when they speak of his human imperfections and his suffering on the cross. We realize that this may be a shocker of a posture! However, the Fourth Gospel can only be understood as the faith statements of its five authors inked in mythic forms.

Think what myth can do; it points to deeper meanings that are full of faith in Yeshua. More than that, the short stories (first 12 Chapters are allegories about each and every person's metanoia, baptism and belief in the message and the messenger, Yeshua. The difficulty we humans have is laboring to discover the nature and meaningfulness of each message. In Chapter Six we'll attempt to unravel the deeper meaning of all those vignettes and the entire Fourth Gospel, i.e., what it means for us all.

Section 2: Will the Twelve Apostles Please Stand Up

Now, let's turn to the names of the twelve, first of the last thousand inconsistencies:

Mark 3: 16	**Matt** 10: 2	**Luke & Act** 6:16 1:13	**John** 21: 2
Simon–Peter	Simon-Peter	Simon–Peter	Simon - Peter
Andrew	Andrew	Andrew	Andrew
James Z	James Z	James Z	James Z
John Z	John Z	John Z	John Z
Philip	Philip	Philip	Philip
Thomas	Thomas	Thomas	Thomas
Matthew	Matthew	Matthew	Unidentified A
Bartholomew	Bartholomew	Bartholomew	Unidentified B
James A	James A	James A	Nathanael
Judas I	Judas I	Judas I	?
Thaddeus	Thaddeus	Judas II	Judas II
Simon C	Simon C	Simon Z	?

Well, well! How about a little quiz! Multiple Choice anyone? Who is at fault for not remembering the correct names of the Twelve?

A. Was it God's forgetfulness?
B. Was it a low battery in the writer's hearing aid?
C. Did the authors forget? (Possibly a confused Source or Oral Tradition!)
D. The Bible is the Word of God and there are no mistakes!

And, the answer is ... here's a hint, go back to page 100 and *"see"* the answer. Or you could just write the Roman numeral for 100! For those of you who dislike riddles, "see" sounds like "C"; the Roman numeral for 100 is "C". We were surprised to see the facts! The last two names from the Synoptics are problematic, n'est pas? And, looks like the Fourth "Good News" had forgotten who were the last six members of the Twelve!

Section 3. The Three "Our Fathers"

We know you've spoken and read the "Our Father" prayer in Matthew 6: 9-15. This is a very popular and formal prayer. Now read the user-friendly version in Luke 11: 2-4. It's possible that few have ever heard of Luke's prayer. Let's look at it here.

> *"He was praying in a certain place, and when he had finished, one of his disciples said to him, 'Lord, teach us to pray just as John taught his disciples.' He said to them, 'When you pray, say: Father, hallowed be your name, your kingdom come. Give us each day our daily bread and forgive us our sins for we ourselves forgive everyone in debt to us, and do not subject us to the final test.'"*

Next you may have to search the Internet to find the "Teachings of the Twelve Apostles" (it's called "the Didache", its Greek title). The big question is whether God told the authors what to say or did Yeshua actually use those very words? Guess what? Nobody told anyone anything! The authors made it up from the Oral Tradition and the aphorisms spoken by Yeshua along with the written sources each one had. The funniest thing is; the Protestant denominations chose the words from Matthew with the Didache's ending.

For those of you who have difficulty getting to the Internet, here is the Didache's formula:

> *8:2 Neither pray as the hypocrites, but as the Lord commanded in his gospel: "Our Father in heaven, hallowed be your name. Your kingdom come. Your will be done, as in heaven, so also on earth. Give us today our daily bread. And forgive us our debt, as we also forgive our debtors. And lead us not into temptation, but deliver us from evil, for yours is the power and the glory, forever."*
> *8: 3 Pray this way three times a day.*

Notice that the underlined is only in the KJV and its daughter translations! Check the NRSV for a reference to other ancient documents containing that underlined phrase.

And, lo and behold, the Vatican II Council in 1965 suggested that Catholics add that same underlined passage from the Didache! Oh, my soul, what's this world coming to when Protestants and Catholics start praying together? And, we give it "Three Cheers!" Five hundred years is a long time to hold a grudge.

Now, read the line that deals with forgiveness, you know, the "as we also forgive", both in this Didache and in Luke 11: 4. Isn't that a heavy burden, especially if one decides not to forgive others? Mighty powerful prayer that many say out loud but are oblivious to its implications! Personally, Luke's is our preferred format!

Section 4. What errors are in the Four Gospels?

Sub-Section A: Mark

A. Mark 1: 23-26 *In their synagogue was a man with an unclean spirit; he cried out, "What have you to do with us, Jesus of Nazareth? Have you come to destroy us? I know who you are—the Holy One of God!" Jesus rebuked him and said, "Quiet! Come out of him!" The unclean spirit convulsed him and with a loud cry came out of him.*
Yeshua tells a sickness Demon to be quiet. Oh, please, demons don't cause sickness! So if God dictated this, then God has a big problem. If Yeshua really said it, then he must be human, yes, fully human including ignorance. By now, you should understand that Mark's mindset is at the root of all this mumbo jumbo demon stuff! Did you catch the title the demon gave Yeshua? The Holy One of God! That's Mark's faith speaking again.

B. Mark 2: 3-4 *They came bringing to him a paralytic carried by four men. Unable to get near Jesus because of the crowd, they opened up <u>the roof</u> above him. After they had broken through, they let down the mat on which the paralytic was lying.*
A person is lowered through a thatch roof (the Greek word is *stege*, thatch). Now turn to Luke 5: 19 and discover that he calls it a tile roof. There aren't any clay ones in Yeshua's territory but only in Luke's homeland. Oops! Who is correct?

C. Mark 2: 14 *As he passed by, he saw Levi, son of Alphaeus, sitting at the customs post. He said to him, "Follow me." And he got up and followed him.*
Is the call of Levi to discipleship or Apostleship? Luke echoes the same in 5: 27-28 but follows with 29 into a great banquet and let's Levi's discipleship evaporate. Is this a confusion between Levi the tax collector and Matthew the Apostle? It appears that there is in Mark's source a story of Levi which Luke repeats but which Matthew morphs into Matthew the Apostle! Who is correct?

C. Mark 2: 26 *How he went into the house of God when Abiathar was high priest and ate the bread of offering that only the priests could lawfully eat, and shared it with his companions?"*
Yeshua's refers to the High Priest in David's eating the Tabernacle breads; Yeshua said it was Abiathar. But 1 Samuel 21: 2 states it was Abimelech. Yipes, whose mistake was that?

D. Mark 3: 21 *When his relatives heard of this they set out to seize him, for they said, "He is out of his mind."*
If at the Annunciation Mary and Joseph had been informed by the angel, how come they now think him "out of his mind"? Bad Karma, this verse! That's why Matthew and Luke left it out in their Gospels.

E. Mark 4: 34 *Without parables he did not speak to them, but to his own disciples he explained everything in private.*
Yeshua may have said this but for those belonging to the Kingdom of God it has veracity. The Bible does speak in myth to those who can interpret it! But the real reason that Mark wrote this is that early Christians believed that God deliberately made certain people hard of hearing. That's "folk theology" and it's false! It's one's mind's eye that blinds one's heart. (OH, we just made two metaphors, didn't we?)

F. Mark 8: 23-25 *He took the blind man by the hand and led him outside the village. Putting spittle on his eyes he laid his hands on him and asked, "Do you see anything?" Looking up he replied, "I see people looking like trees and walking." Then he laid hands on his eyes a second time and he saw clearly; his sight was restored and he could see everything distinctly.*
This is an example of Yeshua not being able to cure on the first try! What gives here?

G. Mark 8: 27-30 *Now Jesus and his disciples set out for the villages of Caesarea Philippi. Along the way he asked his disciples, "Who do people say that I am?" They said in reply, "John the Baptist, others Elijah, still others one of the prophets." And he asked them, "But who do you say that I am?" Peter said to him in reply, "You are the Messiah." Then he warned them not to tell anyone about him.*
When Yeshua asks his disciples, "Who do people say that I am?" Mark writes his faith statement. We see in Luke 9: 18-22 the same story but without Yeshua's rebuke of Peter found in Mark 8: 32-33. Luke didn't want to embarrass the memory of Peter. The Fourth Gospel makes no mention of this. Yet in Matthew 16: 13-19 the incident is expanded into a great position for Peter. This Catholic mantra from Matthew is read every year in their churches throughout the world. Now, if I were King and desired total adherence to my authority, I would certainly remind my subjects that God gave me that authority. Ergo, the Catholic must be told that mantra every year to justify the Papal authority.

G. Mark 9: 1 *He also said to them, "Amen, I say to you, there are some standing here who will not taste death until they see that the kingdom of God has come in power."*
This is one of those double entendre verses. In one interpretation it implies that some within his hearing will not see death until the Kingdom of God comes in power. Is that the end time? If it were, it hasn't happened! The other interpretation means just the presence of the Kingdom. Well, it appears that neither condition has occurred, except that for some Christians it has happened in their hearts. (Another metaphor.)

H. Mark 9: 9 *As they were coming down from the mountain, he charged them not to relate what they had seen to anyone, except when the Son of Man had risen from the dead.*
Once one accepts the complete humanity of Yeshua then one will realize that Yeshua could not have said this. It is only Mark's Backward-Looking faith speaking.

I. Mark 9:12 *He told them, "Elijah will indeed come first and restore all things,*
So, Yeshua believes in reincarnation. Actually, Mark is the culprit.

J. Mark 11: 13-20 *Seeing from a distance a fig tree in leaf, he went over to see if he could find anything on it. When he reached it he found nothing but leaves; it was not the time for figs. And he said to it in reply, "May no one ever eat of your fruit again!" And his disciples heard it. ... 19 When evening came, they went out of the city. Early in the morning, as they were walking along, they saw the fig tree withered to its roots. 21 Peter remembered and said to him, "Rabbi, look! The fig tree that you cursed has withered."*

This is the famous cursing of the fig tree. In this version Yeshua gives it the evil finger BUT it doesn't die until the next day. Matthew in 21: 19 recognizes this delay as bad Karma for Yeshua. In his plagiarized version it dies immediately. Another" Oops"!

K. Mark 12: 28-34 *One of the scribes, when he came forward and heard them disputing and saw how well he had answered them, asked him, "Which is the first of all the commandments?" Jesus replied, "The first is this: 'Hear, O Israel! The Lord our God is Lord alone! You shall love the Lord your God with all your heart, with all your soul, with all your mind, and with all your strength.' The second is this: 'You shall love your neighbor as yourself.' There is no other commandment greater than these." The scribe said to him, "Well said, teacher. You are right in saying, 'He is One and there is no other than he.' And 'to love him with all your heart, with all your understanding, with all your strength, and to love your neighbor as yourself' is worth more than all burnt offerings and sacrifices." And when Jesus saw that (he) answered with understanding, he said to him, "You are not far from the kingdom of God." And no one dared to ask him any more questions.*
If you believe that the Bible is truth from God, then, this verse should clear up the problem of Trinity and help you to realize that the Holy Spirit (sacred breath) is none other than God the Father! If you believe the Fourth Gospel that Yeshua is equal to God, then, this verse is unintelligible! On the other hand, if you think that the Bible is man made, then Mark and the Fourth Gospel are simply inconsistent because of their human fallibility. Big, very big OOPS!

L. Mark 13: 2 *Jesus said to him, "Do you see these great buildings? There will not be one stone left upon another that will not be thrown down."*
This verse is an impossible statement by Yeshua. It's really Mark's Backward-Looking comment placed on Yeshua's lips. However, it may be that Yeshua is referring to the end times and not to 70 AD when the Romans destroyed the Temple. The remaining verses in this Chapter are totally focused on the end times. And judging by the conditions on this Planet right now, there may be some real concerns for the fate of the Universe! Just kidding, folks! Relax, the Earth has been in worse conditions before and it's still here. And, really, how many times have self-appointed prophets predicted the end and we are still going strong.

M. Mark 13: 9 *"Watch out for yourselves. They will hand you over to the courts. You will be beaten in synagogues. You will be arraigned before governors and kings because of me, as a witness before them.*
Another verse that Yeshua could not have spoken. It's Mark who puts these words on Yeshua's lips because Mark's community has experienced these situations and Mark wishes to aggrandize the words and deeds of Yeshua.

N. Mark 13: 30 *Amen, I say to you, this generation will not pass away until all these things have taken place.*
This is an incorrect prediction by Yeshua. It hasn't happened yet to this very day! And, how many generations have passed?

In concluding the 16 errors in Mark, let us remind you that they will be repeated in Matthew and Luke to some equal or lesser degree. Watch for them. Can it be possible that God was asleep during the writing of these Gospels? It sure does seem to us that the thesis, "God doesn't lie!" in reference to the Bible, is incorrect! The only rational conclusion that one can honestly make is that the Bible is a construct of human hands. And, as we have written previously, the entire Bible was "Made in Israel" by males! It wasn't emailed from <god.org>

Sub-Section B. Matthew

A. The Genealogy is tabulated in Appendix J. A quick review will tell you that somebody got the list all mixed up. Any other conclusion is the result of "Intellectual Dishonesty" or the other word that starts with Ig . . . God can't be blamed any more for the errors in the Bible, don't you think?

B. In Matt 5: 48 *So be perfect, just as your heavenly Father is perfect.*
In the context of the previous verses, the word "perfect" really should imply perfect LOVE. Therefore, the word in Greek, *teleios*, which is translated into English as "perfect" is not only a poor translation but also an unreasonable one. We humans don't have the constitution to be "perfect"; perfection is an illusion for humankind but possible by God's grace (2 Corin 12:9). The word should carry with it a suggestion of "striving to be as loving as ... is Loving" or "working towards loving completely as..." or, as an athlete, "practicing to love maturely" as one's efforts to be fully human, fully in God's image.

C. In Matt 7: 21 it says *"not everyone who cries, "Lord, Lord" will be saved".*
In Matt 25: 34-40 there is a parable of a person who is saved because he clothed the naked and fed the hungry without knowing the name of Yeshua! Can you not see that Matt 7: 21 contradicts Rom 10: 13 *"For everyone who calls on the name of the Lord will be saved*? Yet, Paul wrote 10:13 several years before the Gospels appeared! Tell me which is the word of God? Or is She a fickled God who changes Her mind at a snap of an author's finger? "Ain't" life just full of surprises and unanswerable questions?

D. In Matt 10: 23 *When they persecute you in one town, flee to another. Amen, I say to you, you will not finish the towns of Israel before the Son of Man comes.*
Yeshua sends out his disciples and states that they will not have preached to all the towns in Israel before the Son of Man comes. Wow! First, did some of those disciples ever return to witness the Resurrection and experience the coming of the Son of Man? We think not! Second, it's all just another interjection by Brother Matthew! That Backward-Looking will get you into trouble every time.

E. In Matt 11: 14 *And if you are willing to accept it, he is Elijah, the one who is to come.*
It almost sounds like there is reincarnation because Yeshua says that John the Baptizer could really be Elijah. Boy, those picky things we readers miss!

F. In Matt 11: 27-30 *All things have been handed over to me by my Father. No one knows the Son except the Father, and no one knows the Father except the Son and anyone to whom the Son wishes to reveal him. "Come to me, all you who labor and are burdened, and I will give you rest. Take my yoke upon you and learn from me, for I am meek and humble of heart; and you will find rest for your selves. For my yoke is easy, and my burden light."*

These verses are Backward-Looking faith statements from Matthew's community not the real words of Yeshua. The problem here is the Chalcedon doctrine of Yeshua's humanity. As a human, Yeshua cannot be in possession of such knowledge. Please re-read that doctrine of 451 AD and understand that being human includes ignorance! Have you been counting all these errors? Quite a few, aren't there? Quiet your thumping heart, there's still more to come! Oh, there's one more comment. How come the Holy Spirit doesn't know the Son? And, even these aphorisms are suspect. Yeshua doesn't point to himself, the author is doing the pointing to Yeshua. Matthew's faith in Yeshua is what's at stake here in these aphorisms.

G. In Matt 13: 11 *He said to them in reply, "Because knowledge of the mysteries of the kingdom of heaven has been granted to you, but to them it has not been granted.*
It is erroneous to ascribe to God the hardening of people's mind. God wishes that all men and women accept Her-Him. Free will blinds the eyes and clogs the mind of humans! Of course, ignorance does that too. Big mistake! Now, consider this: (a) God isn't dictating anything; (b) Matt is writing folk tales he saw in Mark or in his sources; (c) Yeshua is a fully human being with imperfect 1st century information. Hint, hint: all of these are correct. There is no other choice!

H. In Matt 16: 28 *Amen, I say to you, there are some standing here who will not taste death until they see the Son of Man coming in his kingdom."*
This may very well be a direct reference to the presence of the Kingdom of God and not to the Parousia. If you think it means the Parousia, then Yeshua made an incorrect prediction. Or, is it Matthew who didn't get it correctly? Either way, it's Matthew who is making this statement, not Yeshua!

I. In Matt 18: 22 *Jesus answered, "I say to you, not seven times but seventy-seven times.*
In Luke 17: 4 Yeshua answers every time . Now, get this, the KJV says "70 times 7" because the Greek "seventy times" is one word! That's really a different number. Chalk up one more mistake between NAB Gospels and one mistake between translators of the NAB and the KJV! . It seems to us that it's getting more complicated as we make this list of errors. This one alone is sufficient to conclude that the Bible is "Made in Israel" by human hands and minds. Notice the use of 7; it's a magic number meaning perfection!

In Matt 21: 19 *Seeing a fig tree by the road, he went over to it, but found nothing on it except leaves. And he said to it, "May no fruit ever come from you again." And immediately the fig tree withered.*
We get the fig tree tale again, only this time it dies immediately. Better check Mark 11: 20-22 again! Sho'nuff, another mistake! Wouldn't it be nice if the authors of the Gospels actually sat down together and drafted just one big GOSPEL? Then we could all be happy about these tales of Yeshua and never figure out whether they were true or not. Ah, ignorance can be pure bliss, can't it? And knowledgeable facts a great headache!

J. In Matt 24: 34 *Amen, I say to you, this generation will not pass away until all these things have taken place.*
Hey, this is the same thing Mark wrote! Brother Matty is a copycat! Apparently this prediction never came true. Would you believe that we aren't even finished

and we've collected a hefty number of errors, haven't we? What say you about "inspiration" now? OK! So here are more!

K. In Matt 25: 34-40 *Then the king will say to those on his right, 'Come, you who are blessed by my Father. Inherit the kingdom prepared for you from the foundation of the world. For I was hungry and you gave me food, I was thirsty and you gave me drink, a stranger and you welcomed me, naked and you clothed me, ill and you cared for me, in prison and you visited me.' Then the righteous will answer him and say, 'Lord, when did we see you hungry and feed you, or thirsty and give you drink? When did we see you a stranger and welcome you, or naked and clothe you? When did we see you ill or in prison, and visit you?' And the king will say to them in reply, 'Amen, I say to you, whatever you did for one of these least brothers of mine, you did for me.'*
This is a parable of a person who is saved because he clothed and fed some unknown naked and hungry person. There is a statement (Matt 7: 21) that says *"not everyone who cries, "Lord, Lord" will be saved".* While in Romans 10:13, there is this verse *"For everyone who calls on the name of the Lord will be saved."* Can you not see that each passage contradicts the other? Yet, Paul wrote Romans 10:13 several years before this Gospels appeared! Tell me which is the word of God? Or is She a fickled God who changes His mind at a snap of an author's finger? Did I just write that? Sorry, but it is a good line!

L. In Matt 27: 9 *Then was fulfilled what had been said through Jeremiah the prophet, "And they took the thirty pieces of silver, the value of a man with a price on his head, a price set by some of the Israelites,*
He states that Jeremiah is his source. No! No! Dear Matty, it's found in Zechariah 11: 13, word for word! This certainly proves that God did NOT "inspire" the authors to write absolute truth! Read Zechariah yourself:

> *12 I said to them, "If it seems good to you, give me my wages; but if not, let it go." And they counted out my wages, thirty pieces of silver. 13 But the LORD said to me, "Throw it in the treasury, the handsome price at which they valued me." So I took the thirty pieces of silver and threw them into the treasury in the house of the LORD.*

M. In Matt 27: 56 *Among them were Mary Magdalene and Mary the mother of James and Joseph, and the mother of the sons of Zebedee.*
That list of women does not include Mary, Yeshua's Mom. The Mary, mother of Joseph, can't be Yeshua's Mom; Otherwise Matt would have pointed it out.. We are not sure whether Joseph or Joses is the is one of her four sons. (although it's one of her sons in the Greek source the "Literal Text in Strong's Concordance!" Could it be that Matthew mistook Joses for Joseph? A quick check of our Bible sources reveals that out of 20 Bibles only 6 make the mistake of translating the Greek *Ioses*: KJV, NKJV, AV, Darby's, Young's and Webster's. Remember, no "J" in Greek!

Sub-Section C: Luke

A. 1: 31 *Behold, you will conceive in your womb and bear a son, and you shall name him Jesus.*

What happened to the name, Immanuel, from Isaiah 7: 14? Strong's Concordance says that Immanuel is a compound word meaning "God is with us"; it's generic and could mean anyone but it refers to a King who is called, among other names, the son of God. A construct by Luke!

B 1: 32 *He will be great and will be called Son of the Most High, and the Lord God will give him the throne of David his father,*
According to the Fourth Gospel, he already has it! Another construct of Luke! Yet due to the mythic nature of the Fourth Gospel, we have to give it to Luke. BUT, it's still a contradiction no matter how you slice it or to whom you assign it!

H. 1: 35 *And the angel said to her in reply, "The holy Spirit will come upon you, and the power of the Most High will overshadow you. Therefore the child to be born will be called holy, the Son of God.*
First, the "Holy Spirit" is God the Father (remember "Sacred Breath"). Luke has learned well from Paul whose poetic license has taken hold! The rest is Backward-Looking stuff again! What happened to the Rom 1: 3-4 and the three passages in Acts? Luke had his own agenda!

I. 1: 48 *For he has looked upon his handmaid's lowliness; behold, from now on will all ages call me blessed.*
I don't think she said that! If this be true, how come Mark 3:21? Remember the, "He is out of his mind!" statement? Actually, Luke is plagiarizing Hannah's Canticle found in 1 Samuel 2:1-10 which reads:

> *1 and as she worshiped the LORD, she said: "My heart exults in the LORD, my horn is exalted in my God. I have swallowed up my enemies; I rejoice in my victory. 2 There is no Holy One like the LORD; there in no Rock like our God. 3 *"Speak boastfully no longer, nor let arrogance issue from your mouths. For an all-knowing God is the LORD, a God who judges deeds. 4 The bows of the mighty are broken, while the tottering gird on strength. 5 he well-fed hire themselves out for bread, while the hungry batten on spoil. The barren wife bears seven sons, while the mother of many languishes. 6 "The LORD puts to death and gives life; he casts down to the nether world; he raises up again. 7 The LORD makes poor and makes rich, he humbles, he also exalts. 8 He raises the needy from the dust; from the ash heap he lifts up the poor, To seat them with nobles and make a glorious throne their heritage. He gives to the vower his vow, and blesses the sleep of the just. "For the pillars of the earth are the LORD'S, and he has set the world upon them.9 He will guard the footsteps of his faithful ones, but the wicked shall perish in the darkness. For not by strength does man prevail; 10 the LORD'S foes shall be shattered. The Most High in heaven thunders; The LORD judges the ends of the earth, Now may he give strength to his king, and exalt the horn of his anointed!"*

J. 6: 17-26 *And he came down with them and stood on a stretch of level ground. 20 And raising his eyes toward his disciples he said: "Blessed are ... four Blessed's and four Woe's.*
Here Luke places the event on a plain while Matthew says it took place on the mountainside. Luke also changes four of Matthew's "Blessed's" to Woes. Well, so much for the accuracy of Luke!

K. 8: 30 *Then Jesus asked him, "What is your name?" He replied, "Legion," because many demons had entered him.*
Part of the 1st century folklore!

L. 9: 20-21 *Then he said to them, "But who do you say that I am?" Peter said in reply, "The Messiah of God." 21 He rebuked them and directed them not to tell this to anyone.*
Where is Matthew's "keys to the kingdom" and the Papacy appointment? Not here, nor anywhere else, cause it only existed in Matthew's mind!

M. 11: 29-30 *While still more people gathered in the crowd, he said to them, "This generation is an evil generation; it seeks a sign, but no sign will be given it, except the sign of Jonah. Just as Jonah became a sign to the Ninevites, so will the Son of Man be to this generation.*
The sign of Jonah is 3 days and 3 nights. Yeshua was in the tomb for less than 40 hours! Oh well, must be old math! Actually, it's a Backward-Looking faith statement by Luke using O.T future-looking myths..

N. 13: 16 *This daughter of Abraham, whom Satan has bound for eighteen years now, ought she not to have been set free on the sabbath day from this bondage?"*
Even Yeshua believed in demonology! Doesn't God know the truth?

Sub-Section D. The Fourth Gospel

We will see in our Chapter Six that the entire Fourth Gospel is clearly an allegorical Gospel constructed from the faith of its five authors. That really makes the entire Gospel one big myth, doesn't it? Count the words! Lots of mistakes! However, within that myth lies the deeper meaning of relationships with God, Yeshua and the world of friends, neighbors and those who dislike us.

Section 8. The "Who do you say that I am?" Inconsistency

There are three passages in the Christian Testament that start with this question: Mark 8: 27-33, Matthew 16: 13-20 and Luke 9: 18-21. Let's examine each:

Mark 8: 27-33 *Now Jesus and his disciples set out for the villages of Caesarea Philippi. Along the way he asked his disciples, "Who do people say that I am?" They said in reply, "John the Baptist, others Elijah, still others one of the prophets." And he asked them, "But who do you say that I am?" Peter said to him in reply, "You are the Messiah." Then he warned them not to tell anyone about him. He began to teach them that the Son of Man must suffer greatly and be rejected by the elders, the chief priests, and the scribes, and be killed, and rise after three days. He spoke this openly. Then Peter took him aside and began to rebuke him. At this he turned around and, looking at his disciples, rebuked Peter and said, "Get behind me, Satan. You are thinking not as God does, but as human beings do."*

Matthew 16: 13-20 *When Jesus went into the region of Caesarea Philippi he asked his disciples, "Who do people say that the Son of Man is?" They replied, "Some say John the Baptist, others Elijah, still others Jeremiah or one of the* *prophets." He said to them, "But who do you say that I am?" Simon Peter said in reply, "You are the Messiah, the Son of the living God." Jesus said to him in reply, "Blessed are you, Simon son of Jonah. For flesh and blood has not revealed this to you, but my heavenly Father. And so I say to you, you are Peter, and upon this rock I will build my church, and the gates of the netherworld shall not prevail against it. I will give you the keys to the kingdom of heaven. Whatever you bind on earth shall be bound in heaven; and whatever you loose on earth shall be loosed in heaven." Then he strictly ordered his disciples to tell no one that he was the Messiah.*

Luke 9: 18-21 *Once when Jesus was praying in solitude and the disciples were with him, he asked them, "Who do the crowds say that I am?" They said in reply, "John the Baptist; others, Elijah; still others, 'One of the ancient prophets has arisen.'" Then he said to them, "But who do you say that I am?" Peter said in reply, "The Messiah of God." He rebuked them and directed them not to tell this to anyone.*

The first thing to note is the simplicity and similarity of the passages in Mark and Luke. Mark's passage adds an additional dialogue between Peter and Yeshua that ends in Peter's identification with Satan, a strong accusation to say the least. Luke's reading is just the skeleton of Mark's story. It should be obvious that these are significantly different from the elaborate passage in Matthew. Matthew words the incident in the most complementary construct as though he and his community consider Peter to be the titular and spiritual head of the entire Christian Movement. The last few verses give Peter some mighty powerful authority. It is not at all unreasonable to understand why the Roman Petrine Tradition preaches on that Matthean passage every year. How else can they indoctrinate their flocks to believe in Papal authenticity and authority?

If Matthew is the correct rendition, then how come the Christian community didn't elect someone to replace Peter after his death sometime around 67 AD? The only logical answer is, only Matthew and his community believed it! The Fourth Gospel hints at this respect for Peter by the passage in which Yeshua asks Peter, three times, to feed His flock (John 21: 15-17). But, that is a much weaker assignment of power than what Matthew wrote, isn't it? The Roman Petrine position is extremely tenuous, at best! It is noteworthy that the assignment to Peter is found in the 21st Chapter of the Fourth Gospel that is apparently an afterthought and not part of the original text!

Furthermore, some of the dialogue between Paul and Peter was a very strong rebuke for Peter's hypocrisy when the Jerusalem crowd showed up. Didn't Peter change his behavior for fear of James who actually held the position of authority?

Section 9. The Gospel of Judas

After reading all the hype about this great find, we recognized that it is one of many Gnostic writings and, as such, it's of questionable value in the scheme of things. However, because in the Fourth Gospel Yeshua gives a command to Judas that is out of context with the Seder meal, we became interested in what the Gospel of Judas had to say. The verses in the Fourth Gospel read as follows:

Jn 13: 21-27 *When he had said this, Jesus was deeply troubled and testified, "Amen, amen, I say to you, one of you will betray me." 22 The disciples looked at one another, at a loss as to whom he meant. 23 One of his disciples, the one whom Jesus loved, was reclining at Jesus' side. 24 So Simon Peter nodded to him to find out whom he meant. 25 He leaned back against Jesus' chest and said to him, "Master, who is it?" 26 Jesus answered, "It is the one to whom I hand the morsel after I have dipped it." So he dipped the morsel and (took it and) handed it to Judas, son of Simon the Iscariot. 27 After he took the morsel, Satan entered him. So Jesus said to him, "What you are going to do, do quickly." 28 (Now) none of those reclining at table realized why he said this to him. 29 Some thought that since Judas kept the money bag, Jesus had told him, "Buy what we need for the feast," or to give something to the poor. 30 So he took the morsel and left at once. And it was night.*

Judge for yourself, who was this culprit? Was the first underlined pointing to Peter's denial? Could be! The command to Judas, was it to do something that Yeshua had already planned with Judas?

Think about this. What if Yeshua understood that he needed a face-to-face confrontation with the ruling body of the Sanhedrin? Why, you might ask? Because if he lived to 75, he might die unrecognized! He could write a book! Then, maybe, the people would worship the book! However, if he were to die a martyr, he had the chance to be remembered for many a year! Do you think that Yeshua was smart enough to plan this whole thing with Judas from the day they all entered Jerusalem for the Passover remembrance? It did cross my mind! What do you think? Then when it turned nasty for Yeshua, Judas felt regret and blamed himself.

Section 10. What are some errors in the Hebrew Testament?

Because of the size of this portion of the Bible, we will treat only a few of the most obvious mistakes that help us demonstrate the human origin of the Hebrew Testament.

The mistakes in Genesis:

- Gen 4: 14-15 *Since you have now banished me from the soil, and I must avoid your presence and become a restless wanderer on the earth, anyone may kill me at sight." "Not so!" the LORD said to him. "If anyone kills Cain, Cain shall be avenged sevenfold." So the LORD put a mark on Cain lest anyone should kill him at sight.*
  Cain is afraid that someone will kill him. Duh, Where did these someones come from? Adam and Eve are the first humans and they have two sons. Please explain where these other people came from? This is also the reason why Adam's life must be 1000 years in order to populate the Earth! This hints that the story is fabricated!

- The tale in Gen 6: 4-7 *At that time the Nephilim appeared on earth (as well as later), after the sons of heaven had intercourse with the daughters of man, who bore them sons. They were the heroes of old, the men of renown. When the LORD saw how great was man's wickedness on earth, and how no desire that his heart conceived was ever anything but evil, he regretted that he had made man*

on the earth, and his heart was grieved. So the LORD said: "I will wipe out from the earth the men whom I have created, and not only the men, but also the beasts and the creeping things and the birds of the air, for I am sorry that I made them."
OH, those naughty Angels! We believe that many have overlooked this tale about the sons of God impregnating the daughters of men. Small wonder why Matthew and Luke wrote the same tale about God's Spirit impregnating Mary! Note this: the NAB uses sons of heaven and the KJV translates "sons of God". The Hebrew phrase is, ben *'elohiym*, the common idiom for "of God". Now it should be plain that to be called "a son of God" does not necessarily mean equality to God. And we suspect that the Nephilim may very well have been a reference to the Ice Age Neanderthals, some of whom survived to the time of the beginning of the Oral Tradition that followed the end of the Ice Age. Do you remember that the Israelite King is also called "the son of God"?

- The Flood: Both the Epic of Gilgamesh and the Genesis tale appear to be the remnants of the legends relating to the melting of the Ice Age glaciers around 10-12, 000 BC. The dimensions of the Ark, Gen 6: 15, also appear to be somewhat incapable of the task. Naval engineers analyzing the construction details have concluded that such a boat would not hold the cargo described nor would it stand up to the stresses. Interesting as well is a calculation of the water necessary to flood over the mountains of Nepal and the rest of the world. Hardly enough! We do admit that this contrived re-edition from the Epic of Gilgamesh is a mighty memorable tale of faith and perseverance. Seriously, it was re-edited to fit the Hebrew Theocracy.

- Noah and the animals: There seems to be some confusion about just how many of which type of animals were corralled into the ark. Read Gen 6: 19-20 and compare it to Gen 7: 2-10. Mighty strange that there are three different orders! Does this not twig your curiosity? Could it be that the compiler of the Oral Traditions in 500 BC (that was Ezra's task following the Exile!) didn't know which order was the correct one and just put in three different pairings?

- The Salt Pillars: Gen 19: 26 is just one more attempt to weave an extraordinary geological find into the travels of Abram and his many relatives. Imagine the saga the authors could have written if they knew about the Grand Canyon!

- The Tower of Babel: Read Gen 11: 1-9! Did the Hebrew slaves in Egypt see the great pyramids and used that vision to draft an explanation for the many languages in the known world? Surely a student of historic times understands that there were no pyramids prior to the Ice Age but there were people who spoke a different language then (well maybe, grunted would be a better description of their communication skills).

- The Rainbow: any student of Physics understands that rainbows are a product of the refraction of light by the water droplets in the atmosphere during and after a rainstorm. It is very primitive indeed to think that this phenomenon came about as a Divine sign only in Noah's time! Weren't there rainbows during the previous billions of years?

Exodus:

- As much as this is a respected story of Moses' birth as a Hebrew and his saga to become the Hero of the Israelites, we do feel that it is pure myth to satisfy the Israelite mind that a Hebrew lead them out of Egypt. It would be suicide for any Hebrew to admit that Moses was really an Egyptian Prince (an Arab by birth!). Therefore, we are convinced that the birth narrative is pure fiction and legend. Also, refer back to the Sargon infancy story for the model of Moses' birth; we discovered that on Gerald A, Larue's Internet site.

- EX 2: 18 & 21 *When they returned to their father Reuel, he said to them, "How is it you have returned so soon today?" ... 21 Moses agreed to live with him, and the man gave him his daughter Zipporah in marriage.*
  In the first verse Moses is taken to the father-in-law; in the second verse Moses marries the daughter. However, in a later verse, EX 3: 1, Moses refers to Jethro as his father-in-law! WOW! That's surely one more error!

- There is one event that has occurred that points to a natural phenomenon as the cause of the story about Moses crossing the Reed Sea, EX 13: 18 . On the 26th of December 2004 there occurred a tsunami as a result of an ocean bottom earthquake. The ocean-living people in that area immediately recognized the withdrawal of the waters and took to the high land. That was a known sign of ocean floor earthquake previously told to them and they knew that a tsunami was imminent. Researches have discovered that the Mediterranean experienced a similar earthquake sometime between 1500 BC and 1100 BC. This may explain the inclusion of that tsunami as an embellishment of the Exodus story's rendition of the crossing of the Reed Sea. Most Bibles, even the Vulgate, called it the Red Sea except the Jerusalem Bible that has it correct!

- In the passage Ex 19: 16 to 24 it is evident that the Israelites are at the base of a volcano during one of its thermal burps. The entire story is so much like our experience of Mt. St. Helens. No wonder the people were frightened: (a) the smoke on the mountain, (b) the thunder and lightning, (c) the reality of death if they went up the mountainside (sulfurous fumes and maybe lava flows) and lastly, (d) the folk myth of God speaking through the thunder and lightning. All that makes for great theater! And, that's all it was.

- Ex 33: 20 *But my face you cannot see, for no man sees me and still lives.*
  Later it is reported in Deut 5: 4 that the people all saw God's face. How can that be a consistent statement?

Leviticus:

- Well, there may be errors here but is it so ritualistic that we will only comment on that specific error. If these are truly from God then why the first Chapter in Isaiah that condemns it all? The answer may lie in the fact that these explicit regulations for a ritualistic worship are man made, and definitely of Egyptian origin as dictated by Moses himself! In any case, there are two Religious States that have perpetuated these rituals: Israel and the Vatican. There are some times when one experiences the Israelite rituals in the elaborate celebrations of the Roman Petrine Tradition.

- In verse 25: 55 *For to me the Israelites belong as servants; they are servants of mine, because I brought them out of the land of Egypt, I, the LORD, your God.*

That's very strange because in the Fourth Gospel (15: 15) Yeshua tells the reader that he is not our master but our friend. Oh my! Did we get this wrong? No, we are not slaves to God.

Numbers:

- Actually, no comment on so much tedious math! Yep, there were over a million people in that caravan. Would make a great commercial for Chrysler's Dodge Caravan!

Deuteronomy:

- Here is another difficult book to read. Some of the social rules are straight out of a Neanderthal Cave Manual. Imagine, stoning a rebellious teen as prescribed in Deut 21: 18-21? Well, come to think of it, similar thoughts have passed through our minds on occasion when trying to deal with an errant teen! We do recognize the health issues at stake, but really, folks, some are a bit gross for our modern world!

Joshua:

- In the 1930's a woman archeologist proposed an amazing hypothesis: the remnants at the town of Ai indicated that it was the place that the Israelites destroyed first. Most of the male establishment disputed her thesis. You can read about the technical problems disputing that whole Jericho folk tale in Gerald A. Larue's Internet writings. See Appendix L, #9. Not only that but Jericho may very well have fallen apart due to an earthquake rather than a conquest by the Israelites. Ho hum, we've got to include this story in the category of folk myth after all.

Judges:

- Isn't it obvious that there are just 12 Judges of note to write about in this book? Numerology again!

Ezekiel

- 33: 11 *"Answer them: As I live, says the Lord GOD, I swear I take no pleasure in the death of the wicked man, but rather in the wicked man's conversion, that he may live. Turn, turn from your evil ways! Why should you die, O house of Israel?"*

- 33: 14 *"And though I say to the wicked man that he shall surely die, if he turns away from his sin and does what is right and just, 15 giving back pledges, restoring stolen goods, living by the statutes that bring life, and doing no wrong, he shall surely live, he shall not die. 16 None of the sins he committed shall be held against him; he has done what is right and just, he shall surely live."*

In closing this Chapter we thought that we should make a very positive note. These two verses in Ezekiel make the strongest argument for a merciful and forgiving God very much unlike the portrait of a punishing God that has dominated the larger portion of the Hebrew Testament. As a matter of interpretation, these explain why Yeshua ate with and preached to the alleged sinners who were really the very impoverished and helpless of that period.

In addition, we recognized a latent problem. If people are to be punished for eternity, why does God always speak of death: "surely you shall die"? Also, why is God the God of the living not the God of the dead? {See Mk 12: 27, Matt 22: 33, Lk 20: 38

and Wisdom 1: 12-13} Why does the word "destruction" appear in sentences that speak of the death of the obdurate? Could it be that God's justice is NOT like Human Justice? Is it not reasonable to project God's justice to be annihilation rather than eternal punishment? Meditate on this one for a while!

And, thus ends our trek through the Hebrew Testament. There are undoubtedly more errors that we could find but the task is too daunting. To record every error might just run the total number of pages up to the size of an Encyclopedia. Not for this book!

The Summary

The sum and substance of this Chapter is contained in this line: "For a book of this magnitude, the Bible, to be of Divine origin, one error is one too many". We have pointed to more than enough to cast a reasonable doubt about the meaning of "inspiration". For the most part, whether we read the Bible in the original languages or in today's vernacular, humans with all their imperfect, frail and fallible baggage wrote all the Sacred Scriptures and particularly the Bible! However, One must never forget, the Spirit of God does speak through the Bible's mythical composition as does the Spirit of God in all the other Sacred Scriptures! One must be careful not to get caught up in the literal interpretation. There are many verses that are not of God, so wrote the Author of "Satanic Verses:.

In closing this search for errors, mistakes and contradictions, let us quote the mythical Fourth Gospel for an interesting faith statement.

> John 5: 37-40 *Moreover, the Father who sent me has testified on my behalf. But you have never heard his voice nor seen his form, and you do not have his word remaining in you, because you do not believe in the one whom he has sent. <u>You search the scriptures, because you think you have eternal life through them</u>; even they testify on my behalf. But you do not want to come to me to have life.*
> Are the authors telling us that worshiping the literalness of the Bible leads to naught? Is not relationship more important? When the Zen Master pointed to the Sun, his disciples focused on his finger. Are the Literalists worshiping the Son or the finger-written Book?

The real challenge is to discover for yourselves an authentic, serious message from God within the Legends and Myths of all Sacred Scriptures and their implications for living your lives in peace and harmony with your neighbors and your God. Do you understand now why the Zen master had to burn down the Temple?

We have almost destroyed the inerrancy of the Bible but caution you to realize that for the first time you now know why the Sacred Scriptures, with all their problems, are really boos of faith statements made by a sincere group of authors trying to pass on their belief in the teachings of God and Ger prophets. Unless you read them all in that manner you will miss the deep Godly meanings left for you within the legends, myths and aphorisms/parables.

In the next Chapter we'll begin to re-install God's Heart into the people!

281

Here are a couple of thoughts before jumping unto the next Chapter.

In the camp of fundamentalism, people make their own personal doctrinal interpretations. Then they infer that they are saved by means of their own "true doctrines" rather than saved by a redemptive relationship with their God. It follows that all others are incorrect and will not be saved. However, few realize that under this condition none will be saved because there aren't two people who have the same doctrinal interpretation.

R.D. Moon, PhD

The point is that neither worshiping a book or a piece of bread leads to eternal life! Only a relationship with God and with your neighbor leads to wholeness and holiness.

Marcel Etienne Rebelleux, 1931

CHAPTER SIX

WHAT DID YESHUA REALLY TELL US?

The goal of this Chapter is to re-discover the nature of the teachings of Yeshua the Carpenter from Nazareth. We have already demonstrated that the preponderance of the Christian Testament is a fictionalized faith-based remembrance of the life and times of this 1st century prophet and teacher. Because of the confusion between facts and myth there will certainly be significant barriers to our search for the real preachings of Yeshua and, therefore, one's personal meaning. However, there are many bits and pieces, that, when uncovered, will contribute sufficient information to help us achieve what we are setting out to accomplish. Our hope is that this information will lead us to a new meaning to the "Jesus Movement" and, thus, to a new picture of the Face of God.

To begin, we must first put this Yeshua into the context of that 1st century's enculturation. We will have to frame his life experiences in a country of very religious people whose baggage is its history as a Chosen People. Most importantly, we have to understand the backdrop for the teachings of Jesus in a Nation allegedly in relationship with the One God ... the Holy One of Israel ... the Spirit of Holiness. Remember, we are dealing with a people who believe that God chose them. But, could it have been that they chose this Divinity in their desperation as a very downtrodden, suffering, slave nation trapped in Egypt? Could it have been that an Egyptian Arab Prince took it upon himself to lead them to a land full of promise? Could several natural phenomena have occurred that not only permitted the Exodus but also encouraged that desert safari? Whichever you decide, truth or myth, the reality is that a nation of people traversed the Sinai Peninsula, experienced a numinous epiphany that altered their lives and settled in a land they called Israel. The history of that people has been told and read throughout the world ever since. Without this knowledge the life and teachings of Jesus would be incomprehensible!

Therefore, let's spend a few paragraphs reviewing a brief history of these suffering servants of the One God whom they believed chose them to be the Light to the World (Isaiah 44: 21 26).

> *"21 Remember this, O Jacob, you, O Israel, who are my servant! I formed you to be a servant to me; O Israel, by me you shall never be forgotten: 22 <u>I have brushed away your offenses</u> like a cloud, your sins like a mist; return to me, for <u>I have redeemed you</u>. 23 Raise a glad cry, you heavens: the LORD has done this; shout, you depths of the earth. Break forth, you mountains, into song, you forest, with all your trees. For <u>the LORD has redeemed Jacob</u>, and shows his glory through Israel. 24 Thus says <u>the LORD, your redeemer</u>, who formed you from the womb: I am the LORD, who made all things, who alone stretched out the heavens; when I spread out the earth, who was with me? 25 It is I who bring to nought the omens of liars, who make fools of diviners; I turn wise men back and make their knowledge foolish. 26 It is I who confirm the words of my*

servants, I carry out the plan announced by my messengers; I say to Jerusalem: Be inhabited; to the cities of Judah: Be rebuilt; I will raise up their ruins."

PART ONE: The12 Judaic Contributions

1. The Preparation

The nucleus of Israel drew its existence out of Egypt from the very large number of human slaves who were being abused beyond civility. To whom they prayed is not known for certain but those suffering people felt abandoned by the gods of their perception. One day as an Egyptian Prince was passing, he witnessed a brutal beating of an old slave in the mixing pits. He was so filled with compassion that he struck the angry perpetrator and killed him. Immediately his conscience drove him to flee the scene and he disappeared into the mountains. To secure his hiding place this Prince shed his royal clothing and took the garb of the mountain people.

One clear day he spied a burning bush and it spoke to his spirit. The voice demanded that he remove his sandals for the ground on which he walked was sacred. The voice spoke of its concern for those slaves in Egypt who were to be His People. Then the voice pronounced its name, "yod-he-waw-he " in Hebrew, Yahweh in translation, meaning "I AM Becoming". That name has been proclaimed around the world ever since. The epiphany experienced by this Moses changed the man, altered the fate of more than a million foreign slaves and, to most, defined the sacredness of both creation and human life itself.

2. The Passover

Getting out of Egypt was a gargantuan confrontation and the mythic stories of that struggle abound in the Israelite literature, especially the Exodus. Once released, the former slaves felt the presence of a mighty force guarding them; nature provided it in the form of dust devils by day and huge methane flaming bursts by night. Simple people saw a numinous spirit in those eerie displays. The unruly army needed strong leadership and the mighty Moses was very familiar with the affairs of state from his royal days in Egypt. His knowledge of the Laws of Ra provided him with the ingredients to establish order and command of that army. The trek proceeded from water hole to water hole; the desert was unrelinquishingly harsh. Dissatisfaction soon infected the moving column of men, women and children traveling with household goods and their animals. Many times Moses had to quell the confusion, fear and anger that caused this dissention. Then one day they approached an old frothing volcano and, lo and behold, it came to life! It belched black clouds that hid the desert sun for days; it threw burning stone missiles down its ragged slopes; it froze the people in awe and trembling fear. This Moses went up the mountain and there experienced his second epiphany: a supernatural encounter with the thunder and lightning Spirit from whom, it was told, the Laws of a new Nation were spoken and imprinted on two stone tablets. It was then that these twelve tribes of people accepted themselves as one family, one people of one Nation empowered by their One God, Yahweh.

This saga is remembered each and every year in a Passover Ceremony with the unleavened bread and bitter herbs of sacrifice along with the wine of joy to celebrate their entry into the promised land in anticipation of the future eternal Promised Land. Moses had delivered a set of Laws to govern their lives in civility, the Ten Commandments.

3. The Covenant

The Spirit of Thunder spoke clearly of its need for fidelity, trust and ritualistic devotion from this newly formed nation of foreigners. The Spirit of Lightning made a covenant with them. They would be the people of this Spirit who would favor them with gracious mercy and provide a homeland in which they would prosper. Henceforth it would be known as the Covenant of Divine Self-Giving Love. The only requirement in their covenant was the demand for fidelity to the Law, loyalty to the other people of this new Nation and, most of all, absolute trust in "yod-he-waw-he" the I AM Becoming, the Holy One of Israel, the Spirit of Holiness

Then Moses asked to see the Glory of this Yahweh. The Voice said that no one could see its face lest he die. Moses' epiphany consisted in viewing the "behind of God". This extraordinary experience allowed Moses to understand the works of God only much after the event took place. From then onwards, Moses comprehended the meaning of his life, his purpose and the role he played in bringing freedom to the Chosen People ordained by the Holy One of Israel. Thus, we too are able to see God's hand in our daily experiences, but only much after the events.

4. The One God

These sons and daughters of Israel had met the One God of Creation, the Unconditional Self-Giver of Life. The "I AM Becoming" pierced through the wall of silence and entered the consciousness of humankind and re-formed humanity's concept of the Divine.

- "Hear, Oh Israel, the LORD, thy God, the LORD is ONE."(Deut 6: 4)
- "Thus says the LORD, Israel's King and redeemer, the LORD of hosts: I am the first and I am the last; there is no God but me." (Isaiah 44: 6)
- "Fear not, be not troubled: did I not announce and foretell it long ago? You are my witnesses! Is there a God or any Rock besides me? (Isaiah 44: 8)

History was changed in those 40 years of meandering travel to a promised land; the nature-gods were finally interred in the dust of time to be worshipped no more. Life had taken on a new meaning that gave hope to human suffering. The World would soon hear about the communication with the Supreme Creator and each person was soon to be confronted with the choice of God's Way or Destruction's way.

5. The Choice (Deut 30:19)

This mighty "I AM Becoming" spoke once more and placed this supreme choice at the feet of this Nation of foreigners, "I place before you Life and Death, Eternal Existence or personal annihilation, Being or Nothingness, Banquet or Sheol. CHOOSE Life ... Existence ... Be-ing and Banquet in My Eternal Presence!" Know this! It will be your singular choice! "God will not violate your freedom to choose!" The One God of Israel could now communicate with humankind because humankind had passed through physiological, psychological and spiritual puberty making free will an intellectual characteristic of human maturity.

6. **The Promised Land**

And it came to pass that this mighty army of immigrants conquered the new land guided by "I AM Becoming". They settled on both sides of the great Jordan River. Peace permeated the Land for many years. For those years each one of the twelve tribes was ruled by one of the Judges. But true to form, humans became dissatisfied with the status quo and envy raised its ugly head. The people demanded a King and a kingdom like other Nations.

7. **The Kingdom**

The holy prophet, Samuel, chose and anointed a leader, Saul, from among the people. He was followed by a younger man who slew a giant in proof of his potential. This second King of Israel turned out to be the great leader, David by name. He was remembered for his popularity and leadership. It is believed to this very day that David's relationship with God resulted in a promise that through his progeny there would come the greatest King of all. Sadly, David's great power led to great disappointment. Then, Solomon, David's son, became the third King to occupy the throne of Israel. By the last days of Solomon the King was also known as the "Anointed One" and the "Son of God" because he was God's representative to the Nation of Israel. The word for anointing with oil in English is *Messiah*! Later, Messiah, King, Savior and Son of God became synonyms!

8. **The Glory**

Solomon grew into the wisest of all Kings and the Nation thrived on his masterful leadership. The Nation of Israel became the richest of all the Middle East countries. All commerce passed through this thriving junction between the Far East and the Western countries. All the people benefited from the richest to the poorest. The reign and wisdom of Solomon was the Glory of Israel and stories of his greatness were told throughout the lands. In gratitude to the God of Israel, Solomon designed and built a Temple for the LORD of Lords.

9. **The Temple**

In Israel the grandeur of the Temple stood high on Jerusalem's mount. Moses himself designated the tribe of Levi to priest the rituals of atonement and maintain the standards of worship, sin offerings and cleanliness. This monument to the Numinous "I AM Becoming" became the center of Israelite life and worship. Those Levitical rituals have continued to this very day in both Israel's daily prayer and the Vatican's celebrations, ordinations and daily worship.

Because of the duties and responsibilities not only did the Levitical tribe of priesthood become prestigious and wealthy but also did the High Priest become a politically and financially powerful individual.

10. The Failures

Human nature is such that, in the hands of a few, power corrupts and absolute Power in the hands of one person corrupts absolutely. The history of the World Powers confirms it; Israel exemplified it. King after King failed the people. The people disregarded the Laws of Moses and infidelity to the Great "I AM Becoming" spread like the desert winds blowing across the land of Israel.

Catastrophe struck the Nation in the form of conquering marauders who plundered the land and destroyed the Temple. Most Israelites were removed from this Promised Land and dispersed throughout the Eastern and Western nations. Babylon was the destroyer (593 BC); Babylon brought many to its own land and it was there that the captive Israelites were introduced to, the Babylonian Sacred Scriptures. The Sumerian "Enuma Elish" spoke of the beginning of the world. It influenced the authors of Genesis 1 and 2. The gods, Apsu and Tiamat, gave birth to Marduk who became the Creator of the World. There were many nature gods and an evil god formed snakes and dragons to war against the ruling gods but that evil one was eventually overcome. The Epic of Gilgamesh contained a story of a great pre-historic Flood (the end of the Ice Age) that in later years was transcribed into the mythic tale of Noah and his Ark. The Israelites remained in captivity, abandoned by their God. During that exile, called the Diaspora, hope for a new King in the likes of David and Solomon grew in the hearts of every suffering Israelite. They yearned for a savior, a new Anointed One, a Faithful King, a true son of God-- a Messiah.

11. The Promise

By the time the Diaspora ended (539 BC) the returning Israelites had cemented the idea that eventually the great "I AM Becoming" would deliver the scattered peoples of Israel back to their own country. This would take place at some future moment (the End Times) when a human-like person (this Messiah) would descend to the Earth on a cloud.

There followed a period during which the scribes (in the likes of Ezra) documented the history of Israel. First the stories of the Israelite history were assembled into the books of the Torah, then the remaining books of the Hebrew Testament were written over the next 400 years. The preponderance of history recalled was in actuality history mythologized by a faith perceived by the authors in that late sixth century BC. Following that exile the principle books were assembled slowly into the canon called the Hebrew Testament (the TANAK).

The yearnings for an eternal Messiah were simply for an eternal King who would lead the Israelites in battle to conquer the other Nations. Israel would then return to its lost Glory. Through the following centuries the longing became woven into the mythic stories of future justice to be implemented by this God-sent Messiah.

This idea of a Messiah grew into a cult unto itself; the Israelite people still to this very day pray to God that God will establish a Nation headed by this Messiah, this new King, this Anointed One, this Son of God. Then the great Era of peace will certainly follow. The prophetic voices rang throughout the hills of Israel announcing the imminent arrival of the Messiah.

12. The Wisdom and the Prophets

Prior to the onset of the Prophetic movement in Israel there were collected several literary books that became known as the Wisdom Literature. These preserved the knowledge and experience of the Israelite sages and people through the centuries. In certain books there were writings in a mythic style that put forth personification of spiritual abstractions. Proverbs 8, for example, praised wisdom as though it were a person. It gives an honored position to wisdom and recommends that she be pursued and captured. Then there is the pessimistic book of Ecclesiastes, the humor of Proverbs, the love story of the Song of Songs, the trials of Job, the musical poetry of the Psalms that praise God, the machinations of the philosopher in the book of Wisdom and, finally, the book of Sirach whose author wrote:

> ".. With indulgence for any apparent failure on our part, despite earnest efforts, in the interpretation of particular passages. For words spoken originally in Hebrew are not as effective when they are translated into another language. That is true not only of this book but of the law itself, the prophets and the rest of the books, which differ no little when they are read in the original."

All these words give clear evidence of the real nature of the Old Testament that was translated into Greek and became the Septuagint of the Christians. That book was also the singular Bible for all the Greek-speaking Israelites throughout the Mediterranean Basin from 270 BC until 400 AD.

There were two classes of Prophets who spoke for the Great "I AM Becoming": the major ones and the minor ones. The word prophet is a Greek word meaning to speak for someone. The themes of each of the prophets were remembered, elaborated and mythologized over those last 5 centuries BC. Their stories were penned decades and centuries after the death of the prophet. Only the ones whose words were found to speak for the Great "I AM Becoming" were honored and written into the books we find in the Hebrew Testament. All others were either forgotten or lost.

Isaiah spoke of the worthlessness of ritual, the meritorious suffering of the servant people of Israel, (noted above) and the eventual salvation of the just and punishment of the unjust. Jeremiah was chartered to caution the actions of Israel and then announce the New Jerusalem under the new covenant with God (31: 31-34). Ezekiel is again a speaker for the God of Israel; Ezekiel eats the scroll of knowledge. Ezekiel defines the fate of the evil ones who choose freely to perish (whole Chapter 18) but who will be forgiven if they choose to do good. These are surely the words of the forgiving and merciful God of Israel.

One final prophet is necessary to quote because he ushers in the last great thought for the people of Israel. The new King would come to Israel as spectacularly as a human descending from heaven on a cloud. According to the NAB, "Daniel the hero of this mythic tale lived before 538 BC but the actual writings were composed about the time of the persecution by Antiochus IV Epiphanes (167-164 BC)" and it resounded in the minds and hearts of all of Israel and still fills scholars and religious followers in this 21st century with futuristic wonderment.

PART TWO: The Last Prophet

We have finally arrived at the demarcation of history; BC was reset to the approximated birth of Yeshua and AD begun from that point (even though he was born between 6 and 4 BC, go figure!). The moment was ripe with Messianic expectation in Israel and boiling with anger at the Roman conquest. Israel had weathered the conquering Greeks and was now facing a brutal Roman government. The One God was waiting anxiously for another prophet to come along. Yahweh always worked with the simple, humble peasants of the world; for God's power was made the more excellent in human weakness (II Corin 12: 9). When a young pregnant maiden was in need because of her condition, a carpenter named Joseph took her into his household as his wife. The child was born in Nazareth under questionable circumstances. God knew that this was the opportune moment for a deeply spiritual relationship with this peasant boy. They, God and Yeshua, became intimate friends and Yeshua grew in age and wisdom. In his early 30's Yeshua, filled with the Spirit of God, laid down his father's tools, left his shop and began the mission of his vision.

Section I: The Yeshua Movement

Yeshua of Nazareth had heard about the Baptist and sought him out. Following his brief discipleship with John, Yeshua proclaimed the "Good News" of God's Kingdom in the here and now, available to all. This "Good News" was demonstrated by Yeshua's table fellowship, his miraculous cures, and his explanations of the meaning of God's commandments. He spoke in parables, allegories and similes; he coined aphorisms, redefined old cumbersome legalisms and presented new insights into the nature of a God of grace, compassion, mercy and forgiveness. The core of his teachings are summarized in what follows:

A. As a faithful Israelite*, Yeshua worked within the Mosaic Tradition;
B. As a prophet*, Yeshua spoke authoritatively for God;
C. As a Teacher*, Yeshua re-defined the spirit of the Law;
D. As a psychologically mature adult*, he walked his talk;
E. As a spiritual person*, he performed mighty deeds;
F. As a man of wisdom*, he spoke poignant aphorisms and told memorable and meaningful parables

*To read more about these, see the writings of Marcus Borg in Appendix R, specifically, "Meeting Jesus Again for the First Time"

Section II: Re-discovering the Historical Yeshua

We will now delineate the core teachings of this most important prophet, that is, take out the mythologizing and examine the central teachings of Yeshua. Before we move into the history, let us mention that the first thing the listeners understood about Yeshua was the title they gave him—**the** Messiah and **the** Christos. With those titles (each meaning the "Anointed One") came the additional titles of the King of Israel: the son of God and the son of David! Also, associated with the anointing are the words of Psalm 2 (see Appendix S).

We will begin by discovering the authentic teachings of Yeshua within the Synoptic Gospels. You know, that's the material in Mark, Matthew and Luke. Well, we did this very exercise over twenty-five years ago in one of our Bible Study groups. First we had to identify, in the Greek text, what was from Mark and remove it from both the Greek texts of Matthew and Luke. This was necessary because each had distorted what they had copied from Mark. Second, we had to extract the similar material in Matthew and Luke; that we did in the English. Now, we assembled the words allegedly spoken by Yeshua. What we had should, in all likelihood, be the source for our examination. Why that criteria? Because the criteria eliminates the big mythologized sections in the Synoptic Gospels. We definitely did not consider the Fourth Gospel. You will understand this better after you read our commentary in a later part of this Chapter.

Because of the Chalcedon decision we must try to examine only that which is essentially from the human Yeshua's preachings and teachings. Let's restate our dilemma in these terms: "If one has to be Divine to know and live what Yeshua said and did, then we poor imperfect, frail and fragile humans could not meet the criteria of any of Yeshua's teachings or actions!" Yeshua of necessity must be totally human. Then Romans 1: 3-4 resonates with authenticity and only a human person could be promoted in accordance with Ephesians 3: 17-19:

> *... and that {the} Christ may dwell in your hearts {the metaphor means spirit} through faith; that you, rooted and grounded in love, may have strength to comprehend with all the holy ones what is the breadth and length and height and depth, and to know the love of {the} Christ that surpasses knowledge {experience}, so that you may be filled with all the fullness of God.*
> { } are this author's additions for clarity.

Once you decide what the "fullness of God" is, we can agree that it will be the reward for your faith and fidelity to God's WAY of doing business in this life. As far as we are concerned that's exactly what Romans 1: 3-4 means! Oh yes, don't forget the three passages in Acts that repeat the Apostolic preaching of, essentially, the same conviction.

Aphorisms, parables and stories that can be authenticated will be the essential clues to defining what Yeshua preached and taught: the "Jesus Movement". Following that process we'll highlight the Christian Movement after which we've placed our commentary and interpretation of the Fourth Gospel. We hope to demonstrate how a mythologized Gospel of the authors' Faith can be an important contribution to the meaning of the "Jesus Movement".

Therefore, we now have the ingredients to establish the nature of this so-called "Jesus Movement". The following are what we've extracted from the Synoptic Gospels. In most cases we've taken the liberty to modernize the deeper significance for our 21st century readers. Enjoy!

THE TRUE TEACHINGS OF YESHUA

A. The Aphorisms:

"Do to others just like you would want others to do to you"
"Love God with your whole being and your neighbor as yourself"
"Know thyself. Remove those cataracts from your own eyes first,"
"If someone asks you to walk a mile with him, walk two miles"
"Sell all you have and give the proceeds to the poor and follow me"
"Choose NOW, change your behavior"
"Pray for your enemies; forgive those who hurt or hate you"
"If you do not forgive, neither will God forgive your transgressions"
"Humans who seek justice are mostly those who cannot forgive"
"Where your treasure is, there is where your heart will be"
"Store up treasure for the hereafter, you can't take anything with you"
"Help the poor, the sick, the widows and the orphans"
"Go in peace, your sins are forgiven; get with it, dude, you're well again."
"Go wash the prejudice from your own eyes, and you'll see again"
"Give me your loaves and fishes. Food is for sharing not worshiping"
"Do not fear change; make a leap of faith; slake your spiritual hunger with the new wine!"
"Do not build your faith on Sacred Scriptures, build on God."
"Pay attention to the signs of the Kingdom, the blind see, the sick are healed and the deaf hear"
"Come one, come all to God's wedding feast"
"I did not come to call not only the righteous but also the sinners."
"Come to God, all who thirst and hunger; God will refresh you"
"God's grace is sufficient for you"
"Render to civil authorities what is their due and to God, what is God's"
"There is a Power that is greater than anyone you know "
"Seek first the Community of God and all else will be provided"
"Hey, just ask, seek and knock, you'll get it, find it and a door *will* open"
"The Sabbath doesn't rule Humans; humans rule the Sabbath."
"A clean mind is more important than clean hands"
"Daughter, your faith has saved you. Go in peace and be cured of your affliction."
"Do not be afraid; just have faith."
"Take courage, it is I, do not be afraid!"
"How well you have set aside the commandment of God in order to uphold your traditions!
'This people honors the Father with their lips, but their hearts are far from Him;
"But what words come out of the mouth, that is what defiles."
"From within people, from their minds, come evil."
"Watch out, guard against the leaven of the Institutionalism and the leaven of Wealth."
"What profit is there for one to gain the whole world and forfeit his eternal life?"
"Everything is possible to one who has faith."
"If anyone wishes to be first, he shall be the last and the servant of all."
"The gate to life is narrow. And those who find it are few."
"It is easier for a camel to pass through (the) eye of (the) Needle than for one who is rich to enter the kingdom of God."
"Go, sell what you have, and give to (the) poor and you will have treasure in heaven; then come, follow me."

"Suffering builds character, but it usually ends after 39 hours! [Friday at 3 pm to Sun at six am]
"Love your enemies, do good to those who hate you"
"Bless those who curse you, and pray for those who spitefully use you."
"To him who strikes you on the one cheek, offer the other also."
"From him who takes away your cloak, do not withhold your tunic either."
"Give to everyone who asks of you."
"From him who takes away your goods do not ask them back."
"Just as you want men to do to you, you also do to them likewise."
"Love your enemies, do good, and lend, hoping for nothing in return."
"Judge not, and you shall not be judged. "
"Condemn not, and you shall not be condemned. "
"Forgive, and you will be forgiven."
"Not everyone who cries, 'Lord, Lord,' will enter the kingdom of heaven "
"Give, and it will be given to you."
"A good tree does not bear bad fruit, nor does a bad tree bear good fruit."
"For every tree is known by its own fruit"
"For out of the abundance of one's compassion the mouth speaks."
"The harvest truly is great, but the laborers are few."
"You cannot serve God and money."
"Whoever seeks to save his life will lose it, and whoever loses his life will preserve it."

B. The Parables

The parable of the wedding invitations.
The parable of the seeds thrown on good soil and on rocks.
The allegories of the lost coin, the lost sheep and the lost son.
The parable of sewing a new cloth on an old garment.
The parable of pouring new wine into old skins.
The parable of a house divided against itself
The simile of the Kingdom of God and the mustard seed.
The simile of the salt losing its savor.
The parable of the landlord traveling and the end time.
The parable of the blind leading the blind.
The parable of the houses built on rock vs. on sand.
The parable of the lamp placed where it can be seen.
The parable of the thief at night.
The parable of the wise and faithful servant.
The simile of the Kingdom of God being like leaven.
The parable of the great feast and the refused invitations.
The parable of the talents.
The parable of the Good Shepherd.
The Metaphor of the Vine and Branches
The parable of the workers in the field and the day's wages
The simile of the mustard seed.

B. Miscellaneous

The Beatitudes
The "Our Father" (Of the three, Luke's is nearest to Yeshua's teachings)

Section III: The Interpreted Meaning

Now that you've read all those authentic sayings and parables of Yeshua, do you understand what is asked of you?

A. Is there any reference to Institution?
B. Are there any "must believe" doctrines?
C. Are there any Dogmas?
D. What rituals did they prescribe?
E. Did Yeshua assign any hierarchy?
F. Does God communicate through any special priesthood or gatekeeper?

The answer to each and every question is **NO!** Men created Institutions! Men, and we do mean males, created doctrines. Males concocted Dogmas. Self-serving Temple elitists devised rituals. It was Paul's (See 1 Corin 12:28) interpretation that ordered a hierarchy to maintain Christian order just as was done in the time of Moses. That was followed by Constantine's assignment of Church Officials to be the Judicial Supreme Court of his Empire. Only in one person's understanding (1 Peter 2: 9) was the topic of priesthood shot down but revived in later centuries. What exists today is man-made! It is a structure of control and power over the people! None of it was Yeshua's intention!

Because of Yeshua's announcement of the Kingdom of God and the people's association of Yeshua with the expected Messiah, an uncomfortable fear rose in the minds of the ruling Levites and the Roman authorities who in consort with the High Priest of Jerusalem crucified this local revolutionary. And, then, there was the Resurrection and the complete *metanoia* of Yeshua's small group of followers. The World has never been the same since that Sunday, the first day of the spiritual revolution.

PART THREE: Implementing the Message of THE Christ

Section I: The Beginning of the Apostolic Movement

Have you ever paused for a moment and contemplated that the existence of Christianity is the result of one single event in history? That's true, you know! That event was the Resurrection. Had it never occurred, there wouldn't have been a group of men and women so motivated and empowered that they chose not to return to their mundane existence but rather chose to bring their discovery to the rest of the world. For millennia upon millennia the majority of humankind suffered in ignorance of any life-giving meaning to their existence. Writing was invented 6000 years ago and since then there have been many prophets claiming to possess the absolute meaning of LIFE. The Sacred Scriptures are their teachings. Two thousand years ago a small group of men and women came out of an insignificant (but troubling) conquered country and offered their answer to life's purpose. This Satori, Peak Experience, Epiphany (or any other defining term for this event you can use) of the Resurrection spoke clearly of a new dawn in human relationships with the Divine. We have a record, albeit, a slightly mythical one, of the impact of that singular event. That record is the Christian Testament that describes, with a literary style prevalent in that first century culture, the teachings of one Yeshua the Carpenter. He, and he alone, proposed a lifestyle that turned the conventional way of doing business upside down. He spoke in such simple terms that no one can misinterpret him; one can only reject him out of hand! Who he was and what he did and said appear to have been authenticated by means of that Resurrection. God raised Yeshua from the dead and gave Yeshua titles so profound that some find them too extraordinary and refuse to acknowledge what Yeshua taught during his ministry.

There was total chaos among the disciples when Yeshua was crucified and died. Whatever happened on that Sunday morning changed their fear and discouragement into courage and motivation. The disciples proclaimed the good news of Yeshua's Resurrection! Many people came to believe in Yeshua and acknowledged him as the anticipated Messiah of God. Allegedly, Yeshua was reported to have explained everything concerning his life and its meaning using Hebrew Testament passages. The Apostles in turn proclaimed it to the people who held to "what the Apostles handed down". The Apostles preached that this man, Yeshua, was raised from the dead by God and given titles and the "Name above all names" by means of that Resurrection, the Divine authenticated the teachings of Yeshua!

Section II: The Pauline Movement

Paul's ministry to the gentile world converted thousands and established many Christian communities. Paul wrote many epistles containing his own interpretations of the meaning of Yeshua's teachings. Paul was a complex person and his theological explanations equally difficult to understand. Those letters confused many, including Peter, James and many men and women throughout the following centuries. Many folk tales, phony Epistles and distorted Gospels circulated among the Christian communities, the result of which produced a deeply polarizing confusion between communities. Along with that state of affairs, Paul assigned people to a charismatic order of authority (1 Corin 12: 28) in hopes of controlling those misunderstandings. This turned out to be the worst decision that any Apostle could have made. Power was placed in the hands of a few with the administrator second from the bottom. Thus did Paul leave this earth with the seeds for one more Institution. That initiated the Episcopal Period.

Section III: Episcopal Period

Then toward the end of the 60's (69 AD, that is) the order of responsibilities flipped over and the administrator (at nearly the bottom of the ladder) became the Bishop (at the top of the ladder). Bishops along with their communities developed a variety of doctrinal theologies from the myriad folk stories haphazardly circulating through Christian communities. [Remember, no email or Post Office Service and worse, the majority of the first century Christians couldn't read or write!] Several of the roving missionaries were not permitted to preach in some communities because of their conflicting theology. Disagreements arose quickly but quietly within each community. A doctrinal crisis of confusion was born in spite of the Bishop's defense of "What the Apostles handed down." After forty years of varying oral traditions, apocryphal Epistles and distorted Gospels, the Bishops hardly remembered what it was that "the Apostles handed down".

Section IV: The Gospel Period

To make matters more complicated, the first Gospel (Mark) changed the Christological moment from what the Apostles preached; Matthew and Luke followed Mark's lead but pushed an earlier Christology with their contradictory Infancy Narratives. The Fourth Gospel, somewhat Gnostic in character, promoted Yeshua to the epitome of being; Yeshua was declared eternally God. From the late 1st century until the early 4th century, theological chaos ruled supreme over the Empire and Christian communities argued and fought with their Christian neighbors with intellectual and physical fervor (sometimes far too physical).

Section V: The Meanings within the Mythologized Fourth Gospel

By the time of the writing of this Fourth Gospel, in one corner of the Empire, the actual recollections of the life and times of Yeshua had dissolved into a mythical historical mist. The faded memories of Yeshua's humanity were replaced with mythologized tales of a Divine Being who spoke and acted in total control, much like a Gnostic rendition of a god-man of infinite knowledge and power. The five authors (suspected because of five distinct literary styles) appeared to have had no personal contact with the pre-Resurrectional Yeshua even though one alleged author of this Gospel bears the name of John the Apostle. The tone and style of the Gospel is one of mini-stories (vignettes, even!) each of which having great theological significance to the authors who penned their personal belief in Yeshua's meaning rather than in his actual history. The dialogues of Yeshua are not that of a fully human person (be mindful of 1 John 4: 2-3 and Chalcedon, 451 AD); no human possesses such knowledge and control of events as this constructed characterization of Yeshua in this Gospel. One wonders why it was chosen and given such honor as to be the fourth biography. But, then, after our re-interpretations, you may see its true value.

We believe that reading the Introduction to the Fourth Gospel in the NAB is necessary for you to really understand what our interpretations will unfold about this complicated Gospel. Please, take the time now. If you're using another version of the Bible, you can read the New American Bible from the Internet at:
http://www.nccbuscc.org/nab/

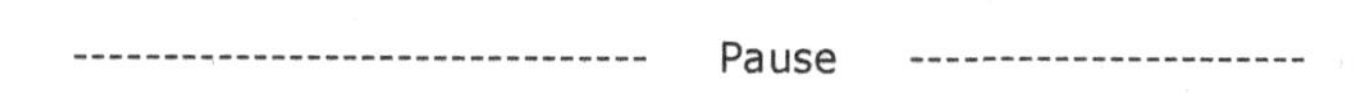

OK, now that you've read the Introduction, settle comfortably in your chair and prepare yourself to re-discover another perspective of the deeper meaning intended by those authors who hid much between the printed lines. In other words, the key to unfolding the spirituality of the Fourth Gospel is to put aside the literal story of each Chapter and focus only on its significance. This challenge is like analyzing itsy bitsy pieces of a jigsaw puzzle to find the relating colors and the slots into which each piece fits. There are hints (signs) pointing to a meaningful picture. However, in this Gospel the picture is about the eternal landscape. In truth, each Chapter of the Fourth Gospel simply presents a piece of the theological and spiritual puzzle in disguised allegorical and metaphorical vignettes that express the faith of the five authors, their belief structure and their world-view.

Oftentimes we humans are not aware of the plethora of signs of eternal life that are all around us. Every town has a sign; each street has its own sign; every home has its numbered sign; there are directional signs on all our highways. There are advertising signs all over the countryside; each business has signs at the entrances; inside there are signs for the stairways, elevators and the location of the key personnel. We humans could not live without signs! If we are intelligent enough to place signs all over the highways, byways and city streets helping us to our destination, don't you think that God wouldn't place an abundance of signs pointing to eternal life?

The pattern, in which the signs are posted in each Chapter (vignette) of this Gospel, is generally like this: (1) an introduction to the event; (2) the major sign presented in an allegorical setting; (3) a contrived discussion with Yeshua's opponents or his disciples; (4) and an epilogue or summary as the author's theological revelations that clearly identify Yeshua as God's definitive sign or pathway leading to eternal life. In spite of the author's contrived stories, the meaning is what is important whether one is a literalist or a modernist. The discussion that follows focuses solely on the interpreted meaning! Of course, all this is only our humble researched opinion. You are not obliged to accept what is proffered.

One next observation is to take some of the confusion out of the peculiar designations of chapter and verse. The original manuscripts were written in Greek uncials (no spaces, no punctuation) without designating chapter and verse. We are convinced that the monks who separated the letters into words and wrote in the numbers for chapter and verse had either no concept of literature or before they did their job had imbibed a bit of the "juice" (grape, that is, with 12 % vinegeistgehalt, "the ghost of the vine"!). At times the punctuation was poorly chosen and confusing. At times principal thoughts were divided into separate verses.

Lastly, one must understand that Gnosticism is a religion of secrecy: secret information handed down by the Ancients for the select few who could benefit by understanding the mysteries of life. This Gospel hints at the secret knowledge possessed by Yeshua that he dispensed cautiously in allegories, parables and similes to the general public and the Pharisees in particular. Then, Yeshua explains the meaning of those stories to his disciples in the same manner as the Gnostics. The key to this puzzlement is that Yeshua is not the speaker in this Fourth Gospel; the authors are the writers and all the words from the lips of Yeshua are the faith statements of the authors! The authors understand Yeshua in a paradigm of Gnosticism. Yeshua as the Eternal Divinity, as the Infinite Creator, must possess, by definition, all knowledge because He IS God and that's who the encultured person of the 1st century AD perceived God to be. Our only explanation of that view is that the authors had no experience of the human historical Yeshua. After close to 70 years of oral traditions and wild stories (including apocryphal Epistles and Gospels) the authors constructed their own faith stories to explain their personal perceptions and meaning of the Yeshua event. Mind you, it really appears that they may have never read any of the Synoptic triplets—the Gospels allegedly penned by Mark, Matthew and Luke! Their mission was to pass on the MEANING of Yeshua's life and teachings, as only they understood it. This Fourth Gospel is abundantly spiritually nourishing but it is NOT historically accurate nor in any way the real words and deeds of Yeshua. So, as before, you have just read our personal theological perception and are in no way required to incorporate it into your private belief structure. But, you must examine it for its novel interpretation of its so-called Gnostic character.

It's time now to read our adrenaline pumping commentary. Be still your heart and experience a mind's eye-opening portrait of Yeshua's ministry!

The Fourth Gospel:
A Contemporary Re-Analysis of a faith-based allegory

Chapter 1:

An allegory is a made up tale to convey the author's intentions. This "Good News" is that author's belief and deep faith speaking in a meaningful way exactly what he believes in story fashion with threads of facts from the Oral Traditions he has heard. One must understand that even the conversations of Yeshua are the faith expressions of these five authors.

We immediately read an amazing introductory part in which the author states his theological position. But, the first 18 verses constitute an addition to the original text, though much after it was written. Let's examine its contents and meaning.

God's thoughts existed from eternity. God put these thoughts to words (the wind-breath-spirit from the Hebrew word, *"ruwach"*). The Universe was created by means of God's breath speaking those words that instantaneously became what God spoke. Creation was an act of total self-giving; it is now the SELF of the Infinite Being that sustains all in existence. Unless God sustains all matter in existence, there would not be this Universe because the Universe is not self-sufficient. God's passion was creation; God's compassion was for all that became. As humankind evolved God watched over them with a besottedness that only a mother could appreciate. These Divine emotions found expression in the world through the Prophets of old when they spoke those words but the primitive audience recognized them not. When we met Yeshua we experienced the personification of God's words in his teachings. When Yeshua spoke those words and performed his deeds, the mind's eye of his listeners was dazzled by his wisdom and the soul's ears were bathed in the peaceful sounds of an eternal heavenly choir.

Verses 19 to 51 form the true introduction to the gospel guiding us to the story. First comes John the Baptist's tale that points to Yeshua's relation to the world.

As God planned, a prophet by name of John preceded this Yeshua. John too spoke familiar words of God, just as those previous prophets did. He pointed to the brilliance to come. John pointed to God's works and God's words by which all things were created. And then, these works and words appeared in the personhood of Yeshua. God's glory shone through this real human person whom the humble, the poor and the suffering came to regard as a reflection of God's true nature. The people experienced God's compassion through Yeshua's actions and teachings, his works and words.

The first of the signs (we'll number them) occurred when John baptized Yeshua and a bolt of light (metaphorically speaking) flashed into their spirit (first sign). Both he and John felt its intellectual presence. They both were deeply affected, to such an extent that John knew that this man would be great and Yeshua felt himself imbued with the Spirit of God. Yeshua's very presence enticed the people to "come to see" and hear him (sign 2). They found in Yeshua a spiritual attraction of affection and acceptance! And they followed him. They were certain that this man held greater meaning to their lives. Those were the signs of grace: John's pointing to Yeshua and the shouting, "Come and see for yourself". The Nathanael story supplies the theological definitions and Yeshua's discourse.

Chapter 2:

The wedding feast is a fable of finding a new life, greater than the one experienced in the present. Your life may be exhilarating, as it was for those who attended this celebration, but the new life brought to you by your experience of the man, Yeshua, will be greater still by orders of magnitude. The new wine is the physical sign (3) of a greater celebration; Yeshua is the human sign of a new spirituality (4). Woven into the story is the contrast between old wine and new wine, old skins and new skins to hold that wine.

These similes are comparing the old traditions of the Israelites towards the Mosaic Laws and the teachings of Yeshua about the new WAY to God. Wrapped up in this simile is the teaching that one cannot put the OLD ways into Yeshua's new WAY, just like new wine doesn't go into old skins. This entire wedding story at Cana is the author's strongest message that Yeshua is a corrective to the distortions of the Mosaic Laws and Rituals. Did you catch the comment by one of the guests? Why was the old wine served first and then, when all were drunk (with the old rituals!), the better wine (Yeshua) was served? Wasn't it a cleaver metaphor that Yeshua was the one who made that new wine? And, the sub metaphor of people being the old skins or new skins!

The next scene consists of Yeshua's visit to the Temple where he cleans out the crooked moneychangers. [Note: this Temple cleansing occurs at the beginning of his ministry, but it's not what the Synoptic Gospels reported!] This cleansing is the precipitator of the tension between Yeshua and his critics. Now the critics challenge the behavior and wisdom of this rebel prophet. And, Yeshua suspects their treachery in their questions and their need for magical signs. Verse 25 states that the mature Yeshua understood his humanity well enough not to share his nature with those men! Remember, "pearls to swine"?

Did you catch the opening phrase, "On the third day"? A very subtle reference to the Resurrection actually occurring on the third day, not three days in the tomb! These authors were pretty crafty, weren't they?

So, here we have two tales each telling the same thing, Yeshua is the messenger who is to correct the old traditions: first, the new Law must be stored in new hearts and, second, the Temple cleansing is the metaphor for cleaning up the distortions of the Law and Rituals of the Torah. The scene is now set for the reader to explore the nature of the new Law from God spoken through Yeshua, the man whom we can see and touch.

Chapter 3:

The next sign develops within the discussion with Nicodemus who asks Yeshua, "Where is the doorway to this new eternal life?" because he recognizes the works of Yeshua as coming from God. Yeshua moves directly into the "born again" topic and points to the simile of physical washing with water compared to a spiritual cleansing by God's grace. Yeshua is alluding to entering physical life in human birth-waters (5, an outward sign) and to spiritual life anointed by the Spirit of God (6, an inward sign). Then comes the challenge to Yeshua who then makes a lengthy discourse (actually the author's theology). At this point the author develops his theology about the true baptizer, Yeshua. [Note verse 22! The Synoptics never touch on the subject of Yeshua's disciples baptizing!]

The author puts all the correct theological words in John's mouth redirecting us to Yeshua, the true person who baptizes with the Spirit of God. Remember, John the Baptist was considered by many to have been the Messiah. The author(s) is (are) making a strong point of identifying John the Baptist as a precursor only.

Chapter 4:

This intro makes the transition by stating the baptizing done by the disciples and moves Yeshua into Samaria. There his thirst propels him to seek out Jacob's Well. Oh, surprise, there is a Samaritan woman at the well! Is this author too obvious? Now he baits the hook and casts the line with this request, "Give me a drink." The scene is now set for the real purpose of this story. There are two signs. The first is that one must recognize that Yeshua is the person (7) through whom salvation and eternal life can be obtained. The second is that women have a rightful place in the discipleship and ministry (8) of Yeshua. It's the identical message found in Luke with respect to Mary Magdalene / Magdala. Unfortunately, some of the large Christian Institutions still can't see their way to placing women on a ministerial and management par with males. {Read 1 Corin 9: 5 in the NRSV, sister-wife! A name for an unmarried woman who traveled with a man both preaching the Good News throughout the Empire. Eat your heart out Rome!} The more important verses in this chapter are 9 to 15. The dialog is so beautifully Shakespearian that they need to be repeated here.

> Jn 4: 9-15 *The Samaritan woman said to him, "How can you, a Jew, ask me, a Samaritan woman, for a drink?" (For Jews use nothing in common with Samaritans.) 10 Jesus answered and said to her, "If you knew the gift of God and who is saying to you, 'Give me a drink,' you would have asked him and he would have given you living water." 11 (The woman) said to him, "Sir, you do not even have* a bucket and the cistern is *deep; where then can you get this living water? 12 Are you greater than our father Jacob, who gave us this cistern and drank from it himself with his children and his flocks?" 13 Jesus answered and said to her, "Everyone who drinks this water will be thirsty again; 14 but whoever drinks the water I shall give will never thirst; the water I shall give will become in him a spring of water welling up to eternal life." 15 The woman said to him, "Sir, give me this water, so that I may not be thirsty or have to keep coming here to draw water.*

True to human curiosity, the woman takes all this conversation literally! She questions Yeshua's ability to get water out of the well. That's the literal and blind response of many who encounter Yeshua's teachings. The banter proceeds. It's quite humorous yet perceptive of the author. We think that this author was re-incarnated and he turned out to be Shakespeare himself. (Chuckle!) Yeshua's response stuns the woman. "HE is that living water!" Again the woman thinks that his living water will quench her physical thirst. Of course, this is all allegorical and very much the author's theology! And, positively not the words of Yeshua! And, to make matters worse, Yeshua never did go to Samaria!

Yeshua challenges her with one of his Divine bits of knowledge about her marital status. [Don't get upset, no human has that ability and Yeshua is totally human. **It's the author's faith speaking again!]** Then the light goes on; she perceives his meaning. She leaves and proclaims to her townspeople that here is a prophet. She is the first disciple to preach in Samaria. Now comes the theology! Verses 22 and 26 contain two important incorrect statements yet ends with a confirmation of Yeshua's mission.

> Jn 4: 22-26 *You people worship what you do not understand; we worship what we understand, because salvation is from the Jews. 23 But the hour is coming, and is now here, when true worshipers will worship the Father in Spirit and truth; and indeed the Father seeks such people to worship him. 24 God is Spirit, and those who worship him must worship in Spirit and truth." 25 The woman said to him, "I know that the Messiah is coming, the one called the Anointed; when he comes, he will tell us everything." 26 Jesus said to her, "I am he, the one who is speaking with you."*

The first underlined is a common folk tale among those early Christians, but it suggests that Yeshua was not trying to establish a new Institutional Religion—for Yeshua, Judaism was already the true religion! The middle underlined is not what God desires (re-read Isaiah 1: 10-20). Notice the last thought of verse 25, "when he comes, he will tell us everything." The author is exposing his intentions for this entire Gospel! Man, this guy can't keep a plot secret! Most importantly, the author uses the last verse to make the major sign (9) of this Chapter.

Then the story moves on to get Yeshua back to Judea and Galilee where he performs a cure. This, the author writes, is the second sign. We suspect that not only has he miscounted, but also missed his own really important signs. We're up to nine signs (and they're all between the lines! Maybe we should call them "sign-lines" or "line-signs").

Chapter 5:

This fifth Chapter contains very potent theology and Christology. It seems to start slowly with a simple healing of a bedridden man (the 10th sign, humanity is ill) but because it occurs on the Sabbath, it attracts a pack of attackers like wolves to raw meat. The sick man doesn't know who healed him. Isn't that typical of us all? When we encounter the healing grace of God, we're never quite sure whether it was the erythromycin or God's graceful interruption. Only with the passage of time do we recognize the giver. (Sound familiar?) Re-read Exodus 33: 18-23! Moses only sees the behind of God. Thus, the author writes of this man's second meeting with Yeshua. To raise the stakes of this story the man shares the good news with the people. Yeshua then begins a lengthy discourse on the powers and centrality of the Son. Obviously, it's the author speaking!

Notice the Christology in verse 18 in which Yeshua is accused of "calling God his own Father, making himself equal to God." Do you recognize the impetus to draft the Nicene Creed, especially when the hierarchs believe that this Gospel is a literal record of Yeshua's spoken words? In verses 21, 22 and 23 there are three staccato powers assigned to the Son: raise the dead, judge the world and worthiness of honor. Now, verse 24 is a tricky one; Yeshua points not to himself but to God and the necessity to believe in God to receive eternal life. In verse 29 it is quite clear that good deeds will earn eternal life! Makes one re-think Paul's "faith alone" position vs. that of James' "faith without good works is dead!"

In verse 39 the author adds a bit of advice for scripture worshippers; the Bible points to Yeshua, not to itself!

John 5: 39 *You search the scriptures, because you think you have eternal life through them; even they testify on my behalf.*

And Yeshua points to God! (Double signs, 11 & 12). Verse 44 is a powerful statement about the Father being the only God.

John 5: 44 *How can you believe, when you accept praise from one another and do not seek the praise that comes from the only God?*

Whoa, folks, does this mean that there is only one God? We suspect a bit of contradiction as well as confusion in the author's theology. The opening verses of Chapter 1 state that Yeshua is the eternal Word but now in 5: 44 the author states that the Father is the only God! What say you now, Oh Reader?

The Chapter ends with the question, "If you place your hope in Moses, Moses will be your accuser in the end.

Thus, this Chapter has covered a lot of theological and Christological ground. Have you come to recognize the simplicity in the pattern of each Chapter? Its four components are: (1) set the scene, (2) get to the situation or provoke a problem, (3) state the sign and (4) develop a mighty lengthy discourse or Sunday sermon.

Chapter 6:

Here the author uses several symbolic activities in the intro leading to the multiplication miracle (the first physical sign-13): the crossing of the sea like in Exodus, the seven foods (seven is the perfect number), twelve baskets of left-overs (even after the bountiful teachings of Yeshua there will be blessings left over for the people of Israel—the twelve tribes) and Yeshua's escape to the mountains (Moses going up Mt Sinai). Now the disciples take a boat ride across the sea and Yeshua walks on water (the sign (14) of Divinity). We suspect that this was more than likely a post-Resurrectional event brought into this story..

Once the people experience the sign of the loaves and fishes they follow Yeshua across the sea for more. That "more" turns into a great dissertation on the Eucharist (the sign and metaphor (15) of food—physical and spiritual). The crowd is confused by the literal words of Yeshua who is alluding to their spiritual manna. The discourse is meant to be metaphorical and not to be taken literally. However, even the Apostles get caught up in the harshness of Yeshua's sayings. People today do not understand the metaphor that God is bread and they miss the reverse, bread is NOT God. The sixth chapter is a mythical writing of the author's belief structure that, when taken literally, confuses his true intent. The flesh eating and blood drinking are just shocking to the literalist but meaningful when viewed metaphorically. When one reads the expression, "eats a book" in Ezekiel, it means that one absorbs the meaning of the book. Likewise, celebrating Eucharist means absorbing the teachings of Yeshua, who is like a living spiritual nourishment just as bread is physically nourishing. But alas, some ears don't hear!

John 6: 27 *"Do not work for food that perishes but for the food that endures for eternal life, which the Son of Man will give you. For on him the Father, God, has set his seal."* (Sign (13) above.)

This puts forth two concepts to the reader: (a) not to get confused by the literal words; (b) focus on this "human being" (a *bar enach* in Aramaic) because God has put a seal of approval on him. The supreme sign of approval was the Resurrection by which God gave Yeshua all the Messianic titles and the Name above all Names! Right on, Romans 1: 3-4 and Phil 2:9!

Verse 35 contains Yeshua's great metaphor (remember, it's the author speaking!):

> John 6: 35 *Jesus said to them, "I am the bread of life; whoever comes to me will never hunger, and whoever believes in me will never hunger, and whoever believes in me will never thirst.*

Yeshua feeds one's hunger and thirst for spiritual food! Remember, it's one's soul (spirit) that hungers and thirsts for this spiritual food; one's body will always need physical food and drink. Verse 35 is purely metaphorical. The remaining Verses 36 to 71 echo verse 35. The author plays with the metaphor of real flesh vs. spiritual flesh and real blood with spiritual breath (like God's breath creating in Genesis). It is a tantalizing passage; please read it yourself! The author makes a very strong argument for focusing on Yeshua and absorbing his teachings: a magnificent teaching about Eucharist!

On a more historical note, drinking the blood and eating the flesh of an animal one has killed has always been a symbol of taking on the spirit of the animal. Check it out yourself; it's documented in the Eskimo and American Indian history books as their cultural traditions!

Chapter 7:

Remember what we've said about the number "seven", that it's the perfect number? Well, this is probably the most complicated of the Chapters! This author is certainly a gifted writer!

Yeshua is drawn to the Temple for the second time in his ministry. It seems the people there are getting to know this teacher! And guess what happens? Yes, another great situation, challenge and discourse! It's about why he was sent. Of course, the human Yeshua had to figure it out himself! But this author has a Backward-Looking knowledge with his own BIG perceived picture. He is telling us what he believes and the meaning is indeed powerful.

The story is kindled by three key verses: 15, 27 and 31. Let's examine them:

> *15 The Jews were amazed and said, "How does he know scripture without having studied?"*
>
> *27 But we know where he is from. When the Messiah comes, no one will know where he is from."*
>
> *31 But many of the crowd began to believe in him, and said, "When the Messiah comes, will he perform more signs than this man has done?"*

In v. 15 the author points out the "wisdom" of Yeshua. In 27 the author tells us that the prophecies about Yeshua coming from the lineage of David is faulty because he knows that Yeshua was born in Nazareth and there really might not be any genealogical connection to David. In 31 the author points to the fact that Yeshua did perform many signs of healing. Stop a minute and catch your breath! Focus on the mythologized nature of this Fourth Gospel. What is written is "meaning" not historical facts, and the discourse is certainly not from the lips of Yeshua!

Then comes the passage in which Yeshua reveals himself (37-39) and the resultant questions from the crowd (40-43). Let's pause to analyze them.

37 On the last and greatest day of the feast, Jesus stood up and exclaimed, "Let anyone who thirsts come to me and drink.
38 Whoever believes in me, as scripture says: 'Rivers of living water will flow from within him.'"
39 He said this in reference to the Spirit that those who came to believe in him were to receive. There was, of course, no Spirit yet, because Jesus had not yet been glorified.

In 37 and continuing in 38, there is the great announcement by Yeshua, a definitive statement by the author. In 39 there is that shocking last sentence: There is NO Spirit yet!!! WHAT IS THIS SAYING? It's not tough to figure, is it? There is no Trinity! Say it again to yourself or out loud so you can absorb it fully. THERE IS NO TRINITY! There is only ONE God; ONE man promoted to the fullness of God; ONE Spirit of GOD—God's Spirit, God's Holy Spirit, God's Spirit of Holiness.

Now, "ain't" that a shocker? Hold it; don't get yourself in a knot! This is only our humble opinion based upon our reading of the Christian Testament in its chronological order and the fact that the Gospels are indeed mythologized, ironically, by those very same authors with a literal and fundamental mindset. The early Christians were people who believed that: (1) God was a puppeteer! (2) God caused people to act at the end of Her-His strings; and (3) the Hebrew Testament was totally factual, and last, but certainly the most thought provoking, the term "Holy Spirit" was used in the Hebrew Testament 500 years before Yeshua's birth!! Later on, after 400 AD, they held to the same belief about the newly canonized Christian Testament. OK Folks, welcome to the 21st century, the information century!

Now let's look at 40-43:

40 Some in the crowd who heard these words said, "This is truly the Prophet."
41 Others said, "This is the Messiah." But others said, "The Messiah will not come from Galilee, will he?
42 Does not scripture say that the Messiah will be of David's family and come from Bethlehem, the village where David lived?"
43 So a division occurred in the crowd because of him.

These verses capture the confusion among the listeners. Some expect the Messiah but others deny that he will be from Galilee (they believe in futuristic prophecy). They know that Yeshua was not born in Bethlehem and not of the Davidic lineage. Well, does it really matter? No, of course it doesn't! And the last verse acknowledges the reality of the author's time and certainly knows how people behave. Those divisions reflected in these verses have taken on a life of their own and have increased exponentially since the 1st century, haven't they?

Then the author punctuates the middle of the discourse with this from the guards:

John 7: 46 *The guards answered, "Never before has anyone spoken like this one."*

How amazing, even the guards acknowledge Yeshua! And then the Chapter ends with Nicodemus' observations:

50 Nicodemus, one of their members who had come to him earlier, said to them,
51"Does our law condemn a person before it first hears him and finds out what he is doing?"
52 They answered and said to him, "You are not from Galilee also, are you? Look and see that no prophet arises from Galilee."
53 Then each went to his own house,

Here again is our friendly night visitor, Nicodemus, from Chapter 3. This time he speaks out to the council who immediately accuses him of being from Galilee. Then a council member says, *"Look and see that no prophet arises from Galilee."* This is another recognition that Yeshua's birthplace is unknown and that Luke and Matthew made up their Infancy Narratives out of their belief that the Hebrew Testament was factual. Oh Boy, are we hitting paydirt, or what?

The signs of this Chapter are the division that Yeshua causes among the crowd (17) and the hatred brewing among the officials (18) whose positions are threatened by these new teachings—one doesn't need Institution. Community, yes; Institution, NO!

Chapter 8:

As we mentioned earlier, the scribe who punctuated this Gospel made several errors, among them is separating verse 53 in the previous Chapter from the remainder of its sentence in Chapter 8. Verse 2 should be the beginning of Chapter 8. The intro is the transition to the sign (19) of forgiveness of the adulteress, 8: 2 to 8: 11.

Immediately following is the larger theological message yet not independent from the topic of forgiveness. Forgiveness brings one out of darkness into the light. There is one not so incidental consideration about forgiveness: people who are hung up on justice as a primary requirement of eternal life are usually those who cannot forgive. Ponder that one for a day or two!

Of course, the readings thusfar are all metaphors and allegories! Please don't forget that! Then, a typical theme of Gnosticism appears here—light vs. darkness. In verse 12 the author initiates the challenge with one more aphorism:

12 Jesus spoke to them again, saying, "I am the light of the world. Whoever follows me will not walk in darkness, but will have the light of life."

It is the simile relating Yeshua to light that guides one through life's dark problems. Have you noticed that Good vs. Evil pairs show up frequently? You know, light vs.

darkness, white vs. black, day vs. night, order vs. chaos, truth vs. lie, God vs. Satan. Note carefully, these are all pre-historical ideas emphasized in Sumerian literature that the Israelites were exposed to during the Exile and brought into the H.T. and C.T. writings. They are the fodder of Gnosticism! But, great metaphors!

Now the game is on! The Pharisees challenge Yeshua. He responds that they refuse to acknowledge that He comes from God. The officials disagree; another debate. In verse 15 Yeshua challenges them again:

15 You judge by appearances, but I do not judge anyone.

Another dig by Yeshua; another response. And Yeshua (the author's belief!) sticks it to them once more in v. 18:

18 I testify on my behalf and so does the Father who sent me."

The debate heats up with v. 21:

21 *He said to them again, "I am going away and you will look for me, but you will die in your sin. Where I am going you cannot come."*

Then the second discourse, v. 22 to 29. The third and final lengthy discourse starts at v. 30 to 58. Let's examine the topics in each section and identify the theological signs.

8: 22-29 This is such a powerful dialogue that it needs to be quoted here:

22 So the Jews said, "He is not going to kill himself, is he, because he said, 'Where I am going you cannot come'?" 23 He said to them, "You belong to what is below, I belong to what is above. You belong to this world, but I do not belong to this world. 24 That is why I told you that you will die in your sins. For if you do not believe that I AM, you will die in your sins." 25 So they said to him, "Who are you?" Jesus said to them, "What I told you from the beginning. 26 I have much to say about you in condemnation. But the one who sent me is true, and what I heard from him I tell the world." 27 They did not realize that he was speaking to them of the Father. 28 So Jesus said (to them), "When you lift up the Son of Man, then you will realize that I AM, and that [I do nothing on my own], but I say only what the Father taught me. 29 The one who sent me is with me. [He has not left me alone], because I always do what is pleasing to him."

V 23 is the contrast of Sheol below and heaven above, the accepted flat earth cosmology.
V 28 in [ ] Does this mean that God does the miracles not Yeshua?
V 29 in [ ] If God is always with Yeshua, how come this contradicts the "Eloi, Eloi ... " in Mark 15: 34?

See how the author's words (aphorisms) bait the audience. Then, notice the two "I AM" revelations, v. 28 and v. 58, which constitute the single sign (21). And, don't lose sight of the fact that all this is the author's belief structure, his perception of the "Yeshua Event".

The 30th verse in 8: 30-58 is the transition statement and 31 & 32 are the bait to the third and last discourse. The sign is "Truth will make you free" (22). The remainder of this Chapter is devoted to Truth and Freedom both of which reside absolutely in God who is the source of Yeshua's words. Notice the sarcasm in verse 41 in reference to Yeshua's illegitimate birth! And, read the great "Before Abraham was, I AM" in verse 58; that is the flag of Trinitarianism. But it is a statement that no human could ever say, nor could Yeshua. This entire Gospel is the author's voice, not Yeshua's!

Chapter 9:

This is a story based on Yeshua's actual cure of a blind person. However, the event is described as an elaborate allegory about us humans in our personal transition from no belief to deeply personal metanoia (change of mindset) leading to a total conviction and belief in Yeshua as the reflection of God. Please read this Chapter slowly and then we'll dissect it.

... pause ...

Welcome back! Now, here's what it all means.

The tension is immediately brought into focus by a miracle performed on the Sabbath! Yeshua surely knows how to get under the skin of those legalists, doesn't he? Even the disciples get into the act with their challenge of sickness equated to sinfulness. The reply (verse 3) is a great one; it dispels the idea that sin produces illness and puts an end to original sin! However, it does hint that God made him blind to show off later on; that's not who God is. Oh, what a statement in v. 5! Yeshua as the light now gives some of it to the blind man. The miracle is the physical sign (23). Great drama! But bad timing; it's the Sabbath. Here come the "who is this man and who did this to him" bystanders. Then the former blind man stands up and shouts defensively, "OK guys, I was blind, now I see!" Well, the crowd shoots back, how did this happen? And the man replied, "The wet clay put in my eyes, the washing in the pool and, holy light, I can see."

There follows the same old attack: he's not from God because he did this on Sabbath. The thinking crowd makes a point: no sinner can do that sign. The Pharisees question the man again: tell us what you think. Bright eyes respond that the prophet did it. Notice that at this point in the story the man cured is shifting his belief to the next higher level. He is met with disbelief; the Jews call the parents. Before we go too far down this path, we should repeat what we've written previously. The term "the Jews" does NOT refer to the common Jewish people, it refers to the Jewish authorities! Back to the path! The parents plead ignorance; they tell the Jews to talk to their son, he's of age. So the Jews recall the son and tell him to praise God for this miracle, Yeshua is a sinner. Bright-eyes makes a stronger affirmation: it's him and he did it! Verse 27 is a great rebuke to their intelligence or is it their stupidity. It reads: "I told you already and you did not listen. Why do you want to hear it again?" And ends with this shot: "Do you want to become his disciples, too?" Wow, do those Jews jump on this, or what? They make a huge denial, like always. The tempo beats on! Out comes the large profession of faith:

> *30 The man answered and said to them, "This is what is so amazing, that you do not know where he is from, yet he opened my eyes. 31 We know that God does not listen to sinners, but if one is devout and does his will,*

he listens to him. 32 It is unheard of that anyone ever opened the eyes of a person born blind. 33 If this man were not from God, he would not be able to do anything."

One more step-up in faith by Bright-Eyes! His spiritual vision is improving, right? Now he sees with his soul! What follows is arrogance from the really blind Jews and they dismiss the former blind man. Having heard this, Yeshua returns with the BIG question, "Do you believe in the Son of Man?" Our newly "born again" says, "I do believe, Lord." The verse ends with, "And he worshiped him."

Finally, the discourse arrives, but a tiny one, followed by a condemnation of the disbelievers. Verse 41 means that physical blindness is not from sin and not demon caused. Intellectual or spiritual blindness is sinful because it's a free choice; it is a sin of intellectual dishonesty or something more serious!

How did you like this story? It's really about us, born without spiritual eyes. We meet Yeshua and see him vaguely. As we get to dialogue with Yeshua (reading the Bible with a keen eye for the meaning and bit of common sense) our understanding comes slowly (or is it, soul-ly?) into focus. But, as expected, there are dissenters all around challenging our perception. Gradually, our insight improves and we recognize the prophet. More objectors speak out against what we believe. Then, our faith and personal integrity strengthen and we profess a strong belief in the "Lord, Yeshua" with conviction and without fear. So it is; Yeshua is the spiritual sign of light (24).

We are grateful to Frs. Ray and Al: the former for sharing the skeletal concept for this Chapter; the latter for showing us how to live it.

Before we leave this Chapter, there is one thing that must be explained. The term, the Jews, has a bad connotation here and we must understand that at that time in history the authors did not want to accuse the Romans because there would be increased persecutions. So they pointed to the powerful and wealthy Jews who aligned themselves with the Romans. All those persecutions of the Jewish people through the ages were a mistranslation of the term, the Jews. Isn't it obvious that the common Jewish people actually formed the base of the believers?

Chapter 10:

Now we take a slightly different approach to discovering who Yeshua is. Again you are requested to read this whole Chapter before proceeding.

The author places on Yeshua's lips several "I AM" claims in verses 1 to 21: Yeshua is the gate through which all must pass; Yeshua is the shepherd who knows his sheep by name; Yeshua lays down his life and takes it up as he wishes (although this is contrary to Rom 1: 3-4). All because the listeners, and us readers, need to contemplate who Yeshua is. The divisions are created. Verses 20 and 21 conclude the section with the disbeliever's rationale and the believer's logical faith.

One verse stands out for its shift in focus:

"16 I have other sheep that do not belong to this fold. These also I must lead..."

It refers to those outside the State Religion of Judaism. But it also implies the same for Christian Institutions as well! Just think, some don't have to belong to any specific Institution to be in Yeshua's flock!

Verse 22 leads us into a third visit to the Temple for the discussion and dissertation sections. My goodness, Yeshua must have been a very annoying prophet. Right off, the Jews gather around him and demand to know whether he is the Messiah or not. True to form, Yeshua states that he has already told them in his words and deeds that proceed from the Father. Then, as if to rub salt in their wounds, Yeshua provokes them with, "You are not of my flock." Then he repeats the sheep allegories of v. 1-21 to which he ends with, "*30 The Father and I are one.*" That sets the Jews off to the stone pile. They accuse him of blasphemy! In v. 36 Yeshua makes his defense with, why accuse me, I only said, "I am the Son of God?" [Point of interest here]. "Son of God" is the Jewish equivalent for a divine being but not God, just an angel. And, like this case, can we not refer to ourselves as (lower case) sons and daughters of God?] Could it be that the author is playing with us with this double entendre? Then in v. 38 Yeshua follows with a second innocent concept, "...the Father is in me and I am in the Father." They try again to get him but he escapes to the Jordan. Based on what John the Baptist said about him convinces some to believe in him. So, did you pick out any covert signs? How about the spoken signs, Son of God and One-ness of Father and Son (25)?

A most important point here, the words that are assigned to Yeshua are only the faith statements of the authors of this Fourth Gospel. Don't get into a tizzy because we quote them as though Yeshua really spoke them; we know he didn't!

Chapter 11:

This is a story of death and resurrection, a tension that hangs heavy on every one of us. This Chapter presents a mini-resurrection foreshadowing the BIG Resurrection to come later on in this Gospel. The principal signs are Faith in Yeshua as the true shepherd (26) and the Power of Yeshua in whom the Father resides (27). The principle aphorism in this Chapter is in verses 25-26, underlined below. The author creates tension in the story line by means of key dramatic expressions placed on Yeshua's lips. Let's list the high lights and please note the author's "faith" statements (the double pound signs, ##):

v. 3 "Master, the one you love is ill."
v. 4 "This illness is not to end in death, but is for the glory of God, that the Son of God may be glorified through it." ##
v. 6 "he remained for two days in the place where he was.
v. 8 "Rabbi, the Jews were just trying to stone you, and you want to go back there?"
v. 11 "Our friend Lazarus is asleep, but I am going to awaken him."
v. 14 then Jesus said to them clearly, "Lazarus has died".
v. 17 Lazarus had already been in the tomb for four days.
v. 21 Martha said to Jesus, "Lord, if you had been here, my brother would not have died." ##
v. 23-24 Jesus said to her, "Your brother will rise." Martha said to him, "I know he will rise, in the resurrection on the last day." ##
v. 25-26 Jesus told her, "I am the resurrection and the life; whoever believes in me, even if he dies, will live, and everyone who lives and believes in me will never die. Do you believe this?" ##

v. 27 She said to him, "Yes, Lord. I have come to believe that you are the Messiah, the Son of God, the one who is coming into the world." ##
v. 34-35 "Where have you laid him?" They said to him, "Sir, come and see." And Jesus wept.
v. 39 Jesus said, "Take away the stone." Martha, the dead man's sister, said to him, "Lord, by now there will be a stench; he has been dead for four days."
v. 43 "Lazarus, come out!"
v. 44-45 "Untie him and let him go." Now many of the Jews who had come to Mary and seen what he had done began to believe in him.

At this point the story moves to the Jewish leaders in conference, planning to eliminate Yeshua as a sacrifice for the many to preserve the Jewish nation from the Romans. Actually they were scheming to save their position, power and wealth. [Interesting that the second Star Trek movie uses the line (the meaning paraphrased) "the needs of the many exceed the needs of the one".] Strangely enough, that 's exactly what happened. Just ask any Christian!] Yeshua then made very few public appearances. The Leaders now reflected on whether Yeshua would come to Jerusalem for the Passover for they were anxious to murder him.

There is an interesting story associated with the underlined in v. 35. It goes like this:

> There was a Guru from India preaching and teaching the principles of Buddhism in America. On one of his trips he met a truly Fundamentalist Baptist Minister who ask this Guru if he knew about Jesus. The Guru replied that he knew everything about the Master, Jesus. "Oh", replied the Baptist preacher, "so you are an expert on the Bible too?" "Definitely not" the Guru answered. Then, you must have at least read the Christian Testament?" questioned the Baptist. "Oh, no!" responded the Guru. "Then, how can you say you know all about Jesus?" returned the Minister. "I only read verse Jn 11: 35, *And Jesus wept.* And I immediately knew the true nature of this prophet. He was a very compassionate and forgiving person, just as your God is!?"

Chapter 12:

Apparently the NAB puts the book of signs between 1: 19 to 12: 50, simply because v. 37 says that Yeshua did no more signs from that time on. There are two important final signs within these first 19 verses: The celebration (28th sign) of Lazarus' resuscitation at the dinner (as symbolic of the Heavenly celebration in the next life) and the physical oiling (29th sign) of Yeshua by a woman (symbolic of the Divine anointing by the Father-Mother, as well as the fact that "Messiah" means that this person is the "Anointed One" and "King". Did you forget those synonyms?). Upon further examination we would suggest that the book of signs ends at 12: 20. Those first 19 verses appear to be the remnants of Chapter 11 that tie up the Lazarus event and then from 12: 20 begins a series of theological pronouncements by the authors concerning the nature of this Yeshua followed by the re-direction of the story towards the Passover feast.

In verse 23 Yeshua announces the end of his mission. Then, in each of the following verses, the author (remember, this is all Backward-Looking faith statements) has Yeshua say some mighty thoughtful aphorisms:

23 Jesus answered them, "The hour has come for the Son of Man to be glorified.
24 Amen, amen, I say to you, unless a grain of wheat falls to the ground and dies, it remains just a grain of wheat; but if it dies, it produces much fruit.
25 Whoever loves his life loses it, and whoever hates his life in this world will preserve it for eternal life.
26 Whoever serves me must follow me, and where I am, there also will my servant be. The Father will honor whoever serves me.

31 Now is the time of judgment on this world;
32 And when I am lifted up from the earth, I will draw everyone to myself."

35 Jesus said to them, "The light will be among you only a little while. Walk while you have the light, so that darkness may not overcome you. Whoever walks in the dark does not know where he is going.
36 While you have the light, believe in the light, so that you may become children of the light."

In the following verses 28 to 30, note the resemblance to Moses on the mountain in Exodus and the people's interpretation of the thunder (God speaking).

28 Father, glorify your name." Then a voice came from heaven, "I have glorified it and will glorify it again." 29 The crowd there heard it and said it was thunder; but others said, "An angel has spoken to him." 30 Jesus answered and said, "This voice did not come for my sake but for yours.

We suspect that this next v. 34 is a challenge that precipitates the remainder of the Chapter. But the last sentence is puzzling! Does this mean that all the "Son of Man" references in the other Gospels, and especially here, is simply a faith profession by the authors? Mighty peculiar!

34 So the crowd answered him, "We have heard from the law that the Messiah remains forever. Then how can you say that the Son of Man must be lifted up? Who is this Son of Man?"

Next, verse 37 is a lament or comment on the many signs that did not produce believers. How is it that all the other signs result in belief but here they don't? Is this to illustrate the resistance of many to the teachings of Yeshua? Maybe so!

37 Although he had performed so many signs in their presence they did not believe in him,

Verses 38 to 41 are H.T. prophecies (from Isaiah) that are not applicable here because each is a reference to either Isaiah's visions or words of the Lord spoken directly to Isaiah. [Recall that the authors of the C.T. believed that the C.T. was the fulfillment of the predictions in the H.T.]

38 in order that the word which Isaiah the prophet spoke might be fulfilled: "Lord, who has believed our preaching, to whom has the might of the Lord been revealed?" See (Isa 53: 1 & Rom 10: 16)
39 For this reason they could not believe, because again Isaiah said:

40 "He blinded their eyes and hardened their heart, so that they might not see with their eyes and understand with their heart and be converted, and I would heal them." (See Is 6: 9)
41 Isaiah said this because he saw his glory and spoke about him. (See Is 6: 1)

There is one comment further here. These so called predictions of the future are really mythologized discussions between Isaiah and God but in no way are they reference material for the Yeshua story. The author's objective has been to correlate the Hebrew Testament with Yeshua to prove that Yeshua is the Messiah but they have distorted many of these H.T. verses. Once again, many passages in the H.T. can be used to refer to just about anyone's life situation because of the mythologizing of those stories. The very enculturation of these 1st century writers is in itself the cause of the confusion between faith and facts. The Gospels themselves confirm this observation. What complicates this mindset is that confusion is alive and active in this 21st century also. The Lord knows that some of us humans haven't yet joined the Scientific and Technological community, let alone the biblical scholarly arena.

This Chapter ends with the author's demanding belief in Yeshua, stating the commissioning of Yeshua by God and describing Yeshua as the Light dispelling the Darkness, an Evil (the theme of Gnosticism straight out of the Babylonian Exile).

Thus we have counted 29 symbolic signs along with the ones identified by the authors of this Fourth Gospel. The balance of this Gospel now turns to the Passion and Resurrection of Yeshua.

Chapter 13:

Verses 1 to 17 tell of the true service that all disciples must practice if they are to follow Yeshua—the washing of the feet, an act of a servant! It symbolizes the relationship of a Master to his disciples, of a shepherd towards his flock, of Ministers to their congregations, of parents to their children, of neighbors to neighbors. See Luke 22: 24-27 for material in support of this interpretation.

Verse 18 appears to have dropped out of the sky with its new thought and aphorism. More than likely, this is an editorial addition to the original manuscript that clues us to the handiwork of other authors. Notice the "I AM" profession in v. 19. Then in verse 21 the plot turns to the deceptions of Judas. We seriously disagree with v. 27 in which Satan enters Judas. That is pure folk lore of the ancient times, yet demonic possession still remains in the dark recesses of the human mind in this 21st century. This vignette ends in v. 30. The plot veers again!

Verses 31 & 32 are hard to fathom as real statements by Yeshua. They may very well be faith statements again by the author. However, they point directly to the Backward-Looking style of the Gospels. Verse 33 addresses "My children" and Ministers have used the same address to their parishioners. We find that a haughty attitude, arrogant and humiliating, especially when ministers consider themselves in possession of all worthy knowledge. We recall one priest pompously telling his congregation that engineers and scientists need to come to him for the answers to life's difficulties because he was the ordained of the Church. Gads, that posture had gone out of fashion when Luther posted his disagreements, around 1525 AD.

More aphorisms follow and then we get to the Peter profession. Ah, Peter does reflect our behavior in many ways, doesn't he? And, Yeshua tells him straight from the shoulder, "Pete, you may eat those words before the week end is over!"

Chapter 14:

It does seem that 13: 31 is the beginning of this very long discourse by Yeshua about his relationship with the Father and that he is the mirror that reveals the nature of God. The aphoristic dialogue fills the entire 14th Chapter. Understand this; it is the theology of the author(s) that we are reading! These are not the words of a human Yeshua. Two particular verses (16 & 26) leave one with a recollection of Jer 31: 31-34, such that God the Father is the Advocate (the Spirit of Truth in v. 17)!

Did you notice the second Judas among the disciples in v. 22? He is also mentioned in Luke's list (Lk 6: 16) presented in our Chapter Five

This Chapter ends with "Get up, let us go" to the sacrifice!

Chapter 15:

What we will read here is a later addition by an unknown editor. It comes out of the blue and is really quite out of place. It's like a little pause for a meditation or sermonette.

We are bombarded with a constant list of aphorisms. But in v. 15 there is a most revealing one:

> *"I no longer call you slaves, because a slave does not know what his master is doing. I have called you friends, because I have told you everything I have heard from my Father."*

Please take serious note of the first underlined. Have you ever called your friend by the address of "my child"? Here Yeshua (no, the author!) is calling his disciples "FRIENDS". Can you imagine the magnitude of that relationship; it's the relationship that brings God present, right up close and personal, as present to you as your beating heart, as your thoughts are in your mind. God may be out there but She is as available as any one of your friends! It should astound your mind that this God of ours is besotted with humankind to the extent that Yeshua thinks of us as friends. This verse alone should bring us to tears of joy! Next time you pray, try replacing the words, "Our Father," with "Dear Friend". It'll give you goose bumps! Then again, how about using "Mommy" or "Daddy"?

The second underlined is somewhat surprising! If Yeshua told the disciples everything that the Father has passed on to Yeshua, then Rom 1: 3-4, Acts 2: 36, 5: 30-31, 13: 33 and Phil 2: 9 are accurate theological statements. The Resurrection is the correct moment of God's appointment of Messiahship to Yeshua with all the titles stated in those five references! Those Titles are:

- Rom 1: 3-4 *Son of God in power according to the spirit of holiness*; remember now! That's God!

- Acts 2: 36 Lord and Messiah;
- Acts 5: 30-31 exalted him at his right hand as leader and savior;
- Acts 13: 33 today you are my Son;
- Phil 2: 9 the name that is above every name.

All of which reflect the content of Eph 3: 17-19! Those do challenge and give new meaning to "What the Apostles handed down"! Those make an inquiring person question the doctrinal postures of the next few centuries. They specifically challenge Trinitarianism!

Check out the parable-metaphor in the beginning; it's the famous, I am the vine, you are the branches. It, too, is an excellent thought on which to meditate! The rest of the Chapter is loaded with juicy aphorisms. Enjoy!

Chapters 16 & 17:

These two represent the great theological dissertations of the author's belief structure about the meaning of Yeshua's mission. The words are lofty and outside the purview of a human Yeshua, specifically because of the Chalcedon definition and the many statements in Paul's and John's letters. The entire dialogue within these two Chapters is extraordinarily counter to the Yeshua we find in the Synoptics. It raises our suspicions that the authors wrote allegedly under the name of the Apostle John but he was not alive or was too feeble to proofread the manuscript when it was finalized. In spite of this shortcoming, many readers, including me, actually resonate with the mythical Yeshua and find great warmth and solace in this version of an all-knowing God-man. It reminds us of the Rudyard Kipling story, The Man Who would be King, when the Indian English-trained soldier asked, "Who would you rather follow; A man or a god?" Our authors must have realized this when they concocted this fictitious tale about a person who was almost 70 years dead.

In spite of this mythologized Fourth Gospel, you should know that Yeshua was a real man who did exist and who did marvelous deeds and spoke enlightening parables, allegories, and metaphors, who died a horrific death at the hands of the Romans. But most of all, his discouraged and disbanded disciples had such an extraordinary experience of the man, Yeshua, and an epiphany of the Resurrected Lord, the Christos, that it gave new meaning to the sign-ificance of Yeshua's prophetic life. The Resurrection transformed history forever! Yet, however human history was altered, there are still very few who walk that narrow "Road less Traveled".

Here are some highlights from 16:

- Catch the admission of Yeshua v. 25 (the author's Freudian slip), *"I have told you this in figures of speech . . . "* Now Folks, this time, that's the truth; it's all been mythologized! Revisit Appendix M.
- Then in v. 29 and v. 30, His disciples said, *"Now you are talking plainly, and not in any figure of speech. Now we realize that you know everything."* Doesn't this sound like a Post-Resurrectional scene? If not, certainly a Backward-Looking conviction.
- In v. 32 Yeshua says, *"But I am not alone, because the Father is with me."* That surely is a great metaphysical thought but not from the lips of Yeshua; one more statement of Faith by the author. Personally, it is a comforting truth about God's presence in our own being.

- And, there is the understatement of the entire Bible, v. 33: *"I have told you this so that you might have peace in me. In the world you will have trouble ..."* Oh, you bet you will!

  And now from 17:

- Then the author (17: 3) blatantly puts this on the lips of Yeshua, *"Now this is eternal life, that they should know you, the only true God, and the one whom you sent, Jesus {the} Christ."* Notice the "only" and at the end the author adds, "one whom you sent, Jesus *{the}* Christ". Now, that's a bit phony, don't you think? Yeshua doesn't have to name his own name when he is talking to his Father; the Father knows who is talking! Yeshua is not using a cell phone! The author let the cat out of the bag here. He really is sharing his own theology in these allegorical stories. That's what we mean by mythologizing.
- The rest of 17: 4-26 is certainly one big personal talk Yeshua has with the Father that is quite extraordinary. We suspect that it's simply the author's soliloquy.

Chapters 18, 19 and 20:

Ending this Gospel is Ch 20 (21 is an editor's addition), the world renowned Passion Narrative made even more famous by the recent Hollywood rendition of Mel Gibson's, "The Passion of the Christ".

- In 18: 2 we finally see Judas entering stage Right to begin the final hours.
- Did you catch the three "I AM" confessions in 18: 5, 6 and 8? Most importantly, in v. 6 at the words, I AM", they all turn away and fall down. Sounds like Mt. Sinai all over again, doesn't it?
- The name of the released revolutionary, Barabbas? (18: 40) Few recognize the irony that it is a name composed of *"bar"* meaning "son" and *"abba"* meaning "daddy!" How cute of the author to have the people pick the phony son of Daddy and kill the genuine person!
- Did you recognize the introduction of Yeshua in 19: 5, "*Behold the man*!" An admission by the authors that Yeshua was a MAN, a human person, including human ignorance! Well, in the other Gospels, not here.
- Do you understand that the statements by Pilate in 19: 4, 5 & 6 are put on Pilate's lips so the blame is directed to the Jews and the Romans are absolved in order to avoid any further persecution during the 90's?
- The famous INRI inscription on the cross in 19: 19 is, I for Iesus (no J in Latin), N is for Nazarean, R for Rex (Latin for King) and I for Iedorum (again, no J in Latin).
- Mary of Magdala (20: 17) was the first to see the risen Yeshua and in the ensuing conversation Yeshua announces, "I am going to my Father and your Father, to my God and your God." Now, is it possible that Yeshua is admitting that he is NOT God! Then again, was it the author's belief or just a literary mistake? Isn't it strange that the other Gospels identify Mary Magdalene yet the Fourth Gospel calls her Mary of Magdala! What gives with the name confusion? Note that she is at the cross, the first to see the empty tomb and the first to announce the Resurrection to, of all people, the disciples! Gives new meaning to "Ladies first!" doesn't it? Is she the Beloved Disciple?

- Here in 20: 22 & 23 is the power to forgive sins, a power that the Catholic Church claims is theirs! Maybe they have a point, but only if this Gospel is taken literally. Unfortunately ... it "ain't" a literal document! Besides, every Protestant knows that God does the forgiving, even before one errs!
- Chapter 20 appears to end with the doubting Thomas story and the last verse is about us,
  "31 *But these are written that you may (come to) believe that Jesus is the Messiah, the Son of God, and that through this belief you may have life in his name."*

Chapter 21:

This final Chapter is definitely an addition to the original manuscript. Its story line is about the assignment of responsibility to oversee the spiritual life of those who would become the flock of the "Jesus Movement". The story of the large fishing catch is symbolic of the great number of people that the disciples would convert and who would then become the "*ekklesia*", usually translated as Church, but really means "called out people". [A note of interest: The KJV translates "*ekklesia*" as community! Nice going Jimmy VI. Church is so ... hierarchical, community is more leveling!]

In the Synoptics there was only one event (Matt 16: 13-19) that placed Peter in a leadership position. Since the Fourth Gospel appeared to have ended with Chapter 20, this last Chapter v. 15-17 is suspiciously an attempt to put Peter back in leadership by means of the three phrases: "Feed my lambs", "Tend my sheep" and "Feed my sheep." As we've seen in our analysis of the Chronological Christian Testament, the leadership grew in chaos rather than orderly. By the 9th decade some author recognized the importance of a single leader and therefore perpetuated the Matthean Myth in this 21st Chapter, added at some later date.

Yeshua told Peter three times to care for the flock in his name! That symbolism took hold after Constantine became the new King in 312 AD. A growing Church quickly incorporated this for its own purposes up to the next 700 years until the Eastern Schism and became further disrupted in 1525 A.D. when Martin Luther sounded the trumpet for reform. The many separated denominational Christian Institutions now live in a broken relationship, very much to the sadness of Yeshua.

This is followed by a prediction of the manner of Peter's death. It's a clear Backward-Looking tale; after all, the author already knew about Peter's death in Rome.

To give the entire Gospel authenticity the authors signed the name of the Beloved Disciple in verse 24. Who he (or is it she?) is remains a mystery and obviously an unanswered question!

Epilogue to the Fourth Gospel

Now, let's wrap this up with a brief summary of this Fourth Gospel. The first thing to mote is the literary style of this Gospel: it is Backward-Looking, full of sophisticated and learned Greek, the contribution of five distinct authors and, finally, containing several later additions which add to the already massive complexity for any reader to determine the true nature of this Yeshua, the humble carpenter from such an obscure town as was Nazareth. **Most of all, the entire Fourth "Good News" is an allegory of the Author's faith woven with threads of history from what the Author heard in the Oral Traditions that reached his ears. Therein lies its power and meaning.**

We dismissed the first 18 verses of Ch 1 because it was a later addition that seriously contradicts all the other books of the Christian Testament. Ch 1: 19 is the original starting point and simply introduces Yeshua and points immediately to a personal challenge to "come and see for yourself" which is our invitation to come and read and study the Bible. Ch 2 is the principal reason for Yeshua's ministry: he is the new Wine; he is the new prophet; he is the corrective to the mis-understood Mosaic Law and rituals. Ch 3 starts by asking, "If Yeshua is here to introduce a new Way, where is the door that opens up to the new Way?" That's easy says Yeshua, "Wash away your old lifestyle and be born again (*metanoia*) in the new Way." Physically and spiritually clean up your act! Ch 4 takes the next step, not only wash yourself but take a drink of "living water". Drink and eat the scroll of Yeshua's teachings. And, mind you, both males and females can be the teachers, prophets and hierarchs! Ch 5 directs the reader to Yeshua as THE speaker for God and that his teachings and preachings are the central true Words of God. Yeshua is God's Emissary! Ch 6 turns our attention to the great metaphor that Yeshua is not only the bread and protein of physical life but also the nourishment for spiritual life, eternal life. Ch 7 then turns to the mission and the message. Yeshua says that the people should not get totally invested in the Old Scriptures with their alleged future predictions concerning the Messiah and where he will come from. **This is the first rebuke of treating the Scriptures literally.** The message is the important thing not the messenger! Ch 8 gets right to the core of who the messenger is with a barrage of aphorisms. Yeshua is the Light in the darkness, the light of the world, the light of life. Yeshua is "Living Water". Yeshua is spiritual nourishment. Yeshua is the central messenger, 'I AM HE". But notice that God is the force behind Yeshua. God sent Yeshua; God does the miracles through Yeshua. Ch 9 is an aside that points to the people's experience of Yeshua as a progression through and a growth in belief and faith in Yeshua. Metaphorically speaking, it is everyone's story of spiritual blindness being transformed into faith through the grace of Yeshua's preachings. Ch 10 redirects us to Yeshua with the "I AM" claim. Then the shepherd allegories begin with a surprising twist. The Shepherd, Yeshua, has other flocks, not in Israel or in any specific place. Those who live the meaning of Love are OK! Ch 11 treats the big picture of life after death. Yeshua is the Resurrection which gives life to whomever follows him. Yeshua is more that drink, more than food, more than light. Yeshua is the gate to eternal life. However, if Yeshua is the Resurrection, it follows that he is the death first. And the plot turns to the murderers. Ch 12 now begins the march to the cross. Yeshua speaks of the end of his mission at length in allegories of the seed dieing and its rebirth to yields much fruit. And, he speaks of our dying to self, resulting in our rebirth to eternal life. Ch 13 is the great servant paradigm demanded of the followers of Yeshua. Leaders are to serve the members! Ch 14 summarizes the aphorisms of the previous chapters and then ends in the pathway to the cross. Ch 15 thru 17 are additions made much after the original writing of this Fourth Gospel and, as such, are out of place, not pertinent to the theme. However, in 15: 15 is a powerful theological statement. Yeshua is not our master; he is our friend! Also, Yeshua has told the disciples everything that he heard from his Father! That is a certification that the Apostles handed down nothing but the TRUTH they heard from Yeshua. Yet, the Synoptics and the first 18 verses of the Fourth Gospel contradict the Apostolic teachings! That's food for the gristmill! Ch 18, 19 and 20 do the Passion thing. Noteworthy is 20: 17 in which Yeshua says to Mary of Magdala that he is going to his Father and to "my God and your God"! Doesn't that put a hole in 1: 1-18? The story ends here but Ch 21 is another editor's later addition. Seems someone wants to get Peter into the papacy again. And finally, the author hides the true authors' identities with the title, the Beloved Disciple.

Now, back to our list!

Section VI: The Church-State

In 312 AD Constantine gained total power over the Roman Empire. He appointed the Christian Authorities (the Bishops) to the Supreme Court as his administrators of Justice. However, on account of the chaotic theological dis-order, Constantine found it necessary to force the Christian Bishops into Council to resolve that problem. Thus was created a pecking order of authority and influence; Christian Church leaders were now firmly entrenched as the Judicial Arm of the Empire – Constantine's Church-State.

Section VII: The Dogmatic Solution at Niceae

The Bishops gathered at Nicaea in 325 AD (well, give or take a few years) and the struggles began and continued for several years under the influential Athanasius who dominated the Council with his forceful defense of the factuality and primacy of the Fourth Gospel. The Council of fundamentalists Bishops succumbed to the strong arm of Athanasius and photocopied the Trinitarian Nicene Creed to the ends of the Empire via foot power. The results quieted the factious Christian world for the time being. Nevertheless, the seeds of dissention went dormant for a century of winter seasons only to burst forth in the middle of the fifth century under a different cause: the lost humanity of Yeshua!

Concurrently, in the political world of the burgeoning Church-State, Constantine moved the capital of the Empire to Constantinople and only after 330 AD did the Court and Government settle permanently in the new capital. That centered the throne and the entire government operation in that city. Rome no longer ruled! Constantinople ruled Rome! Where the Emperor sits is where the cronies thrive. The Bishop of that city took a promotion and the "no-love-lost" towards the Roman Patriarch took on a new life. Then, round two of the Trinitarian conflict popped out of the four corners of the Empire; the voice of dissention asked, "What happened to Yeshua's humanity and/or Divinity?"

Section VIII: The Formation of the Canon and the Development of Patriarchy

The principal cities now had Patriarchs in charge of the local area and the leaders of the Christian towns and villages—their Bishops. The strongest of the Patriarchs held as many as 60 to 70 Bishops under their authority. The two most powerful patriarchs were Rome and Constantinople. {Small wonder why the Great Eastern Schism came into being in the 11th century!} Throughout the Empire Patriarchs and their own Bishops held to slightly different theories and doctrines concerning the nature of this Christ—their Christology (Was Yeshua human or divine?). It was those unique postures that led to the re-examination of the writings and traditions about Yeshua.

At the start of the 5th century the effort to authenticate and establish an acceptable collection of Christian writings took place under the guiding hand of Jerome. There were many individual writings abounding throughout the Christian centers that were strangely erroneous in that they contained fantastic tales about Yeshua. Jerome assembled as many as he could and compared them to what he and the Council of Patriarchs and Bishops considered normative to what was remembered of "what the Apostles handed down". The Catholic Church finalized their selection and Jerome compiled the Latin Bible: the Hebrew and the Christian Testaments into the Vulgate. The four apocryphal books from the Septuagint were added to the Hebrew Testament. The Christian Testament material was approved by the Patriarchs and Bishops who, in consort with Jerome, put the 27 books in an order that suited the needs of the Catholic Church of the fifth century. Because Matthew's testimonial passage (Chapter 16) was perceived to authenticate the primacy of Peter, his Gospel was given first place among the four Gospels and first place in the New Testament. Acts followed, then Paul's Epistles and the other Epistles with Revelation ending the Testament. It is the thesis of our writing that the unique order of the Christian Testament has been the prime cause of the Christological confusion that has plagued the Christian Movement since its inception. That was the purpose of re-reading it anew in our Chapter Four according to its natural chronological sequence of authorship.

Section IX: The Dogmatic Backlash at Chalcedon

Help! Christianity was in chaos again! Neighborliness was in the process of being assassinated by a new Christological uprising. So they called another Council in 451 AD and resolved this by declaring Yeshua to have been a total human, including human ignorance. Wow! Did that decision cut deep? You bet it did. The reverberations penetrated so deeply into the Christian belief structure, that even to this very day, most Christians do not accept the dogma from Chalcedon. Fortunately, in a letter by John, the Chalcedon decision was certified!

> 1 John 4: 2-3 *This is how you can know the Spirit of God: every spirit that acknowledges Jesus Christ come in the flesh belongs to God, and every spirit that does not acknowledge Jesus {come in the flesh} does not belong to God. This is the spirit of the antichrist that, as you heard, is to come, but in fact is already in the world.*

Section X: The First Schism, Eastern Orthodoxy

Was that the cause of the devastating Eastern Schism? No! The separation of Christianity into an Eastern and Western Institution led to the Schism; it was simply a matter of who held the larger number of dioceses. The pomposity of the Patriarchs and the power within the Eastern Patriarchies blinded the two factions, Rome vs. Constantinople. Each demanded absolute power over the other. Thus, "pride cameth before the falling out!" Christendom split in two and has not reconnected. Vatican II in 1965 made a feeble attempt at ecumenism that quickly dissolved because Rome chose to retain and maintain its position as the Infallible Ruler, the Absolute Gatekeeper, requiring obeisance from the East rather than become a humble Christian partner.

Section XI: The Second Schism, The Protest

Once the Infallible Ruler ball got rolling, it gained far too much momentum. Dissention peeked out gradually after the Eastern Schism and peaked in the 16th century over the financial corruption and spiritual vacuum of Rome. Well, Rome didn't have its hearing aid on and wasn't in the mood to re-assess itself. On the European sidelines stood several local Princes who were also coiled to spring out at Roman Power. They isolated Luther and protected him, not because of his new theology of the Pauline "Faith alone" Epistle but because of a need to liberate themselves from Papal jurisdiction over European monarchs.

Enough said, you know the history; Christians discovered "Freedom of Conscience" and ran with it to establish the Protestant denominations that exist today.

Section XII: The Great Divisions and the Modern Age of Discovery

The history of the Protestant Reformation is documented in every library in the world. No need to exhume it here. What happened to the world during the ensuing years was both a diversification of Protestantism followed by a scientific revolution unparalleled in history. Archeology stumbled on the Rosetta Stone. Scientific investigation produced instruments that could now unlock the secrets of Nature. The world wasn't ready to accept neither the scientific observations nor its conclusions. For that matter, neither is a large portion of today's world population in a receptive mood. The flat earth doctrine of Genesis 1 & 2, Job 38 and Psalm 104 was challenged and found to be just mythologized poetry. Christianity hardened its mind and condemned Science. But truth marched on! Chemistry, Physics, Biology, Archeology, Cosmology and others discovered the HOW's of creation and some of Nature's Secrets. The average Christian confused the HOW with the WHO and thereby condemned Modern Science for its unveiling the Natural Law and its truths but also the mythology of Sacred Scriptures, especially the mythic content and constructions in the Bible. Humans believe what they perceive! And what humans perceive is nothing more than what they were taught. What they were taught is prejudicial knowledge. Therefore, one can only conclude that prejudicial knowledge has its basis in ignorance! Yet, ignorance is not evil or sinful, that is, until it becomes the energy for hatred and violence.

There is so much theological diversity within the Christian denominations and throughout the religious world in this 21st century that it is going to take an extraordinary infusion of Divine Grace to re-unify Christianity with itself and with the other religions. A major obstacle has been and will be the refusal of the Roman Petrine Tradition along with Islam and Judaism not only to relinquish their allegedly perceived absolute religious powers but also to honor the remaining religious traditions of all other perceived theological truths. On the other side of the coin, there are many memories of the Church-State fiasco of the past and, particularly, the unwillingness of the Protestant Churches, who championed freedom of religion in Europe and America, to share leadership or, "heaven forbid", to submit to Rome or any non-Christian perception.

OH well, maybe in the next millennium! But we are getting ahead of ourselves. It's the moment to discover the ingredients of spirituality and find our own personal WAY, vector and velocity towards the Center, the Source of all Being.

PART FOUR: The Path and Pain to Unification

The very first step would be to isolate the authentic sayings that most closely approximate the teachings of Yeshua. This should force this century's scholars to re-think the process by which traditions were distorted through the so called (sacred?) 'Oral

Tradition'. Following this there must be a lengthy symposium to come to some agreement concerning the psychology of the religious mind of a literalistic community that pronounced all those doctrines, dogmas and rituals over the past two thousand years. Of course, the symposium must include Church leaders, lay theologians of every denomination, both male and female.

If you get the Shepherds, the sheep and the Scholars together, you will have accomplished a monumental step. The next item on the agenda will be to re-introduce the concept of the Patriarchal format of equal vote; each Denomination (the membership, not just the dignitaries) elects its own three representatives to a Christian Governing Council. Maybe we could design it to be like our House of Representatives. Then, the advisory board (a Supreme Court thing) could be the "Jesus Seminar" members. The point of this exercise is to unite, in equal participation, the Christian People like Moses did to the Egyptian slaves of old. (You know, like 12 tribes!) Who knows, God's grace might just be sufficient and up to the challenge. After all, in the early Church everyone subsisted under one title, give or take a few doctrinal practices and rituals, didn't they?

Do you think this too naïve or impossible? Have you never considered that God is actually capable of such a feat? Don't forget human free will! Then, read Jeremiah 31: 31 to 34! Hey folks, give it a try at the grass roots level, the water may be much warmer than you think! Recall the advice of God (aka, George Burns in the movie, OH, God); it's up to us humans to clean up our act! Besides, don't you believe that God really did tell Adam to take care of this place (Genesis 2: 15)? Literally or figuratively, we are responsible for each other and this planet!

PART FIVE: A New Spirit of God and the WAY of Spirituality

If humans can be inspired to write so many meaningful books like the Bible, then why can't God inspire and motivate the modern scholars or present day church leaders? Whether you accept it or not, God has been working overtime, first at Vatican II Council, then the Charismatic movement and lately in the "Jesus Seminar". All this activity is not bubbling out of some mist on the mountain tops, is it? Did you really sink your teeth into that Jeremiah passage above? Well, look at it again!

> Jer 30: 31-34 *The days are coming, says the LORD, when I will make a new covenant with the house of Israel and the house of Judah. It will not be like the covenant I made with their fathers the day I took them by the hand to lead them forth from the land of Egypt; for they broke my covenant and I had to show myself their master, says the LORD. But this is the covenant which I will make with the house of Israel after those days, says the LORD. I will place my law within them, and write it upon their hearts; I will be their God, and they shall be my people. No longer will they have need to teach their friends and kinsmen how to know the LORD. All, from least to greatest, shall know me, says the LORD, for I will forgive their evildoing and remember their sin no more.*

The new covenant may very well be the WAY of Spirituality and Love in which God whispers the direction, the time and the place for renewal. That time is NOW, not tomorrow! That place is in your spirit, not in any Temple! The directions are in our Chapter Seven (another use of numerology!).

The Summery: Conclusion and Significance

Denominationalism is the product of perception and its claim of absolute truth. Unfortunately,human truth is relative, making no single denomination the sole owner of absolute truth. All are relative and as such none is fully correct. Each sees only one facet of the big picture (just like a jigsaw puzzle). People can only solve the puzzle if all work together and put their pieces on the same table from which we, all, can form the portrait of a Loving People. We are all brothers and sisters seeking the same God, no matter what name we use for Her.

In this Chapter we tried to present a "heads up" of Israelite history so that you could understand the influence it had on Yeshua's enculturation. Who Yeshua was in life, speech and deed is directly related to his being an Israelite with all its baggage. What his ministry consisted of was his own re-interpretation of that history as it impacted on Israel's relationship with its God. As fractured as that relationship was, Yeshua felt in his spirit that God had not abandon Israel. Rather, the people of Israel were misled by the ruling religious leaders and especially by the stern hand of the conquering Nations: the Babylonians, the Greeks and, in the 1st century, the Romans.

It was not out of place for Yeshua to commence his preaching by seeking John the Baptizer and filling his own spirit with the timely prophetic words of this contemporary prophet. After the symbolic cleansing in the waters of the Jordan (his Epiphany), Yeshua took to the highways with his newly imbued energy from the Loving God of Israel. His own sense of God's mercy, forgiveness and grace translated into his outcry of "good news" for all humankind; "straighten out your lives and God will forgive your sins and forget them completely." The Kingdom of God on Earth had arrived for the common Israelite; this was surely the best news. For the modern mind we would use the metaphor, "the Community of God": God's celebrating table fellowship and wedding feast. With the world of the 1st century full of corruption, greed, suffering, oppression and plague, these were welcoming words. What convinced most was the manner with which Yeshua cured sickness and confidently forgave sins. Those awesome, compassionate, miraculous healings equated to God's forgiveness of sins. That was faith inspiring. Men and women were attracted to Yeshua and most became followers, for the message he brought was contrary to the old rigid and ritualistic ways. It was time for the new wine! The Resurrection was that intoxicating drink!

The most deliciously exhilarating wine is found in the Fourth Gospel, not in spite of its predominantly mythical composition but because of it. The synoptics have their good points also: the drama of Mark's "secret" about the human Yeshua; Mathew's new Moses approach (his re-write of the Moses story for the birth of the Messiah and the new law of the Beatitudes), aphorisms and parables; and Luke's focus on the prophetic side of Yeshua and the prominence of women in discipleship. All of those writings, even with the Christological confusions, are worthy of intense study.

Those four Gospels recommend what every mortal needs to believe and practice in his or her life. Their significance is exactly what you decide it to mean, no more and no less. That, strangely, is the spirit of the WAY of Spirituality and Love. Neither God nor Institution can violate your personal WAY by demanding your belief in this or that doctrine, dogma or ritual.

***

It's time to GO directly to Chapter Seven; pass "GO" and collect the gift of your LIFE!

CHAPTER SEVEN

SPIRITUALITY
IS
CHOOSING THE INTELLIGENT PATHWAY TO LOVE

Part One: Human Nature

We have already discussed the psychology of our human nature and its five characteristics along with the seven behavioral profiles and the three factors that govern our imperfect and fallible perceptions. That was an exercise I call "divide and conquer"! We must first understand the different components that constitute what we are as Homo Sapiens. The total human operates with all those parts functioning together; no single part operating all by itself. We are a complex being running in auto-drive firing on all fifteen cylinders [five plus seven plus three] in accord with the control center, our brain. Even though we are constituted with multiple characteristics, behaviors and perceptual factors, we function as a single unit.

Humans are a little like automobiles and computers. A car won't operate unless there is a driver in control. The body parts and organs are under the hood; the brain is the driver. But it takes gas to make that car run; God is the distributor of that gas. A computer is a very complicated electronic device; but it doesn't operate unless plugged in to a Power Source. When it runs it must have the correct programming. We humans are pre-wired by nature's DNA and programmed through our enculturation.

Spirituality, then, depends on our coordinating our SELF as a single unit. Thus, the metaphor we use to state that must reflect our total being. We are first and foremost distinguished by our unique abilities to think about and freely choose our own way in life. We are guided by our likeness to the Creator; a superior force always present to our needs. We are compassionate because of our divine spirit. The only catch to this is our freedom to choose, good or evil. History has shown that this second choice has been the more popular direction of humankind.

Humankind's highest behavior is that of intelligently choosing the pathway of God—Love, the unconditional act of self-Giving. The best model we have is that of Yeshua, a model that needs unraveling from the mythologized Christian Testament.

Part Two: The Meaning of Yeshua's Teachings

We hope that by now you've come to the realization that it must be "God's Way" or the "Lost Way". God's WAY is unquestionably found in the teachings of Yeshua summarized by his aphorisms, parables and some of what the Christian Testament authors have collected about Yeshua. Of course not all is factually from the lips of Yeshua but that which flows from the mythologized memory of what he spoke. Most of it is available for analysis. We believe that Modern scholars (those who came after the discovery of the Rosetta Stone in 1799 AD) have done their homework and so we can pretty well assemble the skeleton of what is called the "Jesus Movement". It is important to clarify one issue. The "Jesus Movement" is not an exclusive spirituality; it is the guide for an inclusive community of people who choose to have a relationship with God and their neighbors. The corollary to this is that it includes all men and women no matter which Sacred Scripture they profess and who live a life of Integrity in keeping with the ideals of "what Yeshua taught".

Our basic thesis is that this "Jesus Movement" contains God's most accurate ingredients to the Way of Spirituality and Love, better than the teachings of any other Sacred Scripture known to this day! {Our humble opinion, please!}. Just relax, it's not a new Religion nor is it the only Way. On the contrary, the "Jesus Movement" is just the best of the many pathways to eternal life! However, we shall see that it's not necessarily the easiest way or, again, not the only way. The prime responsibility for accepting and putting any system into practice will be your intellectual, free choice, and yours alone. There is NO INTERMEDIARY to tell you how to run your unique race of life. You, and only you, can decipher Yeshua's challenge and choose what is best for yourself. That's for certain! Now, let's see what we can share with you in your pursuit. But first, here is a re-ordering of some of Yeshua's specific teachings that we have assembled and considered to be the essentials of this "Jesus Movement":

Section One: The Teachings of Yeshua

The procedure we have used to unravel the most accurate collection of the authentic teachings of this Yeshua, the prophet from Nazareth, is to strip away the non-essential material from the aphorisms and parables. All 27 books of the C.C.T. have one thing in common: it's the consistency of the aphorisms and parables. What is written around those aphorisms and parables is, more often than not, mythologized history remembered by the Oral Tradition. We humans have a penchant for embellishment. Here now we have re-assembled the aphorisms and parables in a pseudo ordering that gives some semblance to an organized, logical presentation that one would expect from that original thinker. Thus our ordering consists of three topics: Yeshua's Invitation to membership, the Requirements of membership and, finally, the personal Results of such a membership. And now, let's review the true teachings of Yeshua.

I. The Aphorisms:

A. Yeshua's Invitation

"I have come to call everyone, not only the righteous but particularly the sinners."
"Come to God, all who thirst and hunger; God will refresh you"
"Do not be afraid; just have faith."
"Everything is possible to one who has faith."
"Do not fear change; make a leap of faith; enjoy the new wine!"
"What profit is there for one to gain the whole world and forfeit his life?"
"Where your treasure is, there is where your heart will be"
"It is easier for a camel to pass through (the) eye of (the) needle than for one who is rich to enter the Community of God."
"Store up treasure for the hereafter, you can't take anything with you"
"You cannot serve God and political power."
"Do not set aside your relationship with God in order to uphold your traditions!"

"Choose NOW, change your behavior"
"Seek first the Community of God and all else will be provided"
"God's grace is sufficient for you"
"God is the Power that is greater than anyone or anything you know"
"Sell all you have and give the proceeds to the poor and follow me"
"For out of the abundance of one's compassion the mouth speaks."
"Know thyself. Remove those cataracts from your own eyes first"
"A clean mind is more important than clean hands"
"Go wash the prejudice from your own eyes, and you'll see again"
"But what comes out of a person, that is what defiles."
"From within people, from their free will, comes evil."
"For every tree is known by its own fruit"
"A good tree does not bear bad fruit, nor does a bad tree bear good fruit."
"Do not build your faith on Scriptures, build on a Divine relationship."
" Recognize the signs of the Community of God, the blind see, the sick are healed and the deaf hear"

B. Membership in the Community of God

"Go in peace, your sins are forgiven; get with it, dude, you're well again."
"Daughter, your faith has saved you. Go in peace and be cured of your addictions."
"Hey, just ask, seek and knock, you'll get it, find it and a door will open"
"Love God with your whole being and your neighbor as yourself"
"Do to others just like you would want others to do to you"
"But to you who hear, I say love your enemies, do good to those who hate you, bless those who curse you, pray for those who mistreat you."
"Watch out, guard against the leaven of Institutions and of Wealth."
" Render to civil authorities what is their due and to God, what is God's"
"The harvest truly is great, but the laborers are few."
"The Sabbath doesn't rule humans; humans rule the Sabbath."
"Give to everyone who asks of you."
"Give, and it will be given to you."
"Help the poor, the sick, the widows and the orphans"
"Judge not, and you shall not be judged."
"Condemn not, and you shall not be condemned. "
"Forgive, and you will be forgiven."
"God is loving, merciful, forgiving and fair"
"If you do not forgive, neither will God forgive your transgressions"
"Pray for your enemies; forgive those who hurt or hate you"
"Humans who seek justice are mostly those who cannot forgive"
"Love your enemies, do good to those who hate you"
"Bless those who curse you, and pray for those who spitefully use you."
"To him who strikes you on the one cheek, offer the other also."
"From him who takes away your cloak, do not withhold your tunic either."
"From him who takes away your goods do not ask them back."
"Love your enemies, do good, and lend, hoping for nothing in return."
"If someone asks you to walk a mile with him, walk two miles"
Character is built through suffering, but it ends after 40 hours! [The badest time is Friday at 3 pm to Sunday just after sunrise]
"Do not build your faith on Sacred Scriptures, build on God."

C. Celebration

"Give me your loaves and fishes. Bread is for sharing not worshiping"
"If anyone wishes to be first, he shall be the last and the servant of all."
"Truthfully, Yeshua is the Way of Spirituality and Love leading to eternal life."
"Take courage, it is Daddy, do not be afraid!"

II. The Parables

A. Identifying the Community of God

The parable of sewing a new cloth on an old garment.
The parable of pouring new wine into old skins.
The parable of the seeds thrown on rocky soil.
The allegories of the lost coin, the lost sheep and the lost son.
The Metaphor of the narrow gate leading to life and the wide Gate to annihilation.

B. Membership in the Community of God

The parable of the talents.
The parable of the wise and faithful servant.
The parable of the blind leading the blind.
The parable of the lamp placed where it can be seen.
The parable of the houses built on rock or on sand.
The parable of a house divided against itself
The simile of the salt losing its savor.
The simile of the Kingdom of God and the mustard seed.
The simile of the Kingdom of God and leaven.
The Parable-Metaphors of the Vine and Branches.
The parable of Workers and the one Talent as the day's pay.
The parable of the Good Samaritan
The parable of the thief at night.
The parable of the landlord traveling and the end time
The "Our Fathers"(Luke's is nearer to Yeshua's teachings)

The Beatitudes of Matthew

- Blessed are the poor in spirit, for theirs is the kingdom of heaven.
- Blessed are they who mourn, for they will be comforted.
- Blessed are the meek, for they will inherit the land.
- Blessed are they who hunger and thirst for righteousness, for they will be satisfied.
- Blessed are the merciful, for they will be shown mercy.
- Blessed are the clean of heart, for they will see God.
- Blessed are the peacemakers, for they will be called children of God.
- Blessed are they who are persecuted for the sake of righteousness, for theirs is the community of heaven.
- Blessed are you when they insult you and persecute you and utter every kind of evil against you (falsely) because of me.

The Beatitudes of Luke

- Blessed are you who are poor, for the community of God is yours.
- Blessed are you who are now hungry, for you will be satisfied.
- Blessed are you who are now weeping, for you will laugh.
- Blessed are you when people hate you, and when they exclude and insult you, and denounce your name as evil on account of the Son of Man. Rejoice and leap for joy on that day! Behold, your reward will be great in heaven. For their ancestors treated the prophets in the same way.
- But woe to you who are rich, for you have received your consolation.
- But woe to you who are filled now, for you will be hungry.
- Woe to you who laugh now, for you will grieve and weep.
- Woe to you when all speak well of you, for their ancestors treated the false prophets in this way

Paul's discourse on Charity-Love (1 Corin 13)

C. Celebration

"Remember, God is the God of the living, not the God of the dead."
The parable of the wedding invitations.
The parable of the great feast and the refused invitations

Section Two: Yeshua's Daddy?

Did you know that the Pauline quote "Abba, Father" is an inaccurate translation? Check it out! It's in Gal 4:6 and in Rom 8:15! There are some corrections necessary. First, God sends the spirit of His son into our hearts. Now is it possible that the spirit of someone is another person within that person? No! And what about the spirit entering our heart? The heart is a pump; it doesn't think; it doesn't emote either; it just pumps. It's a metaphor for Love, passion and compassion. Second, the word "Abba" should really be "Daddy". Now, that puts a slightly different spin on things! Don't you think? Yeshua did use that word, Abba, and that is historically accurate! Well, what does this mean? Very simply, we should pray thusly: "Dear Daddy, how do you feel today in heaven. You know, how much I need you at my side Daddy and it seems like you're so far away. Please, Daddy, help me with my life and those things I need most to be a better person. Keep me away from peril, always." Now that should tell you something special about the God of Mercy, Forgiveness and Compassion. Daddy is such a tender and comforting name. We would suggest that you could call God by another name, Mommy! Those are very intimate names and they reveal why there is such a profound statement found in the letter by John: "God is LOVE!" The passage is:

> 1 John 4: 7-8 *Beloved, let us love one another, because love is of God; everyone who loves is begotten by God and knows God. Whoever is without love does not know God, for God is LOVE.*

"God is LOVE" in Greek is "*theos agape esti*" and reads, "God LOVE is". Love is a word that has been mutilated for several decades in recent times. What, pray tell, did our author mean by that profession? First of all, let's examine the Greek words used in some parts of the Christian Testament..

John 15: 12-13 12 *This is my commandment: love one another as I love you. No one has greater love than this, to lay down one's life for one's friends.* {*agape* in Greek}

1 Corin 16: 14: *Be on your guard, stand firm in the faith, be courageous, be strong. 14 Your every act should be done with love.* {*agape* in Greek}

Luke 6: 27-35 27 * *"But to you who hear I say, love your enemies, do good to those who hate you, 28 bless those who curse you, pray for those who mistreat you. 29 To the person who strikes you on one cheek, offer the other one as well, and from the person who takes your cloak, do not withhold even your tunic. 30 Give to everyone who asks of you, and from the one who takes what is yours do not demand it back. 31 Do to others as you would have them do to you. 32 For if you love those who love you, what credit is that to you? Even sinners love those who love them. 33 And if you do good to those who do good to you, what credit is that to you? Even sinners do the same. 34 If you lend money to those from whom you expect repayment, what credit (is) that to you? Even sinners lend to sinners, and get back the same amount. 35 But rather, love your enemies and do good to them, and lend expecting nothing back; then your reward will be great and you will be children of the Most High, for he himself is kind to the ungrateful and the wicked.* {everyone is *agape* in Greek}

1Peter 1: 22 *Since you have purified yourselves by obedience to the truth for sincere mutual love, love one another intensely.*{first is *phila-delphia*, brotherly love; the second is *agape*}

Mark12: 30-33 *You shall love the Lord your God with all your heart, with all your soul, with all your mind, and with all your strength.' 31 The second is this: 'You shall love your neighbor as yourself.' There is no other commandment greater than these." 32 The scribe said to him, "Well said, teacher. You are right in saying, 'He is One and there is no other than he.' 33 And 'to love him with all your heart, with all your understanding, with all your strength, and to love your neighbor as yourself' is worth more than all burnt offerings and sacrifices."* {*agape* in Greek}

Matthew 5: 43-46 43 * *"You have heard that it was said, 'You shall love your neighbor and hate your enemy.' 44 But I say to you, love your enemies, and pray for those who persecute you, 45 that you may be children of your heavenly Father, for he makes his sun rise on the bad and the good, and causes rain to fall on the just and the unjust. 46 For if you love those who love you, what recompense will you have? Do not the tax collectors do the same?* {*agape* in Greek}

James 2: 8-9 *However, if you fulfill the royal *law according to the scripture, "You shall love your neighbor as yourself," you are doing well. 9 But if you show partiality, you commit sin, and are convicted by the law as transgressors.* {*agape* in Greek}

John 13: 34-35 *I give you a new commandment: love one another. As I have loved you, so you also should love one another. This is how all will know that you are my disciples, if you have love for one another."* {*agape* in Greek}

Matthew 22: 37-40 *He said to him, * "You shall love the Lord, your God, with all your heart, with all your soul, and with all your mind. 38 This is the greatest and the first commandment. 39 The second is like it: * You shall love your neighbor as yourself. 40 The whole law and the prophets depend on these two commandments."* {*agape* in Greek}

In all these passages only two Greek words appear: *philos* (brotherly or sisterly love, meaning friendship) and *agape* (an unconditional self-giving, a Divine Love). However, according to Vine's Dictionary there are a few other Greek words in the C.T. that mean or imply love, the good or evil kinds:

hedone --pleasure, sometimes lusts; today's use: hedonistic behavior, (the excessive seeking of physical pleasures above and beyond those necessary for survival in the sense of Maslow's "Physical Needs").

eros, erotao or *erotikos* caused by love, desire of love, given to love, erotic love or lust.

pathos--meaning passion, lust. {Trench describes *pathos* as "the diseased condition out of which *epithumia* springs."}

epithumia-- "The word is used for a good desire in Luke 22:15; Phil. 1:23, and 1 Thess. 2:17 only. Everywhere else it has a bad sense. In Rom. 6:12 the injunction against letting sin reign in our mortal body to obey the "lust" thereof, refers to those evil desires that are ready to express themselves in bodily activity. They are equally the "lusts" of the flesh, Rom. 13:14; Gal. 5:16, 24; Eph. 2:3; 2 Pet. 2:18; 1 John 2:16, a phrase which describes the emotions of the soul, the natural curiosity for things evil. Such "lusts" are not necessarily base and immoral, they may be refined in character, but are evil if inconsistent with the will of God." That is a direct quote from Vine's Dictionary. We think the word "will" should be replaced with "love".

epipotheo—to long after, to lust{2 Corin 5: 2}.

orexis–lust {Rom 1: 27}.

The Greek language is certainly more sophisticated in that it has those many Greek words expressing love yet for the most part the authors chose *phileo* to describe brotherly or sisterly love as in social responsibility (like the city named Philadelphia, the city of brotherly love). Now, *agape* represents the Love that generates unconditional self-giving: a definition of Divine LOVE that the Fourth Gospel claims to be the nature of God. It is the word that the Gospel authors use to explain Yeshua's teachings, "Love God with your whole body and soul and {love} your neighbor as yourself."

It does seem that, for all their primitiveness, the C.T. authors had a very modern concept of the many facets of love as we have! The point of this foray into Greek is simply to emphasize the biblical notion of God's attitude towards humankind—Unconditional Self Giving or Divine LOVE—expressed in the single word *agape*. That understanding was perceived through the experiences of Yeshua's life, his deeds, teachings and death on the cross. For them, the prime directive in that experience is "to love God totally and one's neighbor as one's SELF". Your "mind's eye" is truly blind if you cannot comprehend the magnitude and power of that Divine Love!

Dear Reader, there is no other Sacred Scripture that even comes close to that perception of the Creator! NONE! There are two problems most people have in rejecting the Bible as the single most "counter cultural" WAY to God and spirituality:

(1) the inability to distinguish between the myths and legends and the clarity of the meaning of the mythologized message,
(2) the perceptions of radical fundamentalists that every word in their Sacred Scripture is directly from God's lips and those who don't totally accept their belief are doomed to eternal torture.

We trust you can now understand the existence of DIFFERENCES. It's not the Sacred Scriptures in themselves that cause differences. The true cause is IGNORANCE; ignorance of the myths and legends around which the Scriptures are constructed by the imperfect and fallible perceptions of well meaning disciples and one's ability to know what is sugar and what is saccharine! Maybe re-reading Chapter Five will help.

Section Three: What is God's Justice?

It behooves all who seek spirituality to re-examine their behavior to determine how many of these aphorisms and parables have been a part of their everyday life. It would appear that many Christians have succumbed to the foibles of Institutionalism, doctrine, dogma and ritual. Far too frequently we have heard condemnations from those steeped in doctrines of Fundamentalistic Christianity. Is it that some are too adamant about their perceived doctrines to be compassionate of another's perceptions? Has their "pre-critical naiveté" blocked their intelligence and burrowed deeply into their pre-judgements? Do they not know that seekers of spirituality must constantly evaluate themselves! But evaluate before they engage in judging others! Yet they who pronounce such judgments out of hand may not be true seekers of spirituality. Nevertheless, there is ONE WHO will eventually place the eternal mirror of behavioral and intellectual honesty up to everyone's mind's-eye forcing the stark reality of an objective judgment of SELF! Then, we will make our ultimate choice for Eternal Life or whatever God places before us.

Now, that brings up a very interesting concept of God's Justice. Remember that in Mark we read:

Mk 12: *27 He is not God of the dead but of the living. You are greatly misled."*

What do you think of this quote? It's something quite profound! Especially when you put all the other similar quotes together. Read on.

In Deuteronomy we find the following pronouncements:

Deut 30: 15 (NIV) *See, I set before you today life and prosperity, death and destruction.*
Deut 30: 19 (NIV) *This day I call heaven and earth as witnesses against you that I have set before you life and death, blessings and curses. Now choose life, so that you and your children may live.*

Then in Matthew there is the following metaphor about a narrow and a wide gate:

Matt 7:13-14 *"Enter through the narrow gate; for the gate is wide and the road broad that leads to destruction, and those who enter through it are many. How narrow the gate and constricted the road that leads to life. And those who find it are few."*

Have you ever wondered what the authors meant by "destruction". So we did a word search for it in the NIV Bible, including its cognates: destroy, destroyed, and destructive. See Appendix AF.

First. Let's review Random House Webster's Unabridged Dictionary that defines "destroy" as:

1. to reduce (an object) to useless fragments, a useless form, or remains, as by rending, burning, or dissolving; injure beyond repair or renewal; demolish; ruin; annihilate.
2. to put an end to; extinguish.
3. to kill; slay.
4. to render ineffective or useless; nullify; neutralize; invalidate.
5. to defeat completely.
6. to engage in destruction.

Synonyms:

1. smash, level, waste, ravage, devastate. DESTROY, DEMOLISH, RAZE. To DESTROY is to reduce something to nothingness or to take away its powers and functions so that restoration is impossible: *Fire destroys a building. Disease destroys tissues.* To DEMOLISH is to destroy something organized or structured: *to demolish a machine.* To RAZE is to level down to the ground: *to raze a fortress.*
2. extirpate, annihilate, uproot.

Those underlined are very revealing! The biblical implication is more than "to make useless". There is a hint at reducing something to nothingness that translates to Absolute Annihilation! Now, let's look at the word search. Take a moment and read Appendix AF, a word Search for Destroy and its many uses. As you read the selections, notice the many definitions implied in those verses. Of special note is the many different Hebrew and Greek words that give several nuances to the concept of destroy, destroyed, destruction and destructive.

People have wondered about the nature of eternity since the time of their earliest cognition; will there be life after death and what will it be like. Will there be a Divine Justice to compensate for human cruelty?

We know that throughout history the cry for justice has been heard for the many cases of barbaric injustices. Even in our own time that plea resounds from every country on this globe. May we suggest that the answer lies in these specific verses found in one of our Sacred Scriptures. Read these that follow:

Wisdom 1: 11-13 *Therefore guard against profitless grumbling, and from calumny withhold your tongues; For a stealthy utterance does not go unpunished, and a lying mouth slays the soul. Court not death by your erring way of life, nor draw to yourselves destruction by the works of your* hands. ***Because God did not make death, nor does he rejoice in the destruction of the living.***

Ester 16: 21-23 *For God, who rules over all things, has made this day to be a joy to his chosen people instead of a day of destruction for them. 'Therefore you shall observe this with all good cheer as a notable day among your commemorative festivals, so that both now and hereafter it may mean salvation for us and the loyal Persians, but that for those who plot against us it may be a reminder of destruction.*

2 Peter 3: 7 *But by the same word the heavens and earth that now exist have been stored up for fire, being kept until the day of judgment and destruction of ungodly men.*
OH my goodness, women are not subject to this! Sweet justice for the Feminist!

Psalm 92: 6 II *How great are your works, LORD! How profound your purpose! A senseless person cannot know this; a fool cannot comprehend. Though the wicked flourish like grass and all sinners thrive, They are destined for eternal destruction;*

Psalm 55: 24 *But you, God, will bring them down to the pit of destruction. These bloodthirsty liars will not live half their days, but I put my trust in You.*

Hosea 13: 14 *Shall I ransom them from the power of Sheol? Shall I redeem them from Death? O Death, where are your plagues? O Sheol, where is your destruction?*

JOE 1: 15 *Alas for that day! For the day of the Lord is near; it will come like destruction from the Almighty.*

MATT 7: 13 "*Enter through the narrow gate. For wide is the gate and broad is the road that leads to destruction, and many enter through it.*
The Greek word is *apolonia*, that translates to "annihilation".

ROM 9: 22 *What if God, choosing to show his wrath and make his power known, bore with great patience the objects of his wrath-- prepared for destruction?* Again, *the* Greek, *apolonia*, annihilation

2 Thessalonians 1: 5-10 *This is evidence of the righteous judgment of God, that you may be made worthy of the kingdom of God, for which you are suffering-- since indeed God deems it just to repay with affliction those who afflict you, and to grant rest with us to you who are afflicted, when the Lord Jesus is revealed from heaven with his mighty angels in flaming fire, inflicting vengeance upon those who do not know God and upon those who do not obey the gospel of our Lord Jesus. They shall suffer the punishment of eternal destruction* ***and exclusion*** *from the presence of the Lord and from the glory of his might, when he comes on that day to be glorified in his saints, and to be marveled at in all who have believed, because our testimony to you was believed.*

After much contemplation, we believe that the God of Mercy, Forgiveness and Love will not choose eternal physical or spiritual torture but will choose what the underlined passage quoted above in 2 Thes 1: 9. Now read Revelation 20, which is a great allegory that requires de-mythologizing. It talks about two deaths: the first is the death of the body, the second death occurs at the Final judgment of humanity. Let's put those 11 passages along side of Rev 20 and see what we get as our personal interpretation. The first death comes and the righteous sees God in all HER Glory and chooses to live with Him for eternity. {Understand that Heaven is not like a Sports Stadium with the best seats for the "goodest" and the bleachers for the borderlined!} It is a one seater, up front—personal--intimate, for all who make the cut! The unrighteous do not see the Face of God but are given the opportunity to make their choice to accept or reject God's Forgiveness, Mercy and Love extended on God's terms not theirs. In other words, our sense of justice is not God's plan for justice. Those who reject God's Forgiveness remain dead until the Universe reaches maximum Entropy (Zero Degrees Kelvin—absolute zero, no more material Energy (and nothing blinking). That is the Day of the Lord when all are physically raised to the Final Judgment. The Good stand along side of God and the Dead awake for their last choice (Deut 30 15 "I set before you Life and Death, Choose Life!"). Those who reject God's Forgiveness for others will choose Annihilation rather than accept the fact that some, whom they think deserve punishment, have been forgiven. In their stubbornness they choose to be outside of God's Presence and Power. {Do you remember, "The sin against the Spirit"?} Since God holds all in existence, those who wish to be outside of that existence can only chooses the second death ---"non-existence"— annihilation. Recall Mark's sentence: *He is not God of the dead but of the living.* The dead are no more! There are only the living who remain.

To think, you now have an opportunity to set your sails in the right direction. Choose God's Way to LIFE!

Part Three: The Nature of Spirituality

Spirituality is a person's aura (like, behavior and attitude) produced by the mind-spirit's acceptance and acknowledgement of the reality of the basic goodness of creation and being at peace with it. Yes, there is evil and there's BIG TIME EVIL. The existence of evil is freely chosen by those individuals who refuse or reject goodness. There are no demons tempting us. On the other hand, BIG TIME EVIL is a consummate effort by many individual evil choosers of such a magnitude that it ends in grievous harm to many innocent people. Does the name "ENRON" give you any clues to what constitutes BIG TIME EVIL? Have you seen "The Passion of the Christ" yet? Was that or was it not BIG TIME EVIL? Think of it! That was only one of thousands of crucifixions! And, how about ethnic cleansing? Are you aware of the national struggles and slaughter in Africa, Afghanistan and Iraq? Have you read the history of the 20th century and all that happened in Europe and Asia in the two World Wars? Have you forgotten or disbelieve the horrors of the Holocaust? Are we unaware of the near annihilation of the American Indian? Need we cite any more examples? Is not the history of humankind rife with the agony of not following God's Way of peace?

Isn't it time humans tried God's Way as espoused in the "Jesus Movement"? It surely is evident that the Christian Movement with all its infallible doctrines, dogmas and rituals has been a failure! And, that's not mentioning all the other Institutional Religions that have done likewise! There are two others that we would categorize as successful competitors to the "Jesus Movement": Buddhism and Zen. Personally, those three are quite similar in intent, being present to the needs of others, in spite of Zen's penchant for "nothingness".

Thus, Spirituality can be one's only security, sanity and salvation. Some have chosen Zen to reach inner peace; others Buddhism and many, Zen Buddhism. Unfortunately, the others (Islam, Christianity, Judaism ... etc) contain justifications for the Jihad, Crusades and Inquisitions, eye for an eye and similar human distortions. Yet Spirituality is independent of Institutional Religions even though spirituality occasionally precipitates from them.

If you are still reading this book, you have already been exposed to the ingredients of what we call Spirituality! You have just finished reading about this "Jesus Movement" ... the core structure of spirituality. You have read excerpts from the other Sacred Scriptures that contribute certain beneficial aspects to spirituality. .

In the beginning of your journey, you will have to make that choice to pursue your unique PATHWAY and patiently await your very own "moment of clarity" and the "metanoia instant" as your initiation. We have just one last consoling quote from the great Humphrey Bogart: "Lighten up, Friend, it ain't gonna hoit!"

The "Jesus Movement" that we touched upon was directed to the 1st century world. With hardly any words changed for this 21st century, we believe it will work just fine in the here and now.

The search is the dynamic of the PATHWAY to Spirituality. First off, it is an attitude that utterly accepts the beauty and ugliness in the world as the reality of one's surroundings. Somehow, people have gotten the impression that spirituality is a faith-based creed or a religious institutional posture of ritual, dogma or hierarchical leadership. Let's clear the air, right now! Spirituality is NOT faith-based, NOT creedal, NOT institutional, NOT ritualistic, NOT dogmatic and definitely NOT hierarchical.

Part Four: The Nature of a PATHWAY

The PATHWAY to Spirituality is a unique, internal effort of free-willed, imperfect and frail human beings who are in a vibrant relationship with their Higher Power as best they comprehend it. Secondly, the attitude exhibited by a person "in the PATHWAY" is the manner by which he or she seeks to relate to this Supreme Cosmic Creator whose existence and nature is intellectually and emotionally perceived and understood by the person's own natural faculties. That attitude emanates from within the individual who experiences the world, as he or she grows bodily and mentally in discrete physiological and psychological stages. Therefore, that attitude changes in consort with those very demarking stages, or levels if you will, and reaches an internally acceptable and mature profile at a time when the person satisfies the five "Maslownian Needs" of life. Tell me you remember their names! Ok, if you need a hint: (1) Physiological, like food, cleanliness and comfort; (2) Security, like parents who care, having a place to chill out (one's home base) and feeling protected in that place; (3) Belonging, being part of, knowing and known and like the lyrics say:

"The greatest thing you'll ever learn,
is to love and be loved in return."

(4) Self-esteem, like knowing and accepting your SELF and possessing a solid self-worthwhileness; (5) Self-Actualizing, like, doing your best with integrity in all things. Satisfying the last two "Needs" is what we know as maturity. However, every single person reaches a level of equilibrium that differs significantly from all others. Each seeks and elevates to his/her own comfortable level of development, like a little bit of each in unique proportions.

What is one's PATHWAY is not necessarily the same for any other. Now that we've begged the question, how can we propose that there is a unique PATHWAY? Can there be a multitude of PATHWAYs? Which is correct, a single PATHWAY or many PATHWAYs? Is the Taoist better off than the Christian? Better off than the Muslim? The Jew? The Hindu? The Buddhist?

The answer is so simple. The correct PATHWAY is one's own chosen path leading to the very best he or she can be. That unique PATHWAY is what each individual develops for his or her growth towards maturity, inner peace and Spirituality. You're now going to ask a lot of questions! You're puzzled, aren't you? Stop a minute; what we presented above (the Jesus Movement) is, in fact, the foundation for peace, both personally and worldly.

Find your Higher Power; give it a name, any friendly name will do. Mommy or Daddy sounds good! Do what the Zen Master said to the Lady; dump your false notions and pre-judge-ments. Think how you would like to be treated; think about the other person and how he or she would like to be treated. Give to others what you would like to receive. Receive graciously. Remember what the Tao Te Ching said, "What goes around, comes around!" Peace begets peace! Serenity begets serenity. And think clearly about the opposite, because a punch begets a club. A club begets a spear. And spears beget arrows which beget guns. Then come cannons, followed by little bombs. And, finally, the Nuclear Bomb! The "Jesus Movement" aphorisms are simple yet accurately God's WAY to Spirituality. The Fourth Gospel contains a treasure chest of impressions of the Prophet Yeshua. The authors wrote what they perceived and believed to be the meaning of the life and times of the MAN, Yeshua, and they described their faith in allegorical vignettes.

But it is not with the literal words that we find the path to God. It's with the MEANING behind the mythologized writings. In other words, we must not draw our battle lines at the literal statements. We have to remove the frosting to get to the cake; dig out the significance and impact of the meaning. Yeshua's discourses frequently end with the expression, "Let him or her who has ears, hear what has been said!" Yeshua spoke in story-fashion to force the listener to dig into the parable for the inner, covert meaning. So now, we will try to formulate our own parable to set the stage for spiritual growth in "choosing the intelligent pathway of love".

Part Five: Pathways? Let's be Practical!

Here we'll just devise our own 12 steps (symbolic metaphors) describing the process of becoming:

1. The One of Silence and Weakness (read Appendix X+Y)
2. The Universe: awe, beauty, power and grandeur!
3. Turning on the Light in your Library!
4. Gifts from beyond!
5. You'll be able to see forever!
6. Which road to OZ?
7. Is there anyone to catch me?
8. Community without Institutionalism!
9. From barriers to open doors
10. Responsibility is ...
11. Training for the Tour de LIFE.
12. Ah, the race!

Now let's translate those 12 symbolic steps into a more serious practical process that applies them to the WAY of Spirituality. The biggest obstacle to starting is ... not choosing to start. Recall, "the best laid plans of mice and men ... quickly dissolve if not started!" OK, jump in! The water appears cold and foreboding but it'll warm up as long as you keep on swimming and searching vigorously.

1. A Higher Power of Silence and Weakness
   So in this case there's four steps :
   One: Facing the existence of a Higher Power (H.P.);
   Two: Accepting that reality;
   Three: Dealing with the Silence of the Universe's Creator; and
   Four: Realizing that the nature of this Being is Weakness—the H.P.'s inability to violate your freedom to choose.

Look, if you found a fully functional typewriter in the middle of the South Pole, what would your first thought be? Someone left it there! Typewriters don't make themselves. Who would that someone be? Yes, a person with the smarts to build it and use it at the South Pole. That person had to be a Human whose name was Royal, whose address used to be New Park Ave, Hartford, Connecticut (in 1945, that is). Now, focus on the Universe. Who put it there? Don't try to pull a fast one and say it's self-sufficient! If it were so, then how come its nuclear furnace is burning itself out? Gotchya!

You'd be right on, if you said a powerful Being; that's our Higher Power. You don't have to be a Stephen Hawking to figure it out! Some of you may refuse to accept the challenge. But if Aristotle in 300 BC could figure it out, so can you. Well, you will after you read his book's Logic or take Philosophy 101 (Logic)! There are others who would claim that it's impossible to know anything about the Spirit world. Our answer is Psychology 102 (the Capabilities of the Human mind)! Folks, our brain may be a hemisphere of delicate jelly but it works on abstract concepts. A Higher Power is an abstract concept; so you can think about it!

Acceptance is the operative word here and, really, it is mentally taxing to do. Don't dilly-dally; just get on with it! OK, here's a thought. Say to yourself, I exist and am not self-sufficient; my parents conceived me. My parents are not self-sufficient. Their parents made them. Repeat the last sentence seven million times. Just because you said it that many times doesn't explain the existence of parents. Parents are not self-sufficient. That chain exists and it is very long. In order to explain its existence one has to admit to a creator, a Higher Power, an Uncaused Cause. Th ... Th ... That's all folks! The acceptance is up to you. Yes, that Creator is One ... Infinite ... and very smart!

But before we leave this topic, what about that Silence and Weakness thing? One's Higher Power doesn't shout. It only whispers and even then one has to dial up the hearing aid to full sensitivity. Weakness comes from the fact that the Higher Power imbued us with free will and SHE/HE cannot violate our freedom! We are made to be our own pilot; we control the flight stick. The Higher Power cannot role back the clock of time or of nature; the entire Universe is speeding towards zero energy and cannot be stopped. OH, please don't get weepy eyed. The end of our Solar System will occur in about 5 billion years from now. That means, not in your lifetime. But, the clock continues ticking and tocking! We are evolving! Just look at your family pictures!

2. This Universe is one BIG place, full of Power and Wonder!
Have you ever thought of where our Sun gets its power? My Nuclear Science professor told us that it comes from Helium formation starting with Hydrogen; it's a fusion reactor! You know something? He's right! And not only our Sun but also the whole Universe is a NUCLEAR power plant! Our own Earth has a liquid core! How do you think is stays that way? It is the molten remnant of the Big Bang, a Nuclear Fusion.

Our Sun is an ongoing fusion reactor producing some mighty large fusion flares. Do you realize that if the Earth were 10, 000 miles away from the Sun, it would evaporate during the next solar flare that hit it? Contemplate this! How come the Earth is just far enough away to be warmed by the Sun's radiation and not so far as to become a snowball? Math, Physics and Chemistry have the answer. The design of our solar system is about as perfect as a Higher Power could make it. Next time you take out your trusty telescope, get up close and personal with the cosmos. Consider thanking your Higher Power! Since everything has a function and a purpose, so also are we here for a purpose! So, go figure ... it out!

3. OH, Please turn on the Light in your Library
For as far back as we can recall, turning on a light was necessary to read in the dark. Well, does that strike a familiar simile? Our brains need intellectual light. Intellectual light is found in Libraries. Go get a card and start training your mind to expand its awareness in and of this 21st century and the wonders of this age, medicine, technology, the basic sciences, etc. READ! READ! Remember our little parable, Johnnie and the Owl? Get educated and listen for the Owl's echo. Read some Zen, some of Buddha's writings, some Darwin, etc. The light of understanding bathed John the Baptist and Yeshua. The same light struck Paul on his way to Damascus. That light bounced about for a while and hit Muhammad, Martin Luther, Gandhi and others. Your efforts can flip the light switch and get you started in the correct direction too. Need a book? See Appendix R for some refreshing ones !

4. Gifts from Beyond!
How much do you love the Christmas Season? The spirit of giving abounds and gifts are plentiful. The joy of discovering what's inside that special gift is heart warming. Folks, all that is dross compared to the grace and peace that puts a smile in your soul ... forever! What you should realize most is that these smiley gifts are FREE – for the asking and seeking. It's truly a spiritual gift! Yes, because it comes with no strings. OK, so there's one, but only one! Your life has to be, "God's WAY or the wrong way!" And there is no negotiating about it, none at all. Take it or leave it! Its yoke is not heavy; the burden is shared with THE In-Spiriting ONE. Have you so soon forgotten 2 Corin 12: 9? "My grace is sufficient for you!" Understand that there are some powerful messages in that best seller. Maybe it's time to re-read it since we've gotten rid of all the smoke and mirrors! Spiritual gifts are aplenty in that Bible ... as long as you don't get too attached to the literal sense. AND, there are other books that will quench your soul's thirst. Again, check out my personal reading list in Appendix R.

5. You'll be able to see forever!
There are discrete moments in our lives when we experience a mental jolt that gives us an answer to a problem that has been troubling us. It's like a creative solution to a homework problem, to a relationship, to a construction difficulty, to your art project, etc. Psychology has a name for that moment; it is called a Peak Experience. The Greeks called it a "Eureka" moment; a Zenist calls it a Satori; some of our contemporaries call it a "born again" experience. We prefer the name, "moment of clarity". Why use this different name? First of all, this one is slightly more accurate because it is a simple experience without all the jargon that makes it mysterious. Secondly, a small "moment of clarity" is, in fact, an everyday experience of simple proportions and content happening to common folk. There is nothing mysterious, nothing magical and very little associated with Institutional Religion. It's just an experience of some real event that produces a clearer understanding of something spiritual concerning one's life.

However, when it occurs in relation to your Higher Power, the meaning of such a moment is very powerful, personal, absolutely private and truly unshareable with anyone else. Why? Because no other person can possibly comprehend that unique instant when you experienced your Higher Power in such a way that your life begins to change and your behavior is moderated along with your vision of SELF and its relationship with others. Your adjustments are not dramatic in the way you might expect (Moses' vision of the burning bush).. A "moment of clarity" is a dynamic power that initiates miniature character re-appraisals. It's like a child's first steps that lead to falling, new attempts, re-falling and renewed attempts at walking eventually followed by running. Powerful "Moments of Clarity" occur infrequently and produce a series of quantum changes (you know, like in Quantum Physics, each infinitesimally small). But they continue to cause changes! So, you will experience these personality changes and feel them move you into new territory. Understanding will rise up as an actualizing force within you.

Many have a "moment of clarity" but few people act upon it in the manner that produces true dialogue with their Higher Power. Oftentimes an individual will seek counseling from a friend who hasn't a smidgen of an idea about what that individual has experienced. If one asks a minister or priest to explain the event(s), the typical response may very well miss the nature of that deeply personal experience. Not many will be able to translate it for you. The veracity of that "moment of clarity" lies only in the individual who responds to it, deciphers it and acts on its meaning. Therein lies the difficulty! You're on your own to work it out, to become a seeker, in terms of what you can unravel about the meaning of that experience which interrupted your lifestyle. Recall, Paul was blinded for a time; his mind's eye was shut. It lasted several years during which he meditated! A "moment of clarity" descends on you at a specific instance in your life and its meaning has to be interpreted by you in the context of your life situation and the apparent significance of that "moment".

Do you remember the Moses story at the burning bush? It started Moses on a journey to a very different life. That burning bush was symbolic of Moses' spirit being ablaze with curiosity and consumed with passion but not harmed. Later in Exodus Moses speaks to his Higher Power (Yahweh, in this case) and asks to see Yahweh's glory (face). Yahweh says that anyone who sees His face will die. Then She says to Moses, "Go hide between the rocks and I will pass by, my hand will cover you and not let you see my face. As I pass, you may look at my behind". These two incidents (the bush and the view from behind) are the "moments of clarity" for Moses. Now, whether these stories are absolutely tape-recorded events is questionable by today's standards of biblical scholarship. The community recognized two "moments of clarity" in Moses' life that produced two drastic changes: courage to lead the Israelites out of slavery and intimacy with Yahweh. So too did other heroes of the Hebrew Testament have their "moments". And thus, courage and intimacy resulted. You may also have a similar occurrence. Be ready!

One of my favorite stories involves an old prospector having a moment of clarity. It goes like this:

> "There was an old prospector who left civilization in his twenties to search the mountains of Colorado for gold. He worked over the ranges for many years with no great luck at all. One spring day after he had spent a very hard, cold winter prospecting, the rains came and were so lasting that he finally decided that he would leave the mountains. After all, he was well over 70 now and had not made his fortune. With what gold he had accumulated he would like to rest during his last years. On the way down he slipped on the slimy paths and fell several times. He felt discouraged and depressed. "God", he shouted out, "where have you been? You've left me all alone, tired and poor. Where are you?"
> "He got up and walked ahead to the bend in the worn-out trail. He looked over the prairie below. Suddenly, the rain stopped and the sky opened up to let the sun shine through. Then it looked like the land was drying out. The green grass was sprouting thickly and flowers were budding. Then, a warm breeze blew across the grass and the flower buds began to open. Within minutes flowers of all colors bloomed and painted a beautiful rainbow of hues across the prairie as if to say, "Look at my creation! Here I am with you always." The old prospector smiled and went his way ... contented."

What would you have thought had this happened to you? Was that a "moment of clarity" for the old man? Being silent is the best way to prepare yourself; mental silence is the secret of meditation; be present to the moment; be patient. Spirituality begins in your life with "moments of clarity"! What happens after is the decision you must make. To understand the event you'll have to ask yourself these questions: "Why now?" "What's the relationship to my present circumstances?" "Where am I to go with this?" "How shall I proceed?"

6. Which way to OZ?

Our lives are confronted with choices at every tick and tock of our heart, at every corner we turn and at every junction on life's highway. Who we are today is the result of an almost uncountable series of decisions that we've made over our past. Try to count yours for just one day. Bet you'll lose count after a few hours! Getting up is your first choice, shutting the alarm is the second, then breakfast, shower or just a face wash, and so on throughout the day. Can you imagine NOT making any choices in a 24-hour period? What's to do to minimize all those choices? Or, is that what makes life challenging? Then, one day as your hectic pace roles on like a ball bearing down an infinite slide, you are hit with a gigantic major turning point forcing you to choose between your present life style and turning to a new path, somewhere joyful, peaceful but thoroughly "unknown". We call that a "Metanoia Instant".

You are frozen in that instant of decision as though your world stopped spinning: the waves unmoving, the sky clear blue with clouds motionless and time not ticking. The "unknown" will have penetrated your being and put you at a supreme intersection where you must choose the appropriate PATHWAY. That instant is very Biblical indeed. It's the Moses story; it's Yeshua's decision to preach the Kingdom of God and the Good News; it's the Paul story; it's the Peter story after the cock crowed three times; it's the Nicodemus night visit. And yet, you're experiencing an identical spotlight in the 21st century.

"*Metanoia*" is the Greek word that appears very often in the Christian Testament and signifies a change in mindset (*meta* is change and *noia* is one's mindset). It's the Greek word we often translate as "repentance" but the correct translation is "to rethink one's psychological and spiritual state", to turn to another way of moral and ethical behavior. In the Bible the demand of this "Metanoia Instant" is to refocus your life in a Godly direction or to commence a more serious relationship with your Higher Power. [After a while you, too, will use "Loving Daddy" instead of "Higher Power".]

Needless to say, that "Metanoia Instant" can put your psyche into a major tailspin beyond your immediate control and comprehension. And, know this for certain; no single person can truly explain what is happening to you because that "Instant" belongs to you as a gift ... wrapped just for you, a gift compelling you to openness. To embrace it, in spite of its confusion and mystery, will alter your present way and lead you to the Divine WAY.

The meaning of that numinous visit will be intelligible only from the "behind of it" (it means you'll understand the event much later).

This "Metanoia Instant" is the first contact, sometimes a monumental confrontation, with the Ephemeral demanding that, at this cross road in your life, you must make a choice because your present pathway is either bland, empty or in chaos. It may well be a gentle knock on your soul's door but more often it's a symbolic lightning strike that disrupts the quiet of your day, whether morning, noon or night, it matters not. In any event, your psychological foundation will be shaken like the vibration of an earthquake, sometimes a Richter 3, more often closer to a Richter 7. Funny, we humans do have a tendency to build on unsteady ground not realizing the dangers that lie silently around the curve and over the hill. Maybe the knock is God's way of alerting you to the not-so-good you continually choose. Your response, then, begins the dance with a mysterious somebody, the dance floor at an unknown place, strange and ethereal. But maybe the knock is just a growth bump on the pathway you have been walking all along. Either case, it IS that Instant of Choice.

7. Is there anyone to catch me?
Whenever we humans make a significant shift in careers we often bounce our choice off of a respected person. In the case of FAITH the choice is totally up to the individual! And many times we balk at the choice. Take the case of the mountain climber who took the bet to climb El Capitan.

> As he was six feet from the top, he slipped and plummeted down the sheer rock face. Half way down his thrashing arms caught a sturdy branch. The shock and the surprise rushed to his brain. It took almost 5 minutes for him to regain his composure. He looked sheepishly down and then immediately focused upwards. A death fear surged through his veins. He thought for a moment and shouted for help, "Is there anyone up there?" Over and over his voice pierced the silence. He was close to giving up. Suddenly, a quieting voice came down from somewhere at the top. "Don't be afraid, I'll save you." OH, relief, he thought. Then the voice said, "Just let go and I'll catch you." He shouted out, "Who are you?" The voice replied, "I'm God!" Our climber went silent for what seemed an eternity. His mind ran through what he had heard, "just let go and I'll catch you. I'm God!" After a moment of thought, he looked up and shouted, "Is there anyone else up there?"

No, if you decide to step off a cliff, God "ain't" gonna catch you. But, if your soul is in jeopardy, God will catch you with a mental, spiritual grace that demands a choice. That choice is whether you have the faith to accept that "God's grace is sufficient" for you. Don't flub it!

8. Community without Institutionalism!
Have you ever noticed how many times the number 12 shows up? Twelve months in a year, 12 sons of Jacob, 12 tribes of Israel, 12 pieces in a dozen, 12 Apostles, 12 Steps in the AA, 12 inches in a foot, 12 ounces in a pound! Opps, the last one is wrong, the momentum was hard to resist. Well, the Alcoholics Anonymous organization has a 12-step program that is really great. No, it's not just for alcoholics, it's not an Institutional thing, it's not brain washing and it's not a religion. What it does is make people whole who were broken and suffering. Why don't we take a good look at those 12 Steps and see for ourselves the stuff they're made of.

"Here are the steps ... suggested as a program of recovery:

1. We admitted we were powerless over alcohol— that our lives had become unmanageable.
2. Came to believe that a Power greater than ourselves could restore us to sanity.
3. Made a decision to turn our will and our lives over to the care of God, as we understood Him {Her}.
4. Made a searching and fearless moral inventory of ourselves.
5. Admitted to God, to ourselves, and to another human being the exact nature of our wrongs.
6. We're entirely ready to have God remove all these defects of character.
7. Humbly asked Him {Her} to remove our shortcomings.
8. Made a list of all persons we had harmed, and became willing to make amends to them all.
9. Made direct amends to such people wherever possible, except when to do so would injure them or others.
10. Continued to take personal inventory and when we were wrong promptly admitted it.
11. Sought through prayer and meditation to improve our conscious contact with God as we understood Him {Her}, praying only for knowledge of His {Her} will for us and the power to carry that out.
12. Having had a spiritual awakening as the result of these steps, we tried to carry this message to alcoholics, and to practice these principles in all our affairs."

The Big Book, p 59 and it's available at this URL:
http://www.aa.org/bigbookonline/

These are indeed very specific to AA. Let's translate them into a format that focuses on its essential spirituality. Instead of Alcoholism being the key idea, we'll focus on personal spirituality; although these two may often overlap in the Diagnostic & Statistical Manual that most psychotherapists use as their reference text defining human dysfunctionality. Here we go!

1. Admit that we are going nowhere with our choices— that our lives have become bland, meaningless or chaotic.
2. Believe that a Higher Power greater than ourselves can help us become a mature spiritual person.
3. Make a decision to turn our lives over to that Higher Power's WAY of doing business as best we understand Him/Her.
4. Make a searching and fearless moral inventory of our behavior.
5. Admit to that Higher Power, to ourselves and to our significant other the exact nature of our problem.
6. Be ready to ask our Higher Power to remove all these defects of character.
7. Humbly ask our Higher Power to remove our shortcomings.
8. Make a list of all persons we have offended and hurt, and be willing to make amends to them all.
9. Make direct amends to such people wherever possible, except when to do so would injure them or others.

10. Continue to take personal inventory and when we are wrong, promptly admit it.
11. Seek through prayer and meditation to improve our conscious contact with our Higher Power as best we understand Her/Him, pray for knowledge, compassion and the will power to carry out resolutions.
12. Having had a spiritual awakening as the result of these steps, we try to live this message and to practice these principles in all our daily affairs.

Then, we find a community of accepting and affectionate people.

9. From barriers to passage ways
For years now in search of God, some (or many) have been bored out of their pews:
By empty rituals that have lost their meaning in the dust of time;
By doctrines that make no sense in the 21st century;
By dogmas that are inconsistent with Yeshua's intent;
By arrogant leaders who intercept and covet the whispers of God to the people.

These barriers must be removed to let God's intimate conversation come directly through to us recipients. Only a severe face-lift can do the job. [One more metaphor!]

Ok, here's what we propose. Let's face-lift the message! Remember the "good news"? It's the message that there's life after death! It's available to anyone just for the asking, praying and reading. God has been knocking on our doors since humans could hear. Clean out your ears! God is asking you to choose; choose life or choose death but understand, you're the one who is choosing. God wants no one to choose death. We humans were always destined to share eternal LIFE with God. {And to set things right, God wills only one thing---to share eternal life with us! God wills NOTHING else for us ... except happiness!} The catch is; eternal life will occur only if we choose to follow God's way of doing business. Uh-Oh, there's that hook again!

The next issue is, "What's God's way of doing business?" Well, you have to read what the prophets have been screaming for years and centuries. Actually, what has been preached is no mystery! Take a new look at the teachings of the "Jesus Movement" for the REAL road signs. Ah, road signs, just like in the Fourth Gospel. We've just pointed them out, haven't we? So, go back and read the basics of the "Jesus Movement" and understand that it is NOT the same as the Christian Movement as it exists today!!

The last of the barriers is just the three R words: Relationship with God, Respect for your neighbors and Robert's Rules of Moral and Ethical Order. You know, those three R's cover a lot of ground. Didn't we read in the Fourth Gospel that Yeshua came as a FRIEND? Do you need a PhD to figure what it's like to be a friend? Take a sheet of paper and write ten things that define a good friend! You'll get the picture. Now, let's consider our neighbors. As soon as we decide to offer respect to all others, the World will change. And, if humans can figure out a set of rules to maintain order at meetings (Robert's Rules of Order), is it so far fetched to consider that God has a set of rules for civility and spirituality? As was written in all the Gospels, Love God fully, and your neighbor likewise!

Just think for a moment, that's all there is to it! No Institution, no rituals, no doctrines, no dogmas, no anything ... but one ... celebrate the Good News and enjoy your life to the fullest!

10. Responsibility is ...
And that is at the center of the chaos existing in this 21st century. People act and then pass the buck. CEO's steal and blame it on the Accountant; the rapist blames it on the woman; the druggie kills and excuses him or herself by saying, "Is was just an accident!" As the one with the gun standing over the blood of a spouse tells the officer, "we were just having a domestic quarrel." Sounds like the Adam and Eve myth had some substantial meaning to it after all. Nothing happens by accident; happenings are chosen. If you're the one choosing, then you're the one accountable. So simple! Every play has a principal actor; in the play called, THIS IS YOUR LIFE, you are that principal actor. OH yes, you are the one writing the script ... daily! When the play ends, take the roses or the tomatoes! Choose now!

11. Training for the Tour de LIFE
Lance Armstrong has certainly not sat on his thumbs for the eleven months prior to the Tour de France. Arnold Schwartzennegger didn't get to where he is today by staring at those weights. Doctors don't get qualified by reading paperback novels. Everyone prepares for a life career. Why is it so inconceivable that a Sacred Scripture is essential for training for the WAY of Spirituality? Look around! There are plenty of spiritual gymnasiums. They all have spires that can be seen for miles around. OH, but we are not talking about Church steeples; we meant God's trees pointing to heaven's abode! Yes, a metaphor! Nature is the Church! Earth is the Church! Did you forget Moses' first epiphany when God said, "Remove your sandals, you are walking on sacred ground!" After all, God did construct this Chapel. Go take an extended trip into a deep forest. Listen to the whispers of nature, absorb its meaning and ask yourself: Why is it so peaceful? It's because the whispering pines and hemlocks are speaking softly of their creator. A note of interest: oaks, maples and ash don't speak; so don't stick your ear on their bark. Some barking things bite!

Some Institutional Religions conduct retreats-- extended periods of spiritual introspection. Attendees spend their time reading the Bible or other spiritual books and listening to sermonettes on the meaning of life with God and your neighbors. Check with your local spiritual center to see if they offer retreats. Or, you could find a quiet place and read one of the Suggested Reading Books in Appendix R!

12. Ah, the race!
We're not talking about the Olympics. We're talking about the race to LIFE. You'll need:

a. A stable foundation from a Master or Avatar;
b. Spiritual direction from a book or The Book;
c. The right moral and ethical attitude (behavior)

Essentially, you'll need to walk your talk along God's moral and ethical WAY of doing business. God's WAY is to build not to destroy, to share not to hoard, to help not to ignore, to accept others not to reject them, to be compassionate not cynical, to hold up not to push down, etc. Re-read the parable of the Good Samaritan!

Since when do our possessions take priority over poverty? Since when do corporate investments take priority over paying an honest wage? Since when does power take priority over integrity? Since when does illicit sex take priority over spousal fidelity? Since when does profit take priority over medical attention? Those kinds of decisions are in total contradiction to God's WAY. And each one took place because of someone's deliberate choice! Don't you be the one to do that! Run your race with integrity!

All this is heavy stuff, isn't it? Maybe you should sit back for a moment to absorb what's been presented so far in this Chapter. You know, a little sip of the juice might just help you relax yourself so you could contemplate for a while **...**

Time's up!

What's this all about?

Let's say that your LIFE is one giant jigsaw puzzle in which each piece represents a single choice you've made. Then, put the several thousands of these chips on a table where you can take a good look at the picture side and re-arrange them into a more meaningful self-portrait whose edge pieces define the boundaries of your encultured life. The rest belong to those daily choices you've made throughout your life up to today. That's correct; you cannot see the whole picture yet until you begin to sort out which choices belong to the beginning of your life, framing the landscape. Those earlier ones were made without you ever considering what portrait you desired. From the beginning of your maturity your choices constituted the brush strokes of your portrait. Those thousands of chips on the table will eventually form that picture.

The more you assemble those individual pieces (choices) into their proper place, the more you will understand what direction you are taking with your choices to paint your life. Watch closely as you add more choice pieces; the portrait is beginning to take form. But still, you can't visualize the whole picture of your life. It takes many different trials and errors to get the pattern to develop. Have you noticed that there are a few holes left unfilled? Yes, some of your choices at that time seem to have been without plan or reason. You continue to find pieces whose scant coloring look out of place. It takes you hours to fit them into your life style. And, even then, you get no clearer idea of the outcome. You work a few more hours and become exhausted. Your mind needs rest; while you sleep your subconscious works feverishly to feedback its findings and activates your dream world. In the middle of the night you bolt up in a cold sweat. You've received a vision; it appears to be a small view of a very large maze. Before you could take in its entirety, the vision disappears. You slide under the warm covers and fall back into a deep sleep.

Morning arrives and you take breakfast to the puzzle-table to continue working on the portrait of your life. Suddenly you are picking out the very next group of pieces that fit perfectly, filling in more clues to the final image. It's incomplete but you're driven on by your desire to get to that last piece. You want to know what your portrait is so you can discover your meaning. You study each piece very carefully and find still more correct places where each choice fits.

Days pass by and there is no complete solution. Weeks pass by and the end is not in sight. Months follow swiftly and then years; in spite of your efforts, many pieces have not been placed. After several decades of concentrated exertion you place the last piece. Finally, the portrait is clear! You see the meaning of your life!

You sigh deeply in awe and feel yourself slipping off the chair and hitting the floor. When you rise, a tunnel appears and there is a brilliant light at its end ...

That brief allegory about putting a jigsaw puzzle together is somewhat true to life but it also speaks to deeper meaning as only a mythical story can. First, it says that we humans do make more choices than we are willing to admit, many thousands as a matter of fact. Secondly, most of the "not-too-bright" choices are made in our youth. [Notice, we didn't define at what age youth ceases! These days, it lasts far longer than the teen years.] Thirdly, when (and if) maturity begins, our many choices establish the nature of our character and integrity. Some of our choices are exemplary, some good and some "not-so-beneficial." Fourthly, that Integrity by which we choose determines the Technicolor of our life portrait. If only our vision could encompass the future? Alas, it doesn't! Fifthly, humans desperately wish to understand the meaning of the portrait. However, like Moses getting a glimpse of God's behind, we only understand God's hand in our life much later ... after the event occurs. We only see our completed portrait -the meaning of our life--at the last moment just before we meet our Maker!

In other words, your life had been a series of choices taking you on many different paths that brought you to many places. When you lost focus of your goals, these little choices may have corralled you into unpleasant and undesirable situations. Were your choices haphazard, without direction and ultimately self-destructive? The problems with letting a coin toss guide you are those dead ends that go nowhere.

Life needs a guide. Your best guide is your Higher Power, God. When God is busy, you'll have to rely on godly friends (spouse, personal friends and maybe a spiritual Master). Choose them wisely and listen for whispers. Let your free will pick out a PAYHWAY that leads to your personal well being. Follow the signs along your WAY that bring peace to your heart and the hearts of those around you. Choose with a determination and destination in mind. Be present to those in your circles; be a sharing person.

The PATHWAY you travel will only paint a portrait with strokes of your personal choices. Keep the final goal always within view; make your choices with it in mind. When the moment arrives for your walk through the tunnel, the portrait you leave behind will inspire those who see it hanging in the Gallery of Lives.

The End may be nearer than you think. Choose responsibly!

Part Six: What Now? The proper place of ritual!

1. Ritual is an activity we humans perform to keep a modicum of meaning in our lives. In that sense it's important to our well being and acceptance of life.

2. Repetitive Ritual has meaning but it also becomes commonplace in its frequency and often loses its purpose and meaning.

3. The Rituals of Religion are meant to be spiritual reenactments to reinforce the influence of powerful and meaningful people and events from human history and traditions. Without a vibrant ritual that remembers and motivates, boredom sets in and the ritual loses its significance.

4. Church services tend to fall into boredom rather quickly when the leader neglects or loses fervor for the Way of Spirituality.

5. This is painfully true in the case of the Catholic, Anglican, Episcopalian and Eastern Orthodox Mass and Christian Services of Protestant Churches. Poor energy, poor sermons, lackadaisical motivation, but particularly, failure to understand the deeper meaning of its originator, all of these making the participants fall rapidly into mental and spiritual unconsciousness.

6. The symbolism of the Mass is the Passion event -- last supper and the crucifixion. Both themes in their present performance definitely lack the color and the pathos of "Jesus Christ Superstar" or "The Passion of the Christ". The Biblical celebration of the Eucharist has, for the most part, been lost in many Christian denominations.

7. In the case of the Eucharist, the meaning is lost because the formula is not that of the "Seder" meal! The significance is not fully understood by Catholics or the eating of flesh and the drinking of blood by Protestant Christians. God may well be represented by bread but bread is not God! The act of eating the unleavened bread and bitter herbs in a seder meal must be truly associated with recalling the tasteless food and the bitter suffering during the Exodus trek to the Promised Land. The aromatic wine represents the joyful exhilaration anticipating entry into the Promised Land. The alcohol is the intoxicating arrival there. The eating of the bread signifies the taking of spiritual food like the verse in Ezekiel 3: 1 being told to "eat the scroll ". The effect of the wine signifies the heavenly (the true promised land) celebration--- the consummate joy of eternal freedom from all ills.

8. Eating flesh and drinking blood has, from the very first breath of humans, been symbolic of taking on the strength and spirit of the animal one has killed. It was no small wonder that the early Gentile Christians translated their "Collective Unconscious" traditions into the taking in the spirit and glorified life of Yeshua when they symbolically ate his flesh and drank his blood! Does this make sense to you? Try reading Joachim Jeremias' book, "The Eucharistic Words of Jesus"; he was the first to make all these connections. In his book he restated, as best his research could, the words that Yeshua may very well have spoken at his Seder, "The breaking of this bread is like the breaking of my body for God's work of salvation for all humankind. Take and eat so that you may share with me this effort for salvation. The pouring of this wine is like the pouring of my blood for the salvation of humankind. Take and drink so that you may pour out your blood with me to bring about salvation." [Give or take a few words!] Proverbs 9: 4-5 reads:

> *"Let whoever is simple turn in here; to him who lacks understanding, I say, Come, eat of my bread, and drink of the wine I have mixed!"*

Since wisdom is metaphorically associated with Yeshua, the early Christian Jewish members intertwined this passage with the Eucharist service. Of course, Paul helped. In I Corin 10: 1-4 we read:

> *"I do not want you to be unaware, brothers, that our ancestors were all under the cloud and all passed through the sea, and all of them were baptized into Moses in the cloud and in the sea. All ate the same spiritual food, and all drank the same spiritual drink, for they drank from a spiritual rock that followed them, and the rock was the Christ."*

How close can you get to the intended meaning of the Eucharist? Nevertheless, chew on this; the focus is on the meaning not the worship of a piece of bread or a cup of wine! Eucharist is METAPHOR! Eucharist is not God! Eucharist is the call to share in the salvation of humankind!

9. Now for the Sunday Mass! It is in no way a re-enactment of the passion weekend. Actually it started out to be the gathering time of the members to teach, to motivate, to celebrate and maintain a dialogue within the Christian communities. Today's Catholics are burdened with the pain of mortal sin if they miss it. BUNK! For the first few hundred years of Catholic history there was no sin attached to missing the Sunday Celebration. Attendance dropped when the Sunday gathering became too ritualistic. The obvious reason was that it lost its significance. And income decreased at the same time. The leaders then decided that the lack of money was of such import that they had to do something drastic. Guess what? It then became the Doctrine of Attendance (the DA) under the penalty of BIG SIN. If you missed Mass on Sunday and died on Monday, Hell - eternal torture - awaited you –so it was preached. In the meantime, collections improved greatly. And today the coffers are very full indeed. We, personally, fail to understand how the wealth of the Vatican helps the poor, abandons poor parishes, closes schools, pays lower wages to their hospital employees or pays off the lawsuits against the sexually abusive priests. OH, did we forgot to mention their alleged controlling interests in the birth control Drug Companies in Italy and those shady deals with some organized special-interest groups, both of which incidents were reported in the weekly magazines decades ago. In the 1960's the Catholic Council of American Bishops took a survey of the sexual activity of the American priesthood and found that 60 of every 100 priests who responded were sexually active and of the sixty, 40 were homosexual. That was some tough job sweeping all that dirt under the sacristy for the last forty- or so years. Does the aphorism, "What goes around, comes around!" ring your moral bell? Or, did you not hear it? Remember, it first was written in the Tao Te Ching! Those Chinese prophets really hit that nail, didn't they? We think we've got to gargle something to get this bitter taste out of our soul. We'll be back shortly!

Ok, shortly has passed, we're back. We're seeing clearer now. In all fairness to the Roman Tradition, it did produce such people as Francis of Assisi, Benedict, Thomas

Aquinas, Robert Bellarmine, and more. Don't forget, the Church buildings in Europe, which produced a high employment rate, the Universities of Europe and the Vatican's art collection. Then there was sanctuary provided by a local Bishop for Galileo Galilee. However, we must not lose sight of the proper time and place for ritual as a means to spiritual development.

Here are some suggestions for all Institutions and Denominations:

1. The day of rest must be a celebration. Make it so! People falling asleep in the back aisles is not our idea of a celebration!

2. That day must include adult education. There are a plethora of cinematic materials that would simply knock your spiritual socks off!

3. Don't forget the kiddies; but don't get serious with them! Make it a fun time. "Little House on the Prairie" is an excellent teaching tool; get the CD's or DVD's of all the shows, show them and discuss them.

4. Make that day a picnic service for the whole family. Help people get some sunshine into their lives. Build a barn, refinish a home for the elderly or needy and invite the whole community. Hire, or accept a volunteer as an Entertainment Manager (spiritually endowed, if you please) for your Community (and maybe consider firing the Minister or Priest and getting a Counseling Psychologist who is in the Spirit).

5. Establish your own group. Not with a Minister or Priest, preferably a College Professor, like Marcus Borg, to provide an intelligent adult discussion focusing on the wholeness and holiness of spirituality.

6. Use a loaf of real bread and a bottle of the fermented grape (a little alcohol won't hurt) and please, explain what you're doing in terms of (a) sharing yourself with the community in the present, (b) remembering the significance of the Passover Seder and (c) taking in spiritual food.

7. And, by all means, communicate yourselves as a caring, sharing, forgiving and compassionate group.

8. Give your group a good name, like "The Community of Spiritual Renewal".

Spirituality is a three-dimensional portrait of (a) your relationship with God (b) the love of those with whom you socialize, including spouse, children, extended family, neighbors and strangers and (c) the state of your SELF-knowledge. Spirituality is expressed rather clearly in Paul's definition of Charity (KJV) or Love (NAB and RSV) in 1 Corin 13:1-13:

1 If I speak in human and angelic tongues but do not have love, I am a resounding gong or a clashing cymbal.
2 And if I have the gift of prophecy and comprehend all mysteries and all knowledge; if I have all faith so as to move mountains but do not have love, I am nothing.
3 If I give away everything I own, and if I hand my body over so that I may boast but do not have love, I gain nothing.

4 Love is patient, love is kind. It is not jealous, (love) is not pompous, it is not inflated,
5 it is not rude, it does not seek its own interests, it is not quick-tempered, it does not brood over injury,
6 it does not rejoice over wrongdoing but rejoices with the truth.
7 It bears all things, believes all things, hopes all things, endures all things.
8 Love never fails. If there are prophecies, they will be brought to nothing; if tongues, they will cease; if knowledge, it will be brought to nothing.
9 For we know partially and we prophesy partially,
10 but when the perfect comes, the partial will pass away.
11 When I was a child, I used to talk as a child, think as a child, reason as a child; when I became a man, I put aside childish things.
12 At present we see indistinctly, as in a mirror, but then face to face. At present I know partially; then I shall know fully, as I am fully known.
13 So faith, hope, love remain, these three; but the greatest of these is love.

Spirituality, then, is a state of LOVE for God, Self. and People. Each of us lives in a world perceived and acknowledged by our own relative truth. We are, after all, imperfect, frail, fragile, emotional, needy animals with free will and the capacity for intelligent and logical thinking. That means we are human, each different and each uniquely encultured into a specific time and place. Most of all, pay attention to verse 11. We need adult education to bring God's people to maturity in heart and mind. (Metaphor! Metaphor!)

Spirituality is fundamentally the submission of SELF to the needs of others in balance with our own needs and understanding. Which one is more important at the moment? It means being present to others in a manner that is not arrogant, not pedantic, not superior, not one hint of these. Rather, spiritual behavior is respectful, compassionate and self-giving. Spirituality is, then, an attitude and a behavior of SELF-respect and "other centeredness" in relation to one's Higher Power and to one's neighbor near and far. Spirituality is being present to the needs of others. The fundamental problem for us humans is clearly, "How does one get there?" Just consider that everyone is riding on a unique vector moving at different speeds towards the Center of all Being---God.

A Fable: The Card Game of Life

Life begins when a Mom and Dad create a new life and give it a shell, you know, our DNA's physical features. Now these features are totally different with each life that is created and this shell is unique to each individual because it's like the throw of the dice, very statistical. In this fable our shell doesn't really determine who we are; who we are comes about by the set of cards we receive.

Life then is like a card game whose players are born with 10 cards, one each from 10 different decks: (1) motor skills, (2) energy consumption, (3) growth, (4) speech, (5) perception, (6) emotions, (7) needs, (8) intelligence, (9) choice and (10) relationships. Every player is like an empty bucket, which gets one card from each of these 10 decks. The individual then plays the Life Game with the cards he or she has been given as best he or she can.

The problem (our shared human condition) is that there are 1 trillion trillion cards in each of those 10 decks and within a deck no two cards are alike. Those statistically assigned 10 cards (one from each deck) comprise our code that gives each player a potential to become whatever he or she chooses in playing the Life Game. However, the new player is not given any clue to the nature of that game that he or she must play! We players have to figure it out as the Life Game progresses.

If those are the ground rules, it's no wonder life is thought of as a game of chance and we frail and flawed humans are prone to err in our choices by our very imperfect constitution!

How's a person to make it to the end game? Some players get the idea that we are to strive to be perfect. What? It's near impossible, isn't it? Look around; see imperfection played out in 3-D and stereophonic sound. You'll see chaos and confusion, disease and depression, greed and poverty, war and misery and so many other horrible conditions that people have chosen for themselves or have permitted others to choose and impose those conditions on us.

What's going on? This isn't a very nice game, is it? Who made up such cruel set of rules for the human race?

Have you figured it out yet? There's only one answer! It's the Creator!!

That's it folks, a Super Mathematician has created (a) the Nuclear Fusion Universe based on statistics and probability (b) a supreme maze of Nuclear Powered stars and planets that could or could not become and (c) the beings who inhabit planet Earth and possibly inhabit other planets out there somewhere, and, finally, (d) the Universe to be an evolving creation moving towards the OMEGA Point when All will be in the presence of the Creator and know HER ... face to face.

OH my goodness! That certainly was a mouthful! What's a body to do in such a deeply shadowed, depressing environment? Is this Creator a sadist, a comedian or just plain mad? Or, is there something peculiar to this puzzle that we're missing?

Did you get the clues? The game is called, "Statistical Spirituality". We are free-willed, frail and imperfect beings who have to discover and choose our personal unique pathway that leads us to the point of inner peacefulness, serenity and a dance of joy. Living totally in that journey is what we call one's spiritual journey. The choices one makes during the trip are completely random, yes, statistical choices that we must make. God doesn't make a single choice for us! God has placed the responsibility clearly on US to fix ourselves and the World around us. We humans are the captains of this spinning and circling planet. God has given US the free will to cure the sickness. God cannot interfere with our freedom!

Note carefully while you read this truism!

"Each person, without hurting others, must choose to act each moment as best he or she can, based on who he or she is at that moment." Personal integrity is its name!

Every single day for the rest of your life say this forgiving prayer to yourself out loud to your image in a mirror; "I have done my very best for who I was at each moment of my past choosings." We cannot forgive others until we have forgiven ourselves!

That is truly a perfect confession acknowledging one's frail, flawed and imperfect human nature. That nature formed your past, determines your present and will influences your future. Hopefully, the image in the mirror reflects your true SELF and your soul/mind hears the words of SELF-acceptance and understands your need for forgiveness. Strength and wisdom develop in proportion to the number of days you make that confession to yourself in the mirror. That's why strength and wisdom are an age thing!

Finally, you may consider this: Pray to your Higher Power thusly, "Dear H.P., I give my life over to You so that you may do for me what I can't do for myself."

This author prays that your Spirituality fosters strength of character and of conviction for your beliefs as well as the wisdom to respect the Way of your neighbors -- near and far!

Again, act and choose wisely with forgiving compassion, just as God acts wisely, mercifully and compassionately!

The End of Ignorance
and
The Beginning of Whole, Holy and Loving Relationships

The APPENDICES

APPENDIX A

A Brief History of the World's Religions

Author's Note: Each of the following Sacred Scriptures or newly established institutions represents a significant event in the development of Eastern and Western Religions. The approximate dates are important only in that they mark a shift in theological posturing that divided a culture into two or more rival sects. An excellent review of western civilization is the Richard Tarnas book, "The Passions of the Western Mind".

Ebla
A city unearthed in Syria (circa 2500 BC): it contained a written dictionary and business writings. The writings from Ebla led scholars to decipher those Sacred Scriptures, historical writings and tales that preceded the Hebrew Testament.

Hinduism of India
Aryan Nature religion in the third Millennium BC
The Vedic texts ~ second Millennium BC Rig Veda, songs of knowledge
***The Upanishads*:** 800 to 500 BC; Scriptures of Hinduism which explained existence and meaning for everyday living.
***Bhagavad Gita*:** 500 to 200 BC Scriptures which combined Hindu and Buddhist teachings.

The Shang
First historical dynasty of China (1751-1050 BC) whose religion was that of spirits and power.

Enuma Elish:
The earliest (~1200 BC) written text out of Tigris / Euphrates Region of Sumerian origin

Jainism
B. Mahavira leaves mainstream Hinduism and rejects revelation and based his religious scheme on logic and experience. Affirms a plurality of Divine beings: 610 BC

The Torah, OT
The first five books of the Old Testament, allegedly written by Moses (1400-1100 BCE), but documented by Ezra about 500 BC and added to as late as 167 BC.

Buddha
Leaves Hinduism and develops a New Way of Four Noble Truths and Eight-Fold Paths - 560 BC.

Socrates
The Athenian philosopher who was executed in 399 BC after the courts of democratic Athens tried and convicted him on a charge of corrupting the youth and disbelieving in the ancestral gods.

Confucius
Based on ethical respect for others, originated around 450 BC.

Legalism
Chinese philosophy of political control by might, later emulated by Mao. (425 BC).

Plato
Spirit trapped in a body, Platonism, the theology of the early Christian movement. 428-347 BC.

Taoism
Chinese (Lao Tzu) philosophy related to the Dao de Jing: 400 to 300 BC, now known as the Tao Te Ching.

Aristotle
Developed Logic and the basic tenets of modern Western Scientific principles (384-322 BCE).

State Religion
Legalism and Confucianism form State ideology of the Chinese Empire under Qin and Han dynasties: 206 BCE.-220 A.D.

Old Testament
Writings by Authors who lived during and after the Book's named principal character. 600 BC to 200/100 BC (Greek translation of existing Hebrew OT, the Septuagint, Alexandria ~270 BCE).

New Testament
Writings of Letters and Gospels by 2nd generation Christians. NOTE: the Mediterranean Christians had only the Septuagint as their Sacred Scripture.

Christianity
Religion that grew from the teachings of Yeshua, the Nazarene. Originally a part of Judaism but expelled in 85 AD as heretical.

Ritual Orthodoxy
The first hierarchically organized "Taoist Church" with the establishment of social ideals through moral precepts and public liturgical ceremonies.

312 A.D. Constantine
Roman Ruler who politicized the leaders of Christianity.

325-350 AD Council of Nicaea:
Constantine demands a Council to stop Christianity's politically disturbing infighting. The Triune Godhead and the Divine Carpenter formulated the core Dogma of the political Roman Petrine Tradition (Catholicism).

China
In the years 365-370 A.D. the birth of two of the main Taoist traditions, representing mysticism and ritual, respectively, takes place.

China
In 402 A.D, the Taoist, Ge Chaofu, compiles new scriptures and attributes them to the Numinous revelation, received by his ancestor Ge Xuan. This school incorporates the doctrine of rebirth and retribution and develops the ideal of universal liberation in contrast to individual immortality.

China
In 424 Taoism becomes the official religion at the Northern Wei court. This period of glory lasts until the first half of the 6 century.

Chalcedon 451 AD
Christianity's 2nd Dogma: the Carpenter was totally Human including ignorance.

The Qur'an
Spoken by Al'lah (Islamic God) to Muhammad -610 AD

China
Tang Dynasty emperors (618-907) generally support Taoism, but the tendency of the period is towards syncretism. The Dao de Jing re-defines Taoism

Eastern Schism
Christianity's conflict Re the Center of Authority: Rome vs. Constantinople, ~1000 AD.

China
Song and Yuan Dynasties (960-1368) are the most supportive of the Redefined Taoism. Other schools, such as that of Filial Piety incorporate Confucian moralism.

Reformation:
Luther challenges Roman Catholic fiscal and theological corruption that ended Roman Catholic' rule over Western Europe: ~1517 A.D.

Council of Trent
Dogmatized Thomas Aquinas' theological works as the permanent theological basis justifying Roman Catholicism. 1545-63 AD

New Christian Sects:
Lutherans from Martin Luther: Original and Missouri Synod.
Baptists from Calvin and His Five Points: Five No. American Sects.
Church of England: Anglicans / Episcopalians .
Misc. Denominations: See Appendix B.

Enlightenment Era:
The Scientific and Philosophic Period: 17th to 18th Centuries.

Vatican I
Council of 1869-1870 defining Papal Primacy and Infallibility, thus polarizing Catholicism against the Eastern and Protestant Churches..

Scientific Revolution:
The Great Challenge to Biblical History and Cosmology.

Evolutionists:
Science's Challenge to Genesis' Creation Story, 1900's.

Nuclear Age:
The Great Wars of 20th century; Einstein, $E=MC^2$, the Atomic Bomb and Nuclear Reactors.

The Space Age:
The Beginning of the Exploration of the Universe. 1960's.

Vatican II Council:
Synod of Catholic Hierarchy in an effort to catch up with Science, Modern Psychology, Biblical Scholarship and Theology (1965).

Age of Technology:
Biological, Medical and Communications - 1975.

The 21st Century
Cloning and the Expanding Universe; the rise of Fundamentalism
and the Wars over Dictators, Terrorism and Oil.

APPENDIX B

A Denominational Listing from the Internet

CHRISTIAN	NON-CHRISTIAN
Anglican and Episcopal	American Indian Assemblies of God
Associated Gospel (Philpott)	Buddhism (3 Sects)
AWANA*	Scientology
Baptist (Canada)	Zen (2 Sects)
Baptist (reformed)	Taoism
Baptist (Southern)	Eskimo
Baptist, (BBFI-independent)	Islam (3 Sects)
American Baptist Association	
Bible Chapel	
Catholic (Roman)	
Christian Church (Disciples of Christ)	
Christadelphian	
Christian Missionary Alliance (Canada)	
Church of God, International (Cleveland TN)	
Church of God (7th Day)	
Church of God of Prophecy	
Church of God, International (Tyler)	
Church of God, World Wide (after 1995)	
United Church of God, an international association	
Evangelical (First)	
Evangelical (Free)	
Evangelical Church	
First Church of Christ Scientist	
Foursquare**	
Independent Fundamental (IFCA)	
International churches of Christ	
Inter-varsity Christian Fellowship	
Jehovah's Witnesses	
Lutheran	
Mennonite Brethren	
Methodist	
Mormons (Latter-day Saints)	
Ministers Fellowship International (MFI)	
Nazarene	
New Apostolic	
Orthodox	
Pentecostal Assemblies of Canada (PAOC)	
Pentecostal Assemblies of God	
Pentecostal: Massive Encyclopedia of Pentecostal churches	
United Pentecostal Church International UPCI	
Plain Truth Magazine	
Presbyterian	
Quakers, Shaking	
Reformed (Dutch/Christian/Canadian)	

Religious Science (Offshoot of Unity)
Salvation Army
Seventh-day Adventist's
Shakers (Mother Ann Lee)
Toronto Airport Christian Fellowship
Triumph Prophetic Ministries, William Dankenbring
Two by Two's (2x2's) **
Unitarian Universalist Church
United Church of Canada
United Church of Christ
Unity Church
Vineyard (AVC)
Wesleyan (Arminian)

* Approved Workmen Are Not Ashamed (2 Timothy 2:15).
** Whether or not this is some sort of twisted humor escapes us.

Appendix C

The Infancy Gospel of Thomas

From "The Apocryphal New Testament" M.R. James-Translation and Notes Oxford: Clarendon Press, 1924

I, Thomas the Israelite, tell unto you, even all the brethren that are of the Gentiles, to make known unto you the works of the childhood of our Lord Jesus Christ and his mighty deeds, even all that he did when he was born in our land: whereof the beginning is thus:
II. 1 This little child Jesus when he was five years old was playing at the ford of a brook: and he gathered together the waters that flowed there into pools, and made them straightway clean, and commanded them by his word alone. 2 And having made soft clay, he fashioned thereof twelve sparrows. And it was the Sabbath when he did these things (or made them). And there were also many other little children playing with him. 3 And a certain Jew when he saw what Jesus did, playing upon the Sabbath day, departed straightway and told his father Joseph: Lo, thy child is at the brook, and he hath taken clay and fashioned twelve little birds, and hath polluted the Sabbath day.
4 And Joseph came to the place and saw: and cried out to him, saying: Wherefore doest thou these things on the Sabbath, which it is not lawful to do? But Jesus clapped his hands together and cried out to the sparrows and said to them: Go! and the sparrows took their flight and went away chirping. 5 And when the Jews saw it they were amazed, and departed and told their chief men that which they had seen Jesus do.
III. 1 But the son of Annas the scribe was standing there with Joseph; and he took a branch of a willow and dispersed the waters which Jesus had gathered together. 2 And when Jesus saw what was done, he was wroth and said unto him: O evil, ungodly, and foolish one, what hurt did the pools and the waters do thee? behold, now also thou shalt be withered like a tree, and shalt not bear leaves, neither root, nor fruit. 3 And straightway that lad withered up wholly, but Jesus departed and went unto Joseph's house. But the parents of him that was withered took him up, bewailing his youth, and brought him to Joseph, and accused him 'for that thou hast such a child which doeth such deeds.'

IV. 1 After that again he went through the village, and a child ran and dashed against his shoulder. And Jesus was provoked and said unto him: Thou shalt not finish thy course. And immediately he fell down and died. But certain when they saw what was done said: Whence was this young child born, for that every word of his is an accomplished work? And the parents of him that was dead came unto Joseph, and blamed him, saying: Thou that hast such a child canst not dwell with us in the village: or do thou teach him to bless and not to curse: for he slayeth our children.

APPENDIX D

Selected Passages from 114 verses in the Gospel of Thomas

7. Jesus said, "Lucky is the lion that the human will eat, so that the lion becomes human. And foul is the human that the lion will eat, and the lion still will become human."

8. And he said, "The person is like a wise fisherman who cast his net into the sea and drew it up from the sea full of little fish. Among them the wise fisherman discovered a fine large fish. He threw all the little fish back into the sea, and easily chose the large fish. Anyone here with two good ears had better listen!"

13. Jesus said to his disciples, "Compare me to something and tell me what I am like." Simon Peter said to him, "You are like a just messenger." Matthew said to him, "You are like a wise philosopher." Thomas said to him, "Teacher, my mouth is utterly unable to say what you are like." Jesus said, "I am not your teacher. Because you have drunk, you have become intoxicated from the bubbling spring that I have tended." And he took him, and withdrew, and spoke three sayings to him. When Thomas came back to his friends they asked him, "What did Jesus say to you?" Thomas said to them, "If I tell you one of the sayings he spoke to me, you will pick up rocks and stone me, and fire will come from the rocks and devour you."

19. Jesus said, "Congratulations to the one who came into being before coming into being. If you become my disciples and pay attention to my sayings, these stones will serve you. For there are five trees in Paradise for you; they do not change, summer or winter, and their leaves do not fall. Whoever knows them will not taste death."

37. His disciples said, "When will you appear to us, and when will we see you?" Jesus said, "When you strip without being ashamed, and you take your clothes and put them under your feet like little children and trample then, then [you] will see the son of the living one and you will not be afraid."

77. Jesus said, "I am the light that is over all things. I am all: from me all came forth, and to me all attained. <u>Split a piece of wood; I am there. Lift up the stone, and you will find me there."</u>

107. Jesus said, "The (Father's) kingdom is like a shepherd who had a hundred sheep. One of them, the largest, went astray. He left the ninety-nine and looked forthe one until he found it. After he had toiled, he said to the sheep, 'I love you more than the ninety-nine.'"

109. Jesus said, "The (Father's) kingdom is like a person who had a treasure hidden in his field but did not know it. And [when] he died he left it to his [son]. The son [did] not know about it either. He took over the field and sold it. The buyer went plowing, [discovered] the treasure, and began to lend money at interest to whomever he wished."

[A saying probably added to the original collection at a later date:]
114. Simon Peter said to them, "Make Mary leave us, for females don't deserve life." Jesus said, "Look, I will guide her to make her male, so that she too may become a living spirit resembling you males. For every female who makes herself male will enter the kingdom of Heaven."

Author's note: One has to admit that some of these passages are not what one would expect from the Synoptic Gospels nor the Fourth Gospel! No. 77 is a good one, especially the underlined.

APPENDIX E

URL's to some Apocryphal Writings

http://www.gnosis.org/naghamm/nhl.html{To read any of these, simply get on the Internet, open this file and click on any Title.}

An Overview of the Nag Hammadi Texts

1. **Writings of creative and redemptive mythology**, including Gnostic alternative versions of creation and salvation: The Apocryphon of John; .The Hypostasis of the Archons; .On the Origin of the World; The Apocalypse of Adam; The Paraphrase of Shem. (For an in-depth discussion of these, see the Archive commentary on Genesis and Gnosis.)

2. **Observations and commentaries on diverse Gnostic themes,** such as the nature of reality, the nature of the soul, the relationship of the soul to the world: The Gospel of Truth; The Treatise on the Resurrection; The Tripartite Tractate; Eugnostos the Blessed; The Second Treatise of the Great Seth; The Teachings of Silvanus; The Testimony of Truth.

3. **Liturgical and initiatory texts**: The Discourse on the Eighth and Ninth; The Prayer of Thanksgiving; A Valentinian Exposition; The Three Steles of Seth; The Prayer of the Apostle Paul. (The Gospel of Philip, listed under the sixth category below, has great relevance here also, for it is in effect a treatise on Gnostic sacramental theology).

4. **Writings dealing primarily with the feminine** deific and spiritual principle, particularly with the Divine Sophia: The Thunder, Perfect Mind; The Thought of Norea; The Sophia of Jesus Christ; The Exegesis on the Soul.

5. **Writings pertaining to the lives and experiences of some of the apostles**: The Apocalypse of Peter; The Letter of Peter to Philip; The Acts of Peter and the Twelve Apostles; The (First) Apocalypse of James; The (Second) Apocalypse of James, The Apocalypse of Paul.

6. **Scriptures which contain sayings of Jesus as well as descriptions of incidents in His life**: The Dialogue of the Saviour; The Book of Thomas the Contender; The Apocryphon of James; The Gospel of Philip; The Gospel of Thomas.

APPENDIX F

An Outline of Christian History

YEAR (AD)	ACTIVITY
~30 to 34	The Yeshua Movement
35	The Apostolic Movement
40's	The Pauline Mission
50	Organization of Communities
60's	The Episcopal Times
70	Markan Community
80	Lukan & Matthean Communities
~85	Bishops Rule
90	Johannine Community
100	The Growth of Theological Confusion
200	The Great Heresies
312	Constantine's Church-State
	The Seeds of Roman Control
325	Council at Nicaea
400	The Christian Canon
451	The Council at Chalcedon
~500	Roman Petrine Tradition becomes the Power
	The Patriarchal Times
1057	The Great Eastern Schism
1517	Luther & the Beginning of the Reformation
1537	The Council of Trent: Counter Reformation Protestantism Flourishes in Europe:
	Lutheran Church
	Anglican Church
	Presbyterian - Calvin
	Baptist Church,
	And many more
1611	The King James English Bible
1799	Discovery of the Rosetta Stone
1800's	Biblical Scholarship Flourishes
1870	Vatican Council I
	Papal Authority & Infallibility:
	Condemnation of (a) Modern Democracy (b)
	Freedom of Conscience & (c) Public Schools
1900's	Ordination of Women
	The Great Expansion of Biblical Scholarship
1965	Vatican II Council-Rome Reforms:
	Rome Centers itself under the Bible
	Traditionalism Takes a Back Seat
	Biblical Scholarship Encouraged
	Ecumenism Begins & Rituals Change
2005	The Death of Vatican II Resolutions
2006	Rome Returns to Traditionalism

APPENDIX G

THE GEOLOGICAL TIME SCALE

http://www.ucmp.berkeley.edu/

If you wish to explore more, simply get on the Internet,open this file and L-click on any underlined! Time scale is that mya = million years ago.

I. **Precambrian Time**-4,500 to 543 mya
  A. Hadean Era-4500 to 3800 mya
  B. Archaean Era-3800 to 2500 mya
  C. Proterozoic Era-500 to 543 mya
    1. Paleoproterozoic Period-2500 to 1600 mya
    2. Mesoproterozoic Period-1600 to 900 mya
    3. Neoproterozoic Period -900 to 543 mya

II. **Phanerozoic Eon** -543 mya to present
  A. Paleozoic Era-543 to 248 mya
    1. Cambrian-543 to 490 mya
    2. Ordovician-490 to 443 mya
    3. Silurian-443 to 417 mya
    4. Devonian-417 to 354 mya
    5. Carboniferous-354 to 290 mya
    6. Permian-290 to 248 mya
  B. Mesozoic Era-248 to 65 mya
    1. Triassic-248 to 206 mya
    2. Jurassic-206 to 144 mya
    3. Cretaceous-144 to 65 mya
  C. Cenozoic Era-65 mya to the present
    1, Tertiary-65 to 1.8 mya
      a. Paleocene-65 to 54.8 mya
      b. Eocene-54.8 to 33.7 mya
      v. Oligocene-33.7 to 23.8 mya
      d. Miocene-23.8 to 5.3 mya
      e. Pliocene-5.3 to 1.8 mya
    2. Quaternary-1.8 mya to today
      a. Pleistocene-1.8 mya to 10,00
      b. Holocene-10,000 years to today

APPENDIX H

Time Scale of Creation and the Fossil Record

{Just remember, the Hebrew word "yowm" means "a long time".}

YEARS AGO	EVOLUTION	GEOLOGIC TIME	
	The BIG BANG	**About 14 to 16 BYA**	
14 Billion	**THE FIRST DAY of CREATION (Starts Here)**		
13 Billion			
12 Billion			
11 Billion			
10 Billion			
	THE SECOND DAY of CREATION		
9 Billion	Galaxies Form		
8 Billion	**Stars Form**		
7 Billion	Solar System		
6 Billion	Sun		
5 Billion	Molten Earth		
	THE THIRD DAY of CREATION		
4 Billion	Solid Earth	Hadean	4.5 BYA
3 Billion		Archaean	3.8 BYA
2 Billion		Protoerozoic	2.6 BYA
1 Billion	Oxygen Increases		
0.9 Billion	Plant Life		
0.8 Billion			
0.7 Billion			
0.6 Billion	Bacterial Life		
	THE FOURTH DAY of CREATION		
0.5 Billion	Sift Shell life	Paleozoic	544 MYA
0.4 Billion	Fish		
0.3 Billion		Permiam Extinction	290 MYA
0.2 Billion	Amniote eggs	Triassic	248 MYA
	THE FIFTH DAY of CREATION		
100 Million	Dinosaurs	Jurassic	206 MYA
90 Million	Mammals	Cretaceous	144 MYA
80 Million			
70 Million			
60 Million	Meteor Extinction	Paleocene	65 MYA
50 Million		Eocene	54.8 MYA
40 Million	Age of Mammals		
30 Million	Large Mammals	Oligocene	33.7 MYA
20 Million	Climate Warming	Miocene	23.8 MYA
10 Million			
9 Million	Stable Continents		

8 Million			
7 Million	Pre-Humans		
6 Million	Grasslands		
5 Million		Pliocene	5.3 MYA
	THE SIXTH DAY of CREATION		
4 Million	Multi-Genesis of Humans		
3 Million	The Garden of Eden (Lasted 28 days)		
2 Million	Lucy		
1 Million	Ice Age Starts	Plistoceme	1.8 MYA
0.9 Million	**THE DAY GOD RESTED from CREATION**		
0.8 Million			
0.7 Million			
0.6 Million			
0.5 Million			
0.4 Million	Neanderthals		
0.3 Million	S. Africans Migrate		
0.2 Million			
0.1 Million			
90 Thousand	Cro-Magnons		
80 Thousand			
70 Thousand			
60 Thousand			
50 Thousand	Cave Pictographs		
40 Thousand			
30 Thousand			
20 Thousand	End of Ice Age	Holocene	10,000 YA
10 Thousand			
9 Thousand			
8 Thousand			
7 Thousand	Egyptian History		
6 Thousand	Writing Begins		
5 Thousand			
4 Thousand	**THE EIGHTH DAY GOD WAS BACK to WORK**		
3 Thousand	Moses		
2 Thousand	Christianity		
1 Thousand	Islam		
TODAY	Space Flight		

The only difference between Genesis and our Geological Evolution-Fossil Record is the time of the origin of the Solar System's SUN. All this confusion because the English (16th century) didn't translate "yowm" correctly !!!

APPENDIX I

Overview of Islam from the Internet

The Arabic word Islam means 'submission' to the will of God (Allah); Islam is the name of the religion originating in Arabia during the 7th-century through the Prophet Mohammed. Followers of *Islam* are known as Muslims, or Moslems, and their religion embraces every aspect of life. They believe that individuals, societies, and governments should all be obedient to the will of God as it is set forth in the Koran, {or Qur'an}, which they regard as the Word of God revealed to his Messenger, Mohammed. The Koran teaches that God is one and has no partners. He is the Creator of all things, and holds absolute power over them. All persons should commit themselves to lives of grateful and praise-giving obedience to God, for on the Day of Resurrection they will be judged. Those who have obeyed God's commandments will dwell forever in paradise, but those who have sinned against God and not repented will be condemned eternally to the fires of hell. Since the beginning of creation God has sent prophets, including Moses and Jesus, to provide the guidance necessary for the attainment of eternal reward, a succession culminating in the revelation to Mohammed of the perfect word of God.

There are five essential religious duties known as the Pillars of *Islam*.

(1) The *shahada* (profession of faith) is the sincere recitation of the twofold creed: 'There is no god but God' and 'Mohammed is the Messenger of God'.
(2) The *salat* (formal prayer) must be performed at five points in the day (varying with time of sunrise and sunset) while facing towards the holy city of Mecca.
(3) Alms-giving through the payment of *zakat* ('purification') is the duty of sharing one's wealth out of gratitude for God's favour, according to the uses laid down in the Koran. There is a duty to fast *(saum)* during the month of Ramadan
(4) The *Hajj* or pilgrimage to Mecca is to be performed if at all possible at least once during one's lifetime.
(5) *Sharia* is the sacred law of *Islam*, and applies to all aspects of life, not just religious practices. It describes the Islamic way of life, and prescribes the way for a Muslim to fulfill the commands of God and reach heaven.

There is an annual cycle of festivals, including the Feast of the Sacrifice *(Id al-Adha),* commemorating Abraham's willingness to sacrifice Isaac, which comes at the end of the Hajj pilgrimage, and the *Id al-Fitr,* marking the end of the month of fasting in Ramadan. There is no organized priesthood, but great respect is accorded to descendants of Mohammed, and other publicly acknowledged holy men, scholars, and teachers, such as mullahs and ayatollahs.

There are two basic groups within *Islam*. *Sunni Muslims* believe that correct religious guidance derives from the practice or *Sunna* of the Prophet. They recognize the first four caliphs as Mohammed's legitimate successors. The *Shiites* believe that correct religious guidance obtains from members of the family of the Prophet, on which basis they recognize only the line of Ali, the fourth caliph and nephew and son-in-law of Mohammed as the Prophet's legitimate successors.

While the Sunnis have through history believed that just government could be established on the basis of correct Islamic practice, the Shiites believe government to be inherently unjust, particularly since the last recognized member of the line of Ali, the Twelfth Imam, became hidden from view in AD 873. There are a number of sub-sects of *Islam*, and in 1995 there were over 1000 million Muslims throughout the world.

APPENDIX J

Genealogies of Yeshua in Matthew and Luke

Matthew's List:
1 The book of the genealogy of Jesus Christ, the son of David, the son of Abraham.
[First Set of 14]
2 Abraham became the father of Isaac, Isaac the father of Jacob, Jacob the father of Judah and his brothers. 3 Judah became the father of Perez and Zerah, whose mother was Tamar. Perez became the father of Hezron, Hezron the father of Ram,
4 Ram the father of Amminadab. Amminadab became the father of Nahshon, Nahshon the father of Salmon, 5 Salmon the father of Boaz, whose mother was Rahab. Boaz became the father of Obed, whose mother was Ruth. Obed became the father of Jesse,
[Second Set of 14]
6 Jesse the father of David the king. **David** became the father of Solomon, whose mother had been the wife of Uriah. 7 * Solomon became the father of Rehoboam, Rehoboam the father of Abijah, Abijah the father of Asaph. 8 Asaph became the father of Jehoshaphat, Jehoshaphat the father of Joram, Joram the father of Uzziah. 9 Uzziah became the father of Jotham, Jotham the father of Ahaz, Ahaz the father of Hezekiah. 10 Hezekiah became the father of Manasseh, Manasseh the father of Amos, * Amos the father of Josiah.
[Third Set of 14]
11 Josiah became the father of Jechoniah and his brothers at the time of the Babylonian exile. 12 After the Babylonian exile, Jechoniah became the father of Shealtiel, Shealtiel the father of Zerubbabel, 13 Zerubbabel the father of Abiud. Abiud became the father of Eliakim, Eliakim the father of Azor, 14 Azor the father of Zadok. Zadok became the father of Achim, Achim the father of Eliud,
15 Eliud the father of Eleazar. Eleazar became the father of Matthan, Matthan the father of Jacob, 16 **Jacob** the father of Joseph, the husband of Mary. Of her was born **Jesus** who is called the Messiah.

Luke's List:
23 * When **Jesus** began his ministry he was about thirty years of age. He was the son, as was thought, of Joseph, the son of **Heli**, 24 the son of Matthat, the son of Levi, the son of Melchi, 25 the son of Mattathias, the son of Amos, the son of Nahum, the son of Esli, the son of Naggai, 26 the son of Maath, the son of Mattathias, the son of Semein, the son of Josech, the son of Joda, 27 the son of Joanan, the son of Rhesa, the son of Zerubbabel, the son of Shealtiel, the son of Neri, 28 the son of Melchi, the son of Addi, the son of Cosam, the son of Elmadam, the son of Er, 29 the son of Joshua, the son of Eliezer, the son of Jorim, the son of Matthat, the son of Levi, 30 the son of Simeon, the son of Judah, the son of Joseph, the son of Jonam, the son of Eliakim, 31 the son of Melea, the son of Menna, the son of Mattatha, the son of Nathan, the son of **David**.
32 the son of Jesse, the son of Obed, the son of Boaz, the son of Sala, the son of Nahshon, 33 the son of Amminadab, the son of Admin, the son of Arni, the son of Hezron, the son of Perez, the son of Judah, 34 the son of Jacob, the son of Isaac, the son of Abraham, the son of Terah, the son of Nahor, 35 the son of Serug, the son of Reu, the son of Peleg, the son of Eber, the son of Shelah, 36 the son of Cainan, the son of Arphaxad, the son of Shem, the son of Noah, the son of Lamech, 37 the son of Methuselah, the son of Enoch, the son of Jared, the son of Mahalaleel, the son of Cainan, 38 the son of Enos, the son of Seth, the son of Adam, the son of God. And, do notice the father of Joseph in Matthew is **Jacob** and in Luke is **Heli.**

Appendix K

Selected Passages from the Q Source

Explanation of the Q Source on the Internet:
http://www.livius.org/q/q-source/q1.htm

The Document:

1. **Annotated from Luke:**
   http://www.religiousstudies.uncc.edu/jdtabor/Qluke.html

2. **Annotated from Luke & Matthew:**
   http://www.livius.org/q/q-source/q2.htm

3. **Selected Passages: The Common Passages from Each Gospel**

Luke 6: 20-23 **Matt 5: 3-12**
The Beatitudes
[Jesus] lifted up his eyes toward his disciples, and said: 'Blessed are you poor, for yours is the kingdom of God. Blessed are you who hunger now, for you shall be filled. Blessed are you who weep now, for you shall laugh. Blessed are you when men hate you, and when they exclude you, and revile you, and cast out your name as evil for the Son of Man's sake. Rejoice in that day and leap for joy! For indeed your reward is great in heaven, for in like manner their fathers did to the prophets.'

Luke 6: 37-42 **Matt 7: 1-5**
Judging others
[Jesus said:] 'Judge not, and you shall not be judged. Condemn not, and you shall not be condemned. Forgive, and you will be forgiven. Give, and it will be given to you: good measure, pressed down, shaken together, and running over will be put into your bosom. For with the same measure that you use, it will be measured back to you.'

And he spoke a parable to them: 'Can the blind lead the blind? Will they not both fall into the ditch? A disciple is not above his teacher, but everyone who is perfectly trained will be like his teacher. And why do you look at the speck in your brother's eye, but do not perceive the plank in your own eye? Or how can you say to your brother, "Brother, let me remove the speck that is in your eye," when you yourself do not see the plank that is in your own eye? Hypocrite! First remove the plank from your own eye, and then you will see clearly to remove the speck that is in your brother's eye.'

Luke 9: 57-60 **Matt 8: 19-22**
The cost of following Jesus
Now it happened as they journeyed on the road, that someone said to him, 'Lord, I will follow you wherever you go.' And Jesus said to him, 'Foxes have holes and birds of the air have nests, but the Son of Man has nowhere to lay his head.' Then he said to another, 'Follow me.' But he said, 'Lord, let me first go and bury my father.' Jesus said to him, 'Let the dead bury their own dead, but you go and preach the kingdom of God.'

Luke 10: 16 **Matt 10 :40**
'He who hears you hears me, he who rejects you rejects me, and he who rejects me rejects him who sent me.'

Luke 11: 9-13 **Matt 7: 7-11**
Ask, seek, knock
[Jesus said:] 'So I say to you, ask, and it will be given to you; seek, and you will find; knock, and it will be opened to you. For everyone who asks receives, and he who seeks finds, and to him who knocks it will be opened. If a son asks for bread from any father among you, will he give him a stone? Or if he asks for a fish, will he give him a serpent instead of a fish? Or if he asks for an egg, will he offer him a scorpion? If you then, being evil, know how to give good gifts to your children, how much more will your heavenly Father give the Holy Spirit to those who ask Him!'

Luke11:33 **Matt 5: 15**
'No one, when he has lit a lamp, puts it in a secret place or under a basket, but on a lampstand, that those who come in may see the light.'

Luke 12: 8-9 **Matt 10: 32-33**
'Also I say to you, whoever confesses me before men, him the Son of Man also will confess before the angels of God. But he who denies me before men will be denied before the angels of God.

Luke 12: 33-34 **Matt 6: 19-21**
'Sell what you have and give alms; provide yourselves money bags which do not grow old, a treasure in the heavens that does not fail, where no thief approaches nor moth destroys. For where your treasure is, there your heart will be also.'

Luke 16: 13 **Matt 6: 24**
Not serving two masters
[Jesus said:] 'No servant can serve two masters; for either he will hate the one and love the other, or else he will be loyal to the one and despise the other. You cannot serve God and mammon.'

APPENDIX L

Suggested Internet Sites for Reference Material

1. **Mesopotamian/Babylonian Creation Myth: The Enuma Elish**
Article by Dennis Bratcher: http://www.cresourcei.org/enumaelish.html

2. **Hinduism**:
(a) GodULike
(b) http://www.hope.edu/academic/religion/reader/reader.html
Select Hinduism
(c) The Bhagavad-Gita
http://eawc.evansville.edu/anthology/gita.htm

3. **Taoism:**
(c) GodULike
(d) http://www.hope.edu/academic/religion/reader/reader.html
Select Chinese Religions

4. **THE DIDACHE (The Teaching of the Twelve Apostles)**
Several Translations
http://www.earlychristianwritings.com/didache.html

5. **Misc. Christian Writings:**
http://www.earlychristianwritings.com/q.html

6. **Historical Jesus**
http://www.earlychristianwritings.com/theories.html
This is a very lengthy article. Please visit this URL

7. **Islam**
http://www.barkati.net/english/

8. **Roman Catholic (Encyclopedia and New American Bible)**
http://www.newadvent.org/cathen/

9. **Old Testament Life and Literature**
http://www.infidels.org/library/modern/gerald_larue

10. **Open the Internet,** then, open either App B or L, then Click on any denomination to view its theology or URL to read the articles.

PART TWO: DOWNLOADING SACRED SCRIPTURES FROM THE INTERNET

Before you start playing with your computer you should know that you can most likely get books from your library for a few weeks at a time and read them

directly. However, when you return the books you no longer have easy access to the material.

If you wish to keep these Sacred Scriptures for your own future reference, you can get copies cheaply from the Internet for yourself. Here's how it's available for free.

Go to your computer, or to a friend's computer, with one ream of paper for yourself or for your friend [maybe have a few dollars to donate to his next ink purchase!]. Get on the Internet and use the search engine of your, or his, choice (We've used Google). Put in one of these titles:

1. Tao Te Ching, and press "go".
   - a. A list of potential sites will then be displayed.
   - b. Pick the one that indicates that the site has the latest English translation.
   - c. Put your mouse arrow on it and left click. Voila! The whole translation of the Tao Te Ching will appear.
   - d. You can now do one of two things:
     - (1) Print all those pages after you make sure of its size and put sufficient paper in the printer tray or
     - (2) Copy [*for Microsoft Word users*] it to a file that you can put on your hard drive:
       - (a) Bring up your word processor and "minimize it",
       - (b) Then highlight all the text and copy *(in Microsoft Word you drag the mouse, with the left click held down, over all the text by starting at the top and simply move the mouse to the very bottom of the text. The text will actually scroll itself and stop at its bottom.)*
       - (c) Then release the left click on the mouse. All the text will now be highlighted.
       - (d) Press the "control" key on the keyboard, and while holding that key down, press the "c" key.
       - (e) This will copy the entire text into a clipboard that you won't see but please know that it's where the text is.
       - (f) Next, go to the lower left of you screen and
       - (g) Left click on the little icon representing your word processor. A blank page of that word Processor will cover your entire screen *(if it doesn't, then click on the expand button located between the "x" and the "minimize" boxes at the top right of your page).*
       - (h) Now press and hold down the "control" key and hit the "v" key. Hooray for you, the text is now onto your word processor and you can change the font and enlarge it as you see fit.
       - (i) You then should "save as" [*its name*] to a favorite folder or make a special folder to hold all the Sacred Scriptures for future reference.
2. Repeat the above for the Sacred text of Islam but start with the words, The Qur'an. Once again you can simply print the text or download it to your folder for future reference. Your choice.
3. Once more repeat step 1 with the word, Upanishads, for one of the Sacred texts of Hinduism. Repeat with the words, Bhagavad Gita, for the other Sacred text of Hinduism.
4. Again repeat step 1, which by now you've mastered, with the words, Enuma Elish, for the ancient Sacred text of the Sumerians. This is getting fun now, isn't it?

5. OK, once more! Put in the words, Four Truths of Buddha, for the Buddhist's Sacred rules.

For any more references material you'll have to go to one of two sites via your search engine: the "GodULike" site which is a somewhat "irreverent" and "humorous" set of commentaries on every religion; it's very informative. Or, go to the "Religion Reader" site put on the web by Hope College which, I think, will present a little different view of the information about the nature and history of religions. Each site will contain a list of referral URL's to which you can go to retrieve reams of additional facts and figures that will amaze you far into the night for many uncountable nights. To use a URL all you gave to do is left click on the title of the link that looks like this, *http://www.godulike.co.uk* Good luck.

Re: Mac procedures to access info...

1. Enter google.com, press return key.
2. Enter Tao Te Ching (or whatever), click on "search".
3. Select any of a zillian choices on subject! (We chose Stan Rosenthal's translation (first on list) because it indicated it was the easiest for beginners.)
4. Anyone who has a Mac will have no problem taking it from there.

APPENDIX M

THE STYLES OF MYTHOLOGY

IN SACRED SCRIPTURES AND IN THIS BOOK

Myth: A traditional tale or legendary story about (a) some superhuman being, (b) some alleged person or (c) event:

The Literary Expressions of Myth:

Allegory:
1. a representation of an abstract or spiritual meaning through concrete or material forms; figurative treatment under the guise of another.
2. a symbolic narrative (**parable**).
3. to speak as to imply something other.

Metaphor:
The application of a word or phrase to an object or concept which it does not literally denote in order to suggest a comparison with another object or concept.

Simile:
A figure of speech in which two unlike things are explicitly compared.

Irony:
A figure of speech in which the literal meaning is opposite of what is spoken (sarcasm, satire or mockery)

Paradox:
A statement seemingly self-contradictory or absurd but in reality expressing a possible truth.

APPENDIX N

Unfolding the Tale of Creation

What is the most impressive is the order of creation in the seven days (*yowm*) of Genesis One. That order starting with plant life, is very close to, if not exactly, what biologists would predict from evolutionary science. Therefore, we're convinced that the hidden message in the Genesis Myth is Natural Evolution. Again and again, one will find myth in the Bible bigger than just scientific facts; it's more than informative and it points to the mystery of our Divine origin. We have sufficient evidence to believe that the natural order does precede closely to the Genesis sequence. Please remember the story of "Johnnie and the Owl" as you read the following:

1st Day: "Let there be Light!"—from a singularity (nothing or something) to the Big Bang, a nuclear explosion that creates the molten elements for the entire Universe!! These would eventually coalesce into stars and planets. As a matter of astronomical fact, we have seen little bangs occurring in distant space; of course that light-show may have taken all this time to traverse the distance between us. This *yowm* took close to 6 to 10 billion years! Hey, this hot radioactive universe took a long time to cool.

2nd Day: Of all that coalesce, one of the stars is the sun in our Solar System and one of the planets in that System is Earth, along with the other planets in our system. [Note: except Venus, which has been hypothesized to have arrived from outside of the Milky Way.] Understand that the planet Earth has not totally cooled to the solid state; our core is still molten to this very day--volcanoes are proof of this molten center. Towards the end, last 0.5 billion, of this *yowm* the solid surface forms and apparently begins the surface contractions that will eventually produce mountains, visible cracks like the Great Lakes and other basins. The land mass is aligned at the equator and begins its extremely slow redistribution of the continents. It will not stop until about 50 million years prior to our present day. Within the past 50 years the US Naval Nuclear Submarine program has photographed the ocean floor visually or with Sonar and the shifting is quite visible. National Geographic has printed maps that illustrate this phenomenon. This interval takes close to 4 billion years. The Universe is now about 9 billion years old and the infant Earth just born only about 0.5 billion years old.

3rd Day: From this period to today represents nearly the remaining 5 billion years of evolution of the Universe while the birth of the planet Earth took place about 4.5 billion years ago. It starts with the surface sufficiently cooled and gaseous atmosphere condensing in severe rainstorms forming seas, lakes, rivers, our Grand Canyon and Great Lakes too (all basins). The ocean covers close to 75% of the Earth's surface and the land mass appears to be one continent at the equator. The water, gases, the heat from excessive internal radiation contributed to the formation of single-cellular life. [Note: This has been verified by a lab experiment on a container filled with Carbon Dioxide, Ammonia, Methane and Hydrogen (the typical atmosphere at that time) exposed to high levels of Gamma radiation. Complex amino acids, the building blocks of DNA, were formed inside the vessel.] Thus, the earliest and simplest life forms were initiated in the condensation when the planet cooled sufficiently. The ocean with its entire mineral content produced a myriad of single-celled microscopic forms that have been classified in the fossil record. This process took close to 2 billion years. The Earth is now 1.5 billion years old and the Universe close to 11 billion.

4th Day: These single-celled microscopic forms evolved into the plant and animal forms, identified as the Cambrian explosion. Eventually the physical and atmospheric conditions caused the evolution of the ocean's and the landmass's plant and animal species to higher forms. In this period some of the water animals migrated to land. There were snakes, lizards, alligators, turtles and all sorts of evolved creatures except mammals. I believe that this mutation process was enhanced by the high levels of radiation that caused DNA changes that gave birth to new species. Here is a good theory: in Physics we learned that there are four forces in Nature: Gravity, Electro-Magnetic, Strong (Nuclear) and Weak (Chemical). I propose that God created another force that we humans have not yet considered, a Life Force. The rules for it are simple, where and when there exists a possibility, no matter the probability, no matter how small the possibility, life will occur. Many atheistic individuals have tried to prove that it is statistically impossible for life to occur in just those billions of years. Could it be that this theory explains the Creators mind? So now after a billion years have passed, the Universe is about 12 billion years old and Earth is 2.5 billion and going strong. The next *yowm* if you please!

6th Day: So now, the Permian Period has ended with such a mass extinction of life that the ground was laid for the rise of the Dinosaurs. They came from the family of lizards, snakes and alligators whose eggs were exposed to far too much radiation that caused excessive mutations and, voila!, the dinosaurs were formed and lived during the Jurassic Era from about 200 to 100 (?) million years ago as determined by radioactive dating and the fossil record. And after the meteorite collided with Earth, the dinosaurs became extinct thus opening the life cycle to mammals. The land and oceans experience a new growth in a variety of plants and animals. Then, about seven million years age the first species of Homo Sapiens appear. Many anthropologists suggest that Homo Sapiens appeared as early as 7,000,000 years ago. The debate is ongoing. Humankind has been writing for only the last 0.4 seconds if the Universe were 24 hours old (i.e., since the Big Bang)! In actual years, it's 6000 out of 14,000,000,000 years. That ain't too long now, is it?

7th Day After all that thinking and holding everything in existence, the Creator fell asleep very exhausted and slept on this *yowm*.

The Big Bang: objective or subjective? Depends on your personal education! The Nuclear Scientists and Geologists say it's objective--provable; the pigmy in New Guinea says it's irrational. And, many fundamentalists call it "the distraction of the Devil". How the Big Bang was started is theory, therefore, subjective. The microwave distribution in the Universe is scientific fact—objective---there was a Big Bang! Who caused the Big Bang is theology! Tell me, "Who was there?" Therefore, it's anyone's subjective belief! Better still, it does depend upon one's perception!

APPENDIX O

Comments on the Enuma Elish

by
Dennis Bratcher
http://www.cresourcei.org/enumaelish.html

Tablet I
The stage is set for the story. The various gods represent aspects of the physical world. Apsu is the god of fresh water and thus male fertility. Tiamat, wife of Apsu, is the goddess of the sea and thus chaos and threat. Tiamat gives birth to Anshar and Kishar, gods who represented the boundary between the earth and sky (the horizon). To Anshar and Kishar is born Anu, god of sky, who in turn bears Ea. These "sons of the gods" make so much commotion and are so ill behaved that Apsu decides to destroy them. When Ea learns of the plan, he kills Apsu and with his wife Damkina establishes their dwelling above his body. Damkina then gives birth to Marduk, the god of spring symbolized both by the light of the sun and the lightning in storm and rain. He was also the patron god of the city of Babylon. Meanwhile Tiamat is enraged at the murder of her husband Apsu, and vows revenge. She creates eleven monsters to help her carry out her vengeance. Tiamat takes a new husband, Kingu, in place of the slain Apsu and puts him in charge of her newly assembled army.

Tablet II
Tiamat represents the forces of disorder and chaos in the world. In the cycle of seasons, Tiamat is winter and barrenness. In the second tablet, to avenge the murder of her husband Tiamat prepares to unleash on the other gods the destructive forces that she has assembled. Ea learns of her plan and attempts to confront Tiamat. While the tablet is damaged, it is apparent that Ea fails to stop Tiamat. Then Anu attempts to challenge her but fails as well. The gods become afraid that no one will be able to stop Taimat's vengeful rampage.

Tablet III
Anshar's minister Gaga is dispatched to the other gods to report the activities of Tiamat and to tell them of Marduk's willingness to face her. Much of this tablet is poetic repetition of previous conversations.

Tablet IV
The council of the gods tests Marduk's powers by having him make a garment disappear and then reappear. After passing the test, the council enthrones Marduk as high king and commissions him to fight Tiamat. With the authority and power of the council, Marduk assembles his weapons, the four winds as well as the seven winds of destruction. He rides in his chariot of clouds with the weapons of the storm to confront Tiamat. After entangling her in a net, Marduk unleashes the Evil Wind to inflate Tiamat. When she is incapacitated by the wind, Marduk kills her with an arrow through her heart and takes captive the other gods and monsters who were her allies. He also captured her husband Kingu. After smashing Tiamat's head with a club, Marduk divided her corpse, using half to create the earth and the other half to create the sky complete with bars to keep the chaotic waters from escaping. The tablet ends with Marduk establishing dwelling places for his allies.

Tablet V
Marduk builds dwelling places for the other gods. As they take their place, they establish the days and months and seasons of the year. Since this is a myth about the natural world, the "stations" that Marduk establishes for the gods correspond to the celestial luminaries that figured in Babylonian astrology. The phases (horns) of the Moon determine the cycles of the months. From the spittle of Tiamat Marduk creates rain for the earth. The city of Babylon is established as the audience room of King Marduk.

Tablet VI
Marduk decides to create human beings, but needs blood and bone from which to fashion them. Ea advises that only one of the gods should die to provide the materials for creation, the one who was guilty of plotting evil against the gods. Marduk inquires of the assembly of the gods about who incited Tiamat's rebellion, and was told that it was her husband Kingu. Ea kills Kingu and uses his blood to fashion mankind so they can perform menial tasks for the gods. To honor Marduk, the gods construct a house for him in Babylon. After its completion, Marduk gives a great feast for the gods in his new house who all praise Marduk for his greatness in subduing Tiamat. The first group of the fifty throne names of Marduk are recited.

Tablet VII
Continuation of praise of Marduk as chief of Babylon and head of the Babylonian pantheon because of his role in creation. The rest of Marduk's fifty throne names declaring his dominion are recited. Final blessings on Marduk and instructions to the people to remember and recite Marduk's deeds.

Appendix P

Oration on the Dignity of Man
by
Pico della Mirandola, 1486 AD

"Neither an established place nor a form belonging to you alone, nor any special function have we given to you, O Adam, and for this reason, that you may have and possess according to your desire and judgment, whatever place whatever form, and whatever functions you shall desire. The nature of other creatures, which has been determined, is confined within the bounds prescribed by Us. You, who are confined by no limits, shall determine for yourself your own nature, in accordance with your own free will, in whose hand I have placed you. I have set you at the center of the world *(Opps! 1486?)*, so that from there you may more easily survey whatever is in the world. We have made you neither heavenly nor earthly, neither mortal nor immortal, so that, more freely and more honorably the molder and maker of yourself, you may fashion yourself in whatever form you shall prefer. You shall be able to descend among the lower forms of being, which are brute beasts; you shall be able to be reborn out of the judgment of your own soul into the higher beings, which are divine."

Quoted from "The Passion of the Western Mind", by Richard Tarnas, whose next paragraph reads:

"To man had been given freedom, mutability, and the power of self-transformation: thus Pico affirmed that, in the ancient mysteries, man had been symbolized as the great mythic figure of Prometheus. God had bestowed to man the ability to determine freely his position in the Universe, even to the point of ascending to full union *(Ephesians 3: 17-19)* with the Supreme God. "

Comments by this book's author in *(Italics)*

APPENDIX Q

Gospel Sources for the Study of Jesus

The Q Source according to the two source theory is at:

http://www.paulonpaul.org/jesus/sources_1.htm#hypothesis

The Q Source based on Luke can be found in the following URL.

http://www.religiousstudies.uncc.edu/jdtabor/Qluke.html

APPENDIX R

Suggested Reading Material

Part One: The 70's and 80's Literature

I Theology

"This Man Jesus" - Bruce Vawter
"Honest To God" - John A. T. Robinson
"The Human Face Of God" - John A. T, Robinson
"The Reality of Jesus" - Dermott Lane
"The Challenge of Jesus" - John Shea
"The Words of Jesus In our Gospels" - Stanley B. Marrow
"Jesus; A Gospel Portrait - Donald Senior
"Jesus God and Man", Raymond Brown

II Scripture

"Who Do You Say That I Am?" -- Edward Ciuba
"Crisis Facing The Church" -- Raymond Brown
"The Critical Meaning of the Bible" -- Raymond Brown
"Peter In the New Testament" -- Raymond Brown
"The Community of the Beloved Disciple" -- Raymond Brown
"Mary in the New Testament" -- Raymond Brown
"These Stones Shall Shout" -- Mark Link
"The Two-Edged Sword" -- John L. MeKenzie
"The Power and the Wisdom" -- John L. McKenzie
"The Birth of the Messiah"-- Raymond Brown
"The Eucharistic Words of Jesus" – Joachim Jeremias

III. Spirituality & Prayer

"Beginning to Pray" - Anthony Bloom
"A Tine For Love" - Eugene Kenedy
"Spiritual Renewal of the American Parish" – E Larsen
"The Renewed Parish In Today's Church" – E Larsen
"As Bread That is Broken" - Van Breeman
"Be Not Afraid" - Jean Vanier
"The Singer" - Calvin Miller
"Letter From the Desert" - Carlo Carretto
"Reaching Out" - Henri Nouwen
"May I Hate God" - Pierre Wolf
"In Search of the Beyond" - Carlo Carretto

IV General

"The People Are The Church" - Eugene Kenedy
"Models of the Church" - Dulles
"Stories of God" John Shea
"To A Dancing God" - Sam Keen.

Part Two: The 90's Literature to Present

Biblical Scholarship and Theology

"Meeting Jesus Again for the First Time"- Marcus Borg
"The God We Never Knew" -Marcus Borg
"Jesus in Contemporary Scholarship"- Marcus Borg
"Jesus and Buddha" -Marcus Borg
"Jesus at 2000" - Marcus Borg
"God at 2000" - Marcus Borg
"Reading the Bible Again for the First Time" – Marcus Borg
" The Lost Gospel, Q" – Marcus Borg, Editor
"The Introduction to the New Testament" – R E Brown
"Introduction to New Testament Christology" – R E Brown
"Giants of the Faith" – Raymond Brown
"Will the Real Jesus Please Stand Up" – Crossan vs Craig
"The historical Jesus" - John Dominic Crossan
"The Birth of Christianity" – John Dominic Crossan
"James the Brother of Jesus" – Robert Eisenman
"The God of Jesus" – Stephen Patterson
"Jesus as a Figure in History" – Mark Allen Powell
"One Jesus, Many Christs" – Gregory Riley
"Liberating the Gospels" – Bishop John S Spong
"This Hebrew Lord" - Bishop John Shelby Spong
"Why Christianity Must Change or Die" - John S Spong
"The History of God" -- Karen Armstrong

Spirituality

"Zen to Go" – Jon Winokur, Editor
"The Way of Life" – Lao Tzu
"Tao Te Ching" – Lao Tzu
"An Introduction to Zen Buddhism" – D.T. Suzuki
"The Empty Mirror" – Janwillem vande Wetering
"Way Farer" – Dennis Schmidt
"Kensho" - Dennis Schmidt
"Satori" - Dennis Schmidt
"Wanderer" - Dennis Schmidt
"Messy Spirituality – Michael Yaconelli
"Spirituality of Imperfection" – Kurtz and Ketcham
"When You're Falling, Dive" – Cheri Huber

Miscellaneous

"The Passion of the Western Mind" - Richard Tarnas-
"Before Marriage, Before Divorce" – Robert E. Mayer
Jerome Biblical Commentary, Brown, Fytzmyer and Murphy
John Dominic Crossan's Article:
http://www.faithfutures.org/Jesus/Crossan1.rtf

APPENDIX S

The Coronation Formula
Psalm 2

1*Why do the nations protest and the peoples grumble in vain?
2*Kings on earth rise up and princes plot together against the LORD and his anointed:
3 "Let us break their shackle and cast off their chains!"
4 The one enthroned in heaven laughs; the Lord derides them,
5 Then speaks to them in anger, terrifies them in wrath:
6 "I myself have installed my king on Zion, my holy mountain."
7 I will proclaim the decree of the LORD, who said to me,
"You are my son; today I am your father."
8 Only ask it of me, and I will make your inheritance the nations, your possession the ends of the earth.
9 With an iron rod you shall shepherd them, like a clay pot you will shatter them."
10 And now, kings, give heed; take warning, rulers on earth.
11 Serve the LORD with fear; with trembling bow down in homage,
Lest God be angry and you perish from the way in a sudden blaze of anger.
Happy are all who take refuge in God!

The important readings here are in bold. These two are repeated in the Gospel stories and in some letters because they are considered to be future predictions about Yeshua. Actually they are simply in reference to the manner in which the Israelites refer to their King, because the Messiah is supposed to be the new Davidic King.

APPENDIX T

A CREATION HYMN

PSALM 104

1 Bless the LORD, my soul! LORD, my God, you are great indeed!
You are clothed with majesty and glory, 2 robed in light as with a cloak. You spread out the heavens like a tent; 3 you raised your palace upon the waters. You make the clouds your chariot; you travel on the wings of the wind. 4 You make the winds your messengers; flaming fire, your ministers. 5 **You fixed the earth on its foundation, never to be moved.** 6 The ocean covered it like a garment; above the mountains stood the waters. 7 At your roar they took flight; at the sound of your thunder they fled. 8 They rushed up the mountains, down the valleys to the place you had fixed for them. 9 You set a limit they cannot pass; never again will they cover the earth. 10 You made springs flow into channels that wind among the mountains. 11 They give drink to every beast of the field; here wild asses quench their thirst. 12 Beside them the birds of heaven nest; among the branches they sing. 13 You water the mountains from your palace; by your labor the earth abounds. 14 You raise grass for the cattle and plants for our beasts of burden. You bring bread from the earth, 15 and wine to gladden our hearts, Oil to make our faces gleam, food to build our strength. 16 The trees of the LORD drink their fill, the cedars of Lebanon, which you planted. 17 There the birds build their nests; junipers are the home of the stork. 18 The high mountains are for wild goats; the rocky cliffs, a refuge for badgers. 19 You made the moon to mark the seasons, the sun that knows the hour of its setting. 20 You bring darkness and night falls, then all the beasts of the forest roam abroad. 21 Young lions roar for prey; they seek their food from God. 22 When the sun rises, they steal away and rest in their dens. 23 People go forth to their work, to their labor till evening falls. 24 How varied are your works, LORD! **In wisdom you have wrought them all;** the earth is full of your creatures. 25 Look at the sea, great and wide! It teems with countless beings, living things both large and small. 26 Here ships ply their course; here Leviathan, your creature, plays. 27 All of these look to you to give them food in due time. 28 When you give to them, they gather; when you open your hand, they are well filled. 29 *When you hide your face, they are lost. When you take away their breath, they perish and return to the dust from which they came. 30 **When you send forth your breath, they are created**, and you renew the face of the earth. 31 May the glory of the LORD endure forever; may the LORD be glad in these works! 32 If God glares at the earth, it trembles; **if God touches the mountains, they smoke**! 33 I will sing to the LORD all my life; I will sing praise to my God while I live. 34 May my theme be pleasing to God; I will rejoice in the LORD. 35 May sinners vanish from the earth, and the wicked be no more. Bless the LORD, my soul! Hallelujah!

APPENDIX U

THE CHRONOLOGICAL AUTHORSHIP OF THE NEW TESTAMENT

1. Apostolic Period: ~33 AD Messiah at Resurrection
{Rom 1: 1-4; Acts 2: 36; Acts 5: 30-32; Acts 13: 30-33}

Approx. Year*	Title of N.T. Book
51	1st Thessalonians
52	2nd Thessalonians
54-55	Galatians
56-57	Philippians
Spring 57	1st Corinthians
Autumn 57	2nd Corinthians
Winter 57-58	Romans
61-63	Philemon
61-63	Colossians
61-63	Ephesians
62	James
64	1st Peter
66	1st Timothy
66	Titus
67	2nd Timothy

2. Baptism Period: 70 AD Messiah at Baptism
{See Mk 1: 9-11}

65-70	Gospel of Mark

3. Conception Period: 80 AD Messiah at Conception {See Mt 1 & Lk 2-Infancy Narratives}

68-80	Gospel of Matthew
70-80	Gospel of Luke
80-85	Acts
81-96	Revelations
90	Jude

4. Eternity Period: 90 AD Messiah from Eternity
{See John 1: 1-18}

70-90	Hebrews**
90+	2nd Peter**
90-100	1st John
90-100	Gospel of John
90-100	2nd John
90-100	3rd John

* Data from the Jerome Biblical Commentary and NRSV
** Contains special "Messiah from Eternity" Material

APPENDIX V

On Legends

!

From "Grandmother and the Priests", Taylor Caldwell, Page 369

Father O'Connor said musingly, "Legends do have a grand way of receding into the past, and becoming tradition, and it is more authentic for a man to say, 'My old Dada heard it from his Dada,' than to say, 1 saw it myself, and I swear it by the saints.' No one believes a man, entirely, but the world has a curious way of believing legends, and the older the better, as if time gave them verity. It was harder for the Apostles to bear personal witness to the life of Our Lord, they who had had the blessed grace to see Him alive among them—and they died for the witnessing—than it is today for a priest to bear the witness through the Church, the Holy Bible and tradition. For the priest teaches what he has been taught, but the Apostles taught what they had known and had seen for themselves and so the people, many of them, did not believe the Apostles, and killed them. Do men fear that all men are liars, then? I do not know. It is very puzzling that men will believe legends, which were first told by dead men, if those legends are old enough.

"It could be," said Father O'Flynn, "that men believe that a story which does not die must be true."

APPENDIX W

The Many Names of God

ALPHABETICALLY

Allah
Brahman
Creator
Deity
El
Father ... Daddy
God
Holy One. Higher Power, The
Isis
Jehovah; Just One, The
Krishna, Sri
LORD, Love
Mother, Mommy
Numinous One, The
One and Only
Punisher, Puppeteer
Queen
Rex
Savior; Spirit of Holiness; Spirit, The Holy
Teacher
Ultimate, The
Victor
W
X
Yahweh
Zeus

PS: OK, We got 24 letters of the alphabet! You can play researcher and find names for the last two: W and X!

APPENDIX X

THE GOD OF REALTIONSHIP

I. BEFORE THE BEGINNING

ALEPH: THE AWAKENING

Within the deeply black and soundless void I perceive that " *I AM*".

This is my conscious certainty!

All around me is an infinity of length, breath and depth. Everything is ... yet nothing moves; there is just endless stillness.

Matter is here; it is everywhere. I bathe in its persistent, motionless existence and its formless, potential energy.

What is this presence in which I am surrounded? Time-less-ness be-ing? Place-less-ness *be*-ing? Suffocating *be*-ing?

Do I simply *BE* in all of it? How does all of that which I experience as part of me exist as separate from me; how is it that all is *ONE* existence and at the same moment disassociated from my *be*-ing?

What do *I* sense? Total, complete presence!

How do *I* sense? By feeling the presence in me!

When do *I* sense? Only in this NOW?

Where do *I* sense? Every place and no place!

There is NO place; it is ALL place. If there is no movement, why do I experience the whole DYNAMIC of this existence? If no sensation, why is the whole of it in every reach of my *BE-ING*? What is this pervading, boundless internal and external power deep inside my consciousness?

I am a part of the whole and I am the whole. I am and it is. There is but ONE interchangeable existence. I am it and it is I.

"*I AM*" the changelessness existing in eternity.

I am alone in timeless, motionless and soundless infinity!

"*I AM ALONE*"! There is no other beside me; there is only singular aloneness.

Is this all?

391

BETH: The Becoming

What does it mean to be aware of me and the formless matter about me? Is the chaos perpetually NOW? Can there be form from this? Yes!

Can I form it? Let me try!

I have succeeded! But I must remain present in that which forms.

What form shall I make permanent?

I shall create a form of order that shall be eternally in relationship with me. I shall form it to be free and relate freely to it in such a manner that it is at once held in existence by me and held without *obeisance* to me but in its own dimensions must conform responsibly to the form of order and relationship instilled into it by me. That it came from me shall be evident to every being that becomes. That there can be a relationship with me shall become evident to all that come into existence. The highest forms shall possess the likeness of me with a desire to discover me. That all things fashioned shall be like me in form of order and relationship that I have imbued into them so that in the end they can eventually transmute into the ONE-ness of existence with me.

I shall breathe my life and passion into the very core of each and every inanimate, animate, sentient and sapiential, existent being. I will instill my passion in all that is, for I shall share all that I am with each that is. All will perceive me because my profile will be clearly established in all that I form. My compassion for others and my joy will dominate the form of order and relationship which I will placed in the hearts of all that be and become.

What I possess shall be a part of these forms with whom I shall share existence. I shall share freely so that each will exist freely. I shall not be master over them but co-existent with them. They shall be free to experience and choose, as I am free to experience and choose. Their destiny shall be their choice not mine. Yet ... I will always desire their presence ... but only as their equal.

My aloneness will end because of their existence and relationship. Never shall any being experience aloneness. We shall all be destined to relationship but only to an intensity freely chosen by those beings that eventually form. This I deem as GOOD.

I make no predestined purpose for any form that becomes. That is inconsistent with their being freely formed, freely existing and freely choosing. If there is an ardent purpose in this creation, then let it be in the relationship that ensues and the joy and beauty of existence, in and for itself. No other purpose! Let unconditional self-giving prevail over all that becomes. That sharing of existence is LOVE; a LOVE that is free; a LOVE that is in intimate relationship. There is no other way. Mine is the WAY of LOVE. My desire is that ALL discover this WAY. In this WAY ALL and I become ONE even though an appearance of separation. In the WAY of LOVE there is no possession, only friendship. In the WAY of LOVE there is equality of being.

One-ness is the destiny of existence, existence freely offered and graciously accepted. Existence freely caused but not demanding, nor oppressively controlling. Existence willed freely so that each existent is individually, freely willed by itself, choosing freely any action, any direction and any purpose it so desires. Worship shall never be demanded from this act of free creation because worship is a distortion of the WAY of LOVE. I do nothing for personal gain. That is not my WAY. My WAY is to give as in gifting that has no conditions attached. Besides, can a free gift return anything greater than itself? Relationship and respect are the only responses to free gifting! There is no other WAY. All else leads to non-existence!

Thus, shall I act. Thus, shall I gather all chaos into my bosom and breathe into it form, order and relationship!

"Let my WORDS be so!"

II. THE BEGINNING

GIMEL: The Light

At that instant all fundamental matter gravitated into her bosom in a singular infinitesimally small ball that left a vacuum in place of the chaotic infinite fullness. There roared an inferno of energy as reality formed. Elements of gas propelled themselves outward as on a single plane with pillars of gigantic magnetic forces flowing both upwards and downwards as if the whole were a spinning gyroscope. The resounding noise echoed into the infinite void with sufficient intensity to push every gaseous element outward. Change had begun and time initiated. *BEING immersed itself into the creation. BEING,* Herself, had altered Herself in the process; *BEING* is now intimately present in creation, is now a participant of time and change as She holds creation in existence in Her passion for intelligent existence.

Initially the forms appeared chaotic in their outward motion as though searching for stability. Many of the random clouds began to coalesce into a large number of immense balls of molten matter while the void was still saturated with streams of intense radiation. Not all the gases formed molten spheres but much continued to move outwards in individual clouds and later many condensed into galaxies which themselves repeated the initial blast of creation but in lesser proportions. The process seemed never to stop. The void began to fill as time proceeded. The Universe continued to expand.

An age of time passed as the entire Universe cooled. The Ground of all Being rejoiced as change continued moment by moment, little by little. Now there was length, width and depth everywhere; now there were massive cloud formations in all directions moving slowly away from each other.

As the radiation of heat and energy subsided, galactic shapes took form each of the millions separated into individual, immense colonies. Each had one or two large stars in its center with several orbiting, spinning spheres. Some spheres of each colony were ideal for molecular growth, others, far too hot or cold, were barren. On one particular sphere there were ideal conditions: the center star gave off sufficient heat, the atmosphere had cooled enough to precipitate the major portion of its moisture, the surface had separated into earth and water portions. Further development continued.

This blue planet had a very small satellite circling it; it reflected the light given off by the center star.

daleth: THE SECOND EPOCH

Molecular activity produced molecular reactivity because of the still intense levels of radiation. Larger super molecules formed in the large water portions of this unique sphere. Then, as time passed, strange one-celled creatures appeared in the expanse of waters followed by larger celled living things. Because of the large elemental gasses collected by this sphere along with the various elements that coalesced onto this ball and the radiation intensity, the waters showed a green growth occurring within itself. This living green growth was independent of the celled creatures.

And, it continued ...

Larger self-propelled creatures formed ... and ...larger ones resulted ...

Much, much time passed and finally, after almost 4 billion Earth years of growth had passed, there appeared a human-like form walking throughout every portion of the entire planet. It was the glory point of my creation!.

My joy was complete ... I am not alone any more ...

Appendix Y

A Long Fable about Our World

For children to read

Once upon a very, very long imaginary time ago there was an invisible place where lived an invisible person whose name was Aba-Mah. This place is easy to imagine, like thinking about a cake on the kitchen table that really isn't there. The cake doesn't really exist but it's real in your mind. Thus, imaginary is a place in our minds. Since we cannot see Aba-Mah, we don't know whether Aba-Mah is a boy or a girl. Aba-Mah is just a person, not with eyes or arms and feet like you and I have, but an invisible person, maybe like the wind. One thing for sure, Aba-Mah feels and thinks like we do. It's strange but there is no other person living with Aba-Mah.

One imaginary day Aba-Mah became aware that there were very many little, very little, disorderly single dots (like very tiny balls) along with Aba-Mah. These dots filled up the entire invisible world. How many dots, you ask? Well, far more than anyone could count! I might guess that there were as many as the stars in our sky times one hundred. And that's a very large number! If you could count all the grains of sand on all the beaches on Earth, you would end up with a number almost as large as the number of dots in that invisible world. The most important thing to understand is that these dots were like building blocks from which Aba-Mah could build things in the imaginary world.

When Aba-Mah realized that only the little dots and Aba-Mah were in this infinite invisible world, Aba-Mah decided that aloneness was not a good thing. Aba-Mah thought and thought and came up with an excellent idea. Maybe Aba-Mah could make a new world in which lived other persons somewhat like Aba-Mah with whom Aba-Mah could have a relationship

So Aba-Mah thought up a plan that would do just that. Aba-Mah thought up a set of rules that would make order and form out of the disorderly dots. The rules were called "Mathematics and Randomness" and the order was called "Physics" and the form was called "Chemistry". The things in this world would be called physical things; just like the things you see every day. Some physical things would be called rocks because they stand still, others would be plants because they grow in one place, and those creatures that move around would be animals. Now, all animals feel but don't think like Aba-Mah does. The animal that does think and feel in the way that Aba-Mah thinks and feels would be a person. Many persons would make up a people.

While making these plans Aba-Mah had to decide whether Aba-Mah would control the plants, animals and people in every respect. Or would the laws of chance govern them? Now, that was indeed a hard decision to make. Shall the new world become exactly as Aba-Mah wanted or would it become something else? What would Aba-Mah choose? Aba-Mah pondered for a long time.

"Eureka", Aba-Mah thought! "If I make this new world into a set of puppets, there will never develop a relationship with me." And that's when Aba-Mah decided to let the new world be governed by chance and be free to become whatever it would become so that Aba-Mah could have a relationship with the creatures in this new world. All living creatures would have free choice! What necame would only have to follow the rules of order and form. Aba-Mah's energy will be given to the world to become. [*When a person gives so much to another, we call it love.*] Aba-Mah did love this new world and hoped it would love in return so that Aba-Mah would not be alone.

Oh, but wait! This would prove to be very difficult. Freedom meant that Aba-Mah could never interfere with the workings of this creation. The new world would become what was possible for it to become! At that moment Aba-Mah decided to imbue the new world with a fifth force called the "Life Force" that would create life even when it seemed most improbable.

Then, the moment arrived. Aba-Mah performed the initiating act. The infinity of little dots were brought together into a single small ball leaving behind an infinite void. Once in Aba-Mah's bosom all those little dots, because of the rules, order and form, exploded outwards into the new void. The explosion released an infinite amount of matter and energy that produced a very large fire with red-hot, melted physical matter shooting out in all directions. WOW! That was a very bright light that shone for a long time. It was at that exact moment when the light came that space and time began. [*Space means that there is a lot of room, you know, like, "outside has more room than your closet has." Time means that things change. Remember that you have birthday celebrations every year because you grow and change.*]

What was invisible before the big light became visible after the light. That was the beginning of our Universe. Very slowly the matter began to cool. Now, this was the end of the first epoch

As most of the matter and space cooled, some large balls formed to become suns. A sun is a very large ball of fire that stopped cooling because the large mass of matter compressed so greatly that the atoms fused into new matter giving off a lot of heat that causes a sun to burn brightly all the time. We have a sun that does this. You see it every day and feel its warmth.

Then there were small balls that cooled off, formed a hard surface and only burned on the inside. These are almost spherical balls, called planets. It turned out that Aba-Mah's rules, order and form made many different suns and many different planets. In some places a planet could have a little planet circling around it. Our planet, Earth, has a small planet going around it; it's the moon.

When the temperature around our planet, Earth, had cooled sufficiently the steam surrounding it came down as rainwater in such forceful torrents that rivers, lakes and the mighty oceans cut into the dry lands of that planet. The large lands that formed are called continents. The second epoch ended.

Now, as it turned out, the Earth was a special planet circling a warming sun just correctly positioned away from that sun so that very tiny plants and living, moving things formed that were almost invisible to the human eye. Aba-Mah was very happy! The third epoch ended.

A very long time passed. The moisture on the planet encouraged larger plants to grow. If you looked carefully, now you could see creatures living in the waters. It has taken investigators such a long time to figure out that these primal sea creatures and plants were actually created out of the gases in air, moisture, lightning and the radiation from the big light in the beginning. This was the end of the forth epoch.

After several more eons passed, the living water-creatures developed into many different kinds of swimming animals large and small. While most of the living creatures remained in the water some of them migrated to the land. But when they moved to the land they had to change because they couldn't swim anymore. Then the Life Force helped them grow into walking animals. Remember that there were many different kinds of swimming animals in the waters so there became many different kinds of walking animals on the land. A great many of these walking animals lived by eating the plants and as time passed some became very large. There were others of the large walking animals that ate other smaller animals. We know about them from the bones dug from the ground. Have you guessed what the large boned animals are called? Yes, the people who have studied those bones have called those animals "dinosaurs". Did you know that some of these dinosaurs still live today? We know them as birds, alligators, lizards, and others too numerous to list. The reason that none of the very large dinosaurs are alive today is that a rock fell from the sky. The rock was so big that when it hit the Earth it caused a big cloud of dust that circled the Earth blocking out the sun. Well, plants need the sun; without the sun most of the plants on the land died. Yet, the plants in the oceans lived. After that, there was not enough plant food on the land for all the dinosaurs to eat. Most of them died. When most of the smaller animals died out, the larger meat-eating ones died too. However, several of the smaller ones flew away or went back into the oceans. This very, very long time ended the fifth epoch. And here began the last epoch, the sixth.

Once again a very long time passed and the animals grew into many varieties, one of which species was the mammals. You can see examples of mammals in the zoo; there are certainly many varieties there. Most animals walked on four feet. Instead of four legs some have two feet and two hands and walk essentially on hands and feet together for all except special moments of fright and flight. Then, they fled on just two legs. If you have a little brother or sister in your house watch them when they first move around the floor. They crawl on all fours; later they stand up and move on two feet. Pay special attention to the way they begin to walk about. Well, these two-footed walking animals developed in exactly the same manner as your brother or sister did. If you stay a while watching the monkey family at the zoo, you will hear them making a variety of noises to each other. That's their way of talking to each other. Your brother and sister started out with the same garbled noise when they first learned to talk. The difference is that we humans have a greater ability to use a much-improved language to communicate than the monkeys do. Even though we humans are superior in most ways, we would like to have the same tree climbing ability as the monkeys.

In a span of the next million years (that's 100 times 100 times 100 and it's a long time, but shorter than the epochs) some of that species of the ape/monkey family developed a simple capacity to think at a level greater than the monkies and apes of our present age. That was the most wondrous event of Aba-Mah's creation. Aba-Mah took great pleasure in the marvels that came about on this little planet in the Solar system located in the Milky Way Galaxy. The Life Force had indeed fulfilled its pre-ordained destiny.

Some of these two-footed walkers banded together in groups and exhibited a level of communication superior to the other animals. They began to make objects that helped them collect food; they utilized caves for protection against the weather. Well, it didn't take long before some of these groups made spears with which to kill animals that threatened the group. Not only did the group protect themselves from people-eating animals but they also protected themselves from other groups who came to hurt them. As more small groups came together they joined forces to become clans that lived in caves in some lands and thatched huts in other lands. Many centuries passed until the very small clans began to form larger groups. And these large clans became tribes that lived in villages. You can see that some areas of the countryside soon became crowded. When this happened, some people in the villages left to find more space for themselves. They created brand new villages. Just picture the many migrations that had to occur to move so large a number of people from place to place to populate the Earth as evenly as it presently is. So the migrations slowed and the people stayed in the comfort of their villages.

During that very long time the people began to experience physical changes because of the place on Earth where they chose to live. People in the North change to a lighter skin color. People in the Far East had their eye shape change. The skin of people along the equator got darker. All this took place because of the sun's rays. People need a special chemical in their body to be healthy and the sun helps the skin produce that chemical. If your skin is light the sun will make enough for you but in the Northern and Southern parts of the Earth where there is little sun you will need a lot of sunshine. So, people's skin is very light and a little sunshine will do the job. Now people along the equator experience a great deal of sunshine. Well, too much exposure just burns the skin. So over the thousands of years the people's skin got very dark to protect them from too much sunshine. We live on a planet where nature takes care of us humans. It's something like when you are hungry. Your stomach sends noisy signals to you to let you know that it's time to eat. Another example of nature taking care of us occurs when a bright light shines into our eyes. Our eyes have a special shade that closes so our eyes won't get burned by the bright light. Ask your parents to show you the lens of a camera, it's just like the shade in your eye.

Then, there's another kind of change. It's called body features. Have you noticed that your brothers and sisters look differently than you when all of you come from the same father and mother? That's called genetics. When one village combined with another village, different physical characteristics of the new village were passed on to the next generation of villagers. If you ever study anthropology you will find artifacts as evidence of (a) a people, Cro-Magnon, who lived about 300,000 tears ago on the southern tip of Africa and (b) Neanderthal peoples who lived about 400,000 years ago throughout Europe and Asia. They all had physical characteristics that differed significantly from each other. So when some people of one clan moved in to another clan, the features of the whole clan began to change from generation to generation. When you grow up you may visit other countries and see for yourself that the people there have physical features different from the people back home.

Well, I now think you can understand why languages around this planet are different. Sometimes you will find that even in one country the spoken, even the written, languages differ very much. In China no two villages speak exactly the same language! Isn't that surprising? But it's true. When villages become isolated, the people learned to speak with different sounds and that character was passed down to the next generation. It's easy to understand that after ten generations a new language was formed.

While all these changes were taking place, what were the people doing to find food? Some became hunters, while other groups became gatherers of nuts, berries and vegetables. We have learned about these people from the paintings on the walls of the caves they lived in. We also learn about people from different lands by studying the stories and myth that they made up to explain why they are here and what are the mysterious things that occurred on our planet, like thunder and lightening, the movement of the sun and moon, the waves and storms of the ocean, and so much more. Can you name some of the happenings around you that you don't understand?

Finally, just about 6000 years ago the human race learned how to write. The first story that we have is about the many gods who formed the world. Some of these stories are from people who thought that every natural occurrence, like lightning or thunder, was caused by a special god, a super human. Some very smart people began to reason that the world had to come from someone.

That someone is Aba-Mah. In Egypt the people called that person Ra. In India that person is called Brahman. In Babylon they wrote the name of Marduk. In the Bible the Israelites called that person Yahweh. The Arabian peoples used Allah. You can read in any encyclopedia what the peoples of different lands called their God. One thing is certain; every person writing believed that the God of their creation story was a single person.

In this story the name of the Creator is Aba-Mah and in the Hebrew language it means Daddy-Mummy. What is your name for the Creator?

Appendix X + Y

ABA-MAH THE MATHEMATICIAN

Once upon a very, very long imaginary time ago there was an invisible place where lived an invisible person whose name was Aba-Mah. This place is easy to imagine, like thinking about a cake on the kitchen table that really isn't there. The cake doesn't really exist but it's real in your mind. Thus, invisible is a place in our minds. Since we cannot see Aba-Mah, we will make believe that Aba-Mah is like a Mother who takes care of us and shares everything with us. But Aba-Mah is just an imaginary person, not with eyes or arms and feet like you and I have, but an invisible person, maybe like the powerful wind.

In one imaginary moment a very long time ago, a strange thing took place. Aba-Mah became aware of Her thoughts.

"Within the deeply black and soundless void I perceive that ' I AM'.

This is my conscious certainty! All around me is an infinity of length, breath and depth.
Everything is ... yet nothing moves ... there is just endless stillness.
Matter is here ... it is everywhere ... I bathe in the fullness of its persistent, motionless existence and its formless, potential energy. "

"What is this presence in which I am surrounded?
Timelessness ...
Placelessnees ...
Suffocating fullness!"

The most important thing to understand is that this formless mass consisted of very small blocks from which Aba-Mah could build things in the imaginary world. So Aba-Mah thought up a plan that would do just that. Aba-Mah thought up a set of rules that would make order and form out of the disorderly blocks.

The rules SHE called "Mathematics and Randomness"; the order SHE called "Physics"; the form SHE called "Chemistry"; and the five Energies were called the:
Gravitational Force,
Electro-Magnetic Force,
Weak Chemical Force,
Strong Nuclear Force,
and the fifth and last was called "The Life Force".

That mysterious "Life Force" will cause life where it is least possible no matter how improbable!

And Aba-Mah continued to think. "Do I simply BE in all of it?
How does all of that which I experience as part of me exist as separate from me?
How is it that all is ONE existence and at the same moment separated from my be-ing?"
"What do I sense? ... Total, complete presence!
How do I sense? By feeling the presence in me!

When do I sense? Only in this NOW!
Where do I sense? Every place and no place!
There is NO place; it is all place.
If there is no movement, SO why do I experience the ENERGY of this existence?
Why is the whole of it in every reach of my BE-ING?"

"What is this pervading, boundless internal and external power deep inside my consciousness? I am a part of the whole ... and ... I am the whole ...
I am ... and ... it is. There is but ONE interchangeable existence... I am it ...and ...it is I. 'I AM' the change-less-ness existing in the eternal NOW ... I am alone in timeless, motionless and soundless infinity!"

"I am alone! There is no other beside me; there is only ONE-NESS and the SILENCE! "

Aba-Mah became Aware of the POWER within HER and within the formless mass. Could SHE change this? SHE pronounced it! It is changed ... SHE succeeded! However, SHE must remain present in that which formed to keep it permanent.

"I shall create a form of order that shall be eternally in relationship with me. I shall form it to be free and relate freely to it... in such a manner that it is at once held in existence by me and held without obedience to me ... but in its own dimensions must conform responsibly to the form of order and relationship instilled into it by me. "

Aba-Mah made it evident to every being that becomes that it came from HER. Aba-Mah made it evident to all that come into existence that there can be a relationship with HER.

"The highest forms shall possess the likeness of me with a desire to discover me. All things fashioned shall be like me in the form of order and relationship that I will imbue into them. For they shall know that Order is Physics; Form is Chemistry and their relationship is Mathematics. In the end they will be able TO transmute into the ONE-ness of existence with me."

Aba-Mah would breath life into the very core of each and every inanimate, animate, sentient and sapient, existent being. SHE would instill HER passion into all that would be. Aba-Mah would share all that SHE IS with each that becomes. All will perceive HER because HER characteristics will be clearly established in all that would form. Aba-Mah's compassion for others and HER joy would dominate the form of order and relationship which SHE would place in the spirit of all that become.

"What I possess shall be a part of these forms with whom I shall share existence. I shall share freely so that each will exist freely. I shall not be master over them but co-existent with them. They shall be free to experience and choose, as I am free to experience and choose. Their destiny shall be their choice not mine. Yet ... I will always desire their presence and friendship, but only as equals. My aloneness will end because of their existence and our relationship. Never shall any being experience aloneness. All shall be destined to relationship but only to an intensity freely chosen. This I deem to be GOOD."

Aba-Mah made no predestined purpose for any form that would become. That is inconsistent with their being freely formed, freely existing and freely choosing. If there is an ardent purpose in this creation, then it would be in the relationship that ensues in the joy and beauty of existence, in and for itself. No other purpose! Unconditional self-giving prevailed over all that became.

That sharing of existence is LOVE; a LOVE that is free; LOVE that is in intimate relationship. There would be no other way.

Aba-Mah is the WAY of LOVE. Aba-Mah's desire is that ALL discover this WAY. In this WAY ... ALL and Aba-Mah become ONE ... even though an appearance of separation. In this WAY of LOVE there is no possession, only friendship. In this WAY of LOVE there is equality of being.

One-ness is the destiny of existence ... existence freely offered...
Existence freely caused but not demanding nor oppressively controlling ...
Existence willed freely so that each existent is individually, freely willed by itself, choosing freely any action, any direction and any purpose it so desires.

Aba-Mah intended never to demand worship from those who would become.
Worship would be a distortion of the WAY of LOVE.
Aba-Mah did nothing for personal gain. That is not HER WAY.
Aba-Mah's WAY is to give as in gifting that has no conditions attached.
Besides, can a free gift return anything greater than itself?
Relationship and respect are the only responses to free gifting! There is no other WAY.
All else leads to non-existence!

Thus, shall I act. Thus, shall I gather all chaos into my bosom and breathe into it form, order and relationship! Let my WORDS be so!"

At that instant, all fundamental matter gravitated into her bosom in a singular infinitesimally small ball that left a vacuum in place of the chaotic infinite fullness. There roared an inferno of energy as reality formed. Hot gaseous Elements propelled themselves outward on a single plane with pillars of gigantic magnetic forces flowing both upwards and downwards like a spinning gyroscope. The resounding noise echoed into the infinite void with sufficient intensity to push every gaseous element outward. Change had begun and time initiated.

Aba-Mah immersed HERSELF into creation! The Ground of all BEING had altered Herself in the process! SHE was now intimately present in creation.
SHE was now an active participant in time and change ... because SHE MUST hold all of creation in REALITY.

Aba-Mah rejoiced as change continued moment-by-moment, little by little.
Now there was length, width and depth everywhere. Now there was light in all directions.

--- LOVE HAD PENETRATED THE DARKNESS! ---

And that, my friends, was just the Beginning because Aba-Mah now shares creation with those highest forms--the humans who finally arrived some 7 million years ago!

You all know the rest of the story, don't you?

If not, you can read it in the old issues of the National Geographic or Discover magazines.

APPENDIX Z

Knowledge and Wisdom in the NIV Bible

It is important to understand that knowledge precedes Wisdom. Far too frequently people think that knowledge is an evil. In fact, during the first few centuries AD the heresy of Gnosticism confused the issue of good knowledge with secret knowledge. Today the same confusion exists among uninformed people.

PART ONE: KNOWLEDGE

GEN 2: 9 And the Lord God made all kinds of trees grow out of the ground-- trees that were pleasing to the eye and good for food. In the middle of the garden were the tree of life and the tree of the KNOWLEDGE of good and evil.

EXO 31: 3 and I have filled him with the Spirit of God, with skill, ability and KNOWLEDGE in all kinds of crafts—

NUM 24: 16 the oracle of one who hears the words of God, who has KNOWLEDGE from the Most High, who sees a vision from the Almighty, who falls prostrate, and whose eyes are opened:

KI 2: 32 The Lord will repay him for the blood he shed, because without the KNOWLEDGE of my father David he attacked two men and killed them with the sword. Both of them-- Abner son of Ner, commander of Israel's army, and Amasa son of Jether, commander of Judah's army-- were better men and more upright than he.

2CH 1: 11 God said to Solomon, " Since this is your heart's desire and you have not asked for wealth, riches or honor, nor for the death of your enemies, and since you have not asked for a long life but for wisdom and KNOWLEDGE to govern my people over whom I have made you king,

JOB 21: 22 " Can anyone teach KNOWLEDGE to God, since he judges even the highest?

PRO 1: 7 The fear of the Lord is the beginning of KNOWLEDGE, but fools despise wisdom and discipline. PRO 1: 29 Since they hated KNOWLEDGE and did not choose to fear the Lord,
PRO 2: 5 then you will understand the fear of the Lord and find the KNOWLEDGE of God.
PRO 2: 6 For the Lord gives WISDOM, and from his mouth come KNOWLEDGE and understanding.
PRO 8: 8-9 Wisdom speaking: "Sincere are all the words of my mouth, no one of them is wily or crooked; All of them are plain to the man of intelligence, and right to those who attain KNOWLEDGE."
PRO 9: 10 " The fear of the Lord is the beginning of wisdom, and KNOWLEDGE of the Holy One is understanding.
PRO 22: 12 The eyes of the Lord keep watch over KNOWLEDGE, but he frustrates the words of the unfaithful.

ECC 2: 26 To the man who pleases him, God gives wisdom, KNOWLEDGE and happiness, but to the sinner he gives the task of gathering and storing up wealth to hand it over to the one who pleases God. This too is meaningless, a chasing after the wind.

ISA 11: 2 The Spirit of the Lord will rest on him-- the Spirit of wisdom and of understanding, the Spirit of counsel and of power, the Spirit of KNOWLEDGE and of the fear of the Lord--
ISA 33: 6 He will be the sure foundation for your times, a rich store of salvation and wisdom and KNOWLEDGE; the fear of the Lord is the key to this treasure .
ISA 40: 14 Whom did the Lord consult to enlighten him, and who taught him the right way? Who was it that taught him KNOWLEDGE or showed him the path of understanding?

DAN 1: 17 To these four young men God gave KNOWLEDGE and understanding of all kinds of literature and learning. And Daniel could understand visions and dreams of all kinds.

HOS 4: 6 my people are destroyed from lack of KNOWLEDGE. " Because you have rejected KNOWLEDGE, I also reject you as my priests; because you have ignored the law of your God, I also will ignore your children.

HAB 2: 14 For the earth will be filled with the KNOWLEDGE of the glory of the Lord, as the waters cover the sea.

LUK 8: 10 He said, " The KNOWLEDGE of the secrets of the kingdom of God has been given to you, but to others I speak in parables, so that, "'though seeing, they may not see; though hearing, they may not understand.'

ROM 1: 28 Furthermore, since they did not think it worthwhile to retain the KNOWLEDGE of God, he gave them over to a depraved mind, to do what ought not to be done.
ROM 10: 2 For I can testify about them that they are zealous for God, but their zeal is not based on KNOWLEDGE.
ROM 11: 33 Oh, the depth of the riches of the wisdom and KNOWLEDGE of God! How unsearchable his judgments, and his paths beyond tracing out!

EPH 3: 19 and to know this love that surpasses KNOWLEDGE-- that you may be filled to the measure of all the fullness of God.

COL 1: 9 For this reason, since the day we heard about you, we have not stopped praying for you and asking God to fill you with the KNOWLEDGE of his will through all spiritual wisdom and understanding.

2TI 2: 25 Those who oppose him he must gently instruct, in the hope that God will grant them repentance leading them to a KNOWLEDGE of the truth,

PART TWO: Wisdom

GEN 3 6 When the woman saw that the fruit of the tree was good for food and pleasing to the eye, and also desirable for gaining WISDOM, she took some and ate it. She also gave some to her husband, who was with her, and he ate it.

2SA 14 20 Your servant Joab did this to change the present situation. My lord has WISDOM like that of an angel of God-- he knows everything that happens in the land. "

1KI 2 9 But now, do not consider him innocent. You are a man of WISDOM; you will know what to do to him. Bring his gray head down to the grave in blood. "
1KI 3 28 When all Israel heard the verdict the king had given, they held the king in awe, because they saw that he had WISDOM from God to administer justice.
1KI 4 34 Men of all nations came to listen to Solomon's WISDOM, sent by all the kings of the world, who had heard of his WISDOM.
1KI 10 24 The whole world sought audience with Solomon to hear the WISDOM God had put in his heart.

2CH 1 12 therefore WISDOM and knowledge will be given you. And I will also give you wealth, riches and honor, such as no king who was before you ever had and none after you will have. "

EZR 7 25 And you, Ezra, in accordance with the WISDOM of your God, which you possess, appoint magistrates and judges to administer justice to all the people of Trans-Euphrates-- all who know the laws of your God. And you are to teach any who do not know them.

JOB 38 37 Who has the WISDOM to count the clouds? Who can tip over the water jars of the heavens
JOB 39 17 for God did not endow her with WISDOM or give her a share of good sense.

PSA 37 30 The mouth of the righteous man utters WISDOM, and his tongue speaks what is just.
PSA 90 12 Teach us to number our days aright, that we may gain a heart of WISDOM.

PRO 1 2 for attaining WISDOM and discipline; for understanding words of insight;
PRO 2 12 WISDOM will save you from the ways of wicked men, from men whose words are perverse,
PRO 3 13 Blessed is the man who finds WISDOM, the man who gains understanding,
PRO 4 6 Do not forsake WISDOM, and SHE_will protect you; love her, and she will watch over you.
PRO 7 4 Say to WISDOM, " You are my sister, " and call understanding your kinsman;
PRO 8 1 Does not WISDOM call out? Does not understanding raise her voice?
PRO 8 12 " I, WISDOM, dwell together with prudence; I possess knowledge and discretion.

ISA 28 29 All this also comes from the Lord Almighty, wonderful in counsel and magnificent in WISDOM.
ISA 33 6 He will be the sure foundation for your times, a rich store of salvation and WISDOM and knowledge; the fear of the Lord is the key to this treasure.
ISA 47 10 You have trusted in your wickedness and have said,'No one sees me.'Your WISDOM and knowledge mislead you when you say to yourself,'I am, and there is none besides me.'

JER 8 9 The wise will be put to shame; they will be dismayed and trapped. Since they have rejected the word of the Lord, what kind of WISDOM do they have?
JER 10 12 But God made the earth by his power; he founded the world by his WISDOM and stretched out the heavens by his understanding.

MAT 12 42 The Queen of the South will rise at the judgment with this generation and condemn it; for she came from the ends of the earth to listen to Solomon's WISDOM, and now one greater than Solomon is here.
MAR 6 2 When the Sabbath came, he began to teach in the synagogue, and many who heard him were amazed. " Where did this man get these things? " they asked. " What's this WISDOM that has been given him, that he even does miracles!
LUK 11 49 Because of this, God in his WISDOM said,'I will send them prophets and apostles, some of whom they will kill and others they will persecute.'
LUK 21 15 For I will give you words and WISDOM that none of your adversaries will be able to resist or contradict.
ACT 7 22 Moses was educated in all the WISDOM of the Egyptians and was powerful in speech and action.

1CO 1 24 but to those whom God has called, both Jews and Greeks, Christ the power of God and the WISDOM of God.
1CO 1 25 For the foolishness of God is wiser than man's WISDOM, and the weakness of God is stronger than man's strength.
1CO 12 8 To one there is given through the Spirit the message of WISDOM, to another the message of knowledge by means of the same Spirit,

EPH 1 8 that he lavished on us with all WISDOM and understanding.

JAM 3 13 Who is wise and understanding among you? Let him show it by his good life, by deeds done in the humility that comes from WISDOM.
JAM 3 17 But the WISDOM that comes from heaven is first of all pure; then peace-loving, considerate, submissive, full of mercy and good fruit, impartial and sincere.

REV 7 12 saying: " Amen! Praise and glory and WISDOM and thanks and honor and power and strength be to our God for ever and ever. Amen! "
REV 17 9 " This calls for a mind with WISDOM.

APPENDIX AA

the Book of DANIEL
The Many Synonyms of the Aramaic Word "man"

The word "man" (men or human) is found in the English translation (RSV or NRSV) of the Book of Daniel. According to Strong's Concordance, Hebrew Section, there are five distinct words that mean "man" these are:

1. ***Adam,*** Hebrew (# 120) used Two times, a man like Adam, distinguished
2. *Iysh*, Hebrew (#376) used Six times, an individual man
3. ***Enach,*** Aramaic (# 606) by far the most frequently used, a man in general (related to #582 a mortal man)
4. ***Geber,*** Hebrew (# 1397) used One time, a valiant man
5. ***Gebar***, Aramaic *(#1400) used Two times,* a certain person; also men, the plural

Daniel and his use of the Hebrew and Aramaic word for "man":

Enach	2: 10 The Chaldeans answered the king, "There is not a man on earth who can meet the king's demand; for no great and powerful king has asked such a thing of any magician or enchanter or Chaldean.
Gebar	2: 25 Then Ari-och brought in Daniel before the king in haste, and said thus to him: "I have found among the exiles from Judah a man who can make known to the king the interpretation."
Enach	3: 10 You, O king, have made a decree, that every man who hears the sound of the horn, pipe, lyre, trigon, harp, bagpipe, and every kind of music, shall fall down and worship the golden image;
Enach	3: 24-25 Then King Nebuchadnezzar was astonished and rose up in haste. He said to his counselors, "Did we not cast three men bound into the fire?" They answered the king, "True, O king." 25 He answered, "But I see four men loose, walking in the midst of the fire, and they are not hurt; and the appearance of the fourth is like a son of the god(s)." {bar elahh}
Enach	4: 17 The sentence is by the decree of the watchers, the decision by the word of the holy ones, to the end that the living may know that the Most High rules the kingdom of men, and gives it to whom he will, and sets over it the lowliest of men.'
Enach	4: 25, that you shall be driven from among men, and your dwelling shall be with the beasts of the field; you shall be made to eat grass like an ox, and you shall be wet with the dew of heaven, and seven times shall pass over you, till you know that the Most High rules the kingdom of men, and gives it to whom he will.
Enach	4: 32 and you shall be driven from among men, and your dwelling shall be with the beasts of the field; and you shall be made to eat grass like an ox; and seven times shall pass over you, until you have learned that the Most High rules the kingdom of men and gives it to whom he will."

Enach	5: 5 Immediately the fingers of a man's hand appeared and wrote on the plaster of the wall of the king's palace, opposite the lampstand; and the king saw the hand as it wrote.(Picture)
Enach	5: 7 The king cried aloud to bring in the enchanters, the Chaldeans, and the astrologers. The king said to the wise men {no Aramaic word} of Babylon, "Whoever {man} reads this writing, and shows me its interpretation, shall be clothed with purple, and have a chain of gold about his neck, and shall be the third ruler in the kingdom."
Gebar	5: 11 There is in your kingdom a man in whom is the spirit of the holy god{s}. In the days of your father light and understanding and wisdom, like the wisdom of the gods, were found in him, and King Nebuchadnezzar, your father, made him chief of the magicians, enchanters, Chaldeans, and astrologers,
Enach	5: 21 he was driven from among men, and his mind was made like that of a beast, and his dwelling was with the wild asses; he was fed grass like an ox, and his body was wet with the dew of heaven, until he knew that the Most High God rules the kingdom of men, and sets over it whom he will.
Enach	6: 7 All the presidents of the kingdom, the prefects and the satraps, the counselors and the governors are agreed that the king should establish an ordinance and enforce an interdict, that whoever makes petition to any god or man for thirty days, except to you, O king, shall be cast into the den of lions.
Enach	6: 12 Then they came near and said before the king, concerning the interdict, "O king! Did you not sign an interdict, that any man who makes petition to any god or man within thirty days except to you, O king, shall be cast into the den of lions?" The king answered, "The thing stands fast, according to the law of the Medes and Persians, which cannot be revoked."
Enach	7: 4 The first was like a lion and had eagles' wings. Then as I looked its wings were plucked off, and it was lifted up from the ground and made to stand upon two feet like a man; and the mind of a man was given to it.
Enach	7: 8 I considered the horns, and behold, there came up among them another horn, a little one, before which three of the first horns were plucked up by the roots; and behold, in this horn were eyes like the eyes of a man, and a mouth speaking great things.
bar Enach	7: 13 I saw in the night visions, and behold, with the clouds of heaven there came one like a son of man, and he came to the Ancient of Days and was presented before him.
Geber	8: 15 When I, Daniel, had seen the vision, I sought to understand it; and behold, there stood before me one having the appearance of a man.
Adam	8: 16 And I heard a man's voice between the banks of the Ulai, and it called, "Gabriel, make this {man} understand the vision." ben Adam 8: 17 So he came near where I stood; and when he came, I was frightened and fell upon my face. But he said to me, "Understand, O son of man, that the vision is for the time of the end."
ben Ash-	9: 1 In the first year of Darius the son of Ahasuerus, by birth a Mede, who became king over the realm of the Chaldeans

Iysh	9: 21 while I was speaking in prayer, the man Gabriel, whom I had seen in the vision at the first, came to me in swift flight at the time of the evening sacrifice.
Iysh	10: 5 I lifted up my eyes and looked, and behold, a man clothed in linen, whose loins were girded with gold of Uphaz.
Iysh	10: 11 And he said to me, "O Daniel, man greatly beloved, give heed to the words that I speak to you, and stand upright, for now I have been sent to you." While he was speaking this word to me, I stood up trembling.
Adam	10: 18 Again one having the appearance of a man touched me and strengthened me.
Iysh	10: 19 And he said, "O man greatly beloved, fear not, peace be with you; be strong and of good courage." And when he spoke to me, I was strengthened and said, "Let my lord speak, for you have strengthened me."
Iysh	12: 6 And I said to the man clothed in linen, who was above the waters of the stream, "How long shall it be till the end of these wonders?"
Iysh	12: 7 The man clothed in linen, who was above the waters of the stream, raised his right hand and his left hand toward heaven; and I heard him swear by him who lives for ever that it would be for a time, two times, and half a time; and that when the shattering of the power of the holy people comes to an end all these things would be accomplished.

Observation: The "son of man" (*bar enach*) is an Aramaic idiom that implies a human person. When it was translated into Greek, it took upon the implication of a title, the "son of a man". The dictionary says: "a construction or expression of one language whose parts correspond to elements in another language but whose total structure or meaning is not matched in the same way in the second language." The authors of the Christian Testament wrote the Greek designation of an Aramaic expression because they didn't appreciate the generic meaning of the Aramaic phrase. The confusion persisted well into the 21st century. Thus the Greek "son of man" became a biblical title used by the authors to designate Yeshua as that human-like person riding the cloud. All this from the interpretation of a dream in the Hebrew Testament that was believed to predict the future.

APPENDIX AB

NIV Search for Spirit

PART ONE: Selections from the Hebrew Testament

The English word, "spirit", is interpreted from the Hebrew word "*ruwach*" which means wind or, figuratively, breath (used to mean the breath of God or of a person), mind, emotion or even an abstraction. When "*ruwach*" is modified by an emotion (as in GEN 41: 8 below), the NIV omits the word "spirit". Additionally, the Hebrew authors frequently associated "spirit" with an abstraction or emotion like "the spirit of wisdom" or "an angry spirit". These exceptions will be underlined and the literal Hebrew identified with parens ( ). For additional distinctions of "Ruwach", see Appendix AC, Vine's Dictionary. The braces denote {this Author's comments}

GEN 1 2 Now the earth was formless and empty, darkness was over the surface of the deep, and the SPIRIT of God was hovering over the waters. {Actually "Spirit" should read "Breath" and "*elohiym*" is the Hebrew word for God}
GEN 3 8 *When they heard the sound of the LORD God moving
about in the garden at the breezy time of the day (! *ruwach* !), the man and his wife hid themselves from the LORD God among the trees of
the garden.
GEN 6 3 Then the Lord said, " My SPIRIT will not contend with man forever, for he is mortal; his days will be a hundred and twenty years. "
GEN 7 21-22 All creatures that stirred on earth perished: birds, cattle, wild animals, and all that swarmed on the earth, as well as all mankind.
Everything on dry land with the faintest breath of life (! *ruwach* !) in its nostrils died out.
GEN 8 1 and then God remembered Noah and all the animals, wild and tame, that were with him in the ark. So God made a wind (! *ruwach* !) sweep over the earth, and the waters began to subside.
GEN 41 8 In the morning his mind was troubled (the Hebrew reads, a troubled spirit. It is the modern translator who chooses "mind"!), so he sent for all the magicians and wise men of Egypt. Pharaoh told them his dreams, but no one could interpret them for him.
GEN 41 38 So Pharaoh asked them, " Can we find anyone like this man, one in whom is the SPIRIT of God? "

EXO 6 9 Moses reported this to the Israelites, but they did not listen to him because of their discouragement (anguish of spirit) and cruel bondage.
EXO 10 13 So Moses stretched out his staff over the land of Egypt, and the LORD sent an east wind (! *ruwach* !) blowing over the land all that day and all that night. At dawn the east wind brought the locusts.
EXO 10 19 and the LORD changed the wind (! *ruwach* !) to a very strong west wind, which took up the locusts and hurled them into the Red {Reed} Sea. But though not a single locust remained within the confines of Egypt,
EXO 15 8 At a breath of your anger (spirit of anger) the waters piled up, the flowing waters stood like a mound, the flood waters congealed in the midst of the sea.

EXO 28 3 Tell all the skilled men to whom I have given wisdom (a *ruwach* of wisdom) in such matters that they are to make garments for Aaron, for his consecration, so he may serve me as priest.

LEV 20 27 "'A man or woman who is a medium or SPIRIT (a fortune-teller) {a KJV translation} is among you must be put to death. You are to stone them; their blood will be on their own heads.'"

NUM 5 14 and if feelings of jealousy (a spirit of jealousy) come over her husband and he suspects his wife and she is impure-- or if he is jealous (a spirit of jealousy) and suspects her even though she is not impure—
NUM 11 29 But Moses replied, " Are you jealous for my sake? I wish that all the Lord 's people were prophets and that the Lord would put his SPIRIT on them! " {Note: this is God's Spirit, the Spirit of the ONE God, not to be confused with a second person!}

JOS 2 11 At these reports, we are disheartened; everyone is discouraged (! ruwach !) because of you, since the LORD, your God, is God in heaven above and on earth below.
JOS 5 1 Now when all the Amorite kings west of the Jordan and all the Canaanite kings along the coast heard how the Lord had dried up the Jordan before the Israelites until we had crossed over, their hearts melted and they no longer had the courage (the spirit) to face the Israelites.

JUD 9 23 God sent an evil SPIRIT {does this not reveal a Puppeteer God of "Reciprocity"?} between Abimelech and the citizens of Shechem, who acted treacherously against Abimelech.

1SA 1 15 " Not so, my lord, " Hannah replied, " I am a woman who is deeply troubled (pained of spirit). I have not been drinking wine or beer; I was pouring out my soul {a breathing physical being, *nephesh*, in Hebrew but not to be confused with spirit} to the Lord.
1SA 16 13 So Samuel took the horn of oil and anointed him in the presence of his brothers, and from that day on the SPIRIT of the Lord came upon David in power. Samuel then went to Ramah.
1SA 16 14 Now the SPIRIT of the Lord had departed from Saul, and an evil SPIRIT from the Lord {God approving an evil sngel!} tormented him.
1SA 19 9 But an evil SPIRIT from the Lord came upon Saul as he was sitting in his house with his spear in his hand. While David was playing the harp,
1SA 28 7 Saul then said to his attendants, " Find me a woman who is a medium {KJV uses a familiar spirit but in the Hebrew the word is *owb*} , so I may go and inquire of her. " " There is one in Endor, " they said.
1KI 10 5 the food on his table, the seating of his officials, the attending servants in their robes, his cupbearers, and the burnt offerings he made at the temple of the Lord, she was overwhelmed (having more spirit).

1KI 22 23 " So now the Lord has put a lying SPIRIT (a spirit of falsehood) in the mouths of all these prophets of yours. The Lord has decreed disaster for you. "

1CH 10 13 Saul died because he was unfaithful to the Lord; he did not keep the word of the Lord and even consulted a medium {a familiar spirit in the KJV but in the Hebrew, owb} for guidance,

2CH 21 16 The Lord aroused against Jehoram the <u>hostility</u> (spirit) of the Philistines and of the Arabs who lived near the Cushites.
2CH 33 6 He sacrificed his sons in the fire in the Valley of Ben Hinnom, practiced sorcery, divination and witchcraft, and consulted <u>mediums</u> (a familiar spirit) and spiritists. He did much evil in the eyes of the Lord, provoking him to anger.
2CH 36 22 In the first year of Cyrus king of Persia, in order to fulfill the word of the Lord spoken by Jeremiah, the Lord <u>moved the</u> <u>heart</u> (stirred up the *ruwach*?) {This is the beginning of confusing the language by our friendly translators!} of Cyrus king of Persia to make a proclamation throughout his realm and to put it in writing:

EZR 1 1 In the first year of Cyrus king of Persia, in order to fulfill the word of the Lord spoken by Jeremiah, the Lord moved <u>the heart</u> (spirit, *ruwach*) of Cyrus king of Persia to make a proclamation throughout his realm and to put it in writing:

JOB 4 9 By <u>the breath</u> (*nshamah*, vital breath or anger) of God they perish, and by the <u>blast (*ruwach, wind*) of his wrath</u> they are consumed.
JOB 4 15 A SPIRIT glided past my face, and the hair on my body stood on end.

JOB 7 11 " Therefore I will not keep silent; I will speak out in the anguish of my <u>SPIRIT</u>, I will complain in the bitterness of my <u>soul</u> (a breathing creature, *nephesh*).
JOB 15 2 Should a wise man answer with <u>windy</u> (! *ruwach !*) knowledge , and fill himself with the east wind?
JOB 15 13 so that you vent <u>your rage</u> (! *ruwach !*) against God and pour out such words from your mouth?
JOB 16 3 Is there no end to <u>windy words</u> (*ruwach, empty breath*)? Or what sickness have you that you speak on?

PRO 11 29 He who upsets his household has <u>empty air</u> (! *ruwach !*) for a heritage; and the fool will become slave to the wise man.
PRO 14 29 A patient man has great understanding, but <u>a quick- tempered man</u> (short of spirit) displays folly.
PRO 16 32 Better a patient man than a warrior, a man who <u>controls his temper</u> (rules his spirit) than one who takes a city.

ZEC 13 2 " On that day, I will banish the names of the idols from the land, and they will be remembered no more, " declares the <u>Lord Almighty</u> (as in Zec 4: 6 above). " I will remove both the prophets and the <u>SPIRIT of impurity</u> (actually reads an unclean spirit!) from the land. {Could this be the source of the notion of demon-caused sickness as found in the Christian Testament?}

PART TWO: Selections from the Christian Testament

{There are four special notes of importance for this part. We will experience:

1. **The Greek notation, *pneuma theos*, for the Spirit of God;**
2. **The use of the single word, Spirit (*pneuma*), as a synonym for God as it was used in the Hebrew Testament;**
3. **The phrase Holy Spirit, in Greek is *pneuma hagio*, a translation, of the Hebrew, *ruwach qodesh, the Spirit of Holiness;* and**
4. **The arrangement of the order of the books of this Christian Testament will be changed from the Catholic Church's 400 AD order to that found in Appendix U. It is noteworthy to recognize that all Bibles authored under every Christian Denomination uses that Catholic order!}**

Apostolic Period (App. U)

1TH 4 8 Therefore, he who rejects this instruction does not reject man but God, who gives you his Holy SPIRIT (First, God gives His Spirit of holiness. Is this not the same as what was written in the Hebrew Testament? See Appendix AD for the use of the yerm "Holiness in the H.T.).

1TH 5 23 May God himself, the God of peace, sanctify you through and through. May your whole SPIRIT, soul (*psuche)* and body (*soma*) be kept blameless at the coming of our Lord Jesus Christ.

{We get the sense that spirit means the whole person. But, Paul believes that one's spirit has two parts, soul and body. Our problem is, does God have two parts? Or, does the single word, spirit, as it applies to God, mean that God can gave three spirits? Or, is Trinitarianism not true? Does God have a physical body? Then how come the Bible speaks of God's face, hands, etc.? Answer: they're all metaphors!}

2TH 2 2 not to become easily unsettled (The Greek reads, *saleuo nous,* disturbed of mind. *Nous* is a philosophic term used by Plato meaning, the mind of a person. It is related to the term, metanoia, changing your mind or behavior, mistranslated to read, repentance.) or alarmed by some prophecy (The Greek reads, pneuma, spirit, implying an evil spirit. Here one would suspect a mis-translation.), report or letter (the Greek reads, logos, suggesting a single word!) supposed to have come from us, saying that the day of the Lord has already come. (The Greek reads, *theos*, and Lord is *kurios*. This certainly illustrates some confusion in the translator's mind. The majority of Bibles use "Lord".)

2TH 2 8 And then the lawless one will be revealed, whom the Lord (kurios) Jesus (not present in the Greek! One can assume that the translator means God.) will overthrow with the breath (The Greek reads, *pneuma*) of his mouth and destroy by the splendor of his coming (*parousia*) .

GAL 3 5 Does God give you his SPIRIT and work miracles among you because you observe the law, or because you believe what you heard?

GAL 4 6 Because you are sons, God sent the SPIRIT of his Son into our hearts, the SPIRIT (Jesus' ?) who calls out, " Abba, Father. "

GAL 6 18 The grace of our Lord Jesus {the} Christ be with your SPIRIT, brothers. Amen. {Note: there are no references to the Holy Spirit in this book. The use of *pneuma*, spirit, in Galatians refers mostly to God the Father as in the H.T. Other interpretations are metaphors.}

PHI 1 19 for I know that through your prayers and the help given by the SPIRIT of Jesus {the} Christ, what has happened to me will turn out for my deliverance.
PHI 3 3 For it is we who are the circumcision, we who worship by the SPIRIT of God, who glory in Jesus {the} Christ, and who put no confidence in the flesh. {Note, there are no references to the Holy Spirit in this book.}

1CO 2 14 The man without the SPIRIT does not accept the things that come from the SPIRIT of God, for they are foolishness to him, and he cannot understand them, because they are spiritually discerned.
1CO 3 16 Don't you know that you yourselves are God's temple and that God's SPIRIT lives in you? {Is this not convincing that it is God's spirit?}
1CO 4 21 What do you prefer? Shall I come to you with a whip, or in love and with a gentle SPIRIT (Greek reads, a spirit of meekness) ?
1CO 6 11 And that is what some of you were. But you were washed, you were sanctified, you were justified in the name of the Lord Jesus {the} Christ and by the SPIRIT of our God.
1CO 12 3 Therefore I tell you that no one who is speaking by the SPIRIT of God says , " Jesus be cursed, " and no one can say, " Jesus is Lord, " except by the Holy SPIRIT {This refers to God the Father –Spirit of Holiness--just like the Hebrew Testament's use!}.
1CO 12 9 to another faith by the same SPIRIT, to another gifts of healing by that one SPIRIT (very clearly, God the Father) ,
1CO 12 11 All these are the work of one and the same SPIRIT, and he gives them to each one, just as he determines.
1CO 12 13 For we were all baptized by one SPIRIT into one body-- whether Jews or Greeks, slave or free-- and we were all given the one SPIRIT to drink.
1CO 14 2 For anyone who speaks in a tongue does not speak to men but to God. Indeed, no one understands him; he utters mysteries with his SPIRIT.

2CO 3 3 You show that you are a letter from {the} Christ, the result of our ministry, written not with ink but with the SPIRIT of the living God, not on tablets of stone but on tablets of human hearts.
2CO 3 6 He has made us competent as ministers of a new covenant-- not of the letter but of the SPIRIT; for the letter kills, but the SPIRIT gives life.

ROM 8 14 because those who are led by the SPIRIT of God are sons of God.
ROM 8 15 For you did not receive a SPIRIT that makes you a slave again to fear, but you received the SPIRIT of sonship (Jesus). And by him we cry, " Abba, Father. " {Actually means Daddy!}
ROM 8 16 The SPIRIT (God) himself testifies with our SPIRIT that we are God's children.
ROM 11 8 as it is written: " God gave them a SPIRIT of stupor (a breath, pneuma, of slumber? Doesn't read well in modern times!) eyes so that they could not see and ears so that they could not hear, to this very day. "
ROM 12 11 Never be lacking in zeal, but keep your spiritual fervor (slothful in spirit), serving the Lord .
ROM 15 19 by the power of signs and miracles, through the power of the SPIRIT (Greek reads, of God!). So from Jerusalem all the way around to Illyricum, I have fully proclaimed the gospel of {the} Christ.

PHL 1 25 The grace of the Lord Jesus {the} Christ be with your SPIRIT.

EPH 1 13 And you also were included in {the} Christ when you heard the word of truth, the gospel of your salvation. Having believed, you were marked in him with a seal, the promised Holy SPIRIT (for Paol, this is God)
EPH 1 17 I keep asking that the God of our Lord Jesus {the} Christ, the glorious Father, may give you the SPIRIT of wisdom (again, a metaphor) and revelation, so that you may know him better.
EPH 4 4 There is one body and one SPIRIT (God) -- just as you were called to one hope when you were called —
EPH 4 23 to be made new in the attitude (the Greek reads spirit) of your minds;
EPH 4 30 And do not grieve the Holy SPIRIT of God, with whom you were sealed for the day of redemption.

JAM 2 26 As the body without the SPIRIT is dead, so faith without deeds is dead.

1PE 1 11 trying to find out the time and circumstances to which the SPIRIT of {the} Christ in them was pointing when he predicted the sufferings of {the} Christ and the glories that would follow.
1PE 4 14 If you are insulted because of the name of {the} Christ, you are blessed, for the SPIRIT of glory and of God rests on you.

1TI 4 1 The SPIRIT clearly says that in later times some will abandon the faith and follow deceiving SPIRITs and things taught by demons. 1TI 4 12 Don't let anyone look down on you because you are young, but set an example for the believers in speech, in life, in love, in faith and in purity. {Some manuscripts have "in spirit".}

2TI 1 7 For God did not give us a SPIRIT of timidity, but a SPIRIT of power, of love and of self- discipline.
2TI 4 22 The Lord be with your SPIRIT. Grace be with you. {If people are referred to as possessing a spirit, is that a second person?}

Baptismal Period (App. U)
MAR 1 23 Just then a man in their synagogue who was possessed by an evil SPIRIT (a demon) cried out,
MAR 1 26 The evil SPIRIT shook the man violently and came out of him with a shriek.
MAR 2 8 Immediately Jesus knew in his SPIRIT that this was what they were thinking in their hearts, and he said to them, " Why are you thinking these things ?
MAR 3 30 He said this because they were saying, " He has an evil SPIRIT. "
MAR 5 2 When Jesus got out of the boat, a man with an evil SPIRIT came from the tombs to meet him.
MAR 5 8 For Jesus had said to him, " Come out of this man, you evil SPIRIT! "
MAR 6 49 but when they saw him walking on the lake, they thought he was a ghost (spirit or phantasm). They cried out,
MAR 8 12 He sighed deeply (groaning in the spirit) and said, " Why does this generation ask for a miraculous sign? I tell you the truth, no sign will be given to it. "
MAR 9 25 When Jesus saw that a crowd was running to the scene, he rebuked the evil SPIRIT. "You deaf and mute SPIRIT," he said, "I command you, come out of him and never enter him again."

Conception Period (App. U)
MAT 3 16 As soon as Jesus was baptized, he went up out of the water. At that moment heaven was opened, and he saw the SPIRIT of God descending like a dove and lighting on him. {This is not a third person!}

MAT 4 1 Then Jesus was led by the SPIRIT (of God) into the desert to be tempted by the devil.
MAT 5 3 " Blessed are the poor in SPIRIT, for theirs is the kingdom of heaven.
MAT 10 20 for it will not be you speaking, but the SPIRIT of your Father speaking through you.
MAT 14 26 When the disciples saw him walking on the lake, they were terrified. " It' s a ghost (some Versions have *pneuma*), " they said, and cried out in fear.
MAT 22 43 He said to them, " How is it then that David, speaking by the SPIRIT (of God), calls him Lord? For he says,

{NOTE: Luke is a disciple of Paul and as such continues the same confusions of Paul in his Gospel and Acts. Paul and Luke's use of the word spirit constitutes over 80 % of the C.T.'s use of spirit}
LUK 1 17 And he will go on before the Lord, in the SPIRIT and power of Elijah, to turn the hearts of the fathers to their children and the disobedient to he wisdom of the righteous-- to make ready a people prepared for the Lord .
LUK 1 47 and my SPIRIT rejoices in God my Savior,
LUK 1 80 And the child grew and became strong in SPIRIT; and he lived in the desert until he appeared publicly to Israel.
LUK 2 40 And the child grew and became strong (some Greek reads, waxed strong in the spirit); he was filled with wisdom, and the grace of God was upon him.
LUK 4 18 " The SPIRIT of the Lord (of God) is on me, because he has anointed me to preach good news to the poor. He has sent me to proclaim freedom for the prisoners and recovery of sight for the blind, to release the oppressed,
LUK 9 42 Even while the boy was coming, the demon threw him to the ground in a convulsion. But Jesus rebuked the evil SPIRIT, healed the boy and gave him back to his father.
LUK 13 11 and a woman was there who had been crippled by a SPIRIT for eighteen years. She was bent over and could not straighten up at all.
LUK 23 46 Jesus called out with a loud voice, " Father, into your hands I commit my SPIRIT. " When he had said this, he breathed his last.

ACT 2 17 "'In the last days, God says, I will pour out my SPIRIT on all people. Your sons and daughters will prophesy, your young men will see visions, your old men will dream dreams. {Noy a third person!}
ACT 5 9 Peter said to her, " How could you agree to test the SPIRIT of the Lord? Look! The feet of the men who buried your husband are at the door, and they will carry you out also. "
ACT 7 59 While they were stoning him, Stephen prayed, " Lord Jesus, receive my SPIRIT. "
ACT 8 39 When they came up out of the water, the SPIRIT of the Lord suddenly took Philip away, and the eunuch did not see him again, but went on his way rejoicing.
ACT 11 28 One of them, named Agabus, stood up and through the ACT 16 7 When they came to the border of Mysia, they tried to enter Bithynia, but the SPIRIT of Jesus would not allow them to.
ACT 16 16 Once when we were going to the place of prayer, we were met by a slave girl who had a SPIRIT by which she predicted the future. She earned a great deal of money for her owners by fortune- telling.
ACT 17 16 While Paul was waiting for them in Athens, he was greatly distressed (Greek reads, his spirit was pained) to see that the city was full of idols.
ACT 18 5 When Silas and Timothy came from Macedonia, Paul devoted (pressed in the spirit) himself exclusively to preaching, testifying to the Jews that Jesus was the Christ.

ACT 19 15 One day the evil SPIRIT answered them, " Jesus I know, and I know about Paul, but who are you? "
ACT 20 22 " And now, compelled by the SPIRIT(of God), I am going to Jerusalem, not knowing what will happen to me there.
ACT 23 8 (The Sadducees say that there is no resurrection, and that there are neither angels nor SPIRITs, but the Pharisees acknowledge them all.)

REV 11 11 But after the three and a half days a breath (pneuma) of life from God entered them , and they stood on their feet, and terror struck those who saw them.
REV 17 3 Then the angel carried me away in the SPIRIT (more like in a trance) into a desert. There I saw a woman sitting on a scarlet beast that was covered with blasphemous names and had seven heads and ten horns.
REV 19 10 At this I fell at his feet to worship him. But he said to me, " Do not do it! I am a fellow servant with you and with your brothers who hold to the testimony of Jesus. Worship God! For the testimony of Jesus is the SPIRIT of prophecy. "

Eternity Period (App. U)
HEB 10 29 How much more severely do you think a man deserves to be punished who has trampled the Son of God under foot, who has treated as an unholy thing the blood of the covenant that sanctified him, and who has insulted the SPIRIT of grace?

1JO 4 1 Dear friends, do not believe every SPIRIT, but test the SPIRITs to see whether they are from God, because many false prophets have gone out into the world.
1JO 4 2 This is how you can recognize the SPIRIT of God: Every SPIRIT that acknowledges that Jesus (the) Christ has come in the flesh is from God,

1JO 4 3 but every SPIRIT that does not acknowledge Jesus is not from God. This is the SPIRIT of the antichrist, which you have heard is coming and even now is already in the world.
1JO 4 6 We are from God, and whoever knows God listens to us; but whoever is not from God does not listen to us. This is how we recognize the SPIRIT of truth and the SPIRIT of falsehood.

JOH 3 8 The wind (*pneuma*) blows (*pneo)* wherever it pleases. You hear its sound, but you cannot tell where it comes from or where it is going. So it is with everyone born of the SPIRIT.
JOH 4 23 Yet a time is coming and has now come when the true worshipers will worship the Father in SPIRIT and truth, for they are the kind of worshipers the Father seeks.
JOH 4 24 God is SPIRIT, and his worshipers must worship in SPIRIT and in truth."
JOH 11 33 When Jesus saw her weeping, and the Jews who had come along with her also weeping, he was deeply moved in SPIRIT and troubled.
JOH 14 17 the SPIRIT of truth (a metaphor for God's grace or God himself). The world cannot accept him, because it neither sees him nor knows him. But you know him, for he lives with you and will be in you.
JOH 15 26 " When the Counselor comes, whom I will send to you from the Father, the SPIRIT of truth (a metaphor for God's grace or God himself) who goes out from the Father, he will testify about me.

APPENDIX AC

Vine's HT & CT Dictionary
of
Wind, Breath, Spirit, Soul, Mind

All this is to show you what the scholar has to determine when translating from Hebrew to Greek to Latin to get to a reasonable meaning in English. Reading this is not for the faint of mind or heart!

HEBREW: Wind, Breath, Spirit;

***Ruwach: reading left to right is three letters in Hebrew [He(pattach) - Wav (chowlem)- Reysh]* written right to left. Sometimes read as *ruwah*.**

The two paewns between the three letters are vowel pointings added about the 7th century by the Masorettes.

No. 1 Strong's Number: 7307; SPIRIT;; Transliterated: *ruwah*; noun

Text: "breath; air; strength; wind; breeze; spirit; courage; temper; Spirit." This noun has cognates in Ugaritic, Aramaic, and Arabic. The word occurs about 378 times and in all periods of biblical Hebrew.

First, this word means "breath," air for breathing, air that is being breathed. This meaning is especially evident in Jer. 14:6: "And the wild asses did stand in the high places, they snuffed up the wind like dragons...." When one's "breath" returns, he is revived: "...When he [Samson] had drunk [the water], his spirit [literally, "breath"] came again, and he revived..." (Judg. 15:19). Astonishment may take away one's "breath": "And when the queen of Sheba had seen all Solomon's wisdom, and the house that he had built, And the meat of his table,... there was no more spirit in her [she was overwhelmed and breathless]" (1 Kings 10:4-5). Ruah may also represent speaking, or the breath of one's mouth: "By the word of the Lord were the heavens made; and all the host of them by the breath of his mouth" (Ps. 33:6; cf. Exod. 15:8; Job 4:9; 19:17).

Second, this word can be used with emphasis on the invisible, intangible, fleeting quality of "air": "O remember that my life is wind: mine eyes shall no more see good" (Job 7:7). There may be a suggestion of purposelessness, uselessness, or even vanity (emptiness) when ruah is used with this significance: "And the prophets shall become wind, and the word is not in them ..." (Jer. 5:13). "Windy words" are really "empty words" (Job 16:3), just as "windy knowledge" is "empty knowledge" (Job 15:2; cf. Eccl. 1:14, 17, "meaningless striving"). In Prov. 11:29 ruah means "nothing": "He that troubleth his own house shall inherit the wind...." This nuance is especially prominent in Eccl. 5:15-16: "And he came forth of his mother's womb, naked shall he return to go as he came, and shall take nothing of his labor, which he may carry away in his hand. And this also is a sore evil, that in all points as he came, so shall he go: and what profit hath he that hath labored for the wind?"

Third, ruah can mean "wind." In Gen. 3:8 it seems to mean the gentle, refreshing evening breeze so well known in the Near East: "And they heard the voice of the Lord God walking in the garden in the cool [literally, "breeze"] of the day...." It can mean a strong, constant wind: "... And the Lord brought an east wind upon the land all that day, and all that night ..." (Exo 10:13). It can also signify an extremely strong wind: "And the Lord turned a mighty strong west wind ..." (Exo 10:19). In Jer. 4:11 the word appears to represent a gale or tornado (cf. Hos 8:7). God is the Creator (Amos 4:13) and sovereign Controller of the winds (Gen. 8:1; Num. 11:31; Jer. 10:13).

Fourth, the wind represents direction. In Jer. 49:36 the four winds represent the four ends of the earth, which in turn represent every quarter: "And upon Elam will I bring the four winds [peoples from every quarter of the earth] from the four quarters of heaven, and will scatter them toward all those winds; and there shall be no nation whither the outcasts of Elam shall not come." Akkadian attests the same phrase with the same meaning, and this phrase begins to appear in Hebrew at a time when contact with Akkadian-speaking peoples was frequent.

Fifth, ruah frequently represents the element of life in a man, his natural "spirit": "And all flesh died that moved upon the earth,... All in whose nostrils was the breath of life ..." (Gen. 7:21-22). In these verses the animals have a "spirit" (cf. Ps. 104:29). On the other hand, in Prov. 16:2 the word appears to mean more than just the element of life; it seems to mean "soul": "All the ways of a man are clean in his own eyes; but the Lord weigheth the spirits [NASB, "motives"]." Thus, Isaiah can put *nepes*, "soul," and ruah in synonymous parallelism: "With my soul have I desired thee in the night; yea, with my spirit within me will I seek thee early ..." (26:9). It is the "spirit" of a man that returns to God (Eccl. 12:7).

Sixth, ruah is often used of a man's mind-set, disposition, or "temper": "Blessed is the man unto whom the Lord imputeth not iniquity, and in whose spirit there is no guile" (Ps. 32:2). In Ezek. 13:3 the word is used of one's mind or thinking: "Woe unto the foolish prophets, that follow their own spirits, and have seen nothing" (cf. Pro 29:11). Ruah can represent particular dispositions, as it does in Josh. 2:11: "And as soon as we had heard these things, our hearts did melt, neither did there remain any more courage in any man, because of you ..." (cf. Josh. 5:1; Job 15:13). Another disposition represented by this word is "temper": "If the spirit [temper] of the ruler rise up against thee, leave not thy place ..." (Eccl. 10:4). David prayed that God would "restore unto me the joy of thy salvation; and uphold me with thy free Spirit" (Ps. 51:12). In this verse "joy of salvation" and "free Spirit" are parallel and, therefore, synonymous terms. Therefore, "spirit" refers to one's inner disposition, just as "joy" refers to an inner emotion.

Seventh, the Bible often speaks of God's "Spirit," the third person of the Trinity. This is the use of the word in its first biblical occurrence: "And the earth was without form, and void; and darkness was upon the face of the deep. And the Spirit of God moved upon the face of the waters" (Gen. 1:2). Isa. 63:10-11 and Ps. 51:12 specifically speak of the "holy or free Spirit."

Eighth, the non-material beings (angels) in heaven are sometimes called "spirits": "And there came forth a spirit, and stood before the Lord, and said, I will persuade him" (1 Kings 22:21; cf. 1 Sam. 16:14).

Ninth, the "spirit" may also be used of that which enables a man to do a particular job or that which represents the essence of a quality of man: "And Joshua the son of Nun was full of the spirit of wisdom; for Moses had laid his hands upon him ..." (Deut. 34:9). Elisha asked Elijah for a double portion of his "spirit" (2 Kings 2:9) and received it.

No. 2 Strong's Number: 178; SPIRIT (OF THE DEAD), a NECROMANCER; Transliterated: *'ob*

Text: "spirit (of the dead); necromancer; pit." This word has cognates in Sumerian, Akkadian, and Ugaritic, where the meanings "pit" and "spirit of one who has died" occur. In its earliest appearance (Sumerian), ob refers to a pit out of which a departed spirit may be summoned. Later Assyrian texts use this word to denote simply a pit in the ground. Akkadian texts describe a deity that is the personification of the pit, to whom a particular exorcism ritual was addressed. Biblical Hebrew attests this word 16 times.

The word usually represents the troubled spirit (or spirits) of the dead. This meaning appears unquestionably in Isa. 29:4: "... Thy voice shall be, as of one that hath a familiar spirit, out of the ground, and thy speech shall whisper out of the dust."
Its second meaning, "necromancer," refers to a professional who claims to summon forth such spirits when requested (or hired) to do so: "Regard not them that have familiar spirits, neither seek after wizards" (Lev. 19:31, first occurrence). These mediums summoned their "guides" from a hole in the ground. Saul asked the medium (witch) of Endor, "Divine for me from the hole [*'ob*] (1 Sam. 28:8, author's translation).
God forbade Israel to seek information by this means, which was so common among the pagans (Lev. 19:31; Deut. 18:11). Perhaps the pagan belief in manipulating one's basic relationship to a god (or gods) explains the relative silence of the Old Testament regarding life after death. Yet God's people believed in life after death, from early times (e.g., Gen. 37:35; Isa. 14:15ff.).
Necromancy was so contrary to God's commands that its practitioners were under the death penalty (Deut. 13). Necromancers' unusual experiences do not prove that they truly had power to summon the dead. For example, the medium of Endor could not snatch Samuel out of God's hands against His wishes. But in this particular incident, it seems that God rebuked Saul's apostasy, either through a revived Samuel or through a vision of Samuel. Mediums do not have power to summon the spirits of the dead, since this is reprehensible to God and contrary to His will. ???

No. 3 Strong's Number: 1892; BREATH; Transliterated: *hebel*
Text: "breath; vanity; idol." Cognates of this noun occur in Syriac, late Aramaic, and Arabic. All but 4 of its 72 occurrences are in poetry (37 in Ecclesiastes).
First, the word represents human "breath" as a transitory thing: "I loathe it; I would not live always: let me alone; for my days are vanity [literally, but a breath] (Job 7:16).
Second, *hebel* means something meaningless and purposeless: "Vanity of vanities, saith the Preacher, vanity of vanities; all is vanity" (Eccl. 1:2).
Third, this word signifies an "idol," which is unsubstantial, worthless, and vain: "They have moved me to jealousy with that which is not God; they have provoked me to anger with their vanities ..." (Deut. 32:21, the first occurrence).

Greek: SPIRIT, BREATH, WIND; *PNEUMA*

No. 4. Strong's Number: 4151; SPIRIT; Transliterated: *pneuma*
Text: primarily denotes "the wind" (akin to *pneo*, "to breathe, blow"); also "breath"; then, especially "the spirit," which, like the wind, is invisible, immaterial and powerful. The NT uses of the word may be analyzed approximately as follows:

(a) the wind, John 3:8; Heb. 1:7; cf. Amos 4:13, Septuagint.;
(b) the breath, 2 Thess. 2:8; Rev. 11:11; 13:15; cf. Job 12:10, Septuagint.;
(c) the immaterial, invisible part of man, Luke 8:55; Acts 7:59; 1 Cor. 5:5; Jas. 2:26; cf. Eccl. 12:7, Septuagint.;
(d) the disembodied (or 'unclothed,' or 'naked,' 2 Cor. 5:3, 4) man, Luke 24:37, 39; Heb. 12:23; 1 Pet. 4:6;
(e) the resurrection body, 1 Cor. 15:45; 1 Tim. 3:16; 1 Pet. 3:18;
(f) the sentient element in man, that by which he perceives, reflects, feels, desires, Matt. 5:3; 26:41; Mark 2:8; Luke 1:47, 80; Acts 17:16; 20:22; 1 Cor. 2:11; 5:3, 4; 14:4, 15; 2 Cor. 7:1; cf. Gen. 26:35; Isa. 26:9; Ezek. 13:3; Dan. 7:15;
(g) purpose, aim, 2 Cor. 12:18; Phil. 1:27; Eph. 4:23; Rev. 19:10; cf. Ezra 1:5; Ps. 78:8; Dan. 5:12;

(h) the equivalent of the personal pronoun, used for emphasis and effect: 1st person, 1 Cor. 16:18; cf. Gen. 6:3; 2nd person, 2 Tim. 4:22; Philem. 25; cf. Ps. 139:7; 3rd person, 2 Cor. 7:13; cf. Isa. 40:13;
(i) character, Luke 1:17; Rom. 1:4; cf. Num. 14:24;
(j) moral qualities and activities: bad, as of bondage, as of a slave, Rom. 8:15; cf. Isa. 61:3; stupor, Rom. 11:8; cf. Isa. 29:10;
(k) timidity, 2 Tim. 1:7; cf. Josh. 5:1; good, as of adoption, i.e., liberty as of a son, Rom. 8:15; cf. Ps. 51:12; meekness, 1 Cor. 4:21; cf. Prov. 16:19; faith, 2 Cor. 4:13; quietness, 1 Pet. 3:4; cf. Prov. 14:29
(l) the Holy Spirit, e.g., Matt. 4:1 (see below); Luke 4:18;
(m) 'the inward man' (an expression used only of the believer, Rom. 7:22; 2 Cor. 4:16; Eph. 3:16); the new life, Rom. 8:4-6, 10, 16; Heb. 12:9; cf. Ps. 51:10;
(n) unclean spirits, demons, Matt. 8:16; Luke 4:33; 1 Pet. 3:19; cf. 1 Sam. 18:10;
(o) angels, Heb. 1:14; cf. Acts 12:15;
(p) divine gift for service, 1 Cor. 14:12, 32;
(q) by metonymy, those who claim to be depositories of these gifts, 2 Thess. 2:2; 1 John 4:1-3;
(r) the significance, as contrasted with the form, of words, or of a rite, John 6:63; Rom. 2:29; 7:6; 2 Cor. 3:6;
(s) a vision, Rev. 1:10; 4:2; 17:3; 21:10."

From Notes on Thessalonians, by Hogg and Vine, pp 204, 205. Notes: (1) For *phantasma*, rendered "spirit," Matt. 14:26; Mark 6:49, KJV, see APPARITION.
(2) For the distinction between "spirit" and "soul," see under SOUL, last three paragraphs.
The "Holy Spirit" is spoken of under various titles in the NT ("Spirit" and "Ghost" are renderings of the same word, *pneuma*; the advantage of the rendering "Spirit" is that it can always be used, whereas "Ghost" always requires the word "Holy" prefixed.) In the following list the omission of the definite article marks its omission in the original (concerning this see below): "Spirit, Matt. 22:43; Eternal Spirit, Heb. 9:14; the Spirit, Matt. 4:1; Holy Spirit, Matt. 1:18; the Holy Spirit, Matt. 28:19; the Spirit, the Holy, Matt. 12:32; the Spirit of promise, the Holy, Eph. 1:13; Spirit of God, Rom. 8:9; Spirit of (the) living God, 2 Cor. 3:3; the Spirit of God, 1 Cor. 2:11; the Spirit of our God, 1 Cor. 6:11; the Spirit of God, the Holy, Eph. 4:30; the Spirit of glory and of God, 1 Pet. 4:14; the Spirit of Him that raised up Jesus from the dead (i.e., God), Rom. 8:11; the Spirit of your Father, Matt. 10:20; the Spirit of His Son, Gal. 4:6; Spirit of (the) Lord, Acts 8:39; the Spirit of (the) Lord, Acts 5:9; (the) Lord, (the) Spirit, 2 Cor. 3:18; the Spirit of Jesus, Acts 16:7; Spirit of Christ, Rom. 8:9; the Spirit of Jesus Christ, Phil. 1:19; Spirit of adoption, Rom. 8:15; the Spirit of truth, John 14:17; the Spirit of life, Rom. 8:2; the Spirit of grace, Heb. 10:29."_ From Notes on Galatians, by Hogg and Vine, p. 193. The use or absence of the article in the original where the "Holy Spirit" is spoken of cannot always be decided by grammatical rules, nor can the presence or absence of the article alone determine whether the reference is to the "Holy Spirit." Examples where the Person is meant when the article is absent are Matt. 22:43 (the article is used in Mark 12:36); Acts 4:25, RV (absent in some texts); 19:2, 6; Rom. 14:17; 1 Cor. 2:4; Gal. 5:25 (twice); 1 Pet. 1:2. Sometimes the absence is to be accounted for by the fact that *Pneuma* (like *Theos*) is substantially a proper name, e.g., in John 7:39. As a general rule the article is present where the subject of the teaching is the Personality of the Holy Spirit, e.g., John 14:26, where He is spoken of in distinction from the Father and the Son. See also 15:26 and cf. Luke 3:22. In Gal. 3:3, in the phrase "having begun in the Spirit," it is difficult to say whether the reference is to the "Holy Spirit" or to the quickened spirit of the believer; that it possibly refers to

the latter is not to be determined by the absence of the article, but by the contrast with "the flesh"; on the other hand, the contrast may be between the "Holy Spirit" who in the believer sets His seal on the perfect work of Christ, and the flesh which seeks to better itself by works of its own. There is no preposition before either noun, and if the reference is to the quickened spirit it cannot be dissociated from the operation of the "Holy Spirit." In Gal. 4:29 the phrase "after the Spirit" signifies "by supernatural power," in contrast to "after the flesh," i.e., "by natural power," and the reference must be to the "Holy Spirit"; so in 5:17. The full title with the article before both *pneuma* and *hagios* (the "presumptive" use of the article), lit., "the Spirit the Holy," stresses the character of the Person, e.g., Matt. 12:32; Mark 3:29; 12:36; 13:11; Luke 2:26; 10:21 (RV); John 14:26; Acts 1:16; 5:3; 7:51; 10:44, 47; 13:2; 15:28; 19:6; 20:23, 28; 21:11; 28:25; Eph. 4:30; Heb. 3:7; 9:8; 10:15.
The Personality of the Spirit is emphasized at the expense of strict grammatical procedure in John 14:26; 15:26; 16:8, 13, 14, where the emphatic pronoun *ekeinos*, "He," is used of Him in the masculine, whereas the noun *pneuma* is neuter in Greek, while the corresponding word in Aramaic, the language in which our Lord probably (!) spoke, is feminine (*rucha*, cf. Heb. *ruwach*). The rendering "itself" in Rom. 8:16, 26, due to the Greek gender, is corrected to "Himself" in the RV. The subject of the "Holy Spirit" in the NT may be considered as to His divine attributes; His distinct Personality in the Godhead; His operation in connection with the Lord Jesus in His birth, His life, His baptism, His death; His operations in the world; in the church; His having been sent at Pentecost by the Father and by Christ; His operations in the individual believer; in local churches; His operations in the production of Holy Scripture; His work in the world, etc.

No. 5. Strong's Number: 4152; SPIRITUAL; Transliterated: *pneumatikos*; Adjective
Text: "always connotes the ideas of invisibility and of power. It does not occur in the LXX nor in the Gospels; it is in fact an after-Pentecost word. In the NT it is used as follows:
(a) the angelic hosts, lower than God but higher in the scale of being than man in his natural state, are 'spiritual hosts,' Eph. 6:12;
(b) things that have their origin with God, and which, therefore, are in harmony with His character, as His law is, are 'spiritual,' Rom. 7:14; 'spiritual' is prefixed to the material type in order to indicate that what the type sets forth, not the type itself, is intended, 1 Cor. 10:3, 4;
(c) the purposes of God revealed in the gospel by the Holy Spirit, 1 Cor. 2:13a, and the words in which that revelation is expressed, are 'spiritual,' 13b, matching, or combining, spiritual things with spiritual words [or, alternatively, 'interpreting spiritual things to spiritual men,' see below]; 'spiritual songs' are songs of which the burden is the things revealed by the Spirit, Eph. 5:19; Col. 3:16; 'spiritual wisdom and understanding' is wisdom in, and understanding of, those things, Col. 1:9; (e) men in Christ who walk so as to please God are 'spiritual,' Gal. 6:1; 1 Cor. 2:13b [but see (d) above], 15; 3:1; 14:37;
(d) the whole company of those who believe in Christ is a 'spiritual house,' 1 Pet. 2:5a;
(e) the blessings that accrue to regenerate men at this present time are called 'spiritualities,' Rom. 15:27; 1 Cor. 9:11; 'spiritual blessings,' Eph. 1:3; 'spiritual gifts,' Rom. 1:11;
(f) the activities Godward of regenerate men are 'spiritual sacrifices,' 1 Pet. 2:5b; their appointed activities in the churches are also called 'spiritual gifts,' lit., 'spiritualities,' 1 Cor. 12:1; 14:1;
(g) the resurrection body of the dead in Christ is 'spiritual,' i.e., such as is suited to the heavenly environment, 1 Cor. 15:44;

(h) all that is produced and maintained among men by the operations of the Spirit of God is 'spiritual,' 1 Cor. 15:46....

"The spiritual man is one who walks by the Spirit both in the sense of Gal. 5:16 and in that of 5:25, and who himself manifests the fruit of the Spirit in his own ways.... "According to the Scriptures, the 'spiritual' state of soul is normal for the believer, but to this state all believers do not attain, nor when it is attained is it always maintained. Thus the apostle, in 1 Cor. 3:1-3, suggests a contrast between this spiritual state and that of the babe in Christ, i.e., of the man who because of immaturity and inexperience has not yet reached spirituality, and that of the man who by permitting jealousy, and the strife to which jealousy always leads, has lost it. The spiritual state is reached by diligence in the Word of God and in prayer; it is maintained by obedience and self-judgment. Such as are led by the Spirit are spiritual, but, of course, spirituality is not a fixed or absolute condition, it admits of growth; indeed growth in 'the grace and knowledge of our Lord and Savior Jesus Christ,' 2 Pet. 3:18, is evidence of true spirituality."* From Notes on Galatians, by Hogg and Vine, pp. 308-319.

No. 6. Strong's Number: 4153; SPIRITUALLY; Transliterated: *pneumatikos*; Adverb
Text: "spiritually," occurs in 1 Cor. 2:14, with the meaning as (j) above, and Rev. 11:8, with the meaning as in (c). Some mss. have it in 1 Cor. 2:13. Notes: (1) In Rom. 8:6, the RV rightly renders the noun *pneuma*" (the mind) of the spirit," KJV, "spiritual (mind)." (2) In 1 Cor. 14:12 the plural of pneuma, "spirits," RV, marg., stands for "spiritual gifts" (text). (3) In 1 Pet. 2:2, the RV renders *logikos* "spiritual."

Greek: SOUL
No. 7. Strong's Number: 5590; SOUL; Transliterated: *psuche*
Text: denotes "the breath, the breath of life," then "the soul," in its various meanings. The NT uses "may be analyzed approximately as follows:

(a) the natural life of the body, Matt. 2:20; Luke 12:22; Acts 20:10; Rev.8:9; 12:11; cf. Lev. 17:11; 2 Sam. 14:7; Esth. 8:11;
(b) the immaterial, invisible part of man, Matt. 10:28; Acts 2:27; cf. 1 Kings 17:21;
(c) the disembodied (or "unclothed" or "naked," 2 Cor. 5:3, 4) man, Rev. 6:9;
(d) the seat of personality, Luke 9:24, explained as = "own self," v. 25; Heb. 6:19; 10:39; cf. Isa. 53:10 with 1 Tim. 2:6;
(e) the seat of the sentient element in man, that by which he perceives, reflects, feels, desires, Matt. 11:29; Luke 1:46; 2:35; Acts 14:2, 22; cf. Ps. 84:2; 139:14; Isa. 26:9;
(f) the seat of will and purpose, Matt. 22:37; Acts 4:32; Eph. 6:6; Phil. 1:27; Heb. 12:3; cf. Num. 21:4; Deut. 11:13;
(g) the seat of appetite, Rev. 18:14; cf. Ps. 107:9; Prov. 6:30; Isa. 5:14 ("desire"); 29:8;
(h) persons, individuals, Acts 2:41, 43; Rom. 2:9; Jas. 5:20; 1 Pet. 3:20; 2 Pet. 2:14; cf. Gen. 12:5; 14:21 ("persons"); Lev. 4:2 ('any one'); Ezek. 27:13; of dead bodies, Num. 6:6, lit., "dead soul"; and of animals, Lev. 24:18, lit., "soul for soul";
(i) the equivalent of the personal pronoun, used for emphasis and effect:, 1st person, John 10:24 ("us"); Heb. 10:38; cf. Gen. 12:13; Num. 23:10; Jud. 16:30; Ps. 120:2 ("me"); 2nd person, 2 Cor. 12:15; Heb. 13:17; Jas. 1:21; 1 Pet. 1:9; 2:25; cf. Lev. 17:11; 26:15; 1 Sam. 1:26; 3rd person, 1 Pet. 4:19; 2 Pet. 2:8; cf. Exod. 30:12; Job 32:2, Heb. "soul," Septuagint "self";
(j) an animate creature, human or other, 1 Cor. 15:45; Rev. 16:3; cf. Gen. 1:24; 2:7, 19;

(k) "the inward man," the seat of the new life, Luke 21:19 (cf. Matt. 10:39); 1 Pet. 2:11; 3 John 2. "With (j) compare *a-psuchos*, "soulless, inanimate," 1 Cor. 14:7.\ "With (f) compare *di-psuchos*, "two-souled," Jas. 1:8; 4:8;\ *oligo psuchos*, "feeble-souled," 1 Thess. 5:14;\ *iso-psuchos*, "like-souled," Phil. 2:20;\ *sum-psuchos*, "joint-souled" (with. one accord"), Phil. 2:2.\

"The language of Heb. 4:12 suggests the extreme difficulty of distinguishing between the soul and the spirit, alike in their nature and in their activities. Generally speaking the spirit is the higher, the soul the lower element. The spirit may be recognized as the life principle bestowed on man by God, the soul as the resulting life constituted in the individual, the body being the material organism animated by soul and spirit....

"Body and soul are the constituents of the man according to Matt. 6:25; 10:28; Luke 12:20; Acts 20:10; body and spirit according to Luke 8:55; 1 Cor. 5:3; 7:34; Jas. 2:26. In Matt. 26:38 the emotions are associated with the soul, in John 13:21 with the spirit; cf. also Ps. 42:11 with 1 Kings 21:5.
In Ps. 35:9 the soul rejoices in God, in Luke 1:47 the spirit.

"Apparently, then, the relationships may be thus summed up 'Soma, body, and pneuma, spirit, may be separated, pneuma and psuche, soul, can only be distinguished' (Cremer)."* From notes on Thessalonians, by Hogg and Vine, pp. 205-207.

Greek: MIND
No. 8. Strong's Number: 3563; MIND; Transliterated: *nous*; Noun
Text: "mind," denotes, speaking generally, the seat of reflective consciousness, comprising the faculties of perception and understanding, and those of feeling, judging and determining. Its use in the NT may be analyzed as follows: it denotes

(a) the faculty of knowing, the seat of the understanding, Luke 24:45; Rom. 1:28; 14:5; 1 Cor. 14:15, 19; Eph. 4:17; Phil. 4:7; Col. 2:18; 1 Tim. 6:5; 2 Tim. 3:8; Titus 1:15; Rev. 13:18; 17:9;

(b) counsels, purpose, Rom. 11:34 (of the "mind" of God); 12:2; 1 Cor. 1:10; 2:16, twice (1) of the thoughts and counsels of God, (2) of Christ, a testimony to His Godhood; Eph. 4:23;

(c) the new nature, which belongs to the believer by reason of the new birth, Rom. 7:23, 25, where it is contrasted with "the flesh," the principle of evil which dominates fallen man. Under (b) may come 2 Thess. 2:2, where it stands for the determination to be steadfast amidst afflictions, through the confident expectation of the day of rest and recompense mentioned in the first chapter.\

No. 9 Strong's Number: 1271; MIND; Transliterated: *dianoia*; Noun
Text: lit. "a thinking through, or over, a meditation, reflecting," signifies (a) like No. 1, "the faculty of knowing, understanding, or moral reflection," (1) with an evil significance, a consciousness characterized by a perverted moral impulse, Eph. 2:3 (plural); 4:18; (2) with a good significance, the faculty renewed by the Holy Spirit, Matt. 22:37; Mark 12:30; Luke 10:27; Heb. 8:10; 10:16; 1 Pet. 1:13; 1 John 5:20; (b) "sentiment, disposition" (not as a function but as a product); (1) in an evil sense, Luke 1:51, "imagination"; Col. 1;21; (2) in a good sense, 2 Pet. 3:1.\

No. 10. Strong's Number: 1771; MIND; Transliterated: *ennoia*; Noun
Text: ""an idea, notion, intent," is rendered "mind" in 1 Pet. 4:1; see INTENT.

Now do you understand why language is so complex?

APPENDIX AD

Search NIV & KJV for "holiness"

PART ONE: The New International Version (NIV)

HEBREW:

EXO 15 11 " Who among the gods is like you, O Lord? Who is like you-- majestic in HOLINESS, awesome in glory, working wonders?
DEU 32 51 This is because both of you broke faith with me in the presence of the Israelites at the waters of Meribah Kadesh in the Desert of Zin and because you did not uphold my HOLINESS among the Israelites.
1CH 16 29 ascribe to the Lord the glory due his name. Bring an offering and come before him; worship the Lord in the splendor of his HOLINESS.
2CH 20 21 After consulting the people, Jehoshaphat appointed men to sing to the Lord and to praise him for the splendor of his HOLINESS as they went out at the head of the army, saying: " Give thanks to the Lord, for his love endures forever. "
PSA 29 2 Ascribe to the Lord the glory due his name; worship the Lord in the splendor of his HOLINESS.
PSA 89 35 Once for all, I have sworn by my HOLINESS-- and I will not lie to David--
PSA 93 5 Your statutes stand firm; HOLINESS adorns your house for endless days, O Lord.
PSA 96 9 Worship the Lord in the splendor of his HOLINESS; tremble before him, all the earth.
ISA 29 23 When they see among them their children, the work of my hands, they will keep my name holy; they will acknowledge the HOLINESS of the Holy One of Jacob, and will stand in awe of the God of Israel.
ISA 35 8 And a highway will be there; it will be called the Way of HOLINESS. The unclean will not journey on it; it will be for those who walk in that Way; wicked fools will not go about on it.
EZE 36 23 I will show the HOLINESS of my great name, which has been profaned among the nations, the name you have profaned among them. Then the nations will know that I am the Lord, declares the Sovereign Lord, when I show myself holy through you before their eyes.
EZE 38 23 And so I will show my greatness and my HOLINESS, and I will make myself known in the sight of many nations. Then they will know that I am the Lord
AMO 4 2 The Sovereign Lord has sworn by his HOLINESS: " The time will surely come when you will be taken away with hooks, the last of you with fishhooks.

CHRISTIAN

LUK 1 75 in HOLINESS and righteousness before him all our days.
ROM 1 4 and who through the Spirit of HOLINESS was declared with power to be the Son of God by his resurrection from the dead: Jesus Christ our Lord.
ROM 6 19 I put this in human terms because you are weak in your natural selves. Just as you used to offer the parts of your body in slavery to impurity and to ever- increasing wickedness, so now offer them in slavery to righteousness leading to HOLINESS.

ROM 6 22 But now that you have been set free from sin and have become slaves to God , the benefit you reap leads to HOLINESS, and the result is eternal life.
1CO 1 30 It is because of him that you are in Christ Jesus, who has become for us wisdom from God-- that is, our righteousness, HOLINESS and redemption.
2CO 1 12 Now this is our boast: Our conscience testifies that we have conducted ourselves in the world, and especially in our relations with you, in the HOLINESS and sincerity that are from God. We have done so not according to worldly wisdom but according to God's grace.
2CO 7 1 Since we have these promises, dear friends, let us purify ourselves from everything that contaminates body and spirit, perfecting HOLINESS out of reverence for God.

PART TWO: King James Version (KJV)

HEBREW

EXO 15 11 Who [is] like unto thee, O LORD, among the gods? who [is] like thee, glorious in HOLINESS, fearful [in] praises, doing wonders?
1CH 16 29 Give unto the LORD the glory [due] unto his name: bring an offering, and come before him: worship the LORD in the beauty of HOLINESS.
2CH 20 21 And when he had consulted with the people, he appointed singers unto the LORD, and that should praise the beauty of HOLINESS, as they went out before the army, and to say, Praise the LORD; for his mercy endureth for ever.
2CH 31 18 And to the genealogy of all their little ones, their wives, and their sons , and their daughters, through all the congregation: for in their set office they sanctified themselves in HOLINESS:
PSA 29 2 Give unto the LORD the glory due unto his name; worship the LORD in the beauty of HOLINESS.
PSA 30 4 Sing unto the LORD, O ye saints of his, and give thanks at the remembrance of his HOLINESS.
PSA 47 8 God reigneth over the heathen: God sitteth upon the throne of his HOLINESS
PSA 48 1 A Song [and] Psalm for the sons of Korah. Great [is] the LORD, and greatly to be praised in the city of our God, [in] the mountain of his HOLINESS.
PSA 60 6 God hath spoken in his HOLINESS; I will rejoice, I will divide Shechem, and mete out the valley of Succoth.
PSA 89 35 Once have I sworn by my HOLINESS that I will not lie unto David.
PSA 93 5 Thy testimonies are very sure: HOLINESS becometh thine house, O LORD, for ever.
PSA 96 9 O worship the LORD in the beauty of HOLINESS: fear before him, all the earth.
PSA 97 12 Rejoice in the LORD, ye righteous; and give thanks at the remembrance of his HOLINESS.
PSA 108 7 God hath spoken in his HOLINESS; I will rejoice, I will divide Shechem, and mete out the valley of Succoth.
PSA 110 3 Thy people [shall be] willing in the day of thy power, in the beauties of HOLINESS from the womb of the morning: thou hast the dew of thy youth.
ISA 35 8 And an highway shall be there, and a way, and it shall be called The way of HOLINESS; the unclean shall not pass over it; but it [shall be] for those: the wayfaring men, though fools, shall not err [therein].
ISA 62 9 But they that have gathered it shall eat it and praise the LORD; and they that have brought it together shall drink it in the courts of my HOLINESS.

ISA 63 15 Look down from heaven, and behold from the habitation of thy HOLINESS and of thy glory: where [is] thy zeal and thy strength, the sounding of thy bowels and of thy mercies toward me? are they restrained?
ISA 63 18 The people of thy HOLINESS have possessed [it] but a little while: our adversaries have trodden down thy sanctuary. JER 2 3 Israel [was] HOLINESS unto the LORD, [and] the firstfruits of his increase: all that devour him shall offend; evil shall come upon them, saith the LORD.
JER 23 9 Mine heart within me is broken because of the prophets; all my bones shake ; I am like a drunken man, and like a man whom wine hath overcome, because of the LORD, and because of the words of his HOLINESS. JER 31 23 Thus saith the LORD of hosts, the God of Israel; As yet they shall use this speech in the land of Judah and in the cities thereof, when I shall bring again their captivity; The LORD bless thee, O habitation of justice, [and] mountain of HOLINESS.
AMO 4 2 The Lord GOD hath sworn by his HOLINESS , that, lo, the days shall come upon you, that he will take you away with hooks, and your posterity with fishhooks.
OBA 1 17 But upon mount Zion shall be deliverance, and there shall be HOLINESS; and the house of Jacob shall possess their possessions.
ZEC 14 21 Yea, every pot in Jerusalem and in Judah shall be HOLINESS unto the LORD of hosts: and all they that sacrifice shall come and take of them, and seethe therein: and in that day there shall be no more the Canaanite in the house of the LORD of hosts.
MAL 2 11 Judah hath dealt treacherously, and an abomination is committed in Israel and in Jerusalem; for Judah hath profaned the HOLINESS of the LORD which he loved, and hath married the daughter of a strange god.

CHRISTIAN

ROM 1 4 And declared (to be) the son of God with power, accorcing to the spirit of HOLINESS, by the resurrection from the dead.
1TH 3 13 To the end he may stablish your hearts unblameable in HOLINESS before God, even our Father, at the coming of our Lord Jesus Christ with all his saints.
1TH 4 7 For God hath not called us unto uncleanness, but unto HOLINESS.
TIT 2 3 The aged women likewise, that [they be] in behaviour as becometh HOLINESS, not false accusers, not given to much wine, teachers of good things;
HEB 12 10 For they verily for a few days chastened [us] after their own pleasure; but he for [our] profit, that [we] might be partakers of his HOLINESS.
HEB 12 10 Our fathers disciplined us for a little while as they thought best; but God disciplines us for our good, that we may share in his HOLINESS.
HEB 12 14 Make every effort to live in peace with all men and to be holy; without HOLINESS no one will see the Lord.

APPENDIX AE

The Heart Metaphors in the Bible (KJV)

A Selection of Metaphors

GEN 6 5 And God saw that the wickedness of man [was] great in the earth, and [that] every imagination of the thoughts of his HEART [was] only evil continually.
GEN 6 6 And it repented the LORD that he had made man on the earth, and it grieved him at his HEART.
GEN 8 21 And the LORD smelled a sweet savour; and the LORD said in his HEART, I will not again curse the ground any more for man's sake; for the imagination of man's HEART [is] evil from his youth; neither will I again smite any more every thing living, as I have done.
GEN 17 17 Then Abraham fell upon his face, and laughed, and said in his HEART, Shall [a child] be born unto him that is an hundred years old? and shall Sarah, that is ninety years old, bear?
GEN 20 5 Said he not unto me, She [is] my sister? and she, even she herself said, He [is] my brother: in the integrity of my HEART and innocency of my hands have I done this.
GEN 42 28 And he said unto his brethren, My money is restored; and, lo, [it is] even in my sack: and their HEART failed [them], and they were afraid, saying one to another, What [is] this [that] God hath done unto us?
GEN 45 26 And told him, saying, Joseph [is] yet alive, and he [is] governor over all the land of Egypt. And Jacob's HEART fainted, for he believed them not.

EXO 4 14 And the anger of the LORD was kindled against Moses, and he said, [Is] not Aaron the Levite thy brother? I know that he can speak well. And also, behold, he cometh forth to meet thee: and when he seeth thee, he will be glad in his HEART.
EXO 4 21 And the LORD said unto Moses, When thou goest to return into Egypt, see that thou do all those wonders before Pharaoh, which I have put in thine hand: but I will harden his HEART, that he shall not let the people go.
EXO 7 23 And Pharaoh turned and went into his house, neither did he set his HEART to this also.
EXO 9 12 And the LORD hardened the HEART of Pharaoh, and he hearkened not unto them; as the LORD had spoken unto Moses.
EXO 9 14 For I will at this time send all my plagues upon thine HEART, and upon thy servants, and upon thy people; that thou mayest know that [there is] none like me in all the earth.
EXO 14 5 And it was told the king of Egypt that the people fled: and the HEART of Pharaoh and of his servants was turned against the people, and they said, Why have we done this, that we have let Israel go from serving us?
EXO 15 8 And with the blast of thy nostrils the waters were gathered together, the floods stood upright as an heap, [and] the depths were congealed in the HEART of the sea.
EXO 23 9 Also thou shalt not oppress a stranger: for ye know the HEART of a stranger, seeing ye were strangers in the land of Egypt.
EXO 25 2 Speak unto the children of Israel, that they bring me an offering: of every man that giveth it willingly with his HEART ye shall take my offering.

EXO 28 29 And Aaron shall bear the names of the children of Israel in the breastplate of judgment upon his HEART, when he goeth in unto the holy [place], for a memorial before the LORD continually.
EXO 35 34 And he hath put in his HEART that he may teach, [both] he, and Aholiab, the son of Ahisamach, of the tribe of Dan.
EXO 36 2 And Moses called Bezaleel and Aholiab, and every wise HEARTed man, in whose HEART the LORD had put wisdom, [even] every one whose HEART stirred him up to come unto the work to do it:

LEV 19 17 Thou shalt not hate thy brother in thine HEART: thou shalt in any wise rebuke thy neighbor, and not suffer sin upon him.
LEV 26 16 I also will do this unto you; I will even appoint over you terror, consumption, and the burning ague, that shall consume the eyes, and cause sorrow of HEART: and ye shall sow your seed in vain, for your enemies shall eat it.

DEU 9 4 Speak not thou in thine HEART, after that the LORD thy God hath cast them out from before thee, saying, For my righteousness the LORD hath brought me in to possess this land: but for the wickedness of these nations the LORD doth drive them out from before thee.
DEU 10 16 Circumcise therefore the foreskin of your HEART, and be no more stiffnecked.
DEU 11 16 Take heed to yourselves, that your HEART be not deceived, and ye turn aside, and serve other gods, and worship them;
DEU 17 17 Neither shall he multiply wives to himself, that his HEART turn not away: neither shall he greatly multiply to himself silver and gold.
DEU 28 28 The LORD shall smite thee with madness, and blindness, and astonishment of HEART:
DEU 28 47 Because thou servedst not the LORD thy God with joyfulness, and with gladness of HEART, for the abundance of all [things];
DEU 28 65 And among these nations shalt thou find no ease, neither shall the sole of thy foot have rest: but the LORD shall give thee there a trembling HEART, and failing of eyes, and sorrow of mind:
DEU 28 67 In the morning thou shalt say, Would God it were even! and at even thou shalt say, Would God it were morning! for the fear of thine HEART wherewith thou shalt fear, and for the sight of thine eyes which thou shalt see.
DEU 29 4 Yet the LORD hath not given you an HEART to perceive, and eyes to see, and ears to hear, unto this day.

JOS 5 1 the LORD had dried up the waters of Jordan from before the children of Israel, until we were passed over, that their HEART melted, neither was there spirit in them any more, because of the children of Israel.
JOS 24 23 Now therefore put away, [said he], the strange gods which [are] among you, and incline your HEART unto the LORD God of Israel.

JUD 19 5 And it came to pass on the fourth day, when they arose early in the morning, that he rose up to depart: and the damsel's father said unto his son in law, Comfort thine HEART with a morsel of bread, and afterward go your way.
JUD 19 6 And they sat down, and did eat and drink both of them together: for the damsel's father had said unto the man, Be content, I pray thee, and tarry all night, and let thine HEART be merry.

1SA 2 35 And I will raise me up a faithful priest, [that] shall do according to [that] which [is] in mine HEART and in my mind: and I will build him a sure house; and he shall walk before mine anointed for ever.
1SA 10 9 And it was [so], that when he had turned his back to go from Samuel, God gave him another HEART: and all those signs came to pass that day.
1SA 24 5 And it came to pass afterward, that David's HEART smote him, because he had cut off Saul's skirt.
1SA 25 37 But it came to pass in the morning, when the wine was gone out of Nabal, and his wife had told him these things, that his HEART died within him, and he became [as] a stone.

1CH 12 33 Of Zebulun, such as went forth to battle, expert in war, with all instruments of war, fifty thousand, which could keep rank: [they were] not of double HEART.

MAT 5 8 Blessed [are] the pure in HEART: for they shall see God.
MAT 6 21 For where your treasure is, there will your HEART be also.
MAT 12 35 A good man out of the good treasure of the HEART bringeth forth good things: and an evil man out of the evil treasure bringeth forth evil things.
MAT 13 15 For this people's HEART is waxed gross, and [their] ears are dull of hearing, and their eyes they have closed; lest at any time they should see with [their] eyes and hear with [their] ears, and should understand with [their] HEART, and should be converted, and I should heal them.

LUK 2 19 But Mary kept all these things, and pondered [them] in her HEART.
LUK 2 51 And he went down with them, and came to Nazareth, and was subject unto them: but his mother kept all these sayings in her HEART.
LUK 6 45 A good man out of the good treasure of his HEART bringeth forth that which is good; and an evil man out of the evil treasure of his HEART bringeth forth that which is evil: for of the abundance of the HEART his mouth speaketh.
LUK 8 15 But that on the good ground are they, which in an honest and good HEART, having heard the word, keep [it], and bring forth fruit with patience.
LUK 10 27 And he answering said, Thou shalt love the Lord thy God with all thy HEART, and with all thy soul, and with all thy strength, and with all thy mind; and thy neighbour as thyself.

JOH 13 2 And supper being ended, the devil having now put into the HEART of Judas Iscariot, Simon's [son], to betray him;
JOH 14 1 Let not your HEART be troubled: ye believe in God, believe also in me.

ACT 2 37 Now when they heard [this], they were pricked in their HEART, and said unto Peter and to the rest of the apostles, Men [and] brethren, what shall we do?
ACT 4 32 And the multitude of them that believed were of one HEART and of one soul: neither said any [of them] that ought of the things which he possessed was his own; but they had all things common.
ACT 5 3 But Peter said, Ananias, why hath Satan filled thine HEART to lie to the Holy Ghost, and to keep back [part] of the price of the land?
ACT 16 14 And a certain woman named Lydia, a seller of purple, of the city of Thyatira, which worshipped God, heard [us]: whose HEART the Lord opened, that she attended unto the things which were spoken of Paul.

ROM 1 21 Because that, when they knew God, they glorified [him] not as God, neither were thankful; but became vain in their imaginations, and their foolish HEART was darkened.
ROM 10 6 But the righteousness which is of faith speaketh on this wise, Say not in thine HEART, Who shall ascend into heaven? (that is, to bring Christ down [from above]:)

2CO 3 3 [Forasmuch as ye are] manifestly declared to be the epistle of Christ ministered by us, written not with ink, but with the Spirit of the living God; not in tables of stone, but in fleshly tables of the HEART.

EPH 4 18 Having the understanding darkened, being alienated from the life of God through the ignorance that is in them, because of the blindness of their HEART:

PHI 1 7 Even as it is meet for me to think this of you all, because I have you in my HEART; inasmuch as both in my bonds, and in the defence and confirmation of the gospel, ye all are partakers of my grace.

HEB 13 9 Be not carried about with divers and strange doctrines. For [it is] a good thing that the HEART be established with grace; not with meats, which have not profited them that have been occupied therein.

JAM 1 26 If any man among you seem to be religious, and bridleth not his tongue, but deceiveth his own HEART, this man's religion [is] vain.

1PE 3 4 But [let it be] the hidden man of the HEART, in that which is not corruptible, [even the ornament] of a meek and quiet spirit, which is in the sight of God of great price.

1JO 3 20 For if our HEART condemn us, God is greater than our HEART, and knoweth all things

APPENDIX AF

The After-Life: Hell or Annihilation

Word Search for Destroy and its Cognates

DEU 7 23 But the Lord your God will deliver them over to you, throwing them into great confusion until they are DESTROYED. {means extinction}

1SA 5 9 But after they had moved it, the Lord's hand was against that city, throwing it into a great panic (a very great destruction--KJV). He afflicted the people of the city, both young and old, with an outbreak of tumors. {also means extinction}
1SA 5 11 So they called together all the rulers of the Philistines and said, " Send the ark of the god of Israel away; let it go back to its own place, or it will kill us and our people. " For death had filled the city with panic (a deadly destruction--KJV); God's hand was very heavy upon it. {also means extinction}

1KI 20 42 He said to the king, " This is what the Lord says: 'You have set free a man I had determined should die (utterly destroyed—KJV: *cherem*). Therefore it is your life for his life, your people for his people.'"

2CH 22 4 He did evil in the eyes of the Lord, as the house of Ahab had done, for after his father's death (destruction—KJV: *mashchiyth*) they became his advisers, to his undoing.

EST 8 6 For how can I bear to see disaster fall on my people? How can I bear to see the DESTRUCTION of my family? "
EST 9 5 The Jews struck down all their enemies with the sword, killing and DESTROYING them, and they did what they pleased to those who hated them.

JOB 26 6 Death is naked before God; DESTRUCTION lies uncovered.
(abaddown)
JOB 28 22 DESTRUCTION and Death say, 'Only a rumor of it has reached our ears.'
JOB 31 12 It is a fire that burns to DESTRUCTION; it would have uprooted my harvest.

PSA 35 8 may ruin (destruction—KJV) overtake them by surprise-- may the net they hid entangle them, may they fall into the pit, to their ruin.
PSA 55 23 But you, O God, will bring down the wicked into the pit of corruption (destruction--KJV); bloodthirsty and deceitful men will not live out half their days. But as for me, I trust in you.
PSA 73 18 Surely you place them on slippery ground; you cast them down to ruin (destruction--KJV).
PSA 88 11 Is your love declared in the grave, your faithfulness in DESTRUCTION?

PRO 15 11 Death and DESTRUCTION lie open before the Lord-- how much more the hearts of men!
PRO 16 18 Pride goes before DESTRUCTION, a haughty spirit before a fall.
PRO 27 20 Death and DESTRUCTION are never satisfied, and neither are the eyes of many.

ISA 10 25 Very soon my anger against you will end and my wrath will be directed to their DESTRUCTION."
ISA 13 6 Wail, for the day of the Lord is near; it will come like DESTRUCTION from the Almighty.
ISA 49 19 " Though you were ruined and made desolate (DESTROYED--KJV) and your land laid waste, now you will be too small for your people, and those who devoured you will be far away.
ISA 51 19 These double calamities have come upon you-- who can comfort you?—ruin and DESTRUCTION, famine and sword-- who can console you?
ISA 59 7 Their feet rush into sin; they are swift to shed innocent blood. Their thoughts are evil thoughts; ruin and DESTRUCTION mark their ways.
ISA 60 18 No longer will violence be heard in your land, nor ruin or DESTRUCTION within your borders, but you will call your walls Salvation and your gates Praise.

JER 4 6 Raise the signal to go to Zion! Flee for safety without delay! For I am bringing disaster from the north, even terrible DESTRUCTION. "
JER 6 1 "Flee for safety, people of Benjamin! Flee from Jerusalem! Sound the trumpet in Tekoa! Raise the signal over Beth Hakkerem! For disaster looms out of the north, even terrible DESTRUCTION.

LAM 2 11 My eyes fail from weeping, I am in torment within, my heart is poured out on the ground because my people are DESTROYED, because children and infants faint in the streets of the city.
LAM 3 48 Streams of tears flow from my eyes because my people are DESTROYED.
LAM 4 10 With their own hands compassionate women have cooked their own children, who became their food when my people were DESTROYED.

EZE 5 16 When I shoot at you with my deadly and destructive (for ruin—KJV) arrows of famine, I will shoot to DESTROY you. I will bring more and more famine upon you and cut off your supply of food.
EZE 32 9 I will trouble the hearts of many peoples when I bring about your DESTRUCTION among the nations, among lands you have not known.

HOS 7 13 Woe to them, because they have strayed from me! DESTRUCTION to them, because they have rebelled against me! I long to redeem them but they speak lies against me.
HOS 9 6 Even if they escape from DESTRUCTION, Egypt will gather them, and Memphis will bury them. Their treasures of silver will be taken over by briers, and thorns will overrun their tents.
HOS 13 14 " I will ransom them from the power of the grave; I will redeem them from death. Where, O death, are your plagues? Where, O grave, is your DESTRUCTION? " I will have no compassion,

JOE 1 15 Alas for that day! For the day of the Lord is near; it will come like DESTRUCTION from the Almighty.

OBA 1 12 You should not look down on your brother in the day of his misfortune, nor rejoice over the people of Judah in the day of their DESTRUCTION, nor boast so much in the day of their trouble.

ZEC 14 11 It will be inhabited; never again will it be DESTROYED. Jerusalem will be secure.

MAT 7 13 "Enter through the narrow gate. For wide is the gate and broad is the road that leads to DESTRUCTION, and many enter through it. {Greek *apolonia,* annihilation}

ROM 9 22 What if God, choosing to show his wrath and make his power known, bore with great patience the objects of his wrath-- prepared for DESTRUCTION? Greek *apolonia,* annihilation

1CO 5 5 hand this man over to Satan, so that the sinful nature may be DESTROYED and his spirit saved on the day of the Lord.

PHI 3 19 Their destiny is DESTRUCTION, their god is their stomach, and their glory is in their shame. Their mind is on earthly things.

1TH 5 3 While people are saying, " Peace and safety, " DESTRUCTION will come on them suddenly, as labor pains on a pregnant woman, and they will not escape.

2TH 1 9 They will be punished with everlasting DESTRUCTION and shut out from the presence of the Lord and from the majesty of his power

2PE 2 1 But there were also false prophets among the people, just as there will be false teachers among you. They will secretly introduce DESTRUCTIVE heresies, even denying the sovereign Lord who bought them-- bringing swift DESTRUCTION on themselves.

2PE 3 16 He writes the same way in all his letters, speaking in them of these matters. His letters contain some things that are hard to understand, which ignorant and unstable people distort, as they do the other Scriptures, to their own DESTRUCTION.

Hebrew words meaning:
destruction = *goleb, natsah*
destroy = *shachath*
destroyed = *sheber*

Greek words for:
destruction = *apoleia*
annihilation = *apoleia*
destruction = *olethros*

APPENDIX AG

The STAR TREK MOVIES

A
Theological and Psychological Interpretation

Well, if you haven't seen any of these Star Trek movies, it's a good time to rent them and enjoy. First, see the film, and THEN read these.

Now, to the analysis:

The first movie, titled, The Motion Picture, was about a Monster, destructive something or other, entering the Earth's space trying to communicate with someone. All the while it is behaving like a spoiled child destroying everything in its path seeking its Creator. The Star Trek heroes Kirk, Spock, McCoy and company travel in the Enterprise to intercept the Monster, hoping to stop it. One of the crew is literally assimilated by the Monster and then she returns as a hologram to the Enterprise with a message for the heroes. "V-ger wants to connect with the Creator." The heroes actually fly through V-ger's vastness slowly approaching its core. They get to the center, leave the Enterprise and walk to an old space probe, Voyager (number one) whose purpose was to collect information and data about the Universe. There's a broken wire connection that prevents this space probe from downloading its data (knowledge) to the NASA creator. The heroes fix it and now Voyager can connect and download its collected Terabytes of data and disappears happily into the Universe. The End.

Now, what's so great about this story? Its hidden meaning appears to be: if humans operate on intelligence (IQ or facts) alone there will result much destruction. Spock hinted at this hidden meaning when he decided to leave Vulcan, the "Logic" planet, and be a member of the Enterprise's human staff. V-ger was the personification of data-knowledge gone awry. And, of course, the NASA group represents God. Returning to God to get full mature knowledge and meaning for our lives is a theme as old as human nature. Did you catch the "fix the disconnected wire"? Aren't we sort of disconnected from God in today's world? Cannot the Trinity fix us? We'll see this theme again in the later Star Trek Movies.

The second movie, The Wrath of Kahn, is a first rate action film, a story of one man's vengeful obsession. Kahn and his group escape their prison and begin a series of conquests by planting wormlike creatures into the brains of two captured members of the Enterprise. Now, Kirk faces two threats, internal and external. The attacks on the Enterprise are specifically at Kirk. These dysfunctional men make for great theater, as do all films of that genre. Eventually, Kirk and Co. win out. Well, we knew that would happen! However, in the last moments Spock performs an act of self-giving, "The needs of the many are greater than the needs of the one." The hidden meaning is that all revenge is an unreasonable evil of pure emotionality that results in self-destruction of body and soul of the perpetrator(s) as well as significant harm to others. (Does this sound like our present day terrorists?)

The third movie, The Search for Spock, is a direct result of the ending of movie II. Spock is found on and saved from the crumbling re-Genesis planet and taken back to his Shaman, wizened Dame Anderson. Spock's spirit, Katra, which he imbued into McCoy just before he died, is returned by "hocus-pocus" to the regenerated body recovered from the re-Genesis planet. However, it is recovered not without the sacrificial death of Kirk's son. (Can you guess what will play a part in a coming attraction of the series?) The antagonist in this adventure is none other than the evil Klingons who lust after the secret powers of regeneration. OH my, sounds like a cloning dilemma in the making! Then come the fireworks and the special effects but, to Kirk's credit, all are safe and ready for the next Hollywood production.

OK, the allegory is fairly obvious: (a) it deals with resurrection in the theological and physical sense; (b) humankind does possess creative powers to produce life but only *in utero*, not yet *in vitro* nor possibly ever; and (c) there are people who would do great evil if they were to get the genesis power, or, for that matter, any absolute power. But, if Kirk is the Master of the Enterprise, then his son is the one making the sacrifice! Did you miss that Christian allusion?

The forth film, The Voyage Home, has a few intriguing modern topics woven into the plot: personal time travel, our environmental concerns and some strange but powerful third party's concern about our developing planet. The film starts off with a huge probe entering the Earth's space causing all sorts of damage that frightens the natives. Enter the Enterprise and its heroic crew! Is the probe searching for something ... maybe trying to communicate with ... nobody knows. Ah, but once again Kirk's suspicions lead to decoding the transmissions from the probe and Spock has an epiphany. The intruder is trying to speak to whales, humpbacks that is. Well, guess what? There *ain't no* humpbacks swimming around any more! (Bad grammar from the 70's but you get the point!) We, today's food hunters, wiped them all out. What to do? Yes sir, go back to Earth in the 70's and get us a whale. And with beer, pizza and all that swimming they must have had a whale of a time (no pun intended ... well ... yes, I intended a pun!) There is also a slight love interest that turns out to be love of science. I particularly enjoyed Spock's humorous struggle with American slang. The crew captures two whales, cruises, at WARP-9, through the Sun's magnetic field and, behold, lands back to the 24th century right in San Francisco's bay releasing the whales who immediately have a short chitchat with the probe, telling it that they are healthy and happy. Thus, the world is saved again.

This allegory is a bit complex because it's overlapped with some theology and some science. First, the theology, God, the Probe, is the concerned party! God is besotted with humankind but troubled about human behavior in its worldly affairs: wars, terrorism, environment, greed and poverty, whatever else you can think of. Even though the film only speaks to the environment, the allegorical implications lead us to other concerns that exist in the Divine mind. Like the movie, OH God, God gave us total freedom to solve the world's plights and wants us to get with it. So that's the theology. The science part is taking care of our environment. Think about it, we can actually do the job if only each one makes a personal effort and puts pressure on our businesses and governments to act ethically. Certainly not an easy task!

The fifth movie, The Final Frontier, starts slowly and begins to look simply like a Zen Master hypnotist trying to set people free from their misery by revealing their pain in their darkness and forcing the pain into the light and gaining strength thereby. WOW, what a concept; right out of the Fourth Gospel and Gnosticism. Light is of God; darkness is of Evil! The plot quickly shifts and leads one to suspect a rebellion whose purpose is conquest. Then, the plot takes a left turn and becomes a kidnapping. Well, simplicity goes out the window when it becomes clear that there are bigger stakes at play. The story turns to Kirk, Spock and McCoy at Yosemite where Kirk is climbing the face of El

Capitan. Nice symbolism, the Captain climbing El Capitan! Also, a symbol of going up to the top where one's vision observes the whole area, like being in heaven. So, true to form, the Enterprise is called upon to go to "the Planet of Peace". The Enterprise and crew are lured into the trap set by our friendly Zenist-Hypnotist. A battle ensues and the hooded Zenist wins out. Spock approaches and recognizes him. But Spock tells no one of this. The troops are brain washed and go back to the Enterprise. They arrive while the captain of a Klingon Bird-of-Prey is still hot on Enterprise's tail anxious to shoot her down. Upon landing they make a covert attempt to capture the renegades but fail. During the struggle Spock has an opportunity to kill Mr. Zen but stops short. All on the Enterprise are themselves captured. Spock finally reveals that the Zen guy is his half brother, Sybok! A plot thickening moment! Sybok reveals his plan to take the Enterprise through the Great Barrier at the outer edge of the Universe, to find Shakarie, the place where God resides. (Actually, there is a Hebrew word that resembles that name, *Shakanah*, the dwelling place of God in the desert, you know, the Exodus: the dust devil by day and the pillar of fire by night.) Sybok's vision from God has directed him to come to Shakarie beyond the Great Barrier. While in the security cell, Spock explains to Kirk and McCoy who Sybok is, a person who obtains experiential-knowledge through emotions rather than through logic. (Now that is labeled emotional-intellect, a somewhat fuzzy theory in modern educational circles.) Back to the story line! The Enterprise journeys to the Universe's outer rim, the Great Barrier, penetrating it is thought to be impossible. So Sybok convinces the crew to go full speed ahead. Sybok comments that the Great Barrier is a symbol for fear of the unknown, a manifestation of humankind's fear. They push on with the same fortitude that led humankind to flight, break the sound barrier and conquer space. Meanwhile that Klingon Bird-of-Prey stalking Kirk and his mighty space ship has continued to follow the Enterprise, even through the Barrier and to the planet Shakarie. Nice subplot, I thought. As the Enterprise breaks into the other world, a glowing planet is seen and Kirk, Spock, McCoy and Sybok jump into Galileo, the piper cub transporter, to fly to the surface of Shakarie. After roaming around a barren dust bowl they find a little cove. Sybok cries out, "We have traveled a long way!" Zero decibels follows. Suddenly, around the cove huge tall rock columns raise up out of the dust and, voila, a little Stonehenge Church for our visitors. Then, a blue smoky cloud puffs up from the ground with all the suspense of a horror film. A mirage of a face appears out of the cloud giving everyone goose bumps while they listen to the talking Face lust over the Enterprise's usefulness in helping HIM escape this planetary prison. "Whoa!" says Kirk, "Why does God need a spaceship to leave this place?" God gets a bit testy and throws a little hot lightening bolt that knocks Kirk backwards off his feet. Spock asks God the same question again and he, too, gets a shot. Now, McCoy stands up to God and asks, "Who are you?" The face responds, "I am One voice with many faces!" McCoy answers back, "What kind of God are you that inflicts pain for your own pleasure?" The Face shows great anger and then Sybok steps aggressively straight to the mirage and asks, just like in the opening scene, if he can meld with God and help him with his pain. Poof! And Mr. Zen is gone. Kirk, Spock and McCoy high tail it out; Spock and McCoy get beamed up leaving Kirk and a bad-tempered Face to duke it out. You know that Spock had to be brought back to the Enterprise to finagle a Klingon General to pull rank over the Captain of the Bird-of-Prey and let Spock use the super god-killing ray gun to defeat the Face in time to save Kirk and the World for the fifth time. Aren't you glad that the Universe's future is going to be safe and secure when 2400 AD comes along?

The allegorical meaning is probably the simplest of stories. We all seek to know God; it's a built in NEED. Kirk's climbing El Capitan is symbolic of the film's search for the High God and, later on in the story, Kirk and McCoy with Spock wearing the jet shoes shoot up a very long narrow tower-way symbolically going to a High Place—Heaven. Why do you think so many people of every nation and throughout human history have been, are and will be involved with religion? Religion is the most popular WAY for humankind's outreach to the Creator. There's a bit of V-ger and Sybok in all of us! The second meaning to this myth-story is to warn us that you shouldn't trust just any hooded, wandering monk with pointy ears leading you to a punishing God. Tain't so says the Carpenter! Finally, the Church building is not necessarily a place to find God. SHE-He is not out there or just in a building. Kirk ends the adventure with this, "Maybe God is not out there, maybe God is in here!" pointing to his heart, the symbol of compassion and the place within where the true God speaks to us. The End.

The sixth movie, The Undiscovered Country, was, at first, not an easy myth to unfold. It starts with the destruction of the Klingon moon, Praxis. Praxis is the Greek word for acts (it means "doing work"). It's also the title of the second book of Luke in the Bible! Boy, are we off to a good start or what? You bet, good Praxis means good work. Bad Praxis means bad work. And we all know that the Klingons are the mythical representation of evil—bad works! The Klingons report that this accident has blown away the atmosphere of their planet and they have 50 years of Oxygen left. (Take note, this was our first symbol: whenever one does evil works there exists the possibility of great destruction to one's spirit.) The Klingon Chancellor of the High Council approaches the Federation to form an alliance to help his nation secure continual peace and resettle to a new planet. What makes for intrigue is Spock's behind the scene emissary negotiations with the Chancellor and Kirk's sworn hatred for Klingons. Added to the plot is that while the Klingons are so vulnerable, certain Federation official's desire to wipe them out by any ruthless means. Kirk is selected to be the host contact point when the Klingon leader meets for an escort to the upcoming great conference of the two nations. They meet in space at the halfway point. Kirk invites the Leader to a social dinner at which we all meet the principal characters including General Chang, a Klingon who hates the human's Federation. OH, so much hate on both sides! Then, during the meal a lot of Shakespearean quotes are exchanged like people throwing darts at each other. The Klingon contingent returns to their Bird of Prey. At the strike of midnight (always a foreboding moment) two torpedoes are shot at the Klingon vessel disabling their gravity controller. Two men from Enterprise beam over to the Bird-of Prey wearing magnetic boots to give them stability so they can easily pass through to the Klingon Chancellor and kill him. They then return to Enterprise but not without bringing along blood droplets from the weightless Klingon ship. Pandemonium follows. Kirk and McCoy beam over to the Klingon ship to find out what happened. The Chancellor is dying and in his last breath urges Kirk to continue the peace process. His death is the alleged responsibility of the Captain of the Enterprise and Kirk is taken prisoner along with Dr. McCoy. The two prisoners are put on trial and sentenced to Ruah Pente (or so the name sounds). Strange that "Ruah" is a Hebrew word in Genesis meaning wind or breath and the Ruah Pente has a bitter cold atmosphere of blowing snow! As expected, Kirk and McCoy escape and are beamed up by the Enterprise to safety. Well, after all, Spock placed a magic locator button on Kirk just before he left the Enterprise to beam over to the Klingon ship! Spock was able to follow Kirk's movement throughout the trial and assignment to the prison on Ruah Pente. Once back in command, Kirk speeds to the next meeting place for the peace initiative attended by the Chancellor's daughter. All is saved when Kirk rushes into the conference and spoils the assassination of the Federation President and exposes the traitors from both sides. The peace is on.

The psychology of this film is that hatred is the father of prejudice and revenge that are the two cornerstones to violence and self-destruction. The only antibiotic is forgiveness. Remember ever reading something about "seven times seventy"? (Matt 18: 21-22)

The seventh movie: Generations. Enter a totally new cast of characters; the old crew is gone, except for a few bit parts. We are now going to be exposed to a high tech world in which the travel between here and eternity is available through a magic rift that wiggles into the Universe every 39 point something years. Initially, Kirk saved the bad guy, Dr. Tolean Soren, in a previous time period of the story along with Guinan, played by Whoopi Goldberg. Kirk dies. 78 years later the "next generation" crew of new players finds our Dr. Soren along with the Klingons still in the thick of the plot threatening the world again. The ever-evil Klingons are interested in Soren's machine for its military potential. What else is new? So Guinan tells Jean Luc about her experience in the world of the rift, called the "Nexus". The plot is focused on Soren who must destroy a planet to cause a shift in the gravitational field in order to bring the rift within Soren's physical position so he can enter it. (Remember, 78 years is two cycles for the rift to show up!) Then he will be able re enter the Nexus. Of course, Picard intercepts the final moment when Soren shoots a missile to annihilate a planet to draw the rift closer. A fight ensues and Jean Luc Picard loses. Now, both he and Soren are in the Nexus. Picard must return to the place of conflict to save the world, however, it must be a few minutes before the actual missile is shot off. He finds Kirk in the Nexus and convinces him to return and join the fight against Soren. (That's Shatner's last bit part!). They return and, in the fight, Soren is defeated, Kirk dies for the last time and the rift passes bye not taking any passengers. The World is saved still yet again. Three cheers for our heroes!

The symbolism is clear: we humans have a yearning for our heavenly reward, a new Eden without sin and pain, a place of eternal happiness. The Nexus is the myth of Eden that resides in our "collective unconscious". The rift symbolizes the pearly gates. Jean Luc Picard is the symbolic Peter who protects the gates from unwanted intruders. Picard, as well as Kirk, is also the symbol of the Archangel Michael who destroys the worldly Satans personified by the Klingons and, in particular, by Dr. Soren. Actually, the Archangel myth is in all Good vs. Evil literature. Think about it! The biggest lines are: Soren, "Time is a predator that stalks you and brings death" (very pessimistic); Picard's first reply, "It's not mortality that defines us, it's part of the truth of our existence" (very optimistic). Picard's second reply. "Time is a companion that goes with us on our journey to cherish every moment" (great reply!). Picard's third reply, "What we've left behind is not as important as how we've lived (surely you can find that somewhere in Yeshua's preachings!)." Now, please tell me that those three replies are not Biblical, are not full of meaning! The End.

The eighth movie: First Contact. This film is the simplest of all the preceding films. The major theme is: what we humans do today has a direct effect on the future of the planet Earth. That puts the onus on who we are and what we do in our NOWs. Tomorrow is today's responsibility. The minor plot deals with the inventor, Zephram Cochran, who achieved Warp speed centuries ago. He is a very intelligent yet common man who is revered in the future Federation Academy. The plot starts with the very evil Borg attacking the Federation. As the conflict grows the Borg counter by returning to Cochran's time to prevent his accomplishment of Warp speed. The Enterprise follows and lands at Cochran's camp. The crew of the Enterprise tells him repeatedly of his future fame, reverence and his revered statue at the Space Academy. [In short, history tends to deify great men of the past.] Biblical worshipers need to give this concept much thought. Cochran refuses to accept their accolades! There are a series of conflicts with, none other than, the Borg. The special effects industry is getting better every year and did a good job in this film. The details of this story follow every other Star Trek plot with approximately the same number of ups and downs. If you follow the TV series, The Next Generation, you'll be familiar with the Borg and Jean Luc Picard's experiences with them.

In the end Cochran flies his simple, converted refurbished nuclear missile at Warp speed and is observed by a passing Vulcan expeditionary space vessel. The Vulcans land on Earth and the human society is welcomed into the future. The world has a good prognosis. The End.

The ninth movie: Insurrection. There is a planet that was colonized some 300 years previously by a small group of outcasts. It seems the inhabitants got younger and retained that gift as time passed. Yep, you guessed it, the Fountain of Youth and Eden altogether! Now, a race of wizen old warriors discovered this "fountain of youth" planet and wants to export all the people there to a different planet just so that they, the warriors, can also be revitalized to their youthful age. The lines are drawn and Picard refuses to just fly bye and look the other way. So the battle begins and the sparks fly. Well, the spark of mutual attraction between Jean Luc and a beautiful maiden (360 years of age) lights up the screen. In the end Picard causes the whole evil plot to collapse and the evil leader dies in his own Death Machine. Could you not have predicted that the world would be saved yet another time? The moral is right on: who has the right to move a group of people from their homeland without first seeking the people's permission? This is a kick in the pants for us white folk for the dirty deal we forced on the American Indian Nations, on the natives of the Bikini Islands, on the Eskimos in our lust for black gold up North, and other atrocious Holocausts. The myth story carries over to ethnic cleansing and quite possibly to the horrible lie in the Fourth Gospel that "the Jews killed Yeshua." This film is a simple Sci-Fi action movie, true fiction, powerfully mythical, with a deep significance far greater than one's mind can foresee. It is hard to say that the world is saved when we realize what is happening to Catholics hating Protestants in Ireland, Catholics in Yugoslavia hating the Muslims there, Palestinian Muslims hating Israelis, Sunni Muslims hating Shiite Muslims hating Sufi Muslims hating Kurd Muslims and a large portion of Iraqi hating Americans for freeing them from a malicious dictator. What will the future bring if we, today's inhabitants, exude so much religious hated? Ponder that in your next free moment! The End.

The tenth and last movie: Nemesis. The story starts with the Reamans proposing an alliance with the Romulans. However, the Romulan High Council votes their disapproval. Now the treachery begins. The Reamans employ their Green Snow Death Ray in the Council's chamber and eliminate the entire Council in one burst of a miniature replica of the Super Death Ray apparatus. At the end of the story we'll witness the Grand Pappy device on their War Bird space ship when they attempt to use it. The stage changes to the Star Ship Enterprise. They discover a source of positron radiation on a distant planet. The Enterprise goes there and searches a dusty desert finding several parts of an android that when assembled remarkably resembles Data, the human-like robot. When the android is activated, it speaks it's name, B-4, a look-alike prototype of Data. Only after analyzing the film for several hours, did I realized that this was the precursor subplot to the major theme. It seems that the Reaman race (a ghastly skeletal visage with deeply set black eyes and small sharp needle-like teeth) unobtrusively obtained a DNA sample of Jean Luc Picard and cloned him, Shinzon by name. He was captured into slavery and suffered the brutality of the Romulans. His survival was made possible by a Reaman mentor who taught him strength and patience. As he grew to manhood the political sands shifted and the Reamans came into power with Shinzon at the head. So, just as B-4 is a prototype of Data, Shinzon is a young duplicate of Picard. In an attempt to bring B-4 up to Data's stage of development, Jordie downloads Data's accumulated knowledge and experience into B-4. Meanwhile, back to the main theme, Shinzon' s experience and mindset produces an attitude of revenge, hatred and psychopathology. Unfortunately weakened by years of slavery under the Romulans, Shinzon needs Jean Luc's blood to overcome his ailing, rapidly decaying cloned body. Wow, I thought I'd seen every possible convoluted movie plot, but this one was creepy. Meanwhile, B-4 has copied all of Enterprises secret Federation military files and emailed them to Shinzon's War Bird. B-4 was an electronic spy! The remainder of the film consisted of back and forth confrontations, conflicts and subterfuge. Picard is captured but before his bloodletting, B-4 shows up on the War Bird (HA, it's really Data in disguise!) Data frees Jean Luc. A shoot out follows, Data and Picard get to an escape pod, climb into the miniature space vehicle. Oops, the escape-hatch is locked. They energize the pod, blast through the door and a few additional doors and fly the corridors into the central meeting room and crash out a glass dome. They narrowly make it back to the Enterprise. OH, the magic created by the special effects team is truly spectacular and exciting! Shinzon initiates the Grand Pappy Green Snow Death machine to annihilate every planet in sight (well, except his own of course!). Picard takes matters into his own hands. He beams over to the War Bird, a final swashbuckling duel ensues and Picard is forced to a wall. His phasar had fallen and is unreachable. Shinzon draws his trusty, glistening Damascus blade and charges Jean Luc. Just as Shinzon's knife closes in, Picard reaches upward to a racked spear, pulls it horizontally and impales the onrushing Shinzon. At his dying moment Shinzon pulls himself deeper into the spear to stare into Picard's eyes at close range. The Death Ray is about to go off when Data appears, places a transport button on Jean Luc who is immediately beamed to the Enterprise. In the last 10 seconds before the death ray fires, Data shoots at the apparatus, it explodes and the entire War Bird goes up in a disintegrating puff. Data is annihilated. Sadness fills the entire crew of the Enterprise. In the last scene Picard is telling B-4 about Data's life of learning to be human. As he walks out of the room, we hear B-4 trying to sing a song that Data sang at Riker's and Deana's wedding in the opening scene of this picture. It was a song that B-4 never heard. The spirit of Data was in the download!

The meaning in this myth-loaded fiction goes like this. Treachery, Slavery, Brutality, Injustice, Physical and Sexual abuse all factor in the creation of a diseased mind that Psychologists call dysfunction. The Diagnostic & Statistical Manual (DSM) identifies hundreds of mental dysfunctions from the simplest to the extremely complex up to and including socio-pathology—a condition in which the individual acts without moral and ethical restraints. This film is a fictional spotlight exposing the hidden evils of "an eye for an eye" theology derived from ancient Sacred Scriptures that pervades our present world. Revenge is an insidious evil that ultimately produces self-annihilation. Hell is not some far away place of eternal suffering; Hell is the NOW, chosen by our own free will and conceived in the darkness of our very own soul. It is no coincidence that several of the villains in this series of movies have a name that starts with "S": Sybok, Dr. Soren, Shinzon. "S" is the first letter of Satan, humankind's mythical supreme Evil! Is the world really saved?

That's it ... till the next movie !

Printed in the United States
By Bookmasters